INVENTIONS AND DISCOVERIES 1993

WHAT'S HAPPENED, WHAT'S COMING, WHAT'S THAT?

Inventions and Discoveries 1993

Copyright © 1993 by Compagnie Douze-12

Facts On File, Inc.
460 Park Avenue South
New York, NY 10016

ISSN 1064-7600
ISBN 0-8160-2865-6

Facts On File books are available at special discounts when purchased in bulk quantities for businesses, associations, institutions or sales promotions. Please call our Special Sales Department in New York at 212/683-2244 (or 800/322-8755).

Text and jacket design by Catherine Rincon Hyman
Composition by Catherine Rincon Hyman/Facts On File, Inc.
Production by Michael Braunschweiger
Origination by Mandarin Offset
Manufactured by R.R. Donnelley & Sons
Printed in the United States of America

10 9 8 7 6 5 4 3 2 1

This book is printed on acid-free paper.

INVENTIONS AND DISCOVERIES

1993

WHAT'S HAPPENED, WHAT'S COMING, WHAT'S THAT?

EDITORS
Valérie-Anne Giscard d'Estaing
Mark Young

Facts On File
New York

CONTENTS

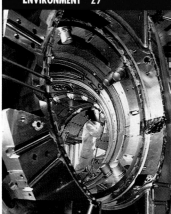

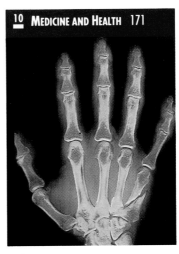

ACKNOWLEDGMENTS

The editors would like to thank the many organizations, companies and individuals that have been contacted during the research of this book. Unfortunately a lack of space prevents us from mentioning everyone by name, but their cooperation and expertise have been invaluable in compiling this book.

Special thanks is extended to the following group of talented professionals who have worked to make this book possible:

Production Manager
Michael Braunschweiger

Art Director
Jo Stein

Managing Editor
Michèle Gavet-Imbert

Editorial Assistant
John W. Hansen

Editorial Contributors
Isabelle Djian
Raymond Hill

Contributing Writer
Karen Romano Young

Photograph Editor
Colombe de Meurin

Index
Marjorie B. Bank

Copy Editors
Virginia Rubens
Joseph Reilly

Translators
Douglas Oliver
Michael Popper
Michael Laraque

Designer
Catherine Rincon Hyman

INTRODUCTION

Historians have been unable to pinpoint the inventor of the wheel, but whoever it may have been, the invention changed the course of history. Without the wheel there could be no mechanical land transportation; without mechanical land transportation there could be no drive-through fast food restaurants; and without drive-through fast food restaurants, how would we survive in the 1990s?

The inspiration, courage and labor of inventors, scientists and researchers touch everything we do. This book highlights the thousands of inventions that influence every aspect of our lives: the food that sustains us, the boxes that entertain us, the drugs that prolong us, the devices that confuse us, the games that energize us, the clothes that describe us, and the machines that could destroy us.

Not all inventions change our lives; there are many examples of ideas and devices that fuel the image of the eccentric inventor, and many of these ideas, such as an umbrella that catches water and suction cups for stimulating hair growth, are featured here.

The essential role of the inventor is to look to the future, and we have attempted to do that too, outlining proposed projects and the progress of research and development under way in all the areas covered in the book. Some of these inventions will be with us in the near future, such as memory plastics, and others will wait until the 21st century, such as the completion of the Human Genome Project. Not all of them may change our lives, but, like their technological ancestors, they will fascinate, enlighten, entertain and stimulate. It is our hope that this book does the same.

Valérie-Anne Giscard d'Estaing
Paris, France

Mark Young
New York City

Editor's Note

The subject of inventions is a controversial one. In numerous cases, many individuals and, often, many nations claim credit for an invention. We have done the best to present the facts as our research has shown them. We welcome readers to write to us with comments and criticism in order that we may correct erroneous information in future editions.

For information concerning the protection of patents, the reader should request the General Information Concerning Patents booklet, stock number 003004006595 from: The Superintendent of Documents, U.S. Government Printing Office, Washington D.C. 20402. At press time a fee of $2.25 was required to obtain the booklet.

If you have invented anything that you feel would be suitable for inclusion in future editions of the book, please send details of the invention and a business-size self-addressed stamped envelope to: The Editor, Inventions and Discoveries, Facts On File, Inc., 460 Park Avenue South, New York, N.Y. 10016. The editors reserve the right to determine at our sole discretion the inventions to be published.

WEAPONS AND WARFARE

HAND-HELD WEAPONS

Prior to Gunpowder

Origins (prehistory)

Weapons were among the first inventions of humankind. The first weapon was undoubtedly a stone, followed by the club, the hunting spear in 500,000 B.C., and the ax in 250,000 B.C. The discovery of metal and gunpowder were the two most significant steps in the progress toward modern weapons.

Spear (prehistory)

The spear was one of the first weapons devised by humans. The first spear was a wooden shaft with a sharp point. The spear was used as a weapon in all cultures. The development of the spear reflects humankind's increasing technological skill, from the first flint-headed spears to the pikes and lances used by European troops up through the 19th century.

Bow and arrow (prehistory)

The invention of the bow ranks as one of the three most important advances in human history, next to language and fire, since it provided humankind with an enhanced means of subsistence. Paleolithic people were the first to use the bow and arrow, and it was used by all cultures until the development of gunpowder made it obsolete.

Sword (Bronze Age)

The development of the sword dates to the Bronze Age, c. 2000 B.C. Historians have been unable to pinpoint the first swords, but it is believed that the sword evolved from the dagger. The development of the sword is tied directly to the development of metallurgy. During the Iron Age, 1000 to 700 B.C., the sword became more durable and therefore more effective as a weapon.

Crossbow (11th century)

There is evidence that a type of crossbow was used by both the Chinese and the Romans. Following the collapse of the Roman Empire, the crossbow was not used in Western Europe until the 11th century, when the Norman army introduced its version. The crossbow was a hand-held ballista that fired metal bolts or arrows. It had the advantage of speed, accuracy and penetration over other bows.

Longbow (12th century)

The longbow, averaging five feet in length, was introduced to England from Wales in the 12th century. It had twice the range of the crossbow—almost 500 yards—and was deadly when used in mass fire at 200 yards. Flights of arrows decimated French knights at Crécy (1346) before they could reach the English lines, and the

Explosives

victory in this battle established the supremacy of the longbow.

Gunpowder (7th century)

The discovery of gunpowder is credited to Chinese chemists, but the timing remains a mystery. Alchemist Sun Simao (China) is reported to have given the first description of how to make gunpowder in the 7th century. China used gunpowder to power primitive rockets in its conflicts with the Mongols in the 13th century. The first use of gunpowder by Europeans in battle was at Crécy in 1346.

Safety fuse (1831)

The safety fuse (or slow match wick) was invented by William Bickford (Great Britain, 1774–1834) in 1831.

Guncotton (1847)

In 1847 Christian Friedrich Schönbein (Germany, 1799–1868), who in 1839 isolated ozone by water electrolysis, developed the manufacture of guncotton or nitrocotton. Guncotton consists of nitrocellulose and is an extremely powerful explosive.

Nitroglycerine (1847)

In 1847 Ascanio Sobrero (Italy) produced nitroglycerine by pouring a half volume of glycerine drop by drop into a mixture of one volume of nitric acid and two volumes of sulfuric acid.

Small Arms

Firing tube (15th century)

With the invention of gunpowder appeared a device that was both an early version of the cannon and the forerunner of the rifle: the firing tube. The design was simple: a metal tube, closed at one end, was loaded with gunpowder and shot. The powder was lit through a small opening in the side of the tube.

Matchlock (15th century)

Through the mid-15th century, light weapons were fired by holding a lighted fuse to the priming hole. The invention of a mechanically activated S-shaped fuse coil freed the marksman's right hand, allowing a better grip on the firearm.

Wheel lock (16th century)

The wheel lock produced the spark necessary to set off the gunpowder, so that the user no longer had to worry about keeping the fuse lit in order to fire the weapon. Johann Kiefuss (Germany) is generally thought to have invented the wheel lock in 1517, but it has also been attributed to

Leonardo da Vinci (Italy, 1452–1519). It was a complicated and costly device that was particularly popular with horsemen, as it enabled them to fire one-handed.

Flintlock (17th century)

The flintlock worked on a principle similar to that of the wheel lock: the charge was ignited by a spark produced by a flint moving against the strike-plate. The flintlock was adopted by the French army around 1660 and it was standard in European armies by 1700.

Breech-loading rifle (1776)

The first breech-loading rifle to be used militarily was developed by Patrick Ferguson, who demonstrated his weapon on June 1, 1776. It was patented in December of that year and 100 rifles were ordered. In March 1777 Ferguson took these to America, where he achieved considerable success.

Samuel Pauly (Switzerland) offered a breech-loading rifle to Napoleon in 1812, but the emperor showed no real interest in it. However, Pauly's pupil Johann Nikolaus von Dreyse did develop the first successful bolt-action breech-loader—the "needle" gun. The Prussian army adopted it in 1842 and used it to good effect in the wars of 1848, 1866 and 1870, when it was finally superseded by the Chassepot.

Percussion lock (1807)

In 1807 Alexander John Forsyth (Great Britain), an avid hunter, invented the method of firing a percussion cap to ignite the priming. Among other things, it eliminated the misfires caused by wet weather.

Revolver (1835)

The idea of repetition by rotation has very early origins. Evidence of it can be seen in a bronze horse pistol, dating from around 1680 and attributed to J. Dafte (Great Britain), which is preserved in the Tower of London, England. A carbine of a very similar design has also survived and can be seen in the Milwaukee Public Museum, Wisc.

In 1814, J. Thomson (Great Britain) patented a flintlock pistol with a revolving magazine-feed mechanism with nine chambers and a single barrel. In 1818, E. Collier, with the help of Capt. Artemus Wheeler and Cornelius Coolidge (all U.S.) followed up with a hunting rifle and a five-shot revolver with a rotating breech. Other inventors followed before a patent was registered on October 22, 1835 by Samuel Colt (U.S., 1814–62).

The Colt (1835)

The intelligent and ambitious Samuel Colt (U.S., 1814–62), a self-educated man, revolutionized the revolver market by making ingenious improvements to the small repeating handgun. He patented his invention in Paris and London in 1835 and a year later in the United States, where he founded the Patent Arms Company in New Jersey.

Dynamite (1866): Alfred Nobel

In 1866 Alfred Nobel (Sweden, 1833–96) invented dynamite, an explosive that retained the power of nitroglycerine but was more stable and therefore safer. Nobel's discovery was the culmination of years of experimentation with the volatile substance nitroglycerine, which had intrigued his father and killed his younger brother.

Nobel inherited his passion for invention from his father, Immanuel Nobel, who had patented several inventions in the mid-19th century. In 1842, the Nobel family moved to St. Petersburg, Russia, where the elder Nobel had set up an armaments factory. Here the Nobels were exposed to the potential of nitroglycerine by two Russian scientists, Nikolai Zinin and Yuli Trapp.

Nitroglycerine had first been produced by Ascanio Sobrero, an Italian chemist, in 1847. Sobrero had been unable to harness the liquid in any practical

Alfred Nobel. (Roger-Viollet)

manner, and had abandoned his research because of the dangers involved in experimenting with the unstable substance. Zinin and Trapp encouraged the Nobels to experiment with the explosive, but Russia's defeat in the Crimean War in 1856 led to the financial collapse of the Nobel family, and Immanuel returned to Sweden.

Both father and son realized the potential impact of nitroglycerine in the emerging fields of engineering and armaments, and each began separate experiments. By 1864 Nobel had rejoined his father in Sweden, where he patented a percussion cap for igniting nitroglycerine. This system became known as the ignition principle and became the standard technique for exploding and controlling explosives. Nobel's glory was short-lived, however. In September, Nobel's younger brother Emil was killed when the family factory was destroyed by an explosion.

The dangers of nitroglycerine frightened the communities where the factories were housed, but its power created a huge demand in the construction and mining industries. As production spread worldwide, so did the accidents. While Nobel was in the United States on a tour promoting the safety of nitroglycerine, his factory in Germany was destroyed by another explosion. Nobel had been working for three years to find a safer version of nitroglycerine, and now he concentrated all his attention on the project.

The solution came by accident. During one of his experiments, Nobel noticed that nitroglycerine leaking from a broken flask was absorbed by *kieselguhr*, a clay-like substance used as an insulator. As an inert material, kieselguhr would absorb nitroglycerine but would not react with it, retaining the explosive force but reducing the volatility. After several experiments Nobel discovered that three parts of nitroglycerine absorbed into one part of kieselguhr formed a solid, plastic explosive that was safe to handle and still extremely powerful. The new explosive was named dynamite (*dynamis* is the Greek word for power), and Nobel obtained patents worldwide.

Dynamite changed the world. Massive engineering projects, previously undreamed of, such as the construction of a railway tunnel through the Alps and the removal of rocks in New York harbor, could be undertaken safely and efficiently. Dynamite also had an enormous impact on warfare. Nobel's invention formed the basis of all explosives until the creation of the atomic bomb.

He began manufacturing the Colt Paterson, but although this was extremely effective, it was not very successful, and eight years later the company went bankrupt. The inventor then worked relentlessly, and the war between the United States and Mexico in 1846 came at a very opportune moment, enabling Colt to re-launch the company and resume production. In 1847 he brought out the Colt Walker, a six-chamber .44 caliber weapon, and in 1848 the Colt Dragoon, the first American Army regulation revolver. Colt was an astute businessman and, in spite of a distinct lack of enthusiasm on the part of the English arms manufacturers, he set up a factory in London. The British involvement in the Crimean War (1854–56) led to the revolver's considerable commercial success and marked the beginning of the Colt empire.

Production in the United States continued to increase. Thousands of revolvers were used by both armies during the Civil War (1861–65), and the westward migration was responsible for a further increase in orders. By the time Colt died in 1862, the future of the company was assured, and in 1873 it brought out the Colt Peacemaker, followed in 1878 by the Colt Frontier. These revolvers, which sold in vast quantities, were of such high quality that they are still produced today with hardly any modifications.

.22 Long rifle (1847)

In 1847 Nicolas Flobert (France) had the idea of fitting a shot pellet onto a case. He had just invented the modern version of the cartridge and in particular the .22 or 5.5mm, which was exported to the United States; there it was greatly improved and extremely successful. This led to the development of the .22 long rifle.

Repeaters (1860)

In 1854 Smith and Wesson, the directors of the U.S. company Volcanic, bought the rights to the Hunt & Jennings rifle, which, with its tubular magazine, was the first repeating rifle to be produced, but which was unusable as it was. The company gave B(enjamin) Tyler Henry (U.S.) the task of making the invention a viable proposition. Unfortunately, his research did not produce any results worthy of note, and it was not until Oliver Winchester (U.S.) bought the business that the Henry rifle came into being in 1860.

The Winchester (1862)

In 1857 Oliver Winchester, a shirt manufacturer and an extremely shrewd businessman, bought from Hunt & Jennings the patents for the invention of a repeating rifle with a tubular magazine. He founded the New Haven Arms Company and engaged the services of B(enjamin) Tyler Henry to perfect the weapon. In spite of an extensive publicity campaign organized by Winchester in 1862 to launch Henry's repeating rifle, the American authorities were in no hurry to purchase it. In 1866 Winchester launched a considerably improved model and renamed his company the Winchester Repeating Arms Company. The new weapon, known as the Winchester Yellow Boy, became extremely popular.

He went on to launch the 1873 model, which became known as "the gun that won the West" and was used by outlaws and sheriffs alike. Produced until 1919, with sales in excess of 720,000, it became an essential piece of equipment for the frontiersman. The 1886 model, the most powerful in the Winchester range, was adopted by the Texas Rangers to help them keep law and order, and the light and handy 1894 model, specially designed for hunters, was so successful that it is still being manufactured today.

Automatic pistol (1872)

The first weapon of this type was patented by Plessner in 1872, followed shortly afterward by Lutze (U.S.) in 1874.

The first true automatic was invented by Hugo Borchardt (Germany) in 1893, and was followed by a version invented by Theodor Bergmann (Germany) a year later.

Semiautomatic rifle (c. 1890)

The first semiautomatic rifles, which used either the recoil or the action of the combustion gases to operate the repeater mechanism, appeared toward the end of the 19th century as a result of an invention by General Mondragon (Mexico). His invention was further developed by the Clair brothers (France), who acquired the patent.

In spite of the fact that a few of these weapons were used on a limited scale during World War I, it was not until much later, with the Pedersen device and then especially the invention of John Garand (U.S.), that the weapon was brought into service in 1932.

Automatic revolver (1895)

The automatic revolver was invented and patented on August 16, 1895 by G. V. Fosberry (Great Britain). It made use of the recoil action to reset the cocking piece and turn the cylinder one notch. It was brought onto the market in 1901 under the name Webley-Fosberry in the English regulation caliber of .455 and in the Colt Automatic .38.

The Browning (1896)

In 1896 John Moses Browning (U.S., 1855–1926) invented the competitor of the Mauser and Lüger, an automatic pistol that used the gases produced by the explosion rather than the energy created by the recoil action. Browning licensed the Belgian National Arms Factory to manufacture his weapon. The compact 1900 model, which held seven cartridges, was an immediate success and was adopted by the Belgian armed forces. By 1920 nearly 725,000 weapons had been produced.

The enthusiasm of the European military for automatic pistols completely disrupted the weapons market, and the Colt factory in the United States called Browning to the rescue. After extensive tests, the American army officially adopted the Colt 1911 model, which was also very popular with the general public. Browning produced a simplified version, the 1911 A1, which also proved extremely successful because of its reliability and solidity.

Browning died in 1926, when his last model, the HP 35, was still in the design stage. This became one of the most popular weapons in the world for both military and civilian use. During World War II the plans of the pistol were removed to Canada for safekeeping. After the war the Belgian National Arms Factory resumed production of the HP 35, which remains standard issue in many countries today.

The Lüger (1898)

When Georg Lüger (Austria) was given the task of improving the Borchardt automatic pistol in 1897, he produced the forerunner of the legendary Parabellum. In 1898 the new weapon was patented. After various tests, the Swiss army officially adopted the Lüger, which already had the famous shape of the many subsequent models. In 1902 Lüger perfected the 9 mm Parabellum cartridge, which was to become the most widely used standard ammunition in the world. In 1904 the German Navy adopted the Lüger P.04 pistol with a 6 in. barrel. American and French forces selected the Lüger for a series of tests.

The Lüger Parabellum, the first pistol to have a significantly increased firing power, became the world's most widely used military handgun. The production of the P.08, which was interrupted in 1942, was resumed in 1960 by Mauser and Interamco.

The Mauser (1898)

In 1871, after the Franco-Prussian War, Kaiser Wilhelm I decided to equip the German infantry with the Mauser, a strong, single-shot rifle. This was a great breakthrough for Peter Paul Mauser, the son of a gunsmith and an extremely clever inventor. He set up his factory in the former Benedictine monastery of Obendorf and devoted himself to perfecting his repeating rifles.

In 1898 he produced the Gewehr 98, which was adopted by the imperial army. The weapon, which had a faultless safety mechanism, proved extremely popular and was soon being used in all areas of combat.

While pursuing this line of research, Mauser also worked on the invention of an automatic pistol. On August 20, 1896 he received the supreme accolade when the Kaiser tried out the Mauser. Although this very accurate pistol did not win the approval of the German military commission, many German army officers adopted it. In 1898 the Mauser 1896 began to be exported all over the world. Today, the Mauser factories mainly produce hunting rifles.

Automatic rifle or light machine gun (1902)

In 1902, Madsen of Denmark developed a light machine gun that could be operated and carried by one man. Other models were subsequently produced by other companies.

The first automatic rifle worthy of the name to be brought into service was the French army's FM 15, also known as the CSRG after its inventors, Chauchat, Suterre and Ribeyrolles, and the company, Gladiator, that had produced the prototypes. Although it was a fairly crude and unreliable weapon, it was produced on a large scale and was adopted by the U.S. Army in 1917.

Submachine gun (1915)

The first submachine gun was manufactured and brought into service in Italy in 1915. It was in fact two combined weapons that used the regulation ammunition for the pistol called the Glisenti 9 mm. The weapon was named the Villa-Perosa after the factory where it was produced, *Officine di Villa-Perosa*. Its inventor, Abiel Revelli, wanted to produce a lightweight machine gun that could be fired on a tripod.

By separating the two weapons and mounting each one on a wooden support in the same way as the carbine, the engineer, Tullio Marengoni, turned it into a *Moschetto automatico* that only fired in bursts. The weapon appeared in 1918 and was immediately followed by an improved version with a double firing level that enabled it to fire shot-by-shot. Both models were produced by the Beretta company. At the same time, in Germany, Theodor Bergmann was developing the MP 18.1, which was the basis for most of the later versions.

Mini submachine gun (1932)

The mini submachine gun first appeared in 1932 in the form of the Mauser 96 (1932 model). It is a very small weapon for special use in certain police and commando units and for the close protection of VIPs. Among the most famous versions are the American Ingram, the Israeli Mini-Uzi, the Czechoslovakian Skorpion and the Polish WZ 64.

Assault rifle (1944)

The first assault rifle to be produced in any quantity was the 1944 German Sturmgewehr 44, a name coined by Adolf Hitler. It was in fact a lightweight machine gun. In 1947 Mikhail Kalashnikov (USSR) used it as the basis for his famous AK-47.

During the 1950s the Belgians developed the first true assault rifle, the F.A.L., which fired 7.62 mm cartridges. The weapon was sold in hundreds of thousands throughout the world.

In 1956 Eugene Stoner (U.S.) invented the AR-15, which was very similar to the Kalashnikov in terms of its use but very different in terms of design. The U.S. army learned to appreciate its true value during the Vietnam War, and the AR-15 (the design of which had been bought by Colt) was adopted at the end of the 1960s under the name of the M-16. A new version of the rifle, the M-16 A2, was brought into service for the U.S. Marines in 1985.

Bullpup (c. 1980)

The bullpup rifle was designed as a modern weapon adapted to new forms of combat, but the system dates back to 1917, when the Burton automatic rifle was invented in the United

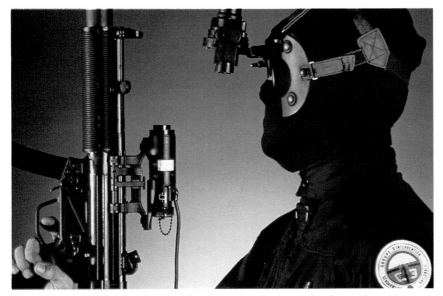

The TN2-1 visor is a lightweight device that improves night vision. It has been adopted by many police forces worldwide. (Gamma/Guichard)

States. The overall length of this compact rifle is much reduced, although the barrel is of the same length as that on a traditional rifle so that its accuracy is in no way affected. The first versions of the rifle were designed in Great Britain in about 1955, but the design was not widely adopted until the end of the 1970s, with the AUG, manufactured by Steyr-Daimler Puch for the Austrian army in 1977; the FAMAS, designed by GIAT for the French army in 1979; and the Royal Ordnance's SA 80 for the British army in 1985.

Stun Gun (1984)

The Stun Gun is an American invention that has the advantage of immobilizing, rather than killing or wounding, by means of a powerful electric charge of between 40,000 and 50,000 v that momentarily dazes and paralyzes the victim.

Glock 17 (1986)

Invented by Gaston Glock (Austria), most of the components of this automatic pistol are made of plastic, except, of course, the barrel. However, this does not, as was originally thought, enable it to pass undetected through the metal detector control systems used in airports. It is a 9 x 9 caliber (= 9 mm Parabellum) lightweight weapon (11 lb 7 oz) that is extremely accurate and reliable.

P.90 (1991)

This weapon is made by the Belgian company Fabrique Nationale de Herstal, and is the first development in the "Small Arms Strategy 2000" system. The P.90 is designed for crews of armored vehicles, tank drivers or weapons systems operators who are unused to handling infantry weapons but who could be threatened by highly trained commandos. Halfway be-

tween the submachine gun and the assault rifle, the P.90 started production in 1991.

CARTRIDGES AND BULLETS

Cartridge (17th century)

The paper cartridge was an early invention. It was in general use by the Swedish army *c.* 1630, but it did not become widely used until the 18th century. Originally it contained gunpowder only, and it did not combine bullets and gunpowder until 1738.

Minié bullet (1836)

The Minié bullet, invented by Henri-Gustave Delvigne and Claude-Etienne Minié (both France) in 1836, was the first to enable the rifled gun to be used efficiently. Gunsmiths realized that the range of the rifle could be substantially increased, but the problem of loading the bullets still had to be solved. The problem was how to obviate tightness caused by rifling. The Minié bullet, with a diameter slightly less than that of the barrel, was automatically propelled by the pressure of the gases. It increased the range of an infantry rifle from 650 ft to more than 3,300 ft.

Integrated priming (19th century)

When rifles could be breech-loaded, inventors had the idea of incorporating the primer into the cartridge. There were many different suggestions, including the pin-fire cartridge invented by Casimir Lefaucheux (France) in 1836, and rim priming, invented by Béringer

and Nicolas Flobert (both France) in 1845. The invention was used intensively during the Civil War (1861–65) and then spread via Europe to the rest of the world.

Metal cartridge (1858)

Among the drawbacks of paper cartridges were that they suffered from the damp and that powder often leaked or was affected by the weather. In 1858, B(enjamin) Tyler Henry (U.S.) devised a self-contained metal-cased rimfire cartridge that eliminated these weaknesses. This was the key to the development of the repeater rifle, the first of which was the Henry rifle. It also opened the way for the first machine guns, such as the Gatling, though there were further technical problems to be overcome in this area.

Center priming (1865)

Center priming was invented in 1865 by both Boxer (Great Britain) and Schneider (France). It was further improved by United States manufacturers, who, from 1867 onwards, produced cartridge cases made from a single piece of brass. The development of this type of cartridge led to the invention of repeating rifles.

The invention of nitro powder in 1884 made it possible to reduce the caliber from 11 mm to 8 mm and subsequently to 7.5 mm, 6.5 mm and 6 mm. These cartridges are still in use today and are effective over a distance of up to 1,095 yd.

Modern research is directed toward developing caseless ammunition; the first trials were carried out during World War II by Germany in 1944. It has already been developed by the German companies Heckler & Koch and Mauser, and the former have even presented the prototype of an assault rifle using this type of ammunition at a NATO exhibition.

Jacketed or armor-plated bullet (1878)

The invention of nitro powder made it possible to obtain muzzle velocities that lead bullets were incapable of. Rubin (Switzerland) invented the composite bullet around 1878. It consisted of a lead nucleus encased in a jacket of a more resistant metal such as cupro-nickel, brass or steel, which was sometimes electroplated with copper or other metals. This type of bullet is used exclusively for military purposes and on rifle ranges. A lead-tipped bullet, known as a semi-plated bullet, is used for hunting.

Dum-Dum bullet (1897)

These hollow-tipped bullets, fitted by the British army to several models of the .303 military cartridges to improve their stopping power, were developed in 1897. Most of the tests on this type of bullet were carried out at the arsenal at Dum-Dum on the outskirts of Calcutta, India during British colonial rule. The Dum-Dum bullet, which causes terrible wounds, was banned by the Hague Convention in 1908, but a certain number were used during the Boer War (1899–1902) and in World War I.

The modern-style mortar was introduced in 1917. Here artillerymen perform a drill with a 120 mortar. (Sirpa/Riehl)

MACHINE GUNS

Mechanical machine gun (1850)

The mechanical machine gun appeared around 1850. It consisted of either a single barrel with a handle which, when turned, propelled and fired the cartridge, or of several barrels that were loaded and fired in rapid succession. The most popular model, invented by Richard J. Gatling (U.S., 1818–1903), appeared in 1862. The same principle was used for the Vulcan cannon, in which an electric motor allows 6,000 20 mm shells to be fired per minute.

Automatic machine gun (1884)

The first continuous-firing automatic machine gun, operated by the effect of the recoil action, was invented in 1884 by Hiram S. Maxim (U.S.). It demonstrated its true value in 1894 when it was adapted for the use of nitro powder. Maxim's basic principle is used today in most types of machine gun.

Researchers introduced different methods of operation based on Maxim's invention. In 1892 John Moses Browning (U.S., 1855–1926) invented the first gas-operated machine gun. In 1893 Captain von Odkolek (Austro-Hungary) patented a very similar invention and sold the rights to the French-based company Hotchkiss. Founded by Benjamin B. Hotchkiss (U.S., 1828–85), the company had already gained a substantial reputation with its rapid-firing cannons. From the beginning of the century, the company manufactured a number of models, culminating in the famous 1914 model used by the French army as well as the armies of many other countries.

Heavy machine gun (1938)

This is the name given to heavy weapons that have to be transported by motor vehicle and operated by an entire team. The most famous version, and the first to receive a baptism of fire, in 1938, was the German four-barrel antiaircraft gun, known as the 2 cm Flakvierling, manufactured by the German company Mauser.

Motorized machine gun (1940s)

Toward the end of the 1940s, General Electric revived the Gatling principle, but replaced the need for "elbow grease" with an electric motor. McDonnell Douglas has developed another model of motorized machine gun known as the Chain Gun. Both weapons have also been adapted as light machine guns.

ARTILLERY

Origins (14th century)

The use of artillery pieces dates to the early 14th century. The earliest "cannons" were simple tubes made of iron, which were used only to attack or defend fortifications.

Gun carriage (15th century)

The gun carriage was designed to support and aim artillery tubes. Jean and Gaspard Bureau (both France) perfected the horse-drawn wheeled gun carriage c. 1440.

Shrapnel shells (1784)

In 1784 Henry Shrapnel (Great Britain) invented the exploding shell.

With his invention, Shrapnel wanted to maximize the effect of artillery fire by having hollow iron balls filled with bullets explode on target. Shrapnel was adopted by the British army in 1803 and came into immediate use against Napoleon, particularly at Waterloo. Shrapnel subsequently became, and remained until very recently, the classic missile of the artillery.

Recoil brake (1897)

Invented in 1897 for the 75 mm French field gun, the hydraulic recoil brake marks the birth of modern artillery. Until then, pieces had recoiled by several yards every time they were fired. The 75 mm field gun was developed by a team of French artillerymen—Gen. Sainte-Claire Deville, Capt. Rimailho and Col. Deport.

Recoilless gun (c. 1910)

This weapon was invented by Davis (U.S.) at the beginning of the 20th century and brought into service for a short time on several English aircraft during World War I. It had two opposing barrels and a central chamber for the propellant charge. Toward the end of the 1930s, the German companies Krupp and Rheinmetall manufactured several models of the 75 mm recoilless gun, one of which was tested by German parachutists in Crete.

Mortar (1917)

The modern version of the mortar was invented by Sir Frederick Stokes (Great Britain), who developed an 81 mm weapon that was brought into service by the British Army in 1917.

In the 1930s Edgard Brandt (France) developed an entire series of mortars ranging from 45 mm to 155 mm. The Stokes-Brandt mortars have been continually improved and form the basis of all modern mortars.

MLRS (1976)

The MLRS (multiple launch rocket systems) program was launched by the Pentagon in 1976 to give the U.S. Army an artillery system using rocket launchers. The MLRS carries 12 227 mm rockets in two banks. They are loaded automatically in less than 10 minutes. Each rocket has a range of 20 miles and is capable of destroying personnel and vehicles within a 32,000-square-foot area. The vehicle fires its 12 rockets in less than a minute. The MLRS is an ideal vehicle for chemical weapons or for laying mines.

ARMORED VEHICLES

Armored vehicles (antiquity)

Horse-drawn chariots were used in ancient times to carry soldiers armed with bows and javelins. They were used by Cyrus, King of Persia, against Croesus, King of Lydia, at the Battle of Thymbreae in 540 B.C. The drawings of Leonardo da Vinci (Italy, 1452–1519) show various projects for armored chariots covered with a conical protection of wood.

Armored car (1902)

In 1902 the French company Charron, Girardot & Voight produced the first armored car combining all the modern technical possibilities: a motorized vehicle, armor-plating, and turret-mounted weapons.

Tank (1908)

Ideas for armored motorized military vehicles can be traced back to the steam era of the mid-18th century. The development of the modern-style tank stems from the late 19th century, when various manufacturers and inventors worked at perfecting a wheel-track system. With the advent of the internal combustion engine, the evolution of the tank proceeded rapidly. In 1900 Frank Brammond patented a track that could be powered by an internal combustion engine. In 1908 an inventor named Roberts (Great Britain) displayed an armor-plated, tracked vehicle at Aldershot, England.

The tank gained military acceptance during World War I (1914–18). With opposing forces bogged down in trench warfare, the need for an all-terrain armored vehicle became obvious. Lt. Col. E.D. Swinton (Great Britain) designed a tank with caterpillar tracks, which enabled it to crush barbed wire and climb over trenches. This first tank was built by the British company William Foster & Co. Ltd., and was first run on September 6, 1915. Tanks were first used in action at the Battle of Flers-Courcelette in France on September 15, 1916.

CHEMICAL WEAPONS

Origins (Middle Ages)

Chemical warfare was well established by the Middle Ages. During that period, asphyxiating missiles made from euphorbia and vine charcoal were stored in the arsenals of most armies. Modern chemical warfare began in 1915 when the Germans released chlorine gas onto the French positions, resulting in 15,000 casualties.

Mustard gas (yperite) (1917)

The blistering and burning chemical warfare gas known as mustard gas was first used in action on July 12, 1917 at Ypres, Belgium, when the Germans fired shells loaded with the gas into the Allies' lines. It was called mustard gas because of its noticeable mustard-like smell.

Nerve gas (1936)

The first of these gases, Tabun, was discovered by the German company I.G. Farben during research on insecticides. Richard Kuhn (Germany) discovered Sarin in 1939, and Soman in 1944. These nerve gases are among the most deadly; absorption of a single milligram of Sarin causes immediate death.

MISSILES

Ballistic missiles (1942)

The first major steps in the field of missiles took place in Peenemünde, Germany in 1937. Most of the theoretical developments took place between 1939 and 1945, and only technological limitations prevented some of these from being put into practice.

The first trial of the V-2, the first operational ballistic missile in history, took place on June 13, 1942. Its form has been adopted for the modern ground-to-ground missile. It was developed by a research team directed by Gen. Walter Dornberger assisted by Wernher von Braun and Hermann Oberth (all Germany).

The main categories of modern missile are the lightweight surface-to-air portable missiles, which are fired from the shoulder, such as the British Blowpipe, or which can be transported on light vehicles—the British Rapier and the American Stinger, for example; the intermediate-range surface-to-air missiles—for example, the Soviet SAM; and the long-range land-to-sea, sea-to-sea and air-to-sea missiles, such as the French Exocet.

Cruise missiles (1944)

Cruise missiles are high-speed, low-altitude pilotless aircraft. They were invented by German engineers in 1944 in the form of the V-1—the *Vergeltungswaffe*, or Vengeance Weapon—which was powered by a ramjet engine.

In 1982 Boeing delivered the first air-launched cruise missiles (ALCM) to the U.S. Air Force. Twelve of these tiny planes with arrowhead collapsible wings are attached to the underside of the wings of a B-52 bomber.

Intercontinental ballistic missiles (ICBMs) (c. 1958)

Intercontinental ballistic missiles (ICBMs) are deterrence or "balance of terror" weapons. They have enormous destructive power—several megatons each; they can be armed with multiple warheads; and they have a range of over 6,000 miles. ICBMs can be launched from either underground silos or submarines. The best-known ICBMs are the Minuteman (United States) and the SS-19 (USSR).

Intermediate-range ballistic missiles (IRBMs) (c. 1970)

Intermediate-range ballistic missiles (IRBMs) are ground-launched missiles (from a silo or the surface), with inertial guidance, usually three separate warheads, and a maximum range of 3,100 miles. The best-known IRBMs are the Pershing (United States) and the SS-20 (USSR).

Submarine-launched ballistic missiles (SLBMs) have the same characteristics as IRBMs. The Polaris (United States–Great Britain), the SS-N-20 (USSR), and the M-20 (France) are the best-known missiles of this type.

Tomahawk BGM-109C (1980s)

The cruise program had a long evolution from 1972, when the idea was first conceived, to its first use in active service in the Persian Gulf War in January 1991.

The Tomahawk is powered by a turbofan jet engine that gives it a range of 800 miles at 500 mph. It cruises along only a few feet above the ground. It is guided by the Tercom system (*ter*rain *con*tour *m*atching), which means that it can hug the contours of the ground and thus avoid detection by enemy radar. As it ap-

ICBMs can be launched from underground silos or submarines. Here a Minuteman III is launched from an underground silo. (U.S. Air Force)

proaches its target, still constantly checking its flight path, it switches to a new guidance system, DSMAC (Digital Scene Matching Area Correlator), which enables it to check that what it "sees" matches the information stored in its computers and to adjust accordingly if there are any discrepancies. Then it homes in on its target with pinpoint accuracy so that the 1,000 lb warhead does the maximum damage. It can be loaded with either conventional or nuclear warheads.

The "invisible" AGM-129/A (1989)

On March 2, 1989, the U.S. Air Force tested the new "invisible" cruise missile, the AGM-129/A, manufactured by General Dynamics and McDonnell Douglas. It has a greater speed than that of the previous generation of cruise missiles and is virtually undetectable by radar.

NUCLEAR WEAPONS

Atomic bomb (1945)

The atomic bomb derives its explosive force from the release of atomic energy through the process of splitting (fission) of the nuclei of a heavy chemical element.

The first stage in the construction of the atomic bomb was the discovery of uranium fission by Otto Hahn and Fritz Strassman (both Germany) in 1939. The production of the atomic bomb was the result of a massive, secret research project, funded by the United States government and its World War II allies, involving a large team of international scientists, that was code-named the Manhattan Project.

President Franklin D. Roosevelt, influenced

by a letter signed by Albert Einstein (1879–1955), authorized a feasibility study in October 1939, and in February 1940 a $6,000 research grant was approved. By 1945 over $2 billion would be spent on the project.

On December 2, 1942 the first self-generated chain reaction of a uranium-graphite pile was put into operation by a research team led by Enrico Fermi (U.S., b. Italy) at the University of Chicago. Following this test, the Manhattan Project was authorized. A factory for the production of uranium 235 was built at Oak Ridge, Tenn., and a secret plant for plutonium preparation was constructed at Hanford, Wash. A laboratory with manufacturing capabilities was established at Los Alamos, N.M., with J. Robert Oppenheimer (U.S.) appointed director in March 1943.

The first experimental explosion of an atomic bomb took place on July 16, 1945 near Alamogordo, N.M. The first military use of the atomic bomb came on August 6, 1945, when it was dropped on Hiroshima, Japan. A second bomb was dropped on Nagasaki, Japan on August 9, 1945. The bombing of Nagasaki resulted in Japan's surrender and the end of World War II. The nuclear age had begun.

Hydrogen bomb (1952)

The hydrogen bomb, or thermonuclear bomb, is the most destructive weapon yet developed by humankind. The hydrogen bomb derives its massive destructive energy from the fusion (joining together) of hydrogen isotopes. Research and development of the first hydrogen bomb was conducted at the Los Alamos National Laboratory, N.M. from 1949–51 under the direction of Edward Teller (U.S.). The United States exploded the first hydrogen bomb on the Pacific atoll of Eniwetok on November 1, 1952 (October 31, 1952 EST). In August 1953 the USSR detonated its first hydrogen bomb.

Neutron bomb (1958)

Research for the development of a neutron bomb began in 1958 in the United States. The theory behind this weapon is that under certain conditions, fusion will generate a neutron flux of billions of radioactive particles—neutron rays—that generate doses of radiation able to kill all forms of life within their range but do not destroy buildings or material and do not create radioactive pollution. The bomb is thus considered a "clean bomb." Once the neutrons have dispersed, the victors are able to seize the enemy's installations intact.

NAVAL WARFARE

Warships

Galley (3rd millenium B.C.)

The Cretans were familiar with the galley by the third millenium B.C. Propelled by oars, the galley dominated the Mediterranean Sea for almost 3,000 years.

Drakkar (or longship) (8th century)

Invented by the Vikings, the drakkar is believed to have first appeared in the 8th century. The drakkar is named for the dragon that decorated the prow of the vessel. Its means of propulsion was both sail and oar, and such was the speed of the ship that the Vikings were able to dominate the North Sea region for centuries.

Man-of-War (1514)

The *Great Harry*, constructed in England, and the *Grande Françoise*, built in France c. 1514, prefigured modern ocean liners. Over the next 300 years the man-of-war became the most prominent naval vessel, with second-rank (two decks) and third-rank (three decks) vessels being introduced. Naval engineer Jacques-Noël Sané (France) is credited with perfecting the man-of-war as a naval weapon by the end of the 18th century.

Battleship

Naval engineer Stanislas Henri Laurent Dupuy de Lôme (France) developed the first high-speed fighting ship, the *Napoléon*, in 1850. This was followed by *La Gloire*, an armored frigate, presented to Napoleon III in 1857. Both were steam-powered and screw-propelled.

In 1859 Dupuy de Lôme was responsible for the construction of two high-tonnage ships, the *Magenta* and the *Solferino*, which, although similar to earlier warships, were armored.

In 1854 John Ericsson (U.S.) developed the revolving turret, which extended the field of fire of a battleship's guns to 360 degrees. His idea was put into practice with the construction of the *Monitor*, which played a decisive role in the

This white froth on the surface of the sea is the only visible trace of an underwater nuclear explosion at Mururoa in the South Pacific. (Sirpa)

Civil War (1861–65), and in particular at the Battle of Hampton Roads on March 9, 1862.

Torpedo boat (1860)

The first torpedo boats appeared between 1860 and 1865. They were basic small craft equipped with a long movable pole in the bow. The pole carried an explosive charge that was set off below the surface near the objective, after a silent approach under cover of darkness.

The first successful use of the torpedo boat dates back to the Russo-Turkish War of 1877–78.

The counter torpedo boat, or destroyer, appeared in 1893—the logical answer to the torpedo boat, which it eventually replaced.

Dreadnought (1906)

The disappearance of rigging from sailing ships made it possible to install turrets on the midship center line, so that, as early as 1906, the modern form of the battleship was established by the HMS *Dreadnought* (Great Britain), which revolutionized naval history. Five armored rotating turrets housed ten 12 in. breech-loading guns.

Aircraft carriers (1911)

The first plane to take off from a warship was piloted by Eugene Ely (U.S.) on November 14, 1910. He took off in a Curtiss biplane, equipped with a 50 hp engine, from the cruiser USS *Birmingham.*

On January 18, 1911 Ely landed the same plane on a specially equipped platform on the quarterdeck of the battleship *Pennsylvania.* He took off again a few minutes later; the aircraft carrier had come into being. The first aircraft carrier built for the purpose was the USS *Saratoga,* launched in 1925.

Landing remained a problem for a long time, and the development of the oblique landing runway was a major step forward. During World War II, the United States built 12 aircraft carriers, extending naval combat into the air.

USS *Arleigh Burke* (1991)

The USS *Arleigh Burke* was commissioned on July 4, 1991, and is the lead ship in a new class of destroyers that utilize the Aegis combat system. Produced by General Electric, the Aegis system is an extensive integrated electronic detection, engagement and control system that is designed to detect and counter all current and projected missile threats to naval forces. The Aegis system, combined with the vertical launching system (VLS), gives the *Arleigh Burke* the capability to fire more missiles and guide them in flight with greater accuracy than any other destroyer.

Submarines

Origins (1624)

Cornelius Drebbel (Netherlands, 1572–1633) was responsible for the creation of the first

The USS *Arleigh Burke* is the lead ship in a new class of destroyers that utilize the Aegis combat system. (U.S. Navy)

submarine. He applied the theories of mathematician William Bourne (Great Britain), who had defined the principle of ballast tanks in 1578. In 1624 Drebbel performed the first trials of his submarine on the River Thames in London, England. The ship was an ovoid, wooden vessel that was propelled by 12 oarsmen. Drebbel was able to renew the air in the submerged vessel chemically, but he refused to disclose his methods.

Bushnell *Turtle* (1776)

This submersible single-place boat was built by David Bushnell (U.S.), and looked like two turtle shells joined together. The *Turtle* was powered by a hand-cranked screw propeller. In 1776, Sgt. Ezra Lee, who had received instructions from Bushnell, piloted the "sub" in an attack on the British ship *Eagle* in New York harbor. The attack failed, but a year later the *Turtle* destroyed a British schooner, and Bushnell was congratulated in person by George Washington.

Nautilus (1797)

In 1797 Robert Fulton (U.S.) designed a propeller-driven submarine that was intended to place explosive charges under the hulls of enemy ships. The *Nautilus* was constructed in Le Havre, France in 1798; trials took place on the River Seine but failed to impress Napoleon. Fulton's invention was also rejected by the British navy, which perceived the submersible as a threat to its naval supremacy.

David (1864)

The first feat of arms performed by a submarine carrying a torpedo—a barrel of gunpowder towed by rope—dates back to the Civil War. During the night of February 17, 1864, a submarine, the *David*, designed by Capt. Horace L. Hunley (U.S.) and piloted by Lt. George E. Dixon with a crew of six men, sank the Union sloop *Housatonic*, which was taking part in the blockade of Charleston, S.C. However, the attack was not repeated, because of the heavy losses aboard the *David* and the security measures deployed by the Union navy.

Submersible (1899)

The *Narval*, built in 1899 by Maxime Laubeuf (France, 1864–1939), was a submersible boat that had ballast tanks on the outside of its thick hull in order to withstand pressure more effectively.

"Classic" submarine (1901)

Diesel-electric–propelled submarines, which are still in use today, were first developed in 1901. The German U-boats that were so effective during both World Wars were of this type.

Nuclear submarine (1954)

The first nuclear submarine was constructed by the U.S. Navy at the instigation of Adm. Hyman G. Rickover. The USS *Nautilus* was included in the naval budget in 1951, was put on the slipway in 1952, and was launched on January 21, 1954. Its first sea mission started on January 17, 1955.

With the advent of nuclear propulsion, submarines, whose original function was to attack ships, have become underwater SLBM (sea-launched ballistic missile) bases.

Retired by the U.S. Air Force in 1991, the SR-71 Blackbird was the fastest aircraft ever built, flying at speeds in excess of Mach 3. (U.S. Department of Defense)

Typhoon (1980)

The Typhoon class submarines of the Soviet fleet are the most impressive strategic submarines ever to be brought into service. They have two nuclear reactors which ensure their virtually unlimited autonomy, and appear to be constructed from two thick hulls joined together. Two vessels of this type have been in service since September 1980.

Pocket submarine (1987)

The crack naval commando units of most forces are currently equipped with 15 or so pocket submarines that enable them to approach enemy ships and coastlines with minimum risk of detection. There is a two-seater and a six-seater version, with a maximum speed of 6 knots.

These submarines, known as SDVs (Swimmer Delivery Vehicles), enable their crews to attach an explosive charge discreetly to the hull of a ship or to take commandos ashore with a minimum of noise. Once its mission has been completed, the SDV heads for the open sea, where it is taken aboard a downgraded nuclear missile-launching submarine specially adapted for the purpose.

Ohio class (1990)

The Ohio class is the latest American nuclear submarine for launching SLBM missiles. Ten vessels are planned, and construction is already underway. Like the Typhoon, the ship is 558 ft long. It will initially carry 24 Trident-I missiles with a range of 5,000 miles and by the end of the 1990s, 24 Trident-II (D-5) missiles with a range of 6,835 miles.

MINES AND TORPEDOES

Sea mine (1861)

There are descriptions of mines in various works at the beginning of the 17th century; however, the prototype of the modern mine was first used in the Civil War, 1861–65.

Self-propelled torpedo (1864)

The self-propelled torpedo was invented in 1864 by Capt. Luppis (Austria). Luppis' design was perfected by Robert Whitehead (Great Britain, 1823–1905) in 1867. The torpedo is a small independent "submarine" carrying a heavy explosive charge in its bow and equipped with a self-steering mechanism that enables it to move itself toward the enemy vessel.

Mine warfare (1939–45)

During World War II (1939–45), several types of mine were developed: the magnetic mine, which was exploded by using the magnetic effect of iron hulls; the acoustic mine, activated by the noise of propellers; and the low-pressure mine, which operated by means of the suction effect caused by the movement of the ship.

AVIATION

Reconnaissance

Kite (2nd century B.C.)

Although it is difficult to say exactly where and how the kite came into being, it is known that it existed in China several centuries B.C. Some sources quote its inventor as being Gen. Han Si, who was the first to use the kite for military purposes, in the 2nd century B.C.

Military airship (1902)

Henri Julliot (France) invented the first military airship in 1902. It was a semirigid airship nicknamed *le Jaune* because of its color (yellow), 187 ft long and equipped with a 40 hp engine. At the beginning of World War I, airships were intended to be used for reconnaissance missions, and eventually on bombing missions. At the end of the war, they came into their own when they were used to protect convoys and combat submarines.

Reconnaissance missions (1911)

Aircraft were used for military operations for the first time in 1911. In October of that year, Italy used Blériot aircraft to carry out reconnaissance missions in Libya. Planes were also used for this purpose during the Balkan Wars of 1912 and 1913. Reconnaissance planes were subsequently transformed into bombers and fighters.

U-2 (1955)

The Utility-2, or U-2 spy plane was designed by Clarence "Kelly" Johnson (U.S.) in 1954. It was the first long-range aircraft designed to fly at high altitude. The U-2's objective was to fly across the Soviet Union photographing military installations. President Dwight D. Eisenhower authorized the project in November 1954, and the U-2 was ready for flight-testing in August 1955. The U-2 had a wingspan of 80 feet and was constructed from lightweight materials in order to reduce fuel consumption. The U-2 completed its first overflight of the Soviet Union on July 4, 1956.

SR-71 Blackbird (1959)

The SR-71 Blackbird is the fastest aircraft ever built. Also designed by Kelly Johnson of Lockheed, the Blackbird was built to fly higher—80,000 feet—and faster—2,000 mph—than the U-2. To achieve speeds of over Mach 3, Johnson designed a special ram engine. Extensive modifications were made to the cockpit to reduce the high temperatures caused by the friction generated at such speeds. Design approval was granted in August 1959, and the Blackbird was made public by President Lyndon Johnson on February 29, 1964. The Blackbird program was retired by the U.S. Air Force in 1991.

AWACS (1977)

The Boeing Airborne Warning and Control System (AWACS), brought out in 1977, makes it possible to carry out airborne surveillance, control and command simultaneously. It is a system that meets the requirements of tactical forces and aerial defense. A new vertical scanning radar, specially developed for the E-3 system, makes surveillance possible at all altitudes.

Bombers

Origins (1911)

The first bomb attack from an aircraft was carried out by Lt. Giulio Gavotti (Italy) on November 1, 1911, from an Etrich-Taube monoplane on an enemy column during the occupation of Tripolitania (Cyrenaica). The bomb was a spherical Cipelli-type device from which the pin was simply removed and the bomb thrown out of the aircraft.

On August 3, 1914 the effectiveness of aerial bombing was demonstrated when, barely six hours after war had been declared, a German Taube dropped three small bombs on the French town of Lunéville.

Ilya Mourometz (1914)

On February 12, 1914 a biplane rose over Moscow, climbed to an altitude of 650 ft and, with 16 passengers on board, flew for five hours at an average speed of more than 60 mph. This biplane, the *Ilya Mourometz*, was to become the first four-engined bomber in service. It was designed by the engineer Igor Sikorsky (U.S.,

b. Russia, 1889–1972), who left the Soviet Union after World War I for the United States, where he became famous as the designer and builder of helicopters.

Ju-87 Stuka (1938)

Designed by Junkers Flugzeug-und Motorenwerke AG, the first Stukas were ready for test flights in 1938. A short- or medium-range bomber, the Stuka, a dive-bomber, was used most effectively during World War II by the Luftwaffe to support ground troops or attack ship convoys. The Stuka carried a maximum bomb-load of one 1,110 lb bomb and four 110 lb bombs. Its maximum speed was 217 mph.

B-29 Superfortress (1942)

Designed by Boeing in 1942, the B-29 became operational in 1944. The B-29 was the largest bomber to enter production during World War II; carrying its maximum payload, it weighed 60 tons. It had a range of 5,000 miles when carrying a 2,000 lb bomb. It was the first production aircraft to have a fully pressurized crew compartment. The B-29 Superfortress *Enola Gay* dropped the first atomic bomb on Hiroshima, Japan on August 6, 1945.

Arado 234B (1943)

Designed by Arado Flugzeugwerke GmbH, the Arado was the first jet bomber. A limited number were used by the Luftwaffe during World War II. The Arado had a span of 46 feet 3½ inches and a maximum speed of 461 mph.

B-58 Hustler (1956)

Designed by Convair, the B-58 was the first supersonic bomber to go into production. The construction and design of the B-58 broke new ground in bomber development. It was the first plane designed with a slim body, so that when the payload was dropped, the aircraft became a much slenderer and therefore much faster aircraft. The B-58's first flight was on November 11, 1956. It had a maximum speed of Mach 2.1 (1,385 mph), and was withdrawn from active service in 1970.

F-111 (1964)

Designed by General Dynamics, the F-111 introduced the variable-sweep "swing wing." The wings of the aircraft could be adjusted from an angle of 16 degrees to 72.5 degrees. The F-111 was developed as a long-range bomber, which pioneered "skiing"—flying 200 feet above the ground at a high speed navigated by terrain-following radar (TAF) to a computer-set bomb target. The F-111's first flight was on December 21, 1964, and it was delivered to the U.S. Air Force in June 1967.

B-1B (1984)

The B-1 was originally designed in 1969 by Rockwell International, but the program was canceled by President Jimmy Carter in June 1977. By 1981, the political climate had

changed and the U.S. Air Force received congressional approval to build a new bomber, the B-1B. The B1-B represents a major advance in aerodynamic design, incorporating early "stealth" technology to reduce its radar signature. Controversy still dogs the B-1B. Numerous technical problems and costs have caused critics to question its value. Most glaringly, all B-1Bs were grounded for repairs during the Persian Gulf War in 1991.

B-2 Stealth bomber (1989)

The B-2 was commissioned by the Carter administration in the late 1970s. The B-2 was designed to be completely undetectable to surveillance apparatus such as radar or infrared. Its shape, paintwork, and construction materials allow the plane to escape detection by radar, as they throw back virtually no electromagnetic waves. The B-2 has no conventional fuselage, but is rather a "flying wing." A long-range strategic aircraft, the Stealth was developed by Northrop and had its maiden flight on July 17, 1989. The Stealth is the most expensive aircraft ever built, estimates rising in 1992 to $850 million per plane. The escalating cost of the Stealth has provoked sharp criticism in Congress. In 1992 the Bush administration agreed to cap production at 20 bombers. The performance of the Stealth has also caused criticism, as it flunked initial radar-evasion tests.

Fighters

Fighter gun (1914)

The first fighter gun, a fixed weapon on the center line of the plane, was an idea put forward in 1911 and tested in 1912 in a Blériot aircraft equipped with a 37 mm revolving gun placed in front of the propeller. In 1914 Raymond Saulnier and Roland Garros (both France) developed a system for firing through the propeller, the blades of which were protected from any impact by steel edges.

In Germany Anthony Fokker (Netherlands) improved the system devised by the two Frenchmen and invented a mechanically synchronized firing system whereby the operation of the machine was interrupted by a series of cogs and rods when one of the propeller blades was in front of the gun barrel. The system was first used at the front in July 1915.

Aircraft machine gun (1914)

The first machine gun was used on an aircraft by Capt. De Forest Chandler (U.S.). The aircraft was a Wright biplane piloted by T. de Witt-Milling, and the gun was a Lewis light machine gun that had to be held at an angle between the knees of the operator. The first planes to use this type of equipment were two Breguet reconnaissance aircraft that took off from the base at Dugny, France in August 1914 equipped with a Hotchkiss 1908 machine gun.

First mounted guns (1917)

The first guns to be mounted in a plane were the German 20 mm Beckers, introduced in 1917 on the Gotha bombers, at the request of the pilots and against the advice of senior officers. The weapons, which were of modern design, reappeared in Switzerland after the war and gave rise to the group of guns known as the *Oerlikon*.

Spitfire (1936)

The familiar World War II Spitfire was the result of a private venture created by a team led by Reginald Mitchell (Great Britain). Without this plane, the RAF would have had nothing to match the German fighters. The prototype Spitfire flew in March 1936.

MiG aircraft (1940)

The Soviet-built MiG aircraft was created in 1938 by Artem I. Mikoyan and Mikhail I. Gurevich (both U.S.S.R.). The first fighter, the MiG-1, was produced in 1940/41. The MiG-9, the first jet aircraft to be mass-produced in the Soviet Union, took to the air on April 24, 1946. The MiG-15 with its arrowhead wings appeared in 1947.

Jet fighter (1941)

The first jet aircraft were developed simultaneously by Frank Whittle (Great Britain) and Ernst Heinkel (Germany). In 1930, at the age of 23, Whittle had registered a patent for a jet engine; he tried to adapt it for fighter planes starting in 1937. The Gloster E28/29 was flown at Cranwell, England on May 15, 1941. But Whittle was beaten by the Heinkel C., which carried out the first secret flight on August 24, 1939 with a Heinkel He 178 piloted by E. Warsitz. The Heinkel He 280, which was the first aircraft to be designed as a jet plane, made its maiden flight on April 5, 1941. Meanwhile, Whittle had vastly improved his engine, making

it possible for the Rolls-Royce Co. to manufacture its first turbojet engine.

During World War II, the only Allied jet aircraft to become operational was the twin-engined Gloster Meteor. A squadron of these planes was used to intercept the V-1 flying bombs. The first German jet fighter, the Messerschmitt Me 262, which became operational on October 3, 1944, could fly at a speed of 540 mph at a height of 30,000 ft.

F-86 Sabre (1948)

One of the most famous and enduring American fighter planes of the post–World War II era, the F-86 advanced both structural and aerodynamic technology. Its design made it extremely fast and maneuverable, and over 9,500 F-86's were built.

F-100 Super Sabre (1953)

The successor to the F-86, the F-100 was the first fighter to exceed the speed of sound (Mach 1) in level flight. Designed by North American Aviation, the F-100 underwent its maiden flight on May 25, 1953.

MiG-25 (1964)

The MiG-25 (code-name: Foxbat) was the fastest fighter plane ever put into service, with a maximum speed of Mach 3.2—2,109.6 mph. Built to intercept the United States's B-70 bomber, a project later canceled by President Lyndon Johnson, the MiG-25 was capable of climbing to 36,000 feet in 2½ minutes, and could operate at 70,000 feet. The maiden flight of the MiG-25 is believed to have occurred in 1964, and it was seen publicly at the Domodedovo air show, USSR in 1968.

F-15 Eagle (1972)

A multipurpose fighter used in aerial combat, interceptor missions and ground attacks, the F-15

could outclimb and out-accelerate MiG fighters. The F-15 was the first American fighter with a total thrust—48,000 lb—that was greater than its weight, 42,300 lb. This allowed it to climb vertically at incredible speeds. It was built by McDonnell Douglas and first flown on July 27, 1972.

F-16 Fighting Falcon (1974)

A multi-mission fighter, the F-16 has a combat range of 600 miles, can carry a 12,000-lb bomb load, has a maximum speed of Mach 2, and is highly maneuverable. The F-16 also introduced several technical innovations, including a tilt-back pilot seat, which reduced the effects of g-forces, and a computerized flight-control system known as fly-by-wire. The plane was built by General Dynamics and had its maiden flight on January 20, 1974.

MiG-29 (Fulcrum) (1977)

A multipurpose fighter and attack aircraft, the MiG-29 is believed to have been built in 1979 and to have been in service with the Soviet air force since the early 1980s. The hallmark of the MiG-29 is its versatility. It can operate as a high-altitude fighter or as an interceptor at low altitudes. To prevent foreign objects from interfering with the engines on takeoff from gravel runways, unique hinged doors were designed to cover the engine intakes. There are more than 500 MiG-29s currently in service.

F-117 Stealth (1981)

The first Stealth airplane in history, the F-117 is a twin-engine, single-seater fighter built by Lockheed. The F-117 project was shrouded in mystery for several years until the U.S. Air Force acknowledged its existence in 1988. The plane had in fact been developed in the late 1970s, with the first test flight in 1981. The F-117 is designed to evade enemy radar, using stealth or "low-observable" technology. The carbon-fiber materials and the positioning of the engines and weapons systems are all designed to reduce heat emissions detectable by radar. The F-117 has been in service since 1983, and was first used in combat during the 1989 invasion of Panama.

The Pentagon did not officially admit the existence of the F-117 stealth fighter until April 3, 1990, but in fact its maiden flight had taken place in June 1981. (Gamma-Liaison /Markel)

Ground-support

Vertical takeoff and landing (VTOL) (1954)

This type of aircraft shares features with the helicopter and the airplane. Its propeller, or propellers, can be used as either a rotor or a standard propeller. In the more recent types of VTOL, such as the Osprey V-22 (see p. 16), the pusher engines that drive the aircraft are able to pivot in such a way that the turbofans function as rotorblades.

The first VTOL craft was the "Flying Bedstead" constructed in 1954 by the Rolls-Royce Co. of Great Britain. Two vertically mounted reaction control jets lifted it off the ground.

DETECTION SYSTEMS

Sonar (1915)

In 1915, Paul Langevin (France) developed a system for detecting icebergs and, by extension, submarines. This formed the basis of the sonar system (the acronym for *s*ound *n*avigation and *r*anging) developed in England in the 1920s. The military derivative, the Asdic (for Allied Submarine Detection and Investigation Committee) was installed in 200 British Royal Navy destroyers and escort vessels in 1939, and was extremely useful to British and American ships during the final stages of World War II.

Radar (1940)

Radar (the acronym for *r*adio *d*etection *a*nd *r*anging) was developed in England in 1940, although a great deal of preliminary research had been carried out previously.

Christian Hülsmeyer (Germany) patented a "detector for objects with a continuous radio wave" in 1904. In 1934 Henri Gutton (France) developed the magnetron, which later became the main component of future radar systems. The director of the company, Maurice Ponte, who was married to an Englishwoman, was able to have Gutton's invention sent to England during World War II thereby enabling the English to develop their own projects.

At the same time, the project of Pierre David (France), an eletromagnetic system for the detection of aircraft, was tested successfully at Le Bourget. The system, based on the idea conceived in 1928, made it possible to detect an aircraft at a distance of 3.1 miles.

Under the pressure of events, research continued during the early stages of World War II and resulted in the invention of radar by a British technical research team under the supervision of Sir Robert Watson-Watt (Great Britain, 1892–1973). Radar proved a determining factor in the antiaircraft defense system during the Battle of Britain.

Strategic Defense Initiative (SDI) (1983)

The SDI or "Star Wars" program was initiated by President Ronald Reagan in 1983. The goal of the program was to create a space-based defense against enemy missile attack. The SDI program has proved controversial, and while not abandoned, the concept has been refocused to provide continuous surveillance and tracking of all ballistic missiles from the time of their launch, using ground- and space-based sensors. This revised concept has been dubbed GPALS (Global Protection Against Limited Strikes) (see GPALS, page 16). The political controversy surrounding the SDI program has hogged the headlines, but there have been some important technological successes that will have an impact on the GPALS program.

In 1989 a high-powered laser called MIRACL shot down a target missile flying at more than twice the speed of sound. In February 1990 a Delta rocket successfully launched two experimental satellites into orbit, the Relay Mirror

Radar was developed in England in 1940. Originally designed for land-based stations, the system was quickly installed on ships for detecting approaching aircraft. (Sirpa/Biaugeaud)

Convair XFY-1 (1954)

On June 2, 1954 the first vertical takeoff and landing of the Convair XFY-1, piloted by J. F. Coleman, took place at Mofett Naval Air Station in California.

This fixed-wing aircraft, equipped with a 5,500 hp Allison turboprop engine, had the peculiarity of landing on its tail with its nose pointing upward. It was known as a "Pogo Stick."

Hawker Siddeley Harrier (1960)

The Hawker Siddeley Harrier made its maiden flight in October 1960. It was designed by Sir Sydney Camm (Great Britain) for the British company Hawker Siddeley. It was the first fixed-wing VTOL fighter plane to become fully operational, and has been in service with the RAF since 1969.

C-5 Galaxy (1968)

In 1965, Lockheed Corp. won a contract to design a transport plane capable of deploying troops and heavy hardware over a range of 8,000 miles. The C-5 Galaxy was tested in 1968 and went into service in 1969. The C-5 had a main-deck width of 19 feet and could transport a maximum payload of 220,000 lb. In 1986, Lockheed delivered an upgraded version, the C-5B, to the U.S. Air Force.

Antonov 124 (1985)

At Le Bourget, France in June 1985, the Soviet-built Antonov 124 *Ruslan* was unveiled. With a wingspan of 240 ft and a length of 210 ft, the Antonov 124 was the biggest airplane in the world when it came into service in spring 1986. Since then, however, an even bigger plane has been built—the Antonov 225, which flew for the first time on December 21, 1988. It reached a speed of 530 mph and can carry a load of 150–250 metric tons for 2,800 miles without refueling. It is 245 ft long and has a wingspan of 285 ft.

Experiment (RME) and the Low-power Atmospheric Compensation Experiment (LACE). The RME satellite carries a mirror with a diameter of 20 in. that is able to reflect back to earth a low-strength laser beam sent out from the ground with a precision of 57 millionths of a degree. The LACE satellite's chief function is to measure the efficiency of a system for correcting distortions of the laser beam caused by its passage through the atmosphere.

A space probe incorporating certain elements of the Brilliant Pebbles system—the deployment in space of 5,000 miniature interceptors that collide with enemy missiles—was launched during the second half of 1990.

Patriot missile system (1985)

The patriot missile was originally designed as an antiaircraft missile. However, it was modified to fit within the framework of the SDI program in 1985. The missile is controlled by a computer and satellite data transmission system assisted by a revolutionary radar system. The missile has a range of 37 miles, a speed of Mach 3, and a mass of 1,550 lb, and can carry a nuclear or conventional warhead. The system gained prominence during the Persian Gulf War when it became known as "the Scud killer."

Sonar dome (1990)

The first "sonar dome" of composite material (fiberglass) appeared on March 1, 1990, a product of the Cherbourg arsenal workshops in France. This submarine nose, designed to protect hypersophisticated monitoring equipment, is the first of its kind in Europe, and is made with an entirely new technology. It is con-

The Patriot missile system gained prominence during the Persian Gulf War. Originally devised as an antiaircraft system, the project was redesigned as a defensive system within the SDI program in 1985. (Gamma-Liaison)

VS-300 Helicopter (1939): Igor Sikorsky

Many inventors have been inspired by Jules Verne, but none so much as Igor Sikorsky. As a boy in the Ukraine, Sikorsky drank in Verne's futuristic vision, especially the book *Clipper of the Clouds*. The Clipper was an aircraft that flew vertically; the idea never left Sikorsky's imagination. At age 10 he built a spring-driven model of a helicopter. He studied Leonardo da Vinci's sketches of flying machines.

At 20, Sikorsky traveled to France and brought home as a souvenir a 25-horsepower engine—the same engine that Louis Blériot had used to power his airplane across the English Channel. Sikorsky used the engine to build a helicopter, but the craft failed. Its structure was too heavy, its engine too weak.

Igor Sikorsky in the VS-300. (Igor Sikorsky)

Encouraged by Tsar Nicholas II, Sikorsky began to build airplanes. He set world records for flight in Russia and later in the United States, where he headed a division of United Aircraft. There, under contract with Pan Am, he launched a series of airplanes, many piloted by Charles Lindbergh. By the late 1930s, however, competition was stiff, and Pan Am considered cutting Sikorsky's division to lower costs. Sikorsky convinced them to let him keep his engineering team and his plant in order to focus on a new project: the helicopter.

The race among inventors for a successful helicopter was hot. Heinrich Focke had flown a twin-rotor chopper in 1936. A series of helicopters were tested in the German military as well. Unlike his competitors, Sikorsky wanted a helicopter lifted by a single rotor. He struggled with the design, building and rebuilding his VS-300 helicopter to find the configuration of major components that would allow the best hovering capability, the highest horizontal speed, and the most precise control.

The VS-300 flew for 10 seconds in the fall of 1939. Sikorsky added a rotor to the tail, simplified the design, and tinkered with pitch. It was a dicey problem: Sikorsky had to build a machine and learn to fly it at the same time. Each process fed the other, through rolls and crashes and crosswinds, until in 1941 the VS-300 flew a record flight of 1 hour, 5 minutes, 14½ seconds. By 1942 the whirlybird traveled 761 miles, from Stratford, Conn. to Dayton, Ohio.

The helicopter was ready to join the war effort. Renamed the R-4 in 1942, it became the first mass-produced helicopter. The armed forces welcomed its help in rescue and transport operations. By the end of World War II, 425 helicopters were in use by U.S. forces.

In civilian life, helicopters became vital in emergency medical situations and in short flights. Many people, including Sikorsky, saw the helicopter as the ultimate replacement for the automobile in everyday life. While it has never achieved that aim, people have found countless uses for helicopters.

structed of successive layers of material pre-impregnated with resin, and is vacuum cooked to give it a homogeneity never previously achieved with composites.

FIGHTER HELICOPTERS

The S 75 ACAP helicopter (1984)

On August 16, 1984 the Sikorsky S 75 ACAP helicopter made its first public flight, which lasted 20 minutes. Constructed from composite materials, the S 75's main interest lies in the fact that it has a lighter structure than conventional helicopters, but nevertheless has a better resistance to bullets.

Apache (1984)

The AH 64 A Apache, built by McDonnell Douglas, is the most powerful, heaviest and most expensive anti-tank helicopter in the Western world. It is equipped with 16 laser-guided missiles, 76 rockets and an automatic 30 mm gun, and flies at a speed of 223 mph. The Apache has been used by the U.S. Army since 1984 and has replaced the AH I Cobra.

Sea Dragon (1987)

In August 1987 the aircraft carrier USS *Guadalcanal* sailed into the Persian Gulf loaded with Sikorsky MH 53 E minesweeper Sea Dragon helicopters, the mine-detecting version of the Super Stallion. The Sea Dragon is the largest helicopter in service. It is 88 ft long and its blades have a diameter of 72 ft. The helicopter's efficiency is largely a result of its speed, which reaches up to 186 mph, and its ability to fly for periods of up to four hours. The mine-sweeping can be either mechanical, when the mine has risen to the surface and is destroyed with guns, or is carried out using magnetic and acoustic systems.

WHAT ON EARTH?

NOT ALL INVENTIONS CHANGE OUR LIVES, SOME JUST MAKE US SCRATCH OUR HEADS.

BEAM DIRECTOR

▼ This giant laser is called the Beam Director. It is designed to track targets in flight and direct a high-power laser beam to selected aimpoints. The Beam Director project is part of the Strategic Defense Initiative program. (Gamma)

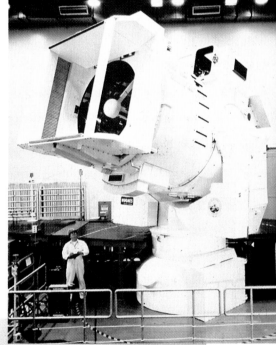

MINE FIELD

▲ The HB876 Area Denial Mine may look as though it has spider legs, but it will give you a lot more than arachnophobia. The HB876 is used to disable enemy airfields. Exploded by randomly timed signals, the mine both causes damage and slows the enemy in its attempts to repair its airfields. (Hunting Engineering Ltd.)

SNOW DANGER HERE

▼ Officials are examining an unarmed cruise missile that had successfully completed a test flight at the Primrose Lake Air Weapons Range in Alberta, Canada. (U.S. Air Force)

COLD STORAGE

▼ This is a photograph of the B1-B undergoing trials at a Florida test facility to measure its resistance to extremes of temperature.(U.S. Department of Defense)

THE FLASHBALL

François Pierre Richert (France) is a professor of ballistics, and has attended many trials as an expert witness. Based on these experiences he decided to create a gun that would stop an attacker in an effective manner without committing murder. In 1985 he received a patent in France for the Flashball, a double-barreled .44 caliber gun that fires foam rubber bullets. These bullets are very powerful at close range and can stop an assailant cold without killing.

GPALS (GLOBAL PROTECTION AGAINST LIMITED STRIKES)

In 1991 the goals of the SDI program were revised by the Pentagon following an extended political debate on its costs, practicality and need. A new purely defensive system called GPALS is now the main program of SDI development. The GPALS program aims to install a system of ground- and land-based sensors that will provide continuous surveillance and tracking of all ballisitic missiles worldwide from the time of launch. GPALS consists of three key segments: Theater Missile Defense (TMD), National Missile Defense (NMD) and Global Missile Defense (GMD).

TMD is a mobile defense system that can be deployed in areas of increased tension. TMD will use space-based sensors and TMD specific radar (known as TMD-GBR) to defend against shorter range missiles. The NMD system is designed to defend the entire United States (including Alaska and Hawaii) from ballistic missile attack. The system utilizes ground weapons and space sensors, including the Brilliant Eyes system. The GMD defense system will consist primarily of space-based kinetic interceptors (the Brilliant Pebbles system) to provide global defense against ballistic missiles. The Brilliant Pebbles system is designed to destroy ballistic missiles during the early phases of flight.

SAAM-SAMP PROGRAM

The SAAM–SAMP (surface-to-air anti-missile and surface-to-air medium-range missile) missile system is a joint French–Italian antiballistic missile program. This system is intended to develop at least two and possibly three interceptor missiles: the Aster 15 and the Aster 30, and an undesignated missile capable of intercepting intermediate-range missiles such as the SS 21. The contract for this system has been awarded to the French companies Aerospatiale and Thomson-CNF, and to the Italian company Selenia.

TORPEDO MINE

The Swedish navy is currently researching a new "intelligent" antisubmarine weapon that could be brought into service during the 1990s. It is a combination of the mine and the torpedo and will be able to distinguish between allied and enemy submarines. The torpedo mine rests on the seabed, from where it uses an acoustic device to record the sounds of passing ships and compare them with programmed sounds in a data bank.

F-22

Promoted as the next-generation American elite long-range fighter plane, the F-22 is designed to be lethal, durable, agile and undetectable. It utilizes advanced avionics, "first look/first kill" and stealth capabilities in its design. In April 1991 the F-22 contract was awarded to Lockheed, Boeing and General Dynamics. In April 1992 the only flying prototype of the F-22 crashed during tests at Edwards Air Force Base in California. This setback, coupled with the program's high costs, has led to calls in Congress for the F-22 program to be scaled down.

New ideas that may change the way we live

LHX (LIGHT HELICOPTER EXPERIMENTAL)

The LHX is to be the American combat helicopter of the 21st century. This light, twin-engined helicopter is being built by a team of manufacturers headed by Boeing and Sikorsky. The LHX will feature the latest in advanced avionics, a flight control panel that features a fly-by-light fiber optic system, and a canted T-tail with a fantail tail rotor. The prototype will make its maiden flight in 1994, and the first delivery is set for 1998.

NH 90

A European project, the NH 90 is a medium tonnage helicopter that is intended to replace the Super Puma. There will be an NH 90 military transport helicopter and a naval version for use as an antisubmarine craft. The first test flight is scheduled for the beginning of 1993 and deliveries should take place in 1998. The NH 90 will weigh 9 tons, be able to fly in all weather conditions, have a range of 435 miles and reach an altitude of 19,700 feet.

OSPREY V-22

This is the first aircraft designed with pivoting rotors. The V-22 program began in 1982, with the Bell and Boeing companies building the prototype, which flew for the first time in 1989.

The V-22 takes off with its propellers rotating horizontally, like a helicopter, and then travels with them turning vertically, like a plane. On September 4, 1991 the V-22 flew with its nacelles tilting at an angle of 45 degrees. During this test the plane reached speeds of 130 knots at 2,300 feet. Ten days later, it carried out a complete conversion at 6,000 feet.

Although it is being developed as a military system, the designers of the V-22 are hopeful that it can be adapted for civilian use. Its maneuverability, passenger capacity and VTOL capabilities indicate that it could be an effective means of transport from airports to downtown urban areas. However, the early success of the V-22 tests has been marred by three separate crashes in 10 months in which seven people were killed. The program is currently under review.

The V-22 is the first aircraft designed with pivoting rotors. (Gamma-Liaison/Jones)

2 AGRICULTURE AND GARDENING

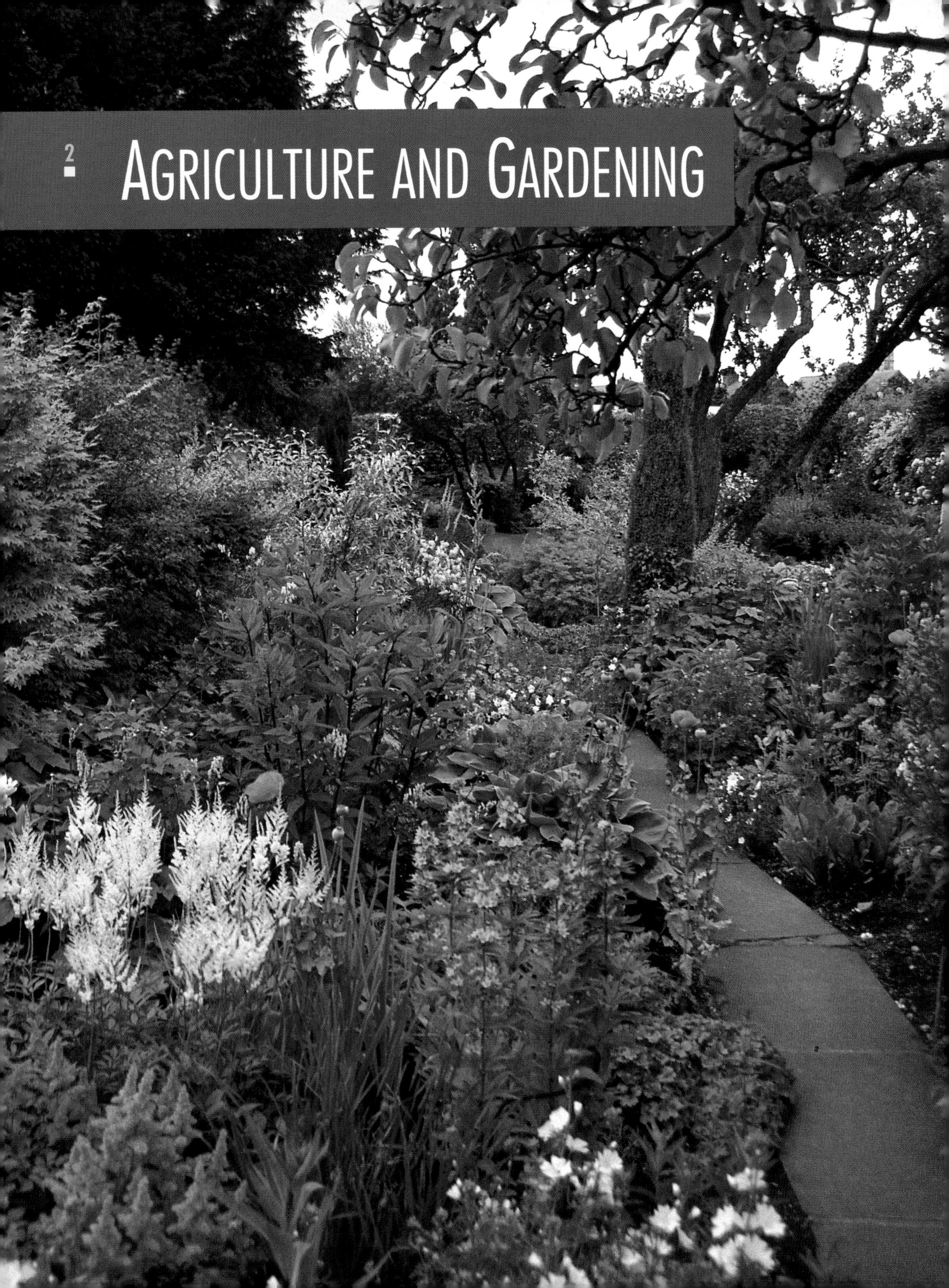

AGRICULTURAL MACHINES

Plowing and Sowing

Origins (prehistory)

Historians believe that agricultural activity dates back to Neolithic times. The first farm machine was the swing plow (c. 4th–3rd millennium B.C.), a symmetrical plowshare that was used to prepare the soil before planting, evidence for which appears in rock engravings and paintings discovered in Europe, Egypt and Mesopotamia. There was little further development of farm machinery until the Industrial Revolution in the 18th century, when new technology developed rapidly.

Seeders (1660)

The use of digging sticks can be traced to the early history of humankind. It is not until the mid-17th century that a mechanical device was first developed to plant seeds. Taddeo Calvani (Italy) is credited with inventing the first seeder, a box device mounted on two wheels, in 1660.

Seed-drill (1700)

In 1700 Jethro Tull (Great Britain) introduced the seed-drill, which allowed seeds to be sown in regular rows. This also made weeding easier, as the farmer could now use a plow with the blades spaced at the width of the rows.

Rotherham plow (1730)

Designed by Joseph Folijambe (Netherlands) in 1730, the Rotherham plow set the standard for plows in northern Europe during the 18th century. The Rotherham was light, with the mouldshare designed as a continuation of the share.

Cast iron plow (1785)

The first plow made entirely of cast iron was built by Robert Ransome (Great Britain) in 1785. In 1789 Ransome received a patent for a self-sharpening plow constructed from interchangeable parts. This breakthrough permitted the development of a standard plow frame, as suitable parts could be attached depending on local conditions.

Steel plow (1837)

John Deere (U.S.) patented the first steel plow, with an all-in-one plowshare and mouldboard, in 1837.

Disc plow (1847)

The disc plow first appeared in the United States in 1847, but it wasn't until 30 years later

The Mass-Production Reaper (1834): Cyrus Hall McCormick

Cyrus H. McCormick. (State Historical Society of Wisconsin)

As long as there's been grain, there's been someone, usually the farmer, who wants it cut down and put away. Ancient Roman farmers considered scything wheat a nuisance. Around 1 A.D., Pliny the Elder mentioned a mechanical reaper. Fifteenth-century Flemish farmers used a cradle to cut stalks of grain and lay them ready for gathering. Scything was backbreaking work, and the cradle added weight to the scythe. Worst of all, ripe wheat must be harvested quickly, before the grain falls to the ground, and even the strongest farmer could only harvest three acres a day by hand.

Cyrus McCormick was not the first to try to invent a reaper. Indeed, necessity created many would-be mothers of this invention. Others hold patents, but McCormick was the first to create a truly practical machine that was mass-produced and sold widely.

McCormick was a Virginia farmer whose father owned a blacksmith shop as well as 1,200 acres of land. The elder McCormick spent much time tinkering with the idea of a mechanical harvester. His son's 1831 design produced a machine that included components found in other reapers: a knife to cut the grain, iron fingers to hold the grain, a reel to push stalks along, and a platform to catch the stalks. The machine was noisy and awkward, but the components were positioned practically. In a few hours it harvested all the oats that three men could cut in a day.

In 1834 McCormick received his patent. From then on the success of the reaper rested on the modern marketing techniques that McCormick pioneered. He advertised heavily, sent out salesmen, sold on an installment plan, and guaranteed his product in writing. The secret to McCormick's success lay in his marketing strategy and in his vision for the Great Plains. In 1844 he traveled across the prairies and envisioned the huge fields of grain that would thrive there someday.

If the reaper's acceptance was smooth, McCormick's own road was bumpy. During the pre–Civil War years he often found himself in court defending his patent against lawsuits. One lawsuit involved John H. Manny, who made reapers in Illinois. Manny hired Edwin H. Stanton as his chief counsel. Stanton included Abraham Lincoln in his staff of lawyers. Manny won the case, and McCormick hired Stanton in his next lawsuit.

When the Civil War began, President Abraham Lincoln appointed Stanton his Secretary of War. During the war McCormick's sympathies lay with the South, yet many hold the reaper accountable for the North's victory. While southern farmers had slaves to cultivate the fields in their absence, northern soldiers relied on reapers. After the war, Stanton said, "The reaper is to the North what slavery is to the South. By taking the place of regiments of young men in western fields, it released them to do battle."

that it gained popularity, following the success of a version built by John Shearer and Sons of Australia in 1877.

Sulky plow (1864)

The invention of the two-wheeled sulky plow is attributed to F.S. Davenport (U.S.), who patented it in 1864. The sulky was supplanted by the Flying Dutchman, a three-wheeled sulky model produced by the Moline Plough Co. in 1884.

Tractor-drawn plow (19th century)

The animal-drawn plow was gradually replaced by machines in the second half of the 19th century. Steam engines were adapted for plowing in the United States as early as 1829. It was not until the 20th century that the tractor-mounted plow first appeared.

Haymaking, Reaping and Harvesting

Threshing machine (1732)

The threshing machine is used to separate grain from chaff. Its origins are unknown, but the most widely known "first" thresher was designed by Michael Menzies (Great Britain) in 1732. It consisted of a set of flails attached by short chains to a horizontal bar turned by an enormous hydraulic wheel.

Meikle threshing machine (1786)

In 1786, Andrew Meikle (Great Britain) developed a threshing machine that became the standard for all future models. The sheaves were channeled between two metal wheels at the front of a drum, where the grain was separated from the chaff by four threshing blades.

Haymaker (1820)

In 1820 Robert Salmon (Great Britain) designed a machine that lifted cut grass and turned it over so that it could be completely dried by exposure to the sun and wind.

Reaper (1822)

Harvesting remained a labor-intensive operation until the early 19th century, when mechanical reapers were introduced. Jeremiah Bailey (U.S.) patented a mechanical reaper-mower in 1822 that used a cutting disc that turned horizontally a few inches above the ground. In 1826 Patrick Bell (Great Britain) built a reaper with a cutter-bar that cut the crop at its roots and laid it alongside the machine. The cutting arm, specific to hay mowing, was invented by William Manning (U.S.) in 1831, but was not manufactured industrially until 1850. The first mass-production reaper was patented by Cyrus H. McCormick (U.S., 1809–1884) in 1834 (for further details see profile on p. 18).

Combine harvester (1828)

The first combine harvester was patented by a farmer named Lane (U.S.) in 1828. His idea was developed by the Moore and Hascall Co., which built an operational machine at its Michigan factory in 1838.

Combined thresher-winnower (1837)

In 1837 Hiram and John Pitt (U.S.) constructed a steam-powered machine that simultaneously threshed and cleaned grain. The grain was separated by a threshing drum equipped with numerous metallic pins, rather than blades, and then fell into a hopper. The straw was swept by a rake and the chaff blown away by a ventilator.

The pollen aspirator, first built in 1988, collects pollen more rapidly and in greater quantities than any other method yet devised. (Cenagref)

Hay baler (1853)

The hay baler was invented in 1853 by H.L. Emery (U.S.). Emery's machine produced five bales per hour, each weighing 250 lb.

Self-propelled combine harvester (1888)

The prototype of the self-propelled combine harvester was built by an engineer named Best (U.S.) in 1888. However, Best did not develop the project, and it was not until the 1930s that the idea was redeveloped by the American company Massey-Harris. In 1944 the company launched its version with great success.

Axial threshing (1975)

The American companies International Harvester and New Holland started development of an axial threshing combine harvester in 1962. The first prototype, called the Axial Flow, was built in 1975 and represents the most important development in harvesting since motorization. The Axial Flow uses a central rotor and new system of separation, permitting the construction of a more compact machine.

Pollen aspirator (1988)

Among other things, pollen is used in medical research on allergies, and in the development of hybrid seeds for reforestation and the genetic improvement of some plants, such as larch. In order to increase and speed up pollen collection, Patrick Baldet (France) and the Seeds and Forest Plants division of CEMAGREF in France developed a self-propelling machine that encloses the tree in a sort of "cage." Collection is carried out by vacuum suction within this cage. It took three years to develop this pollen harvest machine, which was first used in 1988.

Robot coconut-cracker (1990)

The coconut is very labor-intensive and time-consuming to process: it has to be gathered under the tree and dried to recover the copra

The first axial threshing machine was built in 1975. These machines use a central rotor and a unique separation system. (J I Case)

from which the oil is extracted by crushing. The French company Biotropic has developed processing equipment to automate all of these operations. The new machinery has been on the market since 1990.

The coconut is cleaned and then peeled by centrifuge before a second machine removes the kernel from the shell. The fresh kernel is then processed in a sterile atmosphere by separation, then hydro-extraction, to obtain, respectively, oil, milk and coconut cream.

The speed of this processing preserves taste and freshness, expanding the commercial possibilities in the food industry (ice creams, biscuit manufacturing) and in the cosmetics sector (suntan products).

Tractors

Origins (19th century)

Because of the immense size of the farms in the United States there was a large demand for agricultural machinery by the 19th century. As early as 1829 the Case Co. was developing three-wheeled direct traction machines. These tractors consisted of two large rear wheels supporting a boiler, with a small front wheel steered by the vehicle. By the mid-1830s, tractors were widespread throughout the western states.

Burger tractor (1889)

The first kerosene-powered tractor was designed by an engineer named Burger (U.S.) in 1889, and was built by the Charter Gas Engine Co.

Froelich tractor (1892)

In 1892, John M. Froelich (U.S.) asked the Van Duze Gas and Gasoline Engine Co. of Cincinnati, Ohio to build an internal combustion engine that could be used in a tractor. The resulting model was the first operational gasoline-engine tractor and was the precursor of John Deere's tractors.

Hart and Pan tractor (1902)

In 1902 C.W. Hart and C.H. Pan (both U.S.) built a four-wheeled tractor. By 1905 they had founded Hart & Pan, the first American company specializing in tractor manufacture. W.H. Williams, the commercial director, coined the word "tractor" to replace the term "gasoline traction engine," which took up too much space in advertisements.

Caterpillar tractor (1904)

In 1904, Benjamin Holt (U.S.) developed the idea of the caterpillar tractor, which would be able to increase the carrying surface of steam tractors. Holt equipped a steam tractor with a set of wooden caterpillar tracks, creating a larger wheel surface area, which reduced the tendency of the heavy machines to bog down.

Wallis Cub (1913)

The Wallis Cub or Bull Tractor was built in 1913 and marks a breakthrough in tractor design. It was the first of the smaller, lighter, faster tractors and was referred to as frameless since it no longer had the heavy frame common to steam engines.

Farmhall tractor (1924)

Introduced in 1924 by International Harvester, the Farmhall tractor represents a revolution in tractor design. It was a multipurpose machine capable of plowing or harrowing. As new accessories were invented, its functions grew.

Tractor with tires (1931)

In 1928, lemon plantation owners in Florida made improvised rubber tires for their tractors to stop the damage the tires were doing to the roots of their trees. In 1931 B.F. Goodrich invented a solid rubber tire. The Firestone Tire and Rubber Co. introduced a water-filled rubber tire in 1932.

Tool Carrier tractor (1939)

Invented by Harry Ferguson (Ireland) in 1939, the Tool Carrier set the standard for equipment-pulling tractors. Ferguson standardized the three-point hookup and entered into a partnership with Henry Ford (U.S., 1863–1947) to mass-produce a tractor with a hydraulically driven hookup.

AGRONOMY

Soilless gardening (hydroponics) (1860)

The growing of plants without soil, using both hydroponics and aeroponics (in which water and mineral salts are sprayed directly onto crop roots) has been extensively developed in the last decade. It is hoped that hydroponics will help solve the problems of disease and soil erosion. Although this technology sounds futuristic, its origins date to the mid-19th century.

In 1860 two research scientists, Ferdinand Sachs and Gustav Knopp (both Germany), succeeded in growing plants in a simple mineral solution. In 1914 a scientist named Mazé (France) drew attention to the role that rare elements which are present as impurities in water could have in hydroponics. However, it was not until 1940 that molybdenum, a fertilizing element, completed the list of elements thought to be indispensable to the constitution of nutrient solutions.

Sprayer (1884)

The idea for a sprayer was introduced in 1781 by the Abbé Rosier (France) in his book *Cours d'agriculture*. The first prototype was developed by Victor Vermorel (France) in 1884. Vermorel based his invention on a spray diffuser he had

seen demonstrated to wine growers in the Hérault region. Vermorel perfected the device by adding a pump to the spray nozzle. In 1887 he introduced a portable spray, worn on the back. Mechanical sprays first appeared in 1889.

Spray planes (crop dusters) (1921)

In 1921, Curtis JN6Hs were adapted for use as spray planes. They were used to spray arsenate powder on catalpa forests to destroy sphinx grubs that were attacking the trees.

The first planes built expressly for spraying operations were designed by the Huff-Daland Co. of Ogdensburg, N.Y. in 1924, and were used in the Mississippi Delta to kill cotton weevils.

The first liquid larvicides were sprayed in 1930 in New Jersey and California to exterminate mosquito larvae.

INSECTICIDES

Pyrethrin (c. 1st century B.C.)

Reportedly the Chinese were using pounded pyrethrum (chrysanthemum) to kill fleas over 2,000 years ago. The use of pyrethrin as an insecticide took root in Europe in the 18th century.

Arsenic (1681)

In the Middle Ages entomologists prescribed arsenic against insect plagues. The use of arsenic compounds for treating plants was first recorded in 1681.

Sulfur (1843)

Sulfur has been used since 1843 as an insecticide to fight red spiders and plant lice. Today it is used in many synthetic products. Mixed with lime, it is commonly used to treat fruit trees.

Synthetic insecticide (1935)

The first synthetic insecticide, phenotiazine, was obtained by a research team of the Department of Agriculture in 1935.

DDT (Dichloro-diphenyl-trichloro-ethane) (1939)

DDT was synthesized by Othmar Zeidler (Germany) in 1873. Paul Müller (Switzerland) discovered the insecticidal properties of DDT in 1939 and patented his discovery in 1940. DDT was used extensively by Allied troops in the Pacific during World War II to kill malaria-carrying mosquitoes. Because of its stable nature, DDT is a lingering pollutant, and its use has been banned in many countries.

BHC (1940s)

In the 1940s, BHC, a compound of chlorine, was developed in Great Britain. It was particu-

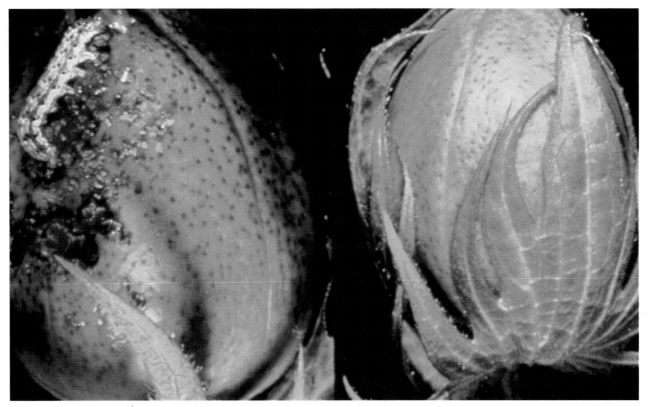

Bacterial gene implant has allowed the cotton ball (right) to stay worm free. (Gamma/Monsanto)

larly useful in controlling locusts, mosquitoes and the tsetse fly. However BHC could not be used as a crop spray because it caused many crops to acquire an unpleasant taint.

vented a process for the synthesis of ammonia from hydrogen and nitrogen. This process, known as the Haber-Bosch process, became the basis for the development of all nitrogenous fertilizers.

soon after without having to plow and harrow the field, which saved both labor and fuel.

Phytotoxins (1991)

To destroy some weeds, very potent herbicides are required, and this can have an adverse effect on the environment. Increasingly, therefore, scientists are looking for ways to combat weeds naturally. In 1991, Gary Strobel of the University of Montana discovered one such substance, maculosin, in a natural fungus that attacks spotted knapweed, a major pest in North American pastures. Such phytotoxins as maculosin act by causing diseases in target plants without harming other plants. Similar steps have been taken to protect rice and citrus plants, but this is the most specific yet developed.

FERTILIZERS

Superphosphate (1817)

One of the first compounds to be added to the soil was superphosphate, originally a mixture of bones and sulphuric acid devised by James Murray (Ireland) in 1817. In 1843 a factory for the production of superphosphate was opened near London, England by a man named Lawes. Lawes's factory was producing 40,000 tons annually by 1847.

Guano (1839)

Guano, the accumulated droppings of seabirds, was first imported to Europe from South America in 1839. During the 19th century guano was an important source of nitrogen. By the late 19th century, caliche—sodium nitrate—was being mined in Chile as a supplement to guano.

Nitrogenous fertilizer (1912)

In 1912 Fritz Haber (Germany, 1868–1934) and Carl Bosch (Germany, 1874–1940) in-

HERBICIDES

Phytohormones (1926)

In 1926 F.W. Went (Netherlands) discovered growth-controlling substances, initially termed auxins but later named phytohormones. Phytohormones could be used to inhibit the growth of weeds, and from this discovery emerged the concept of selective herbicides.

Dinitro-ortho-cresol (DNOC) (1932)

DNOC was patented in France in 1932 and was the first chemical that could destroy weeds but not asssociated crops.

Paraquat (1950s)

During the 1950s the British chemical company ICI developed a new group of herbicides known as bipyridyls. The best-known of these is paraquat, which kills surface weeds but is ineffective once it has seeped into the soil. This discovery caused a revolution in farming, as the farmer could now spray the land and then sow the crop

ANIMAL HUSBANDRY

Beekeeping (3rd millennium B.C.)

The Greeks attributed the invention of beekeeping to Aristaeus, the son of Apollo, and the Egyptians had a myth to explain the origins of bees and honey, according to which honey was the tears of the god Ra. The first Egyptian beekeepers appeared under the Old Kingdom (between 2780 and 2280 B.C.). They made much use of honey, since they did not know about sugar.

Artificial insemination (1780)

Lazzaro Spallanzani (Italy, 1729–99) carried out the first recognized experiment of insemination on a dog in 1780. Despite the success of this experiment, it was not until the 20th century that new research was carried out, notably in Russia with the work of Ivanov in 1907 and Milanov in 1933.

Artificial insemination was mainly developed after World War II and became a common practice, particularly for cattle, when it became easier to keep semen in storage.

Milk refrigeration (1850)

The first system for refrigerating milk was invented in 1850 by Lawrence (U.S.). His invention represented a great step forward. Up to this point, the temperature of milk as it came from the udder (101.3° F, the cow's body temperature) was extremely favorable to the proliferation of bacteria. Fast refrigeration was thus one of the fundamental stages in the preservation of milk for distribution, and permitted the development of the dairy industry.

Milking machines (1862)

The invention of the milking machine dates from the 19th century. The first model was made by L.O. Colvin (U.S.) in 1862. In 1889, William Murchland (Great Britain) developed a constant suction machine.

In 1895 Dr. Alexander Shields (Great Britain) had the idea of using the principle of the pulser, which gave rise to intermittent suction. This was less painful for the cow than Murchland's machine, which caused inflammation. The process was perfected by Hulbert and Park in 1902 and by Gillies in 1903.

Refrigerated abattoirs (1873)

In the latter half of the 19th century, confronted with the problem of supplying meat to the towns of the eastern United States, Daniel Holden (U.S.) and his brother were the first to envisage, in 1873, the preservation of meat in refrigerated abattoirs. Before that, meat was salted or smoked at the slaughterhouses where the animals were actually reared, an operation that was normally carried out in winter, or occasionally in the summer (as in Chicago in 1853) if there was a large supply of natural ice.

Barbed wire (1874)

In 1874 Joseph Gliden (U.S.) built the first machine capable of producing barbed wire in large quantities. This cheap mode of fencing quickly spread throughout vast regions of the western United States. However, disputes soon broke out between farmers who were installing fences and big stock breeders who were accustomed to herding their cattle cross-country as they pleased.

Cream separator (1878)

The cream separator, based on a system using centrifugal force, was patented in 1878 by Carl Gustaf de Laval (Sweden). Before Laval's separator, milk was left to stand and separation occurred as the result of the different weights of buttermilk and cream.

The centrifuge principle was afterward put to use in many industrial fields and in biological laboratories.

Embryo transplantation (1975)

The first genetic experiments in embryo transplantation in cattle were carried out in 1975 in the laboratories of British researchers Rawson and Polch.

Agronomy has much to gain from the identical reproduction of animals of a high genetic value. In the laboratories, the race to perfect cloning is under way. The technique consists of removing the nuclei from the cells of an embryo and transferring them into ovocytes from which the nucleus has been removed. The new "egg" has the same genotype as the initial embryo. It is then transplanted into a surrogate mother. In 1989 it was announced that a research company in the United States had cloned eight calves from a single embryo.

Tele-alarm (1987)

Dennis Carrier (Canada) received a U.S. patent for the tele-alarm in 1987. The alarm is attached to pregnant animals and notifies the farmer when the animal is about to give birth.

Programmed reproduction (1991)

The sexual activity of animals (stock-breeding animals in particular) is normally linked to the seasons: the production of sexual hormones is closely bound up with the photoperiod—the number of daylight hours in a 24-hour period. Hence the use of artificial light, or "luxo-therapy," to stimulate the production of these hormones. The discovery in 1991 by scientists from the French research institute INRA of the essential role of melatonin, a cerebral hormone, in biological rhythms now makes it possible to envisage controlling animals' sexual activity. The use of melatonin combined with artificial light should make it possible to program the reproduction of livestock.

FISH-FARMING

Origins (antiquity)

It was the Romans who first had the idea of farming marine animals, fish or crustaceans, in enclosed waters (fishponds). The Chinese also used artificial spawning grounds.

Oyster farming (2nd century B.C.)

The first oyster farmer recorded by history was a Roman named Sergius Orata. He built an oyster bed on his property, in Lake Lucrin, near Naples at the beginning of the 2nd century B.C.

Orata built fishponds that connected with the sea but protected the oyster brood from waves.

The young oysters were provided with posts to which they could cling and grow in proper conditions of temperature and light. Sergius Orata's know-how was such that he made a fortune selling his oysters. His contemporaries said of him, "He could grow oysters on a roof." Lake Lucrin disappeared in 1583 after an earthquake and a volcanic eruption.

Currently, Japan is the number-one producer of oysters in the world.

Mussel beds (1235)

After being shipwrecked on the French coast in 1235, Patrick Walton (Ireland) settled there. Between tall wooden stakes planted in the sea he stretched nets to catch birds. He soon noticed that these stakes became covered with mussels, which seemed to grow remarkably well there. He had the idea of planting many more stakes, close together and linked by racks. He called these strange barriers "bout choat," which became *bouchot*, the French term for these mussel beds.

Artificial fertilizing of fish eggs (1420)

The invention of the artificial fertilization of fish eggs in 1420 is attributed to Dom Pinchon, a monk at the Abbaye de Réome near Montbard on the French Côte d'Or. Anxious to provide the Christians with sufficient food for the many days of abstinence, the monk thought up a system for fertilizing eggs that would provide enough fish to make it possible to observe the fast days. The fertilization process was described in 1763 by the naturalist Jacobi (Germany), who reinvented Dom Pinchon's box, calling it a hatching box.

In 1701 C.F. Lund (Sweden) invented a spawning box, one of the first of its kind.

Cultured pearls (c. 1899)

At the end of the last century (the patent came into the public domain in 1921), Kokichi Mikimoto (Japan) invented a procedure that made it possible, with pearl oysters, to obtain cultured pearls. Natural pearls are those formed without any deliberate outside action.

Natural pearls were more sought after (and thus more expensive) than diamonds until the invention of cultured pearls. Natural pearls were mainly gathered in tropical seas by divers, who went to a depth of 131 ft without breathing apparatus, helped by weights held between the feet—a dangerous operation.

In the hands of sometimes unscrupulous dealers, the intensive exploitation of pearl oysters was slowly but surely exhausting the natural beds in Ceylon, Japan, the Red Sea, Polynesia and the Persian Gulf when the invention of cultured pearls opened up new horizons.

Pearls have since been cultivated in specialized "sea farms" and have become a product almost like any other. It takes three years for a pearl to form around a core of nacre that is implanted in the pearl oyster. One oyster can take two to three grafts during its life, but no more. In 1990 about 68,000 pearls were produced in this way by Japanese pearl farms, which, since 1968, have faced competition from

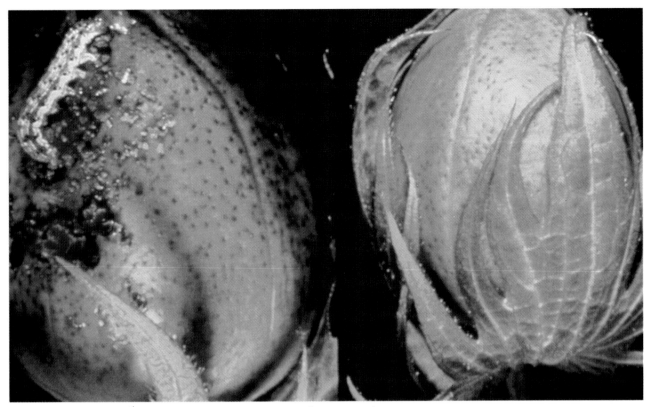

Bacterial gene implant has allowed the cotton ball (right) to stay worm free. (Gamma/Monsanto)

larly useful in controlling locusts, mosquitoes and the tsetse fly. However BHC could not be used as a crop spray because it caused many crops to acquire an unpleasant taint.

FERTILIZERS

Superphosphate (1817)

One of the first compounds to be added to the soil was superphosphate, originally a mixture of bones and sulphuric acid devised by James Murray (Ireland) in 1817. In 1843 a factory for the production of superphosphate was opened near London, England by a man named Lawes. Lawes's factory was producing 40,000 tons annually by 1847.

Guano (1839)

Guano, the accumulated droppings of seabirds, was first imported to Europe from South America in 1839. During the 19th century guano was an important source of nitrogen. By the late 19th century, caliche—sodium nitrate—was being mined in Chile as a supplement to guano.

Nitrogenous fertilizer (1912)

In 1912 Fritz Haber (Germany, 1868–1934) and Carl Bosch (Germany, 1874–1940) in-

vented a process for the synthesis of ammonia from hydrogen and nitrogen. This process, known as the Haber-Bosch process, became the basis for the development of all nitrogenous fertilizers.

HERBICIDES

Phytohormones (1926)

In 1926 F.W. Went (Netherlands) discovered growth-controlling substances, initially termed auxins but later named phytohormones. Phytohormones could be used to inhibit the growth of weeds, and from this discovery emerged the concept of selective herbicides.

Dinitro-ortho-cresol (DNOC) (1932)

DNOC was patented in France in 1932 and was the first chemical that could destroy weeds but not asssociated crops.

Paraquat (1950s)

During the 1950s the British chemical company ICI developed a new group of herbicides known as bipyridyls. The best-known of these is paraquat, which kills surface weeds but is ineffective once it has seeped into the soil. This discovery caused a revolution in farming, as the farmer could now spray the land and then sow the crop

soon after without having to plow and harrow the field, which saved both labor and fuel.

Phytotoxins (1991)

To destroy some weeds, very potent herbicides are required, and this can have an adverse effect on the environment. Increasingly, therefore, scientists are looking for ways to combat weeds naturally. In 1991, Gary Strobel of the University of Montana discovered one such substance, maculosin, in a natural fungus that attacks spotted knapweed, a major pest in North American pastures. Such phytotoxins as maculosin act by causing diseases in target plants without harming other plants. Similar steps have been taken to protect rice and citrus plants, but this is the most specific yet developed.

ANIMAL HUSBANDRY

Beekeeping (3rd millennium B.C.)

The Greeks attributed the invention of beekeeping to Aristaeus, the son of Apollo, and the Egyptians had a myth to explain the origins of bees and honey, according to which honey was the tears of the god Ra. The first Egyptian beekeepers appeared under the Old Kingdom (between 2780 and 2280 B.C.). They made much use of honey, since they did not know about sugar.

Artificial insemination (1780)

Lazzaro Spallanzani (Italy, 1729–99) carried out the first recognized experiment of insemination on a dog in 1780. Despite the success of this experiment, it was not until the 20th century that new research was carried out, notably in Russia with the work of Ivanov in 1907 and Milanov in 1933.

Artificial insemination was mainly developed after World War II and became a common practice, particularly for cattle, when it became easier to keep semen in storage.

Milk refrigeration (1850)

The first system for refrigerating milk was invented in 1850 by Lawrence (U.S.). His invention represented a great step forward. Up to this point, the temperature of milk as it came from the udder (101.3° F, the cow's body temperature) was extremely favorable to the proliferation of bacteria. Fast refrigeration was thus one of the fundamental stages in the preservation of milk for distribution, and permitted the development of the dairy industry.

Milking machines (1862)

The invention of the milking machine dates from the 19th century. The first model was made by L.O. Colvin (U.S.) in 1862. In 1889, William Murchland (Great Britain) developed a constant suction machine.

In 1895 Dr. Alexander Shields (Great Britain) had the idea of using the principle of the pulser, which gave rise to intermittent suction. This was less painful for the cow than Murchland's machine, which caused inflammation. The process was perfected by Hulbert and Park in 1902 and by Gillies in 1903.

Refrigerated abattoirs (1873)

In the latter half of the 19th century, confronted with the problem of supplying meat to the towns of the eastern United States, Daniel Holden (U.S.) and his brother were the first to envisage, in 1873, the preservation of meat in refrigerated abattoirs. Before that, meat was salted or smoked at the slaughterhouses where the animals were actually reared, an operation that was normally carried out in winter, or occasionally in the summer (as in Chicago in 1853) if there was a large supply of natural ice.

Barbed wire (1874)

In 1874 Joseph Gliden (U.S.) built the first machine capable of producing barbed wire in large quantities. This cheap mode of fencing quickly spread throughout vast regions of the western United States. However, disputes soon broke out between farmers who were installing fences and big stock breeders who were accustomed to herding their cattle cross-country as they pleased.

Cream separator (1878)

The cream separator, based on a system using centrifugal force, was patented in 1878 by Carl Gustaf de Laval (Sweden). Before Laval's separator, milk was left to stand and separation occurred as the result of the different weights of buttermilk and cream.

The centrifuge principle was afterward put to use in many industrial fields and in biological laboratories.

Embryo transplantation (1975)

The first genetic experiments in embryo transplantation in cattle were carried out in 1975 in the laboratories of British researchers Rawson and Polch.

Agronomy has much to gain from the identical reproduction of animals of a high genetic value. In the laboratories, the race to perfect cloning is under way. The technique consists of removing the nuclei from the cells of an embryo and transferring them into ovocytes from which the nucleus has been removed. The new "egg" has the same genotype as the initial embryo. It is then transplanted into a surrogate mother. In 1989 it was announced that a research company in the United States had cloned eight calves from a single embryo.

Tele-alarm (1987)

Dennis Carrier (Canada) received a U.S. patent for the tele-alarm in 1987. The alarm is attached to pregnant animals and notifies the farmer when the animal is about to give birth.

Programmed reproduction (1991)

The sexual activity of animals (stock-breeding animals in particular) is normally linked to the seasons: the production of sexual hormones is closely bound up with the photoperiod—the number of daylight hours in a 24-hour period. Hence the use of artificial light, or "luxo-therapy," to stimulate the production of these hormones. The discovery in 1991 by scientists from the French research institute INRA of the essential role of melatonin, a cerebral hormone, in biological rhythms now makes it possible to envisage controlling animals' sexual activity. The use of melatonin combined with artificial light should make it possible to program the reproduction of livestock.

FISH-FARMING

Origins (antiquity)

It was the Romans who first had the idea of farming marine animals, fish or crustaceans, in enclosed waters (fishponds). The Chinese also used artificial spawning grounds.

Oyster farming (2nd century B.C.)

The first oyster farmer recorded by history was a Roman named Sergius Orata. He built an oyster bed on his property, in Lake Lucrin, near Naples at the beginning of the 2nd century B.C.

Orata built fishponds that connected with the sea but protected the oyster brood from waves.

The young oysters were provided with posts to which they could cling and grow in proper conditions of temperature and light. Sergius Orata's know-how was such that he made a fortune selling his oysters. His contemporaries said of him, "He could grow oysters on a roof." Lake Lucrin disappeared in 1583 after an earthquake and a volcanic eruption.

Currently, Japan is the number-one producer of oysters in the world.

Mussel beds (1235)

After being shipwrecked on the French coast in 1235, Patrick Walton (Ireland) settled there. Between tall wooden stakes planted in the sea he stretched nets to catch birds. He soon noticed that these stakes became covered with mussels, which seemed to grow remarkably well there. He had the idea of planting many more stakes, close together and linked by racks. He called these strange barriers "bout choat," which became *bouchot*, the French term for these mussel beds.

Artificial fertilizing of fish eggs (1420)

The invention of the artificial fertilization of fish eggs in 1420 is attributed to Dom Pinchon, a monk at the Abbaye de Réome near Montbard on the French Côte d'Or. Anxious to provide the Christians with sufficient food for the many days of abstinence, the monk thought up a system for fertilizing eggs that would provide enough fish to make it possible to observe the fast days. The fertilization process was described in 1763 by the naturalist Jacobi (Germany), who reinvented Dom Pinchon's box, calling it a hatching box.

In 1701 C.F. Lund (Sweden) invented a spawning box, one of the first of its kind.

Cultured pearls (c. 1899)

At the end of the last century (the patent came into the public domain in 1921), Kokichi Mikimoto (Japan) invented a procedure that made it possible, with pearl oysters, to obtain cultured pearls. Natural pearls are those formed without any deliberate outside action.

Natural pearls were more sought after (and thus more expensive) than diamonds until the invention of cultured pearls. Natural pearls were mainly gathered in tropical seas by divers, who went to a depth of 131 ft without breathing apparatus, helped by weights held between the feet—a dangerous operation.

In the hands of sometimes unscrupulous dealers, the intensive exploitation of pearl oysters was slowly but surely exhausting the natural beds in Ceylon, Japan, the Red Sea, Polynesia and the Persian Gulf when the invention of cultured pearls opened up new horizons.

Pearls have since been cultivated in specialized "sea farms" and have become a product almost like any other. It takes three years for a pearl to form around a core of nacre that is implanted in the pearl oyster. One oyster can take two to three grafts during its life, but no more. In 1990 about 68,000 pearls were produced in this way by Japanese pearl farms, which, since 1968, have faced competition from the pearl farms of French Polynesia, whose pearls are highly prized. A connoisseur may pay up to $10,000 for a single cultured pearl, if it is of the right luster and perfectly formed.

Aquaculture (1933)

In 1933 Prof. Fujinaga (Japan) first solved the problem of getting shrimp (*Penaeus japonicus*) to reproduce in captivity.

Between 1890 and 1910 billions of cod and lobster larvae had been released into the ocean by American biologists to multiply, in the hope of improving productivity, in vain. Prof. Fujinaga's experiments at last opened the way to modern aquaculture, whose production (in fresh and salt water) is today more than 25 million metric tons per year.

Algae farming (1972)

In 1972 Howard A. Wilcox (U.S.) put forward the idea of using algae to produce methane as an energy source. His calculations showed that if a "field" 532 miles long of algae of the species *Macrocystis pyrifera* could be cultivated in the ocean, the entire annual gas requirements of the United States could be produced. The idea is to harvest the algae, which the action of the sun's rays cause to grow very fast, and then to use a bacterium to digest it, with a resulting emission of methane.

GARDENING

Frames and glass cloches (antiquity)

It is thought that the Romans were already familiar with the use of glass shelters and artificial heat to counter the difficulties of producing certain vegetables during the winter months. But it was not until 1600, when Olivier de Serres, the first French agronomist, wrote his *Théatre d'agriculture et mesnage des champs*, that glass cloches were recommended for growing melons. The glass cold frame is probably a 16th-century Dutch invention.

Spade (prehistory)

The first appearance of this digging instrument probably dates back to prehistoric times, when humanity moved from the gathering to the agricultural stage.

The low Latin name for the spade *becca* or *besca* tells us that it was already used by the Romans, who were great horticulturalists and builders of gardens.

Wheelbarrow (12th century)

The origins of the wheelbarrow are obscure. In Europe one of the oldest representations of a wheelbarrow, used on cathedral building sites, dates from the 12th century. But the wheelbarrow must already have been in use in Asia, and more specifically in China. Moreover, China has an astonishing variety of vehicles on the wheelbarrow theme, the common feature of all

The lawn mower was invented in 1831. Edwin Budding's original design has been modified many times since, but his original concept still applies. (Le Livre Mondial des Inventions)

Pruning shears were invented by the Marquis Bertrand de Moleville in 1815. (Le Livre Mondial des Inventions)

Binomial nomenclature (1753): Carolus Linnaeus (Carl von Linné)

The Book of Genesis tells us that Adam sat in the Garden of Eden and gave each animal its name. Unfortunately, the names he gave them were not recorded; if they had been, it would have saved a lot of work for Linnaeus.

Until Linnaeus came along, animals, and indeed all of nature's species, answered to a confusing hodgepodge of names. The name of each species consisted of a generic name followed by a phrase describing it. The trouble was that each naturalist used a different phrase to describe the same plant or animal. None of them knew which species the others were talking about; all might study the same species, believing they were each studying something different.

At age 30, Linnaeus went to Amsterdam to act as house physician and naturalist for a wealthy doctor. The doctor asked Linnaeus to write descriptions of all the plants in his extensive garden. Linnaeus's system of binomial nomenclature grew from this experience.

Binomial nomenclature—literally, naming with two names—is a simple system for classifying species and for storing and retrieving information about them. The first name, as in previous systems, gives the genus. The second name, often descriptive, gives the species name. For example, a house cat goes by the designation *Felis domesticus* and a lion answers to *Felis leo*.

This simple system was accepted immediately and almost universally. The use of Latin, then the language of scholars, helped scientists the world over to share research and other information. The new terminology was concise and easy to understand. It opened zoology and botany to lay people as well, helping them to see the relationship between members of the same generic family.

Primarily a botanist, Linnaeus classified all the known flowering plants in his *System Plantarum*, in 1753. *Systema Naturae*, published in 1758, classified more than 4,000 animals, including, for the first time, human beings. It was Linnaeus who coined the phrase *homo sapiens*—wise man—to classify humans. He was also the first to use the signs ♂ and ♀ to designate male and female.

Begonia grandis "Alba." (Christopher Woods)

of them being that, like all wheelbarrows, they have a single wheel.

Pruning shears (1815)

Forced into exile by the French Revolution, the Marquis Bertrand de Moleville, a former minister of Louis XVI, kept himself busy by developing a tool that has become almost a symbol for gardeners: pruning shears.

Lawn mower (1831)

The invention of the lawn mower in 1831 is credited to two Englishmen: Edwin Budding for the design and Ferrabee for the manufacture. The machine was horse-drawn, and the horses' hooves were covered by rubber boots so that they would not damage the lawn while pulling the cylindrical blades of the machine.

At the beginning of the second half of the 19th century, the steam mower was produced, followed by the motor-driven lawn mower. Black and Decker produced the first successful lightweight model in 1969.

Garden hose (1850)

Making artificial "rain" to provide plants with water is a procedure that was described in 800 by a Benedictine monk. At that time water was poured from a jug and allowed to run between the fingers onto the ground.

Around 1850 the first gutta-percha hoses began to replace watering cans and the watering cart drawn by a donkey.

Hedge-trimmer (1880)

In 1880 R. Hornsby (Great Britain) invented a machine for cutting hedges, made entirely of metal. Drawn by two horses, it was supported on two large wheels and had a seat in the front for the driver and one in the back for the man operating the cutting arm made from two big vertical blades.

Flymo (1963)

A mower based on the hovercraft principle was produced by Flymo in Great Britain in 1963. This mower with a vertical blade has a fan that creates an air cushion under its plastic skirt. The machine is therefore very light and easy to use, even on slopes, and is practical for negotiating obstacles.

Heinz Zipfel (Germany) updated the air cushion system, creating the Fremo GMS in 1977. This machine mows the grass however long it is, collects the cut grass, is not damaged by damp (and can therefore mow in all weathers), and makes it possible to mow even quite steep slopes. The system has been patented in five countries, including France, Germany and the United States.

Automatic water kit (1968)

A real transformation of garden watering techniques was developed by two men, Kress and Kestner, for the German company Gardena in 1968. Using molded plastic components, they developed a system of automatic connections

that could be simply clicked together without any tools (or leaks) to assemble all the equipment necessary for watering (hoses, nozzles, faucets, etc.). Gardena has sold over 20 million of these kits.

Tree replanter (1985)

It is very difficult to transplant an adult tree without damaging it or ruining its chances of settling in its new location. The Hydra-Brute Tree Replanter, an American invention from Lakeshore Industrial brought out in 1985, is very easy to handle and currently has the best performance of any implement of its kind. It does everything—digging up the tree, transporting and replanting it—and it can be operated by one person.

Flowers, Fruits and Vegetables

Lemon (1000 B.C.)

Some say the lemon tree first appeared in the foothills of the Himalayas, others say it was in the Malayan archipelago. Whatever the case, it was cultivated by the Chinese some 3,000 years ago.

The Romans wree the first westerners to introduce it into their gardens. They called the fruit the "apple of the Mede," in reference to a people who lived in what is now Iran. The fruit was used mainly for medicinal purposes, as an antidote to poisons and venom and as an insect repellent.

It was not until the Crusades that the lemon tree became properly established in the Mediterranean countries, even though the Arabs had already done much to spread it during their conquests.

The lemon was one of the few gifts from the Old to the New World, thanks to Spanish and Portuguese navigators.

One of the lemon's greatest glories was that it made possible the prevention of the terrible scurvy that had been decimating ships' crews at sea. In the mid-18th century James Lindt,, a Royal Navy surgeon, discovered the remarkable anti-scurvy properties of this fruit.

It was not until 1932, a century and a half later, that the lemon's anti-scurvy properties were correctly attributed to its high vitamin C content.

Orange (15th century)

For a long time it was believed that oranges were the famous "golden fruit" of the garden of the Hesperides—the three nymphs of the setting sun—which was identified as being at the foot of the Atlas Mountains. But this was just a legend, since neither the Greeks nor the Romans were familiar with oranges.

The bitter Seville orange was no doubt brought to the Mediterranean basin by Arab navigators and was rediscovered by the Crusaders in Palestine. But the sweet orange that we enjoy today is a mutation of a fruit that originated in India or China and did not appear in Europe until the beginning of the 15th century.

Pineapple (1493)

Christopher Columbus and his companions became the first Europeans ever to taste a pineapple, when they landed in Guadeloupe. The natives of the Caribbean had long been growing this fruit, which they called *Nana*, meaning "flavor." Its exceptional qualities soon made it the Nana Nana, or flavor of flavors, from which its Latin name, *Ananas comosus*, is derived. However, the English were more struck by its appearance than by its taste and called it the pineapple.

In Europe the first attempts to grow pineapples under glass took place in Italy at the beginning of the 17th century, and then it was tried in the greenhouses of the Botanical Gardens of Leyden in Holland.

Potato (1554)

The potato was first introduced into Europe in 1554 by the Spanish conquistador Pizarro, who brought it from South America, where it had long been cultivated by the Indians of the Andes Mountains in Chile and Peru. A few years later it was introduced to the British Isles by Sir Walter Raleigh (who also brought tobacco back from the New World). Over the next century or so it spread across Europe, becoming especially important in Ireland and Germany. The French regarded the potato as unfit for human consumption.

Tulip (1554)

Augier de Busbecq, Austrian ambassador at the court of Süleyman the Magnificent, was also an amateur botanist. In 1554 he discovered a flower in Persia and sent seeds and bulbs to Vienna.

A French botanist sent the first tulips to a trial garden in Leyden, Holland some years later, and the reign of the Dutch tulip began.

However, it was not until the 1730s that tulip mania began; fortunes were gained and lost because of the flower as it spread to the gardens throughout Europe and then to the rest of the world.

Carrot (16th century)

The wild carrot came from Afghanistan long before the time of Christ. The Greeks and Romans did not set much store by it, and it was used only for limited medicinal purposes before the 16th century, when the Italians brought it to the world's attention. Although it was tasty, the carrot of the time had almost nothing in common with the vegetable of today. It was a thin white or yellow root and fairly tough. It took centuries of selection and hybridization to give it the orange color it has had since the early 19th century.

Tomato (1596)

Of South American origin, the tomato was brought to Europe in 1596. At first cultivated as a curiosity, it was considered to be a violent poison.

This vegetable–fruit had to wait more than two centuries before its nutritional qualities were recognized. President Thomas Jefferson cultivated the tomato in his garden but didn't eat the fruit.

Begonia (1690)

At the end of the 17th century, Father Plumier, explorer and botanist, was working with plants in Haiti when he discovered the first flowers of a new plant. He immediately dedicated the species to Michel Begon, the governor of Santo Domingo. Despite their virtues, it took nearly an entire century for begonias to be known and cultivated throughout Europe.

Strawberry (1714)

It is to François Frézier (France), an officer of the French navy and author of a *Treatise on Fireworks*, that we owe the pleasure of eating today's fat, juicy strawberries. Frézier had been sent to the South American coast in 1714 to study the fortifications of Chile and Peru. The five plants of *Fragaria chiloensis* (Chilean strawberry) that he brought back to Brittany in France did not bear fruit, but they pollinated other species that had been brought from Virginia, to produce the first of our modern strawberries.

Dahlia (1789)

The first dahlia was sent from Mexico to Madrid in 1789. It was given its name by the botanist Cavanilles (Spain) in honor of the Swedish botanist Andreas Dahl, himself a student of Carolus Linnaeus, the Swedish founder of the modern classification of plants.

Grapefruit (1809)

Count Odette Phillippe (France), a surgeon in Napoleon's army captured at the battle of Trafalgar, was imprisoned by the British in the Bahamas. It was there that he discovered the *Citrus paradisi* or grapefruit, which grew there in abundance. When he was freed two years later, he set himself up as a doctor in Charleston, S.C., before moving to Florida, where, in 1809, he established a citrus fruit plantation using seeds and plants from the Bahamas. Sixty years later, the grapefruit was a major source of revenue for Texas, Arizona and California.

It was not until 1914 that the fruit crossed the Atlantic and arrived in Palestine, where large orchards were planted.

Chicory (1850)

In the underground passages of the Brussels Botanical Gardens, where he was head gardener, M. Bréziers had the idea of forcing a few roots of the chicory used in coffee and then eating the young shoots. The original strain has been extensively hybridized and selected so that today we can enjoy this gently bitter salad vegetable all through the winter.

Granny Smith and Golden Delicious (19th century)

It was Miss Granny Smith who, in Australia in 1868, first grew this green apple flecked with white, with juicy, tart-tasting flesh. As for the famous Golden Delicious, it was born in West Virginia at the end of the 19th century in the orchards of Anderson H. Mullins. By 1914 this apple was already widely known and planted in various parts of the United States.

Orchid (1898)

In 1898 Noël Bernard (France) discovered that orchid seeds, in order to germinate and guarantee the first stage of development of the embryo, needed to be in contact with a microscopic fungus that lives in symbiosis with the plant's roots. Bernard invented a way to allow the seed to germinate independent of the plant.

In 1922 Dr. Lewis Knudson (U.S.) developed an environment that allowed germination without the presence of the fungus.

Kiwi fruit (1959)

Chinese gooseberry and Yang Tao are just two of the names given to *Actinidia chinensis*, a plant discovered on the banks of the Yang-Tse River in 1845 and brought to the West at the end of the last century.

In 1906 this prolific creeper arrived in New Zealand, where it aroused the interest of local farmers who became the first in the world to plant orchards and export this new fruit.

The New Zealanders wanted to emphasize the originality of their product, and in 1959 they chose to give this fruit the name of the symbolic bird of their country: kiwi.

Black tulip (1986)

After its long existence as a legend, the black tulip is now a reality. In 1979 Geert Hageman (Netherlands) put pollen from the "Wienerwald" variety on the stamen of a "Queen of the Night," creating the first black tulip. It was not until 1986 that the bulb he thus obtained and raised produced its first flower. The demands of reproduction meant that only three bulbs existed in 1987 and a dozen in 1988. Fields of black tulips are still some way off.

The Big Boy tomato, named for David Burpee's then-four-year-old son Jonathan, was developed by Ovid Shifriss in 1949. (W. Atlee Burpee & Co.)

WHAT ON EARTH?

NOT ALL INVENTIONS CHANGE OUR LIVES, SOME JUST MAKE US SCRATCH OUR HEADS.

THE ULTIMATE INSECTICIDE?

Left: This "Terminator"-like machine is not the ultimate insecticide, but the latest in soil samplers. Designed at the National Soil Tilth Laboratory in Ames, Iowa, the machine measures the effect that tilling practices have on pesticide seepage. (National Soil Tilth Laboratory)

DESIGNER COWS

▼ This is not the newest line in genetically engineered cattle, but the latest idea in keeping cows warm. Designed by Mosaku Sakurai (Japan), these eye catching synthetic-fiber cow blankets are coated with aluminum and silver. (Gamma/Wada)

QUICKER PACKER

▼ In 1986 Dieter Pfister received a patent for the Quicker Packer, a rake and funnel device designed to take the backache out of the fall cleanup. In 1992, Pfister received a U.S. patent for an updated model. (Pfister Enterprises)

ZOO DOO

Pierce Ledbetter (U.S.) has launched Zoo Doo compost, a product that consists mainly of rhinoceros and elephant manure. Many zoos do in fact recycle their animals' excrement and use it as compost on their grounds. Data on these exotic composts is not available but, as Ledbetter states, "People just get a real kick out of using rhinocerous doo."

PLANTOPHONE

Presented at the Brussels Trade Fair, Belgium in 1987, this "telephone for plants" was invented by M. Heusquin (Belgium). It is shaped like a probe and penetrates into the heart of the plant. When the plant is thirsty, a little red light flashes, accompanied by an audible signal that repeats every five seconds. Once the plant has drunk its fill, the device gives a little bleep, and a green light comes on when the desired level of water has been reached.

New ideas that may change the way we live

EDIBLE COTTON

Cottonseed contains the toxin gossypol, which is harmful to humans. Due to the abundance of cotton in the southern United States, researchers have worked to find a way to remove gossypol from the seed and produce a seed that can be used in cooking. A team of scientists from the Institute of Research into Cotton and Exotic Textiles has managed to extract the gossypol from the seeds and transform them into oils and flour. Besides tasting good, these products are reportedly of great nutritional value.

BEE LANGUAGE COMMUNICATION

In 1973, Karl von Frisch (Austria, 1886–1982) was awarded the Nobel Prize for Medicine and Physiology for discovering how bees communicate. Bees use a language that takes the form of a dance describing a figure eight. The orientation and rhythm of the dance indicate the direction and distance of a food source.

Axel Michelsen (Denmark), a specialist in animal acoustic communication at the University of Odense, Denmark had the idea of building a robot that incorporated all known data about bee language, so as to guide worker bees artificially. In collaboration with Wolfgang Kirchener (Germany) of the University of Würzburg, Germany, Michelsen has built an artifact slightly bigger than an average-size bee, covered with a thin layer of wax from the hive. A very fine shaft linked to a motor makes the robot spin and reproduce the positions of the body during the dance. A tiny plastic tube ending in the robot's head deposits sugary water and stimulates the regurgitations.

These mechanisms are piloted by a programmed microcomputer. Experiments have proved that the system works, and it is hoped that it can be perfected as a practical tool in the production of honey.

HYPERIMMUNE MILK AND EGGS

Over the past decade, the Stolle Research and Development Company has received several U.S. patents for processing methods used in the production of hyperimmune milk and eggs, and compounds that are found in them, such as a natural anti-inflammatory compound that can relieve pain and appears to be safer than aspirin. This futuristic-sounding concept is in fact part of a growing field called *nutriceuticals*—the production of natural-food products that yield medical benefits as well as high nutrition.

Stolle researchers, using the principle that animals naturally produce antibodies to fight disease, have injected cows and eggs with dead bacteria of the types that infect humans. The result has been that milk and eggs have been produced containing antibodies that aid humans in fighting such diseases as tooth decay, stomach infections and salmonella. These products have not been approved by the Food and Drug Administration for human consumption, and they raise so many issues that it is expected to be several years before they are cleared for use by the public.

ANTISENSE POLYGALACTURONASE (PG) GENE

Most tomatoes sold in stores are picked while still green, and ripen in transit to the store. However, consumers often complain that the flavor is not as good as that of fresh-picked tomatoes. Recognizing this problem, the American company Calgene has patented the PG Gene (commercial trademark FLAVR SAVR), which is the critical ingredient in producing a genetically enhanced tomato that can be picked ripe and can last for two weeks before rotting. These genetically engineered tomatoes, it is claimed, retain their flavor when they reach the consumer. This happens because the PG Gene suppresses the production of the PG enzyme, the enzyme that causes the pectin degradation that results in fruit softening. This type of biotechnology research is being applied by many companies to other fruits and vegetables such as carrots, celery and peppers.

BIOINSECTICIDES

The destructive impact of synthetic chemical insecticides on the environment has led to an extensive search for alternative, environment-friendly pest controls. In July 1992 the American company Mycogen received the first federal approval for a genetic- ally engineered insecticide, MVP. This bioinsecticide is made up of biotoxins that are formed naturally from bacteria. These biotoxins kill selected insects but are not harmful to crops, wildlife or humans.

GENETIC MAPPING

A technique to help farmers select the best breeding combinations for commercial dairy and beef cattle, gene mapping is being developed by the American company Genmark. The system identifies traits such as milk proteins, milk-producing potential and growth rates via genetic markers applied during the breeding process. From this data, farmers are able to identify the most commercially desirable types of cattle for breeding.

FRUIT STORAGE

In April 1992 the British agricultural ministry unveiled a new facility at its Horticultural Research Institute that will be used to research optimum conditions for storing fruit crops after picking. Presently, researchers are testing apples for their response to temperature, humidity and gas mixture fluctuations. It is hoped that the results of this research will allow farmers to preserve their crops by holding them in better storage facilities, rather than relying on fungicides.

WHITE MARIGOLDS

In 1954 David Burpee (U.S.) offered a $10,000 prize to the gardener who could breed a white marigold. It wasn't until 1975 that the prize was won. W. Atlee Burpee & Co. has been attempting to produce a perfectly white hybrid from the prize-winning specimen, and in 1992 the company announced that it had succeeded. This pure white marigold, called French Vanilla, will be launched for the 1993 growing season.

The first pure white marigold, French Vanilla, will be launched in 1993. (W. Atlee Burpee & Co.)

3 INDUSTRY, ENERGY AND THE ENVIRONMENT

HYDRAULICS

Vertical water-raising wheel (5th century B.C.)

The first waterwheel was invented in the Middle East sometime between the 5th and 3rd centuries B.C. It was a vertical wheel used to elevate water, not to drive it.

The dam (3000 B.C.)

The oldest dam on record was built in Egypt about 3000 B.C. Initially, dams were used to create reservoirs to supply water to towns and for irrigation, but later they were used to produce energy.

It was François Zola (France), father of the author, who in 1843–59 constructed the first modern arch dam near Aix-en-Provence, but it was a technique that was not widely adopted. There are two other types of dam: the gravity dam and the coffer dam. The first of these, after being studied mathematically, was constructed on the River Furan at St-Etienne in 1861–66, and the first big dam of the second type was the Panama Dam, built in 1912.

Archimedes' screw (3rd century B.C.)

One of the greatest scientists of antiquity, Archimedes (Greece, 287–212 B.C.), invented the hydraulic screw. This device is made of an inclined cylinder that encases a broad-threaded screw. It is used to raise water, to service whatever purpose is needed. The device is introduced into a body of water, then the screw is rapidly turned, so that the water rises from whorl to whorl.

Undershot waterwheel (1st century B.C.)

The undershot waterwheel was the first hydraulic engine invented. It derives from the vertical wheel, but the exact date of its development is unknown. Undershot wheels (moved by water passing beneath) were used to turn grindstones in water mills by the 1st century B.C.

Horizontal waterwheel (1st century A.D.)

The horizontal wheel was developed in the mountainous regions of the Middle East during the 1st century A.D. It was equipped with paddles driven by the force of flow in mountain streams.

Overshot waterwheel (4th century A.D.)

The overshot waterwheel was introduced by the Romans in the 4th century. The design was based on the undershot waterwheel, using buckets instead of paddles. This design was used by all industries up until the end of the 18th century.

Hydraulic ram (1796)

In 1796 Joseph (1740–1810) and Etienne (1745–99) de Montgolfier (both France) had the idea of utilizing the kinetic energy of running water in a pipe to force a portion of the liquid mass to a higher level than its source. The energy was transferred through what they called the ram effect. The principle was to be improved by Amédée Bollée (France, 1844–1917), another builder of hydraulic rams.

Poncelet wheel (1827)

In 1827 Jean Victor Poncelet (France, 1789–1867) published his *Paper on Curved-paddle Waterwheels Driven from Beneath*. This work defined improvements to the design of undershot wheels, leading eventually to the turbine.

Fourneyron turbine (1832)

In 1832, Benoit Fourneyron (France, 1802–67) patented the first water turbine, the outward-flow reaction turbine.

Francis turbine (1855)

In 1855, *Lowell Hydraulic Experiments* was published by James Francis (U.S., b. Great Britain). In it he described the invention of a reaction turbine intended for medium to small falls of water. Today it is the most used reaction turbine.

Hydroelectric power (1869)

On September 28, 1869, Aristide Bergès (France, 1833–1904) became the first to convert the mechanical energy of a waterfall in the Alps into electrical energy, which he used to operate the machines in his factory. He achieved this by the used of forced conduits.

In 1886–87 he organized an extremely dangerous operation. At a depth of 82 ft below the bottom of Lake Crozet, which stands at an altitude of 6,459 ft, he excavated an overflow gallery, to collect surplus water.

ELECTRICITY

Voltaic cell (1800)

The voltaic cell, the first electric cell, was built by Alessandro Volta (Italy, 1745–1827) in 1800. Volta had studied the work of Luigi Galvani (Italy, 1737–98), who had observed that two different metals put in contact with a muscle in a dead frog caused the muscle to contract. Volta attributed the muscle response to an interaction with the two metals. This gave him the idea for building an electric battery. He soldered a copper ring and a zinc ring together, piled them up in a set order, separated them with felt rings soaked in acidulated water, and discovered that chemical energy could be converted into electrical energy. The battery permitted measurement of differences in electrical potential (voltage). The word *volt* was coined as a unit of electrical measurement in Volta's honor.

In 1831 Michael Faraday (Great Britain, 1791–1867) managed to produce an electric current by induction, rotating a metal disc across magnetic lines of force. This was the first induction electric generator and the first machine to convert mechanical energy into electrical energy. The first generators driven by steam engines soon made their appearance. These large and not very powerful machines provided an alternating current.

Accumulator (1802)

Johann Wilhelm Ritter (Germany, 1776–1810) was the first to attribute the generation of current in batteries to a chemical transformation. He succeeded in 1802 in recharging a battery after it had discharged, and so discovered the principle of the accumulator.

It was not until 1860 that the first practical accumulator was built. Gaston Planté (France, 1834–89) developed this accumulator, which consisted of two plates of lead rolled into spirals and bathed in dilute sulphuric acid. In 1880, Camille Faure (France) perfected this accumulator by pasting lead oxide onto the lead strips, thus increasing capacity. At this time, Gramme dynamos appeared (see below), which secured this accumulator's future by offering a high performance method for recharging.

Thermoelectric effect (1823)

In 1823, Thomas Johann Seebeck (Germany, 1770–1831) observed that if heat was applied to the junction of two different metals that were joined in a closed circuit, it had the effect of making the needle of a compass deviate. An electric current had therefore been created within the wiring. The Seebeck or thermoelectric effect found a practical application about a century and a half later with semiconductor techniques.

Magneto (1832)

On the advice of Ampère, Hippolyte Pixii (France, 1800–35) built the first magneto-electric (magneto for short) generator in 1832, which was perfected by Faraday's induction electric generator (see above).

Daniell cell (1836)

In 1836 John Frederic Daniell (Great Britain, 1790–1845) invented the first impolarizable battery. Daniell's battery improved on the volta cell by eliminating hydrogen. Hydrogen present in the volta cell had created a barrier (polarization) at the positive pole, blocking the flow of current.

Lead–acid storage battery (1859)

In 1859, Gaston Planté (France, 1834–89) invented the first electric storage cell: the lead–acid battery.

Johann Wilhelm Ritter (Germany, 1776–1810) had observed in 1803, on a lead plate voltmeter, the principle according to which this kind of secondary cell works.

Lead–acid batteries are still the most common type of battery.

Previous page: The interior of a tokamak. (CEA)

Leclanché cell (1866)

In 1866, Georges Leclanché (France, 1839–82) applied for a patent for a battery with a solid rather than liquid depolarizant. The Leclanché battery had a zinc anode, a mixture of carbon-manganese dioxide for cathode, and a saline electrolyte of ammonium chloride (hence it is sometimes called a saline battery). The Leclanché cell was further developed by Charles Féry (France, 1865–1935) and is still in use today. In 1881, Félix Lalande and Georges Chaperon (both France) developed an alkaline version of the Leclanché battery.

Dynamo (1871)

On July 17, 1871, the French Academy of Sciences gave an enthusiastic welcome to Zénobe Gramme (Belgium, 1826–1901). He had been living in France since 1856 and had invented the dynamo (short for dynamoelectric generator), which was a generator of continuous and completely reversible electric current.

With his invention, which marked the beginning of electrical technology, Gramme combined many of the discoveries and inventions made since the invention of the magneto. Although an early version of the dynamo had been constructed by Antonio Pacinotti (Italy) in 1860, it had not advanced beyond the experimental stage. Gramme's dynamo was developed by Friedrich von Hefner-Alteneck (Germany) in 1873.

Alternator (1878)

In 1878 the French company Gramme, founded by Zénobe Gramme (Belgium, 1826–1901) and Hippolyte Fontaine (France), manufactured the first alternators. A German company founded by Werner von Siemens (1816–92) began producing them at the same time.

An alternator is a device that transforms mechanical energy into electrical energy; it produces an alternating current.

Transformer (1882)

The principle of the transformer, which enables the parameters of electrical current to be modified (i.e., in voltage strength), was demonstrated by Michael Faraday (Great Britain, 1791–1867), who built a transformer in his laboratory.

The modern transformer was invented simultaneously by Lucien Gaulard (France), William Stanley (U.S.) and John Dixon Gibbs (Great Britain) between 1882 and 1885.

Transmission of electricity (1882)

In 1882 Marcel Deprez (France, 1842–1918) carried out the first transmission of electricity through high-voltage cables. On September 25, 1882 he transmitted a continuous electric current from Miesbach to Munich along a telegraph wire. On February 6, 1883 an amazed crowd, gathered at Porte de la Chapelle in Paris, saw an electric motor start up at the same time as an apparently unconnected dynamo situated next to it. In fact the motor was connected by an electricity line that ran to Le Bourget and back to Paris.

Dry cell (1887)

Dry cells are batteries in which the electrolyte is in the state of humid paste. Since no liquid can leak out, the dry cell is portable. Hellesen (Great Britain) is generally credited with building the first dry cell, which he developed in 1887 as a portable version of the Leclanché cell.

Photoelectric cell (c. 1895)

The photoelectric cell was invented by Julius Elster (Germany, 1854–1920) and Hans F. Geitel (Germany, 1855–1923) around 1895. It has the ability to transform a luminous flux into an electric current. Production of the photoelectric cell depends on selenium, a nonmetallic crystalline solid, discovered in 1817 by Jons Jacob Berzelius (Sweden).

Alkaline storage batteries (1914)

Around 1914 the ingenious inventor Thomas Edison (U.S., 1847–1931) developed the first alkaline storage battery, so called because the electrolyte is not acid but basic nickel–iron and nickel–cadmium storage cells.

The iron–zinc battery was developed in 1941 by H. André (France).

The energy storage efficiency of this kind of battery is two to three times better than that of the lead battery.

Fuel cell (1936)

Designed by Bacon (U.S.) in 1936, the fuel cell has a much longer lifespan than normal batteries, as the fuel supply can be renewed. Industrial production of fuel cells did not begin until 1960. Spacecraft use cells fueled by hydrogen, with combustion supported by oxygen.

Magneto-hydrodynamic generator (1959)

In 1959 the Avro Research Laboratories in Massachusetts built the first magneto-hydrodynamic generator in a purely experimental form. The generator was capable of directly transforming calorific energy into electrical energy. It was a practical demonstration of theoretical work carried out 10 years earlier by Hannes Alfvén (Sweden), Nobel Prize winner in 1970.

Lithium battery (1975)

Lithium anode batteries, marketed from 1975 on, proved a great step forward in battery technology. The energy per unit in this generation of batteries was nearly three times that of the previous best. These types of batteries have many applications in many fields, such as medicine (heart stimulators), computer memory banks and telecommunications. Their resistance to extreme temperatures (from -55° Celsius to 175° Celsius) makes them invaluable to the military.

Nickel–iron battery (1983)

The improvement of storage batteries has been a constant preoccupation of car manufacturers. One of the lines of research has been directed toward new galvanic couples, nickel–iron in particular, which had been considered by Thomas Edison toward the end of the 19th century.

Since the appearance of the first electric Nissan Micra at the end of 1983, many prototypes have been produced by Japanese car manufacturers, who are convinced of the superiority of this type of battery in terms of durability and power. But they are not as yet being mass-produced. In Europe similar efforts are being made, notably by Mercedes and Peugeot, the latter in collaboration with Saft, a French company specializing in different types of battery, which provided the battery for the prototype of the electric Peugeot 205.

Marcel Deprez is credited with performing the first transmission of electricity through high-voltage cables in 1882. (Sodel)

PETROLEUM

Origins (antiquity)

Petroleum has been used since the dawn of civilization. The Egyptians used pitch to preserve their mummies, and the Chinese used it for heating houses, cooking and making bricks. In Europe the oil was first used to grease chariot wheels and as an ingredient in medicine.

Drilling (2nd century B.C.)

Drilling exploration was first undertaken in China in the 2nd century B.C. Oil wells were bored using bamboo stems and bronze pipes.

Refining (distillation) (unknown)

Refining permits the breakdown of petroleum into hydrocarbon derivatives, such as propane, gasoline, diesel fuel and lubricating oil. The origins of the refining process are unknown but must be tied to the first uses of petroleum. In 1556 Georg Bauer (Germany, also known as Georgius Agricola) explained how to refine caulking tar from petroleum in his work *De Re Metallica*.

Rotary drilling (1844)

Robert Beart (Great Britain) filed the first patent for rotary drilling in 1844. Beart's method consisted of a boring bit with toothed rollers rotating around a central rod. This was improved by Rodolphe Leschot (France) in 1863 when he introduced a wear-resistant diamond bit.

Oil lamp (1840s)

Outside China, oil was not used as a source of lighting until the mid-19th century, when a colorless liquid was extracted from crude oil—a liquid which, when lit, burned with a flame strong enough to provide light without producing offensive smells. This liquid, used in lamps, was known as burning oil.

Gasoline (1855)

In 1855 Benjamin Silliman (U.S.), making use of studies on the composition of petroleum performed by European chemists, undertook a series of distillation experiments. From this research he obtained a number of new products: tar, lubricating oil, naphtha, paint solvents and gasoline, which was used as a stain remover and considered of minor importance.

Offshore drilling (1869)

On May 4, 1869, Thomas F. Rowland (U.S.) filed the first patent for a fixed drilling platform. The first working offshore oil well was built off the coast of California in 1897.

Also in 1869, Samuel Lewis described the principle of the self-elevating mobile platform, but it wasn't until 1954 that the first platform of this type was built.

Multistep refining (1873)

As the quantities of crude oil to be treated increased, it became necessary to develop processes that would handle all the stages of refining in the same installation. The process known as multistep refining was first developed by A.A. Tavrisov (Russia) in Baku, Russia in 1873. In 1877, unaware of Tavrisov's system, Samuel Van Sycle (U.S.) invented the same process at Titusville, Pa. In 1880–81 the Nobel brothers developed a new multistep method using stills in a cascade arrangement. The refining process column was finally perfected by the American company Power Speciality Co. in 1926.

Oil tanker (1886)

The first tanker designed specifically for the transport of oil was the German ship the *Glückauf*, launched in 1886.

Cracking process (1891)

The cracking process is a refining process that increases the efficiency of fuel production from petroleum. It permits the transformation of a certain number of heavy residues from the refining process into light by-products, principally gasoline and diesel fuel.

Thermal cracking was invented by Vladimir Chukhov (Russia) in 1891. In 1913 W.M. Burton (U.S.), head of manufacturing at Standard Oil of Indiana, patented a cracking process involving high temperatures and high pressure. In 1915 Jesse Dubbs (U.S.) improved the process, and Shell Oil was granted the license in 1919.

Subterranean storage (1916)

The process for storing hydrocarbons in a gaseous form underground was patented by the German company Deutsche Erdöl in 1916.

Turbodrilling (1922)

Turbodrilling was developed by the Soviet Union. The bit was powered by circulating drilling mud "driven" by Kapeliushnikov turbines. The drill shaft no longer turned, thus it did not wear. The first experiment was conducted in 1922.

Well-logging (or electrical core sampling) (1927)

The first attempt at electrical core sampling, the method by which the nature of the substrata is determined by taking electric measurements, was carried out on September 5, 1927. The test was performed by a team from the French company Schlumberger under the direction of Henri Doll.

Catalytic cracking (1937)

In 1937 Eugène Houdry (France) outlined a new cracking process in which the cracking of vaporized oil was promoted by a catalyst; this process became known as catalytic cracking. Houdry had been working on his theory for nearly 10 years. Catalytic cracking proved a success, since it created products far superior to those obtained by thermal cracking.

Catalytic reformation (1949)

Catalytic reformation was invented in 1949 by V. Haensel for the Universal Oil Products Co. This operation permits the composition of gasoline to be modified, specifically to increase the octane levels.

Electrodrilling (1949)

This method was invented by the American company Electrodrill Corp. in 1949. With this

This underwater hydrocarbon production station, situated at the bottom of the North Sea, is the first ever built. Part of the *Skuld* research project, the station became operational in 1988. (Elf Aquitaine)

method, a motor is attached to a cable rather than to the drill shaft.

Horizontal drilling (1980)

In 1980 the French companies Elf Aquitaine and IFP (French Oil Institute) carried out the first successful horizontal drilling (for natural gas) in Lacq. In 1982 these same two companies completed the first horizontal offshore drilling (for crude oil) at Rospo Mare, Italy.

Underwater hydrocarbon production station (1988)

Elf Aquitaine completed the construction of the first underwater hydrocarbon production station, Skuld, in September 1988. Installed in the Norwegian North Sea, it is capable of producing 8 billion cubic meters of gas in 360 feet of water.

STEAM ENGINES

Origins (1st century A.D.)

Hero of Alexandria, a Greek mathematician, outlined his theory for a machine he called an aeolipile in the 1st century A.D. The proposed aeolipile was a steam-operated wheel, but no attempt was ever made to build it.

Connecting-rod system (14th–15th century)

Historians date the connecting-rod system to the turn of the 15th century. The system enabled a continuous circular movement to be converted into a rectilinear up-and-down movement, or vice versa. The system spread rapidly, and its uses were applied to saws, pumps and wheels. Two hundred years later, it contributed to the development of the steam engine.

Atmospheric engine (1661)

The aim of the first steam engines was to utilize atmospheric pressure to generate power. In 1843 Evangelista Torricelli (Italy) discovered and demonstrated the principle of atmospheric pressure, which led to his invention of the barometer. At Magdeburg, Germany in 1654, Otto von Guericke (Germany, 1602–86) performed an experiment that demonstrated the force of atmospheric pressure (two teams of draft horses could not pull apart two 20-inch-diameter close-fitting balls).

In 1661 von Guericke invented a machine that consisted of a metal cyclinder inside which a piston moved up and down. Using his pump, von Guericke created a partial vacuum inside the cyclinder, and the piston plunged downward within the cylinder, lifting a weight by means of a system of ropes and pulleys. This was the first time air pressure was seen to be performing a function.

Newcomen's steam engine, built in 1703, was the first successful steam engine. James Watt used Newcomen's engine as a prototype for his machine, which launched the Industrial Revolution. (Josse)

Papin's engine (1679)

Denis Papin (France, 1647–c. 1712) had the idea of creating a void behind the piston by using the evaporation and condensation properties of water. In 1679 he invented a safety valve for his steam digester (the prototype of the pressure cooker) which gave him the idea of developing a cylindrical machine in which a piston would be steam-operated.

Newcomen's engine (1712)

As mining industries developed in size and scope in the 17th century, the problem of flooding in the mines became a major concern. By the early 18th century several attempts at developing water pumps had been made. In 1698, Thomas Savery (Great Britain, c. 1650–1715) registered a patent for a steam pump that was capable of extracting water from great depths. This machine had no piston or valve and, proving to be unstable, was abandoned. In 1705, Thomas Newcomen (Great Britain, 1663–1729) joined forces with Savery and in 1712

built the first practical steam engine. Newcomen's engine was designed to operate with steam at atmospheric pressure (boiling point) and could be built by the craftsmen of the day.

Watt's steam engine (1765)

After repairing a version of Newcomen's engine in 1763, James Watt (Great Britain, 1736–1819) had the idea of converting the steam engine into a steam motor. In 1765 Watt built a Newcomen engine fitted with a separate condenser, which improved efficiency. He patented this engine in 1769, but could not afford to continue his work alone, and entered into a partnership with Matthew Boulton (Great Britain, 1728–1809), a manufacturer in Birmingham, England. Watt continued to refine the engine, making it double-acting, allowing power in the upward and downward movement, introducing rotary beam motion and sun-and-planet gearing. Such was the efficiency and reliability of the machine that by 1790 over 500 steam engines had been produced by Watt and

Boulton; the steam engine became the instrument of the Industrial Revolution.

Multiple expansion engine (1803)

In 1803, Arthur Woolf (Great Britain, 1776–1837) patented the first multiple expansion engine. This was a machine with two or three cylinders in which the steam expanded consecutively.

High-pressure engine (1805)

Jacob Leupold (Germany) published a design for a high-pressure noncondensing steam engine c. 1723, but there is no evidence that it was ever built. The first high-pressure steam engine was built by Richard Trevithick (Great Britain, 1771–1833) in 1805.

AUTOMOTIVE ENGINES

Piston engine (1673)

Christiaan Huygens (Netherlands, 1629–95) demonstrated the first piston engine in 1673. Huygens's engine was operated by a charge of gunpowder in a cylinder beneath the piston. The force of the explosion pushed the piston up, and it came down as the gas cooled. Huygens's engine proved impracticable, but his concept was sound. However, it wasn't until the early 19th century that his theory was reexamined.

Closed system hot-air engine (1816)

In 1816 Robert Stirling (Great Britain) invented the closed system hot-air engine. However, the first Stirling engine was not manufactured industrially until 1844.

Water-cooled engine (1823)

In 1823 Samuel Brown (Great Britain) invented a water-cooling system. In Brown's engine, water was circulated around cylinders lined with jackets. Water was driven by a pump and cooled when it came into contact with the ambient air.

Open system hot-air engine (1851)

In 1851 John Ericsson (U.S.) patented the open system hot-air engine. Ericsson's engine was an upright in-line, four-cylinder engine rated at approximately 50 horsepower. It was built for a transatlantic ship that bore his name, and was launched in 1858.

Two-stroke engine without preliminary compression (1860)

The first operational internal-combustion engine was invented in 1860 by Étienne Lenoir (France, 1822–1900). Lenoir's engine was characterized by a two-stroke operating cycle fueled by coal gas, with a horsepower rating from 0.5 to 12 hp. Despite its low efficiency, the Lenoir engine gained popularity rapidly.

"Air-breathing" engine (1867)

In 1867 Nikolaus Otto (Germany, 1832–91) and Eugen Langen (Germany) designed the "air-breathing" engine. It became the most widely used internal-combustion engine until the introduction of the four-stroke engine in 1876.

Brayton engine (1873)

In 1873 an engineer named Brayton (U.S.) built the first engine that used preliminary fuel compression as part of its operating cycle. The Brayton engine uses a two-stroke system with combustion at constant pressure, making it the predecessor of the diesel engine.

Four-stroke internal-combustion engine (1876)

In 1876 Nikolaus Otto (Germany, 1832–91) patented the first four-stroke internal-combustion engine. It had a single piston that was horizontally oriented, employed flame ignition, was water-cooled, and operated on coal gas fuel. Otto presented the engine at the 1878 World's Fair in Paris, France, where its smooth performance and high efficiency gained wide acclaim and marked the engine as a landmark in engine development.

Double-piston engine (1878)

The first double-piston engine was built in 1878 by Ferdinand Kindermann (Germany) for the German company Hannverscher Maschinenbau A.G.

Two-stroke internal-combustion engine (1879)

To avoid Otto's patent for the four-stroke engine, Dugald Clerk (Great Britain) designed the two-stroke internal-combustion engine for the British company Sterne & Co. in 1879. The two-stroke engine was less efficient than the four-stroke, but it had a higher fuel rating and is still used in vehicles such as mopeds.

Four-stroke gasoline engine (1883)

In 1883 Edouard Delamarre-Debouteville and Léon Malandin (both France) built the first gasoline-fed four-stroke engine. It was experimental and was not produced commercially. On January 29, 1886, Karl Benz (Germany, 1844–1929) patented the first truly efficient four-stroke gasoline engine.

Revolving cylinder engine (1887)

In 1887 an engineer named Millet (France) developed the first radial, rotating-cylinder engine. It was a five-cylinder engine with electrical ignition and slide-valve timing.

High-power gas engine (1888)

In 1888 Edouard Delamarre-Debouteville and Léon Malandin (both France) built the first gas engine with a single cylinder capable of producing 100 horsepower. The engine was horizontally oriented, and intake and ignition were regulated by a timing slide-valve system. In 1900 a refined version of this engine became the first to break the 1,000-horsepower barrier.

Radial engine (1888)

In 1888, Fernand Forest (France) designed a 12-cylinder radial engine. The 12 cylinders were laid in four parallel banks of three cylinders each. The radial engine was widely used in aviation because of its compact size.

Four-cylinder linear engine (1889)

The straight four-cylinder engine conceived by Fernand Forest (France) in 1889 is characterized by a four-stroke cycle. The four cylinders, situated at the same level, are cast into the engine block and covered by a quadruple detachable cylinder head. This engine is the most commonly used in European-built automobiles.

V-type engine (1889)

The V-type engine was designed and built by Gottlieb Daimler (Germany, 1834–1900) and Wilhelm Maybach (Germany) in 1889. The V-type was made up of two cylinders joined at an angle of 17 degrees. It produced 1.5 horsepower at 600 rpm. The engine was installed in an automobile designed by Maybach, which is now regarded as the first modern automobile.

Separate combustion chamber engine (1890)

The first engines to be designed with separate combustion chambers were built in 1890 by Herbert Ackroyd-Stuart (Great Britain). This system was the forerunner of the surface-ignition engine (also known as the hot-bulb engine) that was perfected by Rundölf (Sweden) in 1902.

Diesel engine (1893)

In 1893 Rudolf Diesel (Germany, 1858–1913) built the first prototype of the internal-combustion piston engine, later termed the diesel engine. This four-stroke engine was mass-produced from 1897 onwards. A diesel engine compresses air to the point where the rise in temperature is sufficient to automatically ignite the fuel, which is injected at the end of the compression stroke. This is the most efficient heat engine and is still widely used today.

Opposed-cylinder engine (1895)

The flat-twin, the first horizontally opposed cylinder engine, was developed by Albert de Dion and Georges Boulton (both France) in 1895. This engine could have several pairs of cylinders. The prototype had two cylinders and produced 1.5 horsepower. The following year,

Karl Benz (Germany, 1844–1929) constructed a similar two-cylinder engine that generated 5 to 14 horsepower.

Two-stroke diesel engine (1899)

In 1899 Hugo Guldner (Germany) developed the two-stroke diesel engine. This permitted a considerable increase in the specific power of the diesel, from 60 to 80 percent for the same displacement. Two-stroke diesels are currently the most powerful internal-combustion engines, producing 50,000 horsepower. They are used to power naval vessels and high-power industrial engines.

Rotary engine (1956)

Developed in 1956 by Felix Wankel (Germany), the rotary engine was first used by the Japanese company Mazda in 1967.

Two-stroke engine (automobile) (1988)

Since World War II, the two-stroke engine has been virtually excluded from the automobile industry, but in 1973 Ralph Sarich (Australia, b. Yugoslavia) invented an ingeniously designed thermal engine that revived interest among the industry leaders. Sarich, with a grant from the Australian government, set up the Orbital Engine Co., which carried out research into the adaptation of the engine for automobiles.

In 1988 Orbital signed agreements with the Ford Motor Co. and General Motors to assist those companies in developing their own two-stroke engines. In 1992 Ford announced that it had built 25 two-stroke-engined Fiestas in England and that an experimental fleet of 60 cars should be running in 1993. Earlier in the year GM had announced the development of a 3.0 liter, V-6 two-stroke engine. The main advantages of the two-stroke engine over the four-stroke are greater fuel economy, better performance, less emissions and styling freedom.

Ignition Systems

Flame transfer (1836)

In 1836, William Barnett (Great Britain) designed the flame transfer ignition system. A constant flame sparked an intermittent flame, thus enabling the precompressed fuel mixture to be ignited at regular intervals. Barnett's system was replaced by the electric ignition system in 1900.

Ignition tube (1855)

The ignition tube was developed by Alfred Drake (U.S.) in 1855. Drake's system used a small, cast-iron tube that, when heated red-hot, provoked ignition on contact with the fuel mixture. The system was widely used from 1880 to 1905, but proved unusable in variable speed engines and was abandoned with their development.

Ignition magneto (1880)

The ignition magneto was invented by an engineer named Giesenberg (Germany) in 1880,

and perfected by Fernand Forest (France) and Nikolaus Otto (Germany, 1832–91). The magneto is a small generator of electric current that transforms the mechanical energy produced by the turning of the wheels into electrical energy. This produces a spark that fires the duel-air mixture. The first magnetos were of low tension.

Electric ignition by battery and spark coil (1885)

In 1885 Karl Benz (Germany, 1844–1929) reintroduced the electric ignition system that he had developed earlier and that had been used by Étienne Lenoir (France, 1822–1900) in his engine research. The Benz system relied on an accumulator to generate electricity, and although initially unreliable, it was adopted and is still the most widely used system in internal combustion engines.

Starter motor (1931)

The first starter motor designed for automobiles was developed by Maurice Gondard (France) in 1931.

Other Engine Components

Induction coil (1841)

The induction coil was invented in 1841 by Antoine Masson and Louis Breguet (both France). The induction coil uses electromagnetic induction to produce a high-voltage alternating current. It is fitted to all ignition systems in internal combustion engines.

Spark plugs (1885)

In 1885 Étienne Lenoir (France, 1822–1900) invented an electric spark plug very similar to the one still used. The igniting of fuel by a spark had been suggested by Alessandro Volta (Italy, 1745–1827) in 1777, and by Isaac de Rivaz for the internal combustion engine in 1807.

Carburetor (1893)

Wilhelm Maybach (Germany) invented the modern injection carburetor in 1893. An indispensable part of the engine, the carburetor is where the fuel mixture is prepared from air and gasoline vapor before being drawn into the cylinder.

The injection carburetor was first used in an engine with two parallel cylinders, known as the Phoenix engine, manufactured by Maybach and Daimler. It was one of the first operational gasoline engines intended for use in automobiles, and was extremely successful.

Throttle valve (1893)

The carburetor was improved by Karl Benz (Germany, 1844–1929) in the same year it was invented. Benz installed a throttle valve to regulate the amount of air and gas supplied to the

In 1992 both Ford and General Motors announced the development of two-stroke automobile engines. The Ford engine (top) will be tested in 60 cars in 1993. The 3.0 liter, V-6 engine (bottom) is also undergoing test trials. (Ford Motor Company, General Motors Corp.)

engine. This allowed the speed and power of the engine to be adjusted.

Radiator (1897)

The radiator was invented by Wilhelm Maybach (Germany) in 1897. After numerous attempts, Maybach perfected a honeycomb radiator, composed of a network of short, straight ducts through which the air blown in by a fan placed in front of it could circulate. The first radiators were built by the German company Daimler Motoren Gesellschaft, where Maybach worked.

Distributor (1908)

The distributor was invented by Edward A. Deeds and Charles F. Kettering (both U.S.) in 1908. While trying to perfect the ignition system of a car he was rebuilding, Deeds requested help from Kettering, who was an electrical engineer. Working together, they perfected what is considered the first distributor. They tested it on Deeds's car and approached Cadillac, who ordered 8,000 of them for the 1909 model. Returning by train from the Cadillac factory, Deeds and Kettering devised the name Delco for the distributor, using the initials of the newly formed company, the Dayton Engineering Laboratories Company.

TURBO ENGINES

Gas turbine (1791)

In 1791 John Barber (Great Britain) patented the design for what could have been the first gas turbine, but his idea never got past the planning stage.

Steam turbine (1884)

In 1884 Charles Parsons (Great Britain, 1854–1931) built the first steam turbine. This turbine was of the axial-flow type, consisted of two parts, and achieved 18,000 revolutions per minute.

Steam action turbine (1889)

In 1889 Carl Gustaf de Laval (Sweden) manufactured the first steam action turbine, a low-power, single-stage turbine.

Turbocompressor (1905)

While building a gas turbine, A. Büchi (Switzerland) envisaged replacing the combustion chamber with an internal combustion engine. This would eliminate the inconvenience caused by high pressure and high temperatures. From his research Büchi developed the supercharged diesel engine. In 1905 he patented the first turbocompressor. In 1908 Büchi joined the Swiss company Sulzer Frères, which manufactured the first turbocharged engine in 1911. It was a four-stroke single-cylinder diesel engine with pneumatic fuel injection.

Turbocompressor for aircraft engines (1917)

In 1917 Auguste Rateau (France) built the first turbocharged aircraft engine. It produced 50 horsepower, weighed 51 lb and turned at 30,000 rpm.

Turboprop (1920)

The turboprop engine, invented in 1920 by A.A. Griffith (Great Britain), is a gas turbine, the energy from which drives one or more propellers. The turboprop was used on aircraft that flew at speeds in the range of 370 to 500 mph.

Closed-cycle gas turbine (1940)

The closed-cycle gas turbine was invented in 1940 and developed by the Swiss company Escher-Wyss under the name of the Escher-Wyss aerodynamic turbine. Prof. Ackeret and Dr. Keller are credited with the invention.

Gasoline turbo (1967)

One of the most important developments in the history of the automobile has been the use of the turbocompressor in private cars. In 1967 the Swedish company Saab was the first to use turbocharging on its standard engine, producing greater power from a smaller amount of energy because of the system of supercharging applied to this type of engine. In 1974, BMW followed suit and subsequently introduced the turbo-diesel in its 5-24 model in 1983.

JET ENGINES

Ramjet engine (1913)

In 1913 an engineer named Lorin (France) patented the first ramjet engine, but it was never produced commercially. After World War I, the project was continued by René Leduc (France), who constructed the first prototype in 1936. It was not until 1949 that a machine propelled by a ramjet engine made its maiden flight. In spite of some impressive performances, the ramjet engine was replaced by the turbojet engine for various technical reasons, such as efficiency, ease of adjustment, etc. But, as a result of recent research by seven engineers from ONERA, the French National Office for Space Study and Research, and Aérospatiale, the ramjet engine has been revived and may well propel the spacecraft of the future.

Turbojet engine (1930)

It was Frank Whittle (Great Britain) who first attempted to construct a turbojet engine between 1928 and 1930.

The turbojet engine is a jet engine: the exhaust gases produced by reaction create the thrust of the engine and consequently propel the machine containing the engine.

The first British plane equipped with a turbojet engine was ready to fly on May 15, 1941. The turbojet engine of the Gloster Whittle E28 used a turbocompressor and produced a thrust of 827 lb. In Germany, Hans Pabst von Ohain started similar research in 1936 and a Heinkel fighter plane made its maiden flight in 1939.

The Concorde is equipped with Olympus turbojet engines, constructed by the English company Bristol Siddeley.

Turbofan engine (1940)

In 1940 the U.S. company Metropolitan Vickers developed a turbofan engine. This engine is intermediate between a turboprop and a turbojet. It has two advantages over these two other engine types: in-flight fuel consumption is 20 percent less, and there is less noise from the exhaust.

The turbofan engine has been widely used. Pratt & Whitney has built turbojets of this type for the Boeing 707, Boeing 720, Boeing 727, the Caravelle and the Douglas DC-8. General Electric and Rolls-Royce have produced turbofan engines as well.

Pulsejet engine (1940)

In 1940 the principle of the pulsejet was discovered by Paul Schmidt (Germany). He was trying to develop a ramjet that could start up under its own power. The pulsejet was immediately put to use on the German flying bomb, the V-1.

Turbojet with afterburner (1945)

In 1945 the British company Rolls-Royce constructed the first turbojet with an afterburner. Afterburning allows greater thrust to be obtained without substantial increase in engine weight. This increased thrust is particularly useful in takeoff.

The biggest drawback of afterburners is the very high fuel consumption. That is why they are used only very briefly, at takeoff, and to obtain peak speeds with fighter aircraft.

Propfan (1985)

After 10 years' research carried out under the auspices of NASA, the "propfan" project was disclosed in 1985. It combines a contra-rotating propeller and turbine that produces a very considerable saving on fuel.

The first demonstration of flight of the turbojet engine with a jet propeller took place on August 20, 1986 in a Boeing 727. However, despite very satisfactory results, Boeing, the world's leading aircraft constructor, seemed to want to shelve the project. It was McDonnell Douglas that continued the trials with the MD-80, resuming flights on May 18, 1987 in the United States, and taking it to the Farnborough Airshow in England in the autumn of 1988.

Today, more than 160 flights have been carried out with machines equipped with propfan, of which 140 were on the MD-80.

The aim is to produce standard aircraft. Currently being studied are the MD-91 and MD-92. The former will carry 114 passengers, is powered by two General Electric GE36 engines and has a fuel consumption estimated at 40 percent less than that of a conventional aircraft.

NUCLEAR ENERGY

Isotopic separation (1922)

In 1922, Francis William Aston (Great Britain) carried out the first isotopic separation in a laboratory. In order to achieve this, he had used a mass spectrograph that sorted the atoms by using a magnetic field. Isotopic separation involves isolating a particular isotope from a given substance. In fact, a substance never naturally presents itself in isolation, but is always accompanied, usually in very small proportions, by substances with the same atomic number but containing different numbers of neutrons.

Heavy water (1932)

In 1932, Harold C. Urey (U.S.) discovered deuterium and heavy water. He was awarded the Nobel Prize for Chemistry two years later for this discovery.

In 1933, using Urey's method of preparation, Gilbert N. Lewis (U.S.) successfully prepared a few milliliters of almost pure heavy water by fractional distillation of ordinary water.

The term heavy water, a chemical compound similar to water, is used to describe deuterium (the heavy isotope of hydrogen) oxide. This oxide is contained in all water in virtually constant proportions—that is, one molecule of heavy water to approximately 1,000 molecules of water.

Nuclear power stations (1951)

The first nuclear power station to produce electricity was the 300 kW ERR-1 in the United States, which opened in 1951. The first civilian nuclear power station was opened in June 1954 at Obninsk in the USSR when a 5000 kW (5 MW) production reactor was started up. Prior to this, the United States had developed a nuclear-powered engine for military purposes, to be used in a submarine, which had an equivalent capacity. But, as it was a prototype and a military project, this first atomic power station did not receive international approval.

Like all machines, nuclear power stations have a limited life span. It is estimated that, after 20 to 40 years' service, the installations of the reactor are worn out and become dangerous. Already 135 installations throughout the world have been shut down.

Breeder reactor (1959)

The first breeder reactor was commissioned at Dounreay in Scotland in 1959. A breeder reactor is one that produces more nuclear fuel than it consumes, so that the depletion of the world's stock of fissile uranium (i.e. 7 percent of natural uranium) does not present a threat.

In 1955 France started to consider the development of such a system and, in 1975, the Phénix (Phoenix) breeder reactor (250 MW) came into service at Marcoule on the River Rhône. The reactor was named after the bird that, according to Greek mythology, was able

Nuclear Reactor (1942): Enrico Fermi

The 1930s were a time of great flux. In the United States the Great Depression raged on. Dictatorships were born and flourished in Germany, Italy and Japan. And in different parts of Europe and America, physicists worked separately, with an eye on each other's progress, to find ways to divide tiny atoms and create large quantities of energy. Many of these scientists would later work in teams in the United States or in Germany in the race to create an atomic bomb.

In 1932 Sir James Chadwick of England discovered the neutron, an electrically neutral particle in the atom. By "bombarding" beryllium with alpha rays from radium, Chadwick was able to split the beryllium atoms, literally knocking neutrons out of their element.

Enrico Fermi, working in his lab in Italy, continued the work on nuclear fission. This is a process by which single atoms of an element are split into atoms of a new element, along with a release of neutrons and energy in the form of heat and light. Fermi used neutrons instead of alpha rays to bombard every element in the periodic table. He concluded that uranium was the most radioactive. Fermi's

Enrico Fermi. (Le Livre Mondial des Inventions)

uranium split into various components, one of which was thought to be a completely new element. The Italian press published news of this "Element 93." Germany physicists picked up the news, and realized that Fermi had succeeded not in creating a new element but in splitting uranium. They set to work to duplicate the process.

In 1938, Fermi was awarded the Nobel Prize. He was sent to Sweden to represent Mussolini and fascist Italy. Instead, after receiving his prize—without wearing a fascist uniform or giving a fascist salute to the Swedish king—Fermi took refuge in the United States. At Columbia University in New York he began planning an atomic pile, literally a pile of uranium that could sustain a chain reaction, creating a constant flow of energy.

Then came the famous letter to Roosevelt sent in 1939 by Hungarian physicists Leo Szilard and Eugene Wiegner and signed by Albert Einstein—all now working in America—warning of Germany's progress toward a nuclear reactor. Government funds flowed in for Fermi's atomic pile. By December 1942, the pile was erected on a top-secret squash court at the University of Chicago. It was a lattice wall of graphite bricks filled with uranium, with spaces into which cadmium rods could be inserted to control the nuclear reaction.

The first nuclear reaction, which occurred on December 2, 1942, was allowed to go on for 28 minutes. It was a chain reaction in which neutrons produced by one atom's fission went on to split the next atom. A coded message of the success went out: "The Italian navigator has entered the New World."

After this, work on atomic weapons proceeded rapidly. A team of scientists including Enrico Fermi—under the code name Eugene Farmer—was assembled at Los Alamos, New Mexico. Among the physicists were Danish physicist Niels Bohr, Germany's Lise Meitner, Robert Oppenheimer and others. Rarely has scientific research produced so much in so little time. By August 1945, Fermi's pioneering chain reaction was streamlined into one incredibly destructive bomb.

Only after the war was Fermi's discovery harnessed to create energy, nuclear devices used in medicine and peaceful applications in nuclear physics.

to rise repeatedly from its ashes. The first breeder reactor in the United States came into service in 1963, in the USSR in 1968.

Mox (1970)

This is a fuel mixture of uranium and plutonium that was first used in the 1970s. Mox (Mixed Oxide) comes from the reprocessing of natural and enriched uranium-based fuels burned in nuclear power stations.

Mox provides a solution for the recycling process of nuclear waste. It contains 0.8 percent of the isotope uranium 235 (more than uranium in its natural state), and is all the more interesting because after spending three years in a nuclear reactor, the waste has been converted into a fuel and can be reprocessed and reused. Experiments have been carried out on this, especially in the nuclear power stations of Germany.

Thermonuclear Reaction

The Bethe cycle (1938)

In 1938 Hans Albrecht Bethe (U.S., b. Germany) discovered the nuclear transformation cycle, named after him, that explains the energy of the sun and the stars.

Magnetic confinement (c. 1949)

Research on thermonuclear reaction controlled by magnetic confinement began independently in the United States, the USSR and Western Europe toward the end of the 1940s. In the early stages the research was carried out secretly, and some definitive work on plasma physics was done at the Kuratchov Institute in Moscow. For the first time, in 1968, physicists at the Institute brought a plasma to a temperature of 12 million K in a tokamak.

The Lawson criterion (1957)

In 1957, John Lawson (Great Britain) stated the conditions that must be fulfilled by a plasma of deuterium or tritium before the phenomenon of nuclear fusion can take place and be maintained without an external supply of energy.

The Lawson criterion defines the relation that must be reached between the density of the plasma and the length of time of its confinement, the temperature having to reach 100 million K before the reaction can take place.

Tokamaks (1963)

The first tokamak (an abbreviation of the Russian name *Toroidal Kamera Magnetic*, a machine for magnetic confinement that enables plasmas to be studied while in a state of fusion) was invented by Lev Andreevitch Artsimovitch (U.S.S.R.) and first used in 1963.

In the 1970s tokamaks were constructed in many laboratories. In 1978 the Princeton tokamak in the U.S. reached a temperature of 70 million K, but was still a long way from the Lawson criterion.

In 1983 the Alcato C tokamak at the Massachusetts Institute of Technology exceeded the temperature threshold of the Lawson criterion, but only by 15 million K. Today, huge tokamaks like JET (Joint European Torus), installed at Culham in England in 1983, are being built in European laboratories. In October 1988 the JET briefly reached a temperature of 100 million K, ten times hotter than the sun. The aim is to exceed both the threshold of the Lawson criterion and a temperature of 100 million K in order to demonstrate the feasibility of controlled nuclear fusion.

Thermonuclear fusion (1991)

The Joint European Torus (JET) project, based in Culham, England, was created to devise a system that would imitate the sun's energy process. On November 9, 1991, scientists made a major breakthrough in their goal of creating controlled thermonuclear fusion. That day, in experiment 26,148, JET researchers used deuterium-tritium in their machine for the first time. With 1.5 grams of deuterium and five milligrams of tritium, they obtained a 2-second flash in a plasma heated to 220 million degrees. This first flash of its kind produced 2 megawatts of energy for 15 megawatts supplied. The program's goal is to reach the "break-even" point, at which more energy is created than the amount supplied to create it. Currently JET has achieved a value of 10^{22} and is only a factor of 5 or 6 short of the goal; however, scientists estimate that it will be 50 years before that target is reached.

ALTERNATIVE ENERGY SOURCES

Wind

Windmill (10th century)

The earliest recorded windmills were those used in Iran during the second half of the 7th century, but the idea did not reach Europe until the 10th century.

"Windmill" is the generic term for any mechanism used to harness the kinetic energy of the wind in order to operate a machine, in particular a millstone.

Wind engines (1876)

A modern version of the traditional windmill, the wind engine or aerogenerator, converts the kinetic energy of the wind into mechanical energy and, more precisely in the case of aerogenerators, into electrical energy. Wind engines were first mentioned during the second half of the 19th century. Since then, far from becoming obsolete, the use of wind power energy has continued to develop, particularly in countries that have very windy regions.

In the United States more than 300,000 aerogenerators provide 300 million kW/h every year. This is the country that, in the 1970s, built the most powerful wind engine: it produces more than 2 MW.

Biomass

Ethanol (antiquity)

This is the technical name for ethyl alcohol, often known simply as alcohol. The method for obtaining it dates back to antiquity, but its use in industry to produce energy has developed noticeably since 1973.

Ethanol is obtained by fermentation and then refined by distillation. The raw materials are often sugars or starches of vegetable origin.

Methanol (1661)

Methanol, or methyl alcohol, was discovered in 1661 by Robert Boyle (Great Britain) among the distillation products of wood. In 1812 Taylor established a connection with alcohol, but it was two chemists, Dumas and Péligot (both France), who determined its composition in 1835. Like ethanol, methanol is a liquid fuel.

Experiments are currently under way to examine the possibility of using wood alcohol to replace lead in gasoline.

Methane (1776)

This gas, discovered in 1776 by Alessandro Volta (Italy, 1745–1827), is produced during the decomposition of organic matter by fermentation. The first use of biomethane dates back to 1857, when a methane plant was built in a leper colony near Bombay in India.

Methane is mainly used in industrial and urban heating. It is currently being tested to decide its suitability as a car fuel.

Geothermal energy (1818)

Geothermal energy is an inexhaustible source of energy produced by the earth's heat. The oldest geothermal installation is in Larderello in Tuscany and dates from 1818. Geothermal energy can be utilized by harnessing underground water that is hot from contact with the rocks.

A distinction is made, depending on the temperature of the water, between low energy geothermics (less than 194° F), used for heating homes, greenhouses, fish farms and the drying of crops; medium energy geothermics (between 194° F and 356° F), used for refrigeration or to produce electricity by the vaporization of an organic fluid such as isobutane, which makes it possible to drive turbines linked to generators producing electricity; and, lastly, high energy geothermics (higher than 356° F), also used for the production of electricity, but in this case the fluid vaporized is the actual jets of water.

Heat pump (1927)

A heat pump is a device that recovers heat from any free source such as air, ground water, etc. It converts mechanical energy into thermal energy. It transfers the heat accumulated through use of a conventional system of radiators and heat pipes. The only energy expended is that needed to run the compressor for transferring the heat. More energy is recovered than is consumed, which makes this a particularly attractive process.

Credit for having thought of the process goes to Lord Kelvin. In 1852 he had already set down the principles of a thermodynamic machine that produced heat as well as cold. Nevertheless it was 75 years before the first heat pump was built by T.G.N. Haldane in 1927. He used it to heat his office in London, England and his house in Scotland.

Solar Energy

Solar furnace (3rd century B.C.)

The idea of the solar furnace can be traced to Archimedes (Greece, 278–212 B.C.). While defending Syracuse, he armed the soldiers with concave shields which, by concentrating the sun's rays, made the Roman troops believe that they were facing "soldiers of fire." The true inventor of the solar furnace is Antoine Laurent Lavoisier (France, 1743–95), the father of modern chemistry. He concentrated the sun's rays in order to achieve the combustion of a diamond in an atmosphere containing oxygen, without the use of fuel. The first large-scale experimental solar furnace was built at Meudon, France in 1946. This plant has been able to generate temperatures as high as 5,430 degrees F.

Solar collector (17th century)

Modern solar collectors use the greenhouse effect discovered in the 17th and 18th century: the sun's energy passes through glass, warming the air, and is trapped beneath the glass. It was during the 17th century that greenhouses first appeared in France, where the Jardin du Roi (the King's Garden), now known as the Jardin des Plantes (the Plant Garden) was created in Paris in 1653.

Photovoltaic cell (1839)

In 1839 Antoine Becquerel (France) constructed the first photovoltaic cells. Also called solar cells or photocells, they directly transform light into electricity. It wasn't until the mid-20th century that manufacture of photovoltaic cells became possible.

In 1954, Bell Laboratories researchers G.L. Pearson, C.S. Fuller and D.M. Chaplin developed a solar battery that consisted of tiny silicon cells. Initially the performance of these batteries was marred by a low rate of efficiency, but in the last decade this situation has been improved. Cells are currently used to supplement weak spots in the world's electricity networks, such as at isolated telecommunication relay stations.

Solar generator (1878)

In 1878 Augustin Mouchot (France) presented a small solar generator at the Paris Exposition. The solar plant furnished enough energy to operate a steam engine.

Solar thermal power plant (1960)

The first solar thermal plant was constructed in 1960 at Ashkhabad, USSR (now Turkmenia). A solar thermal power plant concentrates the sun's rays on a steam boiler using a set of mirrors. The steam runs a classical turbo-alternator. Solar radiation was generated at the Ashkhabad plant using 1,293 flat mirrors arranged in several concentric circles.

Amorton technology (1987)

In 1987 the Japanese company Sanyo announced the development of a photovoltaic cell using the amorphous (noncrystalline) properties of silicon that enables solar energy to be used to an extremely high level of efficiency. This sytem is known as Amorton technology.

Tidal Energy

Wave energy (1875)

The idea of employing the force of water waves as an energy source seems to have been considered scientifically for the first time by R.S. Deverell (Australia) in 1875. He attempted to measure water-wave energy using an apparatus placed on board a ship which recorded roll and pitch. However, the project did not develop beyond the theoretical stage. In 1889 a mechanical wave energy installation was built at Ocean Grove, N.J. The facility generated energy from a system of sluice gates installed between jetty pilings.

Residents of Tokyo check where they are on a solar-powered street map. Solar street maps were introduced in the city in 1990. (Gamma/Nurita)

This tidal station, built on the Rance River in Brittany, France, was the first of its kind. (Sodel)

Tidal power station (1966)

In 1966 Electricité de France (EDF) put into service the first tidal-powered electric power plant in the world. Situated in the estuary of the Rance River in Brittany, the plant has a total output of 240 megawatts.

ARCHITECTURE AND INDUSTRIAL DESIGN

Origins (Neolithic period)

Historians generally agree that the art of architecture was first practiced in the Neolithic period (between the 9th and 4th millennia B.C.) in the Near East, where the claylike earth was used to build the first walls. Two series of inventions were to play a decisive role in the development of architecture: iron tools, whose use became widespread from the 10th century B.C.; and weight displacement machines such as the pulley and the winch, of which even the most modern machines are merely perfected models.

Bridge (Neolithic Age)

In the late Stone Age tree trunks and piles of stone were used to construct simple bridges.

Arched bridge (4th millennium)

The idea of assembling stones in the form of an arch is credited to the Sumerians c.3500 B.C. The Romans became masters in the art of building stone arches due to their discovery of natural cement.

Winches, pulleys and cranes (c. 4th millennium B.C.)

The pulley, together with the crank and the winch, is first mentioned in *Mechanica*, a work of the Aristotelian school (4th century B.C.). The invention of the pulley and tackle block is attributed to Archytas of Tarentum (430-360 B.C.). The origin of the crane is unknown, but a three-pulley crane device is attributed to Archimedes (Greece, 287-212 B.C.).

The first architect (2800 B.C.)

The first recorded architect who is known is Imhotep. He designed the Saqqâra Pyramid in Egypt, the oldest known construction made entirely of stone, for the Pharaoh Zoser c. 2800 B.C.

Plumb line (3rd millennium B.C.)

The plumb line and the set square were known to the Egyptians at the beginning of the Memphite period (2778–2423 B.C.). Both a symbol and a talisman, the mason's hieroglyphic image (a plumb line in a triangle passing through a horizontal line of the base) assured perpetual stability. The Romans were the first to use lead for the weight.

Aqueduct (antiquity)

The aqueduct was first designed out of necessity in the Middle East and the Mediterranean basin. Cultivated land and entire towns were irrigated by artificial channels that crossed bridges and ran underground. In 703 B.C. the Assyrian king Sennacherib had a 31-mile-long aqueduct built to supply Nineveh.

The arched aqueduct, which allowed water to be carried long distances and to span valleys, was developed by the Romans, first in Rome and then throughout their empire.

Suspension bridge (6th century)

The Chinese were building suspension bridges in the 6th century, although they existed prior to that in the form of drawbridges and footbridges made from vines. Suspension bridges were not built in the Western world until the

19th century. James Finlay (U.S.) built the first suspension bridge in the United States in 1801, at Union Town, Pa., spanning Jacob's Creek.

The level (1573)

The water level was described by the geometrician Strumienski (Poland) in 1573. The spirit level was invented by Melchisédech Thévenot (France, 1620–92). He mentions the device in his correspondence with Christiaan Huygens (Netherlands) between 1661 and 1662, but he did not publish his description of the instrument until 1681.

Iron bridge (1773)

The first iron bridge was built between 1773 and 1779 by Abraham Darby III (Great Britain, 1750–91) at Coalbrookdale, England. The bridge was made of cast iron and its central arch spanned 98 feet.

Skyscraper (1885)

The skyscraper was invented in 1885 in Chicago, Ill., by William Le Baron Jenney (U.S.). During the 1850s, Chicago had begun to expand vertically as a means of escape from the water that frequently transformed roads into quagmires. In 1871 the Great Chicago Fire spurred architects to replace wooden frameworks with steel. In this environment Jenney devised an internal structural skeleton that bore the weight of the entire building; the external wall had nothing to support. The first skyscraper, the Home Insurance building, had 10 floors; two more were subsequently added.

Construction Materials

Concrete

Mortars (2nd century B.C.)

Lime has been known to humans since antiquity, but lime mortars—used to bind stones together—appeared only around the 2nd century B.C. when the Romans began adding volcanic ash to lime to produce a more resistant concrete. It was called pozzolana.

Hydraulic cement (1756)

Medieval builders seem to have lost the Roman recipe for making mortars. Their own were of poor quality until the 12th century, when some improvements were made.

Cement was only reinvented in the middle of the 18th century when, in 1756, John Smeaton (Great Britain) rediscovered its principle: the presence of clay in limestone. And, 30 years later, the furnace masters Parker and Wyatts perfected a new cement by burning nodules of clayey limestone.

Portland cement (1824)

In 1824 a mason from Leeds, England, Joseph Aspdin, patented Portland cement, so-called because it was made by burning a mixture of clay and chalk the color of Portland stone.

Reinforced concrete (1892)

The noncombustibility of concrete was used by François Hennebique (France) as a means of fire prevention; this had also been a major factor in the development of iron architecture. He developed a concrete slab and later a monolithic structure similar to timber. These inventions, patented in 1892, led to a widespread use of reinforced concrete and opened new perspectives in architecture.

Prestressed concrete (1928)

Concrete's resilience under stretching and bending can be considerably increased by prestressing it. Eugène Freyssinet (France, 1879–1962) invented this technique in 1928 following his investigation of the deterioration of concrete arches. Freyssinet's technique was first used in 1946 for the construction of five bridges spanning the Marne River. Today prestressed concrete has almost entirely replaced reinforced concrete in the construction of works of art.

Cast-iron fiber (1987)

In 1987 the Pont-à-Mousson Research Center in France launched a new substance designed to reinforce concrete and mortar. It is manufactured from amorphous (i.e. noncrystalline) metallic strips and is known as Fibraflex. This fiber is very light, very supple and very strong. A common application today is to reinforce concrete used for the restoration of major constructions such as aqueducts. Research is being conducted to extend its use to the manufacture of very thin prefabricated elements.

Glass

Origins (antiquity)

According to the Roman naturalist Pliny the Elder (A.D. 23–79), glass (or glazing, to be precise) was discovered accidentally by sailors. An Egyptian ship laden with natron (the Egyptians used this substance—as they did asphalt—to preserve their mummies) ran aground on a Phoenician beach. Unable to find any stones on which to place their cooking pot, the sailors used two blocks of natron. The heat from the fire caused the natron to combine with the sand (silica) on the beach, and thus, by happy chance, they had discovered glass.

The oldest surviving piece of glass was made during the reign of the Pharaoh Amenophis I between 1557 and 1530 B.C. At the time, glass was used for ornamental objects or receptacles, which were sculpted from glass blocks.

Around 300 B.C. in Alexandria the technique was refined thanks to the invention of molded glass, in which molten glass was poured into a mold.

Glassblowing (1st century B.C.)

The great innovation that was to make glass production available cheaply was glassblowing, discovered in the 1st century B.C. The technique of blown glass (whose composition is very similar to that of modern soda/lime glass) was probably perfected in Syria, but it was the Romans who spread it throughout their empire and beyond.

Venetian glass (10th to 15th centuries)

There were glassmakers in Venice as early as the end of the 10th century, and in 1271 the profession gave itself a statute. The glassmakers were obliged to work on the island of Murano because of the pollution caused by their craft. This isolation helped to protect the secret of the glassblowers' craft; indeed, the craftsmen were not allowed to leave the country. The invention of Venetian glass is attributed to a glassmaker named Beroverio in 1463.

Crystal glass (1674)

Industrial production of crystal glass was developed by glassmakers in England in the 17th century. George Ravenscroft (Great Britain) took out a patent in 1674. Crystal had previously been produced by Venetian craftsmen and by the Bohemians (16th century), whose crystal was brighter than the Venetians'.

Tempered glass (1874)

Techniques for the industrial manufacture of toughened glass were patented on June 13 and July 6, 1874, by François Royer de la Bastie (France). The first theoretical analysis of thermal tempering was publishing in 1929 by J.T. Littleton and F. Preston (both U.S.) of the Corning Glass Works, Corning, N.Y.

Wired glass (1893)

In 1893, Léon Appert (France) opened the way to the fabrication of wired plate glass. Around 1910 two engineers, completely unknown to each other, simultaneously developed plate glass: Emile Fourcault in Belgium and Irving Colburn in the United States. In 1952 Alistair Pilkington (Great Britain) developed a manufacturing method that was much cheaper than the preceding ones: a layer of molten glass was poured onto a layer of molten tin to produce a perfectly smooth and shiny glass.

Laminated glass (1909)

In 1903, chemist Edward Benedictus (France) began research on laminated glass, and he patented his invention in 1909. The glass was commercialized in 1920 and was first used for car windscreens. Some laminated glass is resistant even to shots from automatic weapons.

Pyrex (1915)

Toward the end of the 19th century, Otto Schott (Germany) had shown that adding boric acid would make glass better able to withstand heat shock. Several years later, two researchers at the Corning Glass Works laboratory, E.C. Sullivan and W.C. Taylor, invented a new formula of borosilicate (borosilicate glass) while working on the development of glass railway signal lamps. Patented in 1915, this glass possessed good chemical resistance and was soon used for manufacturing kitchen utensils and laboratory glass. It was marketed as Pyrex.

Vycor (1939)

Ninety-six percent silica, the glass trade-named Vycor, used for the coverings of most halogen lamps, was invented in 1939 by two Corning researchers, M.E. Nordberg and H.R. Hood. This glass is reconstructed from a borosilicate that has undergone various treatments to eliminate almost all other constituents except silica.

Chemical tempering (1955)

In 1955, two Corning researchers, H.R. Hood and S.D. Stookey, took out a patent showing that glass surfaces could be very strongly compressed and therefore greatly reinforced. Chemical tempering is limited to products in which extremely high quality is needed, such as the portholes on the Concorde.

Float glass (1958)

This was invented in 1958 by Alistair Pilkington (Great Britain). The production process is still a secret even though patents have been ceded to other manufacturers. The glass has many applications: in car windscreens and glass walls, for example. The latter are made from Kappafloat and Planar, "energetic" glasses that let solar heat in and prevent internal energy from escaping. Extra-thin float glass is being developed for use in optics, photography and aerospace.

It is thanks to float glass that glassmaking, which for a long time was a traditional activity, has become a heavy industry. Float glass is produced in a giant oven capable of producing between 500 and 600 metric tons of glass a day. There are 110 such ovens in the world, 33 of which are in Europe.

Glass without fluoride (1989)

Fluoride facilitates the fusion of glass. Although fluoride fumes in the air are not dangerous for people, they are a threat to coniferous trees. To protect the forest adjacent to its factory in Savoie, Saint-Gobain has developed a manufacturing process in which the use of fluoride is completely eliminated.

Priva-lite (1990)

Launched at the beginning of 1990 by the Belgian company Saint-Roch, Priva-lite glass is a layered glass that is able to become opaque and then transparent again at the press of a button.

It is made up of two panes of glass and a film of Taliq Liquid Cristal (an American invention): when the switch is thrown the crystals are activated and they align themselves in such a way that the glass becomes transparent. When at rest, the crystals return to their positions and the glass becomes opaque again.

Other Materials

Iron (2nd millennium B.C.)

The so-called Iron Age marks the period when iron replaced the use of bronze, toward the end of the 2nd millennium B.C. The discovery of iron was, however, made much earlier. A recent translation of a text from the Fayoum region shows that the Egyptians were capable of extracting iron ore some 3500 years B.C., but the technique used was rather rudimentary.

The use of iron was developed in Asia Minor (Mesopotamia). It was introduced into Greece toward 1200 B.C, where it permitted the growth of architecture: buildings could be made with blocks of stone joined by metal bolts. Iron also allowed beams of great length to be constructed because metal girders spread weight evenly. The Propylaea of the Acropolis in Athens are a magnificent example of this.

Steel (antiquity)

Since antiquity certain blacksmiths—notably among the Hittites—have produced tools and weapons from iron mixed with small quantities of carbon. In 18th-century England, iron-founders, led by Abraham Darby (Great Britain, 1711–63), produced small amounts of steel. But it was the discovery of a direct conversion process by Sir Henry Bessemer (Great Britain, 1813–98) that paved the way for industrial production of steel (see page 45).

Macadam (1915)

Macadam was invented by John McAdam (Great Britain, 1756–1836) in 1815.

At the end of the 18th century the state of European roads was appalling, as they had not been renewed since the Middle Ages.

Born in Ayr, Scotland, John McAdam had made his fortune in the United States. On returning to Scotland he started, at his own expense, a series of studies on road surfaces. In 1815 he was appointed Surveyor General of Bristol roads, and was at last able to put his theories into practice. He created a road surface made from crushed stones and sand compacted by road-rollers. Although the name still exists, the McAdam road surfacing system has been almost completely abandoned. Nowadays, mixtures of cement, cinders or slag are used. Tar is no longer used either, having been replaced by asphalt.

Fiberglass (1836)

Contrary to popular belief, fiberglass is an old invention. In 1836 Ignace Dubus-Bonnel (France) deposited a patent for the "weaving of glass, pure or mixed with silk, wool, cotton or linen, and made pliable by steam." He also included a sample with his patent request, woven on a Jacquard loom. He could thus produce imitation gold or silver brocades by combining silk with a weft of glass fibers that had been colored with metal particles. Dubus-Bonnel's fabrics won him prizes at the 1839 Paris Exhibition, and the inventor produced the draperies that decorated the hearse used for the reburial of Napoleon's ashes at the Invalides in 1840.

Despite its success on that occasion, the new fiber was subsequently forgotton, probably because of the high costs of production, and would only reappear around 1950.

Currently, most composite materials are made lighter and stronger by the addition of fiberglass. Its uses vary from automobile fenders and hoods, to rocket engine parts, to the masts of sailboards. Some 300,000 objects are today manufactured with fiberglass.

Cinder blocks (1846)

To make it possible to build a wall by simple assembly, with bricks placed rapidly and continuously, Jean-Aimé Balan (France) developed a system of hollow blocks made of brick or hydrated sulphate of lime mortar which he patented on February 2, 1846. This invention opened the way for the cinder blocks that we use today.

Corrugated iron (1853)

In the 18th century painted sheets of metal and tin were used for the roofs of baroque churches. But they rusted easily and lacked rigidity. On September 2, 1853 Pierre Carpentier (France) took out a patent for a "machine to rib galvanized metal sheets." He had invented corrugated iron, and he went on to exhibit it at the Paris World's Fair in 1855. The galvanization process, perfected earlier (1837) by Sorel (France), provided excellent protection against rust and made it possible to produce very cheaply metal structures and roofs that could resist bad weather.

Carbon fibers (1880)

The first carbon fiber was obtained by calcining a bamboo stalk. This was done by Thomas Edison (U.S., 1847–1931), who used the fiber as a filament for his glow-lamp in 1880.

The fiber currently used for the manufacture of composite material was invented in Japan by A. Shindo in 1961 and was later perfected, also in Japan, in 1969. This fiber is obtained by burning very pure polyacrylonitrile fibers in a vacuum. The resulting fiber is 15 times tougher than the best steel, weight for weight. Its principal applications are in sports and aeronautical engineering.

Prefabricated panels (1888)

On December 12, 1888, Georges Espitallier (France) patented the first prefabricated panels: standard-size units made of varnished compressed cardboard and slag-wool. This wool is derived from blast-furnace slag and was developed by Edward Parry (Great Britain).

The idea of prefabrication was not, however, completely new: the Crystal Palace in London, England, built in 1851 for the Great Exhibition, was a gigantic prefabricated conservatory that was designed by Sir Joseph Paxton (Great Britain, 1801–65), a pioneer of iron architecture. It took six months to assemble the parts, which came from a number of different factories.

Stainless steel (c. 1912)

Stainless steel was developed between 1903 and 1912 thanks to the simultaneous efforts of Harry Brearly in Great Britain, F.M. Buckett in the United States, and Benno Strauss and Edward Maurer in Germany.

Composite materials (1964)

Composite materials are made from two or more elements that have complementary properties: often one material withstands traction and the other compression. These compounds have been used for centuries: the first one was probably daub, a mixture of hay and mud. Reinforced concrete was the first modern composite material.

The first very high-performance composites were produced in 1964 but have only had industrial applications since 1970. In 1972, aramide fiber was created by Du Pont. It is lighter and tougher than carbon fiber but may soon be replaced by an even stronger polythene fiber developed by the Dutch manufacturer DSM (1984). Metallurgists have also discovered the benefits of reinforcing metals with carbon fibers.

Besides these spectacular "super" materials, which are used only in small quantities (a few thousand tons per year), numerous low-cost composite materials are also being developed. The most recent of these are FITs, which appeared in 1984. These are thermoplastics reinforced with long fibers. The resulting material is very strong and easy to manipulate.

Carbon-carbon and ceramic-ceramic (1981)

There are two main groups of so-called thermostructural materials. The first group is made up of carbon-carbons, which are composed of carbon material covered by carbon fibers; Carbone Industrie, a subsidiary of the company SEP (Société Européenne de Propulsion), is the second largest manufacturer of these in the world. The second group is made of composite materials based on a ceramic matrix (ceramic-ceramic and ceramic-carbon). These were developed by SEP in 1981, and their license was sold to the American company Du Pont in 1987.

Unique plants have been built to manufacture these materials, which are used in fields ranging from space research to medicine. Some types of biocompatible carbon compounds are excellent as bony artificial materials for use in surgery.

This photograph clearly illustrates the effect of absorbent road surfacing in reducing standing water. (Beugnet)

Absorbent road surfacing (1983)

The latest innovation in roadway surfaces is an absorbent surfacing that acts like blotting paper when it rains. No more slippery roads, no more danger of aquaplaning, no more fine spray reducing visibility—hence fewer accidents. This process sometimes uses crushed old tires mixed with the asphalt. The pioneer in this surfacing is a French company, Beugnet, which developed Drainochape, perfected in 1983. This is already used at accident "black spots" on a number of French roadways, and by 1995 the whole length of the Autoroute du Nord will be surfaced with it.

MACHINE TOOLS

Drill (antiquity)

Drilling machines and lathes are among the oldest machines developed by humankind. Although the exact date of their invention is unknown, their existence is noted by Homer in the *Odyssey*.

Planing machine (18th century)

The invention of the planing machine is disputed, but its origin dates to the mid-18th century. Joseph Whitworth (Great Britain) is generally credited with perfecting the plane. In 1844 he produced the first perfectly true surface-plate.

Slide lathe (c. 1751)

The oldest known metallic slide lathe was invented by Jacques de Vaucanson (France, 1709–82) c. 1751. He used the machine to

manufacture cylinders that he used in building looms.

Reaming machine (1775)

The reaming machine, a device that polishes and adjusts the diameter of a cylinder while it is being drilled, was invented by John Wilkinson (Great Britain) in 1775. The reaming machine is considered to be the first industrial machine tool.

Hydraulic press (1796)

The hydraulic press was invented in 1796 by Joseph Bramah (Great Britain, 1749–1814). This machine was able to provide a very strong mechanical thrust, with motion that was simultaneously progressive.

Screw-cutting lathe (1797)

The screw-cutting or precision lathe was invented by Henry Maudslay (Great Britain, 1771–1831) in 1797. This type of lathe is one of the oldest machine tools ever built.

Milling machine (1818)

The milling machine was invented by Eli Whitney (U.S., 1765–1825) in 1818. He had been the director of an armaments factory since 1815, and designed the milling machine as a more efficient method of manufacturing rifle parts.

Filing machine (1826)

In 1826, the first filing machine was invented by James Nasmyth (Great Britain, 1808–89). The filing machine replaced cold chisel work as a method of obtaining a fine finished cut.

Steam power hammer (1839)

James Nasmyth was also responsible for the invention of the steam power hammer in 1839. Nasmyth's steam hammer made it possible to forge large pieces of metal, as it could forge steel ingots up to a diameter of three feet.

Steamroller (1859)

Louis Lemoine (France) invented the steamroller on May 27, 1859. The invention of the steamroller revolutionized road construction and marked the beginning of industrially constructed highways.

Jackhammer (1861)

The pneumatic pick, or jackhammer, was invented by German Sommelier (France) in 1861. Sommelier invented the jackhammer while working on the construction of the Mont-Cenis tunnel, a project to link France and Italy that was expected to take 30 years to complete. Sommelier modified steam-powered drills to work with compressed air. The jackhammer was so effective that the tunnel was completed in 1871, 20 years ahead of schedule.

Forms of welding date to c. 3500 B.C. Modern applications include using electron beams and lasers. (Sodel)

METALLURGY

Origins (prehistory)

The date of the invention of metallurgy is unknown, but it is known that as early as the 10th millennium B.C. humankind was familiar with metals.

Welding (4th millennium B.C.)

Heterogeneous welding, which enables two pieces of different types of metal to be joined together, dates back to about 3500 B.C. Autogeneous welding is more recent, dating from about 1500 B.C. Until the end of the 19th century the only method of welding iron and steel was by forging. In 1877 Elihu Thomson (U.S.) invented resistance welding. In 1807 Sir Humphry Davy (Great Britain, 1778–1829) invented the electric or carbon arc. In 1885 Bernados invented the carbon arc torch, which permitted a filler metal to be used in welding. In 1890 Nikolai Gavrilovich Slavianov (Russia) developed the process of arc welding with a consumable electrode, and in 1904 Kjeliberg invented the coated electrode. But it was not until 1920 that arc welding became widely used.

Today, electron beam welding is being used much more extensively. This was a process developed in 1954 by M. Stohr, an engineer at the Saclay Center for Nuclear Research. Since 1970, laser welding has also become more common.

Etruscan furnace (7th century B.C.)

The Etruscans have left us eloquent testimony to their metallurgical techniques. Layers of iron ore and of charcoal were piled over a hollow to a height of about 6 ft. The whole thing was then covered with clayey mud and a flue was made at the top of the dome. Holes were pierced lower down the dome to ensure a good draught. When the smelting was complete, the furnace was demolished and the metal retrieved from the process was then worked by a blacksmith.

Blast furnace (13th century)

The antecedents of blast furnaces date from the 13th century. In the 14th century waterwheels were used to work bellows. The inventor of the modern blast furnace was Abraham Darby (Great Britain, 1711–63), an ironmaster from Coalbrookdale, England. Pig-iron (an alloy of iron and at least 2.5 percent carbon) can be obtained directly from iron ore in a modern blast furnace. The second step forward was made by Karl Wilhelm von Siemens (Great

Britain, b. Germany; 1823–83), who in 1857 had the idea of using the heat from the gases inside the furnace to heat the air sent in by the bellows. The open-hearth process was patented in 1858. Since the 1950s, iron ore has been crushed into pellets before being placed in the furnace.

Coke (1735)

The metallurgist Abraham Darby (Great Britain, 1711–63) in 1735 was the first to use coke as a fuel in blast furnaces. Coke is obtained by heating coal in a confined space at between 1650° F and 2100° F.

Cobalt (1735)

This metal was isolated by the chemist Brandt (Sweden) from copper materials found in the area of Harz, Sweden in 1735. In 1910, it was discovered that this metal improved rapid-cut steel, and metallurgists began to experiment with it. Cobalt is currently used in alloys that are resistant to high temperatures (in parts for airplane motors and gas turbines) and wearing and corrosion (in cutting and drilling tools).

Tungsten (1781)

Tungsten is a dense metal. It is the most refractory element known, since its melting point is 3,410° Celsius. It was discovered by Carl W. Scheele (Sweden) in 1781.

Aluminum (1825)

Aluminum was first obtained in powder form in 1825 by Hans Christian Oersted (Denmark), and in ingot form in 1827 by Friedrich Wohler (Germany, 1800–82). In the mid-19th century, Napoleon III of France granted a research subsidy to the chemist Sainte-Claire Deville (France, 1818–81) to develop a method for the industrial production of aluminum. In 1854 Deville obtained the first pure aluminum metal by reduction of aluminum chloride.

In 1886 two scientists, Charles Hall (U.S., 1863–1914) and Paul Héroult (France, 1863–1914), working independently, discovered an electrolytic process for producing aluminum. This process allowed aluminum to be produced in large quantities at low cost and revolutionized the aluminum industry.

Bessemer converter (1856)

Henry Bessemer (Great Britain, 1813–98) perfected a converter in 1856 that allowed him to remove the carbon from pig-iron and to produce steel of a relatively good quality. This discovery, perfected at Bessemer's own cutlery factory in Sheffield, England, was the basis of the rise of the steel industry.

Thomas converter (1876)

Sydney Gilchrist Thomas (Great Britain, 1850–85) improved the Bessemer process in 1876, making it possible to refine the phosphoric pig-iron and to eliminate the various other impurities thanks to a basic lining of the converters.

The Bessemer and Thomas processes are virtually obsolete today. They have been replaced by new processes based on the LD (Linz-Donawitz) process developed after World War II by Austrian engineers. It consists of refining the pig-iron with pure oxygen, introduced via a vertical blast pipe.

Electric furnace (1900)

The melting of scrap-iron in an electric furnace was made possible by the invention of the arc furnace by Paul Héroult (France, 1863–1914). The first industrial application took place on October 9, 1900. The process makes it possible to produce quality steel and currently provides 26 percent of the world's steel.

TEXTILES

Spinning

Origins (antiquity)

The art of spinning dates to prehistoric times. A spindle—a sort of stick with a conically shaped point—was first used to spin wool and flax. The invention of the spinning wheel, which is thought to have originated in the Middle East, was the next important development in spinning technology. It permitted spinning lengths of thread without interruption. The spinning wheel was introduced to Europe c. 13th century.

Flying shuttle (1733)

In 1733 John Kay (Great Britain, 1704–c. 1778) invented the flying shuttle. Prior to the flying shuttle, it had taken two people to weave a cloth, as the shuttle had to be thrown from one side of the frame to the other. Kay's device returned the shuttle automatically. As a result, the quality of the fabric was improved and a single weaver could work on broad cloth. This saved on labor costs and doubled productivity.

Spinning jenny (c. 1760)

The invention of the spinning jenny, the first mechanical spinning frame, is disputed. Most historians credit James Hargreaves (Great Britain, c. 1720–78) with inventing the device in 1764, but others claim that Hargreaves perfected a model invented by Thomas Higgs (Great Britain) c. 1760.

Water-frame (1769)

In 1769, Richard Arkwright (Great Britain, 1732–92) invented the water-frame, a water-powered spinning frame that made continuous spinning possible and is the basis for modern mechanical spinning.

Mule jenny (1779)

The mule jenny was invented by Samuel Crompton (Great Britain, 1753–1827) in 1779. The mule jenny solved the problems associated with spinning cotton. The machine combined features from Hargreaves' and Arkwright's machines: it spun cotton into yarn and then wound the yarn onto spindles.

Ring throstle (1828)

The ring throstle was invented in 1828 by J. Thorpe (Great Britain) and perfected by W. Mason (Great Britain) in 1833. It is still the most commonly used machine for spinning wool, combed cotton and synthetic fibers.

Looms

Origins (prehistoric)

The art of weaving, like that of spinning, goes back to prehistoric times. Although until the end of the 19th century only the wooden handloom was known, the idea of mechanizing the weaving loom led to a number of further inventions.

In 1606 C. Dangon (France) created the *cassin*, a device that made it possible to activate the healds via a series of pulleys. This system allowed the weaving of larger patterns. In 1725 B. Bouchon (France) improved on Dangon's invention by substituting for the looped string an endless band of perforated paper by which the simples for any shed could be selected, thus making it possible to set aside a pattern and take it up again. H. Falcon perfected the system in 1728, using perforated cards to create the pattern.

Mechanical loom (1785)

The first mechanical loom was invented by Edmund Cartwright (Great Britain, 1743–1823) in 1785. Previously, in 1775, Jacques de Vaucanson (France, 1709–92), a brilliant builder of automatic machines, tried to apply a complex automatic action to the weaving loom using a perforated cylinder. Unfortunately, the capacity of this cylinder was too limited. Cartwright's invention, which was improved in 1786, is the basis for present-day looms.

Jacquard loom (1804)

In 1804 in Lyons Joseph-Marie Jacquard (France, 1752–1834) invented a loom for weaving brocade fabrics and various other machines for weaving and for making fishing nets. Jacquard cleverly managed to combine Falcon's and Vaucanson's devices. Jacquard did not take out a patent for this invention, but it made his name. Traditional weavers' looms still use the Jacquard cards to alternate different types of thread and to vary the interlacing of the fibers.

Automatic loom (1822)

In 1822 R. Roberts (Great Britain) invented a fully automatic loom, which was soon adopted throughout Europe. It was later perfected by various technicians and builders, who developed different mechanisms to accommodate more heads. In 1890 J.H. Northrop (U.S.) designed the automatic loom that, with a few adjustments, is still used today in the textile industry.

CLOCKS AND WATCHES

Origins (3rd millennium B.C.)

The first "clock," the gnomon, was invented in the 3rd millennium B.C. and has been attributed to both the Chinese and the Chaldeans. The gnomon was the precursor of the sundial, invented, according to some sources, by Anaximander of Miletus (Greece) in the 6th century B.C. and, according to others, by the Chinese and the Egyptians at a much earlier date.

The first artificial clock, the water clock or clepsydra, appeared at about the same time. The Egyptians in 3000 B.C. used the clepsydra alongside the sundial.

Hourglass (antiquity)

The hourglass, symbol of the passing of time, is also said to have been invented by the Chinese, although the exact date is not known. The first mention of an hourglass is found in a play by Baton, an Athenian comic poet of the 3rd century B.C.

Candle clock (c. 2nd–5th century A.D.)

In the early centuries A.D. the Byzantines introduced candle clocks. Candles were marked at regular intervals and, as they burned lower, it was possible to calculate how much time had passed by the number of marks that remained.

Escapement (725)

The first escapement mechanism appears to have been invented by I. Hsing (China) in 725. The escapement is one of the most important parts of a timepiece: it controls the transfer of energy from the motor to the hands, and it provides the oscillator with energy that compensates for the energy lost through friction. The most commonly used kind of escapement nowadays consists of toothed wheels and an anchor, invented by L. Perron (France) in 1798.

Weight-driven and pendulum clocks (c. 10th century A.D.)

Gerbert d'Aurillac (c. 938–1003), who became Pope Sylvester II in 999, is said to be the inventor of the weight-driven clock. Christiaan Huygens (Netherlands, 1629–95) invented the pendulum clock in 1657. The first portable spring-driven clock was made by the Florentine

The atomic clock uses the natural frequency of energy changes within atoms to record time more precisely than any other timepiece. The HP5071A, seen here, keeps time accurately to within one second in 1.6 million years. (Hewlett-Packard Co.)

architect Brunelleschi (1377–1446) in 1410. This was the earliest domestic clock.

Spiral spring (1675)

In 1675 Christiaan Huygens (Netherlands, 1629–95) invented the balance wheel and spiral spring oscillator. The introduction of the spiral spring into watch design had an effect analogous to that of the pendulum into clocks—another of Huygens's innovations, dating from 1657.

Chronometer (1736)

The watchmaker and astronomer George Graham (Great Britain, 1673–1751) first used the term "chronometer" as applied to a small portable pendulum. In 1736 John Harrison (Great Britain, 1693–1776) made the first naval chronometer, in wood, and perfected it in 1761. Accurate timekeeping was necessary on the seas to enable sailors to calculate the correct longitude. Harrison's spring-driven chronometer was tested by Capt. James Cook on his voyages from 1768.

Winder (1755)

In 1755 the author Beaumarchais (France) invented a watch for Madame Pompadour that could be wound without a key. She could turn a ring mounted on the face with her fingernail. It was not until 1842, however, that A. Philippe (Switzerland) succeeded in producing a mechanism that allowed the watch to be wound and the hands to be repositioned too. The self-winding watch was invented by A.L. Perrelet (France) in 1775. The first self-winding wristwatches were patented by H. Cutte and J. Harwood in 1924.

Electric clock (1840)

The electric clock was perfected in 1840 by Alexander Bain (Great Britain). At the same time, Sir Charles Wheatstone (Great Britain, 1802–75) invented electric distribution of time from a so-called mother clock.

Alarm clock (1847)

The first modern alarm clock was invented by Antoine Redier (France, 1817–92) in 1847. The Braun Voice Control was the first alarm clock to stop ringing at the sound of a voice. It appeared in 1985.

Wristwatch (1904)

Two designers can claim to have invented the modern wristwatch: Louis Cartier (France), who in 1904 made one for the aviator Santos-Dumont; and, in the same year, Hans Wilsdorf (Switzerland), founder of Rolex. Earlier versions date back to around 1800, but they were essentially items of jewelry rather than a watchmaker's product. Wristwatches quickly achieved widespread popularity among women, but it was not until World War I that they were generally adopted by men. In 1910 Rolex produced the first wrist chronometer.

Quartz clock (1920)

Work on the use of quartz as a resonator in clocks began in 1920, but it was not until 1929 that Warren Alvin Marrison (U.S.) perfected the first clock with a resonator of this type. Quartz watches were made commercially for the first time in 1969 by Seiko. In 1988 there was a major change in the way quartz watches work: the battery was replaced by a tiny dynamo that creates energy to compensate for the energy consumed. Two companies are behind this development: Seiko, which has been working on the project since 1973, and the French company Jean d'Eve.

Waterproof watch (1926)

In 1926 Hans Wilsdorf and his Rolex team developed the first completely waterproof watch case. In 1927 Wilsdorf gave an Oyster watch to Mercedes Gleitz, a typist from London, who swam the English Channel with it strapped to her wrist.

Atomic clock (1948)

The principle of the atomic clock was laid down by Willard F. Libby (U.S., 1908–80), winner of the Nobel Prize for Chemistry in 1960. An atomic clock uses the energy changes within atoms to produce extremely regular waves of electromagnetic radiation.

Talking watch (1987)

The Voice-Master VX-2 replies when its owner asks the time. But it can also obey 27 different commands once they have been put into the memory: credit card number, telephone number and so on. Designed by Citizen and marketed in Japan in November 1987, it has been generally available since 1988.

Aviation chronograph (1990)

An innovation from Seiko for pilots: with its four motors, this chronograph is equipped with navigational aids such as systems for calculating flight time, speed, distance, altitude, climbing speed, etc. It has a double time zone and is accurate to two-tenths of a second.

Radio-controlled watch (1990)

Incorporating the technological innovations of the German company Junghans, the Mega 1 is the first radio-controlled wristwatch. It is per-

manently linked to the most accurate clock in the world, the atomic clock of Brunswick's Federal Institute of Physics, via a DCF77 radio transmitter located near Frankfurt. The long-wave signals are easily picked up anywhere within a 950-mile radius of the transmitter by an ultrasensitive flexible aerial located in the watch strap, then converted by a special microprocessor controlling the digital display on the dial of the watch. This system guarantees accuracy to within one second every million years.

POLLUTION CONTROL

A sensor analyzes acid rain above the Vosges Mountains in France. (Explorer)

Rivers and Oceans

Sewage treatment plant (1889)

The world's first sewage treatment plant was built on the River Thames, England in 1889. The river's 209 miles were so polluted by the mid-19th century that only eels could survive in it. A series of plants were built following the completion of the first sewage plant, and their success could be gauged by the repopulation of the river.

Polynorbornene (1975)

Polynorbornene is a white powder that completely absorbs petroleum on contact, and was adapted in the mid-1970s to clean up oil spills. Developed in 1975 by Claude Stein and André Marbach (both France), researchers for the French industrial group CdF Chimie, the product was originally intended to be used in the manufacture of shock-absorbent rubber. Polynorbornene does not harm animal or plant life,

and has been used extensively in Japan to control oil slicks and pollution in its ports.

Automatic warning station (1988)

In November 1986 a fire at a Swiss chemical plant caused extensive pollution of the Rhine River. Two years after this ecological disaster, an automatic warning station, a chain to be set up along the entire length of the river, was opened on November 18, 1988 at Huningue in the Haut-Rhin, France. The station is equipped with a total organic carbon detector, a dissolved hydrocarbon detector, a heavy metal detector, a fluorometer for detecting dye molecules and a pesticide detector.

The equipment, each element of which is controlled by a selection–rejection mechanism and a coordinator, is equipped with a printer as well as a visual display unit. The station also has a tele-data transmission system linked to stations controlling hydraulic structures such as sluices, locks and dams that have to be adjusted in order to limit the effects of pollution.

Inipol (1989)

Inipol EAP 22 is an oil-absorbing formula, developed by research scientists of the French company Élf-Aquitaine, that speeds up the natural process by which hydrocarbons are broken down in the sea. The originality of this product lies in its positive discrimination in favor of those species of microorganisms living naturally in the sea that are able to break down hydrocarbons without disrupting the environment. Inipol EAP 22 was used extensively in the cleanup operation off the Alaska coast following the *Exxon Valdez* oil spill in 1989.

Acid rain neutralizers (1989)

Following 10 years of research, scientists at the University of Lund, Sweden produced sodium carbonate briquets that have proved capable of neutralizing the acidity at the bottom of their lakes.

Dr. L. Hakka of Union Carbide of Canada Ltd.'s technical center has developed the Cansolv process. This process uses a solvent to remove the sulphur oxide from the fumes of

Inipol is an environment-friendly substance that breaks down hydrocarbons in water. It was used extensively in Alaska following the *Exxon Valdez* oil spill. (Elf Aquitaine)

thermal electric power stations, which are a main contributor to the creation of acid rain.

Antinitrate process (1990)

In 1990 Etienne Tillié (France) developed a technique capable of eliminating nearly all the nitrates and phosphates contained in polluted water, whether it is industrial effluent or sewage. The process is adaptable to existing sewage purification plants.

Air

Ozone (1781)

Ozone (O₃), a gaseous element formed from three oxygen atoms, was discovered in 1781 by Martinus van Marum (Netherlands, 1750–1837), who noticed its smell in air through which electric sparks had passed. In 1840 Christian Schönbein (Switzerland, 1799–1863)

coined the name *ozone*, from the Greek *ozein*, meaning a smell.

Global Circulation Models (GCMs) (1970's)

In order to study the effects of increased carbon dioxide emissions on the atmosphere, scientists have created complex mathematical models called Global Circulation Models (GCMs) that simulate the forces that affect the atmosphere and that project the future. The GCM represents the atmosphere as a three-dimensional grid of horizontal and vertical spacing lines. Using supercomputers that can make a billion calculations per second, modelers calculate climate at the intersection of grid lines created by the GCMs. It is by using these models that scientists have been able to show the effects of increased carbon dioxide on global warming and warn of future dangers if this trend continues.

Antipollution filter (1989)

To combat the problem of eye and nose irritation caused by exhaust fumes, the Swiss company Incen launched the Icleen filter in 1989. Placed in a car's ventilation system, this filter absorbs the toxic particles that cause the irritation.

Environment-friendly chainsaw (1989)

Developed in 1989 by the German company Stihl, this chainsaw is fitted with a catalyst that reduces the amount of exhaust fumes. This is the first time that such a device has been developed for a two-stroke engine.

Environment-friendly refrigerator (1989)

In 1989 the Swedish company Electrolux manufactured the first refrigerator to contain half the usual amount of freon gas in its foam insulators. Freon belongs to the chlorofluorocarbon (CFC) family held responsible for the deterioration of the stratospheric ozone layer.

Surveillance of the ozone layer (1989)

On March 22, 1989 a research program was implemented at the University of Wuppertal, Germany to develop a system for monitoring changes in the ozone layer by satellite. The system, known as CRISTA (a telescope for observing the atmosphere and a cryogenic spectroradiometer), will be on board the German satellite Astrospas, which is due to be launched in 1993.

HFA 22 (1990)

The French company Atochem has developed a CFC substitute for aerosols, HFA 22, which is nonflammable and has a very low level of toxicity. Its adverse effect on the ozone layer is 95 percent less than that of CFC-11 and CFC-12.

Humanity's Effect on Ecology (1962): Rachel Carson

Rachel Carson combined her two greatest loves, nature and writing, to become a best-selling author and the twentieth century's most controversial environmentalist.

The early part of Carson's career found her teaching college biology and writing broadcasts and articles for the U.S. Bureau of Fisheries. This Pennsylvania country girl, who never saw the sea until she was a graduate student, made the ocean the subject of her first best-seller, *The Sea Around Us*. The book was a biography of the ocean, a thorough and exhaustively researched analysis. Thrilled by the vast variety of life in the ocean, and determined to share her understanding of the earth's ecology—a word she popularized—Carson went on to write *The Edge of the Sea*, a best-seller about the seacoast.

Carson used much of the information about the ocean that became available as a result of military efforts in World War II. She also came across data about DDT (dichloro-diphenyl-trichloro-ethane), a poisonous spray that had been dusted on people during the war to kill body lice carrying typhus. DDT had been known to science since 1874. It was first used in 1939 in Switzerland to save the potato crop. After the war it became available to the general public and was advertised as a miracle spray to kill insects that destroyed crops.

As early as 1945, Carson proposed an article about the dangers of DDT to the *Reader's Digest*. She was refused. Carson went on with her ocean work, but continued to study DDT. While many scientists were worried about the spray, none had yet gathered together the many studies done.

In 1957 a group of citizens on Long Island sued the government for spraying DDT to eradicate the gypsy moth. While the trial produced evidence of DDT's risks, the case was lost on a legal technicality. By 1958, $200 million worth of pesticides were sold each year.

At last Carson found a publisher for her book about DDT's potential for destruction. Houghton Mifflin would publish *Silent Spring* in 1962.

The scope of Carson's research was enormous: she used the result of studies done worldwide to make a powerful case for the effects of pesticides on the ecology of the globe. In the process she brought to light the idea of ecology: how industry and, indeed, any human action, affects the balance of life.

In 1960 Carson had a breast tumor removed. Her struggle against cancer fed her fears about pesticides, which had been shown to increase the incidence of cancer in humans. Before her death in 1964 Carson saw the huge controversy that *Silent Spring* inspired. Her ideas were attacked widely by chemical companies, the U.S. Department of Agriculture, individual farmers, and local governments. She was accused of being ill-informed and emotional. The scientific community was supportive, however, and by the end of 1962 more than 40 bills for regulation of pesticides were on the agendas of state legislatures. DDT was finally banned over a two-year period that began in November 1969.

Rachel Carson. (Photo by Eric Hartmann, reprinted by permission of Rachel Carson Council)

Several 1992 model Chevrolet Lumina variable-fueled vehicles, calibrated to use ethanol, are being road-tested in Wisconsin and Illinois to determine ethanol fuel performance. (General Motors Corp.)

UBT insulation (1990)

The German group Bosch-Siemens Hausgeräte has found a substitute for CFC in the manufacture of polyurethane foam necessary for the insulation of refrigerators and freezers. The first appliances, available since summer 1990, contain the insulator UBT.

Suva coolants (1991)

In January 1991 Du Pont announced the launch of Suva, a new line of coolants that are thought to be ozone friendly. These coolants have been designed for a variety of cooling systems, including automobile air-conditioning systems and domestic refrigerators.

Waste

Acornic acid (1989)

KAERI, the South Korean institute for high-tech energy research, has obtained a patent for a process for the treatment of industrial effluent. It consists of an acid, obtained from acorns, that is capable of separating out the heavy metals contained in the effluent, including uranium. Chang-In-Sun and Yun Myong-Hwan discovered the depolluting properties of acornic acid. The new process has proved effective for effluent containing nickel, cadmium, mercury and lead.

Incineration by electron torch (1990)

An experimental plant for the high-temperature incineration (7,200° F) of solid chemical waste using an electron torch has been constructed at Pont-de-Chaix in France. The electron torch, which operates on the basis of a fluid composed of electrically neutral gas molecules, positive ions and negative electrons, was so named by chemist Irving Langmuir (U.S.) in 1928.

Biopol (1990)

On April 25, 1991, the British chemical company ICI announced the first commercial application of Biopol. It was the culmination of 15 years of research to find a plastic material that did not depend on fossil fuels for its manufacture and would be fully biodegradable. Biopol is the trade name for the homopolymer polyhydroxybutrate (PHB), which was first discovered in 1926 by Lemoigne at the Pasteur Institute in Paris, France. ICI uses microorganisms of the genus *Alcaligenes*, which are widely found in nature and convert sugar or starch quickly and safely by a process of fermentation, to produce a plastic in the form of a white powder. Not only can Biopol be produced in a natural way; it is also fully biodegradable. Once buried in the soil, it will totally degrade to carbon dioxide and water over a period of weeks.

Engines and Fuel

Catalytic converter (1909)

On April 17, 1909, Michel Frenkel (France) patented a "method of deodorizing exhaust fumes." Frenkel's invention didn't receive much attention until the mid-1970s when the need for unleaded gasoline revived interest in the catalytic converter. In 1974 General Motors developed the first modern catalytic converter.

The catalytic converter turns the polluting exhaust fumes into harmless substances by means of a series of chemical reactions. At the end of 1988 the Ford Motor Company produced a platinum-free catalytic converter that complies with required standards but is much less expensive.

Unleaded gasoline (1974)

Gasoline obtained by refining crude oil is lead-free. In the 1920s chemists decided to add alkyl leads in order to improve the performance of the internal combustion engine. Exhaust fumes from leaded gasoline proved to have an extremely high level of pollution, and legislation forced oil companies to revert to unleaded gasoline. Under the provisions of the Clean Air Act (1970), the Environmental Protection Agency required that unleaded gasoline must be available in all gas stations throughout the United States by July 1, 1974.

Anti-pollution engine (1988)

In 1988 the Japanese automobile manufacturer Toyota presented a low-pollution "weak mixture" engine at the Geneva Motor Show, Switzerland. The engine conformed to the most demanding antipollution standards of the day and did not need a catalytic converter.

Avocet (1989)

Avocet is an additive that improves ignition, reduces corrosion and also diminishes pollution. ICI launched Avocet in 1989 after seven years' development. In tests with vehicles run on alcohol mixed with avocet, soot emissions were reduced by 80 percent and nitrogen oxide emissions by 50 to 70 percent.

Ethanol fuel automobile (1992)

In June 1992, General Motors delivered the first production ethanol fuel automobile made in the United States, the Chevrolet Lumina Variable Fuel Vehicle (VFV), to the governor of Wisconsin. A fleet of 50 VFVs will be tested in Wisconsin and Illinois. The program is designed to evaluate the fuel economy, emissions performance and durability of ethanol fuel vehicles.

METEOROLOGY

Origins (c. 340 B.C.)

One of the first readings of meteorological observations on record dates back to the Yin Dynasty, c. 1300 B.C. However, the scientific study of meteorology began in about 340 B.C. with the publication of Aristotle's *Meteorologica*, which constitutes the first treatise on the atmosphere. In 278 B.C. Aratus did recommend the use of frogs as a means of forecasting the weather!

From 1855 Urbain Le Verrier (France, 1811–77) was responsible for setting up a network of meteorological data between the various European observatories.

Thermometer (1593)

The first thermometer was invented in 1593 by Galileo (Italy, 1564–1642). It was a gas thermometer that registered changes in temperature but could not measure them. A few years later, in 1612, Santorio (Italy) developed the water thermometer.

The first alcohol thermometers appeared in 1641, in Italy. One of the earliest was made in about 1645 by the enameler Mariani (Italy) to the specifications of Grand Duke Ferdinand II (1610–70) of Tuscany.

Barometer (1643)

The mercury barometer was the invention of Evangelista Torricelli (Italy, 1608–47), a student of Galileo.

Using this apparatus, Torricelli succeeded in demonstrating that air had its own variable weight, and that the weight variations (atmospheric pressure) could be measured by studying changes in the height of the mercury column in the tube.

Anemometer or wind gauge (1644)

The air-speed meter with blades was invented in 1644 by Robert Hooke (England, 1635–1703). The principle of this system for measuring wind speed was established in 1450 by Leone Battista Alberti (Italy). The pressure anemometer was invented in 1775 by James Lind (Ireland), and the windmill type anemometer still used today was perfected in 1846 by Thomas R. Robinson (also Ireland).

Hygrometer (1664)

This apparatus, which makes it possible to measure the amount of moisture in the air, was invented in 1664 by Francesco Folli. It was superseded in 1781 by the hair hygrometer, perfected by Horace Bénédict de Saussure (Switzerland): here the hair increases in length as the moisture content becomes higher. Later came the condensation hygrometer.

Meteorological map (1686)

The first known meteorological map was drawn in 1686 by Edmund Halley (Great Britain, 1656–1742) on his return from a voyage to the southern hemisphere. It was he who provided the first explanation of prevailing winds, monsoons and trade winds.

Fahrenheit thermometer (1715)

Daniel Gabriel Fahrenheit (Germany, 1686–1736) invented his thermometer in 1715. He replaced the alcohol with mercury, which has a very low freezing point (-38° F) and a very high boiling point (675° F), and developed a scale of degrees that is named after him.

Celsius thermometer (1741)

In 1741 Anders Celsius (Sweden, 1701–44) built a mercury thermometer on which he fixed the freezing point of water at 0 and the boiling point at 100. He divided the space in between into a hundred degrees.

The World Conference of Weights and Measures adopted the expression "degrees Celsius" (represented by the symbol °C) in October 1948. Today, under the name Kelvin (the Kelvin scale takes as its starting point not the freezing point of water but absolute zero: -459.69° F), it is one of the six base units of the international system.

Beaufort scale (1806)

This scale, graded from 0 to 12, which is used to record wind force, was proposed in 1806 by Admiral Sir Francis Beaufort (Great Britain, 1774–1857). Used by all Royal Navy ships from 1834, it makes it possible to standardize the information recorded in ships' log books. The Beaufort scale was adopted by all navies in 1854 and then by international meteorology in 1874. It is still of crucial importance for all navigators.

Weather balloons (1898)

The first weather balloons, designed to explore the atmosphere at high altitude automatically, were sent up in 1898. This was when Léon Teisserenc de Bort (France, 1855–1913) launched his first balloons from Trappes and discovered the stratosphere.

Weather radar (1949)

In 1924 E.V. Appleton and M.A.F. Barnett (both Great Britain) demonstrated the existence of the ionosphere (the area of the atmosphere in which the air is highly ionized), using the reflection of continuous waves.

However, the first program using radar for weather study was carried out in 1949 in the United States for the Thunderstorm Project, under the direction of M.H. Byers and R.R. Braham.

Weather radar allows scientists to track weather balloons equipped with reflectors, helps the detection of large storm clouds and rain, and allows the internal structure of some cloud masses to be examined.

Weather satellite (1960)

The first weather satellite was launched by the United States on April 1, 1960. The *Tiros 1* satellite was built by RCA.

On August 24, 1964 *Nimbus 1* was launched; this satellite produced the first good quality night photographs.

The first geostationary satellite was launched over the Pacific Ocean on December 6, 1966.

Sodar (1968/69)

The sodar (*so*und *d*etection *a*nd *r*anging) is a radar that, using sound waves that are emitted vertically and broadcast back by turbulence caused by changes in temperature, allows the three components of wind to be measured. The principle behind this device was described in 1968/69 by L.G. McAllister and G.G. Little (both U.S.).

Lidar (1976)

Lidar (*li*ght *d*etection *a*nd *r*anging) is an optical radar system. The transmitter is a laser and the receiver a telescope supported by a photocell detector. Louis D. Smullin and G. Fiocco (both U.S.) were the first to use Lidar for meteorological purposes, in 1976, in order to detect aerosols at a distance of up to 87 miles.

The French company Crouzet is working in collaboration with the American company Spectron to develop Lidar so that it can be incorporated into the control panel of an airplane and make it possible for air crews to detect wind shear.

Meteosat (1977)

On November 23, 1977 Meteosat, the first European geostationary satellite, was launched in the United States. Initially designed to have a life span of three years, *Meteosat-1* in fact kept working for eight years, providing meteorologists with the maps and satellite pictures seen daily on our television screens. It has not been in use since the end of 1985 and is at present drifting in orbit, having been replaced by *Meteosat-2*, which was brought into service in June 1981.

Doppler sodar (1979)

In 1979 the French company Bertin patented the Doppler sodar as a result of research carried out by J.-M. Fage. Sodar was developed in order to improve the safety of air traffic by providing a continuous measurement of wind by means of teledetection. The thermal structure of the atmosphere at high altitudes—its head—is also measured. Wind shear and the movement of atmospheric pollution can be monitored.

The Doppler effect was described by Christian Doppler (Austria, 1803–53). The effect concerns changes in wavelength that occur when the source of a vibration moves closer or further away.

GEOPHYSICS

Origins (6th century B.C.)

In the 6th century B.C. the Greek scholars Thales and Anaximander of Miletus were the first to collate the known pieces of information about the properties of the earth. In the 4th century B.C. the Greek geographer Pytheas theorized that the earth was round, and attempted to prove his theory by a series of voyages that took him as far north as the German coastline of the North Sea and possibly Iceland. The philosopher Aristotle (Greece, 384–322 B.C.) recounted the geophysical knowledge of his time in two works: *On the Heavens* and *Meteorologica*. These books were the basis of geophysics until the 17th century. Aristotle's pupil Eratosthenes (Greece, 284–192 B.C.) was the first to produce a fairly accurate calculation of the circumference of the earth. His estimate of 29,000 miles is within 4,200 miles of the most widely accepted calculation of 24,800 miles.

Seismology

Seismograph (132 B.C.)

The earliest known seismograph was invented in China in 132 B.C. by Zhang Heng. The device, which he called a seismoscope, registered the direction of the main earthquake tremor. Zhang Heng's system was later abandoned, and it wasn't until the 18th century that seismometers were invented anew in the West. Two men are credited with the invention: Jean de Hautefeuille (France) and Salsano (Italy).

The recording seismograph was perfected at the end of the 19th century. On April 27, 1894, Charles Howard Darwin (Great Britain) observed the tremors of an earthquake in Greece from Birmingham, England with a seismograph system he had developed using a bifilary pendulum.

Plate tectonics (1912)

The theory of continental drift was outlined by Alfred Wegener (Germany) in 1912. He proposed that the shape of the eastern coastline of South America indicated that at one time it fitted into the Gulf of Guinea on the west coast of Africa. Wegener's theory was discounted until the 1960s. During a Franco-American scientific expedition in 1974, the rift in the seabed of the Atlantic Ocean that separated the two continents was observed for the first time. Wegener's theory is now accepted by most scientists under the name of plate tectonics. It is believed that the continents are moving in relation to each other on 10 or so plates.

Richter scale (1935)

In 1857 Robert Mallet (Great Britain) had been the first seismologist to attempt to evaluate the intensity of earthquakes. Over the next 50 years various methods were put forward but it wasn't until the development of the Richter scale, in 1935, that one method gained wide acceptance. The work of Charles Richter (U.S.) in collaboration with Beno Gutenberg (U.S., b. Germany), the Richter scale is based on the conversion of the intensity of seismic waves recorded by seismographs into logarithmic calculations. The scale makes it possible for earthquakes to be classified on the basis of energy rather than superficial effects.

VAN method (1983)

The VAN method of forecasting earthquakes was developed in January 1983 by three engineers at the Institute of Physics of the University of Athens in Greece: P. Varostos, K. Alexopoulos and K. Nomicos. Although still in the experimental stage, it has produced some interesting results and can be considered an important step toward an improved method of forecasting earthquakes.

OCEANOGRAPHY

The diving bell (4th century B.C.)

The diving bell, which already existed in ancient times, was described in detail by Aristotle (Greece, 384–322 B.C.). There is no trace of it during the Middle Ages, but it reappears in Italy and Spain during the 16th century. In 1538, to the amazement of several thousand onlookers, including Charles V, two Greeks went to the bottom of the River Tagus in Toledo, Spain, and resurfaced without getting wet and without their lamp being blown out.

In 1552 Venetian fishermen carried out similar experiments in the Adriatic in the presence of the doge and senators. About the same time, the Venetians also invented a "diver's hood" known as the bagpipes.

Halley's bell (1721)

In 1721 Edmund Halley (Great Britain) developed the first diving bell worthy of the name. It was perfected in 1786 by John Smeaton (Great Britain, 1724–92).

The diving barrel (1721)

The progression from the diving bell to the early versions of the diving suit happened almost imperceptibly, so that it is impossible to give a precise indication of the origins of the first equipment that allowed the diver freedom of movement. However, it is generally thought that in 1721 John Lethbridge designed a piece of equipment shaped like a barrel, with two holes for the arms and a glass peephole so that the diver could see underwater. The equipment was not particularly practical, as the diver was forced to lie on his stomach and to return repeatedly to the surface in order to breathe.

A basic diving suit (1796)

The first diving suit in the true sense of the word was invented in 1796 by Klingert of Breslau, Germany (now Wroclaw in Poland). It consisted of a domed cylinder made of thick tinplate that completely covered the head and torso of the diver, leaving his arms free. A short-sleeved bodice and a pair of leather trunks protected his limbs from the water pressure, and the whole thing was completely watertight. Two glass-covered holes at eye level enabled the diver to see. A tube, one end of which was above the surface, was fitted to a hole level with the diver's nose, while a second tube, placed next to it, was intended to evacuate exhaled air. Two lead weights were attached to the diver's waist to provide ballast.

Diving suit with air pump (1829)

The first really effective diving equipment was invented in 1829 by Augustus Siebe (Great Britain), who was commissioned to supply the French Navy until 1857.

Diving suit with automatic air regulator (1865)

This piece of equipment, which played an essential part in the development of the diving suit, was the result of a collaboration between a mining engineer, Benoît Rouquayrol, and a ship's lieutenant, Auguste Denayrousse (both France), in 1865. The air regulator fulfilled the function of an artificial lung in the sense that the diver's lungs actually regulated the intake of air by acting directly on a distribution valve. This forerunner of the air "bottle" was developed in 1936 by the French naval officer and inventor Yves Le Prieur (France). Rouquayrol and Denayrousse were also responsible for inventing what can be considered the forerunner of the diving mask and breathing tube in about 1870. The mask was further developed by another naval officer, de Corlieu, who also invented flippers.

Aqualung (1867)

This version of the diving suit was presented at the Paris Universal Exhibition in 1867 by the New York Underwater Company. It consisted of a metal helmet and waterproof suit, but the diver also carried a tank of air on his back. The air was compressed at 17 atmospheres, and was enough to last one person for three hours at a depth of 65 ft.

First oceanic exploration (1872)

On December 21, 1872 the British schooner *Challenger*, the first oceanography ship in history, set sail. The *Challenger* was not to return until 1874, having set up 362 stations in all the seas of the globe. This schooner, weighing 2,306 metric tons, had been chartered by the members of the Royal Society to study everything having to do with the sea, following a purely chance discovery: in 1860 the transatlantic telegraph cable, laid two years previously, had been brought up from a depth of 5,900 ft to be repaired. The scientists and technicians on board were greatly surprised to find it covered with strange forms of plant and animal life, never seen before. It was during the course of *Challenger*'s 1872–74 voyage that polymetallic nodules were first discovered.

Air bottle (1936)

In 1936 Yves Le Prieur (France) developed equipment that consisted of a bottle filled with air compressed at 2,134 lb per sq in. and a pressure-reducing valve linked to the bottle that distributed air at a suitable pressure to a waterproof mask covering the face.

Cousteau aqualung (1943)

The final stage was reached in 1943 with the aqualung, developed by Jacques-Yves Cousteau (France) in collaboration with E. Gagnan.

Bathyscaphe (1948)

This diving apparatus was invented and tried out in 1948 by Auguste Piccard (Switzerland, 1884–1962). The first bathyscaphe descended, without a passenger, off the coast of Dakar, Senegal, to a depth of 453 ft. The American model *Trieste*, built by Prof. Piccard in 1953, holds the depth diving record. On January 23, 1960 it reached a depth of 35,815 ft in the deepest part of any ocean in the world, in the Marianas Trench near Guam in the Pacific.

The *Nautilus* (1985)

The *Nautilus*, weighing only 18 metric tons and able to carry three people, was developed in 1985 by IFREMER, the French institute for oceanic research. It consists of a titanium sphere 6½ ft in diameter and 6 in. thick, and is equipped with remote handling equipment in the form of two carbon fiber arms.

It proved particularly efficient during the exploration of the wreck of the *Titanic* during the summer of 1987. During an 18-month mission in the Atlantic and the Pacific, from Martinique to Japan via Hawaii and New Caledonia, the *Nautilus* made 198 dives, taking about 150,000 pictures of the ocean floor.

Robot diver (1986)

Jason Jnr was the name given to the robot used in the United States in 1986 by the Woods Hole Oceanographic Institute in the exploration of the seabed and in particular of the wreck of the *Titanic*. Attached by a cable to the submarine *Alvin* at a depth of 12,464 ft, *Jason Jnr* was lowered to the wreck, which lay at a depth of 13,120 ft.

The Jason project has been fully operational since 1988. It consists of two interconnected remote-controlled vehicles, equipped with cameras and a control arm. The two robots, controlled from a ship on the surface, can reach a depth of 19,680 ft.

Submarine helicopter (1986)

The first submarine helicopter, known as the *Deep Rover*, was constructed in 1986 by the California firm Deep Ocean Engineering Co. *Deep Rover* is a completely independent unit that can take a diver to a depth of 3,280 ft for a period of up to eight hours. Its main advantage is that the occupant breathes air at normal atmospheric pressure, which eliminates the need for decompression stages. From behind the panoramic window of the cabin, the pilot controls the movement of two remote-controlled arms that can perform such tasks as welding, bolting, sawing, etc. It is designed to carry out inspection and repair work on pipelines and oil rigs.

Mir-1 and Mir-2 (1987)

The Soviets began testing their first two research submarines in the Atlantic at the end of 1987. Mir-1 and Mir-2, capable of operating at a depth of more than 19,680 ft, were constructed by the Finnish shipyard Rauma-Repola under the scientific and technical supervision of the Russian Academy of Sciences. They have several advantages over other submarines of the same type. They have a greater traveling speed and operating range, a large energy reserve, the ability to change depth without discharging ballast, two manipulator arms and underwater drilling equipment. The Mir-1 and Mir-2 each carry a crew of three and have reached depths of 20,237 ft and 20,073 ft respectively.

Shinkai 6500 (1989)

The *Shinkai 6500* is a Japanese oceanographic research submarine that is capable of descending to 21,320 ft, a depth that no other submarine has reached. Constructed by Mitsubishi Heavy Industries Ltd., the *Shinkai 6500* carries three people and can explore 98 percent of the seabed, compared with 97 percent for the *Nautilus*.

WHAT ON EARTH?

NOT ALL INVENTIONS CHANGE OUR LIVES, SOME JUST MAKE US SCRATCH OUR HEADS.

SUPERPRESSURE BALLOON

Right: This monster balloon is not intended for use in the Thanksgiving Day parade, but to provide a new method for studying atmospheric trends. Designed to drift in the stratosphere, the superpressure balloon was patented by Winzen International Inc. of San Antonio, Tex., in 1992. It has a diameter in excess of 100 yards, can ascend to a level of 22 miles above the earth and can retain its position for as long as a year. A prototype has been built, and tests are scheduled for the end of 1992. (Winzen International)

GROWING PLASTIC TREES IN THE DESERT

There have been various attempts to prevent the advance of deserts by planting forests to contain them. After five years of development, in June 1991, Antonio Ibanez Alba (Spain) patented a plastic tree that is designed to overcome these problems.

The trees are about 30 feet high and have large foam leaves that help to pull in any nighttime moisture. This moisture is then transferred down the branches and the trunk by capillary action. In theory, by collecting dew at night and releasing the moisture during the day, the trees should enable the local microclimate to cool off sufficiently to attract clouds, and thus cause rain. This would permit real trees to be planted after about 10 years.

MOON CONCRETE

Right: Mechanical engineer T.D. Lin (U.S.) has developed a concrete that can be made on the moon from lunar soil. In 1986 NASA gave Lin 40 grams of lunar soil to conduct his experiments. Since 1988 samples of concrete have been created, and scientists are hopeful that this research will have a practical use in the near future. (Gamma/Gaillarde)

ONE-HANDED CLOCK

Left: Figuring that one hand is better than two, inventor Scott L. Sullivan (U.S.) decided to change the face of the traditional clock. The result is a "single-handed timepiece" that features a circle that moves around the face to each hourly position. As the circle rotates around the clock marking the hour time, it rotates on its own axis, and a marker indicates the minute time. In this photograph, the time is three o'clock. Sullivan received a U.S. patent for this device in 1992. (Scott Sullivan)

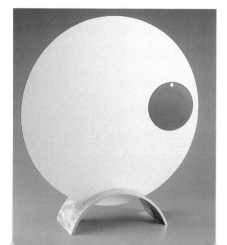

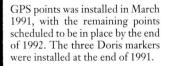

New ideas that may change the way we live

ARMAND BATTERY

Invented by Michel Armand (France), and developed industrially by Michel Gauthier (Canada) and his team at Hydro-Québec, the battery of the future is a filmlike structure no thicker than a sheet of paper. Instead of solid electrodes immersed in a liquid conductor, it consists of three delicate layers: of lithium, polymer-electrolyte and an insertion compound. The result is light, environment-friendly, and inexpensive. It is hoped that this battery will aid in the development of the electric automobile. Companies in Japan and Canada are working to produce the Armand battery commercially. Rival solid-battery designs are being developed by the Danish company Inovision and the British company Harwell.

OVIONIC BATTERY

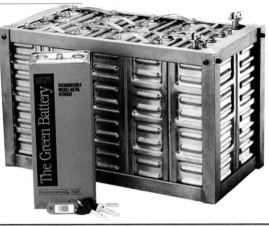

The ovionic battery. (Ovionic Battery Co.)

The ovionic battery, a nickel metal hydride battery, is also being developed for use in electric vehicles. In May 1992 the United States Advanced Battery Consortium (USABC) awarded the battery manufacturers, Ovionic Battery Co., a contract to demonstrate the feasibility of scaling up their battery for use in electric vehicles.

GE-90 REACTOR

Scheduled to be built by 1995, the GE-90 Reactor will be the largest civil engine in the world. It will have a thrust of between 75,000 and 95,000 lb, and is being designed for the new generation of large carrier twin-jet airplanes, such as the Boeing 777, anticipated for launch in the late 1990s. The pioneers of this program are General Electric and SNECMA of France.

SATELLITE EARTHQUAKE FORECASTS

A system of satellites is being installed in space to study the frequency of earthquake recurrence and to correlate data to predict future earthquakes. Covering a zone that measures 250 miles long by 95 miles wide, perpendicular to the coast of Chile, where a major earthquake is expected before the end of the century, this system will comprise a network of geodesic points (the Global Positioning System that is connected to the American satellites of the NAVSTAR network), Doris markers (a system designed by the French National Center for Space Studies [CNES]) and the Spot 2 satellite. The first section of 17

GPS points was installed in March 1991, with the remaining points scheduled to be in place by the end of 1992. The three Doris markers were installed at the end of 1991.

NOAA WIND PROFILER NETWORK

In May 1992 the National Oceanic and Atmospheric Administration (NOAA) announced that a 29-station network of wind profiling systems had become operational. This demonstration program is designed to monitor low-level winds that stir local and regional weather patterns. Located in 15 midwestern and western states, the wind profilers use a new type of Doppler radar to measure wind speed and direction information at 72 different levels in a column of air up to an altitude of 10 miles. This information is transmitted hourly to the National Weather Service for transmission throughout the United States.

The wind profiler machine. (NOAA/FSL)

AQUAPHALT

Aquaphalt is a mixture of asphalt, cement and a water-absorbent polymer— accogel— which can soak up over 300 times its initial volume. The components remain liquid as long as they are kept separate. Once mixed, they instantly form a solid material, strong and of high plasticity, that easily adheres to other substances. Perfected by researchers at Hokkaido University, Japan in collaboration with the Okumura Company, aquaphalt could prove to be an extremely useful building material in areas subject to earthquakes, because of its flexibility and capacity to withstand stress without breaking. It is currently being tested for use in the planned Tokyo Bay Tunnel.

SOLAR SPHERES

A new technology called Spheral Solar Technology is being developed by two American companies: Southern California Edison and Texas Instruments. Very different in appearance from traditional solar cells, this trapping device is composed of aluminum leaves about 25 cm sq on which are planted 17,000 small silicon spheres. Each ball converts solar energy into electrical energy. This new cell has several advantages over current models: it is cheaper to use, can operate using silicon of lower purity levels, and produces higher yields.

ANTIPOLLUTION ARTIFICIAL LAKE

In 1992 David P. Murray received a U.S. patent for an artificial lake designed to erase the problems of pollutants caused by water runoff from residential development. Chemicals used to fertilize lawns or protect building materials often show up in water supplies as a result of runoff following heavy rainfalls. Murray, an aquatic biologist, devised an artificial lake that uses plants, such as pondweeds, to absorb these chemicals. Murray's lake features a flat plateau in the center, where the plants can be cultivated and also cropped if they begin to choke the water system. A trench forms a boundary around the lake, which contains plants, such as coontail, that fight algae.

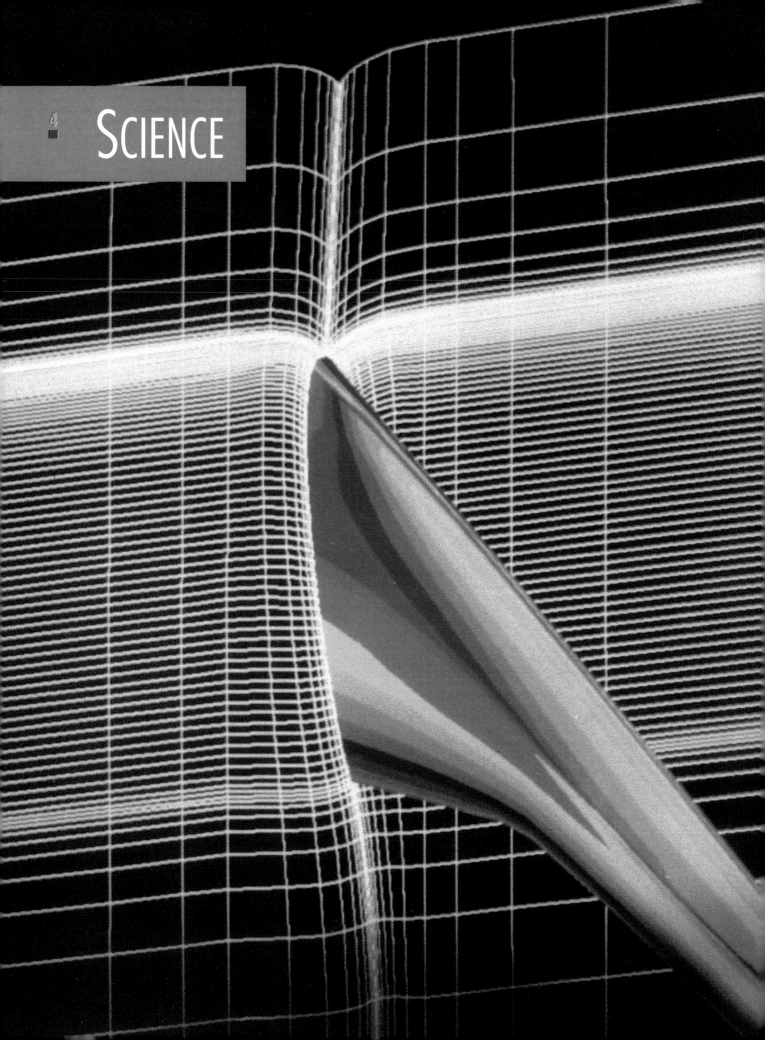

SCIENCE

MATHEMATICS

Numbers

Numeration (3rd millennium B.C.)

Numbers were first written in the 3rd millennium B.C., as is attested to by the clay tablets discovered in Susa and Uruk (currently Warka in Iraq) and those from Nippur (Babylon, 2200 to 1350 B.C.). The Babylonian system of numeration is on a base of 60. Our time divisions are a vestige of this. There was no zero; missing units were simply indicated by a space.

The ancient Mayan system was on a base of 20—the number of fingers and toes. This was a position system and included a final zero which was not an operator.

In the 5th century B.C. the Greeks used the letters of the alphabet. For units of one thousand, the nine first letters accompanied by an inferior accent to their left were used ($\alpha = 1$ and, $\alpha = 1000$). This system, which had no zero, was used for a thousand years. The Hebrews and Arabs adapted it for their own alphabets. Calculations were then made using abacuses. Numbers were represented by pebbles (the word *calculation* derives from the word *calculus*, meaning pebble).

Irrational numbers (6th century B.C.)

Pythagoras (Greece, *c.* 580–*c.* 500 B.C.) demonstrated the impossibility of writing the number $\sqrt{2}$ as a fraction, and hence revealed the existence of irrational numbers. A general form of the theory relating to this exists in Euclid's *Elements*.

Zero (4th century B.C.)

Babylonian numeration was perfected in the 4th century B.C. by the appearance of the zero in mathematical texts. The zero was placed either at the beginning of a number or within a number, but never at the end.

The word *zero* comes from *sunya*, which means "nothing" in Sanskrit; it became *sifr* in Arabic and was Latinized into *zephirum* by Leonardo Fibonacci. It was fixed at zero in 1491 by a Florentine treatise.

Prime numbers (3rd century B.C.)

In the 3rd century B.C. Euclid (Greece) demonstrated that there are an infinite number of prime numbers. The riddle of Eratosthenes (*c.* 284–*c.* 192 B.C.) was the first method used to investigate these numbers systematically. Nonetheless, in 1876 Edouard Lucas (France) developed a method to study the primary nature of some large numbers.

Golden number (3rd century B.C.)

The golden number is the solution, x, of the equation

$$\frac{1}{x} = \frac{x}{1+x}$$

where x is equal to

$$\frac{1+\sqrt{5}}{2} \qquad (\approx 1.618)$$

and exists in an asymmetrical sharing when the ratio between the largest of the two parts and the smallest is equal to the ratio between the whole and the largest. This number was known before Euclid, but it was he who, in the 3rd century B.C., made of it a famous problem by seeking to divide a straight line in mean and extreme ratio or "golden section."

The harmony based on this golden number has been studied in numerous arts: in architecture (Phidias, who worked on sculptures in the Parthenon in the 5th century B.C., Alberti in the 15th century; Le Corbusier in the 20th century), in music (Pythagorean research on sound intervals), and in painting (Leonardo da Vinci, Raphael).

The number π (3rd century B.C.)

By using polygons of 96 sides, inscribed and excribed to the circle, Archimedes (Greece, 287–212 B.C.) demonstrated that the number π is located between

$$3+\frac{10}{71} \quad \text{and} \quad 3+\frac{10}{70}$$

Thus, when Ptolemy (Greek mathematician of the 2nd century A.D.) adopted the value of 3.1416 for π he noted, to justify it, that it was nearly the mean of the two Archimedean boundaries.

In 1874 William Schanks (Great Britain) calculated the first 707 decimal places of π engraved in the Palace of Discovery in Paris, France. The first 527 places are exact, but the remainder are wrong. Since then, through the use of the computer, π has been calculated to millions of decimal places.

Modern numerations (5th century A.D.)

Around the 5th century A.D., decimal position arithmetic appeared in India: it used 10 figures from 0 to 9 such as we know today. In 829 Mohammad Ibn Musa al-Khwârizmî (780–850) published a treatise on algebra in Baghdad in which he adopted this decimal system. A French monk named Gerbert became interested in the Arabic figures during his voyage (980) to Córdoba in Spain, and was able to spread the use of these symbols when he became Pope Sylvester II in April 999. However, it was not until Leonardo Fibonacci, known as Leonard of Pisa, through his *Liber Abaci*, written in 1202, that Arabic numbering began to spread throughout Europe. In 1440, thanks to the invention of printing, the shape of these 10 figures was definitively fixed.

Decimal numbers (16th century)

Up until the end of the 16th century the system of base 10 had only been developed for whole numbers. Numbers between whole numbers were expressed as fractions over the base of 60, which was used for expressing units of time (minutes in the hour) and angles.

François Viète (France) declared in 1579 that sixtieths should be replaced by thousandths, hundredths and tenths, and in 1582 Simon Stevin (Belgium, 1548–1620) suggested using decimal numbers in calculations, but decimals were not widely adopted during the 17th century. Stevin also proposed the decimal division of units of measurement. But it was not until the French Revolution that a decimal metric system was established (December 10, 1799).

Complex numbers (16th century)

Raphael Bombelli (Italy, 1526–73) gave the first definition of complex numbers, which he called "impossible" or "imaginary" numbers. He defined these numbers from his study of cubic numbers, and introduced the concept of $\sqrt{-1}$. A complex number is the sum of a real number and an imaginary one, e.g. $(a+\sqrt{-1}b)$.

Until 1746 people used these imaginary entities without really knowing how they were structured. In that year, however, Jean Le Rond d'Alembert (France) established their general form as $a + b\sqrt{-1}$, assuming the principle of the existence of n roots of an equation of degree n. Leonhard Euler (Switzerland, 1707–83) introduced the notation "i" to designate $\sqrt{-1}$, a notation taken up again by Gauss in 1801.

Transcendental numbers (18th century)

It was in the 18th century that mathematicians came up with the notion of the transcendental number. We call a number, say ∞, transcendental if there does not exist an algebraic equation with rational coefficients with ∞ as a root.

In 1844 Joseph Liouville (France) gave the first example of a transcendental number. Then in 1873 Charles Hermite (France) showed that "e" (the base for natural logarithms) was transcendental, and in 1882 Ferdinand von Lindemann (Germany) demonstrated the same for π.

Fractals (19th century)

We know that the spatial dimensions of normal geometric objects are always integers. Thus a point has a dimension of zero; a line, or a segment of a line, has a dimension equal to one; a surface element has a dimension equal to two, and so on. Fractals are unusual objects whose dimension, known as the *fractal dimension*, has a non-integer value, for example 4/3 or π. Thus they are objects that are geometrically intermediate between points, lines, surfaces, etc.

Let us take the case of a fractal belonging to a two-dimensional plane, and use a fractal dimension that is bounded between one and two. Such a fractal, which is called a *fractal curve*, occupies (intuitively) "more space" in the plane than a traditional curve, yet without occupying the entire plane. Fractals in fact have an extremely complex structure with many ramifications and convolutions. Some have regular structures whose features are repeated identically on all scales, and others are completely irregular.

The origin of the notion of fractals dates back to the end of the 19th century. The mathema-

---

Previous page: A simulation of the transonic flow around the wing of an aircraft. (Onera)

ticians of the time discovered astonishing mathematical objects possessing some of the qualities of fractals. In 1872 Weierstrass built a curve that was continuous but nondifferentiable on all its points; and in 1890 Giuseppe Peano obtained a curve that completely filled a square. These results were unexpected, and Peano, contemplating his theorem, exclaimed: "I see it, but I don't believe it!" The first known fractal is probably Georg Cantor's triadic set (1883). It is a fractal with a dimension between zero and one.

It was only in 1919 that Felix Hausdorff invented the fractal dimension. The word "fractal" itself is recent: it was introduced in 1962 by Benoît Mandelbrot (France), who suggested that fractals could be useful in the study of natural forms, such as coastlines, for example.

Geometry

Thales' theorem (7th–6th century B.C.)

Before Thales, each surveyor or geometer found gadgets with which to measure distances, surfaces, etc. The Greek philosopher and mathematician of the Ionian school Thales of Miletus (c. 624–c. 546 B.C.) had the very clever idea of measuring heights by using shadow at the same time that the "shadow is equal to the object." That is when the sun's rays are projected at 45°. In order to measure the height of the Great Pyramid, he refined his method by using the rays at any given hour. He might have left it at that, but he wanted to formulate a theory based on his experiments. The use of the sun's rays caused him to study parallel lines and the ratios between the lengths projected and the initial lengths. He then drew up his theorem, called Thales' theorem: "Parallels are projected from a straight line onto another line of proportional length." Thales of Miletus thereby introduced the deductive and demonstrative aspect of mathematics to geometry.

Pythagoras' theorem (6th century B.C.)

Using the work of Thales on parallel lines and projections, and in the same spirit of demonstration, Pythagoras, the Greek philosopher and mathematician of the 6th century B.C., became interested in orthogonal projections and demonstrated the theorem that bears his name. This theorem establishes a relationship between the lengths of the sides of a right-angled triangle: that the square of the hypotenuse is equal to the sum of the squares of the other two sides. This relationship had been known since surveyors had begun to practice, but Pythagoras was the first to demonstrate it.

The circle (3rd century B.C.)

The circle is a favorite mathematical object and it has always been an object of study. Humans have long contemplated the perfect circles of the moon and the sun, and before the invention of the written word, drew and measured the circle. The oldest known written definition of the circle is the 15th of Euclid's 23 preliminary definitions in *Elements* (3rd century B.C.). The oldest satisfactory definition of its surface is given by the Egyptian Rhind Papyrus, dating back to 1700 B.C.

Conic sections (3rd century B.C.)

Conic sections have been studied in very different ways over the centuries, and are a good example of how geometry has evolved from antiquity to the present.

Apollonius of Perga (c. 262–c. 180 B.C.), in his treatise on conic sections, studied various ways of cutting a cone. He then showed how parabolas, hyperbolas and elipses would be obtained: he also originated these terms.

In the 17th century, René Descartes (France, 1596–1650) translated conic sections into equations and showed that they could be obtained from second degree equations.

Blaise Pascal (France, 1623–62) developed the modern aspect by approaching conic sections from an analytical point of view. In the 20th century, they are part of the general theory of quadratic forms.

Euclidean assumption (3rd century B.C.)

The Greek mathematician Euclid (3rd century B.C.) worked mainly on a synthesis of his predecessors' work. In his *Elements*, he structured the knowledge of his era by redemonstrating everything from five assumptions that were considered to be true even though they could not be demonstrated. The foremost amd best known is: given a point exterior to a straight line, there exists a unique line that is parallel to this straight line. The contrary of this assumption had been imagined by Aristotle. Until the 19th century, mathematicians thought that the demonstration of this assumption was possible. Thus, in the 18th century, numerous mathematicians tried in vain to demonstrate it by absurdity. Two possible negations appeared: at least one point exists by which there is no straight line parallel to a given straight line. The other was: at least one point exists by which at least two distinct parallel lines pass. The fact of having clearly expressed these two contrary thoughts allowed the following century to create two new kinds of geometry.

Trigonometry (3rd–2nd century B.C.)

During antiquity, trigonometry developed as a technique annexed to astronomy. Thus, the Greek astronomers Aristarchus of Samos (c. 300 B.C.) and Hipparchus of Nicea (c. 200 B.C.), were the precursors of trigonometry. The Alexandrian Ptolemy (A.D. c. 80–c. 160) summarized all the knowledge of the era in his treatise, the *Almageste*.

It was the Arabs who, during the 9th and 10th centuries, developed trigonometry as a separate science. Al Khwârizmî (780–850) established the first sine tables, and Habasch al Hasib those of the tangents. The *Perfection of the Almageste* (877–929) by al Bâttâni was a veritable treatise on modern trigonometry and was much more complete than Ptolemy's *Almageste*. The studies were taken up and elaborated upon by Johan Müller (Germany, 1436–76) and Georg Rhaeticus (Germany, 1514–76). Abraham de Moivre (1667–1754) and Leonhard Euler (1707–83) made a radius and an angle correspond to each complex number, thus allowing trigonometry to be dealt with by means of the exponential form of complex numbers. Trigonometry was thereby integrated into an algebraic theory.

Coordinates (17th century)

The use of numbers for the univocal location of a point on a surface had been known since the time of Archimedes (3rd century B.C.). But it was not until the 17th century that coordinates were used in a systematic way in problems of geometry. Legend has it that René Descartes (France, 1596–1650) had the idea while watching an insect flying by his window. This discovery allowed geometrical problems to be analyzed using algebraic techniques; thus, with Pierre de Fermat (France, 1601–65), analytic geometry, in which equations and curves were linked, had its beginnings.

Euler's nine-point circle (18th century)

The nine-point circle of Leonhard Euler (Switzerland, 1707–83) is a circle that can be built very simply from a triangle. It passes through the middle of the sides of the triangle, through the bases of the perpendiculars of the triangle, and through the three points that are equidistant from the apexes of the triangle and the intersection of the perpendiculars.

This circle is famous not only because it is mathematically interesting, but also because it is indicative of Euler's talents. Leonhard Euler was actually blind when he discovered the nine-point circle. He lost his right eye when he was young, and he lost the use of his left eye at the age of 50 through cataracts. Therefore Euler had to visualize the positions of the nine points mentally, without seeing them, before recognizing and demonstrating that these points were all situated on the same circle.

Non-Euclidean geometries (18th century)

In the 18th century Giovanni Girolamo Saccheri, Johann Heinrich Lambert, Taurinus, Reid and numerous other mathematicians tried to work out the logical consequences of the negatives of Euclid's postulate; but they came up with no complete theories. At the beginning of the 18th century, these theories took shape and developed into two different geometries, both possible and practicable.

Vectors (1798)

Caspar Wessel (Denmark), in 1798, and Jean-Robert Argand (Switzerland), in 1806, wrote two papers on complex numbers. Both of them had the idea of not only representing complex numbers by points A on a plane, but also of identifying them by the vector from the origin 0 to the extremity A on a Cartesian plane. Thus the notion of $\overrightarrow{OA}$ vector was born: the sum of two complex numbers then allowed the sum of two vectors to be worked out. Vectors, quantities specified by both magnitude and direction, are thus geometrical objects, which can undergo the same sort of operations as number sets.

Structure of vectorial space (1844)

Hermann Grassmann (Germany, 1809–77), in his "theory of linear extension" of 1844, defined vectorial spaces in more than three dimensions. At the same time Sir William Rowan Hamilton (Ireland, 1805–65), with his study of quaternions, elaborated the first vector system. These definitions were very useful to physics at the time when the theory of relativity was developed, in which space-time is considered as a vectorial space in the fourth dimension.

Hyperbolic geometry (19th century)

Jéanus Bolyai (Hungary, 1802–60) and Nicolai Ivanovitch Lobatchevski (Russia, 1792–1856) created a geometry in which the plane is a hyperbolic surface. Each of its points is shaped like a saddle.

Definition of geometry (1872)

Various works on non-Euclidean geometries at the beginning of the 19th century stirred up passionate debate and violent polemics; they revolutionized the philosophy of knowledge, in fact, more than geometry itself.

Thus it was necessary to bring this work together and create a theory large enough to accommodate these coexisting but different worlds of geometry. Christian Felix Klein (Germany, 1849–1925), in his opening address to the Erlangen congress (the "Erlangen program," 1872), defined geometry as the study of "groups" or "collections" of transformations, leaving certain geometrical objects invariable, such as medians and perpendiculars. In studying the structure of these groups, Klein integrated geometries into one algebraic theory.

Elliptic geometry (19th century)

Johann Karl Friedrich Gauss (Germany, 1777–1855) created a geometry in which a plane was defined as the surface of a sphere with an infinite radius.

Bernhard Riemann (Germany, 1826–66), a student of Gauss at Göttingen, continued his work and proposed a revision of classical geometry, allowing elliptical geometry to be considered as a particular case of a more general theory.

Algebra

Origins (3rd century A.D.)

The word *algebra* comes from the Arabic word *al-jabr*: to reduce. It is generally considered that the work of Diophantus of Alexandria (3rd century) was the first step in the history of algebra. It was in his *Thirteen Books of Arithmetic* that mathematicians such as Pierre de Fermat (France, 1601–65) and François Viète (France, 1540–1603) found the starting point for their own research. François Viète is often considered to be the inventor of modern algebra. He founded the algebraic language in 1591 in his work *Ars analytica*. The language uses letters not only to indicate unknowns and indeterminates but also to form words or algebraic expressions.

Algebraic equations

1st and 2nd degree equations (1700 B.C.)

Some examples of the solution to 1st and 2nd degree equations attached to specific problems were found in the Rhind Papyrus (Egypt), which dates back to 1700 B.C. Chinese literature offers examples of solutions to these two systems of equation by two unknown writers, in the work *Nine Chapters on the Art of Calculus* (c. 200 B.C.).

The history of 2nd degree equations goes back to the Babylonian civilization of the 2nd millennium (1800 B.C.). The Babylonian arithmeticians knew how to solve all equations of the 2nd degree but did not express them in real number sets. The Greeks in the 3rd century B.C. made the solution of 2nd degree equations the basis of all their geometry, and in order to make them work for real sets, they replaced the Babylonian calculations with constructions by ruler and compass. The Greek algebraists, however, calculated within the set of positive rational numbers, which left many equations unsolved. It was not until the 16th century and the identification of complex numbers that all 2nd degree equations could be solved.

Algebraic symbols (15th–17th century)

The Egyptians used symbols: addition was indicated by two legs walking in the same direction, and subtraction by two legs walking in opposite directions. Conversely, no symbolism is found with the Greeks, where each reasoning process was written out fully.

It was the Germans, the English and the French, in the 15th to 17th centuries, who introduced symbolic calculation. Our + and – signs, which appear in 1498 in an arithmetic book by Johannes Widmann (Germany) were promulgated by Michael Stifel (Germany) in 1544 in his treatise on algebra, *Arithmetica integra*. The root sign $\sqrt{}$ was invented by Cristoff Rudoff in 1526. The sign × is more recent, and William Oughtred (England, 1637) is credited with using it for the first time. The greater than > and smaller than < signs are due to Thomas Harriot (England, 1631). Finally, in 1637 René Descartes (France, 1596–1650) created the use of figures placed as exponents to designate powers (e.g., $9 = 3^2$), and John Wallis (England, 1656) was responsible for the idea of negative exponents ($1/9 = 3^{-2}$).

3rd and 4th degree equations (16th century)

The Italian school of the 16th century brought solutions to the resolution of 3rd and 4th degree equations. The three pioneers were, successively, Scipione del Ferro, Niccolò Fontana, called Tartaglia (c. 1500–57), and Girolamo Cardano (1501–76).

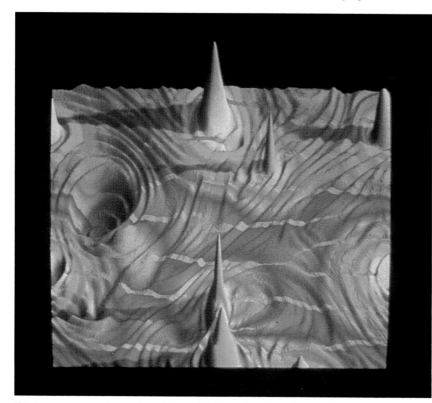

This is a numeric simulation of a turbulence field based on the mathematical concept of "wavelets" as developed by J.O. Stromberg and Yves Mayer. (CNRS-CMOL/Farge)

Fermat's last theorem (1637)

Pierre de Fermat (France, 1601–65) asserted in 1637 that he had demonstrated the following theorem: "There do not exist positive integers x, y, z, n such that $x^n + y^n = z^n$, where n is greater than 2."

In the 17th century mathematicians were not very interested in demonstrating their theorems. So Fermat never published his proofs, simply stating this last theorem, which he believed he had demonstrated. A number of such statements by Fermat were later found to be correct and important, so scientists were accustomed to treat the great mathematician's assertions with considerable respect.

Fermat's "Last Theorem" has never been completely proved after 300 years of research and is the mathematical problem for which the greatest number of incorrect proofs have been published. We only know that the theorem is valid for all the value of n between 1 and 30,000, but a complete proof is remarkably elusive. Mathematicians think that the general theorem is true and hope to prove it eventually.

Theory of probabilities (1656)

The theory of probabilities was born from the study of games of chance. The word *hazard*, transmitted through Spain, comes from the Arabic *az-zahr*, meaning "the die." Blaise Pascal and Pierre de Fermat (both France) were the first, in their correspondence, to try to "mathematize" games of chance.

Christiaan Huygens (Netherlands, 1629–95), aware of this correspondence, published in 1656 the first complete account of the calculation of probabilities, *De Ratiociniis in ludo aleae*. Subsequently, Jacques Bernoulli (1654–1705) wrote the work *Ars conjectandi*, a deeper study of the science than that of Huygens. Finally, it was Pierre-Simon de Laplace (France, 1749–1827) who produced work on the application of mathematical analysis to the theory of probabilities that had a philosophical element.

Statistics (1746)

In 1746 a professor from Göttingen, Germany, Gottfried Achenwall, created the term *statistics*. In fact, the gathering of data goes back to antiquity. For example, the Chinese Emperor Yao organized a census of agricultural production in 2238 B.C.

Adolphe Quetelet (Belgium), in 1853, was the first to think that statistics might be based on the calculation of probabilities.

The appearance of powerful calculators gave birth to methods of analysis of multidimensional data that are currently enjoying wide popularity.

Abel and the 5th degree equation (1826)

While he was still a student, Niels Henrik Abel (Norway, 1802–29) attacked the formidable problem of solving an algebraic equation of the 5th degree. One day he thought he had cracked it, but soon saw that his proof had an error in it. He then decided to prove that it was in fact impossible to solve the general quintic equa-

tion. In 1826 he proved his revolutionary result: that it is indeed impossible to solve equations of degree greater than four by means of radicals.

Abel decided to visit the two greatest mathematicians of the time, Johann Karl Freidrich Gauss (Germany) and Augustin Cauchy (France, 1789–1857), and show them his results. But they did not want to acknowledge the genius of the 24-year-old, and could not be bothered to understand his extraordinary paper. Unrecognized and despairing, Abel returned to Norway, where he died of tuberculosis at the age of 27.

Group structure (19th century)

During the course of the 19th century, many groups were studied at the same time that work was being carried out on various equations. Augustin Cauchy (France, 1789–1857) studied groups of permutations of roots of algebraic equations. Evariste Galois (1811–32) continued this work and developed a theory of groups that unfortunately remains unfinished; he was killed in a duel at the age of 21. His theory, despite some oversights, remained a guide for further research.

During the period 1870 to 1880, Sophus Lie (Norway, 1842–99) formulated the theory of continuous groups of transformation or "Lie groups," notably to study differential equations. These groups were used by Klein in his Erlangen program. Since then, this group structure has been used in all modern mathematics and physics, in research on atomic structures.

Mathematical logic (1854)

The self-taught George Boole (Great Britain, 1815–64) was the creator of symbolic logic. In 1847 he published a short treatise (*Mathematical Analysis of Logic*) in which he maintained that logic must be connected to mathematics and not to philosophy.

In 1854, in his treatise *An Investigation of the Laws of Thought*, Boole set out the results of his thinking. Thus began what is today called Boolean algebra, a system of symbolic logic that codifies nonmathematical logical operations, using the numerical values 0 and 1 only. Logic took its current form in 1879 with Gottlob Frege, whose work was introduced to the public by the philosopher Bertrand Russell in 1903.

Matrices (1858)

The study of systems of equations and linear transformations led Arthur Cayley (Great Britain, 1821–95) to establish tables called matrices, and to define operations on these tables.

Matrix algebra was thus developed, and he published it in a thesis in 1858. His work permitted the further study of the structures of linear transformation groups and prepared the ideas that were put forth by Christian Felix Klein in his Erlangen program (1872).

The set of real numbers (19th century)

In the 4th century B.C. the Greek mathematician and astronomer Eudoxus tried to put into the

form of a set numbers not limited to the rational, which he sensed were insufficient. He was not successful; neither were any number of later mathematicians of antiquity, who were reluctant to deal with irrational numbers.

It was not until the 19th century that Georg Cantor (Germany, b. Denmark, 1845–1918) studied irrational quantities and the notion of "continuity," taking account of the "continuum" aspect of the law of real numbers, formed by an infinity of distinct points, each representing a number. This gave rise to many paradoxes that challenged intuitive ideas. Cantor, aware of the break with traditional good sense, had to struggle for several years to convince his contemporaries of this arithmetic of the infinite. When he died on January 6, 1918, his work had become universally accepted.

Theory of groups (19th and 20th centuries)

Since the work of philosopher and mathematician Gottfried Wilhelm von Leibnitz (Germany, 1646–1716) it had appeared indispensable to create notations and symbols to systematize logic. In his algebra, George Boole (Great Britain, 1815–64) made the union and the intersection of groups correspond to addition and multiplication, on the one hand, and the "or" and "and" on the other. Thus, parallel to logical symbols, symbols and a theory of groups appeared.

Giuseppe Peano (Italy, 1858–1932) introduced in 1895 the symbol $\in$ which signifies "belonging to," $\cup$ for the combination of two sets and $\cap$ for their intersection. Schröder (Germany) in 1877 introduced $\subset$ for inclusion.

With the work of Cantor on real groups, paradoxes appeared that led Peano to define the cardinal number of a group. Emile Borel (France, 1871–1956) introduced the notion of innumerable groupings that opened up 20th century research to topology and the theory of measurement.

Analysis

Logarithm (1614)

Archimedes (3rd century B.C.), in his *Study of the Grains of Sand*, calculated the number of grains of sand necessary to fill the universe, and was close to becoming the inventor of logarithms. Nicolas Chuquet (France, 1445–1500) invented arithmetical and geometrical progressions, as well as negative exponents, but it was John Napier (Scotland, 1550–1617) who invented logarithms in 1614 while doing research on a new method of numerical calculation. His system allows the replacement of multiplications by additions, and divisions by subtractions, using the smallest numbers. However, he did not find his results satisfactory and so developed, together with his friend, Henry Briggs (England, 1561–1631), the decimal or common logarithm. He was then able to calculate each of the first 31,000 prime numbers to 14 decimal places.

Ptolemy's cosmological system (earth at the center of the universe) was first challenged by Copernicus in the 16th century. (Dagli-Orti)

limit. Jules Henri Poincaré (France, 1854–1912) is considered to be the inventor of algebraic and differential topology.

Nonstandard analysis (1960s)

Nonstandard analysis was invented in the 1960s by A. Robinson (U.S.). It is a branch of mathematics that makes it possible to define rigorously, and to use in a practical manner, numbers that are intuitively qualified as infinitely large or infinitely small. Robinson effectively showed that it is possible to construct logically a new analysis, called nonstandard, in which the set of numbers of standard analysis (the usual analysis) are complemented by infinitely greater or smaller numbers that are greater or smaller than all the standard numbers.

This analysis ensures greater rigor in many calculations and makes an important contribution to the study of complex geometric objects such as fractals, and of chaotic physical phenomena.

PHYSICS

Foundations of Physics

Cosmological model (antiquity)

In the 5th century B.C. the Pythagoreans (the disciples of the renowned Greek scholar and philosopher Pythagoras), together with the Greek Eudoxus of Cnidus, imagined a system of concentric spheres, whose rotational axes, variously inclined, passed through a common center: the earth. This cosmological system was systematized by the last astronomer of antiquity, Ptolemy (A.D. c. 80–c. 160) of Alexandria.

The Copernican system (16th century)

Nicolaus Copernicus (Poland, 1473–1543), doctor of law, canon and passionate astronomer, seems to have developed in the early 16th century the cosmogony for which he would become famous: that the earth itself rotates and, like other planets, it rotates around the sun.

Copernicus understood the Church, and he must have anticipated the general outcry from the theologians when his theory ruined their certainty that the earth, and thus man, the "image of God," was the center of the universe. So Copernicus did not rush to publish his book, *De revolutionibus orbium cœlestium libri VI*, and instead put it into the hands of his friend Georg Rhaethicus. The work appeared a few days before Copernicus died, on May 24, 1543.

A little-known but very interesting fact to remember: 18 centuries before Copernicus, Aristarchus of Samos (Greece, c. 310–c. 230 B.C.) had been the first to conceive of a heliocentric universe. Unlike his contemporaries, he thought that the earth and the other planets went around the sun, and not vice versa. Moreover, he had noted the rotation of the earth itself.

Functions (17th century)

Gottfried Wilhelm von Leibnitz (Germany, 1646–1716) had the idea of treating problems by analogy; in effect, he was interested in the similarities between various problems. In particular, he noted in his correspondence with Jean Bernoulli (Switzerland, 1667–1748) that some variables, such as time and distance, might be linked and expressed one as a function of the other. He thus used functions and expressed them using the form $\psi(\chi)$. This discovery was made while researching new methods of calculation that developed during the next century under the name of infinitesimal calculation.

Infinitesimal calculus (18th century)

Jean Bernoulli, professor of mathematics in Basle, Switzerland, explained and disseminated the calculation methods of Leibnitz and introduced them to France around 1691. He was also the professor of Leonhard Euler (Switzerland, 1707–83), who ordered and developed the work of his predecessors. Euler provided the first general theory of variation calculus, clarified the notion of the function, and reassembled all these results in his *Institutiones calculi dif-*
ferentialis (1755) and *Institutiones calculi integralis* (1768–70).

Independently of the work of Leibnitz and of Euler, Sir Isaac Newton (Great Britain, 1642–1727) formulated a theory of calculus that deals with exactly the same problems. Therefore, at practically the same time, infinitesimal calculus made its appearance in various scientific communities. In the 19th century integral calculus made considerable progress thanks to the work of Georg Friedrich Bernhard Reimann (Germany, 1826–66).

Topology (19th–20th century)

Topology is that part of mathematics that studies the ideas, *a priori* intuitive, of continuity and limit. Until the beginning of the 19th century, mathematicians had used these ideas without defining them correctly. David Hilbert (Germany, 1862–1943) sought to make them axiomatic and introduced "neighborhoods." Maurice Fréchet (France) and Frederick Riesz (Hungary), at the beginning of the 20th century, defined respectively the notions of "metric theory" and of "topology." Finally, around 1940, the definition of "filters" by Henri Cartan (France) rounded off the history of the idea of

Laws of dynamics (17th century)

In his *Discourses and Demonstrations Concerning Two New Sciences*, published in 1638, Galileo stated the principle of inertia according to which a body not subject to the action of external forces has a rectilinear and uniform movement. And in the *Principia (Philosophiae naturalis principia mathematica)*, published in 1687, Sir Isaac Newton (Great Britain, 1642–1727) stated the fundamental principle of dynamics, according to which a body, subject to an external force, gathers acceleration in proportion to that force.

The speed of light (1676)

The astronomer Jean Picard (France, 1620–82) of the Observatoire de Paris—who was the first to measure the earth's diameter precisely—had a young Dane, Olaüs Römer, as his assistant. The latter carried out observations of the four large satellites of Jupiter discovered by Galileo some 70 years earlier. He measured the intervals of time between the successive eclipses of the satellites by Jupiter and noted that these were regularly shorter or longer depending on whether Jupiter and the earth were closer together or further apart in their respective orbits around the sun.

Römer understood that this phenomenon was due to delays in the light from Jupiter reaching earth. He then calculated that, to explain all these observations, light traveled at a speed of 186,400 miles per second. At last, after 2,000 years of controversy, it was established that light did not travel instantaneously, but has a finite and measurable speed.

Absolute space (1687)

Sir Isaac Newton (Great Britain, 1642–1727) believed in the existence of "absolute space," in which objects at rest or in motion at a constant speed are not subject to any force of inertia. To illustrate this idea, he carried out the following experiment: having attached a bucket of water to a rope previously coiled upon itself and having waited until the water was at rest in the bucket, he allowed the rope to uncoil itself and thus rotate the bucket. He observed that the surface of the water, which in turn was affected by the rotation of the bucket, took on a concave form.

Newton's interpretation was that the water initially at rest is at rest in absolute space and is therefore not subject to any forces of inertia: its surface is flat. But then, the water in rotation is in rotation in relation to absolute space and is therefore subject to forces of inertia that curve its surface.

Mach's hypothesis (1889)

Absolute space theory was prevalent until 1889 when the physicist and philosopher Ernest Mach (Austria, 1838–1916)—who introduced the famous Mach number for measuring supersonic speed—noted that it was not Newton's absolute space but rather all the matter in the universe, and in particular all the stars, that determine the forces of inertia. Thus the water in Newton's bucket is subject to forces of inertia as it is in rotation in relation to the distribution of distant stars.

This hypothesis, known as Mach's principle, is most certainly correct: Newton's absolute space does not exist.

Quantum theory (1900)

At the end of the last century, no law had been discovered to account for the phenomenon of heat and light radiation by a solid, white-hot body. In 1900 Max Planck (Germany, 1858–1947) guessed that radiation did not occur in a continuous fashion but in small discrete units, separate quantities or quanta. This discovery, which enabled scientists to explain heat radiation, turned physics upside down, especially in the sphere of classical mechanics, which became inoperable in the area of infinitely small quantities.

Thanks to this theory, Albert Einstein (Switzerland, b. Germany; 1879–1955) explained in 1905 the photoelectric effect by showing that light, which comprises both waves and particles, moves by quanta, tiny packets of light, which were later called photons.

Niels Bohr (Denmark, 1885–1962) built on this quantum theory a model of an atom, describing in 1911 the movement of electrons inside the atom. This model enabled him to achieve remarkable results in the fields of the spectroscopy of gaseous matter and of X-ray physics.

Wave mechanics (1924)

In 1924 Louis de Broglie (France) produced the wave theory of matter, which also derived from quantum theory. It was perfected by E. Schrödinger.

Statistical determinism (1927)

In 1927 Werner Heisenberg (Germany) stated that the absolute principle of determinism in classical mechanics (the same causes produce the same effects) was no longer true of wave mechanics. He introduced the idea of statistical determinism, which allowed the calculation of probabilities only.

Today, quantum mechanics has become the basic tool of modern physics, but it has not yet yielded up all its secrets.

Fundamental Forces

Interactions (antiquity)

The elementary particles of matter may act among themselves in various ways, because of forces or what we call "interactions." Four fundamental forces are known at present, of which two were known to antiquity—gravitational and electromagnetic forces—and two are the fruit of 20th century research: weak and strong interactions.

The process of interaction, according to modern theories, is like the superimposition of elementary interactions occurring when a particle is exchanged, characterized by the force called an "intermediary boson." The particles interact a bit like football players, passing the ball later-ally from one to another. In the case of electromagnetic force, the particle that is exchanged (the boson) is the famous light-particle identified by Albert Einstein in 1905, the photon.

In 1986 Ephraïm Fischbach and his colleagues at the University of Washington suggested the possibility of a fifth force, but its existence has not been confirmed since.

Electromagnetic force (1824–64)

It is this force that links atoms and molecules to form ordinary solid bodies. Thus, if your elbow doesn't sink into the wood of your desk while you are writing, it is because the electrons in the atoms of your desk and of your elbow push against each other by means of electromagnetic interaction.

The relationship between electricity and magnetism was discovered in 1820 by Christian Oersted (Denmark) in an experiment during which he noticed that a magnetic needle was deflected by an electric current. André Marie Ampère (France) later generalized these observations, but it was James Clerk Maxwell (Great Britain) who, in 1864, formulated the general laws of electromagnetism and showed that light was nothing but an electromagnetic wave.

Since the 1930s a number of physicists such as P.A.M. Dirac (Great Britain) and Richard Feynman and Julian Schwinger (both U.S.) have developed the modern theory of electromagnetic interaction between electrons (with the exchange of photons).

Force of gravity (1687/1915)

Responsible for the movements of great masses on a large scale (the rotation of the earth around the sun, the movement of the galaxies, the expansion of the universe, etc.), the force of gravity, whose laws were first stated by Sir Isaac Newton (Great Britain, 1642–1729) in 1687, is the weakest of known forces. Today it has a very special status because it has been interpreted since Albert Einstein (1915) as a manifestation of the curvature of space-time. With regard to gravitational force, the boson that plays a role analogous to that of the photon is called the *graviton*.

Weak force (1934/1974)

It has been known since Enrico Fermi's (U.S., b. Italy, 1901–1954) work in 1934 that this force is manifested during certain radioactive processes, such as the spontaneous disintegration of the neutron. In 1974 physicists Sheldon Glashow (U.S.), Abdus Salam (Pakistan) and Steven Weinberg (U.S.) decided that the existence of three particles, the intermediary bosons W+, W– and Z°, played a role analogous to that of the photon and the graviton for weak force. (For this work they won the Nobel Prize for Physics in 1979.) These three particles were observed at the European Center for Nuclear Research (CERN) in Geneva by physicists Carlo Rubbia (Italy) and Simon van der Meer (Netherlands), who won the Nobel Prize for Physics in 1984. Their discovery was certainly one of the most important in particle physics in the second half of the 20th century.

Strong force (1935/1965)

Strong interaction, discovered by Hideki Yukawa (Japan) in 1935, is principally responsible for the cohesion of atomic nuclei: it is this force that maintains the links at the center of the atom between the protons and neutrons that constitute the nucleus. More precisely, the protons and neutrons are made up of quarks and the strong force is what binds the quarks to each other. A difficult theory known as quantum chromodynamics has been elaborated by various physicists since Yoichiro Nambu (1965), and suggests that quarks interact among themselves by the exchange of eight bosons that are called gluons, massless particles that transmit the forces that bind quarks together.

Theory of superstrings (1984)

The concept of superstrings in its present form was invented by Michael Green (Great Britain) and John Schwarz (U.S.). The theory had its origins in the work done by Yoichiro Nambu (Japan) in the late 1950s, while Joel Scherk and André Neveu (both France) were among those who made important contributions to its development. Ordinarily in physics, one thinks of elementary particles as points, without dimensions. The new idea is to replace the concept of the particle, an object with zero dimension, with the concept of a string, which has one dimension. Then one could think of interpreting particles and their associated waves as excited states of a vibrating string, and thus arrive at a classification of particles and a unification of the four fundamental forces.

For example, it has been shown that the lowest state of vibration of a string may be identified with the graviton, the hypothetical particle of the gravitational field. A notable characteristic of superstrings is that they necessarily evolve in a space-time having more dimensions than the four usually allowed to space-time.

Since August 1984, when Green and Schwarz proved a very important result for the theory of superstrings, dozens of physicists have been working on the subject, and thousands of articles have been published. Known as the Theory of Everything, it can answer important questions like: How did the universe begin? What is matter? What is the origin of time? Developments are still being made in the field of superstrings.

Standards

Metric system (1795)

The principle of mandatory units for weights and measures was established in France during the Revolution. A decree issued on April 7, 1795 instituted the metric system, established the names of the units, and, for the first time, legally defined the meter as a fraction of the distance between the North Pole and the Equator, measured on the meridian from Barcelona, Spain to Dunkirk, France.

Begun in June 1792, the measurement of the meridian arc by J.-B. Delambre and Pierre Méchain (both France) was not completed until the end of 1798. For this geodesic operation, the two astonomers used the repeating circle, invented by Charles de Borda, which made it possible to measure angles to the nearest second (each degree is divided into 60 minutes and each minute into 60 seconds). The choice of the word *meter* is attributed to Borda; it is also the word that had previously been chosen by Tito Livio Burattini (Italy) in a treatise published in 1675, in which he suggested using the length of a pendulum marking the seconds as a universal unit of length, and this he called the catholic meter. The unit of weight became the kilogram.

On June 22, 1799 the first standard meter rule and the kilogram weight were placed in the French National Archive in Paris. That same year the metric system became compulsory in France, but its use spread very slowly. It was not considered fully established until 1840.

Planck's constant (1898)

Physicist Max Planck (Germany, 1858–1947), after discovering the quantum of interaction h (see Quantum theory), noted in 1898 that h could be used to establish an absolute scale of units.

These units have no proportional relation to the ordinary physical world. If you wanted to test this scale physically, with the aid of a particle accelerator constructed by present-day techniques, you would need an accelerator the size of our galaxy—that is, about 100,000 light-years in diameter.

It is thought that the Planck constant is the limit on this side of which quantum effects appear in the gravitational field. It is not understood at present, however, how these effects could intervene.

Among Sir Isaac Newton's achievements was the formulation of the laws of gravity. (Dagli-Orti)

International System of Units (1960)

This sytem of units was created in 1960 at the 11th General Conference of Weights and Measures. It is designed to define the seven base units from which all other units are derived. They are: length (the meter); mass (the kilogram); time (the second); electric current (the ampère); thermodynamic temperature (the Kelvin—which is equal to the Celsius degree, but the Kelvin scale begins at absolute zero, not 0 degrees Celsius—0 degrees Celsius = 273.16 K); quantity of matter (the mole); luminous intensity (the candela). In 1986 the definition of the SI meter was changed from the distance between two marks on a platinum-iridium bar to the light meter, which is to say the 299,792,458th part of the distance traveled by light in a vacuum in one second.

Hydrodynamics

Archimedes' principle

Archimedes (Greece, c. 287–212 B.C.) was the first to formulate the principle of floating bodies that bears his name: all bodies weighed when immersed in fluid (liquid or gas) show a loss of weight equal to the weight of fluid they displace.

After having discovered this principle, Archemides cried *Eureka!* ("I've found it!"). Less well-known are the circumstances of this discovery: the ruler of Syracuse, Hiero II, a naturally suspicious man, had given some pure gold to a jeweler so that he could melt it down and make a royal crown. Archimedes was put in control of this work. He then had the idea of immersing, in a receptacle filled to the brim with water, first the crown, then gold and silver equal in weight to that of the crown. After each experiment, so the story goes, he weighed the water that had overflowed. He finally showed that the figure of the first weighing had fallen between the figures of the next two: it weighed less than pure gold and more than silver. Thus it was proved that the crown had been made of a mixture of gold and silver.

Hydrostatic paradox (1586)

The physicist and mathematician Simon Stevin (Belgium, 1548–1620), known as Simon of Bruges, was inspector of dikes for the States of Holland. In that capacity, he was directly interested in the internal forces of liquids, and thus was the first to make a truly scientific study of these forces.

In 1586, Stevin's three books on mechanics were published. These contained his famous hydrostatic paradox: the pressure of a liquid at the bottom of a receptacle depends solely on the depth of the liquid and not on the shape of the receptacle. Conversely, the weight of the liquid depends on the shape of the receptacle.

Fundamental principle (17th century)

Taking the fundamental relationship as a starting point, Blaise Pascal (France, 1623–62) also deduced his fundamental principle: pressure applied to any one point of an incompressible fluid at rest is transmitted without loss to all other parts of the fluid.

Characteristic numbers

Reynolds number

The physicist and engineer Osborne Reynolds (Great Britain, 1842–1912) carried out research in the field of hydrodynamics, studying the flow of viscous fluids. Reynolds number is a dimensionless coefficient expressing the relationship between the inert forces and the viscous forces.

Froude number

The physicist and engineer William Froude (Great Britain, 1810–79) was the first to study by experimental means the resistance of a fluid to motion. To carry out his experiments, he devised the first model tank.

Mach number

The physicist and philosopher Ernst Mach (Austria, 1838–1916) was the first person to recognize the role of velocity in aerodynamic flows. The Mach number (M) is the ratio of the inertial forces to the square root of the forces of pressure. If M is greater than 1, then the object is supersonic (or greater than the speed of sound in air, which is 760.6 mph). If M is less than 1, the object is subsonic.

Gravitation

The center of gravity (3rd century B.C.)

The greatest scientist of antiquity, the Greek Archimedes (born in Syracuse in 287 B.C.), first determined the centers of gravity of homogeneous solids defined geometrically, such as the cylinder, the sphere and the cone. Archimedes developed this idea in his *Book of Balances*. In this book he also displayed his rigorous law of levers.

Falling bodies

Galileo (Italy, 1564–1642) demonstrated by experiment that falling bodies accelerate at a rate that is independent of their nature and composition. According to legend, he threw a wooden ball and a lead ball from the top of the tower of Pisa, and noted that they reached the ground at the same time (disregarding a slight resistance in the air). In 1686, Sir Isaac Newton (Great Britain, 1642–1727) came to the same conclusion as the result of experiments with oscillating pendulums. And in 1888 Lorand Eötvös (Hungary, 1848–1919) showed with the aid of torsion pendulums that the "universality" of falling bodies was correct to within 1 in 10.

None of these experiments was satisfactorily explained until 1915, when Albert Einstein (Switzerland, b. Germany, 1879–1955) discovered the general theory of relativity.

Kepler's laws (17th century)

Johannes Kepler (Germany, 1571–1630) undertook a systematic study of the movement of the planets, in particular that of the planet Mars.

He stated three laws that bear his name. They had the great merit that calculations on the basis of these laws proved to coincide with observations. The first two laws were published in *Astronomia Nova* in 1609, and the third in *Harmonices Mundi* in 1619.

The laws of universal attraction (1685)

One evening in 1665 Sir Isaac Newton (Great Britain, 1642–1727) was musing in his garden. The moon was full. An apple fell at his feet, and Newton wondered why the moon, too, did not fall to earth. This question led the man of science to state in his *Philosophiae naturalis principia mathematica* (1685) the laws of universal attraction. However, the discovery of the laws that govern the universe cannot be reduced to this one anecdote, related by Voltaire, and anyway not verified.

Before Newton, Johannes Kepler (Germany), using as a starting point the notebook of Tycho Brahe (Denmark), had established between 1601 and 1618 the three laws that bear his name and that enable us to calculate a planet's orbit around the sun and its rotation period. At the same time, Galileo issued many observations on the trajectory of projectiles and, for the first time, in 1609 had looked at the sky through an astronomical lens. Before these men, Copernicus and then Giordano Bruno, who was condemned to death and burned at the stake by the Inquisition in 1600, had fallen afoul of official theory that made the earth the center of the universe.

It thus fell to Newton to unify the astronomical knowledge of his time in the famous law of universal attraction.

Space-time (1907)

Space-time is the geometric framework in which the events of nature take place. It has four dimensions: the three usual dimensions of space—length, width and depth—plus an additional dimension, that of time. An event in space-time is therefore the datum of the place where and the moment when the event occurred. Why are space and time, which appear to be of very different natures at first glance, linked in a single entity, space-time? It is because space-time makes it possible to interpret the theories of relativity most fruitfully. In 1907, two years after the publication of Einstein's Specific Relativity theory, Hermann Minkowski—who had taught Einstein at the Zurich Polytechnicum—demonstrated that in his former pupil's theory there was a mathematical quantity that could be interpreted as the distance between events taking place in space and time. In Minkowski's hands Specific Relativity became a geometric theory of space and time, with straight lines, planes, rotations and distances, as in traditional geometry.

Later it was realized that Minkowski's space-time was flat, like the space in Euclid's two-dimensional geometry. And in 1915 Einstein showed that gravitational fields curve space-time in such a way that the true space-time of the universe has a curved geometry.

Theory of Relativity (1905/1915): Albert Einstein

Albert Einstein. (Charnet/Académie des Sciences)

There is an old story that Albert Einstein taught his secretary to explain the theory of relativity in this way: When a man spends two hours with a pretty girl it seems like a minute, but if the same man were asked to sit on a hot stove for a second, it would seem like two hours.

In reality the theory that changed the face of physics, energy, and warfare is less easy to comprehend, yet its central principle remains as simple.

Two hundred years before Einstein, Sir Isaac Newton proposed that light waves pass through space through an ether—a transparent, weightless substance thought to surround the earth. In the late 1800s, the American scientists Albert Michelson and Edward Morley experimented to see if light traveled at different speeds depending on whether it went with or against the earth's movement. Young Einstein studied this work and agreed that the results—that light traveled at the exact same speed regardless of direction or distance—proved there was no ether. Before, physicists had believed that the speed of light varied according to space and time, which never changed. Instead, said Einstein, light is the only constant, and space and time change relative to it.

In 1905 at age 26, Einstein published his theory of "special" relativity in the *Annals of Physics*. The 30-page paper held no references to other experts. In 1915 Einstein went on to express his theory of "general" relativity mathematically: $E = mc^2$. Stated verbally, the energy of an object equals its mass times the speed of light, squared.

The implication is that matter and energy are essentially the same thing in different forms, and that matter can be converted to energy. Matter with great mass can be converted into great quantities of energy.

In his teens, Einstein was a high school dropout who later failed his college entrance exams. He finished school, then researched the theory of relativity while working as a patent clerk in his adopted country, Switzerland. Nazi danger led him to move to the United States in the 1930s.

In 1939 the physicist Leo Szilard and others realized that nuclear energy could be harnessed to create a massively destructive weapon. Szilard wrote a letter to President Roosevelt, warning him that the Germans had the potential pieces to the puzzle. Einstein signed the letter, which moved Roosevelt to establish the Manhattan Project to create the atom bomb. This was the first concrete application of Einstein's landmark theory. After the atom bomb was dropped on Hiroshima, Einstein said, "If I knew they were going to do this, I would have become a shoemaker."

The theory of relativity fueled quantum theory and is today the moving force behind nuclear energy, in which atoms are split to create energy to power entire nations.

Matter

Gases (17th century)

The chemist Jean Baptiste van Helmont (Belgium, 1577–1644) was the first to recognize the existence of different gases, such as carbon dioxide and oxygen, which were identified as such much later. Until the 17th century the knowledge of these states of matter was purely empirical.

The Greeks designated the immense dark space that existed before things began as "chaos." Van Helmont invented the word "gas" from the sound of that word.

Air (17th century)

In antiquity, air was, with earth, water and fire, considered one of the four natural elements. John Mayow (Great Britain, 1640–79) was the first to demonstrate that air was a mixture of gases.

In 1783 Henry Cavendish (Great Britain, 1731–1810) made the first relatively precise analysis of air. He found it to be composed of 20.8 percent oxygen, 78.2 percent nitrogen, and described the presence of a "bubble" that represented about one percent of the volume of gas analyzed.

Oxygen and nitrogen (18th century)

It was in 1777, in a paper that was not published until 1782, that Antoine-Laurent de Lavoisier (France, 1743–94), the founder of modern chemistry—in the wake of Joseph Priestley (Great Britain) and Carl Wilhelm Scheele (Sweden)—named the life-giving air "oxygen" (*oxygène*, literally "that which produces an acid"), and non-vital air "nitrogen" (*azote*, literally "that which does not maintain life"). In 1772 the physician and botanist Daniel Rutherford (Great Britain, 1749–1819) had distinguished between "noxious air" (nitrogen) and carbon dioxide in his doctoral thesis, *De aere mephitico*.

Water (1781)

The physician Paracelsus (Switzerland, 1493–1541) was the first person to draw attention to the existence of hydrogen.

In 1781 Henry Cavendish (Great Britain, 1731–1810) had the idea of burning oxygen and hydrogen together. He measured the quantities of the two gases and observed that they were converted into a quantity of water whose weight was the same as the sum of the weights of the two gases.

Lavoisier repeated and completed Cavendish's experiments. He had the idea of vaporizing the water and separating the vapor into its two constituents, which he then combined to form water again. This series of experiments led him to state his famous law of the conservation of matter in a chemical reaction, which states that the sum total of matter in the universe cannot be changed.

Argon (1894)

In 1894 Sir William Ramsay (Great Britain, 1852–1916) and Lord John William Rayleigh (Great Britain, 1842–1919) detected the presence of an inert gas in the air through spectroscopic analysis. They called it *argon*, which means *lazy* in Greek.

Helium (1895)

In 1895, Ramsay and Per Theodor Cleve (Sweden, 1840–1905) identified the presence of helium in cleveite, an ore. Helium in the atmosphere had been reported by Jules Janssen (France, 1840–1907) at the time of the eclipse of the sun on August 18, 1868.

Neon, krypton, xenon (1898)

In 1898, Ramsay and Morris William Travers (Great Britain, 1872–1966) isolated other rare gases in the air: neon, krypton and xenon.

Radon (1900)

In 1900 Ernst Dorn (Germany) discovered the last inert gas, radon, in the radioactive disintegration products of radium. Radon is a dangerous gas. In the United States it was discovered in 1986 that it could contaminate houses in certain regions. At present, 12 percent of American houses contain enough radon to pose the same risk of lung cancer to their inhabitants as if they had smoked half a pack of cigarettes every day of their lives.

Changes of State

Atmospheric pressure (1643)

The physicist and mathematician Evangelista Torricelli (Italy, 1608–47), a pupil of Galileo,

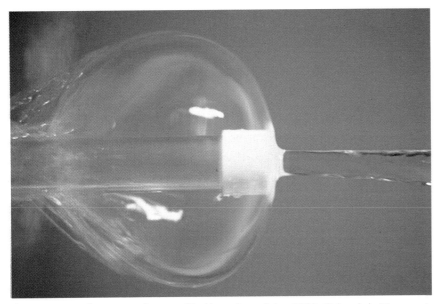

The composition of water was determined by Henry Cavendish in 1781. (Palais de la Découverte)

was the first to measure air pressure, in 1643. To prove the existence of atmospheric pressure, he used mercury, which is 13 times denser than water, so that he could work on more easily measurable heights. He filled a crucible and a glass tube with mercury, and inverted the open end of the tube over the crucible. The mercury level went down in the tube and stabilized at 30 in. from the open surface of the crucible. Torricelli deduced from this that air exercised pressure on this surface, balanced by the hydrostatic pressure exercised by the 30 in. of mercury in the tube. Torricelli's tube was the first barometer. The term *barometer* was invented by Edme Marlotte (France).

Vacuum (1654)

The engineer Otto von Guericke (Germany, 1602–86), a native of Magdeburg, developed the first vacuum pump. In 1654 von Guericke demonstrated it to the nobility of the Holy Roman Empire.

He joined together two hollow bronze hemispheres, each 20 in. in diameter. Creating a vacuum in the sphere, he harnessed two horses to each hemisphere. The horses pulled: nothing happened. He had two more horses added: still nothing. It took eight horses harnessed to each hemisphere to pull them apart.

A man of science, von Guericke was also a showman. During his experiments, he demonstrated that when burning candles were snuffed out in a vacuum, animals in the vacuum quickly expired, and bells no longer rang. These "miracles" caused his fellow-countrymen to take him for a magician.

Expansion of gases (1661)

In 1661 the self-educated scientist Robert Boyle (Ireland, 1627–91) demonstrated that the variation in the volume of a gas is inversely proportional to the variation in its pressure. He was interested in the experiments of van Helmont and Pascal, and directed his research toward the compressibility of gases. Using a simple graduated J tube and mercury, Boyle proved that the volume of the air imprisoned in the tube can be reduced by half by doubling the pressure exerted by the mercury.

Charles' Law (1798)

In 1798 Jacques Charles (France, 1746–1823), a physicist and ballooning enthusiast (he was the first person to think of filling balloons with hydrogen), pronounced the following law: if a gas is held at a constant pressure, its volume is directly proportional to its absolute temperature.

Gay-Lussac's Law (1804)

In 1804 Joseph Louis Gay-Lussac (France, 1778–1850) discovered that the volume of gas at a given temperature t is related to the volume at 32° F (if the pressure is constant) in the same way as the relationship discovered by Jacques Charles.

Ideal gas (19th century)

Emile Clapeyron (France, 1799–1864) was the first to use the notion of ideal or perfect gas. Ideal gas is a purely theoretical perfect fluid, which represents the limit of a real gas state in which the temperature tends towards absolute zero, and where the pressure becomes very high.

Liquefaction of gases

Origins (1818)

In 1818 Michael Faraday (Great Britain, 1791–1867) discovered a means of liquefying gas (i.e., transforming it from the gaseous state to the liquid state) by increasing the pressure when cooling the gas. The son of a blacksmith, Faraday started out as an errand boy in a bookshop and later became a bookbinder. An avid reader, he taught himself physics. To perfect his scientific knowledge, he enrolled in an evening course taught by Sir Humphry Davy and became his assistant at the Royal Institution.

In 1818 Faraday oriented his research in a direction that was entirely new for the day: studying the effects of pressure and cold on gases. Faraday successfully liquefied hydrogen sulphide and sulphuric anhydride but did not succeed with oxygen, hydrogen or nitrogen.

Liquid oxygen (1877)

In 1877 Louis-Paul Cailletet (France, 1832–1913), an ironmaster in Burgundy, invented a pump that enabled him to obtain and maintain pressures of hundreds of atmospheres.

He managed to liquefy oxygen by causing the sudden expansion of gas in a capillary tube in which he decreased the pressure from 300 to 1 atmosphere which dropped the temperature to −182° F.

A few days after the success of this experiment, Raoul-Pierre Pictet (1846–1929), Professor of Physics at the University of Geneva, published the results of similar research.

Thomas Andrews (Ireland, 1813–85) also liquefied gases independently, and discovered the "critical temperature" that Cailletet and Pictet used in their further work on liquefaction.

Liquid air (1895)

In 1895 the inventor and industrialist Karl von Linde (11842–1934) succeeded in liquefying air by compression and expansion with intermediary cooling. He was thus able to separate the gases and prepare almost pure liquid oxygen.

In 1902 Georges Claude (France, 1870–1960) invented another process for liquefying air, by expanding the gas and applying an outside force. From the liquid air, he isolated oxygen, nitrogen and argon in liquid form by fractional distillation. He thus set in motion the first industrial process for liquefying gases.

Liquid hydrogen (1899)

In 1899 Sir James Dewar (Great Britain, 1842–1923) used Linde's air liquefaction process to obtain boiling liquid hydrogen.

Liquid helium (1908)

In 1908 Heike Kamerlingh Onnes (Netherlands, 1853–1926) liquefied helium in his cryogenic laboratory in Leyden. Helium was the last gas to be liquefied. Research did not end there, however. In 1971, in liquefying helium 3 (an isotope of helium 4, the gas's normal form) at less than 2.7m K, it was discovered that this also had the property of superfluidity (already discovered in helium 4); it has almost no viscosity.

Note that Onnes also discovered supraconductivity, now called superconductivity, in 1911: that is, the property of certain metals or alloys, at temperatures close to absolute zero, to lose their resistance to electrical currents.

Thermodynamics

Origins (19th century)

In 1849 Sir William Thomson (later Lord Kelvin; Great Britain, 1824–1907) invented the term *thermodynamics* to describe the study of relations between thermal and mechanical phenomena, but the discipline as such may be said to have been founded by Sadi Carnot (France, 1796–1832). Thermodynamics is the mathematical formulation of the parameters defining a system in the exchange of energy. These parameters are temperature, pressure and volume.

Carnot principle (1824)

After studying the steam engine invented in 1703 by Thomas Newcomen (Great Britain, 1663–1729), Sadi Carnot (France, 1796–1832) stated in his only published work, *Reflections on the Motive Power of Fire* (1824), that mechanical energy could be produced by simple transfer of heat.

Work–heat equivalence (1842)

The physicist Julius Robert von Mayer (Germany, 1814–78), following Carnot, was interested in gases and the motor power of heat. In 1842 he published the results of his research in *Annalen der Chemie und Pharmaciae*. He stated intuitively the theory that was later to be called the principle of work–heat equivalence.

This principle was confirmed by the numerous and exact measurements made by James Prescott Joule (Great Britain, 1818–89), working at the same time (between 1840 and 1845). He turned his famous current meter in an isolated enclosure, filled with a liquid whose temperature he measured as it rose. Thus he was able to evaluate the quantity of heat set free by clearly defined mechanical work.

Temperature (1848)

In 1848 Sir William Thomson (later Lord Kelvin; Great Britain, 1824–1907) stated the zero principle of dynamics. This principle enabled him to define thermodynamic temperature and to establish an objective method of measuring it.

When two systems are each in thermal equilibrium with a third, they are in thermal equilibrium with each other. This equilibrium is expressed by their equal temperatures. If you give a conventional value to the temperature of a system in a given physical state, the other temperatures can be determined by what are called thermodynamic measures.

In 1961 the General Conference on Weights and Measures chose as the standard unit of thermodynamic temperature the Kelvin (K), defined as the degree on the thermodynamic scale of absolute temperatures at which the triple point of water is 273.16 K (the equivalent of 0° C). At this temperature, ice, water and steam can coexist in equilibrium.

According to this convention the freezing and boiling points of water at one atmosphere are, respectively, 273.15 K and 373.15 K. The temperature interval measured by one Kelvin is equal to that which measures 1° C.

Principles of thermodynamics (1852/1906)

In 1852 Sir William Thomson stated the first two laws of thermodynamics based on the work of Carnot, von Mayer and Joule. The third principle was formulated in 1906 by Walter Hermann Nernst (Germany, 1864–1941).

ELECTRICITY AND MAGNETISM

Electrostatics

Origins (c. 600 B.C.)

The Greeks had already observed the phenomenon of electricity, as Thales of Miletus (*c.* 624–*c.* 546 B.C.) relates in his writing, around 600 B.C., describing the electrostatic power of a fossil resin found on the Baltic seashore: amber, which the Greeks called *elektron*. Other phenomena had been recorded, such as the flash or electrotherapical response of a torpedo fish under a drop of water, but no links had been established between them.

First electrical machine (1672)

The first electrical generator was invented by Otto von Guericke (Germany, 1602–86) in the second half of the 17th century. It consisted of a revolving ball of sulphur to which friction was applied by a person's hands. Thanks to this machine, Guericke discovered in 1672 that static electricity could cause the surface of the sulphur ball to glow—that is, he understood electroluminescence.

In 1708, physician William Wall (Great Britain) made the connection between electroluminescence and lightning.

Conductors (18th century)

Between 1727 and 1729 Stephen Gray (Great Britain, 1670–1736) discovered conductivity and carried out the first experiment of transporting electricity over a distance, using silk threads attached to a glass tube, which was rubbed, and an ivory ball.

In 1740 Jean Desaguliers (France) proposed that solids through which electricity freely circulates, such as iron and copper, should be called conductors, and those through which it does not circulate, such as glass or amber, should be called insulators.

Leyden jar (1745)

At this period electrical friction machines were perfected and became more powerful. The possibility was even discovered of accumulating strong electrical charges on a conductor isolated by glass or air. In 1745 Ewald Jürgen von Kleist (Germany) made the first condenser, a few months before the invention of the famous Leyden jar, built by Petrus van Musschenbroek (Netherlands). The jar became a curiosity and an attraction in the courts of Europe, the great and the wealthy across the continent coming to see how electric charges were produced. It is a glass jar coated inside and outside with tinfoil or other conducting material.

Lightning-conductor (1752)

The ground was prepared for Benjamin Franklin's (U.S., 1706–90) famous experiment of 1752, when he flew a kite with a metal tip in a thunderstorm. The tip was joined to a piece of insulating silk holding the wet string, and thereby to an iron key which, dangling free in the air near the technician, filled the role of the condenser. Thanks to this contrivance, a dangerous one, Franklin could charge up a Leyden jar and prove that thunderclouds contained electricity.

Franklin made a fortune by inventing and selling lightning-conductors, and also became the most important public figure in the United States. He is considered to be the first scientist of the New World.

Coulomb laws (1785)

Beween 1784 and 1789, engineer and physicist Charles de Coulomb (France, 1736–1806) invented his famous torsion balance, which enabled him to establish the fundamental laws of electrostatics (1785).

Superconductivity

First discovered in mercury in 1911 by Heike Kamerlingh Onnes (Netherlands), who succeeded in liquefying helium at 4.2 K, that is –425.128° F, superconductivity is the property of certain metals or alloys, at very low temperatures, to lose their resistance to electricity. For a long time it was thought that this temperature would be in the range 0–20 K.

After Onnes's discovery, research stayed at the level of laboratory curiosity for a long time, until suddenly progress was made in a totally unexpected way, because of materials known for their insulating power and not as conductors: ceramics. The first work with these was carried out in the laboratory for crystallography and material sciences in the University of Caen in France.

But it was in 1986 that superconductivity really took off with the results obtained in IBM's Zurich laboratories on ceramic superconductors by two scientists, K.A. Müller (Switzerland) and J.G. Bednorz (West Germany), which earned them the Nobel Prize for Physics in 1987. Their superconductivity record at –396.4° F launched an era of other records, which in turn open up astonishing perspectives on tomorrow's technology: trains running by magnetic levitation, the stockpiling of enormous amounts of energy, new kinds of computers, etc.

Some scientists think that discoveries about superconductors could be as important in the future as was the invention of the transistor or the laser in the past.

Electrodynamics

Ohm's Law (1827)

In 1827 Georg Simon Ohm (Germany, 1789–1854) used a hydraulic analogy to formulate a precise definition of the quantity of electricity, the electromotive force and the intensity of a current, thereby formulating the law that bears his name. Ohm likened electric current to a

Theodore H. Maiman displays a ruby laser which he first built in 1960. (Gamma)

liquid flow and the electric potential created by an electromotive force to a difference in level.

Joule effect (1841)

When a current passes through a homogeneous conductor, the conductor heats up. After 1882 this effect carried the name of James Prescott Joule (Great Britain, 1818–89), who formulated the law in 1841.

The heat engendered by the passage of the current turns the filaments of incandescent lamps red. Elements are still used to produce heat in cookers, electric radiators, etc. The

principle of the fuse is also based on this effect: a metal wire with a low fusion temperature is inserted into an electric circuit; if the intensity increases to an abnormal degree, the wire melts and the circuit is broken.

Electric discharge in gases

An electric discharge corresponds to the passage of charges—that is, to the current in an environment that is a low conductor or insulator.

Paschen's Law

Two physicists, Friedrich Paschen (Germany, 1865–1947) and Sir John Townsend (Ireland, 1868–1957), showed that the breakdown potential of a gas between parallel plate electrodes is a function of the product of the gas pressure and the electrode separation. This potential is minimal for a determined value of the product in question. Paschen discovered this law empirically, and Townsend expressed it scientifically.

Electromagnetism

Polar magnetism (1600)

The magnetic needle of a compass always points toward the North Pole. This phenomenon is due to the existence of a magnetic field around the earth. William Gilbert (Great Britain) in 1600 was the first to realize that the earth is a giant magnet whose magnetic poles are situated not far from the earth's geographic poles, the points through which the earth's rotational axis passes. The lines of the earth's magnetic field run from south to north and form a gigantic structure around the earth.

Magnetic field (1819)

In 1819 Christian Oersted (Denmark, 1777–1851) proved that the passing of an electric current creates a magnetic field in the space surrounding the conductor. This phenomenon is known as induction: the passage of a current induces a magnetic field.

In 1820 François Arago (France, 1786–1853), made the first electromagnet. Also in 1820, André-Marie Ampère (France, 1775–1836) developed his theory of magnetic reactions of live electricity. Ampère studied the mutual interaction between currents and magnets, which led to his rule known as the *Bon homme d'Ampère*. This rule illustrated the direction of magnetic deflection by a hypothetical little man lying on a conducting wire.

In 1830, C.F. Gauss (Germany) theorized that the earth's magnetic field originated inside the earth, and its direct cause was the rotation of the earth. Neither Gauss nor any other physicist has been able to prove this theory, but it is generally accepted as correct.

Induction (1831)

In 1831, while studying the results obtained by Oersted and Ampère, Michael Faraday (Great

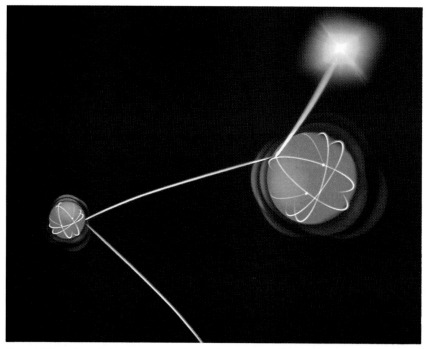

The simulation of a collision between an electron (the orange light) and two atoms, taking place in a metal, is depicted here. (A.N.A./Freeman)

Britain, 1791–1867) discovered the principle of electromagnetic induction. Faraday's discovery had enormous technological ramifications. Among other things, it served as the basis for electricity-producing machines known as generators: the magneto, which produces a magnetic field by a permanent magnet; the dynamo, for producing direct current; and the alternator, for alternating current.

Foucault current (1850)

The self-educated physicist Jean Bernard Léon Foucault (France, 1819–68) was the first to demonstrate the existence of electric currents inducted by an alternating magnetic field in a massive conductor. Named in honor of their discoverer, these currents create a magnetic induction whose flow opposes that of the alternating magnetic field that produces them. The mechanical force resulting from the passage of these currents is therefore always a resisting force.

Foucault currents, also known as eddy currents, have many applications, including induction-heating and electromagnetic braking systems.

Electromagnetic waves (1864)

James Clerk Maxwell (Great Britain, 1831–79), a pupil of Michael Faraday, was one of the most illustrious physicists of the 19th century, and in 1864 was the first to suppose the existence of electromagnetic waves. Although Maxwell was not able to prove his theory experimentally, he hypothesized that light has an electromagnetic nature.

Electronics

Cathode rays (19th century)

Around 1850 Heinrich Geissler (Germany, 1815–79), who had been a glassblower before becoming a manufacturer of laboratory equipment, constructed glass containers equipped with electrodes, in which he created a vacuum. He thus obtained very attractive lighting effects that varied with the shape of the container and the type of gas used. This phenomenon was further observed by Julius Plücker (Germany, 1801–68) in 1854, and Johann Hittorf (Germany, 1824–1914) in 1869.

In 1879 William Crookes (Great Britain, 1832–1912) carried out experiments proving once and for all that rays were emitted by the cathode of such glass tubes.

In 1895 Jean Perrin (France, 1870–1942) demonstrated that cathode rays are charged with negative electricity and that they are deflected by electric or magnetic fields.

In 1897 Sir Joseph Thomson (Great Britain, 1856–1940) calculated the ratio between the charge and the mass of the particles emitted. It then became apparent that these particles were electrons. The existence of electrons was first hypothesized in 1874 by George Stoney (Ireland, 1826–1911), who named them in 1891.

Cathode-ray oscilloscope (1897)

In 1897 Karl Ferdinand Braun (Germany, 1850–1918) perfected the cathode-ray oscilloscope. The trajectory of cathode rays is rectilinear, but, in an electric field, they are deflected in proportion to the voltage applied. The cath-ode-ray oscilloscope can display the transient or repeated wave forms on a fluorescent surface.

The cathode-ray tube is the device that creates an image on television screens. In this case, a signal is induced in the television's aerial by a signal given by the transmitter of the broadcasting network.

Semiconductors (1929)

A semiconductor is a solid with an electrical conductivity somewhere between that of an insulator and that of a metal. An insulator when at low temperatures, a semiconductor becomes a conductor when subject to increased heat or light. The odd phenomenon of electrical conductivity had already been noted by Michael Faraday (1839, in his experiments with silver sulphide) and by Karl Ferdinand Braun (1874, on galenite), without having been explained.

The first coherent theory of conductivity in solids (covering the properties of insulators, conductors and semiconductors) was produced by Felix Bloch (b. 1905), a Swiss physicist who became a U.S. citizen in 1939. In 1929 he suggested a theory of bands. Between 1925 and 1935, Bloch and scientists from various countries perfected the theory of semiconductors.

The understanding of the semiconductor mechanism was the basis for the invention of the transistor, which was to revolutionize electronics.

Electronic gate (1986)

In 1986 Bell Laboratories at AT&T and Cornell University established the speed record for semiconductors: they created an electronic gate prototype, capable of interrupting an electric signal in 5.8 millionths of a millionth of a second (i.e., 5.8 picoseconds). During this time a light ray could only travel 0.063 in. Some parts of the circuit measure just a third of a micron.

Lasers

Origins (1917)

In 1917 Albert Einstein (Switzerland, b. Germany, 1879–1955) formulated the principle that was to lead to the invention of the laser. He declared that it was possible to stimulate the emission of electromagnetic radiation by matter by stimulating the electrons of the atoms of which it is composed. This amplification generates a continuous beam—that is, with a uniform wavelength and particles which are displaced in the same direction.

Maser (1954)

A maser is a microwave amplifier (or oscillator). The first gas maser (*m*icrowave *a*mplification by *s*timulated *e*mission of *r*adiation) was built by the team of J. Gordon, H. J. Zeiger and Charles H. Townes (all U.S.) in 1954.

Laser (1957)

The name laser (*l*ight *a*mplification by *s*timulated *e*mission of *r*adiation) was coined by R.

Gordon Gould (U.S.), who developed the gas discharge laser, 1957–59. In 1958, Arthur Schawlow (U.S.) and Charles H. Townes applied the maser theory to infrared and optical frequencies. The first light beam amplifier was built and tested by Theodore H. Maiman (U.S.) at the Hughes Research Laboratory, Calif. in 1960.

Holograms

Holograms (1948)

The hologram (from the Greek *holos*, whole, and *gram*, something written) is a three-dimensional photograph using the interference produced by the superimposition of two laser beams. Dennis Gabor (Great Britain, b. Hungary) discovered the principle of holography in 1948 in the course of his research into electronic microscopy. But it was not until the discovery of the laser that practical applications could be developed.

E.N. Leith, J.U. Upatnieks and C.W. Stroke (all U.S.) of the University of Michigan carried out the first tests in 1963. Since then, holography has developed greatly in the spheres of research, industry and art. The first examples of holography applied to art were achieved by Prof. Youri Denisyouk (U.S.S.R.) who, toward the end of the 1960s, applied holography to the reproduction of works of art.

Recess holograms (1986)

Thanks to a combination of holography and computing, a team from the Massachusetts Institute of Technology, directed by Stephen Benton, has managed to represent a car in three dimensions. This technique could reduce the design time of a car from five years to 18 months.

Conoscope (1988)

The result of research begun in 1985 (and made public in 1988), in collaboration with D. Psaltis, the Conoscope is a holographic camera functioning with natural light. It is the culmination of a simple idea that is also a revolution in three-dimensional imagery. The hologram and the laser have always been indissolubly linked: only this type of coherent artificial beam makes it possible to produce and collect the interference fringes necessary for the creation of a three-dimensional image.

Scientists Gabriel Sirat and Alain Maruani (both France) from the ENST succeeded in obtaining the same effect by using two beams of natural light dephased by a double refractive crystal. The two beams define a cone in space, hence the name of the device. Since its early applications, the development of the hologram has suffered limitations associated with the use of the laser: taking photos in the dark, the immobility of the subject, and the impossibility of digitizing the image have contributed to the fact that until now, the animated holographic image has remained a laboratory curiosity. The Conoscope, however, works in broad daylight and produces an image that is accessible to video

techniques. And so it is the first-born of the first generation of viable holographic cameras. The three-dimensional film is within its reach.

There are countless other applications: the holographic checking of manufactured articles, the guiding of robots through three-dimensional space and the numbering of objects for computer-aided design, to name only a few examples.

ATOMIC AND NUCLEAR PHYSICS

Atom (5th century B.C.)

Greek philosophers of the 5th century B.C. were the first to suggest that all matter was made up of invisible particles: atoms.

Atomic theories (1801)

The first modern atomic theory was created by physicist John Dalton (Great Britain, 1766–1844), who in 1801 adopted the classical hypothesis of the indivisibility of matter and gave it a scientific basis. In 1810 Joseph Louis Gay-Lussac (France), experimenting with chemical actions in gases, established that gases combined in simple proportions by volume, and that the volumes of the products are related to the original volumes, thus refuting Dalton's theory.

The phenomenon was explained by Amedeo di Quaregna e Ceretto, Count Avogadro (Italy, 1776–1856), who distinguished clearly between the atom and the molecule.

In 1897 the indivisible nature of the atom was taken up again by Sir Joseph John Thomson

(Great Britain) and Jean Baptiste Perrin (France), who won the Nobel Prize for Physics in 1906 and 1926 respectively.

Avogadro's number (1811)

In 1811 Amedeo di Quaregna e Ceretto, Count Avogadro (Italy, 1776–1856), Professor of Physics at the University of Turin, established a law that was named after him. Avogadro assumed that in analogous conditions of temperature and pressure, equal volumes of gas contain the same number of molecules.

Avogadro's hypothesis did not gain immediate recognition. It was not until some 50 years later that Stanislao Cannizzaro (Italy, 1828–1910) demonstrated the necessity for adopting Avogadro's concept as the basis for a coherent atomic theory. Cannizzaro honored Avogadro by giving his name to an atomic constant. He defined the Avogadro number as the number of gaseous molecules contained in a gram-molecule of any substance—that is, the quantity of that substance occupying a volume of 9.48 cu ft in typical conditions of temperature and pressure.

The periodic table of elements (1869)

A fundamental stage in the development of chemistry, and of modern science in general, the periodic table was the work of Dimitri Mendeleev (Russia, 1834–1907) in 1869. It enabled scientists to establish relationships between various chemical elements that had been considered as independent entities, and to understand why certain elements had the same properties.

The interesting thing about this classification is that it shows the periodic variations of chemical and physical properties in the chemical elements when they are classed in ascending order of their atomic mass.

Particle accelerators break down matter into its most elementary particles. This is achieved by bombarding it with particles such as electrons or neutrons at high speed, or by causing head-on collisions of the particles. (Cosmos)

X-rays (1895)

In September 1895 in Würzburg, Wilhelm Conrad Röntgen (Germany, 1845–1923) discovered X-rays. Röntgen called the rays "X" because their nature was then unknown. It was not defined until 1912, by Max von Laue (Germany, 1879–1960), who managed to diffract the rays through a lattice of crystal.

X-rays are electromagnetic waves that pass through material that is normally opaque to light. These rays have a very short wavelength.

The discovery of X-rays immediately created a considerable stir. Röntgen, a national hero before the century was out, was awarded the Nobel Prize for Physics in 1901.

Natural radioactivity (1896)

In nature, some heavy nuclei emit natural radioactivity. Henri Becquerel (France, 1852–1908) discovered this phenomenon in Paris in 1896 while performing experiments on uranium. In fact, it was the discovery of X-rays that led to the discovery of radioactivity.

One cloudy day in Paris, Becquerel set up an experiment designed to verify whether a sample of pitchblende (a black mineral composed of uranium and potassium) exposed to sunlight emitted X-rays. Unable to complete his work because of the weather conditions, Becquerel put his equipment away. He resumed the experiment another day when the weather had improved, placing the samples of pitchblende on a photographic plate that had not been removed from its wrapping. When later developing the plate, he was surprised to see an image appear whose contours followed the outline of the ore sample perfectly. What could possibly be the origin of the "energy" in the mineral that was capable of leaving an impression on a photographic plate? (See radium, below.)

Radium and polonium (1898)

Becquerel took the matter up with his friends Pierre Curie (France, 1859–1906) and his wife, Marie (France, 1867–1934). Examining the pitchblende more closely, Pierre and Marie Curie discovered that the radiation had been caused by at least one substance that was much more radioactive than uranium. Finally, after two years of unrelenting and meticulous work, the Curies revealed the existence of not one but two elements that emitted this strange radiation: radium and polonium. The second one was named in honor of Marie Curie, née Sklodowska, who was Polish by birth. For these discoveries Henri Becquerel shared the 1903 Nobel Prize for Physics with Pierre and Marie Curie.

Radioactive disintegration (1902)

Sir Frederick Soddy (Great Britain, 1877–1956), winner of the Nobel Prize for Chemistry in 1921, explained the phenomenon of radioactive decay of atomic nuclei, thus paving the way for research in nuclear energy.

Rutherford's atom (1911)

The explosion of a radioactive atom discharges alpha particles with great energy. When a beam of alpha rays passes through a thin metal plate, some particles are widely deflected. To explain this phenomenon, revealed by the experiments of Hans Geiger (Germany, 1882–1945) and his team, Ernest Rutherford (later Lord Rutherford; New Zealand, 1871–1937), winner of the Nobel Prize for Chemistry in 1908, in 1911 went back to Jean Perrin's hypothesis of the nuclear structure of atoms. That is that all the mass and all the positive charges are concentrated in a small central nucleus, which creates an intense field of attraction in which electrons revolve around the nucleus in the same way that the earth revolves around the sun.

Rutherford calculated that these positive particles are about 1,836 times the mass of the electrons; he called them protons. The neutral atom helium has a nucleus made up of two protons, around which revolve two electrons.

Bohr's atom (1913)

Niels Bohr (Denmark, 1885–1962), winner of the Nobel Prize for Physics in 1922, inspired by the quantum theory proposed in 1900 by Max Planck (Germany, 1858–1947), suggested in 1913 a theory explaining the radiation emitted by atoms, when under electric discharge, for example.

Arnold Sommerfeld (Germany, 1868–1951), a mathematician and physicist, began in 1915 to apply relativist mechanics and quantum theory to the atom to explain the fine structure of spectral lines from hydrogen. He explained that the circular orbits suggested by Bohr were in fact elliptical orbits.

Geiger counter (1913)

The Geiger counter was invented in 1913 by Ernest Rutherford (New Zealand) and his assistant, Hans Geiger (Germany). This enabled them to locate and count alpha particles, a constituent of the rays emitted by radioactive decay.

The atom in wave mechanics (1925–26)

The Bohr–Sommerfeld model, in which the electrons were precisely located on an orbit, precluded the development of an atomic mechanics that could take account of all the phenomena involving atoms.

Two physicists developed a satisfactory theory from 1925–26. Erwin Schrödinger (Austria), winner of the Nobel Prize for Physics in 1933, applied to the atom an idea of Louis de Broglie (France): an electron, or any other particle, has a wave associated with it.

Werner Heisenberg (Germany), winner of the Nobel Prize for Physics in 1932, formulated his uncertainty principle, which said that it was impossible simultaneously to determine the position and the momentum of a particle with absolute certainty, permitting the combination of Schrödinger's formalist mathematics with a physical interpretation that satisfied the wave–particle duality.

Artificial radioactivity (1934)

In 1934, in Paris, Irène (1897–1956) and Frédéric (1900–1958) Joliot-Curie (the daughter and son-in-law of Pierre and Marie Curie) obtained radioactive phosphorus by bombarding aluminum with alpha particles (the nuclei of helium).

In their natural state, certain elements such as radium, neptunium and actinium are radioactive. Nuclear reactions, on the other hand, bring into play the disintegration of atomic nuclei, thus obtaining radioactive nuclei unknown in nature: these elements are said to have an artificial radioactivity.

This discovery earned the Joliot-Curies the Nobel Prize for Chemistry in 1935, and has allowed the fabrication of isotopes used in medicine, biology, metallurgy, etc.

Transuranian elements (1940)

The discovery of artificial radioactivity in 1934 led physicists of the time to think that there might be bodies with atomic numbers greater than Z92, the number of uranium in the periodic table. These are called transuranian bodies. The first one was discovered in June 1940 at the University of California at Berkeley by E.M. McMillan and P.H. Abelson. They called it neptunium, and it has an atomic mass of Z93. At the end of 1940 G.T. Seaborg, J.W. Kennedy and A.C. Wahl discovered plutonium, of mass Z94.

The latest element was discovered at the Doubna Nuclear Research Institute near Moscow in 1987. Its atomic mass is Z110. Theoreticians such as Sven Gosta Nilsson and the Swedish school think that Z114 could exist.

Nuclear magnetic resonance (1946)

Now a means of medical investigation, nuclear magnetic resonance (NMR) is a physical phenomenon that was discovered in 1946 by the Swiss-born American physicists Felix Bloch and Edward Mills Purcell, who jointly obtained the Nobel Prize for Physics in 1952.

NMR or nuclear induction is a method of measuring the magnetic field of atomic nuclei, using a particular property of the proton whose behavior is closely linked to its environment.

It is especially useful in analysis, as it allows the precise detection of specific atoms in a number of areas: in botany, in geology, in food technology, and so on.

Carbon 14 (1947)

In 1947 Willard Frank Libby (U.S.), a chemist specializing in the radioactivity of living organisms and recipient of the 1960 Nobel Prize for Chemistry, explained the formation of carbon 14 in the atmosphere. Carbon 14 is an isotope of common carbon, carbon 12. It has two more neutrons than carbon 12.

The dating of ancient objects by means of carbon 14 (known as carbon dating) is based on the extent of the residual activity of isotope 14 in carbon.

A number of other radioactive isotopes, contained in samples from a particular event, allow the occurrence to be dated along the same principles (measuring the residual activity of a radioactive isotope whose period is known). Argon–potassium dating is much used. Such a process, used on the charcoal of the Lascaux caves in France, enabled scientists to date the habitation of the caves to 13,000 years B.C.

One of the most famous recent examples of carbon dating has been its use on the Holy Shroud of Turin, considered by many to be Christ's shroud. Three institutions—the British Museum, the University of Arizona and the Federal Institute of Technology in Zurich—took part in this work, the results of which were made known at the end of 1988: in fact, the shroud dates back only to the Middle Ages.

The 110th element (1987)

The 110th element, according to Mendeleev's periodic table, was synthesized for the first time in August 1987 by researchers in the Doubna Nuclear Research Institute near Moscow. This new element was obtained from a U-400 cyclotron, at the end of two years' work by Prof. Yuri Aganessian. Experiments are under way to obtain a 111th element.

Particles

Elementary particles (1929)

An elementary particle is one that is "indivisible," that has neither dimension nor internal structure. Of course, some particles may appear to be elementary at one time in scientific history, and then later be revealed as complex. This was the case, for example, with the proton and the neutron.

At present, elementary particles are organized in two categories: the leptons and the quarks, with which antiparticles are also associated. The existence of the latter was suggested by P.A.M. Dirac (Great Britain) in 1929. Even by observing them closely by the most powerful particle accelerators, no one has been able to detect the slightest internal structure in leptons, quarks and their antiparticles.

Leptons

The electron (1875)

This was the first lepton to be discovered. Its existence was deduced from eletromagnetic experiments made by Sir Joseph John Thomson (Great Britain) from 1875. Its negative electric charge was precisley determined by R.A. Millikan (U.S.) in 1916. The positron, which is the antiparticle associated with the electron, was discovered in cosmic rays in 1932 by C.D. Anderson (U.S.).

The neutrino (1933)

The existence of this lepton was postulated by Wolfgang Pauli (Switzerland, b. Austria) in 1933, to explain certain phenomena in beta radioactivity, and was named *neutrino* (tiny neu-

tron) by Enrico Fermi (Italy). It is an extremely light particle, which can travel through dense matter like the earth without difficulty because it hardly interacts with matter. It was directly identified toward the end of the 1950s by Reines and George Arthur Cowan (both U.S.).

It is now known that there are in fact three types of neutrino, associated respectively with the electron, the muon and the tau.

The muon (1937)

Discovered in 1937 by C.D. Anderson in collaboration with Neddemeyer, the muon has a mass 206.77 times that of the electron. It was created in an accelerator in 1939.

The tau (1976)

This came to the fore during an experiment on collisions between electrons and positrons, run by Prof. Martin L. Perl and his team at Stanford University in 1976. Its mass is 3,600 times that of the electron.

Quarks

Origins (1964)

In 1964 the physicists Murray Gell-Mann and George Zweig independently postulated the existence of quarks (although Zweig called them "aces") as the fundamental constituents of protons and neutrons. There are now thought to be six quarks, known by their English names: Up, Down, Strange, Charm, Bottom, and Top. A team at the European Center for Nuclear Reearch (CERN) found experimental evidence of Top's existence in 1984, and estimated its mass at 30–50 billion electron volts.

The physicist Greenberg proved that quarks must have a new kind of charge, which he called color, that takes the form of three different shades, conventionally blue, red and green.

Composite particles

These are not elementary particles but are made up of elementary particles linked together. There are many composite particles in nature; the proton, the neutron and the pion are the most important examples.

The proton (1886)

The discovery of the proton goes back to an experiment conducted by E. Goldstein (Germany) in 1886. It is the main constituent of the atomic nucleus, with a positive charge, and is made up of three quarks.

The neutron (1932)

This is the second constituent of the atomic nucleus, and it was discovered by James Chadwick (Great Britain) in 1932, building on the work done by W. Bothe in Germany and the Joliot-Curies in France. Its name comes from the fact that it is electrically neutral. It is made up of two Down quarks and one Up.

The pion (1935)

In 1935 Hideki Yukawa (Japan) postulated the existence of a new particle to explain the transmission of nuclear force: the π-meson or pion. He predicted that it would have about 200 times the mass of an electron. The pion was actually discovered in 1947. It is made up of a quark and an antiquark (the antiparticle associated with the quark).

Bosons

These are particles associated with classic waves. They appear also as the particles exchanged during the process of fundamental interactions. Their name derives from the fact that they obey Bose–Einstein statistics.

The photon (1923)

"Invented" by Albert Einstein in 1905 to explain the photoelectric effect, the photon is a light particle. It "carries" the electromagnetic force between charged particles. A.H. Compton (U.S.) found evidence of its existence in 1923.

Gluons (1982)

There are eight gluons responsible for strong nuclear interactions. They have never been seen, but an experiment conducted in 1982 by a group of American research workers from Brookhaven and the City College in New York seems to prove their existence.

Weak interaction bosons (1983)

There are three of these, called W–, W+ and Z^0, which were found to exist by a team of 200 research workers led by Carlo Rubbia (Italy) and Simon van der Meer (Netherlands) at CERN in Geneva in 1983.

The graviton (21st century)

This is a particle in the gravitational field. At present it exists only as an abstract concept. It is thought that gravitational waves may be formed from a large number of gravitons.

CHEMISTRY

Inorganic Chemistry

Ceramics (7th millennium B.C.)

Terracotta pottery, invented simultaneously in Turkey, Syria and Kurdistan in the 7th millennium B.C., was the first technique to transform matter of mineral origin through the use of fire. With pottery, humans had invented the first artificial material.

In general, antique pottery had one major drawback: it was not watertight. Thus, through the centuries, people attempted to perfect a watertight clay as well as watertight exterior varnishing.

Alexandre Brongniart, in the mid-19th century, created the precursor of modern pottery, before the appearance of industrial ceramics around the 1950s, with neoceramics based on the principle of calcination, and oxide ceramics. Because they hardly expand, the latter are very resistant to heat and are thus used in the aerospace industry.

Porcelain (6th century A.D.)

The first porcelain that can be definitely dated was manufactured in China in the 6th century. In 1698, an industrialist, Baron Schnorr (Germany), discovered the first European deposits of kaolin in Saxony. At the same time, von Schirnahaus (Germany, 1651–1708) and Johan Friedrich Böttger (Germany, 1682–1719) perfected the process for making porcelain.

In 1752 the discovery of kaolin deposits in Saint-Yrieix-la-Perche in central France led to the rapid development of porcelain factories in Limoges.

Cobalt (1735)

This metal was isolated for the first time in 1735 by Georg Brandt (Sweden) from copper minerals found in the Harz region. The word *cobalt* is derived from the Middle High German word *Kobalt*, which means "goblin," because the vapors given off during the fusion of copper minerals, which contain cobalt, are toxic.

In 1910 it was discovered that this metal improved high-speed steel, and metallurgists became interested in it. Cobalt is used in alloys that are resistant to high temperatures, in magnetic materials and in hardwearing alloys that resist corrosion.

Sulfuric acid (18th century)

The first sulfuric acid plants were created in England in the 18th century. They used the leaden condensing chamber developed in 1746 by the chemical engineer John Roebuck (Great Britain, 1718–94). For the first time a link was formed between the laboratory and industry.

In 1774 steam replaced water in the process, which changed from discontinuous to continuous.

Chlorine (1774)

In 1774 Carl Wilhelm Scheele (Sweden, 1742–86) discovered chlorine, by causing hydrochloric acid to react with manganese dioxide. From saltpeter Scheele also discovered tartric, oxalic and lactic acids and glycerine.

In 1810 Sir Humphry Davy (Great Britain, 1778–1829) recognized chlorine as a new element. A constituent of all living organisms, it does not exist in a free state in nature. It is found only in the form of chlorides (hydrochloric acid salts).

Tungsten (1781)

Discovered in 1781 by Carl Wilhelm Scheele (Sweden), tungsten is a hard, malleable element. Its name means "heavy stone" in Swedish. Tungsten is the most fire-resistant element known to date, with a melting point of 6,170° F.

Tungsten is used in the manufacture of lamp filaments, and in the composition of silver, copper, zinc, pewter, argyrodite and germanite based minerals. The main sources are found in China, the Korean peninsula, the United States and Russia.

Cadmium (1817)

This silver-white metal, with its slight tinge of blue, was produced for the first time in the laboratory in 1817 by Frederic Strohmeyer (Germany) using its oxide present in a sample of zinc carbonate. In 1818 Strohmeyer proposed the name *cadmium* for this newly discovered metal because it was mainly recovered from the zinc *cadmia fornacum*, flowers formed on the walls of ovens used to distill zinc.

Industrial production of cadmium began in 1827 in Upper Silesia. The main uses of cadmium and its compounds are in electroplating alloys and car radiators. In addition, cadmium rods are used to control the flux of neutrons in nuclear reactors.

Silicon (1823)

This is the most common element on the surface of the earth (28 percent) after oxygen, with which it is associated in the form of silica (flint) or silicates (clay). It was isolated in its pure state for the first time in 1823 by Jöns Jakob Berzelius (Sweden, 1779–1848), one of the creators of modern chemistry. It has important uses in metallurgy, where it increases the resistance of steel to corrosion. It is also used in the making of light alloys, such as alpax (aluminum–silicon), which have many uses: pistols, casings, bicycle wheels, electrical appliances, etc.

It is used in the plastics industry and, of course, in electronics for the manufacture of silicon chips. The name Silicon Valley has been applied to the Santa Clara region in California, where most of the factories using silicon as a raw material in the manufacture of semiconductors are concentrated.

Nitric acid (1838)

The preparation of nitric acid by the catalytic oxidation of ammonia gas was discovered in 1838 by Frédéric Kuhlmann (France); the catalyst used in the reaction was platinum.

Using this method, Wilhelm (Germany, 1853–1932) made nitric acid on a small scale. But when Carl Bosch (Germany, 1874–1940) replaced platinum with a catalyst based on iron, manganese and bismuth, the production of nitric acid on an industrial scale could be considered. The resulting production of nitrates replaced the natural nitrates that had been imported from Chile.

Germanium (1885)

In 1885, while analyzing argyrodite ore, Clemens Winkler (Germany) discovered a new metal, which he named *germanium*, after its country of origin. Germanium is easy to purify and is used as a solid semiconductor in transistors and rectifiers.

Germanium dioxide is used in the composition of glass with a high refractive index. It is also a good catalyst in the polymerization of polyester.

Aluminum (1886)

In 1822 mineralogist Pierre Berthier (France, 1782–1861) discovered, near the village of Les Baux, in Provence, the first deposits of an ore which he named *bauxite*. It was in fact hydrous alumina (aluminum oxide).

In 1825 Hans Christian Oersted (Denmark) obtained aluminum in a powdered form, and in 1827 it was created in the form of an ingot by Friedrich Wöhler (Germany, 1800–82).

In 1886 Paul-Louis Héroult (France, 1863–1914) and Charles Martin Hall (U.S., 1863–1914) discovered independently, but almost simultaneously, the process of electrolysis, still in use, which was to give rise to the aluminum industry.

Since then, because of technological progress, aluminum has never ceased to grow in importance.

Ammonia (1908)

By applying the laws of chemical equilibrium, Fritz Haber (Germany) succeeded in 1908 in synthesizing ammonia, using the elements that make up this substance: nitrogen and hydrogen.

The industrial development of the procedure in 1909 by BASF was the work of Carl Bosch (Germany). By converting atmospheric nitrogen into ammonia, this process ensured a ready supply of fertilizers.

Semicrystals (1984)

A geometric rule requires that the elementary figure of a crystal possess symmetrical axes of the order of two, three, four or six only. Symmetry of the order of five is impossible in practice, for the simple reason that pentagons do not have their edges touching.

In 1984, however, four research workers announced the discovery of a structure in matter symmetrical to the order of five. The discovery was made jointly by Dan Schechtmann and Ilon Blech of the institute of technology, Technion, in Haifa, Israel; by Denis Gratias of the center for metallurgical chemistry at CNRS in France; and by John Cahn of the National Bureau of Standards in Washington. They chose to call this new stable state of matter semicrystal, not entirely a crystal and not entirely amorphous.

In 1985, mathematical models created by computer showed that this impossible structure was feasible in a six-dimensional space, and in July 1986 a team at the Péchiney research center in France managed to create a cupro-manganese alloy made up of single crystals observable by the naked eye.

This discovery enables scientists to envisage the fabrication of new alloys whose resistance and lightness could completely alter the industrial scene. Aircraft manufacturers are watching these new developments with particular attention.

Excellent conductors of heat and very stable up to temperatures of 400° C, semicrystals are ideal to coat hot-plates on cookers and frying pans. The technique was patented in 1988 by Jean-Marie Dubois, a chemist and director of research at the French CNRS. Pans thus coated will be able to cook an omelet in 5–10 seconds and meat in 35–40 seconds.

Transparent ceramics (1988)

A transparent ceramic used in the new scanner-detectors has been commercially produced since 1988 by General Electric. These new detectors are made up of 900 sensitive elements (from photodiodes to silicon) placed side by side and covered with a block of transparent ceramic. This material (HiLight Ceramic) acts as a scintillator when hit by X-rays.

Superconductive ceramics (1988)

Du Pont has applied for a patent for a superconductive ceramic, which is more stable and easier to manage than the nonresistant materials currently in use for carrying electricity.

Expandable ceramics (1990)

Another innovation in the field of ceramics is the development of superplastic ceramics. Fumihiro Wakai (Japan) and the research teams of Mitsubishi and the University of Osaka have produced ceramics that can undergo deformation (elongation) through heating.

Organic Chemistry

Rubber and Plastics

Natural rubber (1736)

In 1736, the naturalist Charles Marie de la Condamine (France, 1701–74) discovered natural rubber while working in Peru. Condamine noticed that native tribesmen made various everyday objects from a black resinous product; he obtained samples of this substance and sent them back to Paris.

Nitrocellulose (1833)

Two chemists, Theophile-Jules Pelouze and Henri Bracannot (both France) obtained nitrocellulose (or cellulose nitrate) in 1833. It was not produced industrially until 1847, when Christian F. Schonbein developed it as cotton-powder.

Vulcanization (1839)

This technique, which stabilizes the properties of rubber and makes it usable, was invented by Charles Goodyear (U.S.) in 1839. Natural rubber becomes stiff in cold temperatures and softens with age, making its industrial use limited. While testing the drying agents of rubber, Goodyear accidently left a piece of gum stabilized with sulfur on a hot stove. When he re-turned he observed that the rubber appeared to be stabilized. Goodyear had invented vulcanization.

Synthetic rubber (1860)

In 1860 Greville Williams (Great Britain) decomposed rubber by heat, thus isolating a substance called isoprene. In 1880 G. Bouchardat (France) became the first to prepare a solid substance from isoprene. In 1884 Tilden synthesized isoprene by decomposing turpentine vapors. This discovery laid the foundation for the production of synthetic rubber.

Cellulose acetate (1869)

In 1869, Paul Schutzenberger obtained an acetyl cellulose (cellulose acetate) by the action of acetic anhydride on cellulose. In 1884 Charles F. Cross and Edward J. Bevan (both Great Britain) took out patents for the industrial production of cellulose acetate. Cellulose acetate is used in the manufacture of varnish, plastics and photographic films.

Celluloid (1870)

Celluloid was invented by the Hyatt brothers (U.S.) in 1870. The Hyatts began their celluloid research in response to an advertisement offering a $110,000 award to anyone who could develop a substitute for ivory in the making of billiard balls. After several years they obtained celluloid by hot-mixing ocellulose nitrate, a macromolecular vegetable substance, camphor and a plasticizer.

Rayon (1891)

In 1891 Charles F. Cross (Great Britain) obtained the patent for fabricating cellulose xanthate, the basis of cellulose. In 1921 Edward J. Bevan (Great Britain) obtained a patent for obtaining rayon from acetate.

Bakelite (1907)

In 1907 Leo Hendrik Baekeland (Belgium, 1863–1944), a chemist living in the United States, invented the first duroplastic resin, bakelite. It was designed as a rubber substitute, since rubber was prone to drying out and cracking. Bakelite could be shaped and set under extreme heat and pressure and would then remain hard and heat-resistant. It was ideal for such objects as pot handles.

Cellophane (1908)

On November 14, 1908 Dr. J.E. Brandenberger, a specialist in the dying and printing of textiles, used viscose to treat cotton. A fine film stuck to the cotton, and cellophane had been invented. In 1912 Brandenberger trademarked the name Cellophane. Initially used in the clothing industry, cellophane is now commonly used for the packaging and conditioning of a wide range of products.

PVC (polyvinylchloride) (1913)

In 1913 Prof. Klatte (Germany) patented the polymerization of the gas vinyl chloride. The German company I.G. Farben was the first company to produce PVC industrially in 1931. PVC is used in a broad range of products, such as shoes, fibers and bottles.

Polymers (1922)

The structure of polymers was discovered by Hermann Staudinger (Germany) in 1922. Polymers are made up of very long chains of thousands of atoms that spread out forming links with each other. Staudinger found large molecules in these chains—macromolecules. The artificial creation of these macromolecules in natural chains is called polymerization, which is the basic procedure for all production of synthetic fibers.

Plexiglass (1924)

In 1924 the chemists Barker and Skinner made an organic glass, the polymethacrylate of methyl. In 1934 this product was produced commerically under the name Plexiglass (from "plastic flexible glass").

Polystyrene (1933)

Styrene was first prepared in 1831. At that time it was already known that when heated or exposed to light, styrene is transformed into a vitreous solid. Polystyrene was perfected in 1933 by the chemist Wulff (Germany). A compound was first marketed in 1938. In 1951 BASF produced stretch polystyrene, one of a family of styrene polymers.

Polyamides (1935)

Polyamides were perfected in 1935 in the research laboratories of Du Pont by Wallace H. Carothers. He patented polyamide 6-6 in 1937, calling it nylon (see below). Polyamides are best known as fibers but also make excellent technical plastics, such as Rilsan and Technyl.

Nylon (1937)

Nylon was perfected and patented in 1937 by Wallace H. Carothers, director of the department of fundamental research in physical chemistry at Du Pont. Nylon is a polyamide obtained from adipic acid and hexamethylene.

Polyurethanes (1937)

Polyurethanes were invented by Otto Bayer (Germany) in 1937. As soft foam plastic, they are used for mattresses and car cushions; as semirigid foam, for dashboard trims and shockproof packaging; as rigid foam, for thermal insulation (refrigerators); as elastomers, for shoe soles, printing rollers and textile fibers.

Teflon (polytetrafluorethylene) (1938)

Known as Teflon, the tetrafluorethylene polymer was discovered by Du Pont engineer Roy

Roy J. Plunkett (right) in the Du Pont laboratory where he discovered Teflon in 1938. (DuPont)

J. Plunkett (U.S.) in 1938. Teflon was first patented in 1939. The idea of spreading it over metal was invented by Marc Gregoire in 1954.

Polyethylene (1939)

The first grams of low-density polyethylene were obtained by the engineers Fawcett and Gibson (both Great Britain) for the British company Imperial Chemical Industries (ICI) in 1935. ICI first produced polyethylene in 1939. These products received immediate recognition as the best material for cable insulation. In 1953 Karl Ziegler (Germany, 1896–1973) developed a process for the manufacture of high-density polyethylene (PEHD).

Lycra (1952)

This elasthane (elastomer of polyurethane) was perfected by researchers at Du Pont in 1952. It is most commonly mixed in small proportions (2 to 10 percent) with normal fibers for clothes that cling to the body, such as bathing suits.

Polypropylene (1954)

In 1954 the polymerization of propylene was perfected by the engineer Natta (Italy). Very resistant, it is used for food packaging, domestic appliance casing (vacuum cleaners), industrial fabrics and carpeting.

Kevlar (1965)

Discovered in 1965 by research scientist Stephanie Kwolek at the Du Pont laboratories, Kevlar is one of the most resistant of all synthetic fibers. Five times more resistant than steel, Kevlar is an aramide fiber, a descendant of bakelite and nylon.

Gore-Tex (1969)

All sports enthusiasts are familiar with clothing made of Gore-Tex, a material that is virtually a second skin, protects against wind and foul weather, yet disposes of perspiration. Bob Gore (U.S.) invented Gore-Tex in 1969, deriving it from Teflon. Apart from textile applications, Gore-Tex is used in electronics (wires and cables), in industry (membranes, filters, waterproof connections) and medicine (prostheses).

Dyneema fiber (1979)

A super-tough polyethylene fiber, this has been perfected by Koos Mencke (Netherlands), an engineer with DSM chemical group. This fiber is 15 times stronger than steel yet floats on water. The DSM group marketed it as Dyneema fiber, developed in 1979 by P. Smith, A.J. Pennings and P.J. Lemstra. It is used for such diverse products as tennis rackets, bulletproof vests and light armor plating for vehicles.

Peba (1981)

This family of synthetic materials was created in 1981 by Gerard Deleens. Peba is halfway between elastomers (rubber) and plastics, and is used for shoes, sports equipment and industrial parts.

Other Carbon Compounds

Nicotine (1828)

In 1562 Jean Nicot (France) extracted a juice from tobacco (brought from America by Christopher Columbus) that accelerated the healing of wounds.

However, it was not until 1828 that R. Posselt and R. Reimann isolated nicotine in its pure state. Ingested, it is a violent poison that has been used for criminal ends, and its toxicity is utliized in plant medicine to destroy parasites.

Urea (1828)

This organic substance exists naturally in the blood (0.20 to 0.50 g per liter) and in urine (2.5 g per liter), where it was discovered. Its synthesis in 1929 by Friedrich Wöhler (Germany) marked a turning point in demonstrating for the first time that an organic substance can be obtained independently of any living organism.

Benzene (19th century)

Benzene is a hydrocarbon with the formula C_6H_6, and the question of its structure was one of the oldest mysteries of organic chemistry. The chemist August Kakule (Germany, 1829–96) had long been searching for an answer to this question when one night he dreamed of a snake biting its own tail. In the morning he understood that to explain all the chemical properties of benzene the molecule had to bite its own tail just like the snake: it had to have a cyclical structure in which the six atoms of carbon are arranged in a circle, their six linkages forming a hexagon.

Formaldehyde (1868)

Discovered in 1868 by August Wilhelm von Hofmann (1818–92), formaldehyde is used in the textile industry, in papermaking, tanning, dyeing, photography and joinery (wood glues). It is also a base of synthetic resins and insulating foam that is injected into partitions.

Moreover, formaldehyde is used, because of its antiseptic properties, as a disinfectant in solution, known as formol. Formol is easily polymerized into metaldehyde, in which form it is used as blocks for lighting barbecues.

Lead tetraethyl (1923)

Lead tetraethyl, put onto the market in America in 1923 by the Ethyl Corporation, is an anti-knock agent which, when added to gasoline, increase its octane level and thus its efficiency. It also prevents deterioration of the engine. However, in 1965, scientist Clark C. Patterson (U.S.) called attention to its harmful effects. Inhaled or accidentally ingested (from polluted plants, for example), lead tetraethyl enters the bloodstream and affects the central nervous system.

Liquid crystals (1929)

In 1929 the physicist Friedel (France) discovered products that could be presented in a stable state and were intermediary between solids and liquids. One family of these products is now well-known: that of liquid crystals. Unlike solid crystals, their molecules can change direction under certain circumstances—in particular, when submitted to a very weak electric current, their transparence is altered. It is this property that is used in watch display panels; any figure can be formed from just seven segments.

In 1971 the Swiss company Hoffmann-La Roche perfected the first panel of liquid crystals.

From 1973 on, liquid crystals made their appearance in many objects of everyday use: watch-dials, calculator screens, electronic games, portable computers and so on.

Synthetic diamonds (1955)

Ever since it has been known that the diamond is nothing more than ordinary carbon in a practically pure state and in a form of very regular crystals, attempts have been made to produce the gem artificially.

In 1894, chemist Henri Moissan (France) thought that he had manufactured diamonds by heating carbon to a very high temperature under great pressure. However, it wasn't until 1955 that General Electric produced true synthetic diamonds by heating carbon to 4,700° F at a pressure exceeding 100,000 atmospheres.

These tiny diamonds (hardly longer than a millimeter) are often black and are used in industry. But it is possible, by increasing the temperature at which they are formed, to create transparent diamonds for use in jewelry. Because of the cost of production and the time it takes, these artificial diamonds are more expensive than natural ones, and not as beautiful.

Analytical Chemistry

Mass spectrography (19th century)

The discovery of the electron in 1897 by Sir Joseph John Thomson (Great Britain) proved that the atom was not single and indivisible but was made up of several particles. Researchers very soon delved into the innermost structure of matter and came up with evidence for the existence, at the heart of the same natural substance, of two or more atoms chemically similar but of different atomic mass. They called these isotopes, and the process used was called mass spectrography. The differences between such

atoms came from the number of neutrons contained in their atomic nuclei, which varied from one isotope to another. Thus uranium ore has three isotopes: uranium 238 (92 protons, 146 neutrons), uranium 235 (92 protons, 143 neutrons) and uranium 234 (92 protons, 142 neutrons). The same is true for most natural bodies, except for a few such as aluminum.

For his work on the nature of isotopes, Frederick Soddy (Great Britain, 1877–1956) won the Nobel Prize for Chemistry in 1921.

Mass spectrograph (c. 1919)

By separating isotopes from a body, it became possible to make a very precise analysis of them. The mass spectrograph was created by Francis Aston (Great Britain), an assistant of J.J. Thomson. It enabled Thomson in 1919 to analyze the neon atom, and to show that it is made up of two isotopes: neon 20 and neon 22. Aston then continued with the analysis of many bodies, and received the Nobel Prize for Chemistry in 1922.

The mass spectrograph, which uses the difference in deflection of isotopes in a magnetic field, remains a powerful analytical tool. In effect, it allows the composition of all bodies to be precisely determined. For example, in the search for traces of explosive in the case of a murder attempt, it is possible to use this technique to find the exact nature of the explosive used, as certain isotopes are explosive and others are not.

BIOLOGY

Genetics

Gametes (5th century B.C.)

The first person to suspect the existence of male and female reproductive cells was the Greek doctor Hippocrates (c. 460– c. 377 B.C.): in effect, he accepted that the formation of the human enbryo involved male and female seeds.

These two seeds are the spermatazoon and the ovum. The former is the characteristic cell of the sperm produced by the testicles. A man produces about 200 million of these per day. The ovum is produced by the ovary. At birth, a girl has about 400,000 ova, whose number then diminishes; by puberty there are only 10,000, of which only 400 achieve maturity.

The cell (1665)

The scientist Robert Hooke (Great Britain, 1635–1703) was the first to use the word *cell* (from *cellula*, little room) to describe the miniature empty structures that he observed in 1665, with the aid of a rudimentary microscope, when he cut into a piece of cork. Cork being a dead tissue, Hooke in fact was only looking at the outer walls of the cells. At the same period, Antony van Leeuwenhoek in Holland was using a somewhat better microscope to observe some

isolated cells, such as those in drops of blood, sperm and bacteria.

It was not until 1824 that René Dutrochet (France) established that living tissue was made up of juxtaposed cells. Then in 1833, Robert Brown (Great Britain, 1773–1858) described the cell nucleus. Today we describe a cell as being made up of a cytoplasm and a nucleus, enclosed by a membrane.

Heredity (1865)

In 1865 the Moravian-born botanist Gregor Johann Mendel (1822–84) demonstrated that hereditary characteristics are transmitted via distinct elements, which are today called genes. Two sets of experiments allowed him to reach this conclusion. The first set consisted of crossing of peas of stable lines that differed among themselves in a couple of characteristics; for example, peas with smooth or wrinkled seeds were crossed with those with green or yellow cotyledons. The crossing of such plants produced the first-generation plants in which dominant characteristics were revealed; for example, the hybrids obtained by the crossing of smooth yellow peas with wrinkled green peas were smooth and yellow. But when the hybrids were crossed, the parental green and wrinkled characteristics appears in a quarter of the second-generation hybrids.

From these observations, Mendel deduced that hereditary factors determining traits went in pairs, and that the recessive characteristic was only expressed in the plant when both parents had that characteristic. Such experiments allowed Mendel to determine that in peas the smooth and yellow characteristics are dominant, while the green and wrinkled characteristics are recessive. He also formulated laws that bear his name and which, by revealing the segregation of characteristics, prove that hereditary factors behave independently: they join together and separate across generations and hybridizations, according to the statistical norms of chance.

Chromosomes (1888)

Chromosomes are short rods, usually curved (measuring 0.000194 in.) in humans, that are found in the cell nucleus. The anatomist G. Waldeyer (Germany) named them in 1888. The essential constituent of chromosomes is DNA.

Mutations (1901)

The first observations of mutations were made by botanist Hugo de Vries (Netherlands) in 1901. In cultivating and studying plants of different species, he observed some that did not correspond to what would be expected from their original seed. These individual plants were different from their progenitors, and their differences were inherited by their offspring. De Vries gave the name "mutations" to these hereditary variations. Later, it was proved that the modifications sprang from alterations in the genes. Mutations are observed among animals as well as vegetables. Today, experimental mutations can be obtained by using radiation and chemical products.

The gene (1910)

In 1909 Wilhelm Johannsen (Denmark) coined the name *genes* for the hereditary units that produce physical characteristics in an organism. The key research in this field was done by Thomas Hunt Morgan (U.S.), in the period 1910–20. While studying the fruit fly *Drosophila melanogaster*, Morgan formulated the chromosomic theory of heredity, which established the correlation between genes and chromosomes.

It is estimated that an individual's genetic inheritance consists of 100,000 genes divided among 46 chromosomes. Genes are segments of DNA, but protein accounts for only 5 percent of total DNA. The role of the remaining 95 percent is still unknown. Moreover, some genes may be unstable and may move around inside the genome. Transposons—mobile genetic elements—were discovered in 1951 by Barbara McClintock (U.S.).

Protein (1953)

A protein can be represented as a chain of amino acids, of which there are 20 different kinds. Frederick Sanger (Great Britain) was the first to work out the sequence of amino acids in various protein molecules, in 1953. He determined the sequence for insulin.

Proteins form the main structural components of most animal cells: they constitute connective tissues, skin, hair, ligaments and tendons. Proteins also take part in metabolic processes, when they are called enzymes. Some hormones are also proteins; insulin is an example. Today, insulin can be produced by synthesis.

Genetic code (1966)

When the structure of DNA was discovered in 1953, physicist George Gamow (U.S.) assumed the existence of a correlation between the sequences of nucleotides in genes and those of amino acids in proteins. He theorized that the former governed the latter by means of a code consisting of combinations of nucleotides. In 1961, Marshall Nirenberg (U.S.) showed that the code functions through triples (three by three combinations of nucleotides). Since DNA contains four different nucleotides, there are 64 different triplets. In 1966, the genetic code was completely deciphered, and it is now possible to link a specific amino acid with each triplet. The cellular machinery can "read" genetic messages and translate them into proteins. The genetic code is universal and is virtually identical in all living creatures.

Oncology (1981)

Cancer genes, or oncogenes, were discovered in 1981 by three separate U.S. research teams: that of Prof. Robert Weinberg at the Center for Cancer Research, part of the Massachusetts Institute of Technology; that of Dr. Geoffrey Cooper at the Sydney Farber Cancer Institute in Boston; and that of Prof. Michael Wigler of Cold Spring Laboratory on Long Island.

Cancer genes are not in themselves generators of cancer. They only become so when they are affected by carcinogenic substances, ionizing radiation, or viruses. Recently, various cancer genes have been isolated, for cancer of the colon, the bladder, the kidneys, and for a form of leukemia.

Ribozymes (1982)

Enzymes are not necessarily proteins. RNA can also act as an enzyme and as a catalyst to biological reactions. This important discovery was made independently by two chemists, Thomas Cech (U.S.) of the University of Colorado and Sidney Altman (U.S.) of Yale University, both of whom received the Nobel Prize for Chemistry in 1989. In February 1991, Cech and USB (United States Biochemical Corp.) patented

---

DNA Structure (1953): James D. Watson and Francis H.C. Crick

"It seemed almost unbelievable that the DNA structure was solved, and that the answer was incredibly exciting, and that our names would be associated with the double helix."

—James Watson, 1953

They met at the Cavendish Laboratory at Cambridge University and discovered that they shared an interest in DNA, the gray material in a cell's nucleus that holds the keys to life, health, heredity and growth. Watson and Crick's shared enthusiasm soon became so audible that before long, they were assigned an office together at a peaceful distance from other scientists. What they uncovered there has been described as one of the two or three greatest achievements in the history of science.

DNA was identified in 1869 by the Swiss chemist Johann Friedrich Miescher. Since then others had tried to determine its role and structure. By the 1940s scientists knew that DNA is a large molecule (a group of atoms) in the form of a long, repeating chain. Linus Pauling, a chemist at California

Two views of the double helix of a DNA molecule. (CNRS-IBAC)

Institute of Technology, began the race to discover how DNA is put together. He was the first to try to create models of DNA, using metal pieces that fit together like tinkertoys to represent the individual atoms.

Watson and Crick knew DNA's components: deoxyribose—a five-sided sugar molecule, a phosphate molecule (hydrogen, oxygen and phosphorus) and a base molecule that could either be a purine (adenine or thymine) or a pyrimidine (cytosine or guanine). Somehow these pieces fit together in a structure shaped like a helix, similar to a spiral staircase.

But how many strands of molecules were there: two? three? four? Both Watson and Crick had studied X-ray differentiated photographs of DNA taken by Maurice Wilkins and Rosalind Franklin of King's College, London. Watson attended a lecture by Rosalind Franklin about the components of DNA. He took no notes, and returned to Cambridge with bungled figures. When he and Crick tried to create a model based on these figures, the "molecule" fell apart. Then Wilkins showed Watson and Crick copies of Franklin's famous "Photograph 51," the clearest representation yet of DNA. Watson sketched the photo and used it to begin a new model.

In 1952, important pieces were still missing. Watson tried using the sugars and phosphates as the backbone of the helix, but couldn't fit the bases into the center space without throwing the spiral off balance. Crick began then to note which bases like "to sit together." He first asked Cambridge mathematician John Griffith to calculate the ways that the four bases might be attracted to each other through electrical forces. Griffith found that adenine would be attracted to thymine, and cytosine to guanine. The biochemist Edwin Chargaff pointed out the 1:1 ratio between the nitrogen bases, in terms of necessary amounts. Chargaff said, "I never met two men who knew so little and aspired to so much."

Watson and Crick needed to know only a little more in order to create a successful model of DNA. In early April 1953, they sent a paper describing their model to the British journal *Nature*. In 1962, they shared the Nobel Prize with Maurice Wilkins. Many scientists agree that Rosalind Franklin would have shared this honor, had she not died in 1957. Her work formed much of the foundation for the discovery of the structure of DNA.

Said Watson, "It is so beautiful, you see, so beautiful."

these new molecular devices, which it is hoped can be used in the treatment of viral diseases, including AIDS.

Genetic Engineering

Clones (1952)

Clones are genetically identical organisms derived from a single individual. Bacteria cultures all derived from a single bacterium are clones. In plants, the technique of cloning is currently used to obtain large numbers of identical plants through asexual reproduction. Propagation by cuttings is also a form of cloning. In animals, cloning is much more difficult because it involves the delicate technique of transferring embryonic nuclei. Carried out for the first time in 1952 on frogs, the technique consists of grafting the nucleus of a donor embryo cell to a previously enucleated recipient ovum by microsurgery.

Synthesis of the first artificial gene (1973)

This was achieved in 1973 by the researcher Har Gobind Khorana (India) at the Massachusetts Institute of Technology. It involved a double helix of DNA, corresponding to the precursor of ribonucleic acid, the gene for tyrosine transfer-RNA. The artificial gene was a 207-base long chain created to be the same as a known gene in a virus. It worked as well as the natural one, and this technique has become essential in genetic engineering.

Genetic engineering (1974)

It was in 1974 that the term "genetic engineering" made its first appearance in the scientific world. The association of the word "engineering" with "genetics"—or the science of genes—came about because of the new possibility, open to researchers, of breaking up DNA, separating out the genes and recombining them in another DNA molecule.

Genetic engineering is thus the collection of techniques that enables scientists to break into DNA, isolate genes, identify their structure, modify them if necessary, and finally, introduce them into an organism that might be different from the one from which they were originally taken.

Genetic engineering quickly established itself as a basic technique in all areas of biology. But alongside these fundamental activities, it has also made possible the manufacture of rare substances, or those difficult to extract. Medicine and industry have found new methods of production by using organisms—most often genetically modified bacteria—to work on such projects as the synthesis of insulin, a new vaccination against hepatitis-B, or alcohol from biomass for use as a fuel. A new technique, genetic engineering is far from having exhausted all its opportunities.

Ultra-rapid sequencers (1985)

The first robots capable of sequencing DNA were perfected in 1985 by Prof. Lloyd Smith (U.S.) at the University of Wisconsin. The technique at that time involved getting DNA fragments to migrate on acrylamide gels by applying electric currents of 40 volts/cm. The various positions of the bands of DNA are read by laser and transmitted to a computer that calculates the sequences. In 1990 the same team developed a robot 25 times faster using quartz capillaries and currents of 450 volts/cm. Nucleotides are read at a rate of 10 per minute. This invention has been patented in association with the company Applied Biosystems.

Chain polymerization (1985)

PCR (Polymerase Chain Reaction) is a biological technique for reproducing at will a specific fragment of DNA without cloning—that is, without having to introduce DNA into a microorganism. This method, perfected by the U.S. company Cetus in 1985, uses an enzyme, DNA polymerase, capable of swiftly synthesizing up to 100 billion identical molecules of DNA from a single "starter" DNA molecule. The technique has a great many applications: diagnosis of genetic or viral diseases, cancer research and forensic medicine.

Genetic barrier (1989)

The mechanism of the genetic barrier, a phenomenon that prevents different species from interbreeding, was explained in 1989 by a research team led by Miroslav Radman (Yugoslavia). The separation of the species is due to the action of enzymes that are able to recognize DNA of foreign origin and eliminate it. In selecting mutants without these enzymes from various different bacterial species, the team managed to break this barrier: *Salmorichia* was created from the pairing of *Salmonella thymimurium* and *Escherichia coli*.

Genetic Identification

HLA system (1958)

In 1958 Jean Dausset (France) first described the HLA system (for Human Leucocyte Antigen) in white globules. The HLA system is a series of proteins present at the surface of all the cells of an individual. These proteins are analogous to fingerprints. They vary from one individual to another and in some way may be thought of as a person's identity card. Today it is known that tolerance to grafts depends on the resemblance of the HLA systems of the donor and the recipient.

Genetic fingerprinting (1985)

In 1985 Prof. Alec J. Jeffreys (Great Britain), head of the genetic laboratory at the University of Leicester, England, developed a revolutionary procedure for detecting criminals by analyzing their blood, sperm, skin, hair or saliva: genetic fingerprinting.

The method involves locating cells, repetitive sequences or mini-satellites in DNA that are unique to every individual. The chains of mini-satellites make up molecular imprints, forming a kind of genetic identity card.

Evolution Theories

Lamarckism (1809)

In 1809 the botanist J.B.P.A. de Monet de Lamarck (France, 1744–1829) published his *Zoological Philosophy*, in which he set forth his theory of evolution: transformism.

According to Lamarck, the species are transformed with time, under the influence of their surroundings, and through the intermediary of their habits and needs. This theory of mutability had its hour of glory, then fell out of favor. However, there has been a revival of interest since studies carried out by biologists at Harvard Medical School on mutant *Escherichia coli* bacteria.

Darwinism (1859)

In his book entitled *On the Origin of Species by Natural Selection*, published in 1859, the naturalist and biologist Charles Darwin (Great Britain, 1809–82) studied the problem of evolution of species. According to him, the species are not unchangeable, the result of distinct creations, but are progressively transformed by selection of the individuals who are best adapted to their environment (survival of the fittest).

Microbiology

Microbiology (1857)

In 1857, Louis Pasteur (France, 1822–95) discovered yeast (microscopic fungi) and explained the fermentation process. Pasteur extended his research to bacteria; this was the beginning of microbiology.

Bacteriology (1870)

From 1870 on, Louis Pasteur cultivated and identified *Staphylococcus*, *Streptomyces* and *Streptococcus*. He was thus the inventor of bacteriology.

Pasteur proved that, if the environment was favorable, all cultivated germs could multiply. Since then, many culture environments have been experimented with, thus allowing the isolation of many germs, which these days are known and identified.

Immune system (1877)

In the last century Louis Pasteur came up with the idea that living beings possessed within themselves the means of fighting against sickness. When in 1877 Ilya Metchnikoff, who had discovered that certain cells in living organisms were capable of "eating" and "digesting" microbes, passed through Paris, Pasteur asked him whether he would join his team. So many stages were involved in the progressive discovery of the immune system, such as "tissue immunity" described in 1922 by Levaditi and Nicolau, that it was not until the 1950s that a clear idea was formed of the defense system belonging to each organism.

Virology (1898)

Between 1880 and 1885, while working on rabies, Pasteur realized that he had come up against an illness, then incurable, whose agent he could not cultivate. In fact, this was not a bacterium, but a virus. Eventually he was able to develop the vaccine.

In 1898 Martinus Beijerinck (Netherlands, 1851–1931) discovered microorganisms even smaller than bacteria: they passed through the finest porcelain filters. Beijerinck also discovered the virus that caused tobacco mosaic disease. This was the birth of virology. In 1935 Wendell Stanley (U.S., 1904–71) succeeded for the first time in crystallizing a virus.

In 1959, thanks to electronic microscopy, X-ray diffractions and biochemical methods, André Lwoff (France) established a definition of the virus based on the presence of nucleic acids, which made for progress in virology. The AIDS virus, discovered in 1983 by Luc Montagnier (France), is an RNA virus, or retrovirus.

Synthesis of a virus (1968)

In 1968 two researchers, Arthur Kornberg and Robert L. Sinsheimer (both U.S.), succeeded in completely synthesizing a virus, using only two enzymes—a polymerase DNA and a lipase DNA—extracted and purified from colonies of colon bacilli.

In Vitro Cultivation

In vitro culture (1907)

In vitro cultivation is a method by which a living organism, animal or vegetable, or a part of this organism (cells, tissues, organs), is sustained outside its natural environment.

The culture in vitro of animal cells and tissues was invented in 1907 by R.G. Harrison (U.S.) and perfected in 1910 by Alexis Carrel (France). This method as applied to vegetable cells and tissues was invented between 1931 and 1938 by Roger Gautheret and Pierre Nobécourt (both France) and by Philip White (U.S.).

In vitro cultures are used in research to obtain medical products (serums, vaccines, antibiotics), to produce plants that are protected against viruses and to propagate plants from buds or cuttings.

One of the most spectacular recent successes of in vitro culture is the saving of the date palm, which has been afflicted since the beginning of the century with a terrible blight. Bayoud disease is a fungus that attacks the roots and eventually kills the tree. In Morocco, which is particularly affected, the disease destroys between 150,000 and 200,000 trees a year, bringing devastation and the progressive destruction of the palm groves. This has a domino effect on the microclimate and thus on the crops and on animal rearing, leading eventually to the exodus of the population.

In vitro plant propagation (1952)

In 1952 G. Morel and J. Martin (France) of INRA (National Institute of Agronomical Research) obtained from a few cells, placed in an artificial environment, a genuine dwarf plant, that could be transplanted to serve as the basis for producing perfect plants.

The success of Morel and Martin's method enabled diseased plants to be regenerated and to proliferate rapidly in their improved form. It is used now to produce roses, orchids, potatoes, fruit trees, etc.

In vitro synthesis of proteins (1954)

The biochemist Du Vigneaud (U.S.) achieved the first synthesis of two proteins in 1954. This concerned hormones usually secreted by the postpituitary gland: oxytocin and vasopressin, each of which is made up of nine amino acids. In 1969 the first efficient artificial synthesis of a large molecule was achieved by Bruce Merrifield (U.S.) of the Rockefeller Institute, N.Y. They created a string of 1,211 amino acids. Thanks to genetic engineering techniques, proteins such as human insulin, marketed by the Eli Lilly Co. under the name Humulin, or the growth hormone Protopin, developed in 1985 by Genentech, can be produced industrially from recombined bacteria. Today three-dimensional molecular modeling by computer or molecular graphics makes it possible to visualize artificial proteins on-screen and hence manufacture made-to-measure medicines.

BIOTECHNOLOGY

The term *biotechnology* was first coined by Profs. F. Gros, F. Jacob and R. Royer in a paper they wrote on the "biological revolution." The term describes a technique whereby the properties of living organisms are manipulated for practical and industrial purposes. Biotechnology is a fast-developing field that provides a link between several disciplines: genetic engineering, enzymology, microbiology, biology, molecular biology, immunology, biochemistry and animal and vegetable biology.

Monoclonal antibodies (1975)

Early research in the field of biotechnology led to the development in 1975 of monoclonal antibodies by Georg Koehler (Germany) and César Milstein (Argentina). This discovery permitted early diagnosis of hereditary illnesses such as mucoviscidosis.

Food additives (1980)

The creation of food additives from biotechnology research is a rapidly growing field. In 1980 the French company Pernod Ricard produced a flavoring agent, anethole, that is obtained from fennel plants cloned in vitro. In 1986 B. Zyrbriggen developed the preservative aspartam glycerol, using mutated yeast cultures.

Researchers have been able to genetically manipulate the sex of unborn mice by injecting them with the gene Sry, which stimulates male development. Here the mouse on the right should have been a female, but was genetically altered and is a male. (Gamma/Hoffman-Spooner)

Giant mice (1982)

Genetic engineering had made it possible to select the most productive strains of plants and animals and to develop transgenic organisms. The first of these were the "giant mice" into which R. Brinster and R. Palmiter (both U.S.) transplanted the growth hormone in 1982. The experiment used a method developed in 1980 by M.R. Capecchi (U.S.) for injecting a gene into eggs that had just been fertilized, a method that is used effectively in fish-farming but that has proved less efficient with pigs and rabbits.

OncoMouse (1984)

The first animal to be patented as a result of genetic modifications was the OncoMouse, bred by Philip Leder and Timothy Stewart (both U.S.) and patented in 1984. These mice carry human oncogenes that are used in cancer research.

Transgenic plant (1984)

The first plant of this type was produced as a result of research carried out at the University of Ghent, Belgium in 1984. It was a kanamycin (antibiotic) resistant tobacco plant. In 1986 the Swiss company Ciba-Geigy and the American company Monsanto developed tobacco plants resistant to triazines. In 1987 a toxin was produced that enabled tobacco to combat the *Manduca sexta*, a caterpillar that is particularly harmful to tobacco. The first large-scale experiments were undertaken in 1988, and have proved that it will be possible for farmers to grow tobacco without the use of insecticides.

Biolipstick (1984)

By placing cultures from vegetable cells in bioreactors, large quantities of substances with coloring, aromatic and medicinal properties are obtained. This method is replacing the extraction of such substances from plants. The first of these products to be marketed was shikonine, used in "Biolipstick," produced by the Japanese company Kanebo and developed by Mitsui Petrochemical Industries, also of Japan, in 1984.

WHAT ON EARTH?

NOT ALL INVENTIONS CHANGE OUR LIVES, SOME JUST MAKE US SCRATCH OUR HEADS.

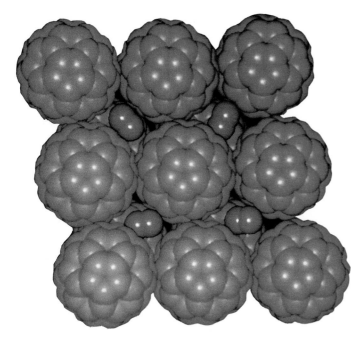

CHAOS THEORY

This is not a project to determine how teenagers decorate their bedroom walls, but the study of unpredictable phenomena based on solid mathematical theorems. In 1892 Jules Henri Poincaré (France) demonstrated that most dynamic systems exhibit chaotic behavior patterns. It was not until 1954 that A.N. Kolmogorov outlined the theorem for the condition under which chaos exists, which was proved conclusively by V.I. Arnold and Jurgen Moser in the 1960s. In 1963 Michel Hénon (France) discovered the first "strange attractor," the point that attracts all the trajectories of a chaotic system.

RADIATION ROBOT

This robot, devised by Dr. Uchiyama (Japan), detects the amount of ▼ radiation absorbed by different parts of the human body. Known as "the phantom," the robot can be exposed to all types and levels of radiation. (Gamma/Wada)

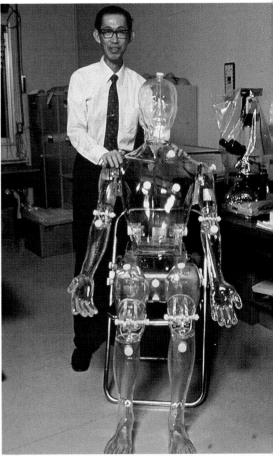

BUCKYBALLS

▲ Buckminsterfullerenes or buckyballs, hollow molecules of 60 or 70 carbon atoms, were discovered in the mid-1980s. Experiments have shown that spaces between the atoms allow an efficient means of filtering, separating and storing certain gases, such as oxygen and hydrogen. (Sandia National Laboratories)

THE PLASTIC HOUSE

▼ Perhaps the ultimate cure for dry rot is the plastic house. Designed by David George, this house is built entirely from plastic materials, including all the joints and windows. The house weighs 23 tons and cost $3 million to build. (Jerrican)

STEP PROJECT

As part of a joint project of NASA and the European Space Agency, Galileo's observance of the equivalence principle, which later became a cornerstone of Einstein's general theory of relativity, will be conducted in space. The project, known as STEP (Satellite Test of the Equivalence Principle), retests Galileo's observation that "all bodies fall with uniform acceleration, irrespective of their weight and internal composition." The basis of the test will be to control very precisely the distance between two bodies of different composition loaded on board a satellite. The satellite is counterbalanced in orbit by the earth's force of gravity and centrifugal force. Everything occurs as in "free fall" within the gravitational field of the earth. The experiment is to be performed from a height of 4,300 miles, the distance between the satellite and the center of the earth. NASA officials expect satellite construction to begin in 1995, with a launch in 1999 or 2000.

ACOUSTIC LEVITATION

Designed by Charles A. Rey and Dennis R. Merkley of Intersonics, Inc., the acoustic levitation system is designed to allow scientists to test new materials without their being affected by other materials holding them in place, such as a container or clamp. The system is designed specifically for testing ceramic materials for their value as high-temperature superconductors, but also has applications for glass and aerospace materials. Patented in the United States in 1992, acoustic levitation combines the use of air pressure and acoustics to suspend materials for testing. An air cushion elevates the object, which is then bombarded by sound generators, which immobilizes it in mid-air.

MEMORY PLASTICS

The Japanese group Nippon Zeon is developing a plastic with a memory. It has the same properties as the metal alloys, but thanks to a greater molecular mass and to its particular chemical links, it is as elastic as rubber. So, for example, in the future dented car fenders will re-shape themselves when heated to the temperature of manufacture. It may be the super-material of the future.

THE HUMAN GENOME PROJECT

The Human Genome Project was launched in the United States in 1985 and since 1990 has been overseen by HUGO (Human Genome Organization). The goal of the project is to map the location of the 100,000 genes among the 23 pairs of chromosomes present in every human cell and then determine the order, or "sequencing," of the 3 billion base pairs of nucleotides that make up these chromosomes. Initially estimated to take 15 years to complete, research published by Daniel Cohen in September 1992 shows that the project is well ahead of schedule.

Cohen, the director of the Center for the Study of Human Polymorphism (CEPH) in Paris, devised a new research strategy that has seen a rapid acceleration of results in the mapping of the genome. Cohen's work has forced other scientists to revise their mapping strategies. Instead of studying each chromosome separately, Cohen's method consists of cutting, by restriction enzymes, the whole genome, producing thousands of fragments that are analyzed by computer to reconstitute the order of the fragments on the chromosome.

In October 1992 the first maps of two human chromosomes, the Y chromosome (constructed by David Page of the Whithead Institute, Cambridge, Mass.) and chromosome 21 (constructed by Cohen), were published in *Nature* and *Science*. At the beginning of 1993, Cohen's research had resulted in the completion of 97 percent of the physical cartography of the human genes, four years ahead of schedule.

ODOR GENES

A team of researchers at Johns Hopkins University, led by Solomon H. Snyder, received a U.S. patent in 1992 for the gene of a protein they had identified that may be able to help in restoring or enhancing an individual's sense of smell. Experiments have shown that the protein attaches itself to various odor-causing molecules, and transports them to receptors at the back of the nose. It may have applications for people who have lost their sense of smell, such as the elderly and patients undergoing chemotherapy.

GENE GUNS

Ballistics came to the aid of biologists with the creation of the gene gun, invented in 1988 by Prof. John Sanford (U.S.) of Cornell University. In 1990 Du Pont de Nemours obtained the rights to the gun and produced a "biolistic" device that used gunpowder to insert foreign genes directly into plant or animal cells. More recently, pressurized gas has replaced gunpowder as the driving force (see photo at left). This technique uses tiny gold "bullets" coated with a film of genetic material that penetrates the cells, at speeds exceeding 670 mph. In 1992 the U.S. company Agracetus obtained a U.S. patent for a particle-acceleration system for a gene gun they had developed. The Agracetus "weapon" uses a slightly different technique to fire microscopic particles of DNA-coated gold into living cells. Du Pont and Agracetus have negotiated a cross-licensing agreement that gives Agracetus the rights to human and animal applications, and Du Pont the rights to other applications, including plants.

Biolistic Particle Delivery System. (Bio-Rad)

OSTEOGENIN

Osteogenin is a protein that induces bone formation in mammals. In experiments conducted on rats, Dr. A. Hari Reddi of Johns Hopkins University applied a layer of osteogenin to soft muscle tissue fragments, and clamped the muscle to a silicone mold. In a few days this experiment generated a bony formation with its own blood network. If the protein involved can be isolated, purified and synthesized, it is hoped that a system could be developed for creating bone from muscles. It will be seven to ten years before osteogenin can be used for human purposes.

New ideas that may change the way we live

An artist's representation of the cosmos as known in the Middle Ages: a scientist breaks through the celestial vault to discover how the stars move. (Dorka)

ASTRONOMY

Origins (antiquity)

Astronomy, together with mathematics, is the oldest science studied by humankind. The first rudimentary astronomical observations were carried out in the ancient civilizations of Mesopotamia, Egypt and China. In order to observe the stars, the first astronomers used an index bar that was a simple rectilinear rod, and a compass, a double articulated index bar. They also had the astrolabe, an instrument that measured the position of the stars above the horizon, which is said to have been invented by Hipparchus, the Greek astronomer, in the 2nd century B.C.

Planets

First identification (antiquity)

Five planets—Mercury, Venus, Mars, Jupiter and Saturn—were known at the time of the Roman Empire. All five are named for Roman gods.

Uranus (1781)

Uranus was the first planet to be discovered that was not known to the ancient world. It was detected by Sir William Herschel (Great Britain), who reported his find in 1781.

Neptune (1846)

Two men, working independently, predicted the existence of Neptune in papers published in 1846. Based on their observations of irregularities in the motion of Uranus, John Couch Adams (Great Britain) and U. Jean Joseph Leverrier (France) produced theoretical calculations that proved the existence of Neptune. To prove his theory, Leverrier contacted John G. Galle (Germany, 1812–1910) at the Berlin Observatory and suggested that he look for the planet. Galle observed Neptune on September 23, 1846.

Pluto (1930)

In a paper published in 1914, Percival Lowell (U.S.) predicted the existence of Pluto. In 1919, W.H. Pickering (U.S.) published independent calculations that confirmed Lowell's prediction. On February 18, 1930, Clyde Tombaugh (U.S.) confirmed Pluto's existence, having systematically compared astronomical photographs taken on January 23 and 29 of that year.

Lenses and Telescopes

Galileo's lens (1609)

In 1609 Galileo Galilei (Italy, 1564–1642) built a magnifying lens to observe the sky. Although Galileo is often credited with being the inventor of the telescope, his lens was in fact only an improved version of an existing lens invented in the Netherlands in the late 16th century. Galileo's instrument used a concave lens, and with it he made an extraordinary number of discoveries: the sunspots marking the sun's surface; the four large moons of the planet Jupiter—Io, Europa, Ganymede and Callisto; the phases of the planet Venus, which gave substantial support to the theory that the earth revolved around the sun; the rings of Saturn; the myriad of stars that make up the Milky Way; and the contours of the moon. From his observations, Galileo produced his theory of elliptical planetary rotation, which was condemned by the Pope. In 1633 Galileo was forced to renounce his theory by the Roman Catholic Church and was placed under permanent house arrest at his home in Florence, where he spent the last nine years of his life.

Telescope (1672)

The first telescope was built in 1672 by Sir Isaac Newton, the famous physicist, mathematician and astronomer (Great Britain, 1642–1727), who set out in the *Principia* in 1687 the laws of universal gravitation. The instrument was perfected in the 17th and 18th centuries, in particular by astronomers William Herschel (Great Britain) and Johannes Hevelius (Germany). In 1842 William Parsons (Great Britain) built the first giant telescopes in the garden of his house.

Giant Telescopes

Mount Palomar (1948)

The huge telescope on Mount Palomar in California is equipped with a lens that has a 16 ft 5 in. aperture. It was brought into service on June 3, 1948.

The telescope was initiated by George Ellery Hale, an astronomer and inventor of the spectroheliograph, and built with the aid of a $6 million donation from the Rockefeller Foundation. Hale's giant telescope has become difficult to use because of the increasing level of pollution coming from the neighboring city of Los Angeles.

Galileo's development of the lens led him to a number of discoveries from which he derived his theory that the earth revolved around the sun. (Palais de la Découverte)

Previous page: The view from an orbiting space shuttle. (Le Livre Mondial des Inventions)

Zelentchouk (1974)

The Zelentchouk observatory telescope, located at an altitude of 6,728 ft in the Caucasus Mountains, Russia, was the largest in the world up to 1992. The telescope, with its 19 ft 8 in. aperture, was designed by Dr. Icannissiani. It went into operation in 1974 after extreme difficulties in manufacturing its enormous 42-metric-ton lens. This was made by the Lomo center in Leningrad and is 1½ million times more powerful than the human eye.

Infrared telescope (1977)

The largest infrared telescope in the world, equipped with a lens with a 12 ft 6 in. aperture, was installed in 1977 by British scientists at an altitude of 13,780 ft on the top of Mount Mauna Kea, an extinct volcano on the island of Hawaii.

Multiple-lens telescope

The world's first multiple-lens telescope was installed at the Mount Hopkins Observatory, Arizona by the Smithsonian Astrophysical Observatory (SAO) and the University of Arizona. It comprised six lenses with a 6 ft 1 in. aperture and is the equivalent of a single-lens telescope with a 14 ft 9 in. aperture. This new kind of optical telescope was devised by astronomers in order to reduce the size as well as the cost of the instruments without sacrificing performance.

Keck Observatory (1990)

A sum of $70 million was offered by the Keck Foundation at the California Institute of Technology for the construction of the largest optical telescope in the world. Work began on September 12, 1985 on the summit of Mauna Kea, an extinct volcano on Hawaii.

The mirror of this enormous telescope, which allows astronomers to observe objects of magnitude 26—in other words, 200 million times smaller than objects discernible by the naked eye—was built using 36 identical hexagonal parts, juxtaposed in order to form a single mirror measuring 32 ft 10 in. in diameter.

In December 1990 it took its first photograph of the galaxy NGC 1232, some 65 million light-years away, to test the parts of the telescope that were already in operation. The final element of the Keck-1 mirror was installed on April 2, 1992. An identical second telescope, the Keck-2, is scheduled for completion in 1996. Linked electronically, the telescopes should allow objects 13–14 billion light-years away to be observed.

Radio Astronomy

Radio telescope (1932)

Radio astronomy involves the study of radio waves, whose wavelengths range from a few millimeters to several meters, using special instruments called radio telescopes. The first radio telescope was developed in 1932 by Karl Jansky (U.S., b. Czechoslovakia).

Employed by Bell Laboratories to trace the origin of parasitic signals causing obstructions to radiotelephonic traffic over the North Atlantic, Jansky built a receiver that he had invented himself in Holmdel, N.J. With this apparatus he captured the first unfamiliar noises coming from outer space: "a continuous whistle" coming from the constellation of Sagittarius, at the center of our galaxy 155,350,000 billion miles away.

This discovery received enormous publicity; however, Jansky abandoned radio astronomy in 1938 because of the indifference with which the scientific community greeted his discovery. However, his name is remembered in the unit of measurement of the radioelectric flux of the stars.

Reber radio telescope (1937)

The first true radio telescope was built in 1937 by the engineer Grote Reber (U.S., b. Netherlands). An avid radio buff, he used his savings to build an instrument in his garden in Wheaton near Chicago. It comprised a parabolic antenna with a diameter of about 9 ft 10 in., and was azimuthal, like all modern radio telescopes. After two years of patience and unsuccessful experimentation, Reber finally received a signal with a wavelength of 6 ft 2 in.

With this success behind him, Reber tried in 1941 to draw the radioelectric map of our galaxy. This document, published in 1944, marked the beginnings of radio astronomy as a new scientific discipline, officially recognized by astronomers, who were eager to use it.

Radar astronomy (1946)

Radar astronomy is a particular technique in which radio telescopes are no longer used simply as passive receivers but like radar—that is, in an active manner, first as transmitters, then as receivers.

Since 1946, radar echoes with rather weak transmission power have been obtained from the moon, as well as from other bodies, in order to measure their distance and their movements. This same technique was recently used with the Arecibo radio telescope to establish the first topographical map of the surface of the planet Venus.

Radio-astronomic observatories (c. 1950)

The first radio-astronomic observatories were created in Cambridge, England and in Sydney, Australia after World War II, thanks to the progress made in the areas of radar and electronics during that conflict.

The International Union of Telecommunications (IUT) contributed valuable aid to radio astronomers by deciding, in 1959, to reserve a frequency band of approximately 1420 MHz exclusively for the study of signals emitted by cosmic hydrogen over 8.3 in. in wavelength.

One such transmission, which had been announced by the young astronomer H.C. van de Hulst (Netherlands) in 1944, was indeed detected in 1951 by physicists H.I. Ewen and E.M. Purcell (both U.S.), with the help of a spectroscope.

Synthesized aperture interferometer (1960)

The synthesized aperture interferometer was developed in 1960 by radio astronomer Sir Martin Ryle (Great Britain), who in 1974 received the Nobel Prize for Physics with his colleague Antony Hewish. Synthesized aperture interferometry is a method which, using two or more antennae, allows one to gather simultaneously with a single receiver several signals from the same source and to make a true chart of the area observed with a resolution similar to that which would have been obtained by using a very large instrument.

The first large radio interferometer was developed by Sir Martin Ryle in 1964 at Cambridge, England, by using three telescopes 1 mile apart.

VLA (1977)

The largest radio interferometer is the Very Large Array (VLA), built near Socorro in the New Mexican desert.

The VLA comprises 27 metal parabolas measuring 82 ft in diameter, distributed along three bases 15½ miles long arranged in a Y shape. The whole unit forms the equivalent of a giant dome measuring 16¾ miles in diameter.

Giant Radio Telescopes

Jodrell Bank (1957)

The first giant radio telescope was built in Jodrell Bank, near Manchester, England. Designed by Sir Bernard Lovell (Great Britain), it began operation in 1957. Equipped with a mobile antenna 76 meters in diameter, it was capable of detecting radio waves having lengths in excess of 50 meters.

Eifelsberg (1962)

The world's largest radio telescope with a mobile antenna was built in Eifelsberg, Germany in 1962. This instrument is equipped with a parabolic antenna measuring 328 feet in diameter.

Ratan 600 (1974)

The Ratan 600 is a radio telescope with a diameter of 600 meters, made of approximately 900 rotatable reflectors arranged in rings. The largest radio telescope ever built by the former Soviet Union, it went into operation in July 1974.

Arecibo (1974)

The Arecibo radio telescope was installed in Puerto Rico in 1963 and put into service in 1974. A fixed-antenna apparatus, Arecibo's reflector comprises 38,778 aluminum panels. On November 16, 1974, within the framework of the SETI (Search for Extraterrestrial Intelligence) program, a 169-second message was sent at a frequency of 2,380 MHz toward the M13 global star cluster in the Hercules constellation. The message has to travel a distance of 25,000 light-years, and astronomers are not expecting a response until the year 51974, 500 centuries from the date the signal was transmitted.

Satellite—earth station telescope (1986)

In July and August 1986 astronomers from NASA's Jet Propulsion Laboratory created the largest radio telescope ever built, by electronically linking aerials on earth with those aboard an orbiting satellite. The parabolic aerials, measuring 230 feet in diameter, located in Japan and Australia, were in contact with one measuring 16 ft 5 in. belonging to the TDRS communication satellite in a geostationary orbit 22,300 miles above the earth. The telescope thus created measured 11,185 miles in radius. It has made it possible to observe three quasars that astronomers believe to be between 15 and 20 billion years old.

Airborne telescopes

First observations (1927)

The first astronomical observations carried out by airplane date back to June 29, 1927, when a twin-engine British Imperial Airways plane was used to photogrpah a total eclipse of the sun from above the London fog. This observation technique has since been used successfully with the Concorde.

Kuiper Observatory (1975)

Since 1965, NASA has been equipped with observatory jet aircraft, the Learjet and the Convair 990, which have enabled scientists to discover, most notably, the infrared emission from the center of our galaxy. Since 1975 NASA has also used a giant four-engined C 141 Starlifter, specially equipped for astronomy and for research into the infrared radiation. This plane, named the Kuiper Observatory after the famous astrophysicist Gerard P. Kuiper (U.S., b. Netherlands; 1905–73), may be used on more than 200 nights a year. It is capable of flying for three hours with nine metric tons of observation equipment, at an altitude of more than 46,000 ft. The Kuiper Observatory, equipped with a telescope with a 35.8 in. aperture, has already made several important discoveries—such as, for example, the rings of Uranus, in 1977.

Space Astronomy

Astronomic satellites (1946)

The first observations by means of astronomic satellite were carried out in 1946 by Americans who used V-2 rockets salvaged in Germany. However, this technique did not allow for long observations. The first astronomic satellites were launched by the United States (notably *Explorer 1* in 1958, under the direction of Joseph Van Allen, enabling the radiation rings circling the earth to be discovered—the Van Allen rings) and by the USSR (the Cosmos satellites, beginning in 1962, which are not exclusively for the purposes of astronomy).

Space radio astronomy (1968)

The first radio astronomy satellites were those of the Radio Astronomy Explorer (RAE 1 and 2) from NASA, launched in July 1968 and June 1973 respectively.

The first radio telescope in space was put into orbit by the USSR in July 1979 on the orbital station of *Salyut 6*. This radio telescope, KRT 10, weighing 441 lb, had an antenna with a diameter of 33 ft, carried by a cargo vessel called *Progress*, and sent into orbit for the purpose of observing centimeter and decimeter waves. The Soviets carried out their interferometry observations of various radio sources in this way in conjunction with an observation station in the Crimea.

Uhuru (1970)

Launched from Kenya on December 12, 1970, *Uhuru* was the first satellite to be dedicated to X-ray astronomy.

After *Uhuru*, other X-ray satellites were launched. In 1978 the *Einstein* satellite was launched in commemoration of the centennial of the birth of the great physicist in 1979. The European satellite *Exosat*, launched in 1983 by an American Delta rocket, completed its mission in 1986.

The next X-ray mission, that of NASA's AXAF satellite (Advanced X-Ray Astrophysics Facility), is planned for the 1990s and is expected to last 10 years.

COS-B (1975)

Launched in August 1975, the COS-B satellite, developed by the European Space Agency (ESA), was wholly dedicated to gamma astronomy or high-energy astronomy. The mission finished at the end of April 1982.

The COS-B's mission will be continued during the 1990s by NASA's GRO satellite (Gamma Ray Observatory).

IUE (1978)

The IUE (International Ultraviolet Explorer) was launched on January 26, 1978 as a joint venture between NASA, the European Space Agency and the Engineering Research Council.

Its mission was to observe the stars and the sun within the wavelengths of the ultraviolet spectrum. Among the data received by this satellite are some of prime importance with relation to the origin of life on earth.

It was the only ultraviolet explorer in operation and remained so until work was completed on the Hubble Space Telescope.

IRAS (1983)

Launched on January 26, 1983 by a Thor-Delta rocket, the IRAS (Infra-Red Astronomy Satellite) stopped functioning on November 22 of the same year. Built through the cooperation of the United States (NASA), Great Britain and the Netherlands, its purpose was to transmit data on bodies in the universe too cold to emit light visible to the human eye.

In the 10 months it was in operation, IRAS drew up a cartographical map of the whole sky and found some 200,000 sources of infrared rays.

The continuation of its mission will be guaranteed from 1992 on by the European Space Agency's (ESA's) satellite observatory.

Astro-C (1987)

On February 5, 1987 the Japanese Institute of Space and Astronomy Sciences (ISAS) launched the Astro-C satellite, the purpose of which was to observe neutron stars and perhaps black holes. The satellite, equipped with X-ray and gamma equipment, is presently in orbit at an altitude of about 330 miles.

Hipparcos (1989)

The European Space Agency's scientific satellite, *Hipparcos*, called the "surveyor of the stars" by astronomers, was launched by the European rocket *Ariane 4* on the night of August 8–9, 1989.

When it was unable to fire its apogee motor, which should have sent it into geostationary orbit at an altitude of 22,370 miles, its mission was revised, and since then *Hipparcos* has worked on a modified orbit. This satellite is due to measure the positions of more than 100,000 stars and to draw up a map of the sky with a precision never seen before.

Hubble space telescope (1990)

Planned for several years, the Hubble Space Telescope (NASA's space telescope in collaboration with the ESA) was put into orbit 318 miles above the earth on April 25, 1990 by the space shuttle *Discovery*. Its mission was to transmit to earth pictures free from atmospheric impurities, that is to say, exceedingly clear images. Two cameras, two spectrometers and a photometer allowed the telescope to function within the visible, infrared and ultraviolet spectrums. Hundreds of experiments were planned for the 15 years it was expected to be in operation.

Its effectiveness has been temporarily reduced, however, as one of the mirrors is defective and produces blurred images. Thanks to computerized corrections, this flaw—which should be repaired during a space mission scheduled for 1993 or 1994—has not prevented the Hubble from transmitting excellent photos of Pluto and Saturn.

ASTROPHYSICS

White dwarfs (1779)

Some stars, whose mass does not exceed that of the sun by more than one and a half times, cave in at the end of their lives, giving rise to celestial bodies called white dwarfs.

It is not possible to give a date on which a white dwarf was first discovered, but that of the planetary nebula, the Lyre, was sighted by Antoine Dargulier in 1779. The existence of

Sirius's companion, Sirius B, was calculated in 1834 by Friedrich Bessel (Germany) and observed in 1862 by Alvan Graham Clark (U.S.). Neither of these men understood the exact nature of the subject of their observations.

Cepheid stars (1784)

The cepheid stars take their name from the first among them: Delta Cephei, discovered in 1784 by John Goodricke (Great Britain). These relatively rare stars (today only 700 of them are known) have a variable luminosity or magnitude.

They are of great importance since they enable scientists to calculate distances within the universe. In fact, there is a linear relationship between the rhythm of the variation of their brightness and their average luminosity. This relationship was proven by Henrietta Leavitt (U.S.) in 1912.

The Pole Star is a cepheid star whose period of variation is approximately four days.

Eridani B (1910)

It was in 1910, with the discovery of Eridani B, that scientists became curious about this object with its peculiar temperature and density.

In 1917 it was established that Sirius B and the Van Maanen star had the same characteristics as Eridani B.

A short time afterward, the quantum theory was to provide answers to questions posed by astronomers: it is a quantum principle called the Pauli principle that enables the white dwarf stars to be stabilized.

Hidden mass in the universe (1913)

Since the time of the pioneering work by Fritz Zwicky (U.S.) in 1913, it has been very widely believed that 90 percent of the total matter in the universe is invisible. In fact, all the indications would lead one to believe that, surrounding the galaxies, and in particular our galaxy, there is a giant spherical halo composed of invisible matter. What is the composition of this matter? Black holes? Neutrinos? Numerous theories have been put forward over the last few years, none of which is entirely satisfactory.

Big Bang theory (1930)

Big Bang theory explains the formation of the universe from the explosion of an original atom, about 15 billion years ago. The hypothesis was formulated in 1930 by astrophysicist George Gamow (U.S., b. Russia; 1904–68) and physicist Georges Lemaître (Belgium, 1894–1966). In 1949, Gamow predicted that this explosion would have left a residue in the form of a regular, omnipresent background noise in all directions of the universe. In 1965 the discoveries of Arno A. Penzias and Robert Wilson (both U.S.) (see Cosmic background radiation, p. 86), seemed to support Gamow's theory.

The enigma of solar neutrinos (1938)

Since the work of Hans Bethe (U.S., b. Germany) in 1938, it is believed that the nuclear reactions occurring inside the sun, which also serve to supply the latter with light and energy, are well understood.

All the calculations demonstrate that the sun must emit, because of its nuclear reactions, a certain quantity of very light particles that are called neutrinos. The detection of neutrinos coming from the sun has been undertaken by several laboratories throughout the world, in particular the Davies Laboratory in the United States.

All the experiments show that the sun, mysteriously, emits only a third of the calculated number of neutrinos. Could this be because neutrinos exist in three different forms and that not all these forms are recognized? Astrophysicists are puzzled, and some of them have their doubts as to our understanding of the inside of the sun.

Solar wind (1951)

The solar wind was discovered by Biermann in 1951. He noticed that part of the tail of comets was pushed by a wind of particles (electrons and protons) coming from the sun and moving at speeds of some hundreds of kilometers per second. The presence of this solar wind was explained as follows: the attraction of the sun is too weak to retain completely the outer region of the sun known as the solar corona, which therefore tends to escape naturally into space and to inundate the solar system with particles.

In the future, the solar wind could be used to drive space vessels equipped with enormous solar sails, in the same way that a normal wind drives sailboats.

Van Allen belt (1958)

A remarkable region of the magnetosphere is the Van Allen radiation belt, discovered by Dr. James Van Allen (U.S.) at the very beginning of the space age, in 1958. This region is situated at an altitude of some 9,300–12,400 miles and is the center of oscillatory movements of high-energy electrons and protons trapped in the magnetic field. The existence of the Van Allen belt may be a fascinating phenomenon, but the radiation can also damage the electronic equipment of satellites and endanger the health of humans in space.

Quasars (1961)

During the 1950s and 1960s radio astronomers drew up a chart of celestial radio sources. At Cambridge University a catalog of them, entitled 3C, was drawn up; it is considered to be the most important on the subject. By observing, in 1961, one of the radio objects discovered by Cambridge, the astronomer Matthews managed to locate it very precisely. Using a telescope, he discovered a star that was shown to be rather special. In 1963 Hazard, Mackey and Shimming made a second similar discovery. After examination of the results of the objects observed, which were named quasars (quasistellar radio sources) in reference to their stellar form, they were identified as being very remote and very bright galaxies.

Quasars have extremely high luminosity and so can be seen at great distances, despite their relatively small size. Their luminosity can exceed that of the sun by many billions of times. More than 20 years after their discovery, it is not known which source of energy feeds the quasars to make them so bright and so active.

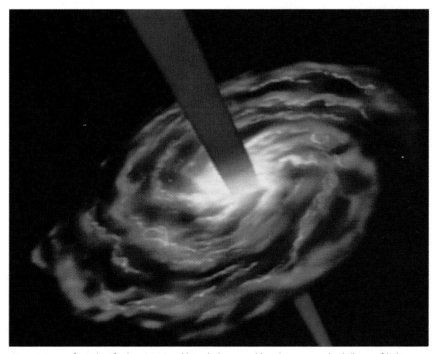

Quasars were first identified in 1961. Although these starlike objects may be billions of light-years from earth, their luminosity, several billion times that of the sun, allows them to be observed from earth. (ESA)

At present about 3,000 quasars have been recognized and recorded by astronomers, one of which, discovered in 1987 by Stephen Warren, is the most distant object ever observed.

The distance separating us from the quasars is such that it cannot be measured either in light-years or in parsecs (1 pc = 3.26 light-years), because there is no point of reference on which to base a measurement. To express their remoteness astronomers use the quantity of red in the light we receive from them. However, estimates are in terms of billions of light-years.

Cosmic background radiation (1965)

In 1965 physicists Arno A. Penzias and Robert Wilson (both U.S.) discovered the existence of cosmic background radiation, an ocean of identical invisible microwave radiation permeating all of space. This discovery supported Gamow's theory of omnipresent background noise created by the Big Bang.

Black holes (1967)

The existence of black holes comes within Einstein's theory of general relativity, but was predicted by astronomer and mathematician Pierre de Laplace (France) in 1796.

Black holes are the collapsed remains of giant stars the extreme gravity of which would prevent even electromagnetic waves from escaping, including light waves. Their mass would bore a hole in space from which nothing could escape. Such objects could only be detected by the effect produced on objects in the area surrounding them.

Astrophysicists are therefore carrying out research on systems where stars seem to orbit around invisible bodies the mass of which must be greater than that of a neutron star. At present there are three systems that could be considered serious candidates: Cygnus X-1, LMC X-1 and LMC X-3. However, they all lend themselves to different interpretations and cannot at present be considered undeniable proof of the existence of black holes.

The name "black hole" was first coined by Prof. John Wheeler at a meeting in New York City on December 29, 1967.

Gravitational mirages (1979)

One day in 1979 the astronomers Carswell, Walsh and Weymann (Great Britain) were extremely surprised to find that two quasars close to each other in the sky were each emitting an absolutely identical light.

It was not long before this phenomenon was explained. It is known that light is not generally propagated in a straight line but is sent off course by the field of gravitation of heavy bodies. The astronomers were seeing two images of one and the same quasar, the light of which had reached earth following two different trajectories passing on either side of an enormous galaxy situated between the quasar and us, and acting as a light deflector.

This quasar is now called the double quasar and the phenomenon of the multiplication of images is called gravitational mirage. Many other examples have been discovered since 1979.

Pulsars (1967): Jocelyn Bell

From hall closets to intergalactic astrophysics, some of the best discoveries are made while you're looking for something else. This was the case with Jocelyn Bell, a 19-year-old graduate student who made one of the most important astronomical discoveries of the century.

Bell was an assistant to Antony Hewish, an astronomer at Cambridge University in England. Hewish constructed a radio telescope, an intricate structure of aerials that was designed to study the twinkling of stars, called scintillation. Radio telescopes, like radio receivers, pick up static—rapid variations in the strength of a signal. Most radio astronomers adjusted their telescopes so that they would not record any signal variation shorter than about a second. The only fast variations they expected were from the twinkling of stars. Since Hewish wanted to study this twinkling, he tuned his telescope to pick up the rapidly varying star signals.

In the middle of the night, scintillation is usually weak. But Jocelyn Bell noticed that this was exactly when a particularly strong set of signals appeared. She quietly observed the signals for a month. She determined that each signal was actually a set of quick pulses, very regularly spaced, occurring every 1.3373011 seconds. Even more unusual, the signals remained constant with respect to the stars, rather than with respect to time. The radio telescope received them only when the portion of the sky from which the signals originated passed over.

Bell's discoveries made Hewish nervous. The pulses came much as the beam of a lighthouse strikes a ship at sea: arriving suddenly and briefly and then disappearing for a definite period of time before arriving again. Could the pulses be a signal from a planet in a far galaxy?

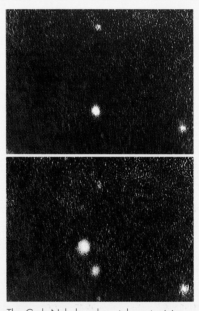

The Crab Nebula pulsar, taken at minimum and at maximum light. (Lick Observatory)

This possibility led Hewish and Bell to dub the signal, and the three more that Bell soon located, LGM 1, LGM 2, LGM 3 and LGM 4. LGM stood for "little green men." The discoveries were kept quiet at first, because the astronomers were reluctant to release news that seemed to suggest the existence of extraterrestrial life. A frustrated Bell said later, "I went home very cross. Here I was trying to get a Ph.D. out of a new technique, and some silly lot of little green men had to choose my aerial and my frequency to communicate with us."

But the little green men were soon discounted. Any planet must revolve around a sun, and signals coming from it would be affected by its orbit. No such changes were found in the signals, so another source was suggested: neutron stars, at the core of supernova stars. Neutron stars, the result of the collapse of the inner core of a supernova, are said to be incredibly dense. Up to this point neutron stars existed only in theory. Now astronomers claimed that rotating neutron stars exuded the regular "lighthouse" signal. Only they could have the huge power required for such a strong signal. As such, pulsars proved the existence of neutron stars.

Einstein's rings (1987)

A different type of gravitational mirage was discovered in 1987 by an observation team in Toulouse, France. This team made the observation that the arc of light in the cluster of galaxies Abell 370 comes from further afield than does the star cluster itself. It is very likely, therefore, that this is what is called an Einstein ring, that is to say, a deformed image that looks like the ring of a distant quasar as a result of a gravitational mirage due to Abell 370. An image such as this, in the shape of a ring, very occasionally appears in cases where the quasar, the star cluster and earth are perfectly aligned along the same line of sight.

Cosmic ripples (1992)

On April 23, 1992, astrophysicist George F. Smoot (U.S.) announced that his team had discovered "tiny ripples in the fabric of space-time put there by the primeval explosion process." Dubbed cosmic ripples, their discovery was based on data supplied by the COBE satellite (see also Space Probes, "COBE" p. 92). In order to map the microwave sky, special instruments

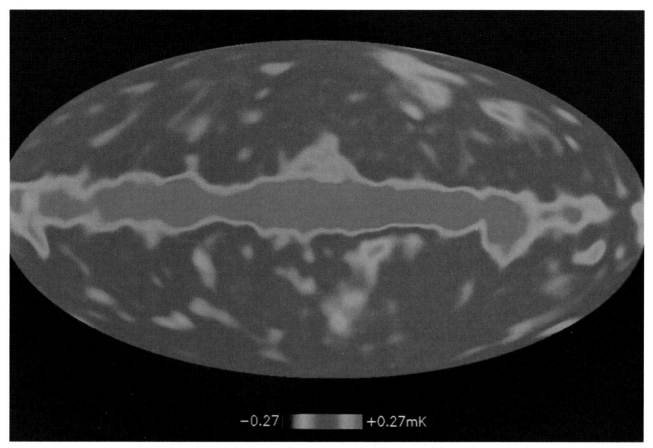

This 360-degree map of the whole sky shows minute variations in the cosmic microwave background, believed to be relic radiation from the Big Bang. The discovery of these "cosmic ripples" was reported in April 1992. (Lawrence Berkeley Laboratory)

called Differential Microwave Radiometers (DMR) were installed on COBE. Smoot and his team of researchers at the Lawrence Berkeley Laboratory, Calif., analyzed millions of precision measurements provided by the DMRs and created maps of the microwave sky showing vast areas of space with minuscule temperature variations. These variations had been predicted by Big Bang theorists, and it is claimed that this discovery offers evidence to support that theory of the origin of the universe.

ROCKETS

Origins (13th century)

According to Chinese legend, a mandarin once attempted to fly hanging from two paper kites driven by a large number of rockets. The earliest known accepted use of rockets is the 13th century, when Tartars used them in 1241 at the Battle of Legnica.

Liquid-fueled rocket (1926)

The exact date of the launch of the first liquid-fueled rocket is widely debated. The earliest claim dates to 1895, when Pedro P. Poulet (Peru) built and patented an engine with a 4-in. diameter into which was injected a mixture of nitrogen peroxide and petroleum, lit by a candle. The most widely accepted claim as to the first liquid-fueled rocket is that of Robert H. Goddard (U.S., 1882–1945). On March 16, 1926, he launched a small rocket a distance of 12.5 meters. The flight lasted 2.5 seconds, but Goddard did not publish details of the launch until 10 years later. As early as 1919 Goddard had published a work describing "a method for reaching extreme altitudes," and during his career he applied for more than 200 patents for liquid-propelled rockets. However, he rarely published details of his work, and did not gain the respect of his peers until much later in his career.

The first European to launch a liquid-fueled rocket was Johannes Winkler (Germany), whose small rocket HW I (fueled by liquid oxygen and methane) was launched on February 21, 1931 in Breslau, Germany (present-day Wroclaw, Poland).

V-2 (1942)

The most powerful of the rockets used during World War II was the German A-4, alias V-2, which inspired all postwar rocket builders. The V-2 was developed under the direction of Gen. Walter Dornberger, assisted by Wernher von Braun and Thiel. The first test launching took place on October 3, 1942. Over 4,000 V-2s were directed at London during the period 1944–45.

Korolev rocket (1957)

The first rocket that escaped from the earth's gravitational pull was a Korolev rocket launched on October 4, 1957, which sent *Sputnik I* into orbit. The Korolev rocket was designed by Sergei Korolev (USSR, 1906–66), and details of its construction were not revealed until 1967. The rocket's revolutionary design consisted of a series of stages comprising numerous engines, each having a weak unit of thrust. The Korolev measured 30 meters in length, weighed 300 tons and developed a thrust of 514 tons at liftoff.

Atlas rocket (1957)

Shocked by the launch of *Sputnik I*, the United States rapidly deployed its resources to join the space race. The Atlas rocket, produced by General Dynamics, was first launched on December 17, 1957. The Atlas was the most widely used rocket in the United States space program.

The Atlas is derived from the long-range MX774 missile designed by Karel Bossart (Belgium) at the Jet Propulsion Laboratory at Caltech, in Pasadena, Calif. The rocket weighed 147 tons and was propelled by a kerosene and liquid-oxygen fuel mixture. For its upper stage it used the Agena rocket built by Lockheed. This was the first rocket stage that was able to be reignited in flight. On February 20, 1962 John Glenn's first orbital flight was powered by an Atlas rocket.

Titan rocket (1959)

The Titan rocket was developed by the Martin Marietta Corp., and is one of the most powerful rockets in the United States arsenal. The first version, *Titan 1*, first flew in February 1959. It was equipped with two kerosene and liquid-oxygen engines, with a thrust of 136 tons at liftoff.

Titan technology spawned the first intercontinental missile, the *Titan 2*. Numerous upgrades have been designed for both military and scientific purposes.

Delta rocket (1960)

The McDonnell Douglas Delta rocket, which flew for the first time on May 13, 1960, has been used extensively by NASA in placing geostationary satellites into orbit. The Delta rocket was propelled by Rocketdyne kerosene and liquid-oxygen engines with a thrust of 90 tons, backed up by nine Thiokol powder-propulsive engines with a unit thrust of 23 tons.

Yanguel rocket (1962)

The Yanguel rocket has been used to launch many of the Cosmos satellites sent up by the former USSR. The rocket is 20 meters in length and was derived from the Soviet ballistic missile Sandal. The rocket was designed by Mikhail Yanguel, and first launched in 1962.

Chelomei rocket (1965)

The most powerful Soviet-built rocket is the Chelomei, a 1,000-ton machine. It has been used since 1965 to place large scientific and geostationary satellites into orbit. The rocket was built by Vladimir Chelomei, and is also known under the name of "Proton-launch" after the large scientific satellites that it put into orbit when it was first created.

Saturn 5 rocket (1967)

The largest American built rocket is the gigantic *Saturn 5*, developed by NASA and built under the direction of Wernher von Braun. This rocket weighs 2,900 tons and develops 3,400 tons at liftoff. The rocket's first trial was carried out in November 1967 at Cape Canaveral, Fla. *Saturn 5* was subsequently used for all the moon flights between 1969 and 1972, and in 1973 launched the first American space station.

Ariane (1979)

Launched for the first time in December 1979, the Ariane rocket was invented and perfected for a very precise task: to place satellites in geostationary orbit. For this task, which requires a satellite to be positioned at an altitude of 22,370 miles above the equator, the rocket is assisted by the location of its launching site, Kourou in French Guiana, which is only five degrees from the equator.

Although it has a launching capacity of 3,860 lb for the geostationary orbit (GTO), *Ariane 1* was abandoned in February 1986, at the time that Spot was launched, in favor of models 2 and 3, which were capable of launching 5,733 lb GTO.

It is worth noting that Ariane is the European space rocket, built with the participation of 10 western European countries: Belgium, Denmark, France, Germany, Great Britain, Italy, Netherlands, Spain, Sweden and Switzerland. Members of the European Space Agency (ESA) decided in 1973 to build Ariane, and construction was carried out by about 60 companies from the 10 participating countries.

Ariane 4 (1988)

Ariane 4 came into operation in 1988, the first launcher in the world to provide different options. According to the wishes of the customer

The Saturn 5 rocket was used to launch all Apollo missions that went to the moon between 1969 and 1972. (NASA)

A "star's-eye" view of Italy as seen by the satellite Landsat. (ESA)

and the mass and form of the satellites to be launched, there could in theory be about 40 different versions of the rocket. In practical terms, however, Arianespace will market six different versions; the differences between them will be based on the form and volume of the cap containing the satellites, and on the extra engines that will run on either solid or liquid fuel. Depending on the version, the rocket has a capacity of between 4,190 lb and 9,260 lb GTO.

Pegasus (1990)

On April 5, 1990 NASA launched a commercial rocket, *Pegasus*, to send two small satellites into orbit (one experimental satellite for the U.S. Navy and PEGSAT), from a specially converted B-52 bomber. *Pegasus* is the fruit of the efforts of an American company formed jointly by the Orbital Science Corporation and Hercules Aerospace. It is innovative in that it is the first launcher rocket to use an airplane for the liftoff phase (hence saving fuel), and also because it is the only machine currently performing as a light launcher, as opposed to the very powerful launchers, which are costly for small loads.

SATELLITES

(See also Communications, p. 204)

Sputnik I (1957)

The first artificial earth satellite, *Sputnik I* (*companion* in Russian), was launched on October 4, 1957 by a Korolev rocket. This simple sphere, made of polished steel, had a diameter of 58 cm and weighed 84.5 kg. *Sputnik* was designed under the aegis of the USSR Academy of Sciences, directed by Mistslav Keldych.

Explorer I (1958)

The *Explorer I* was launched on January 1, 1958 by a Jupiter C rocket built by the U.S. Army. This small satellite (14 kg) was built under the direction of James Van Allen of the Jet Propulsion Laboratory at Caltech. It was this mission that led to the discovery of the radiation belt that surrounds the earth, known as the Van Allen belt.

Transit 1 (1960)

This satellite, launched by the United States in 1960, was the first to provide navigation aid to vehicles on earth. Using special equipment, a vehicle on earth can ascertain its position through triangulation.

Cosmos satellites (1962)

On March 16, 1962, the USSR launched the first in an extensive series of satellites under the name Cosmos. The Cosmos program was used to launch satellites for a variety of tasks, among them military space missions, reconnaissance, electronic spying and navigation.

Landsat (1972)

In 1972 NASA launched *Landsat 1* under the name of ERTS-1 (Earth Resource Technology Satellite). Observation satellites like *Landsat 1* are used for a variety of purposes, such as cartography, the search for minerals and water, and even to follow the movements of swarms of locusts.

Mission "Planet Earth" (1991)

This is a vast satellite observation program to study the earth's environment. A series of satellite launches is planned, extending to the year

2020. The first, *UARS* (Upper Atmosphere Research Satellite), was launched on September 12, 1991, to study the upper atmosphere. Under this Mission Planet Earth program, NASA announced its EOS project at the end of 1991. This also consists of a series of average-sized satellites each carrying four to six instruments, the first to be launched in June 1998.

MANNED SPACECRAFT

Vostok (1961)

The first manned spacecraft, *Vostok 1*, was also the first artificial satellite with a human on board. On April 12, 1961 Yuri A. Gagarin (USSR, 1934–68) circumnavigated the earth at an altitude of 203 miles in 108 minutes. The Vostok series were 4.7-ton vessels, and the inhabitable cabin was a simple sphere measuring 2.3 meters in diameter. The cosmonaut was installed in the cabin, in an ejectable seat.

Mercury (1961)

The first American manned spacecraft, *Mercury*, was built by McDonnell Douglas for NASA. These were small, simple capsules (1.2 tons, 2.9 meters in length) and they could carry one suited astronaut for a short-duration flight. The capsules were launched by Atlas rockets.

On May 5, 1961 the first American astronaut, Alan B. Shepard, was launched into space for a suborbital flight lasting 15 minutes. On February 20, 1962 John Glenn became the first American to circle the earth, during his 4-hour-55-minute flight aboard another Mercury vessel, *Friendship 7*.

Voskhod (1963)

Voskhod was the successor to the Vostok program. A 5.7 ton vessel, *Voskhod* was capable of carrying two cosmonauts, as a result of a rearrangement of the cabin interior. On March 18, 1965, during the second and last *Voskhod* mission, Alexei Leonov (USSR) performed the first space walk. It lasted 20 minutes, during which time Leonov's spacesuit expanded, making it difficult for him to reenter the vessel.

Gemini (1965)

The Gemini cabins were also constructed by McDonnell Douglas. Like *Voskhod*, Gemini increased the cabin capacity to two astronauts. The Gemini cabins also were designed with a propulsive compartment allowing rendezvous with an Agena rocket, previously sent into orbit.

Gemini cabins were launched with two Titan rockets. The first orbital flight of a Gemini cabin, *Gemini 3*, took place on March 23, 1965, with astronauts Virgil Grissom and John Young on board. Using these manned vessels the United States carried out the first orbit transfers (*Gemini 3* in March 1965) and the first space docking of two vessels placed in earth's orbit (*Gemini 6* with Agena in March 1966).

Apollo (1967)

The Apollo vessel, built by North American Rockwell, was a manned satellite with an entirely new concept, designed specifically for moon flights. The Apollo cabin linked up with the lunar module to form the "lunar train" launched by the giant *Saturn 5* rockets to the moon. The space cabin, conical in shape, was occupied by three astronauts and weighed no more than 5.7 tons on reentry into earth's atmosphere.

NASA launched 11 Apollo cabins, nine of which were for voyages to the moon. On July 29, 1969, during the *Apollo 11* mission, humans first landed on the moon. Neil Armstrong was the first human to walk on the moon, joined by Edwin "Buzz" Aldrin. Armstrong and Aldrin stayed on the moon for 21 hours 36 minutes.

Soyuz (1967)

The *Soyuz* ("union") was a 6.7 ton vessel designed for linkups with the *Salyut* orbital space station. *Soyuz* comprised three parts: a propulsion module for orbital maneuvers, a pressurized cabin for work in space, and a reentry module equally pressurized and used for crew reentry. The *Soyuz* was the most widely used manned spacecraft over a period of 15 years, 1967–81.

Orbital Stations

Salyut (1971)

The USSR was the first country to launch a manned orbital station. Since April 1971 the Soviets have put into orbit seven Salyut orbital stations. The last to date, *Salyut 7*, was launched on April 19, 1982. Its crew was made up of seven Soviet cosmonauts, one of whom was the second woman cosmonaut ever.

Although clearly smaller than the American orbital station *Skylab*, this station is capable of carrying a crew of four cosmonauts for one week. However, long flights lasting several months generally have a two-person crew.

Skylab (1973)

On May 14, 1973 the United States launched *Skylab*, the biggest orbital station ever built. Eleven days later, a team of three astronauts transported by an Apollo craft took up their positions aboard it. The 75-metric-ton *Skylab* was built by McDonnell Douglas and Martin Marietta with elements recovered from the Apollo program. Built into the S-IVB stage of a *Saturn 5* rocket, *Skylab* had a living space of 1,300 cu ft of unprecedented comfort for a spacecraft (kitchen, beds, shower, etc.). Sent into circular orbit around the earth at an altitude of about 310 miles, *Skylab* contained a vast amount of scientific equipment, including an astronomical observatory.

The station was occupied by three successive teams of three astronauts. *Skylab* made it possible to take more than 175,000 photos of the sun and more than 46,000 of the earth. *Skylab*'s mission was completed at the end of 1973. After

the station had been momentarily placed in a higher orbit by the last crew, it was not possible to bring it back to earth. During an attempt to do so in 1979, the orbital laboratory burst into flames as it reentered the atmosphere and crashed into a sparsely populated part of Australia.

Spacelab (1983)

Europe has also built a habitable orbital laboratory. *Spacelab*, built by the German firm ERNO and industrialists from 10 European countries (Belgium, Denmark, France, Germany, Great Britain, Italy, the Netherlands, Spain, Sweden and Switzerland), comprises a pressurized module where up to four astronauts can work, and pallets carrying instruments directly exposed to the space vacuum. The whole laboratory weighs a maximum of 11.3 metric tons, of which 5.5 to 9.1 metric tons constitutes scientific and technical instruments.

Spacelab's first flight was in November 1983. The shuttle *Columbia*, which launched the laboratory, had a crew of six men, including the first non-American astronaut, 42-year-old Urf Merbold (Germany), an expert in crystallography. The project cost $1 billion. *Spacelab* is now run by NASA.

Experimental space station (1984)

Christened *LDEF* (Long Duration Exposure Facility), this experimental space station was released in 1984. It was the size of a coach, weighing 12 metric tons and was to have been returned to earth 10 months later. However, it had to stay in space much longer because of delays that had built up in NASA's program. It was therefore recovered by the space shuttle *Columbia* on January 12, 1990 after spending more than five years in space, exposed to meteorites, cosmic rays and corrosion.

LDEF is the first satellite of its size to be brought back to earth without being burned by the dense layers of the atmosphere. The wealth of information gathered will have a direct impact on the choice of materials to be used for the construction of the station *Freedom*, which has to last for 30 years.

Mir orbital station (1986)

The *Mir* orbital station (*Mir* means peace in Russian) has been going around the earth at an altitude of between 186 and 249 miles since February 20, 1986. The station—which is locked alongside the astrophysical module *Kvant*—has many uses: first, to analyze changes undergone by the human body during a long period in a weightless state (reduction in muscles, weakening of bones, etc.), in order to prepare for long interplanetary trips such as the one to Mars in around 2020; second, to carry out observations of earth, as well as of the planets and stars that surround us; finally, to carry out experiments in an atmosphere that is weightless—the creation of alloys and new crystals, preparation of ultra-pure medicines, experiments on the growth of plants, and so on.

In order to enhance still further the performance of the orbital station, the Soviets sent up a second scientific module, *Kvant 2*, in 1989, while in June 1990 *Kristall* was launched to make semiconductors in a weightless environment.

Space Shuttles

Space shuttle (1981)

The NASA space shuttle is the first rocket in the history of astronautics that can be recovered and used again. It is a real aerospace vehicle that weighs more than 2,000 metric tons and lifts off like a rocket: vertically. The main part, the orbiter, is a kind of delta-winged aircraft that weighs 100 metric tons and is placed into orbit around the earth at low altitude (100 to 683 miles). The orbiter reenters the atmosphere as a glider, and lands on the runway horizontally, like a plane. The shuttle can carry a 39-metric-ton payload and a crew of between four and seven people, two of whom are the pilots.

Thanks to its jointed arm, the shuttle can place all sorts of satellites into orbit. This revolutionary rocket prefigures the spaceships of the future, which, like all other means of transport, will be reusable.

Initiated by President Richard Nixon in 1972, the shuttle (as well as its prototype *Enterprise*, which was used for test landings) was constructed principally by Rockwell International.

The first shuttle, *Columbia*, had its maiden flight on April 12, 1981, with John Young and Robert Crippen at the controls. *Columbia* lifted off from Cape Canaveral, Florida, and landed 54 hours later at Edwards Air Force Base in California.

The second shuttle, *Challenger*, had its first flight in April 1983 but was destroyed in a tragic accident on January 28, 1986. The third shuttle, *Discovery*, had its first flight in August 1984, and the fourth, *Atlantis*, in 1985. The fifth shuttle, *Endeavor*, built to replace *Challenger*, was launched on May 8, 1992.

Soviet shuttle (1988)

The Soviet space shuttle, *Bourane* or "snow storm," was first launched on November 15, 1988. Propelled by a giant rocket called Energia, *Bourane* (which weighs 105 metric tons at takeoff) lifted off unmanned, in automatic mode. Forty-seven minutes later, the shuttle was circling in orbit. After going twice around the earth at an altitude of 155 miles, *Bourane* switched on its retrorockets and returned to a runway 7½ miles from its launch site.

If the landing of the Soviet shuttle can be compared to that of its U.S. cousins *Discovery*, *Atlantis*, *Columbia* and *Endeavor* (all land without an engine, gliding down), the liftoff is very different. Unlike the U.S. shuttles, at the moment of liftoff *Bourane* is in a totally passive state: the four engines on the first stage of Energia (800 metric tons of thrust each) ignite at the same time as the rockets on the second stage (200 metric tons of thrust each). The first burn kerosene and oxygen, the second, liquid hydrogen and oxygen.

After 10 min 30 sec of propulsion *Bourane* separates from the rest of the rocket at an alti-

Pressurized suit (1934): Russell Colley

Wiley Post. (B.F. Goodrich)

Wiley Post was a flamboyant, high-flying aviator who traveled the world setting flight records and winning races. To Post, high altitude equaled high speed. Determined to win a race from London, England to Melbourne, Australia, Post set out to find a safe way to fly in the stratosphere, at an altitude of 47,000 feet.

Such a height was unheard-of. In order to survive his flight, Post needed to supply oxygen to his body at constant pressure. The race was slated for October 1934. Early that year, Post made a request of B.F. Goodrich in Los Angeles for a pressurized rubber suit.

The first suit was made of six yards of double-ply rubberized parachute cloth. Its total cost was about $75. The project engineer was William R. Hucks, assisted by John A. Diehl. Post took the suit to Wright Field, Ohio, to test it in a pressure chamber there. The suit sprang a leak and blew apart. Instead of traveling back to L.A., Post went to Goodrich's Akron plant, and enlisted the help of engineer Russell Colley.

In late July, the second suit was ready. Unfortunately, Post wasn't. During the wait, he had gained a few pounds. It was a hot, humid day, and Post became stuck inside his suit. Colley led the laughing Post to a refrigerated room, to no avail. The suit had to be cut off.

Suit number three was finished in August. Colley sewed it at home at night on his wife's sewing machine, which became a casualty of the process. Another casualty was Post's wallet. While waiting to try on the suit, he taught Colley's 11-year-old daughter to play craps—and wound up owing her $60,000.

They tested the suit at Wright Field that month, with success. It was made of two separate layers of fabric: an inner rubber bag contained oxygen under pressure, and an outer fabric shell controlled the inner bag's shape, to allow Post to move. (Post wore his long johns under the suit.) When Post took a trial flight into the stratosphere in his plane *Willie Mae*, suit number three became the first full-pressure suit to fly.

Post began making plans to fly to London for the start of the race, daydreaming about the $50,000 prize. Sadly, in September the *Winnie Mae* developed engine trouble, and Post had to drop out of the race. The following year he died in Alaska in the same plane crash that killed Will Rogers.

Before long, engineers developed pressurized cabins for airplanes. Pressurized suits were used by military pilots who flew at high altitudes. They became the basis for space suits, as well. In 1954 Goodrich began designing and building life-support suits that went into space with Alan Shepard and John Glenn.

tude of 68 miles. Finally, at 100 miles altitude, *Bourane*'s principal engine comes into action and propels the shuttle to its circular orbit, at an altitude of 155 miles, which it reaches 47 minutes after liftoff.

The *Bourane* program has experienced many technical setbacks. There have been no missions in recent years and the program is currently under review.

Space Vehicles

LEM lunar module (1968)

The Lunar Exploration Module (LEM), nicknamed "space spider" because of its shape, was developed by Grumman to enhance the safety of those phases that are without a doubt the most critical in space travel—landing and takeoff. This 15-metric-ton "space lift," built of aluminum and covered with gold leaf, allowed a crew of two astronauts to land on the moon within 12 minutes and to take off within seven. They could then rejoin the *Apollo* cabin, which was revolving around the moon at an altitude of about 62 miles, with the third astronaut on board.

The LEM performed without breaking down throughout all the Apollo flights. On April 11, 1970 it even saved the crew on the *Apollo 13* mission after the explosion in midflight of an oxygen tank in the cabin.

Lunakhod (1970)

The first mobile lunar robots, Lunakhods, were designed by Soviet engineers to carry out moon explorations. Two Lunakhods were used by the USSR. The first, carried by the *Luna 17* probe, explored the area of *Mare Imbrium*, from November 1970 to October 1971. The second, placed by the *Luna 21* probe in the Sea of Tranquility, operated between January and July 1973. The Lunakhod was equipped with numerous scientific instruments, which included a spectrometer, telescope and a panel of reflector-maser prisms permitting the distance between the earth and the moon to be measured precisely.

Lunar Rover (1971)

The first moon vehicle, the Lunar Rover, was manufactured by Boeing. It was used during the last three Apollo missions, 15, 16 and 17, in 1971–72. The vehicle measured 10 feet in length and 8 feet in width, but could be folded for transport in the lunar module. The four wheels were made of a fine supply-wire netting and each was activated by an electric engine placed in the hub and supplied by a 36-volt battery. The vehicle had a cruising range of 60 km and a maximum speed of 14 km/h. Driven like any ordinary automobile, the Lunar Rover was equipped with a color television camera, which transmitted images of the landscapes, and an antenna which allowed the crew to remain in constant contact with the earth.

Manned Maneuvering Unit (MMU) (1984)

In February 1984 a *Challenger* mission enabled the astronaut Bruce McCandless, aged 46, to use the MMU or Manned Maneuvering Unit for the first time. This $10 million project allows the astronaut complete independence. McCandless was away from the space shuttle for 90 minutes while the latter was more than 168 miles above Hawaii.

It was the first time that a human had "wandered" in space in this way without being tied to anything. The freedom it gave was extraordinary but it was not without its dangers. If there was a breakdown or defect in the equipment, the astronaut would have been completely on his own in space.

SPACE PROBES

Origins (1920s)

The idea of sending space probes to the planets goes back to the beginning of space exploration around 1920.

Hermann J. Oberth (Germany) described in two published works (appearing in 1923 and 1929) the broad principle of interplanetary space flight. During this time, Walter Hohmann (Germany) became the first person to calculate the conditions of such space flights (flight time, mass of propellants, etc.) as well as the best orbits for reaching the planets. Some of these orbits are still used today and are known by the name Hohmann orbits as a tribute to their inventor.

Luna 9 (1966)

It was on February 3, 1966 with the Soviet space probe *Luna 9* that an artificial satellite landed on the moon for the first time.

The United States achieved this feat on June 2, 1966 with the landing of the automatic probe *Surveyor 1*, which transmitted 11,150 photographs of the surroundings (Sea of Tempests). This was followed in 1967 by the probe *Surveyor 5*, which carried out the first analyses of lunar soil.

Then, in September 1970, the USSR sent the *Luna 16* probe, which carried out the first core-sampling of lunar soil.

Venera 7 (1970)

The USSR also launched the probe *Venera 7*, which landed on the planet Venus for the first time on December 15, 1970, and then *Venera 9* and *10*, which landed on Venus on October 22 and 25, 1975, transmitting the first images from Venus's surface.

The United States successfully carried out the first flights over Jupiter and Saturn, the largest planets in the solar system. First, it was *Pioneer 10* and *11* that flew above the two planets, in December 1973 and December 1974, respectively. Subsequently, it was the probes *Voyager 1* and *2* that flew over Jupiter and Saturn, this

time getting even closer, as well as over their numerous satellites, before continuing on their flights toward Uranus and Neptune.

Voyager (1977)

Launched on August 29, 1977 by a Titan-Centaur rocket, the *Voyager 2* space probe overflew the planet Neptune on August 25, 1989 after a journey of 2.8 billion miles. The information and images gathered by the two Voyager probes have provided a rich stock of data. Among the phenomena discovered during their prolonged exploration of the universe are 17 previously unknown moons—three around Jupiter, four around Saturn and ten around Uranus. They also revealed that there are rings around these planets. The images transmitted also showed that there were active volcanoes on *Io*, one of Jupiter's moons. This is the one other planet in the solar system, apart from earth, to have volcanic activity.

Voyager 2 then set out to explore the frontiers of the solar system in order to gauge more accurately where the influence of the sun gives way to the galactic flow of the Milky Way. Like *Voyager 1*, launched on September 5, 1977, it will disappear forever into the universe and gradually cease to transmit photographs.

Magellan, Galileo and Ulysses (1989)

The first of these probes, *Magellan*, was launched toward Venus during the *Atlantis* mission in May 1989. It began its orbit of Venus in September 1990 and provided some extremely interesting images of the planet, including a crater large enough to hold Los Angeles and a river of solidified lava 185 miles long.

The second, *Galileo*, set off toward Jupiter on October 18, 1989. The crew of the shuttle *Columbia*, during the December 1990 mission, observed the probe as it passed 589 miles from earth, which it was to use as a gravitational springboard to take off toward Jupiter. It is scheduled to reach that planet in December 1995.

The European probe, *Ulysses* (built jointly by France and Germany), was successfully launched by the shuttle *Discovery* on October 6, 1990. It will enable scientists to observe and analyze the flow of electrons, protons and helium from the primary cosmic base of Jupiter and the sun.

COBE (Cosmic Background Explorer) (1989)

Launched by NASA in 1989, the *COBE* is an observation satellite for studying the cosmic background radiation discovered in 1965 by Arno A. Penzias and Robert Wilson (both U.S.). The satellite has made more than 300 million measurements, some which show minute variations in the density of matter (930 millionths in degrees Celsius), which bear witness to the structure of the universe. On April 23, 1992, astrophysicist George Smoot announced the discovery of cosmic ripples at the edge of the universe. This discovery was based on data provided by COBE (see also Astrophysics, "Cosmic ripples," p. 86).

WHAT ON EARTH?

NOT ALL INVENTIONS CHANGE OUR LIVES, SOME JUST MAKE US SCRATCH OUR HEADS.

ROCKY IV

▲ A prototype mini-rover, dubbed *Rocky IV*, is being tested by NASA engineers for use on Mars. The vehicle is 2 feet long, 15 inches wide and 14 inches high. Powered by motors in each of its six wheels, *Rocky IV* uses sensors to avoid such hazards as cliffs, dropoffs and excessive tilt angles.

MESSAGE ON A SPACE PROBE

▼ Recognizing the vast potential of the *Pioneer 10* voyage, three journalists approached Carl Sagan with the idea of designing a message to extraterrestrial beings that would describe the earth and its inhabitants. Sagan and his wife designed this plaque and presented it to NASA. The 6 x 9-inch gold-anodized frame was bolted to *Pioneer 10* when it was launched on March 2, 1972.

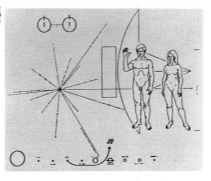

SPACE SHOWER

This is not a reference to meteors or shooting stars, but to the astronauts' favorite place to sing. NASA is developing a special shower for use in weightless conditions, which will be fitted on board the orbital station. Designed by Rafael Garcia, the completely enclosed shower cell will use 7 pints of water per minute, compared to 35 pints on earth, and a special attachment will suck up the water and recycle 93 percent of it. It is hoped that astronauts will be able to shower every two days. Currently, astronauts aboard the space shuttle are limited to washing themselves with a sponge.

"TURBO ROVER"

In 1992 the Fairchild Space and Defense Corporation received a patent for a nuclear-fueled turbocompressor dubbed "Turbo Rover." This machine is designed to generate heat and electricity on the planet Mars. Capable of operating at surface temperatures of 1,900° Celsius, the Turbo Rover is powered by a nuclear reactor fueled by four plutonium pellets.

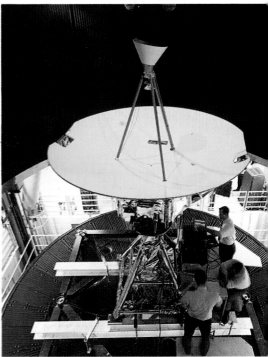

THE ULTIMATE SATELLITE DISH

Right: Although the number of channels is limited, the reception from this satellite is out of this world. This is the *Pioneer 10* space probe, which was launched in March 1972 and is still functioning more than five billion miles away from earth. Here the probe is undergoing a test in a space simulation chamber.

VERY LARGE TELESCOPE (VLT)

In 1987 the European Southern Observatory (ESO) announced the planned construction of the world's largest telescope, named VLT (Very Large Telescope). The project is expected to be completed in 1997, with the first-phase completion scheduled for 1994–95.

The VLT will comprise four astronomic lenses with 26-ft-3-in. diameter mirrors. A 52-ft-6-in. chamber will extend it further. The aim of the VLT is to allow scientists to observe stars inside interstellar clouds, and even to look into the center of galaxies, and possibly locate potential black holes.

LOISA

Loisa is the name for an American project for a telescope to be constructed on the moon. Based on an idea of the astronomer Antoine Labeyrie (France), Loisa will comprise 30 small telescopes transported to the moon in detached pieces. It is hoped that the project would allow views of distant galaxies. No dates for implementation have been set at this time.

New ideas that may change the way we live

at different altitudes; and a platform in polar orbit containing meteorological and observational instruments.

The space station will be built and tested on the ground and then assembled in space. It is expected that construction in space will begin in 1995, and *Freedom* will be fully operational by the end of the century. *Freedom* will comprise four pressurized modules, attached to a long truss. Three of the modules are laboratories, designed separately by the U.S., Japan and Europe. The fourth module provides living quarters for the crew. When completed, *Freedom* will be 353 feet in length and 243 feet high, and will weigh 296 tons. A maximum crew of four astronauts will live in the station.

MARS ENVIRONMENTAL SURVEY (MESUR)

In May 1992 NASA announced its plans to send 16 small, low-cost landers to the surface of Mars. The landers will be launched in three stages, the first scheduled for 1999, the second for 2001 and the final phase for 2003. Known as the Mars Environmental Survey, the project aims to complete a global reconnaisance of the surface of Mars. Experiments will provide details of the planet's weather, chemistry and seismic activity.

AX-5 AND ZPS Mk-3 SPACE SUITS

These two new types of space suits are designed for use during missions on the space station *Freedom*. Tested since February 1988 by NASA, they should allow astronauts to work outside the station for up to eight hours. The ZPS Mk-3 weighs 150 lb, and the AX-5 85 lb.

CASSINI SPACE PROBE

Planned since 1982, the space probe *Cassini* should be launched in April 1996. It will reach Saturn in October 2002, after a journey of 900 million miles.

Cassini will orbit around the system formed by Saturn and its large satellite *Titan*, the only moon in the solar system with an appreciable atmosphere. The European Huygens probe will then be detached from *Cassini* and released into *Titan*'s dense nitrogen atmosphere. After being slowed down by an aerodynamic shield, it should reach the unknown surface of *Titan* and carry out numerous measurements. The density of the probe has been calculated so that the probe will float if Titan's surface is formed by an ocean composed of ethane, methane and liquid nitrogen.

The *Mars Observer* will reach the planet in fall 1993. (NASA)

MARS OBSERVER

Launched on September 25, 1992, the *Mars Observer* will study the surface and atmosphere of Mars. It should rendezvous with the planet on August 24, 1993.

FREEDOM SPACE STATION

The orbital space station project *Freedom* was launched in 1984 by President Ronald Reagan. An international civil program, it is being built by a partnership of the United States, Japan, the European Community and Canada.

Freedom is designed to be a permanently manned research facility in space. It includes such features as a permanently habitable module laboratory linked to the station; an autonomous module, which will fly in conjunction with the station but

Cassini is scheduled for launch in 1996. (ESA)

6

EVERYDAY LIFE

THE KITCHEN

Food and Drink

Sugar (antiquity)

The extraction of cane sugar goes back to antiquity, and the plant was probably first cultivated in India: the Greeks and Romans referred to sugar as "Indian salt" and "honey of India." The Christians probably brought it to the West during the Crusades. It has been proven that during the 12th century there were mills in Siciliy that made "honey canes." Centuries ago the Chinese knew not only how to extract cane sugar but also how to refine it, an operation that was developed much later in the West.

Beer (4th millennium B.C.)

People have been drinking beer for thousands of years: in India (c. 3200 B.C.), in China (c. 3000 B.C.) and above all in the Middle East, where the Sumerians reserved 40 percent of their cereal crop for brewing. In Egypt beer was considered to be the national drink. It was, however, very different from the beverage we know today. Less liquid than our beer, it resembled a kind of drinkable "bread" but had nonetheless a high alcohol content (13 to 15 degrees proof) and was generally made from barley. In the Middle Ages monks introduced hops into the recipe, and in the 12th century professional brewers appeared.

Tea (c. 2737 B.C.)

Two different legends recount the discovery of tea. Shang Yeng was the Emperor of China around 2737 B.C. As a health measure, he ordered his subjects to drink nothing but boiled water. One day, leaves from a nearby tree fell into his own simmering water and the Emperor was delighted by this new drink.

The second legend is set circa A.D. 520. According to Japanese tradition, an Indian prince, Bodhidharma, who had become an ascetic, went to China to teach Zen Buddhism. To keep himself awake during long hours of meditation, he cut off his eyelids and threw them away. At the place where they fell there soon grew a bush. When the master's disciples came to meditate with him, they picked the leaves of this tree and made an infusion from them to keep themselves awake. It was a tea plant.

Mustard (4th century)

In the footnotes of history we find the story of how the Gauls introduced the Romans to the mustard seed when they occupied Rome in the 4th century. When these seeds were ground up with vinegar or wine must, the result was *mustum ardeo*, from which our name mustard comes. It was not until the Middle Ages that mustard found its way onto every table.

In the 13th century the town of Dijon first became famous for the quality of its mustards using verjuice, an extract of unripe grapes, to make this most sought-after condiment.

As centuries passed and tastes changed, mustard was flavored in different ways: with vanilla in the 17th century, then with orange blossom or violet water, then, in the 19th century, with various spices or herbs like tarragon, chervil, chives, lemon or red fruit.

Coffee (15th century)

According to legend the stimulating qualities of coffee were discovered by a goat herder in the Yemen. He noticed that his herd would not sleep at night after eating the red fruit of the coffee bush. We know for a fact that coffee was drunk in Aden in 1420. It was adopted in Syria and Turkey, and by 1615 coffee had reached Venice. Coffeehouses became popular in the 18th century; perhaps the most famous is Edward Lloyd's in London, where underwriters and merchants carried out much of their insurance business.

Whiskey (1494)

The first mention of a spirit made from malted barley dates from 1494. The monk John Cor distilled it for his abbey.

Following the civil and religious wars that ravaged Scotland for centuries, the production of malted barley spirit, in other words, whiskey, remained secret until 1823, when a certain John Smith established an official distillery in the valley of Glenlivet.

Croissant (1683)

The crescent roll was invented in 1683 in Vienna, Austria by the Pole Kulyeziski. The city had been under siege by an immense Turkish army led by Kara Mustafa. The famished Viennese were finally saved by Charles de Lorraine

The brewing of beer dates to the 4th millennium B.C. Commercial breweries first appeared in the 12th century. (Le Livre Mondial des Inventions)

Previous page: Washing machines on the line. (Explorer/Howarth)

and the King of Poland, John III Sobieski. Kulyeziski, having taken a decisive part in the final victory, was given the stocks of coffee abandoned by the routed Turkish army and was authorized to open a cafe in Vienna. This he did, and to accompany his coffee, he had a baker make small milk bread rolls in the shape of crescents to commemorate the victory over the Turks. They were immediately successful.

Champagne (around 1695)

Until the end of the 17th century the wine of Champagne was kept in barrels. It then became clear that it was easier to keep the wine in bottles, and it was decided to preserve the young wine systematically in bottles, even before fermentation was complete. The fermentation continued in the bottle: the still active fermenting agents transformed the sugar into alcohol and carbon dioxide. The carbon dioxide caused the champagne to fizz when the bottle was opened. The phenomenon was observed collectively and it is impossible to attribute it to one person. It is only in recent years that Dom Pérignon has been hailed as the person who discovered champagne. Although he was known for his skillful blending of different grapes to enhance his wines, these were mostly red wines, and there is no proof that he took an interest in the bubbly wine from Champagne.

Carbonated mineral water (1741)

Fizzy mineral water was invented in Whitehaven, England by William Brownrigg in 1741. He had the idea of adding carbonic acid (which produces bubbles) to ordinary spring water and then bottling it. The bubbles would appear when the bottle was opened.

Sandwich (1762)

John Montagu, fourth Earl of Sandwich (Great Britain, 1718–92) is said to have invented the sandwich in 1762. A devoted gambler, the earl one day refused to leave his gambling table for lunch. His cook prepared a small snack for him consisting of a piece of meat between two slices of buttered bread. The sandwich rapidly became very popular throughout the British Isles, but did not spread to continental Europe until the following century.

Bourbon (1789)

This beverage, the American cousin of Scotch and Irish whiskies, was invented in 1789 by Pastor Elijah Craig in Bourbon County in northern Kentucky. The refinement of this whiskey, distilled from corn mash and malted barley, was carried out by Dr. James Crowe in Franklin County, Kentucky.

Camembert (1790)

It is not known whether Marie Harel got the recipe from her mother, Marie-Catherine Fontaine, or from a priest from the Brie district whom she sheltered at the start of the Revolution. What we do know is that her cheese was very successful at the Camembert markets in Orne, France. Her daughter and son-in-law, who were excellent business people, took over from her, establishing the cheese's reputation and giving it its name.

Canned food (1795)

In 1795 Nicolas Appert (France, 1749–1841) invented a brilliant method for preserving food. *Appertization* consisted of sterilizing foodstuffs in hermetically sealed containers away from circulating air. This process was not yet that of canning food, and involved jars covered with five layers of cork.

Tin cans (1812)

In 1810 Pierre Durand patented a metaled vessel for preserving food. The patent was bought for £1000 by Bryan Donkin and John Hall (both Great Britain), who combined Durand's preserving process with Appert's. Tin cans were first made in 1812 in a preserving factory built at Blue Anchor Lane, Bermondsey, London.

Sugar beet (1812)

During the Continental System (Napoleon's attempt to counteract British maritime power), he considered it of the utmost importance that France should be able to manufacture sugar, by extracting it from beets. On January 2, 1812 he was overjoyed to hear that the manufacturer Benjamin Delessert (1773–1847) had succeeded in doing this at his factory in Passy.

Napoleon went to Passy that very day and decided to establish imperial factories and to devote 600,000 acres to sugar beet cultivation.

Delessert's predecessors were the chemist Margraff (Germany), who started his work in 1747, and Achard (Germany, b. France), who began in 1799. The juice was extracted by rupturing the cell walls of the root. But it was impure; people did not like the sugar and productivity was low. In 1864 Robert (France), a sugar manufacturer in Moravia, obtained the juice by diffusion, which did not require rupturing the cells.

Chocolate (1819)

Twenty-three-year-old François-Louis Cailler (Switzerland) made the first bars of chocolate at Vevey in 1819. Small-scale production of chocolate had begun in France and Italy after the Spaniards returned from South America with the recipe. At that time it was a drink prepared from roasted, crushed cocoa beans.

In 1879 Rodolphe Lindt (Switzerland) built a chocolate factory in Berne. In those days blocks of chocolate were hard and had to be crunched; they also left a gritty sensation in the mouth along with a bitter aftertaste. Even when heated up, the chocolate remained thick and heavy. Because of this, Lindt invented a machine that kneaded the chocolate for a long time; he then had the idea of adding cocoa butter to it. The chocolate we know today was born, and Lindt patented his invention in 1880.

Cocoa powder (1828)

Cocoa powder was made for the first time by Conraad Johannes van Houten (Netherlands) in Amsterdam in 1828. He invented a way of obtaining a soluble cocoa powder that could be used to make a hot drink. Up to that time the only way to make it was by melting pieces of chocolate.

Tonic water (1840)

In 1840 the British company Schweppes, founded by Jakob Schweppe (Germany), developed Indian tonic water. Schweppe had begun making soda water from distilled water charged with carbon dioxide in 1792.

Tonic water is a soda containing sugar and quinine. The idea of putting quinine in soda originated in the Indian Army as part of the fight against malaria.

Condensed milk (1858)

Although Nicolas Appert (France) had the idea of condensing milk in 1827, the process was not applied industrially for another 30 years. It was not until 1858 that Gail Borden (U.S.) set up the first factory producing sweetened condensed milk in the United States.

In 1884, work by Meyenberg made it possible also to produce evaporated milk that contained no added sugar.

Chewing gum (1869)

In 1848, J. Curtis (U.S.) marketed spruce resin for the first time. Spruce is a native tree of Maine.

In 1860 spruce resin was abandoned in favor of chicle, a gumlike substance obtained from the sapodilla, a tree that grows in Yucatan. This resin was a popular chew among the Aztecs and was brought to Staten Island, New York by Gen. Santa Anna (Mexico), who led the attack on the Alamo. He showed it to Thomas Adams, and Adams began selling this gum in 1871. It was not until 1875 that John Colgan came up with the idea of flavoring it. However, it was only in the 1890s that chewing gum became truly widespread, thanks to William Wrigley.

Margarine (1869)

Margarine was invented in 1869 by Hippolyte Mège-Mouriès (France) following a contest launched by Napoleon III to come up with a replacement for butter. An artificial butter that would be economical and would not go rancid represented an undeniable advantage when providing food for the army and navy.

Mège-Mouriès's method consisted of processing animal fat (essentially tallow), from which he obtained a paste of a color and consistency close to butter and which did not have a disagreeable odor. He christened his product *margarine* because of its pearly color (pearl is *margaron* in Greek). Later, thanks to improvements in Mège-Mouriès's process, margarine was made from vegetable fat.

Coca-Cola (1886): Dr. John S. Pemberton

Dr. John S. Pemberton. (Coca-Cola)

Sugar. Caffeine. Vegetable extracts. Coca leaves. The ingredients of the world's most popular soft drink are known to many, but the exact proportion of each is a closely guarded secret locked away in a safe at Coca-Cola's headquarters. Dr. John S. Pemberton's original formula has never been patented but has been closely imitated since it made its debut in 1886 in Atlanta, Georgia.

Pemberton was a pharmacist known for developing an array of chemical compounds useful for treating many human ailments: Globe of Flower Cough Syrup, Indian Queen Hair Dye and Triplex Liver Pills, to name a few. This enterprising man spent much time in his chemical laboratory, looking for new flavors to make his pharmaceutical products more palatable.

Around 1880, Pemberton began to experiment with a tasty "soft" drink that could be sold at the soda fountain. Shortly after founding the Pemberton Chemical Company, in 1886, Pemberton hit on a syrup which, when mixed with carbonated water, would be a thirst-quenching drink. He added caffeine for a pick-me-up, put in coca leaves (with the cocaine removed) for flavor, and mixed his brew in a brass kettle.

The first taste-tester was Willie Venable, resident "jerk" and "soda-water king" of Jacob's Drugstore in Atlanta. Venable bought the mix on a trial basis, and it wasn't long before customers began wanting to ask for the drink by name. Pemberton and his three company partners put their heads together, and one, Frank Robinson, suggested Coca-Cola. Next, Robinson tried writing the moniker in an adaptation of the elaborate Spenderian penmanship script of the day. The famous Coca-Cola label has barely been changed since; likewise Coke still uses the slogan coined them: "Delicious and Refreshing."

From inauspicious beginnings—the first Coca-Cola factory was a three-legged pot at the rear of Pemberton's lab, stirred by his son Charlie—Coca-Cola has conquered the world.

Artificial flavoring (1874)

In 1874 Dr. Wilhelm Haarman and Prof. Ferdinand Tiemann (both Germany) synthesized vanillin, the principal component in vanilla beans. Two years later, Karl Reimer conceived a chemical compound that fully reproduced the flavor of vanilla. This was the beginning of artificial flavoring.

Ketchup (1876)

The ketchup we know today was invented by Henry Heinz (U.S.) in 1876, but its origins go back to ancient times. The Chinese were probably the first to prepare a sauce called ketchup or *ke-tsiap*, a sort of brine marinade for fish or shellfish.

It was introduced into Europe at the end of the 17th century by the British, who had come across it in Malaysia, where it bore the name *ketchap*, and adapted it to the ingredients available in Britain. It was then taken to the United States by long-distance navigators from Maine. Tomatoes were not introduced to the recipe until the 1790s.

Saccharin (1879)

Saccharin was discovered by Constantin Fahlberg (U.S.), who was working under the direction of Prof. Ira Remsen at Johns Hopkins University in Baltimore. He published the results of his work on February 27, 1879. Recent studies seem to prove that saccharin can be hazardous to health, but only if consumed in extremely large quantities.

Breakfast cereals (1898)

Corn flakes were popularized in 1898 by Will Keith Kellogg (U.S.). Before that, Henry D. Perky of Denver, Colo. was the first, in 1893, to have the idea of making ready-prepared breakfast cereals. Having met a man who nursed his stomach pains by eating boiled wheat soaked in milk every morning, Perky came up with a product made from wheat, which he called Shredded Wheat.

Will Keith Kellogg was employed by his elder brother, a doctor at the Battle Creek Sanitarium in Michigan. Working at night in the hospital kitchen, Will boiled wheat in an effort to help the doctor find a digestible substitute for bread. One day in 1894, after a batch of boiled wheat accidentally was left to stand, the brothers tried again. Unknowingly, they had tempered the wheat by letting it stand. The compressed wheat was flaked off rollers with blades devised by Will. Thus was the modern-day breakfast cereal born. Granose Flakes were launched in 1894; they became Corn Flakes in 1898.

Instant coffee (1937)

The first attempts at the production and marketing of instant coffee took place in the United States in 1867, but with no great success.

It was the Swiss company Nestlé that gained the lion's share of the market by creating Nescafé in 1937. Nowadays there are 100 different varieties of Nescafé in the world.

Espresso (1946)

Espresso coffee has been around since the late 19th century, but it only became popular in Europe with the invention of the Gaggia coffeemaker in Italy in 1946.

Freeze-dried food (1946)

In 1946–47 E.W. Flosdorf (U.S.) demonstrated that the process of freeze-drying, which was already known and used, could be applied, under proper conditions, to products such as coffee, orange juice and meat.

Freeze-drying achieves dehydration through refrigeration: the water content solidifies faster than the other elements in the product and is eliminated in the form of ice.

Freeze-drying was invented by Arsène d'Arsonval and F. Bordas (both France) in Paris, in 1906, and rediscovered by Shackwell (U.S., 1851–1940), in St. Louis, Mo., in 1909. The process was first applied medically.

It was not until 1955 that freeze-drying entered the food industry, where it was applied to Texas shrimps and Maryland crabs.

Carton (1951)

It was Ruben Rausing (Sweden), an industrialist specializing in packs for dry foodstuffs (flour, sugar, etc.), who revolutionized the packaging of liquids and drinks in 1951. Combining the most highly developed paper, aluminum and plastic technologies, he created the tetrahedral carton, a form of packaging that was totally new in form, manufacture and cost.

In 1961 Rausing and his Tetra Pak company began their decisive expansion with the first aseptically filled cartons of UHT-treated long-life milk. Following dairy products, a whole range of goods including fruit juices, soups, cream and wine were packaged in "brick" form.

This has brought about a real revolution in our daily life, with Tetra Pak now present in 98 countries. If all the packing sold by Tetra Pak in 1991 were placed end to end, it would reach 14 times further than the distance between the earth and moon.

Cooking Utensils and Appliances

Plate (ancient times)

The plate was known to peoples of the ancient world, especially the Romans. But it disappeared during the Middle Ages and was replaced by bowls and wooden trenchers.

Plates reappeared in 1530, in silver, at the banquet celebrating the marriage of King Francis 1 of France (1494–1547) to Eleanor of Habsburg.

Fork (6000 to 3000 B.C.)

Distant precursors of the modern fork have been unearthed at diggings at the site of Çatal-Hüyük in Turkey. It then seems to vanish, and the first indication of its "reinvention" is its mention in certain inventories drawn up in the 14th century. It was probably brought to the West by Italians. The 1307 inventory of Edward I mentions seven forks, including one in gold.

It was not until the first half of the 17th century that the fork reached English dining tables.

Corkscrew (17th century)

Toward the end of the 17th century, the use of watertight corks made corkscrews indispensable. We do not know who invented the first ones, but in 1795 Samuel Hershaw (Great Britain) developed the screw and nut corkscrew.

Coffee grinder (1687)

The invention of the coffee grinder in 1687 contributed to the diffusion of this brand-new drink. The electric coffee grinder was invented in 1937 by the Kitchen Aid division of the Hobart Manufacturing Co. of America. The first model sold for $12.75.

Matches (1826)

The first primitive matches were developed at the end of the 17th century. They were simply small sticks of wood dipped in melted sulphur and were developed by Robert Boyle (Ireland, 1627–91). They needed to touch something burning in order to catch fire. The first real matches that lit without contact with fire were invented by John Walker (Great Britain) in 1826 while he was working on developing a new explosive. He failed to see the commercial potential, but Samuel Jones did, and set up a factory. These matches were foul-smelling, and so Charles Sauria (France) and Stephen von Roemer (Austria) independently came up with cleaner and more efficient matches based on phosphorus. The first factories were set up in Vienna in 1833.

The substance used (white phosphorus) was highly toxic to the workers and the product was dangerously inflammable, which led chemists to continue their research.

Safety matches (1847)

The discovery of red phosphorus in 1847 enabled Lundström (Sweden) to create so-called safety matches, which need to be struck against a special material. These new matches first gained recognition at the Universal Exhibition in Paris in 1855.

Vacuum flask (1892)

In 1892, Sir James Dewar (Great Britain, 1842–1923) invented a thermal isolation device that made it possible to liquefy gases. He did not patent the device, nor did he see its wider commercial application. Reinhold Burger, a glass-blower (Germany), cased the fragile vacuum flask in metal and eventually decided to call it a Thermos flask. He patented it in 1903 and by 1906 the invention had crossed the Atlantic.

Coffee filter (1908)

In 1908 Melitta Bentz (Germany) wanted to improve the quality of the coffee for her family. She pierced holes in the bottom of a tin container, then cut out a disc from absorbent paper,

---

Toll House Cookie (c. 1930): Ruth Wakefield

The Toll House Inn was built in 1708 as a tollgate for travelers between Boston and the whaling town of New Bedford, Massachusetts. The Whitman, Massachusetts inn was bought and renovated in 1930 by Ken and Ruth Wakefield.

Mrs. Wakefield was chief cook. She liked to use a favorite American recipe for after-dinner cookies—Butter Drop-Do's. One day she added Nestlé's semi-sweet chocolate, thinking it would melt during baking and marble into the cookie dough. Instead, the chocolate chunks remained intact, softening only a little, and lo! The chocolate chip cookie was born.

A good friend, Marjorie Mills, was food editor of a Boston newspaper. She gave out Mrs. Wakefield's cookie recipe on a Boston radio show. Toll House cookies were an instant hit.

At the time, Nestlé was considering discontinuing its semi-sweet bar, which seemed to sell only in the Boston area. They dispatched a company representative to investigate, and found that Boston was mad for chocolate chip cookies.

Nestlé set out to lighten the chopping chore for cooks by scoring the semi-sweet bar. The company even sold a special chocolate chopper. By 1939 Toll House cookies were a national craze. That sparked another invention, Nestlé's semi-sweet morsels. In 1940, Nestlé bought the Toll House name from the Wakefields, promising them a lifetime supply of free chocolate. The company printed Ruth Wakefield's recipe on the wrappers of its chocolate bars and morsels.

Today, chocolate chip cookies are baked with morsels that are large, small, milk chocolate, mint chocolate, and—as part of the back-to-basics movement?—chopped semi-sweet chocolate. Year after year, chocolate chips top the cookie best-seller list. That famous recipe follows. Enjoy!

Original Toll House Chocolate Chip Cookie

Toll House Cookies. (Nestlé)

2¼ cups all-purpose flour
1 teaspoon baking soda
1 teaspoon salt
1 cup (2 sticks) butter, softened
¾ cup sugar
¾ cup firmly packed brown sugar
1 teaspoon vanilla extract
2 eggs
One 12-oz pkg. (2 cups) Nestlé-Toll House semi-sweet chocolate morsels
1 cup chopped nuts

Preheat oven to 375 degrees F. In small bowl, combine flour, baking soda and salt, set aside.

In large mixer bowl, beat butter, sugar, brown sugar and vanilla extract until creamy. Beat in eggs. Gradually blend in flour mixture. Stir in Nestlé Toll House semi-sweet chocolate morsels and nuts.

Drop by rounded measuring tablespoonfuls onto ungreased cookie sheets. Bake 9–11 minutes until edges are golden brown.

Makes 5 dozen 2¼-inch cookies.

which she placed in the bottom of the container. She placed it over the coffee pot, filled the container with coffee and poured boiling water over it. The result was excellent, and that was how the Melitta coffee filter was born.

Toaster (1909)

The first toasters were marked by the General Electric Co. in 1909. The machine quite simply consisted of bare wires wound around mica strips.

The first prototype of the pop-up toaster that grills on both sides was developed by Charles Strite (U.S.), and patented in May 29, 1919. The toasters began to appear in homes in 1926.

Electric mixer (1923)

In Racine, Wisc. in 1910, Fred Osius, Chester A. Beach and L.H. Hamilton launched the first electric household motor compatible with both alternating and direct current. Drawing on this invention, Air-O-Mix Inc. of Wilmington, Del. designed in 1923 the Whip-All, a portable mixer. Another first was the Mixmaster, from Sunbeam of Chicago. This was the first fixed mixer (like the present-day food processors) to be commercially successful: in 1930, the year it was put on the market, sales reached 60,000.

Microwave oven (1945)

On October 8, 1945 Percy Le Baron Spencer (U.S.) applied for a patent for what was to be the microwave oven. He was following in the tracks of Sir John Randall and Dr. H.A. Boot (both Great Britain), who developed an electronic tube that produces microwave energy— the magnetron. As they came up with their invention in 1940 it was put to military use in improving radar defenses. Spencer, who was a physics engineer at Raytheon, one of the world leaders in radar equipment, noticed one day that the energy given off by the tubes used for radar produced heat.

This electromagnetic energy gave him the idea of putting a handful of corn in a paper bag and placing the bag within the field of the tube. The corn immediately burst, transforming itself into popcorn. He melted chocolate in the same way. Raytheon developed a cooking program for microwaves and patented the first cooking apparatus of this type, the Radar Range. This machine had a power of 1600 watts. It was heavy, awkward and expensive and was originally intended for use in hospitals and military canteens. In 1952 the Tappan Company put the first household microwave oven on the market.

Tupperware (1945)

The little airtight plastic boxes were the brain-child of Earl W. Tupper (U.S.). He was a former chemist at Du Pont and invented Tupperware in 1945. The unusual feature of Tupperware is that items are not sold in the traditional way but through "parties," and are guaranteed for 10 years. Their ease of use and pleasant design brought them immediate popularity.

Food processor (1947)

This kitchen appliance, destined to equip millions of kitchens throughout the world, has its roots in a 1947 design by Kenneth Wood (Great Britain). Marketed as the Kenwood Chef, it was composed of a powerful and sturdy engine block to which a large number of accessories could be fitted: mixer, citrus squeezer, mincer, slicer and shredder, pasta and ravioli maker, food mill, can opener, etc. Its multiple uses allowed it single-handedly to replace many small appliances.

Nonstick pan (1954)

The nonstick pan was invented by Marc Grégoire (France) purely by chance. Grégoire, a research engineer, was trying to perfect his fishing rods in 1954 when he discovered the processes that make it possible to encrust metal with Teflon. His patents were applied to kitchen utensils, and with these he founded the T-Fal company in 1956, which went on to produce its famous frying pan. T-Fal is still the uncontested leader in nonstick utensils, having sold 25 million frying pans, casserole dishes, etc.

Teflon itself had been discovered by accident in 1938 by Roy Plunkett of Du Pont (see page 73). It is both very slippery and impervious to corrosion. The name "Teflon" comes from tetrafluoroethylene. Du Pont found many uses for it, but did not think to use it for cooking utensils.

The electric frying pan dates back to 1911, when it was launched by Westinghouse.

Refrigeration

Water vapor refrigeration machine (1755)

William Cullen (Great Britain) first obtained ice from water vapor in 1755. Cullen's experiment produced small amounts of ice in a vacuumed bell jar. In 1777 Gerald Nairne (Great Britain) accelerated the process by adding sulphuric acid. In 1866 Edmond Carré (France) developed the first machine capable of making ice in large quantities, and it was an immediate success.

Compressed-ether refrigeration machine (1805)

In Philadelphia, Pa. in 1805, Oliver Evans (U.S., 1755–1819) presented his prototype for a compressed-ether refrigerating machine. Its chief innovation lay in the introduction of a closed-cycle system. This process was patented by Jacob Perkins (U.S., 1766–1849) in 1834. The first industrial machines were designed by James Harrison (Australia), who received his first patent in 1855.

Expanding-air refrigerating machine (1844)

The principle of reducing air pressure was known as early as the 18th century. John Gorrie (U.S.) applied the principle to the construction of an expanding-air refrigerating machine in 1844. Gorrie, a Florida doctor, built the machine to comfort his patients. He obtained a British patent in 1850 but the invention caused a scandal in the United States, where he was accused of competing with God by using his machine to make ice year-round. It wasn't until the following year, 1851, that Gorrie finally received a U.S. patent.

Absorption refrigerating machine (1859)

In 1859 Ferdinand Carré (France) patented an absorption refrigerating machine, in which the fluid, having generated coldness, is absorbed by another substance rather than being drawn up by a compressor.

Ammonia compressor refrigerating machine (1872)

David Boyle (U.S.) obtained the first patent for a compressor using ammonia in 1872. However, Karl von Linde (Germany, 1842–1934) built the first successful models in 1876.

SO₂ compression refrigerating machine (1874)

In 1874 Raoul Pictet (Switzerland, 1846–1929) used sulfur dioxide (SO_2) as the working fluid in a compression refrigeration system. Cold was produced by vaporizing a fluid. Pictet's machine was installed in 1876 at the first artificial skating rink in London, England.

Refrigerator (1913)

The Domelre, manufactured in Chicago in 1913, was the first functional household refrigerator. In 1918 Nathaniel Wales (U.S.) designed a device that was widely marketed under the name Kelvinator. The Frigidaire trademark appeared one year later, in 1919.

Carl Munters and Balzar von Platen (both Sweden) succeeded in constructing a silent and functional refrigerator. They filed their first patent in 1920, and developed a condenser device in 1929. Mass production began in 1931 with Electrolux, in Stockholm.

In 1926 General Electric manufactured a hermetically sealed unit, and in 1939 it introduced the first dual-temperature refrigerator. This allowed frozen foods to be kept in a separate compartment.

Deep-freezing (1924)

Industrial deep-freezing was launched by Clarence Birdseye (U.S.) in 1924. He applied preservation techniques used by the Labrador Inuit, which he had observed in 1912 and 1915. In 1924 he set up the Freezing Company to deep-freeze up to 500 metric tons of fruit and vegetables a year. In 1929 he realized that the deep-freezing process would have to be speeded up and invented a freezing machine with two plates, which chilled the product on both sides. Lastly, in 1935, he invented his multiple plate freezer, which is still used today.

This flat iron made completely of bronze dates to the 18th century. (Gamma/Beinat)

Dehydration (1945)

The dehydration process, designed by Howard (U.S.) in 1945 and patented in 1949, put the finishing touch on freezing techniques. It made it possible to reduce the mass to be transported by about 50 percent.

Precooked frozen meals (1945)

In 1945 Maxson (U.S.) was the first to offer precooked frozen meals to airline passengers. These were followed by "TV dinners," which started to develop in a spectacular way in 1954. In the United States in 1960, 215 million dishes were prepared.

THE HOME

Household Appliances

Iron (4th century)

It is known that the Chinese were using a kind of receptacle with a brass shaft containing embers in the 4th century. In the West the ancestor of the iron was the "smoother" made of wood, glass or marble. Various types of irons were designed from the 17th century onwards: irons that were heated on the fire, hollow irons filled with embers, and the classic laundry irons heated on stoves. Other means of heating the iron were tried, using hot water, gas or alcohol, until the first electric iron was perfected in 1882 (see below).

Carpet sweeper (1876)

The history of the mechanical sweeper starts at the end of the 17th century. In 1699 Edmund Hemming (Great Britain) invented a broom of this type to sweep the streets. James Hume in 1811 and Lucius Bigelow in 1858 (both Great Britain) can also be considered as creating forerunners of the carpet sweeper. The first efficient carpet sweeper was invented by Melville R. Bissell (U.S.), who patented it on September 19, 1876. He was the owner of a porcelain shop in Grand Rapids, Mich. Mr. Bissell suffered from an allergy to the dust produced by the straw he used to pack his pots. To cure this, he designed a broom with a cylindrical brush that pushed the dust into a container. The local success of this device led Mr. and Mrs. Bissell to set up the Bissell Carpet Sweeper Company to market their product. Their name became synonymous with carpet sweeper, much as Hoover is now linked with vacuum cleaners.

Electric iron (1882)

The electric iron was invented and patented by Henry W. Seeley of New York on July 6, 1882. However, it could not be used at the time as homes were not then connected to an electricity supply. The first electric steam iron was brought out in 1926 by Eldec Co. of New York.

Dishwasher (1886)

The first model of a mechanical dishwasher was developed between 1850 and 1865 in the United States. However, it was not until 1886 that Josephine Cochrane of Illinois came up with an efficient design, albeit crude and cumbersome. Her main aim was to reduce the number of breakages of crockery by her servants, rather than as a labor-saving device.

The electrically powered dishwasher first appeared in 1912.

In 1932 an appropriate detergent, Calgon, was discovered. This facilitated the dishwasher's development.

The automatic dishwasher first appeared in 1940, also in the United States. It was not exported to Europe until about 1960.

Washing machine (19th century)

Replacing the steam boiler, which itself replaced the washtub of the Middle Ages, the washing machine appeared during the 19th century. Composed of a wooden bin that was filled with soapy hot water, the first mechanical washing machines used heavy blades to stir the washing. This principle of tossing clothes inside a rotating cylinder still governs the operation of modern machines. One of them operated in 1830 in an English laundry. Around 1840 in France an industrial model with double sheathing, four compartments and a draining plug was designed; it was driven by means of a crank.

Electric washing machine (1901)

The first electric washing machine was invented and developed by Alva J. Fisher (U.S.) in 1901. It was not until the start of World War II that electric vertical-tub machines with built-in turbo-washers or with a vertical axle fitted with blades began to be mass-produced in the United States. Horizontal drum machines appeared in 1960.

Vacuum cleaner (1901)

Hubert Cecil Booth designed and patented the first vacuum cleaner in London in 1901. His Vacuum Cleaning Co. provided a cleaning service with uniformed employees.

A much lighter machine was developed by Murray Spangler (U.S.). He sold the rights to his vacuum to William B. Hoover, who launched the Hoover Model "O" at the end of 1908. His device was much lighter than that of Booth and it was an immediate success. Its ability to suck up dust brought remarkable results, greatly simplified cleaning and even improved sanitary conditions.

Air conditioning (1911)

Willis Carrier (U.S.) invented air conditioning in 1911. In 1902 he had studied the regulation of air humidity at a Brooklyn printing press. By 1904 this led him to devise an air-conditioning system in which he modified a steam heater to accept cold water and circulate air. This system both cooled air and removed its humidity and is still in use today. Continuing his research, in 1911 Carrier devised an air humidity graph that allowed him to make a rational estimate of air-conditioning requirements.

Central Heating

Hot air (antiquity)

Hot-air heating was used in China in ancient times. In most peasant dwellings the entire family would sleep on a slab heated by a hearth placed below it. This heating system was also widely used by the Romans in thermal baths (hypocaust) and private houses.

Hot-air heating installations in Roman houses were mentioned by Seneca in the 1st century A.D. He describes "tubes embedded in walls for directing and spreading, equally throughout the house, a soft and regular heat." This system reappeared in Europe during the 19th century under the name "cellar heating installations."

Steam heater (18th century)

The steam heater was able to carry heat further and more surely than the hot-air system. The first known model was the one installed by James Watt (Great Britain, 1736–1819) in his factory on the outskirts of Birmingham, England in the 18th century.

Hot-water heating (1777)

This system was known to the Romans, who occasionally used this central-heating system. The modern hot-water heating system was first installed in a castle near Pecq, France in 1777.

An architect named Bonnemain (France) designed the heating system. In 1899 the radiator made of assembled parts first appeared in the United States.

Electric radiator (1892)

The first electric radiator was patented by R.E. Bell Crompton and H.J. Dowsing (both Great Britain) in 1892. They attached a wire to a cast iron plate and protected the whole with a layer of enamel.

In 1906 Albert Marsh (U.S.) invented an alloy of nickel and chrome that could be heated red hot without melting. This resistant alloy proved to be an ideal element for the construction of electrical heating apparatus.

In 1912 C.R. Belling (Great Britain) perfected a refracting clay around which a nickel-chrome alloy wire could be wound. The same year he built the first "Standard" electric radiators.

Lighting

Origins (3rd millennium B.C.)

Lighting lamps existed as early as the 3rd millenium B.C. Small dishes that held oil and a wick have been discovered dating from this time. Glass lamps appeared in the 18th century. In 1784, braided wicks replaced cotton wicks.

Oil lamp (1804)

Aimé Argand (Switzerland, 1755–1803) was the inventor of the oil lamp. The first Argand-style lamp was manufactured in England in 1804. It was a draft oil lamp containing a glass chimney and a braided wick shaped like a hollow cylinder. The oil supply was located on a level above the wick. Argand's system eliminated smoke while also increasing light intensity.

Safety lamp (1816)

Sir Humphry Davy (Great Britain, 1778–1829) invented the safety lamp for miners in 1816. In 1811, Davy had discovered the principle of the electric arc (see below), and based on this work a physicist named Changy (France) developed an electric lamp for miners in 1858.

Arc lamp (1847)

In 1811 Sir Humphrey Davy had demonstrated the luminous properties of the electric arc. Davy produced the first model, but his "egg" remained at the experimental stage. The first effective arc lamps were created by W.E. Staite (Great Britain) in 1847. W. Petrie (Great Britain) perfected Staite's lamp in 1848.

Yablochkov's candle (1876)

In 1872 Pavel Nikolayevich Yablochkov (Russia) was asked to light the Moscow–Kursk railroad line, on which the Czar was to travel, thus preventing any potential terrorist from taking advantage of the dark. Yablochkov studied the arc lamp and developed an improved version, the Yablochkov candle, in 1876. This invention

Incandescent lamps were developed almost simultaneously by Thomas Edison and Joseph Swan. They later joined forces to perfect the invention. (Photothèque EDF)

paved the way for the electic lighting of public places, then streets and houses.

Incandescent lamp (1878–79)

The incandescent lamp was invented simultaneously during the years 1878–79 by two men: Thomas Edison (U.S., 1847–1931), at Menlo Park, N.J.; and Sir Joseph Swan (Great Britain, 1828–1914) at Newcastle-upon-Tyne, England. After a series of lawsuits against each other, the two men joined forces in 1883.

The principle of the incandescent lamp rested on a physical law set forth by James Prescott Joule (Great Britain, 1818–89), called the Joule effect, which proves that if a sufficiently powerful current passed through a sufficiently resistant conductor to bring it to white heat, the thermic energy would be converted into luminous energy. The practical problem was developing a filament able to withstand high temperatures. In 1865 H. Sprengel invented a pump that created a satisfactory vacuum inside the bulbs.

On December 18, 1878, Swan presented the carbon-filament lamp, but was unable to perform a public demonstration since the filament had burned out. On November 1, 1879, Edison patented his lamp, but his carbonized cotton filament also burned too quickly. Simultaneously in October and November 1880, the two inventors produced marketable lamps with cotton filaments that were steeped in carbon.

Neon tubes (1909)

The neon tube was invented by Georges Claude (France, 1870–1960) in 1909. It directly applied the principle of electric discharge in gases. The first neon tubes were used to illuminate the Grand Palais in Paris, France on December 3, 1910.

Tungsten filament (1910)

William David Coolidge (U.S.) of the General Electric Co. succeeded in 1910 in drawing out tungsten into thin filaments for producing incandescent-lamp filaments. These filaments, which solved the problem of resisting high temperatures, were patented on December 30, 1913.

Fluorescent tubes (1934)

Fluorescent tubes were developed after 70 years of research by numerous scientists. Fluorescent tubes made use of the properties of certain materials to emit light when subjected to ultraviolet radiation. This radiation is produced by an electric discharge in a gas at low pressure. The first fluorescent lamps were installed in cities in 1934.

Litec bulb (1965)

In 1965, Donald Hollister (U.S.) developed the Litec bulb, a non-electrode fluorescent lamp. It resembles an ordinary incandescent lamp, but the filament is replaced by a minuscule electromagnet that receives the current via an electronic device built into the bulb's base.

SL Lamp (1980)

The SL Lamp was invented by Philips N.V. engineers at its laboratory in Eindhoven, Netherlands in 1980. It is based on the principle of the fluorescent tube, but it can produce the same amount of light as the incandescent lamp using 25 percent of the energy, and lasts five times as long.

Halogen lamp (1980)

An incandescent lamp with a tungsten filament, the halogen lamp was developed by Philips N.V. in 1980. The atmosphere of the lamp contains argon or krypton and a percentage of halogen.

THE BATHROOM

Bath (antiquity)

The ancient Greeks and Romans used baths made of marble or silver. In the Middle Ages people bathed in simple wooden tubs. The ancestor of the individual bath with heated water is the steamroom designed in the second half of the 16th century by Ambroise Paré (France, c. 1509–90).

Paré, a surgeon, built his bath for hydrotherapeutic purposes. In the 18th century metal baths became more common. By the end of the 18th century a craftsman named Clément (France) had developed a varnish that could be applied to sheet metal. This made possible the manufacture of bathtubs at an accessible price, which led to their quickly replacing the traditional wooden or marble tubs.

Comb (antiquity)

It is believed that some form of comb has been used since the earliest days of humankind. Discoveries in Scandinavia have dated combs back to 8000 B.C. The manufacture of tortoise-shell combs began in the United States in 1780.

Soap (2500 B.C.)

For a very long time people had been aware of the cleansing properties of oily and fatty compounds associated with vegetable ash. A form of soft soap, probably of a very indifferent quality, existed in Mesopotamia in 2500 B.C. It reached Rome and Gaul in the 4th century, *sapo* being a word of Gaulish origin.

From the 13th century onwards, it was known how to make a solid soap using such fatty raw materials as soot or oil and alkalis such as plant ash or, better still, ash from seaweed which contains sodium carbonate. Until the end of the 18th century, there was very little development in soap-making techniques, and it remained a rare and expensive commodity.

Marseilles soap came into being in 1791 with the invention of a new process for the manufacture of sodium carbonate by Nicholas Leblanc.

Razor (12th century)

Obviously no one person can claim to have invented the razor. Men have always shaved, with seashells, shark's teeth and, later, bronze blades.

The razor, properly speaking, dates from the 12th century. The steel razor was created in Sheffield, England in the 18th century.

Toothbrush (15th century)

The toothbrush appears for the first time in a Chinese painting from the end of the 15th century. It appeared in Europe in the 17th century.

The first nylon toothbrush was Doctor West's Miracle Tuft Toothbrush, manufactured by Du Pont in the United States in 1938.

The first patent for an electric toothbrush goes back to 1908, but electric toothbrushes did not become popular until the 1930s.

Flushing system (1595)

As early as 1595 a courtier, Sir John Harington (Great Britain) had invented a practical water-flushing system for cleaning toilets, but his invention did not end the reign of chamber pots, despite gaining favor with Queen Elizabeth I.

It was not until 1775 that inventor Alexander Cummings (Great Britain) patented a flushing system. In 1778 30-year-old Joseph Bramah (Great Britain) invented the ball-valve-and-U-bend method still used today. But it was not until the end of the 19th century, with the advent of running water and modern plumbing, that the flushing system found its way into most homes.

Toilet paper (1857)

Toilet paper was invented in the United States by Joseph Cayetty in 1857, but for a long time it remained a luxury item. Walter Alcock (Great Britain) in 1879 became the first to produce a toilet roll. Only by the end of the century did the product really catch on.

Safety razor (1895)

In 1895 King Camp Gillette (U.S.) patented the safety or mechanical razor, whose distinguishing feature was its double-edged replaceable blades. He marketed his product through the company he founded in Boston in 1901, and the first razors went on sale in 1903. The Gillette Safety Razor Co. has undergone steady expansion since then.

Gillette introduced the twin-blade GII in 1971 and the first swivel-head razor in 1975.

Bathroom scales (1910)

Scales for domestic use were invented in 1910 by a German company, Jas Ravenol. They were marketed under the name Jaraso. The first American scale of this kind is attributed to J.M. Weber (patented in 1916). The first scale with a digital display was introduced by the Hanson Scale Co. in 1964. In 1984 H.S. Ong (b. Malaysia) designed a talking scale.

Kleenex (1924)

The first disposable paper handkerchiefs were produced in 1924 by the Kimberley-Clark Co. of Neenah, Wisc., under the name of Celluwipes. The product was later renamed Kleenex-Kerchiefs and then shortened to Kleenex. Originally, however, the tissues had been used as face wipes for women.

Aerosol (1926)

In 1926 Erik Rotheim (Norway) invented the aerosol. He discovered that a product could be projected in a fine spray by introducing a gas or liquid into the container to create internal pressure.

On August 22, 1939 Julian S. Kahn of New York invented a disposable spraycan that could contain an aerosol. But this idea did not have its first commercial application until 1941. In that year L.D. Goodhue and W.N. Sullivan (both U.S.) manufactured an insecticide in aerosol form.

Aerosols are now out of favor because of popular concern about the damage being done to the ozone layer by CFCs.

Electric shaver (1931)

The first electric shaver was developed by Colonel Jacob Schick (U.S.). The first model was patented and marketed in 1931. After a slow start, the electric shaver caught on, and by the end of the 1930s Schick was selling millions every year.

Disposable razor (1975)

The disposable razor was invented in 1975 by the French company Bic, the famous ballpoint pen manufacturers. The company was directed by Baron Bich, who was of the opinion that half a razor blade was sufficient for a shave and that with the saving made on the other half, it was possible to manufacture a handle.

Lubricating razor (1986)

Launched simultaneously in 1986 by Schick (Schick Pivot Plus) and Gillette (Contour Plus), this razor is designed with a blade containing a lubricating substance that gives a smoother shave without scraping the skin.

CLOTHING AND ACCESSORIES

Clothes

Shoe (antiquity)

A museum in Romans, France has a pair of Egyptian shoes made of papyrus, dating back to 4000 B.C. But the shoe was undoubtedly invented much earlier, although the distinction between the right and left foot dates only from the middle of the 11th century. Until then, footwear had to be made to measure.

The pump, which was originally a basic type of slipper for wearing indoors, appeared in the 16th century. Its popularity increased during the 19th century when it became extremely fashionable. From 1900 it played an important part in the emancipation of women by replacing the ankle boot and becoming a comfortable town shoe.

It was not until the 1890s that mass production of standard-sized shoes became possible, and the Manfield Shoe Company of Northampton, England took the lead.

Bra (antiquity)

There is proof that the bra existed in ancient Rome. It is depicted on ceramics, where the female gymnasts wear the *strophium*, a sort of scarf wound over the breasts in order to provide support.

In 1805 a band of elastic material was worn below high-waisted muslin dresses to keep the bust firm. It crossed at the front and was fastened at the back of the neck. In 1889 Herminie Cadolle invented the bra as we know it, but it did not become widely used until the 1920s. In 1913, Mary Jacob of New York devised a backless bra to suit her ball gown. It was patented on November 3, 1914 and, after some early problems, became a success. According to current statistics, the average American woman buys five bras per year, compared with 1.3 and three bought by her French and British counterparts.

Tie (ancient Rome)

The tie originally formed part of a military uniform. Roman soldiers wore a focale, a kind of tie, around their necks. It was not until the 17th century that the tie became more widely worn. The introduction of this fashion is attributed to either the Swedes in c. 1600 or the Croatian army in *c.* 1668.

Stockings (ancient Rome)

In ancient Rome, women wore bandages wrapped around their feet and legs. These "stockings" were also used by men, and their use was widespread in Europe up to the Middle Ages. In the 16th century knitted hose was developed. At the end of the 16th century W. Lee (Great Britain) invented the stocking loom, which revolutionized the production of stockings.

Handkerchief (2nd century B.C.)

The handkerchief is thought to have appeared in Rome during the 2nd century B.C., but it did not become part of everyday life. It did not reappear until the 15th century in Italy, where a distinction was made between the handkerchief used for the nose, which was slipped into the pocket, and the handkerchief used for the face, which was held in the hand. The handkerchief reached France during the 16th century and was immediately adopted by the Court and by actors, becoming as indispensable to tragedy as the fan was to comedy. It became widely used during the 17th century.

Pockets (16th century)

Surprisingly, pockets are a rather late development in clothing. Prior to the 16th century, if a man was carrying personal items, he would most usually place them in a codpiece at the front of his trousers. Toward 1600 these items became less popular and, instead, a small opening was made in the seam of a pair of trousers into which a pouch could be placed. Eventually this became a permanent fixture—and the pocket was invented.

Top hat (1797)

Although the French lay claim to having devised the top hat in 1796, the credit for creating it is usually given to a London milliner, John Etherington. On January 15, 1797 he emerged from his shop wearing a tall, hard, black hat. A crowd quickly gathered to have a look at this new item, and there was even some unrest. However, despite this controversial start, the hat was an immediate success.

Macintosh (1823)

It was Charles Macintosh (Great Britain, 1760–1843) who, in 1823, was the first to succeed in producing a waterproof cloth that could be used in the manufacture of clothing. His cotton fabric, imbued with a mixture of rubber and turpentine, maintained its full flexibility. The Macintosh became *the* waterproofed overcoat worn by men during the 19th century.

Jeans (1850s)

Jeans were created around 1850 by Oscar Levi Strauss for pioneers of the Californian gold rush. These hard-wearing trousers were originally cut out of a blue cloth that served for tenting. This cloth had been imported from Nîmes, France's traditional production center, where it was known as *serge de Nîmes*, hence the term *denim*. The famous copper studs first appeared on the pockets in 1873 to prevent splits down the seams caused by keeping tools in the pockets.

The earliest mention of the word *jean* dates from 1567 and appears to be a corrupt form of the word *genoese*—from Genoa. A twill cotton fabric was also manufactured in Genoa, where sailors wore pants made of this material. Denim is a heavy cotton cloth having an ecru woof and an indigo warp.

Nylon stockings (1940)

The stocking market was revolutionized by the appearance of nylon in 1938. Nylon was developed by a team of researchers from Du Pont led by Wallace H. Carothers (1896–1937), who committed suicide a year before nylon appeared. The potential for use as stockings was quickly seen, and Du Pont prepared to launch the new fashion item on May 15, 1940. The first nylon stockings reached Europe in 1945.

Bikini (1946)

On July 5, 1946 Louis Réard (France) presented an extremely daring two-piece in his swimwear collection. He called it the bikini because he considered it as explosive in its own way as the American atomic bomb that had been exploded four days earlier on the Pacific island of Bikini. The novelty was such that none of his professional models would wear it and Réard had to appeal for help to a dancer from the Casino in Paris, Micheline Bernardini. His creation was patented and, duly protected, the word *bikini* soon entered the dictionary.

Miniskirt (1965)

The miniskirt was created by the dress designer Mary Quant (Great Britain) in her store, Bazaar, on King's Road, London, England, in the spring of 1965.

Almost simultaneously, the fashion designer Courrèges (France) was creating a line that was very architectural, quite short and futuristic. Wearing Courrèges miniskirts, opaque tights and small helmets, fashionable women resembled astronauts. But his was an haute couture collection, whereas Mary Quant's skirts were enthusiastically taken up by a generation of young women.

Inflatable bikini (1992)

"Top Secret" is an inflatable bikini due to be launched in 1993. The designers, Hot Coles, applied for a U.S. patent in 1992. A small air pump inside the bikini bra connects to an inflatable lining in the bra cups. The pump fills air chambers in both sides of the bra and is adjustable. A release valve deflates the bra.

Tailoring and Sewing

Needle (antiquity)

The needle dates from prehistoric times. The first needles were made of fishbone or a piece of bone with an eye pierced in the middle or at the tip. Ivory needles have been discovered in Greece, and copper and bronze needles in Egypt. By 1370, Nuremberg, Germany was already a center of production for manufacturing burnished iron needles. These types of needles gained general circulation in France only in the mid-16th century, and in England in the 18th century.

Pin (1817)

While pins have been made for thousands of years, it was not until 1817 that Seth Hunt (U.S.) informed the Patent Office of his invention of an automatic machine for manufacturing one-piece pins, with body, head and point. His machine began operation in 1824, when Samuel Wright filed a patent in England. England had been the home of the industrial pin since John Tilsby had founded the first large pin works in Gloucester in 1625.

Hunt's machine was improved in 1838 by Henry Shuttleworth and Daniel Foote Taylor (both Great Britain) from Birmingham, England. Their pin was less dangerous.

Sewing machine (1830)

In 1830 Barthélémy Thimonnier (France) invented the first sewing machine to work in a regular and useful way. It already included all the elements of today's machines.

The following year Thimonnier set up a company in Paris making military uniforms. But he met with violent opposition from workers. Thimonnier had to return to his native town of Amplepuis, and to his trade as a tailor.

In 1834, at the same time as Thimonnier was carrying out his research, Walter Hunt (U.S.) designed a machine with two threads and a shuttle. Twelve years later Elias Howe replaced the hook on this machine by a needle with a hole.

In 1845 Thimonnier and his new partner Magnin made a second application for a patent for a machine that could do 200 stitches a minute and then, on August 5, 1848, another application for a machine made of metal, the *couso-brodeur*, which could do chain stitch. A little earlier Thimonnier had applied for a British patent, which he almost immediately gave over to a Manchester company. In 1849 Morey and Johnson (both Great Britain) bought an American patent. The American machine had a hooked needle, like Thimonnier's. In 1851 the Great Exhibition was held in London. By an unbelievable stroke of bad luck, the *couso-brodeur* arrived in London two days after the judges had examined the exhibits.

In 1851 Isaac Singer (U.S.) was the first to build and market a sewing machine for domestic use, in Boston, Massachusetts. His needle was taken from Howe's machine. Singer became far more famous than Thimonnier, who died a ruined man in 1857, after finally having the consolation of presenting his machine at the Universal Exhibition in Paris.

Safety pin (1849)

The invention of the modern safety pin is attributed to Walter Hunt (U.S.), who developed it in 1849. It appears that fibulas and brooches, used in ancient Crete to attach draped clothes, were made according to a related principle.

Snap fasteners (1886)

The snap fastener was invented on May 29, 1886 by an industrialist from Grenoble in France, Pierre-Albert Raymond. The patent was requested in the name of the company Raymond & Guttin, the latter being the co-inventor. The metal press-stud was initially used as a fastener in the local glove industry.

Many imitations were produced worldwide, but the company always fought to protect its patent and won its case. It extended its products to the international level, and is still in existence today.

Dry cleaning (1855)

The first dry cleaner's was founded in 1855 in Paris by J.-B. Jolly (France). He discovered the principle of dry cleaning accidentally when he tipped a bottle of turpentine over a dress. He noticed that the dress was not stained but, on the contrary, cleaned. Ludwig Anthelin of Leipzig, Germany made a further step forward in 1897. He discovered the use of carbon tetrachloride, which is much less flammable than turpentine. Unfortunately this product attacks the respiratory tract, so it was replaced in 1918 by trichlorethylene.

Accessories

Fan (antiquity)

The fan has been known since earliest antiquity. In ancient Egypt, fans were made from giant lotus leaves, and in Greece and Rome from peacock feathers. The folding fan appears toward the end of the 16th century.

Button (3000 B.C.)

An ancient invention, buttons have been discovered in the Indus Valley dating to 3000 B.C., and in Scotland dating to 2000 B.C. It was not until the Middle Ages that the button came to be used with a buttonhole as a fastening device; prior to that the button had merely been a decoration.

Umbrella (2nd century B.C.)

It would seem that the umbrella was a Chinese invention from as early as the 2nd century B.C. However, some claim that umbrellas were used a thousand years previously in Egypt as sun shades. The Greeks and the Romans were both using them in the 1st century A.D., but as a rain shield it was seen as a woman's item.

The umbrella was considered effeminate as recently as the mid-18th century, when Sir

Jean-Paul Balou has invented a funnel umbrella that not only keeps the holder dry, but catches the water as well. (Michael Jolyot Reims)

A close-up view of a strip of Velcro. The hooks were inspired by burdock seed heads. (Cosmos)

Jonas Hanway (Great Britain) began to popularize its usage for men. So, by the time of his death in 1786, they were often referred to as "Hanways" and their future was assured.

Zipper (1893)

Around 1890, Whitcomb Judson (U.S.) devised a quick zipper system based on interlocking small teeth. The idea was ingenious but its practical application not simple. Judson filed his patent on August 29, 1893 and entered into partnership with a lawyer, Lewis Walker, to found a company.

In 1905 machines to manufacture zippers were in operation, but their products were far from perfect. It was not until 1912 that Judson's invention provided full satisfaction to its users: this was due to the improvements made by Gideon Sundback (Sweden).

The American zipper was marketed by the Goodrich Company, which used it on snow boots.

Velcro (1948)

Velcro is a Swiss invention whose discovery dates from 1948. Returning from a day's hunting, the engineer Georges de Mestral noticed that burdock seed heads clung to his clothing. Under the microscope he discovered that each of these heads was surrounded by minute hooks allowing them to catch onto fabrics. It then occurred to him to fix similar hooks on fabric strips that would cling together and serve as fasteners.

Eight years were needed to develop the basic product: two nylon strips, one of which contained thousands of small hooks, and the other even smaller loops. When the two strips were pressed together, they formed a quick and practical fastener. The invention was named Velcro (from the French *velours*, velvet, and *crochet*, hook). It was patented worldwide in 1957.

BEAUTY AND COSMETICS

Mirror (antiquity)

The exact date of the invention of the mirror is unknown, but many mirrors have been discovered in the tombs of the pharaohs. The philosopher Aristotle (Greece, 384–322 B.C.) mentions in his writings the existence of glass mirrors lined with burnished metal. The invention of the crystalline mirror is attributed to the Venetians during the 18th century.

Perfume (antiquity)

Perfume originated in Asia and the Far East, but the exact dates are unknown. It is believed that cultural disciplines and the abundance of vegetation made experimentation with perfume possible in that part of the world. Initially, wood and scented resins were burnt on altars, and then perfumes were put into dishes to enhance the flavor of food or to act as an aphrodisiac.

The modern perfume industry was well developed in France by the 17th century. By the end of the 19th century perfumes were being produced from synthetic products.

Lipstick (17th century)

At the beginning of the 17th century, women colored their lips with a fairly harsh, slightly scented pomade, colored with the juice of black grapes and alkanet (dyers bugloss).

Later, cerates, a kind of salve, were produced that had a base of wax and oil. The same principle is used in the manufacture of Rosat, a product used to prevent lips from becoming sore and cracked.

In the 20th century, chemists came to the rescue of the cosmetologists. They succeeded in manufacturing sticks of rouge that were easily moulded and did not have any adverse effects on the lips or mouth.

Eau de Cologne (1709)

The Italian Farina family is credited with creating eau de Cologne in Germany in 1709. It was an alcohol-based mixture blended with fresh-smelling products like mint oil.

Hairsetting (c. 1870)

The modern set was invented by Lenthéric of France around 1870. The waves were no longer obtained by heating the hair with curling tongs, but by drying them with warm air. During the 1920s the Parisian hairstylist Rambaud realized the advantages of combining the techniques of the permanent wave and the set. After cutting and perming the hair, Rambaud rolled it and secured it with curling pins. It was then dried under a hot air drier.

The result was surprising. The hot air permanent applied on its own had produced tight little curls that had the advantage of not uncurling, but that were not particularly attractive. Rambaud had replaced it with a soft and loosely waving hairstyle.

Shampoo (1877)

The term *shampoo* originated in England in 1877. It was derived from *champo*, a word in Hindi that means "to massage" or "to knead."

Originally brewed by hairdressers, shampoos were made by boiling soft soap in soda water. It was not until after World War II that shampoos came into general popular use.

Vaseline (1879)

Robert Chesebrough, a chemist from Brooklyn, N.Y., became worried by the growth of the petroleum industry, which was threatening his own sales of kerosene. So he visited the oilfields of Pennsylvania and there discovered a gummy residue that stuck to the drilling bits. The workers had found one use for it—it encouraged a cut or a burn to heal quickly; otherwise it was a complete nuisance to them and hindered their work.

Chesebrough took some samples of the paste back to his home. There he tried it out and, having confirmed its healing qualities, began to manufacture it, calling it Vaseline Petroleum Jelly. It quickly became enormously popular and soon was being used not only for medicinal purposes but also as a cleaning agent, an anti-rust device and so on. So, by the time he died in 1933, his product was in use the world over.

Hot air perm (1906)

On October 8, 1906 Nestle, a German hairstylist living in London, England, demonstrated a new method of curling hair. He then went to live in the United States, where his new invention, permanent waving, was extremely successful.

Hair color (1909)

The first conclusive tests were carried out in 1909 by the chemist Eugène Schueller (France) based on the chemical paraphenylenediamine. He founded a company that in 1910 became L'Oréal. In 1927 the hairdressing industry was revolutionized by the invention of Imédia, a dye that was manufactured from organic coloring agents and that offered a wide range of natural shades.

Nivea cream (1911)

In 1911 a chemist from Hamburg, Germany, Paul Beiersdorf, invented a skin cream. It was marketed by the company he set up in 1882. The cream, which was white as snow, was called Nivea.

Hairdryer (1920)

The two earliest models appeared in Racine, Wisc. in 1920. They were the Race, made by the Racine Universal Motor Co., and the Cyclone, made by Hamilton Beach. They were manual models.

In the winter of 1951 Sears, Roebuck & Co. marketed the Ann Barton, the first helmeted model for home use.

Dry perfume (1984)

The first dry perfume was invented in 1984 by Franka Berger (France). In 1985 she commercialized it under her own name in America and Japan, where it was immediately successful.

In 1989 Berger invented the first mousse perfume for the body.

Hairstyle video (1988)

You can now see yourself on a screen with the hairstyle of your choice, without losing a single lock of hair. This has been made possible by the use of a video and a graphics sheet linked to a microcomputer, designed for use by professional hairstylists and beauticians and for beauty counseling. The Video-Look was invented in 1988 by Alain Saulnier (France).

HOME IMPROVEMENT

The hammer (prehistory)

This is one of the oldest tools. A stone may have been the first hammer. The first decisive improvement was the addition of a handle. The stone axe hammer of the Neolithic Age had a handle just as hammers do today. However, stone was a fragile material. It was not until the Bronze Age that the metallic hammer made its appearance and its widespread utility became understood.

Vise (prehistory)

The earliest vise is considered, rightly, to have been the human jaw (paleolithic). The primitive object itself was made of wood. At the end of the Bronze Age (c. 3500–c. 1200 B.C.) the discovery of the screw completed an invention that has survived broadly unchanged to the present day. It was greatly simplified by the discovery of iron (c. 1200 B.C.).

The first screw vises similar to ours seem to have appeared in the 14th century. They were perfected in the 16th and 17th centuries.

Saw (antiquity)

The saw would appear to have been invented by the Egyptians during the Bronze Age, around 3500 B.C. to 1200 B.C. Roman craftsmen produced a wide variety of saws, including the frame saw, which until the 14th century formed the basis for this type of equipment. The metal saw appeared in the 15th century.

Plane (c. 1200 B.C.)

The plane appeared during the Iron Age, around 1200 B.C. The earliest depictions date back to the Gallo–Roman era, in countries occupied or influenced by the Romans.

A variation of the plane, the trying-plane, is one of the earliest tools. The best preserved are those that were carefully worked, sculpted and polished between the 16th and the 18th centuries.

Brace (15th century)

The forerunners of the brace—that is, all tools used for piercing—existed in prehistoric times. The Egyptians used an instrument derived from the hand drill. The auger, which dates only to the middle of the Bronze Age, found its final form during the Iron Age.

The screw auger, from which the brace was developed, seems to have been used in Scandinavia from the 11th to 13th centuries, mainly on the structures of rivergoing vessels. The brace, in the form that we know it, appeared in the first quarter of the 15th century. The first known depiction of it is on the painting *The Annunciation* by Robert Campin, Master of Flémalle.

Screwdriver (17th century)

This is a tool that has been continually developed since it was first used at the end of the 17th century. The screw has become more important since the middle of the 19th century, with the development of machine tools. For a long time, producing screws was a laborious task since the grooves had to be filed by hand.

John Whitworth (Great Britain) was responsible for the standardization of the thread in 1841.

Nail (18th century)

The first machines to make nails date from the 18th century (patents of Ezekial Reed [U.S.] in 1786 and Thomas Clifford [Great Britain] in 1790). However, the artisan's nail goes back even further in time, since the oldest known nails were found in Mesopotamia and date from approximately 3500 B.C.

Electric hand drill (1917)

After developing presses for postage stamps, machines for attaching boot buttons and machines for printing banknotes, two young inventors, S. Duncan Black and Alonso G. Decker (both U.S.) revolutionized the do-it-yourself field in 1917 by manufacturing the first rotary hand drill. Their portable drill weighed 24 lb. After World War II much lighter and greatly improved hand drills enjoyed a rapid and widespread popularity, to the point of becoming a basic and indispensable item for all do-it-yourself enthusiasts.

Portable workshop (1968)

The Workmate, a portable workshop, was developed by Ronald P. Hickman and Michael J. Roos (both U.S.) in 1968. The Workmate was designed to be a stable workbench that can be equipped with all the traditional tools and accessories, yet can be folded up and transported from room to room. Marketed by Black and Decker since 1977, the Workmate has been an enormous success worldwide.

Gas-operated drill (1986)

This new wireless hand drill was invented in 1986 by the Japanese company Tanaka Kogyo. It has a two-stroke engine, a fuel tank, and is completely safe to use, even in damp weather. The absence of electrical wiring makes it safe and easy to use.

Pouring lip for paint (1987)

The pouring lip was invented in 1987 by the American company Spill Bill, and makes life a lot easier for painters and do-it-yourself enthusiasts. It is made of flexible plastic and fits onto the rim of the paint can once the lid has been removed. The paint can be poured easily and cleanly into another receptacle and the brush can be rested on it without the paint running down the side of the can. Once the paint is dry, it is easily removed from the lip.

BUSINESS AND COMMERCE

Money and Banking

Bill of exchange (4th century B.C.)

In the 4th century B.C. the Greeks invented the bill of exchange. Isocrates' (436–388 B.C.) *Discourse on Banking* bears witness; he refers to this means of payment as allowing one to travel without taking along large sums of money.

Travelers handed over a sum of money to their local banker. In return, the banker gave them a letter. Upon presentation of this letter to a banker at the traveler's destination, the traveler would be given the money required.

The bill of exchange was the forerunner of the banknote.

Coins (7th century B.C.)

Coining, i.e. the affixing of an official mark to a gold ingot, was invented in the middle of the 7th century B.C. in Asia Minor during the reign of Ardys, king of Lydia.

The coins were small ingots made of a mixture of gold and silver known as *electrum*, found in its natural state in the river that flowed through Sardis, the capital of Lydia. The name of the river, the Pactolus, later became synonymous with abundance and wealth.

The first coins to be made from this mixture were shaped like flattened pellets. On one side they bore a triangular or square hallmark and on the obverse side, an Assyrian-style lion whose nose was decorated with a sort of shining globe.

Stock exchange (c. 1450)

The stock exchange—that is, a place where financial transactions occur—was created about 1450. Until then, merchants and bankers got together at fairs. In the middle of the 15th century, a family of bankers in Bruges, Belgium, the Van de Bursens, opened its house to these transactions. Over the entrance portal was a frontispiece depicting three engraved purses. Antwerp opened an exchange in 1487, and it soon became the largest in Europe. Sir Thomas Gresham (Great Britain, c. 1519–79) founded the Royal Exchange in London in 1568; it became known as the Stock Exchange in 1773.

Banknotes (1658)

Originally, bankers at medieval fairs delivered registered receipts to their depositors. Then, in about 1587 in Venice, it became possible to transfer these receipts through the practice of endorsement. It was this endorsement that helped spread the use of paper money.

The first bank to issue banknotes was the Riksbank of Stockholm in 1658. The Bank of England was founded in 1694.

Traveler's check (1891)

The traveler's check was invented in 1891 by American Express. The first check was countersigned on August 5, 1891 and the system spread rapidly throughout Europe, contributing to the development of tourism and international exchanges.

Credit card (1950)

The first company to organize payment by credit card was founded by Ralph Schneider (U.S.) in 1950. The first 200 members of the Diners Club were able to dine on credit in 27 New York restaurants. The Bank of America was the first to introduce a bank credit card, the Bankamericard, in 1958.

Business

Department stores (1824)

The first department store was the *Belle Jardinière*, founded in Paris in 1824 by Pierre Parissot. His publicity and sales methods revolutionized commercial practice. He insisted that his merchandise be sold at "a fixed price and for cash," whereas trade had always been based on two main principles: the negotiation of the price between the seller and the buyer, and buying on credit. Harper's Building, designed by the architect John B. Corlies, opened in New York in 1854, followed in 1858 by the Crystal Palace Bazaar, the first department store to be opened in London.

Mail order (1850)

Direct mail-order sales date back to the 17th century. But it was not until about 1850, when postal charges came down, that the practice became widespread. Mail-order catalogs appeared simultaneously in France (Manufacture des Armes et Cycles of Saint-Etienne) and in the United States (Sears Roebuck).

Supermarkets (1879)

The first stores of this type were born in the United States in 1879. In those days, they had a plain and rather drab appearance, not at all like the wide-aisled, well-lit stores today.

Cash register (1879)

The cash register was invented by James J. Ritty (U.S.) on November 4, 1879. He owned a saloon in Dayton, Ohio, and the constant quarrels with his customers exasperated him.

During a boat trip to Europe, he noticed a machine that registered the number of times a propeller turned. This machine triggered the idea for his cash register, which served both as a printing–adding machine and a till.

Counter displays (1913)

The counter display was invented by Edward J. Noble (U.S.), a candy salesman. Noble and his partner, J. Roy Allen, had bought the patent to Life–Savers candies, but the product was not selling as well as Noble had hoped. To help spur sales, Noble had the idea of creating a counter display so that retailers could position the candies next to their cash registers. The ploy proved successful.

Car rental (1918)

Car rental was introduced in 1918 by a second-hand car dealer from Chicago. He rented out 12 vehicles. His company was bought in 1923 by the president of a Chicago taxicab company, John D. Hertz, who renamed the unsteady business the Hertz Self-Drive System.

Franchising (1932)

Franchising was invented by Howard Johnson (U.S.). Johnson owned a small drugstore in Wollaston, Mass., where he sold his own brand of ice cream, which proved very popular. As a result of the success of his ice cream, Johnson converted his store into a restaurant and purchased another store. Johnson believed that a chain of restaurants nationwide would be popular stops for travelers, but he was unable to finance his plan. Instead he decided to sell his techniques to other restaurants. They would use his name and buy his specialties against a royalty. The first franchised restaurant opened in Cape Cod, Mass. in 1932.

Shopping cart (1937)

In Oklahoma City, Okla., the owner of the Humpty Dumpty Store invented the first shopping cart on June 4, 1937. He had noticed that his customers had trouble lugging all their purchases through the different departments. He converted folding chairs into cars: the feet were mounted on wheels, a basket replaced the seat, and the back served to push the vehicle.

McDonald's (1948)

In 1940 Maurice and Richard McDonald (both U.S.) set up a hamburger stand next to their movie house in Pasadena, Calif. In 1948 they had the idea of making it self-service, stressing the quality of the hamburgers served there.

By 1952 they were known throughout southern California, where they had set up several branches. Ray Kroc, a restaurant equipment contractor, offered to sell franchises for them throughout the country. In 1962, when 200 branches had been opened, Kroc bought the McDonalds' share. Today there are McDonald's franchises in over 50 countries.

TV shopping (1985)

The first television shopping channels were introduced in the United States in 1985. Viewers are invited to phone in their orders for items shown on the screen.

Alarms, Identification and Security Devices

Lock (antiquity)

The oldest locks seem to have first appeared in ancient Egypt. These massive locks made of hard wood worked using combinations of cylindrical pins of different lengths, which fitted into grooves cut in immobile components that acted as keys.

Safety locks (18th century)

Safety locks date from the 18th century (Robert Barron's throat lock in 1778, the pump lock by Joseph Bramah [both Great Britain] in 1784). They were perfected in the 19th century, notably by Alexandre Fichet (unhookable lock patented in 1829 and 1836). Charles-Louis Sterlin and Eugène Bricard (two-bolted lock, 1829) and Linus Yale (pin lock, called the Yale lock, patented May 6, 1851, which was inspired by the ancient Egyptian locks).

The skeleton key was first displayed at the Chicago Exhibition in 1894 by Alfred and Jules Bricard.

Safe (1844)

In 1844, Alexandre Fichet (France), a locksmith, invented the first modern safe. Previously, strong boxes with secret compartments had been used, but they were not fire-resistant and could be stolen. Fichet had been working on his idea for some time, having applied for a

This video screen shopping cart provides the shopper with a recipe for any meal, and a directory of where the ingredients can be found in the store. (Cosmos/Woodfin Camp-Abramson)

patent for a burglarproof lock for this invention in 1829.

Fingerprints (1892)

Identification by fingerprinting was invented by Sir Francis Galton (Great Britain, 1822–1911) in 1892.

Eye prints (1984)

"Eye Printing" was launched in September 1984 by the American company Eye Dentify. It is a rapid system of identification by a retinal image that sweeps the back of the eye, and allows a more accurate identification than by the standard fingerprinting method.

Falcon Eye (1985)

The Falcon Eye, named after its inventor, Bob Falconer (U.S.), is an automatic light that comes on when it detects a human presence, illuminating an area of up to 2,700 sq ft, and switches off when the room is empty. Invented in 1985 and patented in 1988, this light is equipped with an infrared detector adjusted to the frequencies of the human body. It cannot be activated accidentally by a pet or any other source of heat, and it only comes on if there is insufficient natural light. The Falcon Eye is a useful burglar deterrent, energy saver and aid for the handicapped as well as a general household convenience.

IDX 70 (1987)

The IDX 70 system was produced by the American company Identix in 1987. This is a system for the identification of fingerprints, recorded on a memory card. The invention is based on a process known as global vision developed by researchers at the University of California at Berkeley and Rockwell International for the FBI in 1962.

Palm Recognition System (1987)

A device based on the geometry of the hand, known as the Palm Recognition System, was developed by the Japanese company Mitsubishi in 1987.

Securiscan (1987)

Securiscan is a remote-controlled electronic system for the home that was launched by Thomson in 1987. Thanks to a tiny computer the size of a radio, you can switch on the central heating, the garden hose and household appliances. It also provides surveillance of the home and sends a telephone warning in the case of a breakdown, flood or fire, while speakers for relaying spoken messages and an alarm system make Securiscan a burglar deterrent.

Anti-asphyxia alarm (1988)

In 1988 two American doctors, Kurt Shuler and Gerhard Schrauser (both U.S.), horrified by the increasing number of accidents caused by carbon monoxide, developed a series of alarms using warning lights that come on when the level of CO in the air becomes dangerous. These are the world's first battery-operated alarms that can work anywhere.

THE OFFICE

Typewriters

Origins (17th century)

Various descriptions of ancient typewriters have been uncovered, dating as far back as the "two-quill mannual system" created by William Petty (Ireland) in the 17th century. On January 7, 1714, Queen Anne of England granted a patent to Henry Mill for a "machine capable of replacing handwriting by the printing of letters similar to those used in print shops." As far as is known, Mill never built the machine. In the 19th century various prototypes were designed, generally to aid blind people. One of the best known was that built by Pellegrini Turri (Italy) for Countess Caroline Frantoni, who was blind, in 1808. Several letters between the two still exist, but no details of the construction of Turri's "typewriter" are known.

First modern typewriter (1833)

The first modern typewriter, also conceived for the blind, was invented in 1833 by Xavier Progin (France). It featured a circular basket of bars bearing characters that converged and struck at the same point.

Typewriter ribbon (1841)

The familiar inked ribbon was devised by Alexander Bain (Great Britain) in 1841.

First marketed typewriter (1870)

In 1870, Malling Hansen (Denmark) had the first typewriter built that was intended for commercial production. Built by Jurgens, a mechanical company in Copenhagen, it was marketed in October 1870 under the name Skrivekugle.

Remington Model I (1874)

Christopher Latham Sholes (U.S.) devised the idea of a "literary piano" in the early 1870s. He built more than 30 models before perfecting the machine, with the help of James Densmore (U.S.). They sold the machine to rifle manufacturer Remington Small Arms, which marketed it as the Remington Model I in 1874.

Portable typewriter (1889)

In 1889, George C. Blickensderfer (U.S.) built the first portable typewriter. Known as "the Blick," the machine was stored in a case.

Chester Carlson invented the process of xerography in 1938, when he was just 32. (Rank Xerox)

Electric typewriter (1901)

Dr. Thaddeus Cahill (U.S.) developed an electric typewriter in 1901. The company he created went bankrupt after having built 40 models at a unit cost of $3,925.

Electromatic (1933)

After 11 years of research and experimentation, R.G. Thomson (U.S.) built the Electromatic. The machine was successfully launched by IBM in 1933.

Electronic typewriter (1965)

IBM launched the 72BM in 1965. The 72BM was the first typewriter with a memory, which was stored on magnetic tape. In 1972 Rank Xerox developed the first electronic typewriter with a live memory. This machine also featured the first daisy wheel, which was invented by Dr. Andrew Gabor (U.S.). In 1978 the Italian company Olivetti and the Japanese company Casio marketed the first electronic typewriters with rapid-access memories. They featured "type wheels" rather than balls.

Keyless typewriter (1984)

In 1984 the Japanese company Matsushita produced the first typewriter without keys. The Panaword keyboard that operates the machine is a sensitive sheet. The "typist" writes messages by hand, on a screen.

Silent typewriter (1989)

In 1989 Dr. Andrew Gabor perfected the first silent typewriter at the Xerox Palo Alto Research Center (PARC). Marketed as the Xerox Piano, the machine was launched in 1990.

Photocopying

Carbon paper (1806)

Carbon paper, used to obtain several copies from one document, was invented by R. Wedgwood (Great Britain), who patented it on October 7, 1806. The process he described employed a thin sheet of paper saturated with ink and dried between sheets of blotting paper.

Photocopy (1903)

Photocopying refers to the process of rapid reproduction of a document by the instantaneous development of a photo negative. It was invented by G.C. Beidler (U.S.) in 1903. Beidler, an office clerk, noticed the constant need for copies of documents, so he developed a machine for replacing laborious manual or typed copies and patented it in 1906. The first photocopy machine was marketed by the American company Rectrigraph in 1907, but it was not until the 1960s that the photocopier became commonplace.

Xerography (1938)

On October 22, 1938 Chester Carlson (U.S., 1906–68) produced the first xerographic image (from the Greek *xeros*, meaning dry, and *graphein*, to write). He called the new process Xerography and patented it after several improvements had been made. Between 1939

and 1944, 20 companies refused his patents. In 1944 the Battelle Memorial Institute, a non-profit-making organization based in Columbus, Ohio, signed an agreement with Carlson and began to develop xerography.

In 1947 Battelle signed an agreement with a small photographic business, Haloid, which later became Xerox.

In 1959 the first photocopier, the Xerox 914, was brought onto the market.

For a long time Xerox had no competition in the photocopying market, making $15 billion in 1987, but in the last few years its virtual monopoly has been threatened by the Japanese. Toshiba, for example, makes machines that can produce 100 copies per minute.

Color photocopier (1973)

The Japanese company Canon developed the first color photocopier, which was brought out in Japan in 1973.

Pocket photocopier (1986)

This tiny, extra-light photocopier, the KX Z40X, is an ideal size, barely 6.2 in. long by 2.7 in. wide. It was developed by Panasonic in 1986. It can reproduce any kind of document and operates for up to 20 minutes. It has no wires, no batteries and can be recharged from a storage battery.

Other Office Equipment

Paper clip (1900)

The paper clip, a metallic clip that allows one to attach sheets of paper together, was invented in 1900 by Johann Waaler (Norway), who patented his invention in Germany.

Scotch tape (1925)

Dick Drew (U.S.) invented adhesive tape in 1925. Then a young assistant at the 3M laboratory in St. Paul, Minn., Drew asked car manufacturers to test the first samples of waterproof adhesive paper. At that time, car-body builders had to paint cars in two tones. Paint was applied by spray gun, and the difficult part was to separate the colors clearly and distinctly. Glued-together newspapers were used, but it often happened that when the bands were removed, the fresh paint also came off. Drew studied the problem and, with the encouragement of management, sought a solution: adhesive masking tape. Five years later cellulose adhesive tape appeared.

The name Scotch tape arose because initially only the edges of it were self-adhesive. Car-body workers, who were asked to use it, suspected that this was done to save glue and money, rather than to make it easier to stick on and peel off. So they called it Scotch tape, maligning the reputation of the Scots.

This spiral escalator serves 10 floors. Enough to make even the most avid shopper's head spin! (Gamma-Liaison/Boyd)

"Post-it" notes (1981)

This invention has invaded our daily lives, in the office, at home, everywhere. It was invented purely by chance in 1970. Dr. Spencer Sylver of 3M was involved in research on a completely different product when he discovered an adhesive that "sticks without sticking." He sent samples of his discovery to other laboratories in the 3M group, but no use could be found for this surprising product.

It was not until 10 years later than Arthur Fry, another research worker in the 3M group, found a use for what was to become the Post-it, again purely by chance. He was a member of a choir and was trying to find a way of marking the pages of his music book without damaging the paper. And this was why, in 1980, he put a thin layer of this famous "unknown" adhesive onto the page markers of his score . . . and it worked! The little pastel-colored pieces of paper that stick, unstick and can be re-stuck at will came into being. The name Post-it was invented in 1981.

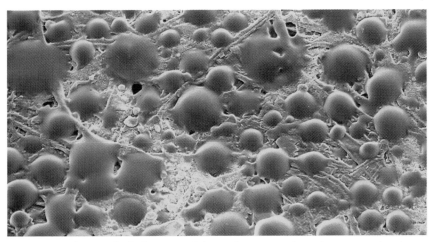

A microscopic photograph of a Post-it note. Spheres of resin are sunk into the paper, and each time the paper is pressed, bubbles burst and glue is released. (Cosmos)

BUILDING FACILITIES

Elevator (1743)

The first known elevator was built at the Palace of Versailles, France in 1743 for King Louis XV. It was installed on the outside of the building, and enabled Louis to go from his apartments (on the first floor) to those of his mistress, Mme. de Châteauroux (on the second). Using a system of counterweights, it was possible to move the elevator without too much effort.

Fire extinguisher (1816)

In 1816 Capt. George Manby (Great Britain) developed a fire extinguisher that worked using compressed air. The first fire extinguisher using a chemical base was invented in 1868 by François Carlier (France). His extinguisher contained bicarbonate of soda and water. A bottle filled with sulfuric acid was attached inside, near the cap. To use the extinguisher, one had to break the bottle, thus freeing the sulfuric acid. A chemical reaction produced carbonic acid, which forced the water out.

In 1905 Alexander Laurent (1905) experimented with mixing a solution of aluminum sulfate and bicarbonate of soda with a stabilizing agent. The bubbles so formed contained carbonic acid. They floated on oil, gasoline or paint and prevented contact with the air, thus with oxygen.

Mechanical elevator (1829)

The first elevator of this type was built in London in the Coliseum in Regent's Park, in 1829. It could carry 10 passengers. The public was invited to go up to visit a replica of the dome of St. Paul's Cathedral and admire a panorama depicting London. It was thus more of a tourist attraction than a means of locomotion.

Otis elevator (1857)

The first elevator installed in a department store began operation on March 23, 1857 in New York. It was built by Elisha Graves Otis (U.S.) for R.V. Haughwout & Co., a five-floor store on Broadway. Otis had already introduced the first safety elevator with a brake in 1852 in New York.

Hydraulic elevator (1867)

Léon Edoux (France, 1827–1910) installed two lifting devices using hydraulic pistons 69 feet high at the Paris Exhibition in 1867. He called them *ascenseurs* (elevators).

The lifts using hydraulic pistons, which became widespread in the United States after 1879, went 20 times faster than Otis's 1857 elevator. Their development was stalled by the difficulty of digging very deep foundations. Nevertheless, in 1889 Edoux managed to build an elevator that traveled 525 feet up the Eiffel Tower.

Electric elevator (1880)

The first electric elevator was built by the German company Siemens & Halske, for the Mannheim Industrial Exhibition in 1880. It reached a height of 72 feet in 11 seconds. In one month it carried 8,000 passengers to the top of an observation tower overlooking the exhibition.

Escalator (1892)

The escalator was the invention of two men: Jesse W. Reno and George H. Wheeler (both U.S.). The escalator was originally designed as a sloped moving conveyor, which proved too dangerous. Reno perfected the conveyor by replacing it with movable stairs. He patented his invention on March 15, 1892. He subsequently designed ribbed platforms that passed through the teeth of a comb fixed to the ridge of each step.

The name *escalator* was coined by Charles D. Seeberger (U.S.) in 1899. The first public escalator was used at the 1900 Universal Exhibition in Paris, before being installed in the United States in Gimbel's Department Store in Philadelphia. From 1922 onward Reno and Wheeler's escalator was installed in numerous stores and offices.

The first spiral escalator was put into operation in 1985 in a Japanese store by the Mitsubishi Electric Corp.

Escape chute (1972)

Gerard Zephinie (France) designed an original method for evacuating 25 to 35 people from a building in the event of a fire: the escape chute. The device was patented in 1972 and is manufactured by the Otis Company. It consists of a concentric fiber sheath. Escapees slide into it; their fall is braked by the body's friction against the elastic walls.

LEISURE

Calendar

Origins (antiquity)

The earliest known calendars were devised in ancient Egypt and were based on the lunar cycle of 29½ days. The months began with the full moon and had alternately 29 and 30 days. Egyptian society was an agricultural one, and the lunar calendar was dropped in favor of a solar system, since this better reflected the seasons, and thus the harvest.

Julian calendar (45 B.C.)

The Romans initially used a calendar based on 10 lunar months, known as the calendar Romulus, and it is from this calendar that we get the names of the months. Numa Pompolius was responsible for adding two more months and creating a 355-day year. Periodically the Romans adjusted their calendar to the solar year, which led to a great deal of confusion. In 45 B.C. Julius Caesar finally revised the calendar. The Greek astronomer Sosigenes of Alexandria advised Julius Caesar. The new calendar, known as the Julian calendar, was independent of the moon, and comprised months of 30 and 31 days, and leap years, like the present one.

Gregorian calendar (1582)

The Julian calendar required that one day be subtracted every 128 years, in order to be in perfect harmony with the sun. In 1582 Pope Gregory XIII decided to subtract all at once the 10 days accumulated since the Roman era, so Thursday October 4, 1582 was followed by Friday October 15, 1582. The Gregorian calendar is so precise that it is only one day off every 3,000 years.

Driving

Traffic lights (1868)

The first traffic light was set up at the junction of Bridge Street and Palace Yard in London, England on December 10, 1868. It was a gaslight mounted at the top of a 23-foot steel pole. One side was red and the other green, and a lever system made it rotate. Red meant "Stop" and green meant "Be careful." The light proved dangerous—a policeman was badly injured when it exploded as he was turning it.

The first electric traffic light was set up at Alfred A. Benesch's insistence at the junction of 105th Street and Euclid Avenue in Cleveland, Ohio on August 5, 1914. The manufacturer, the Traffic Signal Co. of Cleveland, had fitted the light with a bell that rang when the color changed. The first three-color traffic light was installed in New York City in 1918.

Automobile registration (1893)

The first numbered plates were introduced in Paris, France in 1893.

Parking meters (1935)

The first 150 parking meters were put into operation on July 16, 1935 in Tulsa, Okla. A journalist, Carlton Magee (U.S.), had devised the parking meter system and shortly afterward founded the first company that was to build them, the Dual Parking Meter Co.

Relaxation

Pipe (prehistory)

Pipes were already in use in prehistoric times. Archeologists have unearthed various models in clay or iron. In Mexico, it was long customary to hand out ready-filled pipes at the end of meals to guests. In Europe, the pipe was first established in England. At first made of terracotta, pipes began to be made of wood toward the end of the 18th century.

Sauna (1st century B.C.)

The principle of the sauna was conceived in Finland in response to the need for relaxation and body hygiene. The most recent research shows that its origin dates to c. 2000 B.C. Initially the sauna was a hole in the ground containing a pile of stones that could be heated. Water was thrown over the stones and transformed into steam. When the sauna became a building adjacent to the main house, it also served as a place for drying meat and grain.

Cigarette (16th century)

The cigarette was invented by beggars in Seville, Spain, at the end of the 16th century. They had the idea of rolling the tobacco salvaged from cigar butts inside a small cylinder of paper. Cigarette use spread to Portugal, Italy, England and France. The first commercial cigarette factory opened in Havana, Cuba in 1853.

Metal detector (1931)

Treasure hunters scouring the beach with beeping metal detectors are a familiar sight. These instruments were invented in 1931 by Gerhard Fisher (U.S.) and were originally intended for industrial and geological use. The chance discovery of some coins dating to the Civil War opened up a whole new dimension for Fisher's product. Extensive design modifications have been made to the detector.

Sun-tan parasol (1984)

In 1984 John Sear (Great Britain) developed a sunshade that makes it possible to sunbathe while providing protection from the sun. The sun-tan parasol is made from Solmax, a filter screen invented in 1982 by J.A. Cuthbert (Great Britain). Tests have proved that this filter, in violet-colored plastic, will, as long as it retains its color, exclude 90 percent of the sun's harmful rays while letting through 75 percent of the UVA rays that tan the skin. In this way it eliminates the risks of sunburn and sore and inflamed eyes.

Beach-towel clamp (1989)

A beach towel spread on the sand is disturbed by the slightest gust of wind and by every movement made. Inventor Christiane Caillat-Maillefer (Switzerland) devised a clamp to hold the towel firmly in place. Patented in 1989, the beach-towel clamp is a single piece of plastic, consisting of a peg, which holds the towel, and a spike with a rough surface, which is planted in the sand.

WHAT ON EARTH?

NOT ALL INVENTIONS CHANGE OUR LIVES, SOME JUST MAKE US SCRATCH OUR HEADS.

BUZZ TOPPER

▲ The "Bee-bee," designed by Carisa Traut, is a novel way of gaining a swarm of attention. Note: The bee earrings are optional. (Gamma-Liaison/Budge)

A HELPING HAND

For all those waiters rushed off their feet, Philip Garner (U.S.) has invented this helping hand. Although unable to snap fingers for the busboy, it is ambidextrous. (Streetporter)

CONVERTIBLE TABLE

The Espace table invented by Armand Faber (France) converts into four types: a low, square occasional table (left), a dining table capable of seating eight people (below), a bridge table, and a long occasional table. (Le Livre Mondial des Inventions)

THE INDUCTION TABLE

Right: The Induction Table is an extraordinary cooking table that does not actually heat up. Food is cooked in normal utensils, such as a frying pan, that create a magnetic field on contact with the table. The accumulated magnetic energy heats the frying pan and cooks the food. Since the table itself does not heat up, people can't burn themselves. Also, the microchip that controls the table can tell the difference between a frying pan and a fork, and will not heat the fork. Thomson launched the Induction Table in 1991 and has taken out 17 patents to protect it. (Thomson)

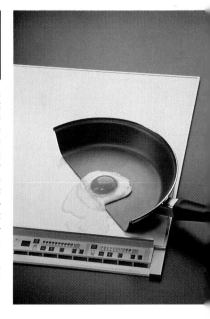

New ideas that may change the way we live

DISPOSABLE COFFEE PERCOLATOR

Kraft General Foods received a U.S. patent for a disposable coffee percolator in 1992. Designed by Maxwell House engineers Warren Rehman and Saul Katz, the invention allows a single cup of coffee to be brewed in a microwave oven in one to three minutes. The device, which looks like an oversize cup, operates in the same manner as a normal percolator. A special lid prevents the coffee granules from being damaged. When the coffee is brewed, the percolator pipe, its pedestal, and the granules basket are all thrown out.

OZONE WASHING MACHINE

Developed by a team of engineers at Tri-O-Clean Laundry Systems, Inc. of Fort Pierce, Fla., the Tri-O-Clean system is a new washing machine system that cleans clothing without using detergent or hot water, and doesn't drain the water away, but recycles it. Intended for commercial use by large institutions such as hospitals, prisons and hotels, the Tri-O-Clean system uses ozone to clean the wash. An electrical generator pumps ozone into the machine during the wash cycle. The ozone breaks down the organic molecules that comprise the stains, dirt and other marks on the laundry, and the force of the water washes the molecules away, leaving the clothes clean. A filter system removes the dirt from the waste water, allowing the water to be recycled. Hot water is not used because the ozone molecules break apart more rapidly at higher temperatures, which would make the system ineffective. A U.S. patent for the system was issued in 1992.

MICROWAVE CLOTHES DRYER

American Micro-Tech, Inc. is developing a microwave clothes dryer. In June 1992 Southern California Edison announced that it had tested a prototype that met U.S. Department of Energy standards. The device, covered by patents in Canada, Japan and the United States, uses 10 percent less energy than conventional electric dryers, operating at lower temperatures with shorter running cycles. Commercial development is some years away.

The Tri-O-Clean laundry system uses ozone to clean the wash. The organic molecules in stains are broken down by the ozone and washed away by the force of the water. (Tri-O-Clean)

COMMODE CONTROL

Spurred by new regulations concerning bathroom water usage, the Neo Rest tankless toilet has been developed by Toto Kiki of Japan. The toilet is designed to reduce the amount of water flushed at one time to 1.6 gallons rather than the typical 3.5 to 5. A microcomputer regulates the volume of water flushed. In addition, a push-button panel allows the user to control such amenities as seat temperature, air freshness, bidet functions and even the raising and lowering of the seat. Toto hopes to market the toilet in the United States in 1993.

E-LAMP LIGHT BULB

The E-Lamp light bulb represents a potential revolution in light bulb technology: the bulb lasts 14 years, uses only a quarter of the electricity used by a conventional incandescent light bulb and fits into regulation household sockets. In the mid-1970s, physicist Don Hollister invented Induction Lighting Technology, from which he developed the E-Lamp. The E-Lamp has no filament; a high-frequency radio signal, generated by a special magnetic coil fixture, converts gas inside the lamp to a plasma that emits an invisible light that reacts with the lamp's phosphorus coating to create visible light. The bulb is not expected to be available for domestic use for some time, but Intersource hopes to start industrial production next year for bulbs to be used by utility companies.

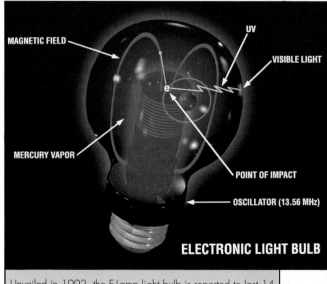

MAGNETIC FIELD
UV
VISIBLE LIGHT
MERCURY VAPOR
POINT OF IMPACT
OSCILLATOR (13.56 MHz)

ELECTRONIC LIGHT BULB

Unveiled in 1992, the E-Lamp light bulb is reported to last 14 years and uses a quarter of the electricity of a conventional incandescent light bulb. (Intersource Technology)

SYMMETRICAL TANNING

In 1992 Alan H. Swing received a U.S. patent for a beach towel that includes a device that indicates the direction of the sun. This beach towel sundial notifies the sunbather of changes in the angle of the sun, allowing the sunbather to move the towel during the day so that the maximum tanning rays are soaked up: a technique Swing calls "symmetrical tanning."

GAMES, TOYS AND SPORTS

GAMES

Board Games

Senet (2nd millenium B.C.)

Senet was the most popular game in ancient Egypt. Ancient scrolls attest to the game's popularity among peasants, artisans and even the pharaohs. A representation of the playing board is depicted on the tomb of Ramses III (1198–1166 B.C.), and the game itself has been found in the sepulcher of Tutankhamen (1370–1352 B.C.).

Alquerque (1200 B.C.)

The forerunner to checkers, alquerque is one of the earliest-known board games; a version was discovered in an Egyptian temple at Kurna that was built in 1200 B.C. The game came into Europe through Spain, introduced by Arab merchants, who called it El'quirkat. Alquerque is mentioned in *The Book of Games* (1283) by Alphonso X, and was popular in France during the Middle Ages.

Backgammon (antiquity)

Types of backgammon are among the most ancient of games. A game board uncovered during excavation of the ancient city of Ur is suitable for playing backgammon, but historians have been unable to prove a link. It is believed that backgammon was played by the Greeks and Romans. In the 10th century the board was changed to its current configuration, and this is often referred to as the origin of the modern game.

Go (1000 B.C.)

Tradition has it that the game of go was invented 3000 years ago by the Chinese Emperor Yao to encourage his children to think logically. Go was introduced to Japan via Korea toward the mid-8th century, and it was in Japan that it had its greatest success. The object of the game is to capture one's opponent's territory.

Go was at its peak of popularity in the 17th century, and a former Buddhist monk named Hon Inbosansa, a go champion, founded an official go academy in Edo (Toyko), Japan.

Chess (6th century)

The earliest mention of the game of chess is made by Karnamak (Persia, 590–628). The game seems to have originated in northern India, around the year 500, but the rules we use today were established in Europe around 1550. The 16 pieces—king, queen, bishop, knight, rook or castle and pawns—are arranged on a checkered board with 64 squares and maneuvered against the opponent.

The expression "checkmate" comes from a phonetic deformation of the Arabic phrase *al shâh mat*, which means "the king is dead."

Monopoly. (Parker Bros.)

Monopoly (1934): Charles B. Darrow

Monopoly used to be a simple word of Greek origin that meant "owning everything." Now it has another definition in *Webster's*: a trademark for a board game. Surely no one who has grown up since 1934 can hear that word without thinking of little green houses and red hotels (in wood or plastic, depending on the age of your set).

It's hard to believe that when Charles B. Darrow first presented Monopoly to executives at Parker Brothers, it was turned down unanimously. It broke the cardinal rules of board games: It was too long. The rules were too complicated. Worst of all, it had no clear-cut conclusion.

With help from a printer friend, Darrow produced the game on his own. After he had sold 5,000 sets to Wanamaker's of Philadelphia, a department store, Parker Brothers reconsidered. By early 1935, 20,000 sets a week were produced.

Parker Brothers figured the game would be a short-lived adult fad, not suited to children at all. It was only successful, they thought, because the Depression made get-rich-quick fantasies so attractive. In 1936, co-founder George Parker ordered production ceased. Yet Christmas yielded huge profits, and sales continued up from there.

Before long, Darrow was the world's first millionaire game designer. His game had innocent beginnings—the streets of his favorite seaside resort, Atlantic City, New Jersey. Marven (actual spelling) Gardens was borrowed from the nearby town of Margate. Three of the railroads were named for train lines that brought vacationers to Atlantic City; the Short Line was named for the local bus company.

Since 1935 an estimated 250 million people have played Monopoly on more than 85 million sets sold worldwide. Monopoly is licensed in 32 countries, and translated into 19 languages as well as Braille. Foreign editions use their own currencies, and property names are taken from popular cities. In England, Boardwalk is Mayfair; in Germany it's Schlossallee; in France it's Rue de la Paix. Any way it's expensive!

Politically speaking, Monopoly stands for capitalism. As such, the anticapitalist nations disapprove. Fidel Castro once ordered all Cuban Monopoly sets destroyed. But Monopoly remains overwhelmingly popular: the six sets displayed at the 1959 American National Exhibition in Moscow mysteriously disappeared.

Stateside, Monopoly is the center of enormous competitions and record-setting events. The game has been played under water (at the New England Aquarium), and a set has been specially engineered for space flights. There has even been a $600 set made of chocolate.

Monopoly remains the backbone of Parker Brothers, which provides services ranging from replacing parts to advising antique collectors to officiating and clarifying rules. Let us provide them a service in return by stating once and for all: When you land on Free Parking, you don't win any money. It's simply a place to rest.

Previous page: Dirt bike skateboarding. (Gamma)

Checkers (16th century)

It is not known when checkers was first devised, but it is believed to be derived from the ancient game of alquerque. It is argued that checkers was played by the Greeks and Romans. The earliest-known book on checkers was written by Antonia Torquemada (Spain) in 1547. The game was popular in Spain, and in 1650 Juan Garcia Canalejas published a book of strategy that is still used today. The rules and size of the board vary among countries. In the United States the checkerboard consists of 64 squares and 12 pieces per player.

Scrabble (1948)

In 1948 James Brunot of Newton, Conn. patented the game of Scrabble. The source of his patent was a game called Criss-cross, in which players had to make up crosswords on a piece of cardboard using wooden letters. Criss-cross was invented in 1931 by Alfred M. Butts to keep himself amused after losing his job in the Depression. It was not until Brunot came along that Butts saw the commmercial potential. By 1953 over a million sets had sold.

Othello (1974)

Goro Hasegawa invented the game of Othello in Japan in 1974. This game of strategy, which pits two players against each other, consists not in eliminating an opponent's men by removing them from the board (as in chess or checkers), but in turning them over to take possession of them. Othello, which also exists in an electronic form, is the most widely played game in Japan after the game of go.

Trivial Pursuit (1981)

Invented in 1981 by three young Canadians, Chris and John Haney and Scott Abbott, this game tests general knowledge of geography, history, art and literature, sports, science and entertainment. From two to 36 players may take part at a time, but the game is usually played by six people. The game was a huge success in Canada and well over 50 million sets have been sold throughout the world.

Card Games

Poker (1000 B.C.)

Contrary to popular convention, poker did not originate in Chicago during Prohibition. In fact the origin of the game goes back almost 3,000 years to a game called As, which was played in Persia. Pairs, three-of-a-kind, full house and four-of-a-kind were all used, as well as the chief element of poker: bluff. The game was introduced to Europe during the Crusades and developed in Spain under the name *primero*. French versions called *bouillote* and *brelan* were imported into Louisiana by French settlers. As the settlers moved west they took the game with them, and many variations were created. It is claimed that poker derives its name from the

style of the game, as the players poke their opponents to make them flare up like a fire.

Cribbage (17th century)

The invention of cribbage is credited to Sir John Suckling (Great Britain, 1609–42), who devised the game in the 17th century. It is believed that Suckling developed the game from Noddy, a popular card game in England at that time.

Whist (1743)

This card game of British origin, the ancestor of bridge, was described for the first time in 1743 by Edmund Hoyle (Great Britain), in a treatise he wrote on the game.

Bridge

Origins (c. 1850)

Bridge developed from whist and is considered to have been first played in Istanbul, Turkey *c.* 1850. The game consists of a battle between two camps, hence the name "bridge," since each player is partnered by the player sitting opposite.

Contract system (1925)

The contract system, which evolved from the French game *plafond*, was devised by Harold Vanderbilt (U.S., 1884–1970) in 1925. His system enabled players to evaluate the strength of their hands. This form of the game gained worldwide popularity, and international competitions were soon staged.

Blackwood convention (1933)

The most widely used convention in contract bridge is the Blackwood convention, devised by Easley Blackwood (U.S., 1903–92) in 1933. Blackwood's method calls for the partner of a four no-trump bidder to show the number of aces held by steps at the level of five.

Puzzles

Jigsaw puzzle (c. 1760)

The jigsaw puzzle, a picture glued on to some kind of backing and cut into irregular pieces that must then be reassembled, came into being simultaneously in France and in Britain around 1760. It was originally an educational toy. Dumas (France) in 1762 began selling cut-up maps which had to be put back together. In Britain John Spilbury stuck a map of England onto a thin layer of mahogany. He cut the jigsaw along the borders between counties, which were then sold separately. Spilbury died at the age of 29, without having made a success of his idea. In 1787 William Darton (Great Britain) produced a puzzle with portraits of all the English kings, from William the Conqueror to George III. The player had to know the order of succession by heart to be able to do the puzzle.

In 1789 Wallis simplified this game and produced a history of England in color, which provided the model for all later puzzles that required more observation and patience.

Crossword (1913)

The crossword puzzle was invented in 1913 by Arthur Wynne, an American journalist born in Liverpool, England.

Wynne worked in the games department of the *New York World* and was always looking for new puzzles. He remembered a game from Victorian times which he had played with his grandfather, called the Magic Square. By reconstructing the square, including black squares and adding a list of 32 definitions, he invented the crossword puzzle, the first of which appeared on December 21, 1913 in the *New York World*'s weekly supplement. His definitions were descriptive and very simple.

Rubik's cube (1979)

In 1979 academic, Erno Rubik (Hungary) invented a fiendish cube, of which more than 100 million have been sold throughout the world. With his royalties, Rubik set up a small design company in Hungary and funded a foundation for inventors. The idea of the cube was to make all nine squares that comprised each face of the cube the same color, and to do this for each of the six faces.

In 1988 he launched the mind-blowing Rubik's clock. The trick is to use the knobs to set all the hands of 18 clocks to midnight when each knob controls several clocks at once.

Video Games

Space War (early 1960s)

The first computer game was "Space War," developed by a research team from the Massachusetts Institute of Technology in the early 1960s. The game required costly and cumbersome equipment and seemed to have little commercial future.

Pong (1972)

The first succesful commercial video game was Pong, invented by Nolan Bushnell (U.S.). Bushnell had witnessed a demonstration of "Space War" and had devoted his energies to creating a practical video game. His first effort, Computer Space, produced in 1971, was a failure, but his second, Pong, was an enormous success. A unsophisticated game by today's standards, Pong was a sort of electronic table tennis game. The first copy of the game was installed in Andy Capp's Tavern in Sunnyvale, Calif., where it broke down after a few hours when the machine became jammed with coins.

Space Invaders (1978)

The Japanese company Taito Corp. introduced Space Invaders on June 16, 1978. The game was a tremendous success and spurred the growth of video arcades worldwide in the late 1970s. The game pitted the player against rows of advancing Martians in close formation.

Video Display Units (1985)

By the early 1980s, microcomputers had lost their impact and the video game market was in a steep decline. For this reason, Atari, Sega and Nintendo developed Video Display Units (VDUs), which were specially designed for video games. VDUs appeared in 1985, and the Japanese company Nintendo rapidly gained the market lead. Nintendo has manufactured such games as Dragon Quest, Super Mario and Zelda.

Game Boy (1989)

This Walkman of video games, developed by Nintendo, is completely autonomous. It is fitted with a small screen and ear plugs and takes game cassettes.

Other Games

Dominoes (c. 2450 B.C.)

In the National Museum of Baghdad (Iraq) there are objects made of bone dating from *c.* 2450 B.C., found in Ur in Chaldea, which archaeologists think are similar to our dominoes.

However, it was not until the 18th century that this game appeared in Europe, reaching Britain via France around 1795. The term *domino* derives from a similarity with the black garment of the same name worn by priests in winter over their white surplice. Dominoes were originally ebony on one side and ivory on the other.

War games (1780)

These are simulations of historical or entirely fictitious military conflicts. The contemporary form of the war game was invented by Helvig, the Duke of Brunswick's master of pages, in 1780. In 1837 von Moltke, the general in charge of the Prussian army, made the playing of war games part of military training. After 1870 all nations followed this example. War games were popularized in the United States in 1953 by Charles Roberts. The mass production of the game Tactics enabled him to set up the Avalon Hill company, which today dominates the war games market.

Pinball (1930s)

The distant ancestor of pinball is the game of billiards, described by Charles Dickens in 1836. The great economic crisis of 1929 and Prohibition favored its development. In 1931 pinball went into mass production and soon acquired the features it still has today: in 1932 the tilt was invented by Harry Williams, and the Ballyhoo was launched by a young Chicago businessman, Richard T. Moloney; in 1933 the machines were electrified, while the Rockelite, created by the American company Bally, was the first to be brightened by luminous scores, and bumpers were invented in 1936.

Electric pinball machine (1938)

It was Samuel Gensberg, a Pole who emigrated to the United States at 18, who invented the first electric pinball machine around 1938, calling it the Beamlight. The first modern pinball machines appeared in 1947, with Chicago Coin's Bermuda and H. Mabs' Humpty-Dumpty.

Frisbee (1948)

Frisbee was invented by students at Yale University in 1947, who played with aluminum pie plates. These came from a Bridgeport baker, Joseph Frisbie, who was a regular supplier to the University. In 1948 a young American just out of the army, Fred Morrisson, applied for a patent for a similar disc in plastic. Later he granted the license to the California firm Wham-O (inventors of the hula-hoop), who, having heard about the origins of the game, called it Frisbee.

Dungeons and Dragons (1973)

Dungeons and Dragons is the first modern role-play game and is the fruit of the imagination of an American traveling salesman, Gary Gigax.

Barbie was created in 1958 by Mattel, and is named after the daughter of the founders of the company. (Le Livre Mondial des Inventions)

Gigax was bored with war games and so, with his friend Dave Arneson, designed a simulation game in which the players would not be obliged to move pieces on a board. Each participant takes on a character. The universe Gigax created was inspired by the famous novel *The Lord of the Rings* by J.R.R. Tolkien.

Having perfected the rules of his game, Gigax tried in vain to sell it to the big U.S. games manufacturers. In the face of so many rejections, he became a part-time shoe repairman before producing and selling his game himself in 1973. Today TSR Hobbies, of which he is managing director, is one of the most successful games manufacturers.

TOYS

Dolls

Origins (antiquity)

Almost as long as there have been children there have been dolls. Originally they were made from wood, terra-cotta, and more rarely, wax and ivory. The ancient Greeks and Romans made dolls with movable limbs. The torsos of Greek dolls were often made of burnt clay to which the limbs were attached by cords. The Romans were fond of rag dolls.

In 19th-century Europe, Saxony in Germany produced most of the torsos for dolls that were made from papier-mâché. In Nuremberg, Germany and London, England, doll-makers became renowned for their porcelain dolls. These dolls would be dressed in Paris before being sent as far afield as China.

Talking dolls (1820s)

The first talking dolls were created in the 1820s by Johann Maelzel, the inventor of the metronome. Thomas Edison (U.S., 1847–1931) adapted a phonograph with round discs to go inside a doll *c.* 1887. Edison's doll said, "Mommy, daddy," using a recording of a real human voice.

Barbie Doll (1958)

Barbie was created in 1958 by Mattel. Elliot and Ruth Handler (both U.S.) had founded Mattel in 1945. They named the doll Barbie after their daughter. It was the first doll to have an adult's body and a complete wardrobe of miniature clothes. Ken, Barbie's boyfriend (named after the Handlers' son), appeared in 1961. In 1963 Barbie's friend Midge came on the market, followed by a younger sister, Skipper, and since then others have been added to the line.

Cabbage Patch doll (1983)

The original Cabbage Patch dolls were created by Xavier Roberts, and launched on November 12, 1983 in Hollywood, Calif. Coleco Indus-

This model of the port at Copenhagen, Denmark was constructed from three million Lego bricks. (Cosmos)

tries produced the mass-market version of the dolls under license from Roberts. Each doll is unique and is sold with a birth certificate and a certificate of adoption.

Other Toys

Teddy bear (19th century)

The Americans, Germans and Russians all claim to be the inventors of the teddy bear.

Toys representing bears have long been made in Russia. Tsar Nicholas II gave a wooden bear to President Loubet of France at the time of the Franco–Russian Treaty of 1892.

According to other sources, while Theodore "Teddy" Roosevelt was president of the United States (1901–09) his son had a real bear cub that he loved. When the bear died, the boy was so unhappy that a handyman had the idea of making him a toy that looked like the bear. The president's son was also called Teddy, hence the name teddy bear.

A third version holds that in 1902 the German Richard Steiff designed the first teddy bear, with shoe-button eyes and gray mohair fur. An American trader bought 3,000 of them. These soft toys appeared dressed as pages at the wedding of Theodore Roosevelt's daughter, hence the name teddy bear. Some of the teddy bears made by Richard Steiff and his wife Margarete

are now highly valuable and have been sold at auction for thousands of dollars.

There is a fourth version of the origin of the name "Teddy," again involving Roosevelt. One day, while out hunting, he saw a young bear and refused to shoot it. The story caught the public imagination and a New York shopkeeper began to make stuffed toy bears and called them teddy bears. Whatever the origins, by World War I over a million were being sold every year.

Model cars (19th century)

The first small model cars appeared at the same times as their life-size namesakes at the end of the last century. The first cars on a 1/45 scale were launched by the British company Matchbox, which became one of the world's leading manufacturers of toy cars.

Construction sets (1900)

The first construction set was Meccano, invented by Frank Hornby (Great Britain) in 1900. Hornby invented the toy for his two sons. He wanted a toy that would encourage children to build things rather than destroy them. Hornby set to work and thought of the different elements needed to construct a crane. In the first stage he thought of making metal strips in similar formats with regularly spaced holes so that they could be assembled. Then he made nuts and bolts that would fit the holes, and designed small pulleys. The idea was a huge

success. Originally calling his toy Mechanics Made Easy, Hornby changed the name to Meccano in 1907.

Silly Putty (1947)

Toward the end of the 1940s, researchers at General Electric discovered a synthetic substance they thought might be able to replace rubber. It was soft, elastic, pliable and moldable, but GE soon realized the material had no industrial potential. In 1947 Peter Hodgson (U.S.), an advertising executive from New Haven, Conn., bought a quantity of the substance from GE and hired a Yale Univeristy student to make 100-gram balls and package them as plastic cubes. In 1949, Hodgson advertised Silly Putty in a client's toy catalog. Silly Putty was an instant success.

Lego (1955)

The Lego bricks we know today first came on the market in 1955. They were designed after World War II by Ole Kirk Christiansen (Denmark), a former carpenter who had retrained in toy manufacturing. He formed the name Lego from the Danish *leg godt*, which means "to play well."

The Lego World Cup took place for the first time in Billund, Denmark, the town where its inventor was born, in August 1988. Some 175,000 children from 14 different countries took part in the contest.

The Indianapolis 500 was first run in 1911. The Indy straightaway is one of the most famous scenes in American sports. (Brian Spurlock)

Hula-hoop (1958)

The plastic hula-hoop was invented in 1958 by Richard P. Knerr and Arthur K. "Spud" Melvin, who owned the Wham-O Manufacturing Co. of San Gabriel, Calif. In six months, the inventors sold 20 million hula-hoops in the United States at $1.98 each, a turnover of about $40 million.

Transformers (1980)

Within a decade of having been launched by the American company Hasbro, Transformers had become one of the world's best-selling toys. They are remarkably adaptable—one moment they are robots, and then they can be reassembled as vehicles in a few seconds. And, with their hi-tech look, they have proved a great hit with many children.

SPORTS

Auto Racing

Origins (1880s)

It is not known who invented automobile racing, and there are various claims as to the first automobile race, the earliest being a 200-mile race from Green Bay to Madison, Wisc., in 1878. The first road race in which official time was kept was in France, from Paris to Bordeaux and back on June 11–13, 1895.

Rally driving (1907)

At the start of 1907 the French daily newspaper *Le Matin* issued a formidable challenge: "Are there any drivers prepared to go from Peking (China) to Paris (France)?" The race began in Peking on June 10, 1907, and the victorious *Italia*, driven by Prince Borghese, reached Paris on August 11, having overcome unbelievable difficulties. The following year an even crazier race was organized: New York to Paris via Alaska and Russia.

Indianapolis 500 (1911)

The Indianapolis Motor Speedway was built in 1909 as a test track for automobile development. The owners of the track repaved the surface within a year of its opening to improve safety conditions for racing. On May 30, 1911 the first Indianapolis 500 was run. The race captured the imagination of the public and quickly established itself as an American institution.

Le Mans 24-hour (1923)

The first 24-hour endurance race at Le Mans was staged on May 26–27, 1923. It was organized by three men: Georges Durand, Emile Coquille and Charles Faroux (all France). Their aim was to create a road-testing ground for mass-produced "improved" cars. The time was set at 24 hours to push the machinery to its limits.

Central engine (1955)

In 1955 the British manufacturer Cooper used its Racer 500 as a basis for developing a sports car with a central Coventry Climax engine, the Cooper Type 60, which was adapted to Formula 1 Grand Prix racing. In 1959 and 1960 Jack Brabham (Australia) won the world driver's championship in a central engine race car.

Direct fuel injection (1960)

In 1960 an engineer named Kugelfischer (Germany) perfected direct fuel injection using a mechanical pump. This system was adopted by all automobile racers within a few years. It was not until 1975 that the system was used on mass-produced automobiles.

Monocoque chassis (1963)

Designed by Lotus manufacturing engineer Colin Chapman (Great Britain), the monocoque chassis was an enormous step forward in race car development. A one-piece aluminum chassis, the monocoque supplanted tubular-style chassis construction, making the car stiffer, lighter and faster.

Ground-effects aerodynamics (1978)

A giant advance in automobile racing technology, ground-effects technology was developed by Colin Chapman (Great Britain) for his 1978 Formula 1 Lotus team. Chapman's Lotus was designed to allow air to flow through the car's side-pods, which had the effect of making them act like inverted wings. To enhance this effect the car was built with skirts that harnessed the flow of air so that the car was sucked to the ground. Such was the impact of Chapman's innovation that his team dominated the Formula 1 season. Ground-effects aerodynamics was rapidly adopted in all forms of racing.

Badminton

Origins (1860s)

Badminton is descended from the ancient racket game of battledore and shuttlecock. The modern version of the game is named after the Duke of Beaufort's country seat, Badminton House, in Gloucestershire, England, where the game was first played in the 1860s. It is claimed that one rainy day a cord was stretched across the hall for an indoor game of battledore, and modern badminton was created.

Baseball

Origins (1839)

According to legend, and officially recognized in 1908 by a special committee of the commissioner of baseball, the game was invented in 1839 by Abner Doubleday in Cooperstown, N.Y. Sports historians reject the Doubleday legend, however, insisting that the game was played at a much earlier time.

The most widely accepted theory on the origins of baseball is that the game began in England *c.* 1750, and that it developed from such games as cricket and rounders. It is uncontested that Alexander Cartwright, Jr. formulated the rules of the modern game in 1845. The first game played under these rules was on June 19, 1846, when the New York Nine defeated the New York Knickerbockers, 23–1, in four innings.

Uniforms (1849)

The first time a standard uniform was worn by all members of the team was in 1849, when the New York Knickerbockers donned old cricket uniforms. The forerunner of the modern uniform was first introduced in 1868 by the Cincinnati Red Stockings.

Bats (1859)

The earliest bats were believed to be modeled after cricket bats, which were flat. In March 1859 the National Association of Baseball Players adopted a rule limiting the bat to a diameter of 2½ inches. It was not until 1862 that rules were passed that required the bat to be round and made of wood.

Catcher's mask (1875)

Fred W. Thayer, a Harvard University student, designed the first catcher's mask in 1875. The mask was a modified fencer's mask, and it took Thayer two years to build a satisfactory model. The mask was first used by Harvard's catcher, James Tyng, during a college game in 1875. It was first used by professionals in 1877.

World Series (1903)

The first World Series was staged in 1903, an unofficial challenge game series, won by the Boston Pilgrims (AL) five games to three over the Pittsburgh Pirates (NL). The World Series was staged officially from 1905 on.

All-Star Game (1933)

The All-Star Game was the brainchild of Arch Ward (U.S.), the sports editor of the *Chicago Tribune*. Ward convinced the owners of the *Tribune* and baseball officials to stage a "Dream Game" between the best players from the American and National Leagues as an attraction for the 1933 World's Fair in Chicago. The game was played on July 6, 1933 at Comiskey Park, Chicago. It proved so popular that baseball officials decided to stage the game annually.

Little League Baseball (1939)

Little League was founded by three men: Carl E. Stotz (U.S., 1910–92), and George and Bert Beeble (both U.S.) in Williamsport, Pa. in 1939. By 1946 there were 12 leagues in Pennsylvania and it was decided to inaugurate a Little League World Series in 1947. Today Little League Baseball is both an American and an international institution, with over 16,000 leagues worldwide and more than 2.5 million players.

Rotisserie Baseball (1980)

Author and baseball addict Daniel Okrent (U.S.) invented Rotisserie Baseball in 1980. The game calls for players to own imaginary teams of real major league players. The rotisserie teams earn points determined by the real statistics of the players in such categories as home runs, RBI's, batting average, wins, saves, ERA, etc. In 1984 Okrent published the rules of the game in a book called *Rotisserie League Baseball*, and new leagues formed nationwide rapidly. The game is named for the restaurant in New York where the idea for the game was born.

Inflatable baseball glove (1991)

In 1991 Spalding launched the airFLEX glove. Inside the glove is an air inflation system that pumps the glove to custom-fit the fielder's hand. On October 20, 1992, Spalding received a U.S. patent for the air inflation system.

Basketball

Origins (1891)

Basketball is one of the few sports that can pinpoint its origins. In 1891 Dr. James Naismith (Canada, 1861–1939), a professor at the International YMCA College in Springfield, Mass., decided to develop a sport that could be played indoors, at night or in winter. In mid-December 1891 Naismith invented basketball. He nailed two peach baskets to the opposite walls of a gym and set down the rules.

The first game took place on January 20, 1892. The teams were made up of seven players each, and the game was played over three 20-minute periods.

24-second clock (1954)

The 24-second clock, which requires that teams shoot the ball within that amount of time after gaining possession, was invented by Danny Biasone (U.S., b. Italy; 1909–92) in 1954. The fledgling National Basketball Association (NBA) had been losing fans because of the slow pace of play. Biasone, owner of the Syracuse Nationals, invented the shot clock to speed up play and make the game more attractive. The NBA adopted the shot clock for the 1954–55 season, and it has been widely hailed as the most important development in league history.

Bowling

Origins (2500 B.C.)

A bowling-like game existed in ancient Egypt *c.* 2500 B.C. Nine pins and a ball of stone were found in the tomb of an Egyptian child. The "bowling alley" was covered by three arches through which the ball had to pass, in a manner similar to croquet. The modern game is closely related to the German game of nine-pins called Heidenwefern. This game was a sort of religious rite, in which sinners would attempt to knock down pins to absolve themselves of sin, hence the game's name, which means "knock

The rules of basketball were devised by Dr. James Naismith. The first game was played on January 20, 1892. (Brian Spurlock)

down pagans." A version of this game appeared in the United States in the 17th century.

10th Pin (1845)

Bowling had been banned in Connecticut in 1841. In order to circumvent the law prohibiting nine-pin bowling, a 10th pin was added in 1845.

Boxing   ⌄

Origins (3000 B.C.)

Boxing is an ancient sport; a decorative fresco discovered in Iraq dating from *c.* 3000 B.C. depicts boxers with their fists wrapped in pieces of leather.

First rules (1743)

The earliest-known rules were established by the champion pugilist Jack Broughton (Great Britain, 1704–89) on August 6, 1743. Broughton established the rules for fighting barefisted, which included the dimensions of the ring and the prohibition of blows below the belt.

Queensberry rules (1867)

The 8th Marquess of Queensberry (Great Britain, 1844–1900) in conjunction with the boxer Arthur Chambers formulated the Queensberry rules in 1867. The Queensberry rules, still in place today, included the wearing of gloves, the three-minute round and the ten-second count.

Cycling

Origins (1868)

Bicycle races quickly followed the machine's invention. The first race was held on May 30, 1868 in the Parc de St. Cloud, Paris, France over a distance of 1 mile 209 yards. The race was won by James Moore (Great Britain, 1847–1935).

Cycle touring (1896)

Cycle touring was first established in Italy in 1896. The first official route was from Rome to Naples, and nine cyclists participated. The first Audax certificates were created by Vito Pardo in 1898. These were awarded to cyclists capable of covering 124 miles between sunrise and sunset.

Tour de France (1903)

The Tour de France, conceived by Henri Desgranges (France), took place for the first time on July 1, 1903. There were six stages, and 20 out of the initial 60 riders completed the course. The first race was won by Maurice Garin (France). In 1919 Desgranges introduced the *maillot jaune*, the yellow jersey, worn by the leading rider during each stage and presented to the eventual winner.

Mountain bike (1973)

The mountain bike was created in Marin County, Calif. in 1973. Aficionados of sports, space and adventure customized their road bicycles so that they could take them on the nearby mountain slopes. Many of them became very skillful, and soon the Canyon Gang was to be seen racing down the steepest slopes.

Gradually, small-scale manufacturers began to build these machines, which were dubbed mountain bikes. These bikes gained popularity rapidly, and today almost all manufacturers in the American market offer this kind of bike.

The Tour de France was the brainchild of Henri Desgranges. In 1919 he also conceived *le maillot jaune*—the yellow jersey—to identify the race leader and to be awarded to the eventual winner. (Cor Vos)

Full-wheel bicycle (1984)

Designed by Prof. Dal Monte (Italy), a specialist in aerodynamics, this unique and futuristic bike was designed to break the speed record. In Mexico, on January 23, 1984, Francesco Moser (Italy) rode 51.151 kilometers in one hour to break his four-day-old record. The bike's performance was so impressive that the full-wheel was rapidly adopted by racers for all speed or sprint races.

Footbag

Origins (1972)

Footbag was invented in 1972 by John Stalberger (U.S.). Footbag is played with a small, pliable, pellet-filled, ball-like object with little or no bounce, used for kicking. The aim is for the player to keep the footbag in the air for as long as possible. The game can be played alone, with two, or as a team. Hacky Sack footbags were patented in 1979.

Football

Origins (1869)

Football is a derivative of soccer and rugby. The first football game was staged on November 6, 1869 at New Brunswick, N.J. between Princeton and Rutgers. This game was a modified version of soccer, and it wasn't until five years later that the modern game began its development. In May 1874, Harvard played McGill University (Montreal, Canada) in a three-game challenge series played under the modified rugby rules introduced by McGill. Harvard officials were impressed by the McGill game and adopted it themselves. Other colleges joined Harvard and the new game spread rapidly in the Northeast.

Modern rules (1880)

The basic format of the modern game was devised by Walter Camp from 1880 to 1885. At various rules conventions during this period, Camp proposed such concepts as the line of scrimmage, 11-man teams, reduction in field size, "downs" and "yards to gain" and the offside penalty.

Rose Bowl (1902)

The first bowl game was the Rose Bowl, staged on New Year's Day 1902 at Pasadena, Calif. The game, in which Michigan defeated Stanford 49–0, was held as part of the Rose Bowl festival. The second game wasn't held until 1916, but the contest has been held annually since.

Forward pass (1906)

The forward pass was legalized in 1906, but it wasn't made popular until 1913, when Gus Dorais and Knute Rockne of Notre Dame used the strategy to great effect in Notre Dame's 35–13 defeat of Army. Army was heavily fa-

The first golf balls were made of leather stuffed with feathers. The modern version was developed from the rubber-corded ball invented by Coburn Haskell in 1899. (William S. Romano)

vored to win the game, but quarterback Dorais and end Rockne had planned and practiced the forward pass during the summer, believing that it would break down the Army defense. Their success inspired other teams to use the pass, and the nature of the game was quickly transformed.

T-formation (1940)

The original designer of the T-formation is unknown, but George Halas is credited with making it popular in 1940. Halas, the coach of the Chicago Bears, lined his quarterback up directly behind the center, while the fullback and two halfbacks were in a line parallel to the line of scrimmage. Halas introduced his system during the 1940 season. The play gained widespread acceptance following the Bears' 73–0 drubbing of the favored Washington Redskins in the 1940 championship game.

Super Bowl (1967)

In 1966, the National Football League (NFL) and its rival the American Football League (AFL) agreed to merge their competing leagues to form an expanded NFL. Regular-season play would not begin until 1970, but the two leagues agreed to stage an annual AFL–NFL championship game beginning in January 1967. Lamar Hunt, owner of the Kansas City Chiefs, suggested that the game be called the Super Bowl, but the other owners rejected the name. The press, however, began to use the name and in 1969 the NFL officially recognized the title.

Arena football (1987)

Invented by Jim Foster (U.S.), arena football had its debut season in 1987. Arena football is a scaled-down version of the outdoor game adapted to indoor arenas.

Golf

Origins (1457)

The exact origins of the game have been lost to antiquity. The development of the modern game is generally traced to Scotland in the 15th century, although some historians think that the game may have been brought to Scotland from the Netherlands. The earliest reference to

Zamboni Machine (1949): Frank J. Zamboni

How did a lowly iceman become the king of ice rinks? The story is a real fairy tale, including an ice princess (Sonja Henie), a quest (a cross-country journey) and a happy ending.

Frank J. Zamboni was an ice maker in Paramount, California, in the 1920s and 1930s, when Paramount's chief inhabitants were dairy cows, not movie stars. His ice kept the milk chilled until the late thirties, when electric refrigerators moved into the market. Frank and his brother, an electrician, took their ice business elsewhere: they built an ice rink across the street.

In 1942 Frank began to tinker with ways to mechanically resurface the rink. Back then, creating a new layer of ice took half an hour and half a dozen workers. By hand, they scraped and sprayed the ice. The process took up all the time between hockey periods, and boasted little charm or entertainment. Then, in 1949, the Zamboni machine hit the ice, providing both. The first Zamboni was a big box built atop a Jeep chassis. It worked, and boy, was it fun to watch!

Olympic skater turned movie–star Sonja Henie lived in nearby Hollywood. One day she and her figure-skating troupe came to skate at Zamboni's rink. It was there that Henie fell in love with a Zamboni—the machine, not the man. She asked for a machine of her own. Zamboni built the machine, disassembled it and set off to meet Henie in St. Louis. When he got there, Henie and her entourage had moved on to Chicago. Zamboni followed her, put the machine back together and said goodbye.

And they rode off into the sunset, Henie and her Zamboni. She used the machine to clean the ice at every rink where she skated. It wasn't long before the rink owners fell in love, too. Soon there were Zambonis everywhere.

These days there are thousands of Zamboni machines in the United States, Canada, South Africa, Europe and Asia. A Zamboni costs upwards of $50,000, but its slow speed—9 mph—and low mileage make it durable. Small, tractor-pulled Zambonis are available for smaller rinks. A super-sized machine was developed especially for the speed-skating oval at the 1988 Olympics. A special Zamboni sucks water out of rain-soaked Astroturf. And, in 1991, an electric Zamboni made its debut.

What more could we ask of the wonderful Zamboni? Major rinks can sell the sides of their Zambonis as advertising space. No wonder everyone loves the Zamboni: it keeps advertisers, rink owners, skaters and little kids of all ages happy, ever after.

How It Works

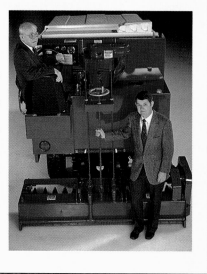

1. A blade shaves the surface of the ice.
2. Shavings are collected and spewed into a tank.
3. Water is fed from a squeegee that smoothes the ice.
4. Dirty water is vacuumed, filtered and returned to the tank.
5. Clean, hot water is spread over the ice.
6. Water freezes to create a smooth new surface.

Frank J. Zamboni (seated at left).
(Zamboni Co.)

---

the game is a decree issued by James II in 1457 prohibiting the game. The king felt his citizens were spending too much time playing golf and had neglected archery practice.

Golf ball (1848)

The first golf balls were made of leather and stuffed with feathers. In 1848, gutta-percha balls were introduced. These balls were made of solid gutta-percha (a rubberlike substance obtained from trees) and had a smooth surface. They could drive further than feather balls but would twist erratically. An unknown golfer noticed that nicked balls tended to travel straighter than smooth balls, and experiments with dimpled balls followed. In 1899 Coburn Haskell (U.S.) invented the rubber-cored ball, which had succeeded the gutta-percha ball in popularity by 1902.

Steel-shafted clubs (1929)

The first golf clubs were wooden and generally handcrafted from hickory. It wasn't until the early 20th century that experiments with steel-shafted clubs were successful. In 1929 the Royal & Ancient Golf Club and the United States Golf Association, the ruling bodies of the game, authorized the use of steel-shafted clubs in their competitions.

Hang Gliding

Origins (1948)

In 1948 Francis Rogallo (U.S.) designed a supple, flexible wing made of woven wire, covered with a silicon-based coating. Rogallo, a NASA engineer, contacted various groups to fund his "glider" but found no backers. Rogallo was one of a long line of inventors who had attempted to find a way for humans to fly. Leonardo da Vinci (Italy, 1452–1519) had sketched a design of a parachute and a wing. One of the pioneers of gliding, Otto Lilienthal (Germany, 1848–96), was killed during testing of one of his machines.

Delta wing (1964)

By 1964 increasingly efficient delta-shaped wings had appeared. That year Bill Moyes (Australia), a NASA engineer, designed a 48-square-foot delta wing. In New York harbor on July 4, 1969 Moyes's partner Bill Bennett (Australia) took off on water skis pulled by a boat, then released himself from the line and flew over the Statue of Liberty.

The autonomous takeoff hang glider, which did not require another vehicle to pull it, replaced the towed version thanks to the work of inventor Dave Kilbourne.

Ultra-lights (1975)

In the 1970s the popularity of hang gliding increased rapidly, but people who lived in flat areas often had to travel long distances to participate in the sport. To solve this problem, enthusiasts experimented with motorized hang gliders. In 1975 the first viable prototype ultra-lights appeared more or less simultaneously in Australia, France and the United States.

Hockey

Origins (c. 17th century)

A hockey-like game was played on the frozen canals of the Netherlands in the 17th century. The modern game developed in Canada, where rules were codified at Kingston, Ontario in 1855.

Stanley Cup (1893)

The Stanley Cup was donated to the Canadian Amateur Hockey Association by Sir Frederick Arthur Stanley, Lord Stanley of Preston, in 1893. The Stanley Cup is currently the oldest competition in North American professional sports.

Horse Racing

Origins (1400 B.C.)

The earliest evidence of horse racing dates to the Hittites of Anatolia in 1400 B.C. The Hittites are said to have participated in frenzied horse races.

English thoroughbreds (1680)

The English thoroughbred stock was created by a group of horsebreeders whose aim was to produce faster horses. They bred selected English mares with Arabian stallions: the Byerley Turk (foaled 1680), the Darley Arabian (foaled 1702) and the Godolphin Arabian (foaled 1734). All English thoroughbreds are descended from these three stallions.

Triple Crown (1930)

The Triple Crown, the legendary prize awarded to the winner of the Kentucky Derby, Preakness and Belmont Stakes, was first won by Sir Barton in 1919. The phrase, however, was not coined until 1930, when *Daily Racing Form* writer Charles Hatton used it to describe Gallant Fox's victories in the three races that year. To date only 11 horses have gained the Triple Crown.

Ice Skating

Origins (c. 2nd century)

Ice skating has existed for centuries in northern Europe. The earliest evidence of the sport dates to Scandinavia in the 2nd century. At first, blades made of bone were fitted into wooden shoes, but by the beginning of the 17th century bone blades had been replaced by metal ones.

Figure skating (1860s)

Jackson Haines (U.S., 1840–75) is regarded as the pioneer of the modern sport of figure skating, a composite of dancing and skating. During the 1860s, Haines toured Europe, where his shows were greeted enthusiastically, and his style of skating was widely copied.

Skating rink (1876)

The first artificial skating rink was built by John Gamgee (Great Britain) in London, England. The rink was opened on January 7, 1876. The surface area was only 400 square feet and Gamgee used Pictet sulphur oxide machines and glycerin water to make the ice.

Axel jump (1882)

One of the most difficult jumps in the skating repertoire, the axel jump is named for Axel Paulsen (Norway), who invented the technique in 1882. The skater takes off from the forward outside edge and lands on the back outside edge of the opposite foot. The axel is easy to spot, as it is the only jump that requires takeoff from a forward position.

Salchow jump (c. 1903)

One of the standard jumps required of any skater in competition is the salchow. It is named for 10-time world champion Ulrich Salchow (Sweden, 1877–1949), who invented the jump c. 1903. To perform the jump the skater lifts off the ice using the back inside edge of one foot and lands on the back outside edge of the opposite foot.

Judo

Origins (1882)

Judo (which means "gentle art" in Japanese) was invented in 1882 by Dr. Jigoro Kano (Japan, 1860–1938). Kano had devoted himself to jujitsu, but he was not physically strong, and sought to compensate for this handicap by developing his mind and spirit. Kano perfected a method of attack and defense that brought victory by using suppleness rather than strength; he called his method judo.

Karate

Origins (1916)

Karate is based on the use of the human body's natural weapons. It is devised from the Chinese art of shoalin boxing, known as kempo, which was popularized in Okinawa in the 16th century as a means of self-defense. Gichin Funakoshi (Japan, 1869–1957) devoted his life to the development of the art. He gave his first demonstration of his new technique at Kyoto, Japan in 1916. At the time this method of combat was known as "Okinawa Te." Funakoshi gave it a more meaningful name: karate (empty hand).

Motorcycle Racing

Origins (1897)

The first motorcycle race limited to two-wheel vehicles was staged on November 29, 1897 at Richmond, England. The race was run on a one-mile oval track and was won by Charles Jarrott.

All-terrain vehicle (ATV) (1967)

In 1967 John Plessinger (U.S.), a student at the University of Michigan, created a motorized tricycle that was designed to cope with rough ground. The first models did not have any suspension but the center of gravity was low, which lent the vehicle greater stability.

Plessinger sold his patent in 1969 to Sperry Rand, which launched the Tri Cart. However, it was the Japanese company Honda that began marketing ATVs in 1973 and made them popular.

Mountaineering

Crampons (1561)

The earliest known use of crampons is by a shepherd, Grataroli (Italy), in 1561. The first "4-points" crampon appeared in the 18th century. In 1908 Eckenstein (Austria) developed a "10-points" version. With the aid of a local blacksmith named Grivel, Eckenstein added two horizontal points to the front of his crampon, which permitted ascension of the face of a slope at more than 45 degrees.

During 1969–70, the Austrian manufacturer Stubai marketed 4-front-point crampons. In 1971, Simond applied for a patent, using the idea of a mountain guide named Walter Cecchinel, in which all the points were aligned to grip everywhere and thus provide greater safety.

Ice ax (1807)

The oldest known ice ax dates to 1807. Jean-Pierre Cachat (France), a guide in the Chamonix region, had manufactured it for his own use.

Down jacket (1932)

During the winter of 1932–33, Pierre Allain (France) invented the down jacket. Previously, mountain climbers took to the mountain equipped with Bonneval cloth jackets and pants.

Vibram sole (1938)

Vittorio Bramani (Italy) invented the rubber sole in 1938. It was to revolutionize mountain climbing, and was named vibram. Prior to the vibram sole, mountain climbers used cleated leather soles, which made climbing on rock very difficult. They also carried shoes with crepe, rope or felt soles, but each was ineffective in certain conditions, such as snow, ice or rain. The vibram sole was effective in all weather and all terrains.

Climbing boots (1947)

In 1947 Pierre Allain (France) developed the first climbing boot. It was molded to the foot, perfectly adjusted and better adapted to let the grips be felt and taken. The sole was smooth. These boots are commonly called P.A.'s, after the inventor's initials.

Olympic Games

Origins (c. 1450 B.C.)

The exact date of the first Olympic Games is unknown, but historians have speculated that the Games go back as far as c. 1450 B.C. The first recorded Olympic Games took place at Olympus, Greece in July 776 B.C. The only contest was a 200-meter race, which was won by Corobius, a cook from Elis. The ancient Games were banned by order of Theodosius I, emperor of Rome, in A.D. 394.

Modern Olympics (1896)

The revival of the modern Olympic Games is credited to Pierre de Coubertin (France, 1863–1937), who was commissioned by the French government to form a universal sports association in 1889. Coubertin proposed a revival of the Games, which led to the creation of the International Olympic Committee (IOC) in 1894. The first modern Games were opened on April 6, 1896 in Athens, Greece.

Racquetball

Origins (1950)

Racquetball was invented in 1950 by Joe Sobek (U.S.) at the Greenwich YMCA, Greenwich, Conn. Sobek designed a "strung paddle racquet" and combined the rules of squash and handball to create the game "paddle rackets," which was later called racquetball.

Roller Skating

Roller skates (1759)

In 1759 Joseph Merlin (Belgium), a manufacturer of musical instruments, invented roller skates. Invited to a ball at Carlisle House, London, England, he had the idea of making a gliding entrance while playing the violin. Merlin's roller skates worked perfectly except for one thing—he had not thought about stopping the skates. He crashed into a mirror at the end of the grand entrance, smashing it and his violin to pieces and seriously injuring himself.

Four-wheel skates (1863)

James L. Plimpton (U.S.) patented the first four-wheel roller skates in 1863.

Rollerblade (1980)

In 1980, two students, Scott and Brennan Olson (U.S.), sought a training device for hockey players to use in the summer. They got the idea of replacing the blades of ice skates with aligning rollers, and founded Rollerblade. In 1992 more than two million pairs were sold in the United States.

Skiing

Origins (antiquity)

Skiing is of Nordic origin, and was used as a mode of transportation for thousands of years. The use of skis was noted at the Battle of Isen in Norway in A.D. 1200. The great Vasa Race commemorates the feat of one of the kings of Sweden, who escaped from Denmark and reached the Dalecarlia Forest on skis with his partisans in 1520.

This invention brings a whole new meaning to the term "jet ski." These turbine skis were invented in 1986 and can reach speeds of 195 mph. (Alain Ernault)

Ski racing (1877)

The first skiing contests were held in Norway in 1877. In 1880, Sondre Nordheim (Norway) had the idea of bending up the front end of the skis. In 1888, Mathias Zdarsky (Austria), inspired by Fridtjof Nansen's (Norway, 1861–1930) trans-Greenland ski expedition, designed shorter skis with metal attachments to hold shoes. The first downhill race was held on January 6, 1911 at Arlberg, Austria, organized by Lord Roberts of Kandahar (Great Britain, 1832–1914). In 1922, Arnold Lunn (Great Britain) organized the first slalom race in Mussen, Switzerland.

Ski boots (1893)

The first ski boots appeared in 1893. They were made of reindeer skin with the fur outside and were inspired by the Eskimo shoes brought back by Arctic explorer Fridtjof Nansen (Norway, 1861–1930) from his Greenland expedition in 1888–89. Boots with hooks were developed in 1962 by Martin (France), who sold his patent to the Swiss company Henke. The principle of the plastic shell was developed in 1968 by the American company Lange. Their boot consisted of an external boot made of epoxy resin and an internal padded slipper.

Artificial snow (1935)

In 1935 the first artificial ski slope, with a ski jump, was built in Boston, Mass.

Bindings (1948)

In 1948, after suffering two broken legs in the same year, engineer and ski fanatic Jean Beyl (France) designed a safety binding and set up the Look Company. In 1966 the French firm Salomon launched the first safety heelpiece that releases the heel when the wearer falls. The following year Salomon marketed the first elastic double-pivoted toe-piece.

Mono-ski (1973)

The mono-ski was invented by surfer Mike Doyle (U.S.). His idea was to find, on snow, the same sliding sensations experienced on water. He built the first single ski in 1973 in only a few hours.

This prototype was transparent and as wide as nearly three normal skis. A pair of standard bindings keep both feet parallel. Doyle inaugurated his mono-ski on slopes in Jackson Hole, Wyo. For the occasion he wore a Hawaiian shirt.

Snowmaker (1976)

The snowmaker came into being by chance. An irrigation company regularly sprayed plants in very cold weather to protect them from being destroyed by frost. During this procedure the water spray created snow, and from this the idea for making artificial snow developed. The most important patent in this domain is that of Armand Marius in 1976. All snowmaking machines are based on Marius's idea.

Snowmax snow inducer (1988)

Snowmax is a protein produced by a subsidiary of Eastman Kodak Corp. It considerably improves the efficiency of snowmakers by raising the temperature at which the water crystallizes into snow to approximately 41 degrees Fahrenheit. It was used extensively during the 1988 Winter Olympics in Calgary, Canada.

Soap Box Derby

Origins (1934)

The Soap Box Derby was the brainchild of photographer Myron Scott (U.S.). Scott had covered a race involving cars built by boys in Dayton, Ohio and was so taken with the idea that he decided to stage his own race, but on a national scale. The first All-American Soap Box Derby was staged in Akron in 1934. The boys and girls competing in the race must build the cars themselves from kits purchased through the organizers of the race.

Softball

Origins (1887)

Softball was invented by George Hancock (U.S.) in Chicago, Ill., in 1887. Rules for the game were drawn up in 1895, and the game was called kitten ball. The name softball was coined by Walter Hakanson (U.S.) at a meeting of the National Recreation Congress in 1926, and adopted nationwide in 1930.

Surfing

Origins (1771)

It is believed that the sport of surfing originated in Hawaii. The earliest description of it was given in 1771 by the explorer Capt. James Cook (Great Britain, 1728–79) during his exploration of Tahiti. Surfing was not known on the U.S. mainland prior to the 20th century. In the 1950s the modern sport developed in Hawaii, California and Australia.

Windsurfing (1958)

A British court ruled in 1982 that Peter Chilvers (Great Britain) had invented the sailboard in 1958. The sport was developed in the United States by surfers unaware of Chilvers's prototype. In 1964 Newman Darby had mounted a sail on a surfboard. In 1968 Jim Drake (U.S.) and Hoyle Schweitzer (U.S.), unaware of previous models, also developed a model. Their model included a keel, articulating joint and wishbone boom, thus giving the sailboard its definitive form.

Morey-Boogie (1971)

The inventor of the Morey-Boogie is Tom Morey (U.S.). In 1971 he created a strange, wide, almost rectangular surfboard, which was also softer, to help prevent accidents without affecting performance. The board is designed so that the surfer lies on the board to ride the wave. Needless to say, gnarly dudes attempt to ride their boards standing up.

Cataplanche (1988)

The cataplanche was brought onto the market in 1990. As its name implies, it is a combination of a planche (surfboard) and a cataraman. Patented by Gilles Mariteau (France) in 1988, it can equal the speed of a surfboard, but has a much greater degree of stability.

Swimming

Origins (antiquity)

In all civilizations the origins of swimming are lost in the mists of time. The first organized swimming competitions were organized in London, England in the 19th century.

English Channel swimming (1875)

The first person to swim the English Channel (from Dover, England to Calais, France) unaided was Capt. Matthew Webb (Great Britain, 1848–83) on August 24–25, 1875. Webb swam approximately 38 miles in 21 hours 45 minutes.

Crawl (1902)

The indigenous peoples of the South Pacific used the crawl stroke in swimming. It was adapted by Syd and Charles Cavill (both Australia), who introduced it to Europe in 1902 and to the United States the following year.

Butterfly (1926)

This variant of the breaststroke, which is the most demanding stroke in swimming, was developed by Eric Rademacher (Germany) in 1926.

Table Tennis

Origins (19th century)

Derived from a medieval game, table tennis developed in Great Britain in the second half of the 19th century. The first known mention of table tennis is to be found in the catalog of a British sporting equipment manufacturer, F.H. Ayres, dating from 1884. In 1890 James Gibb (Great Britain) brought the idea of celluloid balls to England after a visit to the United States. The name Ping-Pong (it derives from the sound made by the ball) was patented by John Jacques (Great Britain) in 1891.

Dimpled bat (1924)

M. Goode (Great Britain) invented rubber bats with small raised points on the surface in 1924.

Tennis

Origins (1873)

Modern-style tennis was invented in 1873 by Maj. Walter C. Wingfield (Great Britain, 1833–1912), who patented the game in 1874. He introduced a number of rules borrowed from an Indian game, in particular the practice of playing on grass. Wingfield called his game *sphairistike*, a Greek word meaning "ball game." The word tennis comes from an earlier French version of tennis called *jeu de paume* (palm game). In this game the server cried *"Tenez!"* ("Here!") to warn the other player that play was about to start.

Tie-breaker (1958)

The tie-breaker was invented by James Van Alen (U.S., 1903–91) in 1958. Traditionalists blocked Van Alen's innovation for several years, but in 1970 the tie-breaker was adopted by the U.S. Open and has been accepted throughout tennis since.

Metal rackets (1960)

The first metal-framed rackets were introduced in the 1960s. The steel racket was patented by Rene Lacoste (France), a former Wimbledon champion, in 1960.

Oversize racket (1978)

In 1976 the American equipment manufacturer Prince introduced the first oversize racket, the "Classic." It was designed by Howard Head. The oversize racket was an enormous success and has revolutionized the sport.

Track and Field

Origins (antiquity)

There is evidence of organized running races in ancient Egypt *c.* 3800 B.C. Running and throwing events were an integral part of the ancient Olympic Games.

Sports shoes (1868)

The Candee Manufacturing Co. of New Haven, Conn. began making canvas sports shoes with rubber soles in 1868.

Marathon (1896)

The first marathon race was included in the first modern Olympic Games in 1896. The race commemorated the run of Phiedippides from the battlefield of Marathon to Athens to announce Miltiades' victory over the Persians on September 13, 490 B.C. Legend has it that the exhausted runner died following the announcement of victory, after having run 24 miles nonstop. The standard marathon distance of 26 miles 385 yards was established at the Olympic Games in London, England in 1924. The race from Windsor Castle to White City Stadium

was lengthened by 385 yards so that the royal children could see the start, and the monarch could see the finish.

Fosbury flop (1968)

By his own account, Dick Fosbury (U.S.) created his famous high-jump technique almost involuntarily. When he could not manage to execute a western roll correctly, he started from a scissors jump and gradually developed the backwards jump. In 1968 Fosbury astonished the world in using the technique to win the high-jump gold medal in Mexico.

Trampolining

T-Model (1936)

Trampolines have been used in circus acts since the turn of the 20th century. The sport of trampolining dates from 1936, when the prototype "T" model trampoline was invented by George Nissen (U.S.).

Volleyball

Origins (1895)

Volleyball was invented in 1895 by William G. Morgan at the YMCA in Holyoke, Mass. American troops introduced the game to Europe during World War I.

Beach volleyball (1940s)

Beach volleyball developed in California during the 1940s. It wasn't until the 1960s that the sport gained a commercial footing, but since that time it has grown rapidly.

Waterskiing

Origins (1922)

In 1922 Ralph Samuelson (U.S., 1904–77) invented water skis. He loved skiing and wanted to have the same sensation in the summer. His first water skis were two curved pine boards that he tried out on Lake Pepin, Minn., during the summer of 1922. Samuelson made no attempt to patent or promote his skis. In 1925 Fred Walker (U.S.), who had seen Samuelson's skis, created and patented Akwa-skees.

Wrestling

Origins (antiquity)

Weaponless combat sports are among the oldest known to humankind. Wrestling was popular in ancient Egypt and Mesopotamia and was practiced in India around 1500 B.C. Indeed, it is mentioned in the epic Sanskrit poem *Mahabharata*.

Wrestling was also a common pastime in ancient Greece, and images of the sport were very

popular. It was probably one of the first Olympic sports, and there are many references to wrestling in Europe in the Middle Ages.

Sumo wrestling (23 B.C.)

The sport's origins are unknown, but the first grand patron was the Suinin, Emperor of Japan in 23 B.C. Sumo continued under imperial patronage until 1185, but under the shoguns, public matches were banned. The ban on sumo was lifted in 1600. In 1684 Ikazuchi Gondaiya, a masterless rikishi (wrestler), proposed rules and techniques to control the sport.

Yachting

Origins (17th century)

Yachting, as a sport, was established in Great Britain in 1661 by King Charles II, who got a taste for navigation while he was in exile in the Netherlands. He challenged his brother to a race that year on the River Thames. Yacht racing spread to other European courts. King Louis XIV of France had mini-ships built to sail on the great lake at Versailles, and ordered a Venetian gondola to be carried over the Alps for his use.

Catamaran (1662)

The catamaran first appeared several thousand years ago off the Coromandel Coast in India. The catamaran was basically a raft made with three tree trunks of different lengths. Its name comes from the Tamil word *kattumaram*: tied timber. The term is now applied only to boats that have two similar hulls. These derive more immediately from the huge canoes used by Polynesians in the South Pacific.

In 1662 William Petty (Great Britain), having learned of the Pacific style of sailing, built two catamarans and raced them successfully against single-hulled yachts. The first person to build a reliable, seaworthy and manageable sporting catamaran was Nathanael Herreshoff, who worked from 1876 to 1881 on the project. The first modern high sea catamaran was launched from Hawaii in 1947 by Brown, Kumalae and Choy. It was called *Manu Kai*, and was the first sailing vessel to exceed 20 knots.

Vertical centerboard (1774)

The lateral centerboard, two streamlined wooden surfaces that could be lifted for tacking, had been developed by Dutch sailors toward the end of the 15th century. In 1774 Lt. Schank (Great Britain), an officer stationed in Boston, Mass. (then a British colony), built a dinghy with a vertical centerboard that ran the length of the keel. Schank had been inspired by small centerboards that Incas had equipped their rafts with.

In 1811 the brothers Joshua, Henry and Jacob Swain (all U.S.) applied for a patent for a pivoting centerboard without ballast that was an immediate success in the United States. The sliding centerboard was popularized by Uffa Fox (Great Britain). In 1928 his Avenger won

52 out of 57 regattas. Since then, the hull shape of centerboard boats has changed very little.

Trimaran (1786)

The first boat with three hulls, derived from the Polynesian latakoïs, was built by Patrick Miller (Great Britain) in 1786. It was essentially a steam-propelled trimaran with a paddle wheel between each hull. In 1868 the first inflatable boat to cross the Atlantic Ocean, the American sailing ship *Non-Pareil*, captained by John Milkes, had three hulls.

The word *trimaran* was coined by Victor Tchechett (U.S., b. Russian) in 1943. It was not until the 1960s that leading designers such as Derek Kelsall (Great Britain) and Dick Newick (U.S.) perfected the trimaran.

Ice yachting (1790)

In 1790 Oliver Booth (U.S.) put a sail and ice skates on a packing case, thus creating the first ice yacht. He traveled on the frozen surface of the Hudson River in winter at Poughkeepsie, N.Y.

Fin keel (c. 1840)

The complexity of centerboards, and the space taken up by their shaft, led boat builders to place fixed centerboards under their keels. These fixed centerboards, made of strong sheet metal to ballast the boat, first appeared in Bermuda *c.* 1840.

At the end of the 1870s a type of boat called the Houari with a nonballasted keel was developed in Marseilles, France. The bulb-shaped ballast at the end of the keel was invented by E.

Bentall (Great Britain) on his 50-foot-9-inch boat *Experiment*, which was launched in 1880. The first designer to make fin keels really effective was Nathanael Herreshoff with his 1891 boat *Dilemma*. This sailing boat brought about a real revolution and was the forerunner of the modern monohulls.

America's Cup (1851)

The first America's Cup was won by the schooner *America* at a regatta at the Isle of Wight, England on August 22, 1851. The New York Yacht Club offered the cup as a challenge trophy, and in 1870 the first defense of the cup for the United States was made by skipper Andrew Comstock. The America's Cup competition is the oldest in any sport, and the expensive cam-

The Fosbury flop is named for Dick Fosbury, who made the technique famous when he won the 1968 Olympics. (Brian Spurlock)

In 1983, *Australia II* became the first challenger to win the America's cup in its 132-year history. Credit for the victory was given to the radical wing keel design of the yacht. (America's Cup Organizing Committee)

paigns in recent history have spurred numerous technical innovations.

Spinnaker (1867)

The spinnaker is a sail set on a pole opposite the main sail. It appeared for the first time during a regatta off Harwich, England on June 9, 1867. In the course of a race between three sailboats, *Sphinx*, *Niobe* and *Vindex*, they each raised a curious round, light sail. The sail was nicknamed Sphinniker after the lead boat, and later became known as spinnaker. In the United States, it was in 1879, during the opening regatta of the Seawanhaka Yacht Club in New York harbor, that the "balloon sail" was first tried aboard the sloop *Schemer*, captained by Lee Smith.

Marconi rigging (1895)

The trapezoid-shaped "leg of mutton" sail appeared in Bermuda *c.* 1820. Sails up to this time had been triangular in shape, and this new design was imported to England *c.* 1880, where it was termed "Bermuda rigging." At the same time it was determined that lengthening the sail influenced the boat's speed.

In 1895 William P. Stephens (U.S.) adapted the Bermuda-rigging mast of his yacht *Ethelwynn* by shrouding the mast to give it greater rigidity. The streamlined shrouded rigging was called "Marconi rigging" since it looked like the design of radio antennas. The first great yacht equipped with Marconi rigging was the *Nyria*, designed by Charles E. Nicholson in 1921.

Winch (1903)

The first winches—mechanical capstans with catches outfitted with a crank—appeared in 1903 in the United States aboard the *Reliance*, the victorious defender of the America's Cup, conceived by Nathanael Herreshoff. This device, today found on sailboats the world over, facilitated climbing and regulating the sheets and halyards of the enormous sails of the *Reliance*, which had a sail area of 16,160 square feet, on a rig 175 feet high.

Rafting (c. 1950)

Rafting is an American invention. At the end of World War II, the U.S. Army Surplus bought small inflatable dinghies designed for disembarkation. Though flexible and easy to handle, they were also long, heavy and motorized. They were first used to carry groups of tourists through the Grand Canyon, but sports enthusiasts quickly saw their potential for racing through rapids. The sport developed in the 1950s when the dinghies were shortened and strengthened and the motor replaced by oars, so that these boats, now called rafts, could take the most impressive rapids.

Jet-ski (1963)

In 1963, Clayton Jacobson (U.S.) designed a piece of equipment that combined the excitement and skills of motocross and waterskiing— the jet-ski. He persisted with his idea and in 1971 approached the Japanese manufacturer Kawasaki. The company liked the idea, and the first jet-skis were produced in 1973.

Hobie Cat (1968)

In 1968, after many years of development, the first Hobie Cat appeared. Invented by Hobart L. Alter (U.S.), the Hobie 14 was an ultralight craft, very strong and easy to handle. Its two highly streamlined asymmetrical hulls were joined by two metal poles and a trampoline. The hobie cat was an enormous success and is used for racing and pleasure.

Speed sail (1977)

Invented in 1977 by the windsurfer Arnaud de Rosnay (France), the speed sail is a kind of land-borne windsurfboard on roller skates. It makes for a spectacular competitive sport, with speeds exceeding 80 mph.

Wing keel (1983)

In 1983 the America's Cup was finally won by a challenger, when *Australia II* defeated *Liberty* (U.S.). The biggest factor in this historic win was the radical wing keel design of the Australian yacht.

A keel functions like the wing of a plane, with a decrease in pressure on one side increasing pressure on the other side. At the extremity of the keel, the depression sucks pressure from the other side and reduces efficiency. The designer of *Australia II*, Ben Lexcen, envisaged fins under the keel to prevent this loss of pressure. This allowed *Australia II* to be fitted with an even more efficient keel than its opponents, and this proved to be the winning edge.

WHAT ON EARTH?

NOT ALL INVENTIONS CHANGE OUR LIVES, SOME JUST MAKE US SCRATCH OUR HEADS.

WALKING ON WATER

Left: This is not the latest vehicle for island hopping, but the summertime version of cross-country skiing. The Aquashoe, invented by Dr. Alan W. Nayes (U.S.), is a unique method of developing aerobic fitness. The "water-walker" uses the same methods as a cross-country skier to stride across the water. The aquashoes can be used in any location that has calm water such as lakes, rivers and harbors. (Aquashoe)

SAND SKIING

Right: Seeking more challenging places to ski than their native Alps, three Austrian skiers turned their attention to the Takla Makan Desert in China. At the end of 1989 the three "Tombas of Arabia" crossed the entire length of the desert. Although the elevation is significantly less than that of Innsbruck, the skiers easily outpaced the camels carrying their provisions. (Gamma Sports/ Contrast)

UNDERWATER HANG GLIDING

▼ Alain Jacques (France), an engineer in fluid mechanics, wanted to see if he could fly his hang glider underwater. Oxygen tank strapped firmly in place, Jacques found that by twisting and turning on his pilot's bar, he could simulate the effect experienced while soaring above the clouds. It is not known if anyone else has tested these waters. (Sipa Press/Margaillen)

DOG RUNS MAN

▲ Perhaps tired of the tame pleasures of walking the dog, Aimé Sauvage (France) invented Trial-Dog racing. Based on the principles of sled dog racing, the "musher" chases after the pack rather than riding behind. Presumably this is not meant to be attempted across the frozen landscape of Alaska. (Le Livre Mondial des Inventions)

INDOOR WINDSURFING

▲ The first known indoor windsurfing competition was the brainchild of Fred Beauchêne (France). He transformed a huge hall in Paris into a gigantic swimming pool measuring 230 feet by 105 feet. Airplane turbine engines situated around the pool produced storm-force winds, powering the windsurfers. (Ernoult Features/Dingo)

SUPER SPEEDWAY NIGHTTIME RACING

With the growing popularity of NASCAR racing, Charlotte Motor Speedway, Charlotte, N.C., decided to stage a nighttime race. However, the technology did not exist that met the safety standards of the drivers or the needs of the television cameras. Speedway officials hired Musco Sports-Lighting, Inc. of Oskaloosa, Iowa to solve the problem. Musco engineers devised the Mirtran Lighting System. The lighting design provides continous lighting on the outside and inside of the track. The outside lighting is primarily conventional pole-mounted lighting, but the inside incorporates new technology that aims the lights away from the track at 6 x 4-foot racks of mirrors. The mirrors are angled to reflect the light onto the track and eliminate glare, thus making the track safe to drive and the lighting quality good enough for television use. The first NASCAR race was staged on May 16, 1992.

New ideas that may change the way we live

Charlotte Motor Speedway staged the first nighttime NASCAR race in May 1992. (Charlotte Motor Speedway)

RACING HELMET DISPLAY (RHD)

Under development by the British Formula 1 racing team Lotus, the RHD allows the driver to monitor key readings of the car's performance, such as engine speed, without averting his eyes from the track. Based on head-up display (HUD) technology used by fighter pilots, the driver reads from a miniature optical lens mounted on special devices extending from the helmet chinpiece. Adjusted to the individual driver's eyesight, the RHD is set at infinity so the driver doesn't have to change focus.

BIODEGRADABLE, WATER SOLUBLE GOLF BALL

In 1990 the International Maritime Organization (IMO) eliminated the dumping of plastic waste into the ocean, a measure that banned the popular cruise-liner pastime of driving golf balls into the ocean. Recognizing the potential market for an environmentally sound golf ball, Patrick E. Kane (U.S.) invented AquaFlyte, a biodegradable, soluble golf ball, for which he received a U.S. patent in 1992. The ball's shell is made from cellulose and water-soluble polymers, and the core's materials include sodium bicarbonate and sodium citrate. The ball looks real, and its flight is two-thirds that of a normal ball. However, unlike the real ball, when AquaFlyte goes to a watery grave it creates fish food, not a one-stroke penalty.

CD VIDEO-GAME

Both Sega and Nintendo have announced plan to launch CD Video-Games in 1993. Sega, in partnership with Sony, is planning to introduce a CD system that provides high-definition animation with a three-dimensional feel and a better quality sound system. This system will also feature actors' real voices and limited-motion video. Nintendo, in partnership with Philips N.V., plans to unveil its new CD Video-Game in January 1993. This system is reported to incorporate full-motion video capability.

GAMOW SLEEPING CHAMBER

Invented by Prof. Igor Gamow (U.S.), the Gamow chamber is designed to enable an athlete training at sea level to gain the fitness advantage of living at high altitude. Research has shown that athletes living at high altitude develop better physiologically for exercise than their counterparts at sea level, but that more strenuous training can be achieved at low altitude because of the greater supply of oxygen available. With his sleeping chamber, Gamow is trying to provide the athlete with the best of both worlds. The 8-foot, 200-lb cylindrical bed chamber can simulate altitudes up to 18,000 feet. A vacuum pump draws air out of the chamber, which is sealed by a latchless Plexiglass door. A valve system devised by Gamow simulates the desired altitude, while circulating fresh air to the sleeping athlete.

GOLF SIMULATORS

With the limited supply of tee times causing long lines at golf courses, ingenious designers have created computer-assisted videos that simulate real golf courses indoors. Golfers can play 18 holes at an indoor range, miles from the nearest blade of grass. The Super Simulator, launched by Golftek, incorporates a video screen and computer software to analyze the swing, and offers the player the chance to play real courses superimposed on the screen, or holes created by computer graphics. The INGOLF system, available since 1990, uses similiar principles. Specially designed balls contain mirrors that allow light sensors to track the trajectory of the ball hit against a 10 x 12-foot video screen.

WORM KLAMP

For the fisherman who is squeamish about handling worms, two brothers from St. Louis, Mo., Frank and Dan Koester, have invented the Worm Klamp. Patented in 1992, the clamp looks like a long-toothed comb. The fisherman lifts up the worm using the plastic arms, and a unique spring-action snaps the worm into the ideal straight-line position held by the teeth of the clamp. The slimy bait is ready to be threaded onto the hook, untouched by human hands.

PICK-UP HOOPS

Invented by Jason Parr (U.S.), Pick-up Hoops is literally basketball on the flatbed of a pickup truck. Unable to find space to play basketball in Detroit, Parr devised his game to be played on the back of a truck. A court frame is bolted to the truck's bed, and two pieces of adjustable four-by-fours allow the rim to be set at the regulation 10-foot height. The backboard extends six feet away from the back of the truck. Parr received a U.S. patent in 1992 and is working with a Florida manufacturer to produce the device commercially.

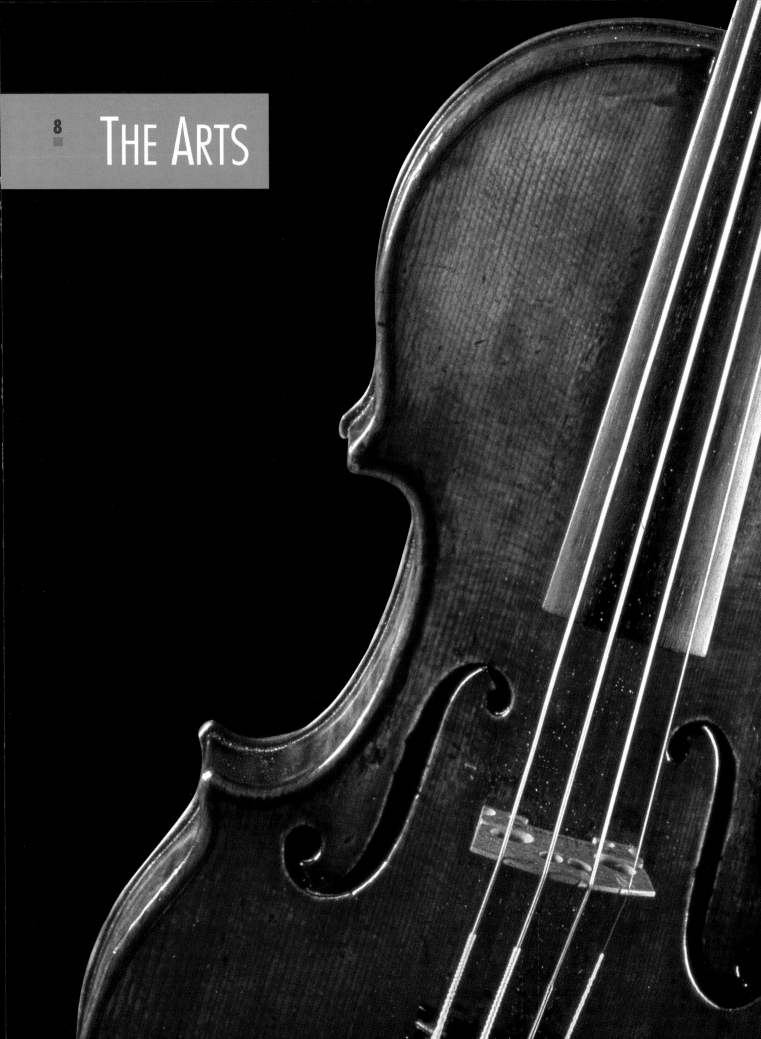

8 THE ARTS

VISUAL ARTS

Painting

Origins (30,000–12,000 B.C.)

It is not known whether humans used paint first on themselves or on other surfaces. Archeologically, the most ancient vestiges of painting are Paleolithic cave paintings dated from 30,000 to 12,000 B.C.

The brush (prehistory)

Like painting, the paintbrush can be traced to prehistory. Paleolithic artists used brushes made of feathers or vegetable fibers, as well as their hands, fingers or sometimes a pad of moss. From earliest times, the peoples of the Mediterranean basin used brushes to apply tempera (paint with water, gum or egg base). The ancient Egyptians used them to decorate tombs as early as 3400 B.C. Today the best brushes are made of silk and fine hair.

Canvas (2000 B.C.)

Canvas (linen, cotton or hemp) is an ancient material. A fragment of linen dating from between 2000 and 1788 B.C. was found in Egypt. Canvas offered a cheaper and lighter base than wood, particularly for large paintings. In the Middle Ages canvas was used for painted processional banners. The use of canvas didn't become widespread until the invention and development of oil paint in the 15th century, when it proved to be an ideal base for the new paint.

Palette (15th century)

The first known palettes were small wooden surfaces used by French painters in the 15th century. Palettes were first used to mix colors for completing the final details of a painting. With the growth of oil painting, the size of the paintings grew larger, a trend mimicked by the palette. The familiar ovoid palette with the thumb hole became popular in the 18th century.

Oil painting (15th century)

The most important technical event in the history of painting was the invention of oil painting at approximately the beginning of the 15th century. Quick-drying oils were known to the Greeks, and texts prior to the 15th century refer to their use, but there were difficulties using oil paints and their use was sparse. However, painters during the Middle Ages wanted a new medium that gave colors greater brilliance and depth, dried slowly and offered resistance to humidity when dry. Historians generally credit the Van Eyck brothers (Flanders) with developing the first successful oil paints in 1420.

Metal paint tube (1841)

In March 1841 John G. Rand (U.S., 1801–73) was granted a British patent for collapsible metal tubes used to store oil paints. Rand, a portrait painter, devised the tubes in order to reduce the time he spent mixing oils. Later the same year he was granted a patent in the United States. In 1846 the British paint manufacturers Winsor & Newton produced the first moist watercolors in tubes.

MUSIC

Instruments

Origins (prehistory)

It is impossible to retrace the origins of most modern-day musical instruments, since they are often the end products of a long evolution whose roots go deep into the history of humankind. However, the innovations made by instrument-makers to perfect and multiply the sound possibilities of their instruments puts them on a level with the greatest inventors.

Percussion instruments

Origins (prehistory)

Percussion instruments were the very first musical instruments to be created by humankind. Their origins go back to prehistoric times, when historians believe people first banged, struck, shook or scraped materials to make rhythmic sounds. Tambourines, maracas, cymbals and numerous other percussion instruments are found in all cultures worldwide.

Drum (prehistory)

The drum is one of the oldest-known instruments. It is common to all cultures, as evidenced by the numerous depiction of drums in the paintings and monuments of all the ancient civilizations, including Egypt, India and Persia.

Drum kit (1910)

The drum kit originated in New Orleans, La. c. 1910. After a long evolution it took its familiar form c. 1950.

Wind instruments

Horn (prehistory)

The horn is one of the oldest-known instruments. Hunters and warriors used primitive instruments carved from animals' horns. The horn was introduced into the orchestra in the 17th century, by which time it was made of metal. In 1815 Heinrich Stölzel (Germany) invented the chromatic valved horn, which he patented in 1818.

Flute (prehistory)

The origin of the flute lies in prehistory. In the Middle Ages a flute with a mouthpiece was generally used, and it was only from the 17th century that the transverse flute began to replace it. In 1832 Theobald Böhm (Germany, 1793–1881), flautist at the Chapel Royal in Munich, Germany, modified and improved the instrument (by covering the holes with keys), to such an extent that one can talk justifiably of a reinvention. It was at this time that wood was replaced by metal.

Trumpet (2nd millennium B.C.)

A bronze trumpet dating from the 2nd millennium B.C. has been discovered in Egypt. The form, for a long time straight, was bent into an S-shape in the 15th century. The art of rolling the tube into a loop was discovered in the 16th century. The valve trumpet, which increased the instrument's chromatic capacities considerably, appeared around 1815. The valve trumpet's invention is attributed to Heinrich Stölzel (Germany).

Oboe (2000 B.C.)

Instruments from the oboe family were played in Egypt around 2000 B.C. Like numerous instruments of this type, the oboe derives from the double-reed aulos, whose invention the Greeks attributed to Minerva and even to Apollo. However, it was not until Frédéric Triébert's (France) refinements in the 19th century that the oboe was perfected.

Organ (3rd century B.C.)

The earliest form of organ consisted of a large set of panpipes fitted with two pumps that forced air through the pipes. The air pressure was created by pumping water by hand, which is why it was known as a hydraulic organ. It was developed by Ctesibius of Alexandria around 220 B.C.

Clarinet (c. 1700)

J. Christian Denner (Germany, 1655–1707) invented the clarinet in Nuremburg c. 1700. However, its origins are ancient; its ancestry has been traced to the arghoul of ancient Egypt. After a series of modifications, the Böhm key system (see Flute) was applied to the clarinet and it reached its technical perfection.

Accordion (1829)

The accordion can claim a large number of ancestors, one of which is the Chinese sheng, invented by a legendary queen, Nyu Wa, c. 2500 B.C. But we owe the invention of the accordion as we know it to Cyril Demian (Austria) who took out a patent on May 6, 1829.

Previous page: The Mendelssohn Stradivarius violin. (Christie's London)

Antonio Stradivarius perfected the art of violin-making in the late 17th century. His instruments are the most admired in the world, with some 500 still in existence. (New York Philharmonic Archives)

Saxophone (1846)

In his attempts to improve the bass clarinet, Adolphe Sax (Belgium, 1814–94) invented a new instrument: the saxophone. Patented in 1846, the saxophone first found success in military bands. It was later to become one of the leading instruments of the jazz era.

Stringed instruments

Harp (3000 B.C.)

The harp is one of the oldest musical instruments, deriving from the primitive musical bow. It existed at the time of the Sumerians and of the Egyptians (3000 B.C.). The harp achieved its familiar form after various modifications which culminated in 1801 when Sébastien Erard (France) put together the first double-action harps.

Violin (17th century)

The violin evolved from medieval instruments such as the *lyra da braccio*. It was in 17th- and 18th-century Italy that the art of instrument-makers such as Andrea Amati and Antonio Stradivari (c. 1644–1737) brought the violin to perfection. Stradivarius built more than 1,100 instruments, half of which still exist. His most famous violin is the Greffuhle, made in Cremona in 1709.

Piano (1710)

The forerunner of the piano is the exchequer. But the inventor of the piano is Bartolomeo Cristofori (Italy, 1655–1731) who in 1698 cre-ated his first *cembalo a martelletti* (a clavichord with small hammers), and toward 1710 his first pianoforte. A number of improvements were later made: G. Silbermann perfected the system of hammers; J.A. Stein invented pedals (1789). But it is Sébastien Erard (France) who, by inventing in 1822 the double escapement that allows a note to be repeated, can be considered the true creator of the modern piano.

Guitar (1850)

The origins of the guitar are disputed. Some historians theorize that the guitar developed from the lute, while others argue that it developed separately in Spain in the mid-16th century. Spanish instrument maker A. de Torres is generally credited with developing the modern guitar in the late 19th century. His work concentrated on improving the upper soundboard, enriching the tone and standardizing the length of the strings.

Electronic Music

Electric organ (1930)

Thaddeus Cahill (U.S.) developed an electro-mechanical organ in 1895. However, the pioneers of the electric organ as we know it were Coupleux and Givelet (both France), who, c. 1930, invented an organ whose sound quality resembled that of the classical organ. Unfortunately, the number of oscillators used (approximately 80) made it rather unstable. In 1943 Constant Martin introduced an improved model.

Electromagnetic organ (Hammond organ) (1935)

The inventor of the electromagnetic organ was Laurens Hammond (U.S., 1895–1973), a former clockmaker from Chicago, Ill., who had been ruined in the Great Depression. In an attempt to revive his business, c. 1935, Hammond decided to convert the unused cogwheels he had in stock to make an organ in which the keys set in motion wheels that released electric currents. The organ had two keyboards, electric tone generation and a wide variety of tone colors.

Electric guitar (1935)

The principle behind the electric guitar was discovered in the United States at the beginning of the 1920s. Lloyd Loar invented the first microphone to be specially adapted for the guitar between 1920 and 1924. If one excepts the electric Dobros (1930) and the Hawaiian electric guitars (Frying pan, 1931), the first solid frame electric guitar was created by Rickenbacher (U.S.), who, in 1935, designed the Electro Vibrola Spanish Guitar, the body of which was made of bakelite.

It was not until 1947 that Paul Bigsby (the inventor of the vibrato system) designed the first modern electric guitar at the request of guitarist Merle Travis. A veritable industry then began thanks to Leo Fender, who marketed the Broadcaster from 1948 on, and the Telecaster from 1950 on. The latter is still popular today in its quasi-original form.

Electric piano (1958)

The first instrument worthy of the name dates from 1958, when the American company Wurlitzer, marketed one intended for use in music schools. It was very quickly adopted by the first rock musicians, as it was easy to transport and had great potential for amplification. It was used for the recording of the Ray Charles classic "What'd I Say?"

In 1963 the well-known Rhodes Fender piano made its appearance. Its particular tonal quality remains a feature of much modern music.

Synthesizer (1965)

Despite a few earlier attempts, the history of sound synthesis (the creation of sounds from electric pulses) did not begin until the early 1950s, with experiments carried out at the University of Bonn, West Germany. The first electronic music studio was set up in 1951 at a West German radio station. Through a complex assemblage of generators and filters, the composers created sounds which they put together manually afterward on magnetic tapes. Because this was a very slow process, the engineer Robert Moog (U.S.) (in collaboration with the composers Herbert A. Deutsch and Walter Carlos) had the idea of bringing together all the necessary equipment in one instrument. His research culminated in the Minimoog, which became available in 1965, and that was when the word "synthesizer" was first used.

Rhythm box (1965)

The organ-maker Wurlitzer developed an electromechanical automatic percussion system (Sideman), probably based on mechanical percussion in 1965.

In 1970 at the Houston Fair, the American company Hammond revealed the first rhythm box to have automatic accompaniment. A few months later the Italian firm Farfisa unveiled its version, which it had been working on at the same time, and it was this one that remained one of the best-performing rhythm boxes for many years.

Digital organ (1971)

In 1971 the American company Allen took up Ralph Deutsch's patent for the use of digital synthesis in musical instruments. The Allen organ does not imitate the sound of an organ but faithfully recreates the sounds of numerous musical instruments from its memory bank.

Guitar synthesizer (1978)

In 1978 a collaboration between the Swedish instrument-maker Hagstrom and the American manufacturer Ampeg provided an opportunity to create a synthesizer based on a guitar. Modern technology has enabled synthesizers to be played using any guitar by means of the MIDI interface.

Electronic drum kit (1980)

The British firm Simmons was the first to replace the skins on a drum kit with electronic sensors that were sensitive to pressure. The patent issued in 1980 was soon taken up by other well-known manufacturers such as Roland, which produced the Octopad, followed by Octopad II in 1990. With its special sound quality, the instrument, played with standard drumsticks, has become a supplement to, rather than a replacement for, the traditional drum kit.

Sampling (1980)

Based on the patent taken out by Ralph Deutsch, sampling marks a turning point in the history of electronic instruments. The process consists of transforming a natural sound, recorded with a traditional microphone, into numerical data (bits). Calculations can then be carried out on these data to play the same sound in different pitches—for example, to mix it with others or to use it as a basic note in a synthesizer. In practice, the sampler is usually made up of a central unit to which a keyboard is connected. Musicians use it mainly to imitate acoustic instruments or to create voice effects.

MIDI interface (1981)

In 1981, at the instigation of American synthesizer manufacturers, the MIDI interface (*Musical Interface for Digital Instruments*) was introduced. This made all synthesizers and their accessories (e.g., rhythm boxes) compatible, whatever their make or functioning method.

A significant aspect of this system of intercommunication is that it has enabled the world of the synthesizer to be linked to that of the computer. The role of the computer in creating music has grown in recent years. The computer has become the musician's assistant if not the composer itself. For instance, a rhythm box marketed by Roland in the United States since the beginning of 1992 can create its own rhythms according to predefined styles. On the Atari ST, Steinberg's Tango software and Creative Sound's Improviser, can automatically improvise on given chords. Automatic accompaniment programs are installed in many keyboards for general use, and are steadily being improved (see Disklavier piano below).

Numeric synthesis box (1981)

In 1981 Linn (Great Britain) patented a rhythm box using numeric synthesis. Thanks to the drop in price of electronic memories, the rhythm box became fully programmable and capable of reproducing the most complex rhythms.

Electronic drumsticks (1986)

In 1986 the Japanese company Casio marketed the first electronic drumsticks. By striking any kind of surface, say a table, wall or saucepan, it is possible to obtain a sound similar to that produced by many percussion instruments. The drumsticks are connected to an electronic case.

Disklavier piano (1988)

The Disklavier is an example of high technology applied to the player piano. An acoustic piano with a built-in computer and playback system, the Disklavier precisely replicates tunes without the pianist touching the keys. Introduced in 1988 by the Japanese company Yamaha, the system is controlled by a 3.5-inch floppy disk, common to most personal computers, which programs all the notes, keys and pedaling for each performance.

Mandala (1990)

Invented by Vincent John Vincent and Frank MacDougall (both Canada), the Mandala is the first video synthesizer. To play it, you just have to move, or dance, in front of a camera. The image is transmitted onto a screen, where virtual buttons are superimposed on it. Each time the image touches one of these buttons, a sound is generated. The relationship between music and movement can be programmed differently for each performance.

MIDI ultrasound controller (1990)

Marketed by Electronic Music Studios (EMS), the Soundbeam system is a MIDI controller based on movement. It projects a cone of ultrasound rays and detects the presence and size of any object. Linked to a synthesizer or a sampler by MIDI, the Soundbeam System makes it possible, for example, to control the pitch notes by placing the hands in specific positions, and to play *glissandos* in harmony with the speed of movement.

SOUND REPRODUCTION

Performance Systems

Phonograph (1877)

Thomas Alva Edison (U.S., 1847–1931) invented the phonograph on August 12, 1877 and patented it on February 17, 1878. The machine

The Disklavier piano is an example of computer technology applied to the player piano. A built-in computer precisely replicates tunes without the pianist touching the keys. (Yamaha)

Thomas Edison invented the phonograph in 1877. His machine produced poor sound quality, and Edison abandoned the project, leaving other inventors to perfect his idea. (The Bridgeman Art Library)

was a revolving drum with spiraled grooves around its circumference. It brought Edison worldwide fame, but the sound quality was mediocre and the cylinders did not last long. Edison preferred to move on to different lines of research and left the task of improving his machine to others. Chichester Bell (cousin of Alexander Graham Bell, the inventor of the telephone) and Charles Sumner Tainter (both U.S.) took out a patent in 1886 for a piece of apparatus similar to the phonograph but using wax cylinders. This was the graphophone.

Speaker (1877)

The first patents relating to the coil-driven speaker, which is virtually the only type in use today, date back to the 19th century. A patent was registered by Ernst Wermer for the German company Siemens on December 14, 1877, and by the physicist Sir Oliver Lodge (Great Britain) on April 27, 1898. But at the time there was no electrical source that would have enabled the mechanism to operate.

In 1924 Chester W. Rice and Edward Kellogg, both of General Electric, registered a patent for a voice coil speaker as well as constructing an amplifier capable of providing power of 1W for their device. The speaker, known as the Radiola Model 104, had a built-in amplifier and came onto the market the following year at a price of $250.

Ribbon speaker (1925)

The technique of the ribbon speaker was invented in 1925. The standard cone was replaced by a very fine aluminum ribbon that was concertinaed and exposed to a magnetic field. The first models were brought out in the United States in the 1940s.

Boxed-in loudspeakers (1958)

It was only later that someone had the idea of putting one or more speakers in a wooden or plaster case to form the loudspeakers we know

today. In 1958 the French firm Cabasse built the first speakers with an incorporated amplifier.

Column speaker (1988)

This speaker was invented by electronics engineer Walter Schupbach (Switzerland), after 15 years of research. It is a single speaker that produces a stereo sound effect and, according to the most highly qualified specialists, makes it possible to achieve an authentic spatial reproduction of sound. It is placed in the center of the room, either on the floor or suspended, and in this way gives an exact reproduction, on the horizontal as well as the vertical plane, of the position of the instruments (or other sources of sound) used during the recording. His invention came onto the market at the end of 1988.

Tape recorder (1888)

The principle of the tape recorder was worked out theoretically in 1888 by Oberlin Smith (Great Britain). Ten years later 20-year-old Valdemar Poulsen (Denmark) put the theory into practice. However, his presentation of the new machine at the 1900 Paris Exhibition did not raise much interest. It was not until 1935 that two German companies, AEG Telefunken and I.G. Farben, made a device based on Poulsen's principle with a plastic tape that ran at 25 ft per second.

Microphone (1925)

In 1925 a team from the Bell Laboratories, directed by Joseph Maxfield, perfected an electrical system of recording. The microphone, by converting sounds into electric currents, replaced the huge horns that had been used until then.

Pulse code modulation (1926)

Pulse code modulation appears to have been invented by Paul Rainey in 1926, reinvented in 1939 by H.A. Reeves (U.S.), and rediscovered during World War II by Bell Laboratories to fulfill the need for secrecy in telephone conversations. The process enables a continuous signal, such as a telephonic signal, to be sampled. The value of each sample is then quantified and converted by coding into a digital signal.

Magnetic recording tape (1928)

Magnetic recording tape was patented in 1928 by Fritz Pfleumer (Germany). As far back as 1888, Oberlin Smith had proposed using strips of fabric covered with iron filings.

In search of perfect sound quality, engineers have created speakers in many shapes and sizes. The revolutionary Technics SST-1 catches the eye as well as the ear. (Le Livre Mondial des Inventions)

AEG became interested in Pfleumer's invention; they concentrated on the development of the tape recorder and passed the work of improving the tape on to I.G. Farben. The first tests were carried out by the two firms in 1932, and in 1934 I.G. Farben was able to produce 164,000 ft of tape.

Performance Media

Record (1887)

In 1887 Emile Berliner, a German living in America, came up with the idea of replacing the cylinder of the phonograph with thin disks of zinc covered with a layer of wax into which fine grooves were cut. Having invented the record, he went on to develop the machine on which it could be played: the gramophone. The record did not replace the cylinder entirely and the two co-existed for many years. On his return to Germany 10 years later, Berliner and his brother founded Deutsche Grammophon Gesell-schafter, which became one of the world's leading recording companies.

Jukebox (1889)

The first jukebox, which worked with cylinders, was installed by Louis Glas (U.S.) at the Royal Palace in San Francisco on November 23, 1889. It was followed by the public phonograph, the Automatic Entertainer, produced by the Gabel Co. in 1906, which offered a choice of music. Unfortunately, the sound quality was poor. The electric gramophone was introduced around 1925, and in 1926 a Swedish immigrant to the United States, J.P. Seeburg, invented the audiophone which offered a choice of eight records.

Stereo record (1933)

The first stereophonic records were produced in Great Britain by EMI (Electric and Musical Industries) in 1933. The research, directed by the physicist Alan Dower Blumlein, culminated in the recording of stereo 78s. The work of Blumlein and EMI remained experimental until 1958, when the American company Audio Fidelity and the British companies Pye and Decca issued the first commercial stereo records thanks to numerous technical advances.

Long-playing record (LP) (1947)

René Snephvangers (Belgium) directed the CBS research team which in 1944 came up with the first 33 rpm record. The long-playing record was perfected in the United States by Peter Goldmark for CBS in 1947 to replace 78s. The patent was taken out under the initials LP (long-playing). The first recordings on a long-player were Mendelssohn's Violin Concerto, Tchaikovsky's *Fourth Symphony* and the musical *South Pacific*. Their fine grooves and slow rpm meant that LPs could hold six times more music than 78s.

Sony WALKMAN (1979): Sony Corporation

Akio Morita and the WALKMAN. (Sony)

So many discoveries are made through serendipity—finding something while looking for something else. But what happens when two deparments of a huge, cutting-edge, hi-tech company work on two parts of one invention, without knowing it?

The company was Sony, and the invention that came about when the left hand found out what the right hand was doing became the WALKMAN. In the late 1970s, a team of engineers was trying to create a portable stereo compact cassette recorder. They needed two components: a stereo recording mechanism and a stereo playback mechanism, which could fit into a small box to make a portable product. As the first step, the team decided to create a prototype of the smallest, lightest stereo cassette player by dropping the recording mechanism.

Meanwhile, another research team worked on making headphones. At the time, the lightest set weighed 100 grams (3.5 ounces). The goal was a set that wieghed half that much.

Sony's honorary chairman, Masaru Ibuka, visited Team 1 and tried out their invention. His opinion? Great, but the headphones were too heavy. And did they know Team 2 was working on lightweight headphones?

By the spring of 1979 two and two were put together, and Ibuka proposed the prototype to Sony's chairman, Akio Morita. The prototype made sense to Morita, whose children played their stereos night and day, everywhere except on the street. He could see the niche where a portable stereo cassette player would fit in. At first, eight of every 10 Sony dealers pooh-poohed the idea. While they hedged, their children and store salespeople tried out the prototypes. College students took the device out for a test-drive, and people followed them around asking where they could get those headphones, that cassette player. Finally, just before the commercial release, this prototype of the portable stereo cassette player was named WALKMAN.

WALKMAN's biggest challenge in the global market was its name. It isn't good English, said dealers in England, Australia and the United States. The English dealers wanted it named Stowaway, Americans opted for Soundabout, and the Aussies dubbed it Freestyle. Nothing doing, said Morita. In 1986, the *Oxford English Dictionary* included WALKMAN as a noun in the English language.

The following year an early WALKMAN took its place in the Smithsonian Institution. In the 1980s the portable stereos were considered one of the top three must-have fashion accessories, along with digital watches and roller skates. In 1989 Sony celebrated production of the 50-millionth WALKMAN. That's 50 million people worldwide walking to the beat of their own drummer, singing along off-key to a song only they can hear. What a movement! Now just imagine: what if they were all hearing the same song?

Tape cassette (1961)

It was in 1961 that the Dutch company Philips developed the first mini tape cassette, which was 3.9 in. long and designed for stereo and mono recordings. This cassette, along with the first cassette recorder, was unveiled in Berlin, Germany in 1963. Philips decided to allow manufacturers to use its patent free of charge so as to encourage the spread of the system throughout the world.

Dolby (1967)

The first noise reducer, designed to improve the signal/noise ratio, was the work of Ray Dolby

(U.S.) in 1967. (Dolby had begun his career working on the tape recorder.) Dolby A was intended for professional use; a few years later, Dolby brought out a simplified system for general use called Dolby B. Dolby stereo, as used in the movies, is produced from four sources, which improve the sound quality and gives the audience a sense of depth and relief.

Compact disc (1979)

The invention of the compact disc (CD) was the result of research carried out on the video disc by the Dutch electronics company Philips NV. Under a joint licensing agreement by Philips and the Japanese company Sony, the CD was first developed in 1979. A process of digital recording is used, rather than the analogue recording process used for the microgroove. The signal is coded in binary form, using the series 0 and 1. The conventional groove has therefore disappeared and has been replaced by millions of microcells known as pits: approximately 4 million per second. The sound is reproduced by a laser beam. The compact disc has a diameter of 5 inches and can hold 75 minutes of music or sound on one side.

The CD was first marketed in 1983, and by 1991 had outstripped both traditional forms of recorded music—records and tapes—in terms of unit sales and values. In the space of a few years, the CD has achieved incredible success, and its applications are many and varied. In 1984 Philips and Matsushita brought out the prototypes of decoders that enabled fixed images, which had been stored on CDs alongside an audio signal, to be viewed on television. In 1985 the extensive storage capacity of CDs was applied to computers. CD players now have the capability of running a disc at twice the normal speed, which makes it possible to record an hour-long disc onto a cassette in just 30 minutes.

Digital audio tape (1987)

Beginning in 1980, several Japanese manufacturers researched the possibility of an audio cassette reader that used digital recordings (Digital Audio Tape or DAT) and offered a quality of sound equivalent to that of the compact disc.

There were two rival models; the JVC fixed-head S-DAT, and the R-DAT, developed by Matsushita and Sony, which has rotating heads and has since been adopted by the majority of manufacturers.

Aiwa was the first company to market the DAT in Japan in February 1987.

Compact disc video (1987)

In 1987 there was a new development. The CDV, the compact disc video, was brought out by Philips and developed in conjunction with Sony. It enables video pictures to be shown on a television screen while laser quality sound is produced simultaneously on stereo. The new readers can reproduce both sound and picture. They will read standard compact discs, while the gold CDVs of the same format (i.e., 5 inches) play pictures and sound for six minutes as well as 20 minutes of music, the 8-inch CDVs offer 40 minutes of pictures and sound and the 12-inch CDVs last for a maximum of two hours, and give additional backing to films and operas. The CDV is one of the answers to the competition offered by DAT (Digital Audio Tape), an audio-digital cassette.

Compil Box (1989)

Patented in 1989 by Pierre Schwab (Switzerland), the Compil Box is a complete audio and video recording studio in a suitcase. Developed using Sony equipment, it works on a battery, a car cigarette lighter socket or standard electric current. It contains no fewer than two speakers,

headphones, a TCD-D10 portable DAT, a CD player, a video Walkman, a camera input point, etc.

CD-MIDI(1989)

In June 1989 the Japanese company JVC brought out a new generation of compact discs, the CD-M, a piece of equipment that contains two types of information: MIDI data for the control of electronic instruments (for example, synthesizers and rhythm boxes), and graphic information related to the different instrumental functions including tempo, tone and so on. Each CD-M contains several pre-programmed musical works by professional artists.

Inserted into a special player, the CD-M reproduces the works on the connected instruments, and the user can add or remove tracks, alter the tempo or adjust the tone at will.

SCMS (Serial Copy Management System) (1990)

The first DAT players equipped with an anti-pirating device appeared in 1990—the SCMS (Serial Copy Management System). This device resulted from the 1989 international agreement reached between publishers and manufacturers. The SCMS system prevents anyone from making a digital copy (known as the second generation) from the first copy.

Double-play CD (1991)

In 1992, Technics announced the development of a laser platen able to read five CDs successively. In 1992 Denon offered the DN 2000 in its semiprofessional range. It is a two-carriage CD player connected to a controller provided with specific commands for each platen. Its advantages include instant start, speed control, rhythm equalizer system and rapid overview of tracks.

PHOTOGRAPHY

Origins (16th century)

Photography results from the combination of two disciplines: optics and photo chemistry. Each followed separate paths through history, the former dating back to the middle of the 16th century, the latter to the beginning of the 18th century. Once they had come together, lenses and films progressed along parallel roads.

It was Sir John Hershel (Great Britain, 1792–1871) who, in 1836, coined the word photography (from the Greek *photos*, light, and *graphein*, to write) to describe the action of light on certain sensitive surfaces.

Camera obscura (16th century)

The Chinese probably knew the principle of the dark room—the *camera obscura*—as early as the 4th century B.C. The Arab scholar Alhazen

(965–1038) used it to observe solar eclipses, and Leonardo da Vinci (1452–1519) described the phenomenon very clearly: a beam of light entering a darkened room through a small hole projects on the opposite wall the reverse image of the outside scene. Daniele Barbaro (Venice, 1513–70) in 1568 placed a lens over the hole, and this gave a sharper image.

However, it seems to have been a Neapolitan dramatist and writer on natural magic, Gianbattista della Porta (1538–1615), who first advocated the use of the *camera obscura* to reproduce images (by drawing them).

In the 17th century several inventors, including Johann Zahn and Athanase Kircher, made portable "dark rooms."

Lenses

Photographic lens (1637)

The famous philosopher and mathematician René Descartes (France, 1596–1650) formulated the principles of modern optics, the law of refraction, in his book *La Dioptrique* in 1637. Descartes' theory explained why the simple glass lens did not give a perfect image. A combination of different lenses, the photographic lens is required to correct distortions of the image formed on the light-sensitive surface when the light has come through a simple lens.

Diaphragm (1816)

The diaphragm regulates the amount of light passing through the objective lens. The iris diaphragm, used in all modern cameras and invented by Nicéphore Niepce (1765–1833) c. 1816, only came into general use c. 1880.

The valve diaphragm was created in 1858 for rapid rectilinear lenses or doublets. The automatic control of the diaphragm's aperture, according to the amount of light available, was the work of Alphonse Martin (France), who patented his invention in 1939.

Compound lens (1830)

An optician named Chevalier (France) developed the compound lens in 1830. This lens did not reconstitute light very well and every photograph required a long exposure time. In 1840 J. Petzval (Austria) produced a much-improved version of Chevalier's lens. It diffused 16 times more light than Chevalier's lens and was perfectly suited to photographing people, as it reduced the exposure time considerably.

Wide-angle lenses (1859)

The panoramic liquid lens conceived by Thomas Sutton (Great Britain) in 1859 covered a 120-degree field at f/12. To reduce refraction, the spaces between the lenses were filled with water.

The first wide-angle lens was von Hoëgh's Hypergon in 1900. Robert Hill's disymetric objective lens, introduced in 1924, gives an even wider field, and is the basis of the modern "fisheye" lens.

Rapid rectilinear lens (1865)

The rapid rectilinear lens consisting of two symmetrical groups of lenses was developed by Thomas Dallmeyer and Steinheil (both Germany) in 1865–66. In 1888 the anastigmatic lens, which corrected aberration by using a new type of glass that greatly deflected highly refracted rays, was developed by Dr. Schott (Germany). This lens gave a sharper image at the edges of the photograph.

In 1893 the Triplet lens was invented by H.D. Taylor. Composed of two convergent elements and separated by a divergent element, the Triplet lens corrected astigmatisms very well. This was the first in a series of rapid lenses, such as Rudolph Zeiss's (Germany) Planar, produced in 1896, and the famous Zeiss Tessar, produced in 1902.

Telephoto lens (1891)

The telephoto lens is an objective lens in which the focal length is greater than the negative image's diagonal and thus produces an enlarged image of a distant object. The first one was used by Thomas Dallmeyer in 1891. Some telephoto lenses with a very long focal length use curved mirrors: they are the catadioptric telephoto lenses perfected by B. Schmidt in 1931.

Lens coating (1904)

Lens coating reduced reflections from the glass surfaces within the lens. In 1904 Taylor patented a method for artificially tarnishing lenses. In 1935 Carl Zeiss patented a method of coating the lens surfaces with fluoride of magnesium.

Since 1945 all lenses have had coated surfaces, improving light transmission and contrast, and making it possible to produce multiple-element lenses.

Zoom lenses (1945)

Zoom lenses are objective lenses with a variable focal length. In 1896 T.R. Dallmayer and J.S. Bergheim perfected a rudimentary lens of this type that can be considered the distant ancestor of the modern zoom lenses. The idea was taken up again in 1945 in the United States with Frank Back's Zoomar, a combination of two sets of mobile lenses. But it was with Roger Cuvillier's Pancinor, developed in France in 1949, that the principle of the variable focal length was finally adopted.

Space objective lenses (1962)

The first space photographs were taken on October 3, 1962 during the Mercury mission with a German Carl Zeiss objective lens (and a Swedish Hasselblad 500C camera). It was also a Carl Zeiss lens that recorded the first steps of the first man on the moon, Neil Armstrong, during the *Apollo II* mission (July 16–24, 1969). During the same period NASA also used the French Angénieux lenses, which can be used in extreme light conditions, to equip the *Ranger* 7, 8 and 9 missions. The Angénieux lenses also went on the first trip to the moon.

Photographic Processes

First light-sensitive surfaces (1727)

As early as 1727 the physicist Johann Heinrich Schulze (Germany) noticed that silver nitrate turned black when exposed to the light. In 1777, the chemist C.W. Scheele (Sweden) made an extensive study of the effect of light on paper with silver chloride. In 1802, Thomas Wedgwood (Great Britain, son of Josiah Wedgwood, the potter) went further and obtained contact images on silver-nitrate coated paper of objects and drawings under glass. But as they were not fixed, these images disappeared when exposed to light.

Photography (1826)

The first attempts by J.W. Ritter (Germany) and Thomas Wedgwood and Humphry Davy (both Great Britain) in 1801 and 1802 to fix an image on light-sensitive paper in a *camera obscura* were unsuccessful.

Nicéphore Niepce (France) was looking for a means of reproducing his son's drawings mechanically. Having thought about the effect of light on some chemicals, in 1816, after many unsuccessful attempts, he managed to capture a picture on silver-chloride coated paper, at the back of a *camera obscura*. But the image was negative and short-lived. He then tried a different process using Jew's pitch, which turns white and hardens when exposed to light. In 1822 he reproduced translucent pictures by contact on a pitch-covered plate. These "heliographs" were the ancestors of photogravures. In 1826, carrying on his research in the *camera obscura*, he captured on the same plate, after eight hours' exposure, the first positive image. Photography had been invented.

Daguerreotype (1835)

It was in 1835 that Jacques Louis Mandé Daguerre (France, 1787–1851), Niepce's partner, perfected a new process to capture the image of an object on a metal plate. In spite of its faults (it was fragile, could be reproduced only by rephotographing and was reversed left to right), the daguerreotype produced a picture of an exceptional quality for the time. On August 19, 1839, Arago, permanent secretary at the French Academy of Science, revealed how daguerreotypes were obtained. They were an immediate success. "Daguerreotypomania" spread like wildfire all over the world: 500,000 plates were sold in Paris in 1846, and more than 3 million in the United States in 1853.

Photography on paper (1839)

The daguerreotype might be perfect from the artistic point of view, but on the technical side it was not the ancestor of contemporary photography. Modern photography has its roots in the work of two men each of whom had no knowledge of the work of the other: William Henry Fox Talbot (Great Britain, 1800–77) and Hippolyte Bayard (France, 1801–87).

As early as 1833 Talbot tried to fix on paper sensitized with silver chloride the image obtained at the back of a camera obscura. The following year, he obtained "photogenic drawings": negative images of the objects placed on the paper. He fixed the images with cooking salt. Improving his technique in 1835—after several hours' exposure and using a wooden box at the back of which he had placed some sensitized paper (a box his wife nicknamed the mousetrap)—he managed to obtain a faint negative image: the first negative on paper.

In 1839, when Daguerre's process was revealed, Talbot started his work again and discovered that by using this negative image as "an object to be copied" he could obtain a positive image on sensitized paper. The negative/positive process had been discovered.

Positive images on paper (1839)

Also in 1839, in Paris, Hippolyte Bayard invented a process that enabled him to obtain positive images directly on paper. They were of such good quality that they were shown at the first photographic exhibition on June 24, 1839. It is undeniable that these unique pictures, obtained after a 15-minute exposure, came before those of Daguerre. However, Arago asked Bayard not to reveal that fact so as to avoid upsetting Daguerre.

Calotype (1840)

In 1840 William Henry Fox Talbot (Great Britain) revealed what Bayard had earlier discovered: that it was possible to make the latent negative image, formed on paper treated with silver iodide that had been subjected to strong light, appear by putting it in a developer. This process meant that a pose could be held for less than 30 seconds, but only Talbot dreamt of using the negative to obtain a positive image through contact. This development led photography into the era of endless reproduction. Talbot called it a calotype from the Greek *kalos*, meaning beauty.

Wet collodion plate (1851)

In 1849 Le Gray (France) light-sensitized his negative materials with a collodion-based preparation—that is, one made of gun-cotton dissolved in ether. Nonetheless, it was Frederick Scott Archer (Great Britain) who first promoted the use of this process in 1851.

Fifteen times faster than the daguerreotype, the wet-collodion process was a resounding success because of the quality of reproduction, and was adopted by all the great photographers, including Roger Fenton and Matthew Brady.

Dry plates (1871)

In 1871 a doctor, Richard L. Maddox (Great Britain), published the first description of a process using really efficient dry plates. Improved by Charles Harper Bennett in 1876, gelatin bromide plates revolutionized the world of photography. And suddenly, industry took over and quickly popularized photography.

In 1879 a young amateur photographer, George Eastman (U.S., 1854–1932), invented a

The autochrome process was perfected by the Lumière brothers in 1903. This autochrome of the Arc de Triomphe in Paris was taken in 1919. (S.F.P.)

machine that could produce dry plates in large quantities. On January 1, 1881 he founded the Eastman Dry Plate Company with Henry A. Strong, a manufacturer of horse-drawn-carriage whips. This small company, based in Rochester, New York, went through a spectacular expansion and is today universally known under the name of Kodak.

Celluloid roll film (1889)

The first celluloid roll film to be used commercially was developed by Henri Reichenbach for George Eastman and marketed in 1889. Already in 1884 Eastman and William H. Walker had invented a container for rolls of negative paper. In 1885 they developed the film Eastman America. Unlike negative paper, it was a thin film that used paper only as a temporary support for the emulsion. The paper was eliminated after development and a thin negative film remained, which was then mounted on glass for the production of prints.

Color Photography

First attempts (1840)

As soon as photography was invented the question of color attracted inventors (colored daguerreotypes, 1840; photographic glazes by Lafon de Carmasac in 1854).

In 1848 Edmond Becquerel (1820–91) managed to photograph color prints but could not fix the images. It was Gabriel Lippmann who, in 1891, obtained the first direct color pictures by the interferential process (the fixation of the luminous vibration traces). That success won its inventor the Nobel Prize for Physics in 1908. The only problem was that his work could only be seen at a certain angle and could not be copied.

Additive process (1855)

This process is based on the discovery made in 1855 by the physicist James Clerk Maxwell (Great Britian,1831–79). Any color can be created by adding together the three fundamental colors, red, green and blue, in appropriate proportions.

Subtractive synthesis (1869)

This is the process from which all modern color photography processes are derived. The announcement of its discovery was marked by a dramatic turn of events: on May 7, 1869 two men, who knew nothing of each other's work, presented similar conclusions to the French Photographic Society. Charles Cros and Louis Ducos du Hauron (who had registered a patent in November 1868) had discovered trichromatic synthesis.

Autochrome process (1903)

It was by applying the principles of additive color synthesis that the Lumière brothers in 1903 perfected the autochrome plate process. Each plate was sprinkled with a mixture of potato starch grains dyed green, red and blue. A single 9 x 12 plate carried nearly 90 million!

This process remained popular until 1932, when it was replaced by Lumicolor and Filmcolor, also Lumière processes. It was subsequently abandoned altogether.

The autochrome technique produced some masterpieces that were very close to paintings in their texture and rich colors.

Modern film

Kodachrome (1935)

In 1911–12 the chemist Rudolf Fischer (Germany) discovered that dyes could be obtained by oxidation or coupling with other chemical substances. All modern color films follow this general principle.

It was not until 1935 that subtractive color synthesis found its first commercial application.

The Kodak Camera (1888): George Eastman

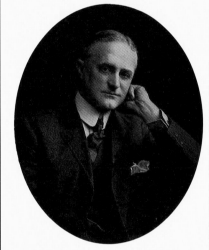

George Eastman. (International Museum of Photography at George Eastman House)

In 1888 George Eastman invented the Kodak camera, a simple, inexpensive, hand-held box that fulfilled his goal of making photography simple and accessible to the general public, or as he best described it, "made the camera as convenient as the pencil."

Eastman's fascination with photography had begun 11 years earlier when it was suggested to him that he photograph his planned vacation to Santo Domingo. Frustrated with the vast array of equipment required to fulfill the task—large camera, heavy tripod, a tent in which to store and develop the emulsions, chemicals, glass plates and plate holders—Eastman abandoned the trip. Instead he turned his mind to another project: making photography simple and available to everyone.

Forced to leave school at the age of 14 to help support his family, Eastman was working as a bank clerk in Rochester, N.Y., when he turned his attention to photography. He studied journals that described the latest ideas for perfecting the dry-plate process of photography.

His first laboratory was his mother's kitchen. He worked for two years developing a formula using gelatin emulsions that would produce a dry plate that could be mass-produced. In 1879 Eastman gained a patent for the plate and for a machine that could manufacture the plates. In January 1881, with the financial backing of Henry A. Strong, Eastman quit his bank job and formed the Eastman Dry Plate Company.

Eastman's next step forward came in 1884, when he introduced transparent roll-film. Instead of using glass plates as the medium for the light-sensitive emulsions that created the photographic image, he had the idea of using long strips of paper that could be rolled on spools attached to the camera. This eliminated the need for photographers to carry glass plates and chemicals, paving the way for mass participation in photography.

In 1888 Eastman unveiled the Kodak camera. A small hand-held box measuring 3.2 x 3.7 x 6.5 inches, the Kodak was equipped with an f/9 objective lens and a shutter with a 1/20 second speed. It contained a roll of film with 100 exposures. The camera was returned to the factory for the film to be developed and the camera reloaded. As Eastman's famous advertisement boasted: "You press the button, we do the rest."

Eastman soon pioneered mass production of his small cameras. By 1900 he was able to launch the Brownie, a simple box camera that cost only a dollar. This made the camera even more accessible: now the price, as well as the technology, was within the range of most people.

Although there have been many refinements to lenses, shutters and rolled film, the modern sophisticated hand-held camera is essentially the same as the original Kodak. Eastman had opened up the world of photography to everyone.

Two musicians, Leopold Mannes and Leopold Godowsky (both U.S.), with Kodak's financial backing, invented Kodachrome.

Agfacolor (1936)

In 1936 the German company Agfa's first reversal film, Agfacolor, came out. It had color couplers present in the emulsion. Subtractive color synthesis then spread all over the world, and improvements were made in rapid succession: in 1939 the Agfacolor negative/positive film appeared, a process that was immediately used by Hitler's propaganda machine (e.g. in the making of prestige films such as the *Adventures of Baron Münchhausen*, which created a sensation at the time).

In 1942 the United States' reply came in the form of Kodacolor. The reversal and negative/positive processes continued to evolve in parallel—the former producing Ektachrome (1945), Anscochrome (1955) and Fujicolor (1948); the latter Ektacolor (1947) and Geva-color. In 1949 a new generation of Kodacolor films, and in 1953 of Agfacolor, applied a technique using color "masks" that gave better color saturation.

In addition to its Kodacolor line, at the end of 1988 Kodak introduced the Ektar 25 and 1000, two types of negative films for print-making, aimed at the amateur wanting very high-quality pictures. These can only be used in 24 x 36 reflex cameras.

Polacolor (1963)

The announcement in 1963 by Edwin H. Land (U.S.) and his Polaroid Corporation that they had created a one-minute color film, Polacolor, caused a sensation. Extremely sophisticated in its conception, this film allowed a color print to be made on paper in only 60 seconds. The emulsion consisted of a negative part half the thickness of a hair, comprising nine distinct layers, and a positive part of four layers, as well as one last layer enclosing a capsule containing an alkaline solution that triggered off treatment. In total there were 14 layers in a single film!

In 1982 Polaroid launched a process for producing instant color or black and white transparencies.

Contemporary color emulsions (1983)

The perfecting of the renowned "T" grain by Kodak in 1983 meant an amazing improvement in sensitivity. This grain makes it possible, among other things, to raise the sensitivity of Kodacolor negative films to ISO 1000. There is also a fantastic improvement for reversal films, and the new Ektachrome comes with ISO 400, 600, 1600, even 3200, which makes it the most sensitive "daylight" film to date. Other companies have researched the same areas: Agfa (use of structured twin crystals) and Fuji (double structure grain SG and Fujicolor that can be used at ISO 3200).

Films with enzymes (1987)

The biotechnological revolution has reached photography with the process perfected by Canon. The enzyme film uses amylase (an enzyme that attacks starch) emulsions on a mixture of starch and color pigments. Light deactivates the enzyme. After reaction and drying, the black and white photo obtained is identical to those obtained with standard film.

3-D Photography

Stereoscopy (1838)

In 1838 Charles Wheatstone (Great Britain) made the first stereoscope, an apparatus that permitted geometric patterns to be seen in three dimensions. Each eye receives an image of the same object from a slightly different angle, and the two images are synthesized by the brain. This gives us the illusion of three-dimensional perception.

In 1849 the physicist Sir David Brewster (Great Britain) built a simple and practical stereoscope (a small closed box with two viewing holes) which, factory-produced by Dubosq (France) was all the rage in London at the Great Exhibition of 1851.

The stereoscopic revolution was all the more important since, because of the lenses' short focal length, exposure time was reduced to about a quarter of a second, which made the first snapshots possible.

Anaglyphs (1891)

In 1891 Louis Ducos du Hauron discovered a new process, anaglyphs, that consisted of superimposing two separate images of the same picture after dying one violet-blue and the other red, and then looking at them through glasses with one lens each of the same two colors. Each eye saw only one of the images, and the brain combined the two to give the illusion of a single three-dimensional picture.

Xography (1964)

This is the basic principle used in three-dimensional postcards. Perfected in 1964, the first 3-D photograph was published in *Look* magazine.

Nimslo process (1980)

This process, perfected in 1980, uses a four-lens camera to obtain four images recorded from different angles. After the film is developed, there are four images captured through 32 components (eight per photo) on the print. The same principle is used for Xography.

Modern Cameras and Processes

Automatic focus (1945)

The first automatic focus device appeared in 1945. It was the Optar, invented by Dr. Kaulmann (Germany). However, the device was too bulky to be fitted on a camera. Automatic focus is now a common feature and the device is an integral part of the camera. There are various principles: the CCD (Charge-Coupled Device), the Sonar by Polaroid (which uses ultrasound), and a system exclusive to Minolta (1983) using an infrared beam. Apart from the auto-focus cameras, the Minolta 7000 was the first reflex camera to use this system. The Minolta 9000 (1986) applies this automatic focusing system to all its range.

Polaroid (1948)

In November 1948 Edwin H. Land (U.S.) launched on the American market the first instant-picture camera, the Polaroid 95. At the age of 28, Land had founded the Polaroid Corporation, which specialized in the manufacture of sunglasses and polarizing filters.

In 1947 Kodak had shown no interest in Land's invention. But, on seeing how popular Polaroid cameras were, in 1976 Kodak decided to launch their own instant-picture cameras. However, Polaroid sued Kodak for patent violation, and after proceedings lasting 10 years, won the case in October 1985. This gave back to Polaroid exclusive use of the process and a minimum of $1 billion damages!

Edwin H. Land holds the second largest number of registered patents in the United States: 533.

Magnetic photography (1981)

On August 24, 1981 Sony introduced its Mavica-Magnetic Video Camera. This camera uses a magnetic disk, representing a revolution in photography: an electromagnetic system now replaces chemicals. The camera does not use film; therefore there is no processing or printing, as the picture can be seen on a screen.

In 1984 Panasonic introduced a camera of this type, but it recorded color pictures on a video floppy disk with a 50-frame capacity. Although it was the pioneer in this domain, Sony only marketed its Mavica MVC 1 (an improved version of the original) at the end of 1988 in Japan.

Kodak disc-film (1982)

On February 3, 1982 Kodak brought out a new type of photographic base: the disc-film. The flat plastic cartridge holds a disc-film that rotates around a hub in front of an exposure window that is behind the objective lens. Thicker than that of ordinary films, the base of the Kodacolor HR Disc film is made of Estar, a thick and rigid material.

DX coding (1984)

The 24 x 36 film cassettes have been coded since 1984; initially perfected by Kodak, the coding system tells the camera the type of film being used, its light sensitivity and the number of exposures. Absent-minded photographers (many devices have been geared to them!) will no longer run the risk of making awful mistakes. All the films on the market at present have such coding, and most modern cameras are fitted with the system.

Quicksnap (1986)

In 1986 Fuji invented a negative color film wrapped in a box that includes the lens and

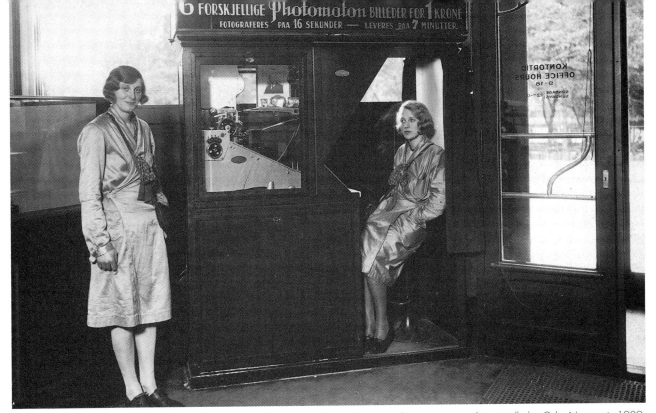

The photobooth was invented by Anatol Josepho in 1924. Here two attendants demonstrate how to use a machine installed in Oslo, Norway in 1929. (Le Livre Mondial des Inventions)

shutter. After the 24 pictures have been taken, the whole package is sent to a laboratory for processing. No adjusting is required; this film-camera is incredibly easy to use. In 1987 it was Kodak's turn to put a camera of that type on the market, the Fling, which joined the Quicksnap, a second-generation Fuji disposable camera. In 1988 Fuji brought out a Quicksnap with incorporated electronic flash.

In 1989 the Quicksnap telephoto lens was brought out. It enlarges the subject two and a half times compared with the standard Quicksnap lens, and provides improved long-distance photographic quality.

Photo CD System (1992)

After three years of development, Eastman Kodak Co. launched the KODAK Photo CD system during the summer of 1992. In September 1990 Kodak, in association with Philips, announced plans to develop the Photo CD, a system for storing photographs digitally on a compact disc. Photo negatives or slides can be converted to Photo CD discs at a photofinisher or photo laboratory. The "electronic photo album" is run on a photo CD player that plays back the photos on standard television screens.

Attachments

Flash (1850)

Toward 1850 it was discovered that the combustion of magnesium wires produced an extremely brilliant light—accompanied, however, by a thick cloud of white smoke. In 1887 Adolf Mietke and Johannes Gaedicke (both Germany) invented flash powder (magnesium powder), an explosive mixture with a base of magnesium, potassium chlorate and antimony sulphate. This process won over most photographers, despite the dangers involved in its use.

Flash bulbs (1929)

In 1925 Paul Vierkotter took out a patent for a new flash method in which the inflammable mixture was contained in a vacuum lamp and set alight by means of an electric current.

But it was in 1929 that the first real flash bulb appeared, thanks to Ostermeier (Germany), who perfected the system and created the Vacublitz bulb. This had the advantage of being both silent and smokeless. Today's flash cubes are miniaturized versions of the flash bulb.

Electronic flash (1931)

The principle used in this invention goes back to the very beginning of photography. In 1851 Fox Talbot succeeded in obtaining an image of a newspaper fixed to a rotating wheel, thanks to a spark supplied by means of a condenser battery.

In 1931 Harold Edgerton of the Massachusetts Institute of Technology invented the electronic flash; the current accumulated at high voltage in a condenser explodes in a tube filled with rare gases.

Underwater Photography

Underwater photographic observations (1856)

The first underwater photograph was shown by William Thompson to the London Art Society in 1856. The photographic apparatus had been placed at the bottom of Weymouth Bay at a depth of 20 ft. The lens, controlled from the surface, stayed open for 10 minutes.

In 1889 zoology professor Louis Boutan (France) took photos at a depth of 164 ft. The photographs thus obtained were published in 1900 in an album that was the first of its kind.

In 1935 William Beebe (Great Britain) took photographs from the porthole of a bathyscaphe at a depth of 2,950 ft.

Ten years later, Maurice Ewing (U.S.) developed an automatic underwater camera to photograph geological formations at depths between 1,310 and 2,300 ft.

Underwater reflex camera (1992)

The Nikonos, from Nikon, is the first self-focusing, watertight reflex model developed for underwater photography. The viewfinder is larger in order to make it easier to use with a mask, and the focusing system is automatic. The camera is made of aluminum alloy with toric joints that can withstand 10 kg per cm pressure, enabling it to be used at depths of up to 100 meters.

Photobooth

Photobooth (1924)

The photobooth is the invention of Anatol Marco Josepho (Hungary), who registered his patent in Germany on January 13, 1924. The machine was marketed in England in 1928. The attendant was replaced by a coin slot in 1968, and in the same year color was introduced.

Prontophot (1991)

The Swiss company Prontophot introduced in October 1991 an electronic photobooth. Thanks to a screen that shows the image, subjects can shoot the photo when they want to. The subject also has a choice of background color. The photo development involves no chemicals, but is done electronically, producing a better quality print.

MOTION PICTURES

Moving Pictures

Magic lantern (1654)

The ancestor of "the movies" is the magic lantern, invented in 1654 by a Jesuit priest, Athanase Kircher (Germany). The magic lantern was a small projector for transparent views. During the 18th and 19th centuries these lanterns were highly popular. Modern slide projectors are nothing more than perfected magic lanterns.

Fantasmagoria (1798)

In 1798, Gaspard Robert (France) opened the first public projection shows—the Fantasmagorias—in Paris, France. Robert's shows were staged in a darkened room, where he projected fantastic luminous images into the dark, terrifying the audience. His method was to project his painted subjects on glass plates behind a screen of translucent percale, which camouflaged the operators and the machines. Robert kept his method a secret for eight years, during which time the fantasmagoria became an enormous success.

Phénakistiscope (1832)

Joseph Plateau (Belgium) demonstrated in 1828 the principle of the persistence of luminous images on the retina, thereby formulating the basis of motion pictures. Plateau invented a phénakistiscope in 1832 that for the first time produced a moving image. A cardboard disc carried a sequence of pictures of a subject such as a dancer. As it revolved, the disc created the impression that the figure was moving.

Stroboscope (1833)

The stroboscope, which works on a principle similar to that of the phénakistiscope, was invented in 1833 by Simon von Stampfer (Austria). It is used today to give the appearance of immobility or slowness to objects that are moving rapidly. The stroboscope has industrial applications, but is perhaps better known for its use in dance clubs for animating the dance floor.

Pictures of movement (1878)

After years of work, photographer Eadweard Muybridge (Great Britain) succeeded in 1878 in demonstrating that a galloping horse does indeed lift all four legs completely off the ground. The horse triggered a series of cameras as it galloped along a track.

Photographic gun (1882)

In 1882, scientist Jules Marey (France) developed "chronophotography" by constructing a repetitive-action "photographic gun" that enabled him to take successive shots of a bird in flight. At the coast in Naples, Italy, Marey chronophotographed the flight of seagulls. Peasants who witnessed the episode told of a madman armed with a gun who aimed at birds without ever shooting and seemed delighted to come back from hunting empty-handed.

Chronophotography on a moving strip (1888)

Dissatisfied with the small size of images obtained with his gun, Marey developed chronophotography on a moving strip in 1888. This allowed him to take 20 images per second on a sensitive strip that stopped running for each shot. It was almost the first ciné camera, but the strip was not perforated and the images were irregularly positioned. While that didn't matter for analyzing movement (the aim of Marey's

George Eastman (left) assists Thomas Edison in demonstrating Edison's kinetograph. This is a rare photograph of the two great inventors together. (L. Christophe)

research), it created insurmountable difficulties for direct synthesis.

Film (1889)

Thomas Edison dreamed for several months of creating a visual equivalent for his phonograph and of linking the two complementary pieces of equipment together. Meanwhile, George Eastman perfected a new, sensitive material for his Kodak camera: nitrocellulose-based film. Edison adopted the nitrocellulose-based principle and in 1889 was able to create and define film in the cinematographic sense of the term, with the perforations and ratings surviving with minor modifications to this day.

While the 35-mm-width format established in 1889 has remained standard for commercial movies, other formats have been tried out: wider formats include the 68 mm Biograph (1896), the 60 mm Gaumont/Demenÿ (1896), the 70 mm Grandeur by Fox (1926) and the 65–70 mm Todd-AO (1955); narrower formats designed for amateurs or special purposes are the 28 mm Pathé-Kok (1912), the 9.5 mm Pathé-Baby (1922), the 1.75 mm Pathé-Rural (1925), the 8 mm Kodak (1932) and the Super 8 Kodak (1965).

Kinetograph (1889)

In 1889 Thomas Edison (U.S., 1847–1931), in collaboration with William Dickson (U.S.), invented the first sound movie camera, the kinetograph, which was patented in 1891. The kinetograph developed from Edison's work on the phonograph. The shutter mechanism was connected to a gramophone, which made it possible to record the sound at the same time as the camera was filming. The kinetograph used perforated 35 mm film, approximately the same as that used today.

Dickson shot the first films for Edison in the world's first film studio, a shed lit by large windows and constructed on a pivot. The whole apparatus turned, following the path of the sun; thus the scenes inside received a constant flow of light.

These first films were shown on a kinetoscope, which Edison had patented at the same time as the kinetograph in 1891.

Movie projector (1894)

Credit is given to Le Roy (U.S.) for having invented the first movie projector that brought together the essential elements of our current models. On February 5, 1894, at 16 Beekman Street, New York City, he publicly projected two of Thomas Edison's kinetoscope films.

Lumière cinematograph (1895)

On February 13, 1895 the Lumière brothers, Louis (France, 1864–1948) and Auguste (France, 1862–1954), took out a patent for "a device for obtaining and viewing chronophotographic prints." They called it the cinematograph.

The first public showing was held on December 28, 1895 in Paris. Their first film was of the entry of a train into La Ciotat station. It was taken at such an angle that the spectators were terrified. This new form of entertainment attracted crowds, and its success led to the growth and development of the motion picture industry.

The Latham "Loop" (1896)

The first real advance in projection technology was a small detail introduced by Maj. Woodville Latham (U.S.). He had the idea of making a loop in the film itself, which was placed between the continuous and the staggered drives of the projector. It enabled movie length to be indefinitely increased without the film breaking.

The "Panorama" (1896)

Filming views of Venice in 1896 for the Lumière brothers, the operator Eugene Promio set up his camera on a gondola. Seeing the success of this moving viewpoint, Lumière operators set out to use all kinds of vehicles (trains, tramways, cars, boats, etc.) to film what they called "panoramas."

Movie camera (1897)

In 1897 Charles Pathé (France, 1867–1957) broke the Lumière brothers' cinematograph into two distinct elements, the camera and the projector. Variable camera speed was developed in 1904 (see slow motion, below). This was done in order to allow speeded-up and slow-motion films. Sixteen images per second were used for ordinary shooting, but 24 per second were necessary for sound films.

Slow motion (1904)

Two students of Jules Mayer—Lucien Bull and Henri Nogues (both France)—invented slow-motion filming in 1904. They understood that by shooting more frames per second than one would normally shoot, one obtains a longer film. Then, projecting this longer film at normal speeds, events are seen to take place less rapidly than they do in reality. That is how slow motion works.

Color Movies

Tinting and coloring (1896)

From the beginning of film history, rudimentary techniques have been used to hide the austerity of black and white movies. The earliest techniques used were tinting and coloring. The tinting process involves immersing the film in a colorant. Coloring consists of hand-painting, frame by frame, color after color, the thousand 18 x 24 mm images that a minute of film contains. Tinting, along with toning (a later process whereby the black in the image is chemically transformed into a given color), were the least costly processes.

Coloring machines (1905)

These machines worked on the stencil principle: areas were cut out of matrix copies (one for each color) and then, on a new copy of film, colors were applied by brush across these matrices. Coloring machines, developed by Charles Pathé (France, 1867–1957) and Léon Gaumont from 1905, were used up to the end of the silent era.

Additive processes (1906)

The first color processes used commercially were called additive: the color synthesis was carried out by succession or addition of colored lights. George Albert Smith's Kinemacolor (1906) passed images alternately through red and green filters. The Chronochrome, developed by Decaux and Lemoine for Gaumont (1911) superimposed three images behind green, red and blue filters. These processes proved inadequate or too complicated to exploit.

Technicolor (1934)

The brand name Technicolor, established in 1915, covers many processes. Important here is Technicolor No. 4, developed by Herbert Thomas Kalmus, Daniel F. Comstock, W. Burton Westcott and L.T. Troland. This was the leading process for 20 years, from 1934 to 1955.

Colorization (1986)

Wilson Markle (Canada) perfected a computer system that makes it possible to color films shot in black and white. The invention of colorization caused a storm of controversy, as film traditionalists insisted that the process violated artistic integrity. However, TV networks and film studios have supported colorization, and the technique continues to be refined and developed.

Sound Movies

Chronophone (1910)

At the 1900 Paris World's Fair, spectators could already take part in a number of imperfect attempts to synchronize the phonograph and the cinematograph. In 1902, Léon Gaumont introduced *phonoscènes*, but without electrical amplification the sound was very weak. Helped by his collaborators Decaux and Laudet, Gaumont perfected his process and in 1910 developed the chromophone, in which the phonographic sound was mechanically amplified by a compressed air flow. In 1912, the Gaumont-Palace, in Paris, showed the movie *Filmparlants* using the chromophone sound system.

Optical sound (1910)

In 1910 Eugène Lauste (France) succeeded with the first photoelectrical sound recordings onto film, called optical sound. Many experiments with optical processes were being tried when *The Jazz Singer* was released in 1927. The first successful "talkie," *The Jazz Singer* focused attention on talking movies (see Vitaphone, below). Various compatible processes—

Movietone (Fox), Photophone (RKO) and Tri-Ergon (Tobis)—were introduced between 1927 and 1929, and replaced optical sound.

Vitaphone (1926)

The introduction of electricity, and especially of triode lamp amplification, created fresh problems. In 1926, Warner Brothers developed the Vitaphone, which synchronized the disc and the projector. That same year they released *Don Juan*, the first long sound movie, and then in 1927 *The Jazz Singer*, the first lip-synchronized movie, whose success spawned the "talkies."

Magnetic sound (1930s)

Invented in 1898 by Valdemar Poulsen (Denmark), magnetic recording was commercialized in Germany in the mid-1930s. Its first applications at the beginning of the 1950s were limited to amateur home movies. Its commercial playback use came with the first CinemaScope (1953, four track layers), then with 70 mm (six track layers). Today, magnetic sound is hardly ever used for movie theater projection but has decisively replaced optical methods for sound recording itself.

Dolby (1967)

This process, invented by Ray Dolby (U.S.), consists, at the time of recording, of suppressing the loudest sounds and amplifying the weakest ones, and then, using a coding system, restoring them to their original levels. Background noise, particularly audible during optical sound silences, is thus erased and overall sound quality enhanced. The Dolby system, in both stereo and mono versions, has helped to improve weaknesses in optical sound at broadcast level.

Modern Movie Cameras

Traveling (1912)

In 1912, the director Giovanni Pastrone (Italy) patented a device to take moving pictures on a cart that he called a carrello. He used the carrello technique extensively in his movie *Cabiria*, released in 1914. The traveling platform (on rails or tires) became an important advance in making movies since it allowed scenes to be shot from different angles and in more elaborate settings. Initially, large cranes were used to hold the cameras, but in 1932 the dolly, a small mobile crane, was developed in Hollywood. The dolly became an essential piece of equipment for shooting movies.

Steady Cam (1970)

Perfected by the technician Garrett Brown (U.S.), Steady Cam allows camera movements without a crane or dolly on rails. The camera is strapped onto the cameraman's body, which means he needs only one hand to hold it. Thanks to a series of controls and balancing devices the cameraman is completely autono-

mous and can move about and even run. Dustin Hoffman's run in John Schlesinger's *Marathon Man* and the little boy's flight through the snowy maze in Stanley Kubrick's *The Shining* were filmed using a Steady Cam.

Shaky Cam (1982)

Devised by Sam Raini (U.S.), a young director, on the set of his film *Evil Dead*, the Shaky Cam is a motorized version of the Steady Cam. The camera is fitted onto a motorbike and protected from bumps by a system of shock absorbers. This allows for very smooth and fast runs at ground level. Raini used the Shaky Cam to give a vision of things from the point of view of a crawling creature crossing a forest at high speed and brushing against the trees.

Sky Cam (1984)

Since perfecting the Steady Cam in 1970, Garrett Brown has perfected two more revolutionary cameras: the Sky Cam (first used in Alan Parker's *Birdy*, 1984), and more recently, the Cable Cam. These two cameras, fitted with video-relays, are fixed on cables stretched at very high altitudes and can glide along them at varying speeds. The result is an amazing sequence of shots that cannot be equaled even from a helicopter.

Special Effects

Origins (1896)

Since the birth of the movies, its creators have used all means of trick photography to evoke fantastic images. Film producer Georges Méliès ((France, 1861–1938) is regarded as the father of "special effects." In 1896, when he was filming the Place de l'Opéra in Paris, Méliès' film jammed in the camera but continued to shoot the scene in front of the opera house. When the film was screened, the jammed footage revealed such amazing phenomena as men changing into women and a bus into a hearse. Méliès, grasping the potential of such a discovery, experimented with the technique, and used it in many of his subsequent films.

Single-frame animation (1897)

This special effects technique is used to give the impression that inanimate objects are moving. Georges Méliès and the American production house Vitagraph first used this technique in the short film *Humpty Dumpty Circus* (1897). In 1913, Willis O'Brien (U.S.) developed the technique further, filming a clay model dinosaur one frame at a time for the film *The Dinosaur*. This technique was called "stop motion." O'Brien used it to great effect in the classic film *King Kong* (1933). O'Brien's pupil Ray Harryhausen improved the technique further, with such famous results as the fight sequences in *Jason and the Argonauts* (1963) and *The Golden Voyage of Sinbad* (1973). In 1981 Denis Murren (U.S.) introduced a new frame-by-frame technique: "go motion." In the film *Dragonslayer*,

the puppets' movements were computer-controlled, which saved time and improved smoothness.

Mask/Counter mask (1898)

In the film *The Corsican Brothers* (1898) the director, George-Albert Smith (Great Britain) introduced to the movies the photographic technique of double exposure—that is, superimposing two images on a single exposure. Georges Méliès perfected the technique, increasing the number of exposures up to seven in his movies *L'Homme-orchestre* (1900) and *Le Mélomane* (1903).

This technique was developed into mask/counter mask by John P. Fulton (U.S., 1902–65), first in *Frankenstein* (1931) and most famously in *The Invisible Man* (1933). In *The Invisible Man*, Fulton used double, triple and quadruple exposure to create the effect of objects apparently moving on their own.

The technique is most widely used in scenes where the actor is confronted by his double, i.e., himself. This process was perfected in David Cronenberg's *Dead Ringers* (1988), in which Jeremy Irons played the roles of twin brothers. In the scenes where the twins are in the same scene, a computer-controlled camera recorded the first shot and then repeated exactly the same movement for a second shot. Meanwhile, Irons had changed character and position, so that on screen, he is having a conversation with himself.

Painting in backgrounds (1920s)

Introduced in the 1920s by the directors René Clair and Abel Gance, this special effect consists of painting certain elements of the background onto a pane of glass that is then placed between the camera and the scene to be filmed. In 1943 Henri Mahé (France) invented Simplifilm, a process based on this technique, which he used in *Blondine*. There were no artificial sets, but drawings and photographs were inserted in the camera between the lens and the actors. This technique is widely used and its uses have grown more sophisticated over time. Stephen Spielberg used the technique to classic effect in *Raiders of the Lost Ark* in 1981.

The two elements—the actual shot and the painting—are filmed separately in order to avoid having an entire crew stand idle during the insertion and removal of the pane of glass. The painted elements are then inlaid into the actual shot by the technique of mask/counter mask (see above).

Blue screen (1950s)

The blue screen is one of the most common principles of illusion in the movies. A subject filmed against a background of a special blue is isolated on a separate film so as to be inserted in a more complex scene. The blue is identified and eliminated in a laboratory process called "separation." This technique was discovered in the 1950s and used by L.B. Abbott to part the Red Sea in Cecil B. DeMille's *The Ten Commandments* (1955).

Vistavision (1977)

Star Wars (1977) represented a milestone in movie special effects. The special effects for the movie were supervised by John Dykstra, who perfected the Vistavision process. This process allowed the film to be used horizontally, instead of vertically, thus allowing a greater surface area of negative to be used. *Star Wars* director George Lucas introduced many innovations in the movie, including linking one of the cameras to a computer which then recorded and memorized each focal plane for the sequences to be superimposed. This system allowed multiplication of shooting angles of the spacecraft models, which could then be intersected in space and seen in movement in relation to the stars from a wide variety of angles.

Zoptic (1978)

Conceived by Zoran Perisic in 1978, the zoptic process was used during the shooting of *Superman* (1978). A camera and a projector are used in unison to give the effect of flight and movement in space. The zoom lens of the projector captures the image of the person or object projected on the background and supposedly flying, while the zoom lens of the camera films the person or object stationary, thus giving the illusion of movement in space.

3-D and Wide-Screen Cinema

Hypergonar (1927)

In 1927, Henri-Jacques Chrétien (France, 1879–1956) conceived a special object lens that allows the image to be compressed in one direction during shooting (anamorphosis) and to be enlarged when projecting so as to recover the original proportions (desanamorphosis). Claude Autant-Lara (France) tried the idea out in a short movie inspired by a Jack London story, *To Build a Fire*. The movie has unfortunately been lost.

CinemaScope (1950s)

At the beginning of the 1950s the success of television began to empty American movie theaters. To stop the exodus, major production companies concentrated on the movies' more spectacular aspects that the small screen could not match. Twentieth Century Fox bought the Hypergonar patents from Chrétien and in a blaze of publicity launched CinemaScope, which almost doubled the width of the screen. The first movie produced by this process was Henry Koster's *The Tunic* in 1953.

During the 1950s several other new developments occurred in wide-screen technology. The imposing Cinerama, introduced by Fred Waller in 1952, revived the triple screen idea developed by André Debrie and Abel Gance in 1926: the huge screen was filled with three images projected side by side. In 1954, Paramount launched Vistavision, which used 35 mm film but ran it horizontally as in 24 x 36 cameras. Todd AO, introduced by Michael Todd in 1955, used wider film: 65 mm for shooting, 70 mm for projection. Panoramic processes, which were cheaper, used lower-height projection windows and shorter-focus projection: the result lengthened images at the expense of an increase in size and a considerable loss of usable film surface.

Natural Vision 3-D (1952)

The Natural Vision 3-D process is similar in principle to anaglyph color systems but, during projection, polarized—not colored—filters select the images to be seen by each eye, which, besides being less tiring to look at, doesn't change the color. Between 1952 and 1954, Associated Aritsts and Warner Brothers produced several movies shot with this process, including Hitchcock's *The Almost Perfect Crime*. Despite periodic revivals, 3-D processes have never really become popular because of the cumbersome installation and the need to wear special glasses.

IMAX (1970)

At EXPO '67 in Montreal, Canada, various multiscreen films gained wide acclaim. Among the crowds astonished by the effect were three filmmakers—Graeme Ferguson, Roman Kroitor and Robert Kerr (all Canada). These men saw the potential of wide- (or giant-) screen technology. They realized that the multiprojector system used at that time limited the practical applications of wide-screen technology. They turned their attention to designing a single projector system that reflected images onto a flat screen, and increasing the practicality of the system. At EXPO '70 in Osaka, Japan, the IMAX system was demonstrated for the first time.

The IMAX image is 10 times larger than the conventional 35 mm frame and three times bigger than a standard 70 mm frame. IMAX projectors incorporate "rolling loop" film movement, which was invented by Ron Jones (Australia) and developed by William Shaw. The rolling loop system advances the film horizontally in a wavelike motion. Each frame moves through fixed registration pins, while the film is held against the rear element of the lens by a vacuum. The combination of the size of the film and the projector technology produces the highest levels of clarity of any film system devised.

OMNIMAX (1973)

The OMNIMAX system is a dome-screen system that premiered at the Reuben H. Fleet Space Theater in San Diego, Calif., in 1973. An extension of the IMAX system, OMNIMAX uses the same rolling loop projection technol-

3-D movies have been the focus of photographic technology since the 1930s, but they are still best known for the special glasses required to view them. (CSI/Baldwin)

The Dream Is Alive screened at an IMAX theater. (IMAX)

ogy, with the images projected through a 180-degree fish-eye lens to fill a domed screen.

Pan-and-Scan (c. 1980)

This is a process perfected by Warner Studios that allows the recentering of a "big screen" motion picture so that it takes up the whole area of a television screen. Pan-and-Scan (from Panavision and Scanner) was introduced in the early 1980s and is used by the video and television industries.

Holographic film (1985)

It was at the Franco-German research institute in Saint-Louis, France that the first convincing *cinéhologrammes* were made. Previously, they had been produced in the USSR (V.G. Komar, 1977) and in the United States (A.J. Decker, 1982).

The holographic cinema principle involves recording on film the light reflected by an object or a person lit by laser and at the same time the light coming from the laser itself. From the meeting of the two lights a 3-D picture is born.

Underwater Filming

The Silent World (1956)

Jacques-Yves Cousteau (France) is generally regarded as the pioneer in underwater filming techniques. His 1956 film *The Silent World* earned him worldwide fame and demonstrated many of the inventions he had created to make underwater filming possible. On the film Cousteau used the underwater industrial television equipment he had invented with André

Laban in 1952, the underwater "sledge" invented with Prof. Harold E. Edgerton in 1954, and the first 35 mm underwater camera invented with Armand Davso in 1955.

Cartoons

Origins (1908)

The forerunner of cartoons was Emile Reynaud's optical theater of 1893. The scenery was projected behind the screen by a magic lantern, the characters painted on a white background and their successive positions transferred onto a perforated translucent strip. In 1908 J. Stuart Blackton and Emile Courtet, known as Emile Cohl, invented filmstrip cartoons. After them, Earl Hurd (U.S.) perfected, in 1914, a system that made it unnecessary to draw in the background each time.

The Cel process (1914)

An important step in animation was the Cel process, created by Earl Hurd (U.S.) in 1914. The technique involved drawing the moving parts of the image on sheets of celluloid, which was then shot while superimposed on a fixed setting. This greatly simplified the drawing and allowed the industrial production jobs to be separated out.

Rotoscope (1915)

Invented by the Fleischer brothers, pioneers of the American cartoon who created *Betty Boop* and *Popeye*, the rotoscope is a technique that consists of filming a real actor and tracing the film so as to give the cartoon character the same

ease of movement. The Fleischer brothers used the system in a feature-length cartoon that has remained famous: *Gulliver's Travels* (1939). Ralph Bakshi (U.S.), a leader in cartoons for adults, used the technique in his film *Fritz the Cat* (1970) as well as in *Lord of the Rings*. The rotoscopy principle is also used to make a "mask" to hide unwanted elements such as the models' stands or even the technicians' heads showing behind miniature scenery. This indispensable process is still in use.

Cartoons by superimposition (c. 1915)

We owe the first superimposition of cartoon characters onto live action films to the Fleischer brothers.

In *Out Inkle* (1915) a small cartoon character was seen coming out of a real inkwell and walking on Max Fleischer's drawing board. Due to the transparency and blue screen processes, the technique has continued to improve. Walt Disney Productions were the first to extend the process to feature-length films.

The technique, enhanced by the use of computer-controlled cameras, found its second wind in Bob Zemeckis's *Who Framed Roger Rabbit?* (1988), co-produced by Steven Spielberg and the Disney Studios.

Disney's Multiplane camera (1941)

It was in a short film starring Mickey Mouse, *The Little Whirlwind*, that Disney Studios tested a revolutionary camera: the Multiplane. Meant to reestablish the laws of perspective in cartoon films and allow shots on several planes, the Multiplane camera has accentuated the realism of scenery and the three-dimensional impression.

Bambi (1942) was the first feature-length Disney cartoon to use Multiplane.

WHAT ON EARTH?

NOT ALL INVENTIONS CHANGE OUR LIVES, SOME JUST MAKE US SCRATCH OUR HEADS.

CRYSTAL CLEAR

▼ "76 crystal trombones in the big parade" would tax the talents of the most successful Music Man, but they really would be "the cream of every famous band." They are the creation of Japanese master glass artist Sasaki Garasu. It took him 15 years to perfect them. (Gamma/ Norimoto)

CLASSIC ROCK

Right: Rock Musician Bob Schlink received a patent for the viotar in March 1992. The viotar is a cross between a violin and an electric guitar, and its sound has been described by one music critic as "like a violin on steriods." The instrument rests on the musician's shoulder and is played with a bow. (Bob Schlink)

WATER MUSIC

▼ Although Handel might have been impressed, he didn't have this in mind when completing his *Water Music* in 1717. Invented by Michel Redolfi, this is believed to be the first percussion instrument capable of resonating properly underwater. (Jerrican/Nura)

THE TWIST

▲ No, this is not Chubby Checker's favorite instrument; in fact, it predates rock and roll by over 350 years. The serpent, a cousin of the cornet, was invented by Edmé Guillaume (France) *c.* 1590. It was first played by religious musicians, particularly in Gregorian plainsong, but by the mid-18th century was widely used by military marching bands. The use of the serpent declined in the early 19th century and it disappeared by the 20th. (New York Philharmonic Archives)

REMOTE CONTROL PIANO

In another version of the computerized player piano, NHK, the Japanese national television network, has developed a process that enables viewers to reproduce recordings of favorite performers on their own pianos, transmitted by satellite via television. It is necessary to fit the piano with a special adapter, so that it can receive and convert the numerical data of the sound. Once this has been done, the keys can play on their own.

INTELLIGENT MUSIC WORKSTATION (IMW)

In the IMW project (Intelligent Music Workstation), 10 researchers and some 20 students from the universities of Milan and Genoa are trying to invent the total instrument of the future. It consists of an open environment based on a Macintosh II computer to which the musician adds specialized modules according to need. Though the project is not yet finished, some modules have already been developed—for example the "Mus-Ser," which generates serial themes; "Temper," an audiovisual application in which animated images can be synchronized with music; "JAM," a versatile improvisation system for light piano music; as well as automatic accompanists, score editors and musical sequencers.

WIDE IMAGING STEREO (1992)

A new speaker system developed by Canon, WIS aims to integrate photography and hi-fi. With traditional speakers the stereo sound is diffused in a diagonal. This device directs the sound downwards onto an acoustic reflector; the stereo image can thus be diffused into a larger environment. Hiro Negishi (Japan) invented the concept, which utilizes the acoustic mirror principle.

"POSTAGE STAMP" CASSETTES

Dubbed Scoopman and marketed by Sony, this is a tiny tape recorder (11.3 x 2.3 x 2.5 cm, operated by a 174 g battery). It uses sonic compression (from 17 to 12 bits) but still gives good sound reproduction. Its postage-stamp-size cassettes can be 60, 90 and 120 minutes in duration.

DIGITAL COMPACT CASSETTE (DCC)

Perfected by Philips in collaboration with the Matsushita group (Panasonic, Technics), the DCC is the recording device likely to succeed the present audio cassette. It offers many advantages, including digital sound (the recording quality is therefore comparable to that of a CDS or DAT). In addition, the platens are compatible with conventional cassettes. A DCC recorder contains two analogue heads as well as nine digital heads.

RE-RECORDABLE CD

In 1989 Sony and Taiyo Yuden began working together to produce the CDR (R for recordable), which can be recorded on once. Other manufacturers have also announced plans to develop re-recordable technology. Thomson of France is developing a CD that could be wiped clean and re-recorded, the MOD (Magneto Optical Disc). Tandy Corp. is also preparing to market a CD which can be wiped clean and re-recorded. It should last almost indefinitely.

CD SCRATCH KIT

In April 1992 Harald Schmid (Germany) received a U.S. patent for a kit that erases scratches from CDs. Although it is claimed

New ideas that may change the way we live

that CDs never wear down, scratches on the disc's transparent plastic coating have interfered with the laser system that reads the data on the disc. Schmid's repair kit includes four grades of sandpaper and guidelines for removing deep scratches.

COMPACT DISC INTERACTIVE (CD-I) SYSTEM

The Dutch electronics giant Philips N.V. launched the CD-I in 1992, after five years of development. CD-I, a home entertainment system, allows CDs to be played on a deck that plugs into a television and stereo system, and can be operated by remote control handsets. CD-I technology is being developed to challenge the video recorder. Philips is currently developing an advanced version of the CD-I that will be able to play motion video-discs, which will include movies and music videos.

MINI DISC

The Mini Disc was inveiled by Sony in May 1991, and was launched on the American market toward the end of 1992. The Mini Disc system, which reproduces high quality sound, features the quick random access function of CDs and the portability of cassette tapes. This system uses an ultra–small magneto–optical disc only 2½ inches in diameter that allows 74 minutes of digital recording and playback. To enhance its portability the Mini Disc is shock resistant.

X-RAY CAMERA

Using technology developed since the 1960s, engineers from Philips N.V. and a team of biologists from the French National Center for Scientific Research, in association with the French National Museum of Natural History, developed a high-speed 16 mm camera using X-rays. X-ray photography makes it possible to analyze the movements of athletes and small animals. The camera can take up to 500 pictures per second.

IMAX SOLIDO

First demonstrated at EXPO '90 in Osaka, Japan, IMAX Solido is the first motion picture system to present full-color 3-D images on a wide-field dome screen. The 3-D images extend in front, above and to the side of the viewer, who observes the screen through cordless electronic liquid crystal glasses. The glasses work as electronic shutters and are synchronized with the projector, decoding the left and right eye images projected onto the screen, giving the effect of stereoscopic viewing. At EXPO '92 in Seville, Spain, the film *Echoes of the Sun*, a 20-minute film telling the story of photosynthesis, was used to demonstrate IMAX Solido.

IMAX Solido glasses. (IMAX)

9 TRANSPORTATION

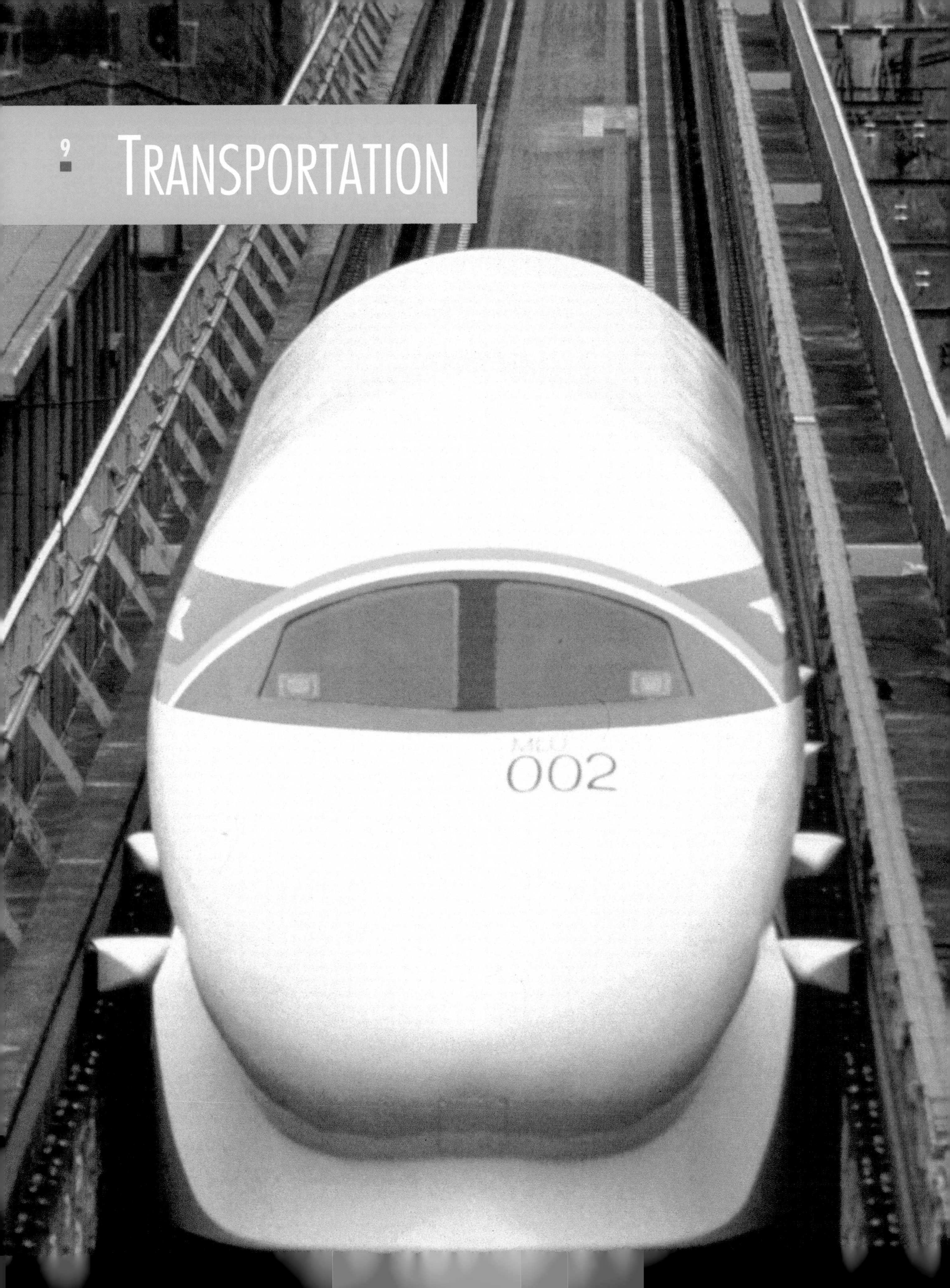

SHIPPING

Steamboats

Boat with a steam boiler (1730)

When use of Newcomen's steam pump had spread into the coal-mining regions of England during the 1730s, a mechanic named Jonathan Hulls used it to equip a tugboat. Placing a crank at the end of the beam of Newcomen's machine, he transformed the back-and-forth movement of the piston into a rotating movement that was transmitted to the paddle wheel of the boat. But the mechanical irregularity of this atmospheric engine and the large quantity of coal it consumed made Hulls's project impractical and it was forgotten.

Steamboat with a paddle wheel (1783)

Watt's invention of the rotative steam engine, which permitted an increase in the driving power of the engine and used less combustible fuel, led to a breakthrough in the progress of steam-powered navigation. It was in the United States that steam navigation was to undergo its greatest improvements.

Steamboat with oars (1787)

A curious demonstration, witnessed by George Washington and Benjamin Franklin, took place on the Delaware River during the summer of 1787. Two builders, John Fitch and James Rumsey (both U.S.), introduced a boat with oars fixed to a horizontal wooden rod, operating in the same way as ordinary oars but powered not by men but by a steam engine.

The *Clermont* (1807)

The *Clermont* was built by Robert Fulton (U.S., 1765–1815) in New York in 1807. It was the first successful commercial steamboat. It measured 164 ft long by 16 ft wide, had a capacity of 150 metric tons and its paddle wheels were 16 ft in diameter. Few people, however, believed that this powerful riverboat would succeed, and even though its trial runs had taken place with no major problems, no passengers showed up for its maiden voyage. Only Fulton and his crew made that first run up the Hudson River from New York to Albany. During its nighttime voyage, the Clermont spread terror: Fulton fired the boiler with pine boughs, which produced a lot of smoke and sparks. This column of flame, along with the noise of the engine and the paddle wheels crashing on the water, terrified the people living along the banks of the river

The *Savannah* (1818)

In 1818 Capt. Moses Rogers (U.S., c. 1779–1821) of Savannah, Georgia planned to build a steamboat intended for regular service between the United States and Europe. A corporation launched the operation, acquiring a handsome sailboat and installing a steam engine and paddle wheels. These paddle wheels could be dismounted and folded on deck.

The *Savannah* left port on May 26, 1819, and arrived in Liverpool, England 25 days later. Its engine had functioned only 18 days of that time, as the captain wanted to take advantage of a favorable wind to economize on coal.

After this successful run, the *Savannah* made its way into the Baltic Sea to Kronstadt and St. Petersburg, Russia, where it was visited by Tsar Alexander I. But the *Savannah* ended up in obscurity. After returning to the United States, it was reconverted into a passenger sailboat and ended its adventurous career on the Long Island coast. It wound up sinking in the harbor during its last voyage.

An English steamer, *Enterprise*, traveled to India in 1825.

Other Shipping

Icebreaker (1864)

The *Ermak* was the first English icebreaker. It was built in 1898 by the Armstrong shipyards, following the design of Russia's Admiral Makarov.

However, the first icebreaker was Russian; the *Pailot* left the shipyard in 1864.

Hydroplane (1906)

Count Charles de Lambert (France, 1865–1944) began studying the idea of hydroplanes as early as 1885, with a system using winches and galloping horses. The first self-propelled hydroplane was produced in 1897, but it was not until 1906 that he developed the first true hydroplane, which was capable of the then astonishing speed of 38 mph.

The hydroplane is a flat-bottomed boat that rises out of the water at high speed. At this point, only the bottom part of its "steps" remain in contact with the water. Driven by an aerial propeller, the craft can travel along shallow rivers but only over calm water.

Hovercraft (1955)

This type of vessel, also known as a Surface Effect Ship (SES), or Air Cushion Vehicle (ACV), was patented on December 12, 1955 by Sir Christopher Cockerell (Great Britain). His hovercraft is a boat that rides on a cushion of air. It does not touch the water but "hovers" over it. The 7-metric-ton prototype, the SR-N1, made its first public appearance at Cowes on May 30, 1959 and caused a sensation. It was highly maneuverable and capable of a speed of over 62 mph.

On July 25, 1959, the 50th anniversary of Blériot's cross-Channel flight, the first hovercraft crossing was achieved.

Lenin (1957)

The *Lenin* was the first atomic-powered surface ship. It was an experimental icebreaker developed by the Russians in 1957. The heart of the *Lenin*, its three nuclear reactors and the associated containment system, weighs 3,000 metric tons. In free water the ship can run at 18 knots and can break an ice-cap 8.2 ft thick at the constant speed of 2 knots thanks to its 44,000 hp engines. It was decommissioned in April 1990.

Atomic-powered ship (1958)

On May 22, 1958 in the United States, construction was begun on the *Savannah*, the first commercial atomic-powered ship. Launched in 1959, it was given the name of its famous ancestor, the first steamer ever to cross the Atlantic. It could transport 9,500 metric tons of cargo and 60 passengers. Attended by a crew of 100, it could develop 20,000 hp and reach speeds of 20.5 knots.

Although the *Savannah* was undoubtedly a technical success, it was a commercial failure. The operating company had to take it out of service in 1967.

Wind-powered cargo ship (1980)

The last large commercial sailing ship disappeared in 1936. The high price of fuel has now reopened the possibility of using the wind as an auxiliary source of power.

In 1980 the Japanese shipyard Nippon Kokan launched the *Skin-Aitoku-Maru*. This is a cargo vessel fitted with two upright wings—each one opening like a book—with a total area of 2,098 sq ft. These wing-sails can save up to 50 percent in fuel costs. Five other cargo vessels to be used in the coastal trade have been launched since. Janda (the association for the development of the Japanese Navy) then instigated the building of a sea-going cargo vessel. The *Usuki Pioneer* was finished in November 1984. Its two computer-controlled metal sails should give this 53.3-ft-long cargo ship a saving of about 30 percent in fuel costs. In the United States the 3,100-metric-ton coasting vessel *Mini-Lace* was fitted in 1980 with a canvas sail that can be made smaller by winding it around the rotating mast. It gives a 20 percent fuel economy.

Turbosail (1982)

The principle of the turbosail was perfected by Prof. Lucien Malavard and his pupil Bertrand Charrier in 1982. A variation on the magnus effect, it makes it possible, among other things, to avoid rotating the cylinder at high speed.

The turbosail was tried out first on the Cousteau Foundation's *Moulin à Vent I* in 1983 and then on the *Alcyone* (formerly the *Moulin à Vent II*).

The *Alcyone* is driven by the combined action of two diesel engines and two turbosails whose efficiency is four times greater than that of the best sail ever made. This system created a 25–35 percent saving in energy on the maiden voyage of the *Alcyone* in May–June 1985. Computers make it possible to adjust these turbosails according to the wind direction, thus obtaining maximum efficiency.

Previous page: Magnetic train. (Gamma)

Sailing liner (1986)

The *Wind Star* (and its twin sister, the *Wind Song*) is the first sailing liner ever built. Produced by the Ateliers et Chantiers du Havre (ACH) at the end of 1986, the *Wind Star*, commissioned by the American company Windstar Sail Cruises, has a sail area of 21,528 sq ft. The masts rise to 190 ft above sea level and the sails are completely computer-controlled. It can carry 180 passengers with a crew of 75. The ship's speed is between 10 and 15 knots. The boats are 440 ft long and have four masts.

The WPC (1990)

Hoverspeed's Wave Piercing Catamaran (WPC) is designed to take over from the hovercrafts that cross the Channel between England and France. It is built like a catamaran (the largest in the world: 240 ft long, 89 ft wide, 450 passengers, 80 vehicles). It came into service in 1990.

Magnetic boat (1992)

It was at the Tsukuba exhibition in Japan that, in 1985, a model of the magnetic boat was first shown to the public. It has no engine (in the strict sense of the term), no sail and no rudder. It is propelled by a system of superconducting magnets arranged along the hull. These create a powerful magnetic field in sea water, which is a good electricity conductor. Its inventor, Yoshiro Saji (Japan), a 60-year-old physicist, has been working on it for about 15 years. The first prototype, the *Yamata 1*, was built by the Japanese Foundation for Shipbuilding Advancement (Tsukuba) and was launched on January 27, 1992.

Navigation Aids

Lighthouse (285 B.C.)

In 285 B.C., one of the Seven Wonders of the World was built on Pharos (an island in Alexandria harbor, Egypt). This was the lighthouse built according to the instructions of Egypt's King Ptolemy II. This lighthouse is said to have measured over 426 ft in height. A wood fire was kept burning all night at its top. It was destroyed by an earthquake in 1302.

The decisive advance in lighthouse construction was the invention, by John Smeaton (Great Britain) in 1759, of a cement that could set in water.

As to the light, it was provided by wood fires until the 18th century. In 1780, Argand (Switzerland) designed the flat-wick oil lamp called the Argand burner. In 1901 a new development appeared: this was the petroleum burner, invented by Arthur Kitsen.

The progress made in optics had an impact on lighthouse design. As of 1752 the parabolic reflector designed by William Hutchinson (Great Britain) increased the power of the light signal.

The most decisive step in the use of lenses was conceived in 1821 by the engineer Augustin Fresnel (France). An optical lens was used to focus the light into a beam aimed at the horizon. Escaping light was collected by concentric rings of prisms.

The use of electric lighting (beginning in 1859 in Dungeness, Great Britain) greatly improved the effectiveness of lighthouses.

Compass (unknown)

No one knows when, where or by whom the compass was invented. It was in China, around the year 1000, that the magnetic needle appeared as an aid to navigation. In China, these first instruments pointed to the south. It was only two centuries later that the compass was mentioned for the first time in Europe in the works of an English monk, Alexander Neckam.

Even the origin of the words *magnetite*, *magnetic* and *magnetism* is obscure. They might be connected to an ancient part of Thessaly (Greece) called Magnesia. A legend tells of a shepherd by the name of Magnes whose metal-tipped crook and hobnailed shoes stuck to the ground and enabled him to discover the magic mineral.

As early as the 12th century the magnetic needle, or steering compass, which in Europe pointed to the north, became essential for sailing in bad weather. In the 14th century, as the steering compass came into general use in the Mediterranean, trade was made easier whatever the weather, all year round.

The compass enabled Christopher Columbus to undertake his westward journey to India which led him to rediscover America, a continent the Vikings had discovered several centuries before and which was probably shown on Süleyman the Magnificent's maps, which Columbus would have consulted.

Tide tables (13th century)

The first know tide tables were drawn up in the 13th century by the monks of Saint Albans, England to give the height of the Thames at London Bridge.

The first printed tables were published in the Nautical Almanac by the Breton Brouscon in 1546. One of the most famous tables is that of Richard and George Holden, published in Liverpool, England in 1773. For a long time, it was used to determine the tides of that harbor, although these are very irregular. In 1858 the Nautical Almanac, published by the British Admiralty, gave a tide table for all of the harbors in the world. As of 1910 it gave tables for only 26 of them.

Octant (c. 1730)

The octant, or Hadley's quadrant, is an optical measuring instrument. Its user points the two edges of the device at distant objects, such as the horizon and the sun, and from the angle thus derived can calculate his position. Conceived by the mathematician and astronomer Isaac Newton (Great Britain, 1642–1727), it was constructed and tested by John Hadley between 1730 and 1732, following the death of the inventor.

It is a forerunner to the sextant that John Campbell constructed in 1757, based on the same principle, but with a few further improvements. The mirrors and the sighting system allow the image of the star or sun and the horizon to be accurately aligned, and the angle obtained can be read directly from this.

Compass card (1876)

It seems that the first compass or mariner's card was made by Flavio Giova (Italy), a craftsman. After centuries of trial and error, the Thomson compass was perfected in 1876; this dry compass had thin cylindrical bars mounted on silk thread and tied to very thin paper—it weighed

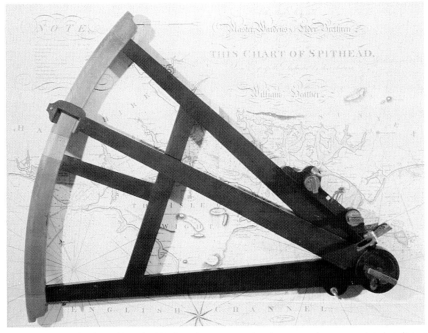

The octant was developed by John Hadley. A navigational aid, its two edges are pointed at distant objects, and from the angle derived, position is calculated. (Dagli-Orti)

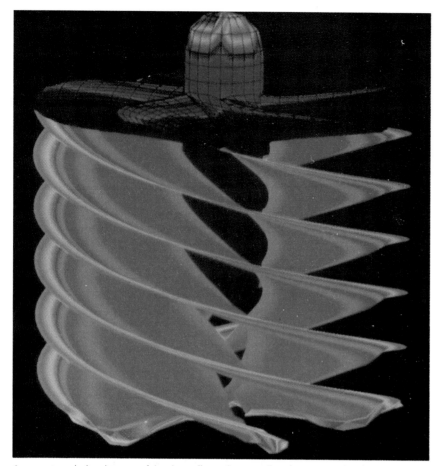

A computer-calculated image of the drag effects of a propeller. The amount of drag effect has an important bearing on the design of a boat. (Onera)

no more than ¾ oz. The liquid compass, a result of the work of Dent (Great Britain, 1833) and Ritchie (Great Britain, 1855), came into general use around 1880. After World War I, it was strongly challenged by the gyrocompass perfected from the work of physicist Léon Foucault (France) and of G. Trouvé.

Propellers

First propellers (1785)

In 1785 Joseph Bramah (Great Britain) patented a 16-blade propeller to drive boats. But the first experiment was made by John Stevens (U.S.) and Sir Marc Isambard Brunel (Great Britain), who coupled two four-bladed propellers to their one-cylinder steam boiler to sail up the Passaic River in New Jersey.

Screw-propeller (1837)

In 1837, engineer John Ericsson (Sweden) patented a screw-propeller in the United States. His propelling system, consisting of two screws, was used on a tugboat, the *Francis Ogden*. In the same period Francis Pettit Smith (Great Britain), a farmer, perfected a similar system and founded a company, the Steam Propulsion Company, which

in 1838/39 built a full-sized, seagoing screw ship called the *Archimedes*, that attained 10 knots.

In 1843, Isambard Kingdom Brunel built the first transatlantic steamship powered by a screw-propeller: the *Great Britain*, measuring 321 ft in length. Two years later, the Royal Navy tied two ships back to back: the *Alecto*, which was a paddle-steamer, and the *Rattler*, which had a screw-propeller. With its paddle wheel at full power the *Alecto* was still pulled by the *Rattler*; the screw-propeller had proved its superiority.

Fully cavitating propellers (c. 1970)

In the 1970s the U.S. Navy, to obtain a greater speed, perfected fully cavitating propellers that exploit the formation of a depression around the blades of the propeller, thus making the most of the pocket of steam created by the whirl of the screw.

Miscellaneous Shipping Developments

Anchor (3rd millennium B.C.)

The first anchors, used by Chinese and Egyptian sailors in the 3rd millenium B.C. and later by the Greeks and Romans, were stones or bags

containing sand or pebbles that could simply be thrown overboard. Pliny, Strabo, and other Roman authors attribute the invention of the metal anchor to several different seafaring peoples. The first approach tried was the single-palm grapnel, used around 600 B.C.

An important improvement was made in the 18th century when better-quality, less brittle iron was used, and when the arms were given a new camber. Around 1770 iron-stock anchors completely supplanted wood-stock anchors. (The stock is a bar perpendicular to the shank of an anchor; its purpose is to make the anchor swing so that one of the flukes grips the bottom.)

In 1821, Hawkins (Great Britain) engineered the mooring hawse-hole anchor with palms. With this system the stock is no longer necessary, the arms being mounted in such a way that they automatically lean to the same side to grip the bottom. This type of anchor was modified between 1872 and 1887 by C. and A. Martin, S. Baxter and W.Q. Byers (all Great Britain).

The CQR anchor, or plough anchor, which G.I. Tayler (Great Britain) patented in 1933, is of an extremely original design. At the extremity of the shank, a double ploughshare is mounted, and the gripping power this provides is twice as great as that of a standard anchor.

Canal lock (14th century)

The double, or chamber, canal lock is an invention attributed by some to 14th century Dutch engineers (later to be improved upon by the Italian genius Leonardo da Vinci) and by others to da Vinci himself around 1480. By regulating the conditions of passage, the invention of the chamber lock solved the problem of getting vessels from one reach of water to another and simplified the often dangerous procedure of lowering and lifting boats.

Weighted keels (17th century)

In order to prevent sailing ships from capsizing under the lateral force of their sails, it was always necessary to concentrate the weight of the ship as low as possible. When fighting ships had no cargo, they had to be filled with stone ballast that acted as counterweight to the sails.

Toward the end of the 17th century King Charles II (Great Britain) had the bottom of one of his yachts covered with lead plates.

In 1796 the British Royal Navy had two frigates built, the *Redbridge* and the *Eling*, which had lead ingots fixed to the outside of the hull. In 1844 the American sloop *Maria*, designed by Robert L. Stevens, had lead-lined wooden hull rails. The first sailing ship to be completely lead-ballasted on the outside of the hull was the *Peg Woffington*, owned by George L. Watson (Great Britain) in 1871.

Lifebelt (1769)

It was a priest, the Abbé de Lachapelle (France), who invented the first lifebelt in 1769. This device consisted of a canvas waistcoat made of coarse hemp and lined with cork, which allowed the arms to be free. He also suggested that sappers wear his belt when reconnoitering fortresses surrounded by moats. The cork breastplate would also act as protection against the sabre and the gun.

Mechanical log (1801)

The mechanical log was created by Edward Massey (Great Britain) in 1801. It standardized an already ancient, but imprecise, system. Originally quite rudimentary, the log was simply a wooden block that was thrown into the water toward the bow of the ship and then recovered when it had reached the stern. The apparent speed of the vessel was calculated by taking into account the time the log took to pass from one end of the ship to the other.

Outboard engines (1905)

Two models appeared in 1905: an American engine designed by Ole Evinrude (Norway), who called it "outboard" because it had the characteristic of being screwed vertically to the boat's outer hull; and a German engine built by Fritz Ziegenspeck, who named it the Elf-Zett.

Distress helmet (1989)

This helmet was designed for sailors by engineer Pierre Fontanille (France). With its highly sophisticated electronic system, it permits the speedy location and rescue of people who have fallen overboard. It is ultra-light and contains an optical system that flashes every three seconds, visible at a distance of 5½ miles, a minute radio transmitter that gives the precise location of the origin of the call, and a valve that releases a colored substance for aerial sighting (and serves as a deterrent to potential aggressors). The various features are triggered the instant a person falls into the water, either automatically or by means of a switch if the wearer is conscious.

RAILROADS

Origins (1753)

In 1753 the British parliament issued a decree relating to the creation of a railroad—a mining line running between Middleton and Leeds. The first public railroad in the United States, the Baltimore and Union Railroad, began operating on May 24, 1830. Used primarily for freight, the cars were drawn by horses.

Locomotives

Trevithick's steam engine (1802)

In 1802–03 the engineer Richard Trevithick (Great Britain, 1771–1833) built the first steam locomotive at the Coalbrookdale ironworks. Soon afterward, urged on by Samuel Monfrey, an ironmaster from the Cardiff area of Wales, he built a second one.

Tests began on February 2, 1804 and they proved conclusive. Trevithick's locomotive,

with a six-ton load, ran on the Pen-y-Darren line (9.3 miles). A few passenger carriages were added. Empty, its speed was 12 mph; loaded, 5 mph.

Trevithick invented high-pressure steam machines and also designed several prototype steam cars.

Blenkinsop locomotive (1812)

The first steam locomotive to be mass-produced was built by John Blenkinsop (Great Britain) beginning in 1812. An engine with an ordinary, non-tubular steam boiler, the Blenkinsop was designed to carry goods and traveled at very low speed. Its special characteristic was that it ran on a toothed rail.

From 1812 the Blenkinsop ran between Leeds and Middleton.

Stephenson's *Rocket* (1829)

In 1829 George Stephenson (Great Britain, 1781–1848) developed the first high-speed steam locomotive. As early as 1813 he had built a steam locomotive equipped with driving wheels joined by connecting rods. These wheels were smooth and rolled on rails. His *Rocket* won the Rainhill trials in 1829, a contest organized by the contractors for the Liverpool–Manchester railway line. Under the competition's conditions (to pull a 40-ton train), the *Rocket* attained a speed of 16 mph, but with no train to pull it could reach up to 35 mph. This exploit marked the birth of the railway.

Crampton locomotive (1846)

In 1846 Thomas Russell Crampton (Great Britain) built the first two locomotives embodying a principle he had conceived three years earlier. Crampton's idea was to build a high-speed locomotive modeled on Stephenson's Long

Boiler but without the latter's major disadvantage—instability resulting from the overhanging position of the boiler furnace in relation to the wheel axles. Crampton shifted one driving axle to the rear of the firebox, leaving only two axles under the cylindrical body of the boiler. His two locomotives, put into service in Belgium on the line running between Liège and Namur, easily reached a speed of 62 mph.

In 1848 Crampton built the *Liverpool*, a locomotive of huge size intended for use on the London–Wolverton line of the London and Northwestern Railway. The engine reached a speed of nearly 79 mph but was nevertheless taken out of service because it put too much strain on the rails.

Electric locomotive (1879)

After various trials by Davenport (U.S.) and Davidson (Great Britain) in 1839, a small train driven by an electric locomotive—developed by Werner von Siemens and Johann Georg Malske—circulated within the walls of the Berlin Fair in Germany in the summer of 1879. Despite its small dimensions, this locomotive is considered to be the starting point for electrically driven vehicles. Preserved by the Siemens Co., this machine still exists.

In 1902 a 124 mph speed record was set by an electric locomotive between Zossen and Marienfelde, in Germany.

The first electric railway in the world was that of Giants' Causeway in Ireland, inaugurated in 1884.

Pacific locomotive (1892)

The famous *Pacific* was put into service for the first time in the United States on the Missouri Pacific Railroad in 1892. The *Pacific* developed 2200 hp and weighed 93 metric tons.

The opening of the Stockton–to–Darlington railway in England took place in September 1825. (Explorer)

Atlantic locomotive (1900)

The *Atlantic* locomotive appeared about 1900 on the Philadelphia–Atlantic City line, hence its name. The use of the *Atlantic* spread to Europe in 1901. It then had 1,500 hp and weighed 64 metric tons.

Diesel locomotive (1912)

The first diesel locomotive was built in 1912 in Winterthur, Switzerland, by the firm Sulzer. It weighed 85 metric tons and developed 1,200 hp; that is weak when compared with the power of steam locomotives of the time.

Tracks

Rails (1602)

The first wheel-guiding rails are believed to have been laid in 1602 in mines around Newcastle-upon-Tyne, England. These rails were made of wood. The first cast-iron rails, laid from 1763 to 1768 between Horsebay and Coalbrookdale, England, were made by Richard Reynolds (Great Britain). These were not railways but tram roads for flangeless wheels.

Raised metal rails (1789)

The first raised metal rails designed for railroad use were invented by William Jessop (Great Britain) in 1789. The first raised rails made from steel were invented by Henry Bessemer (Great Britain, 1813–98) in 1858.

Points (1789)

In 1789 William Jessop also perfected a points system. After the advent of metal tramroads around 1765, forerunners of the points had been invented, but they did not have any moving parts. Jessop's ingenious innovation was to incorporate a moving tongue-rail in this primitive device. His system marked the start of the invention of the points switching system, which remains a collective agreement.

Railroad signals (1849)

The running frequency of trains was originally based on the time interval that separated them. After numerous accidents caused by one train overtaking another, a block-signaling system was adopted by the New York & Erie Co. in 1849. Under this system no train could enter a block until the one in front had left it. In 1856 Edward Tyler (Great Britain) invented an electric signaling device that was adopted for use in the lower Blaisy tunnel on the Paris–Dijon line in France.

The automatic block signal was invented by Thomas Hall (U.S.) and appeared in the United States in 1867. The signals were then operated by the train. In 1871, Franklin Pope (U.S.) installed on the Boston & Lowell Railroad the first signaling system to be centrally controlled.

Rack railway (1862)

In 1862 Niklaus Riggenbach (Switzerland) invented the rack railway that was to be used on slopes of over six percent. He was inspired by John Blenkinsop's system, in which a cog on the locomotive engaged with a toothed rail.

In 1868 Sylvester Marsch (U.S.) built the Mount Washington line in New Hampshire, ascending inclines that reached gradients of up to 30 percent. In 1885 an unnamed Swiss engineer from Lucerne invented a system of triple gears with staggered cogs for the Harz Mountain railway in Germany.

Railroad Cars

Freight car (1801)

Public freight traffic appeared on the Surrey Iron Railway in England in 1801. The cars were drawn by horses.

Passenger car (1830)

The Stockton & Darlington Railway, England, had on occasion carried passengers from its inception in 1825. However, these "passengers" had to sit in coal trucks. The first specifically designed passenger cars appeared in September 1830 on the Liverpool–Manchester line in England. The cars resembled stagecoaches and carried passengers on the world's first intercity service line.

Sleeping car (1836)

Cars with couchettes were in general use on some railroads in the United States by 1836. In 1864 George M. Pullman (U.S., 1831–97) registered a patent for his sleeping car system. The maiden voyage of the first de luxe "Pullman" sleeping car, the *Pioneer*, took place in 1865.

Dining car (1863)

The first dining car was put into service in the United States between Philadelphia and Baltimore in 1863.

Air Brakes (1868): George Westinghouse

On a September day in a trainyard in Pittsburgh, a cart driver darted across the tracks in front of a train that was doing 30 miles per hour. If it had been any other train in the world, the cart driver would have needed to say his prayers, but this train was the four-car train that carried the first air brakes.

This demonstration led to worldwide adoption of air brake systems on trains. Previously, brakemen had had to turn a separate hand wheel in each car of the train. It was an iffy process at best, with trains routinely overshooting platforms. In emergencies, the system was useless. George Westinghouse had observed the wreckage of two freight trains that had a head-on collision just ahead of the passenger train he was traveling on between Schenectady and Troy, New York. Hand brakes had failed to stop the train on time.

Westinghouse was not the first to see the dire need for better brakes for trains, but he

George Westinghouse. (Westinghouse Electric Corp.)

was the first to try compressed air to push the brakes against the train wheels. Westinghouse had read about the use of compressed air—air under pressure— in drilling tunnels in Europe. If air could drive holes through mountains, he reasoned, perhaps it could stop trains.

The air brake worked this way: a tank under the locomotive held compressed air, and pipes led from the tank into each car of the train. At the turn of the brake handle in the locomotive, valves would open to let the air through to the brakes in each car.

That first demonstration train did not stop as smoothly as it might have: the air took time to travel through the pipes. The fourth car bumped into the third car, the third car bumped into the second car, and so on down the line. Yet the daredevil cart driver lived, and air brakes improved rapidly after that. Scores of brakes had been invented since trains gained speed in the 1830s, but none worked as well or as quickly as air brakes.

Westinghouse set out to solve the problems quickly, and soon invented the triple valve, attached to every train car. This valve allowed each car to have its own reserve tank of compressed air, which could be used to set the car's brake and to release the brake as needed.

Just two years after that first demonstration, eight railroads used air brakes for nearly 400 cars. By 1883, Westinghouse air brakes made 50,000 train cars safer and more efficient.

The ICE is fitted with asynchronous motors, powered by triphase current. The train has continuous power of 2,800 kW, with a maximum of 4,300 kW. Under the name of Intercity Express, it runs at a cruising speed of 155 mph.

Magnetic Trains

For the past 20 years, a great number of projects dealing with magnetic levitation trains have been studied in large industrial countries. The trains are suspended a few centimeters above a (very special) track and are propelled by linear induction motors.

The challenge is to go faster than the French TGV within an acceptable cost range. It remains to be seen which line will be the first to dare choose a Maglev (*ma*gnetic *lev*itation) rather than a "wheels on rails" system.

United States (1967)

The first magnetic levitation vehicle was tried out in the United States in 1967, at the Pueblo (Colorado) testing center. In 1973 a linear induction motor engine, developed by Garrett, reached a speed of 250.1 mph.

Transrapid (1972)

As early as 1971, West Germany produced an "electroglider" using the magnetic levitation principle. But the first true Maglev vehicle, the Transrapid, came out a year later. It has been developed by seven large German companies in association with Lufthansa and the German government, which has pledged to subsidize the program over 15 years.

The 177-ft-long train is supported by 64 electromagnets; another 56 help with lateral guidance. Its official maximum speed of 256.4 mph was recorded on January 21, 1988. The Japanese MLU has only managed to reach 251.85 mph.

Great Britain (1983)

Since 1983, a short line (1¼ miles long) using magnetic levitation has linked Birmingham International station to the airport. But the maximum speed on that line is only 15.5 mph.

PUBLIC TRANSPORT

Origins (1661)

Blaise Pascal (France, 1623–62) devised the idea of a public transportation system. In 1661 he proposed a system of coaches that would "circulate along predetermined routes in Paris at regular intervals regardless of the number of people." On January 19, 1662, the King's Counsel authorized the project, and the first coach went into service on March 16, 1662. Despite initial curiosity the project failed, as the coaches were unsuitable for travel on the crowded, narrow streets.

The French TGV is the fastest train built to date. (Texas SUPERTRAIN)

Refrigerator car (1870s)

The invention of the refrigerator car had a significant impact on the United States economy, allowing perishable products, in particular meat, to be transported across the country. The idea for the refrigerator car is generally credited to George H. Hammond (U.S., 1838–1886), who asked William Davis (U.S.) to build one in 1867. Davis's car was crude and was quickly improved upon. In 1877 Joel Tiffany patented his version, which was the first to receive wide acceptance.

High-speed Trains

Japanese bullet-trains (1964)

The Japanese National Railways inaugurated its first high-speed train line, Tokyo–Osaka (320 miles) on October 1, 1964. The maximum speed of these bullet-trains is 130 mph, although during one trial, held on October 17, 1985, a speed of 169 mph was reached.

At present, this high-speed network (*shinkansen*) numbers three lines: Tokyo–Hakat (664 miles), Tokyo–Niigata (184 miles), Tokyo–Morioka (305 miles).

Beginning early in 1992 a new generation of *Shinkansen* came into operation. The Super Hikari reaches speeds of around 168 mph.

British HST (1973)

To increase the speed of trains on non-electrified main lines, British Rail in 1973 created an experimental diesel-electric train comprising two 1,680 kW locomotives with seven or eight passenger cars in between. It could do 125 mph in commercial service and was named the High-Speed Train or HST. In 1979 a mass-produced version was put into operation between London and Bristol. Today there are about a hundred of these trains, known as the 125, in the whole country.

Another high-speed train was researched in 1975–76 by British Rail: the much-talked-about APT (Advanced Passenger Train). But too many unsolved technical problems meant the idea had to be abandoned in July 1986.

TGV (1978)

Research geared to creating a high-speed train, the TGV (*Train à Grande Vitesse*), began in France in 1967, the year in which the first gas-turbine train, the TGS, was produced. This TGS gave birth to two great families of trains: the ETG (*Eléments à Turbines à Gaz*) in 1970, and the RTG (*Rames à Turbines à Gaz*) in 1973, a year after the TGV 001, also using a gas turbine, came out. This reached a speed of 198 mph in 1972. The first electric TGV was delivered in 1978. One of the trains, No. 16, reached 236 mph in February 1981, a few months before the new Paris–Lyons line was put into commercial service. In 1985 the TGV's top speed was 168 mph. However, in May 1990 a TGV reached a speed of 320.2 mph.

The ICE (1985)

The German ICE (Intercity Experimental) is the Deutsche Bundesbahn's (DB) high-speed train. Like the TGV, it is designed to travel at high speed on new lines. Two of these are being built at present between Hanover and Würzburg and between Mannheim and Stuttgart.

DB took delivery of the prototype ICE train in April 1985. Comprising two locomotives with three in between, the train reached speeds of 197 mph in November 1985 and 214 mph in 1986.

Volkswagen Beetle (1934): Ferdinand Porsche

Volkswagen Beetle. (Volkswagen)

Long before it was marketed in the U.S. as the cute "Beetle," Ferdinand Porsche's Volkswagen was the "people's car" of Germany. Created under the aegis of the National Socialist (Nazi) Party in the 1930s, the car was dubbed *KdF-wagen*, in honor of the *Kraft durch Freude* ("strength through joy") movement espoused by Adolf Hitler. Indeed, without Hitler there might never have been a Beetle.

Porsche was an Austrian engineer. He came to Germany in 1923 to design cars for Daimler-Benz. Throughout his long career as the creator of many cars and engines, Porsche envisioned a small, efficient, practical car that would be affordable to many. Several times he proposed the construction design for his Volkswagen, only to have it turned down because car builders would not make a financial commitment to large-scale mass production, or were afraid of the competition a small car would create.

To Hitler, the VW represented a means to stimulate Germany's economy, to create cars that would travel his planned superhighway system, and to make his Nazi party more attractive by offering the first Volkswagens to its members. Accordingly he lowered light metal prices and began construction of the huge plant around which a city—Wolfsburg—grew up.

The Volkswagen's design was truly different: it included an air-cooled engine to allow for Europe's severe winters and to avoid overheating on mountain roads, unit-platform construction for light weight, independent front-and-rear-axle suspension for roadability, and streamlining to allow the one-liter (61 cubic inches) engine to power the car efficiently on a small amount of fuel.

In 1934 Porsche submitted a report to Hitler detailing the effect his car would have on the economy of Germany. The target price was 900 marks ($215). He got his contract, and shortly assigned his son Ferdinand "Ferry" Porsche (who later developed the Porsche 356 and 911) to supervise the test-drive.

During World War II the Wolfsburg plant was used mainly to construct Volkswagens for military transportation; adaptations made the car efficient in Africa's deserts and Russia's snow and ice. Even the amphibious VW was a success.

After the war, Ferdinand Porsche was questioned by Allied forces and ultimately imprisoned by the French. He had been much honored by the Third Reich and highly valued by Hitler, who was quoted as saying, "I have many generals, but only one Porsche."

The German government gave the VW plant over to private industry, and Volkswagen construction boomed. In 1972, the Beetle surpassed the Model T Ford as the world's most-produced car ever. Volkswagen adapted its engine design to trucks, ambulances, multipurpose vehicles, campers, and the famous minibus and Karmann Ghia.

Today, Beetles are manufactured only in Puebla, Mexico, with emission standards that prohibit export to the U.S. Recently Volkswagen celebrated the completion of Beetle number 21 million. For a funny-looking car, it has come a long way.

Taxi (1640)

A coachman, Nicolas Sauvage (France), opened the first taxi business in 1640. He operated along the rue Saint-Martin, Paris with a fleet of 20 coaches. In 1703 the police laid down laws for coach routes and gave each an easily identifiable number, thus introducing the first form of vehicle registration.

The first use of the automobile as an individual means of public transport, with a meter registering both speed and distance, is attributed to Louis Renault (France) who, in 1904, launched small, specially designed two-cylinder cars.

Streetcar (1775)

The streetcar was invented by John Outram (Great Britain) in 1775. Outram's vehicle ran on cast-iron rails and was drawn by two horses.

In 1832 John Stephenson built the first urban streetcar, which operated between Upper Manhattan and Harlem in New York City. In 1852 Emile Loubat (France) thought of embedding the rails in the road surface, and that same year built the Sixth Avenue line in New York City using this method.

Omnibus (1825)

In 1825 Col. Stanislas Baudry (France) devised a system of public transportation using vehicles similar to stagecoaches that could hold up to 15 passengers and a conductor. Although his service was initially designed to transport his bath-house customers, Baudry soon recognized that people living in the Paris suburbs were using it, and he expanded it. His terminus in Paris was located at the Place du Commerce, in front of a store owned by a Monsieur Omnes, whose sign included the words *Omnes omnibus*. Baudry found the word *omnibus* (Latin, "for everybody") appealing, and decided to use it for his transport line.

Motor bus (1831)

Walter Hancock (Great Britain) invented the first motor bus in 1831. The *Infant* was a 10-seat bus powered by a steam engine, and first ran between Stratford-upon-Avon and London that year. The first gasoline-powered bus was built by the German manufacturer Benz in 1895. Put into service on March 18, 1895, the Benz bus carried six to eight passengers.

Subway (1863)

The first underground railroad was inaugurated in London, England on January 10, 1863. It ran between Farringdon and Edgware Road, a distance of four miles, and was powered by steam traction.

Funicular railway (1879)

The first funicular railway operated on the slopes of Mount Vesuvius, Italy in 1879. Pulled by two steam engines of 45 hp each, the funicular ran on slopes where the gradient was over 60 percent.

Trolleybus (1882)

The first trolleybuses appeared in Germany in 1882. They had electric engines that received current from an overhead cable made up of two wires that provided a constant voltage.

Electric tramway (1888)

The first operational electric tramway line was built in 1888 by Frank J. Sprague (U.S.). He obtained a concession for a 17-mile line in Richmond, Va. Sprague's was not the first electric tramway. Siemens and Halske had developed a prototype in Berlin, Germany in 1879, and Thomas Edison (U.S.) had built one at Menlo Park, N.J. in 1880.

AUTOMOBILES

Cugnot steam carriage (1771)

In 1771 Nicolas Cugnot (France, 1725–1804) built what is widely regarded as the forerunner of the automobile. The *fardier* was the first carriage with mechanical traction. Powered by a vertical, simple-effect, two-cylinder high-pressure steam engine, Cugnot's three-wheeled carriage obtained speeds in excess of 2 mph.

Trevithick road steamer (1801)

Richard Trevithick (Great Britain, 1771–1833) was a pioneer in the development of steam engines and their applications. He built several road steamers in the early 19th century. On December 24, 1801, Trevithick ran one of his steamers on a stretch of road near Camborne, England, where it reached a speed of 8 to 9 mph.

Internal combustion engine (c. 1807)

The first attempts at propulsion by an internal combustion engine were made by Isaac de Rivaz (Switzerland). He had built a combustion-engine carriage by *c.* 1807.

Gasoline-powered automobile (1889)

The Daimler-Maybach, built in 1889 by Gottlieb Daimler (Germany, 1834–1900) and Wilhelm Maybach (Germany, 1847–1929), was the first gasoline automobile and is considered to be the first true modern automobile. It had four wheels and a steel chassis; a V-shaped, two-cylinder engine that produced 1.5 hp at 600 rpm, and a four-speed transmission.

Electric automobile (1891)

The first electric cars were developed in the United States in 1891. The Electrobat, manufactured by the Morris and Salom firm of Philadelphia, Pa., was produced only in a small series. In 1892 the Morrison, manufactured by William Morrison of Des Moines, Iowa, was launched.

"Buggyaut" (1892)

The first gasoline-powered automobile built in the United States was designed by Charles and Frank Duryea in 1892. Christened the "buggyaut," it was a carriage driven by a gasoline engine.

Model T Ford (1908)

First built in Detroit, Mich., in 1896 by Henry Ford (U.S., 1863–1947), the Model T Ford was put into mass production on the assembly line in 1908. The 1908 version had developed significantly from the 1896 hand-crafted model, boasting a four-stroke engine and Kane Pennington cylinders. Assembly-line production, a Ford innovation, was an application of the principles of Frederick W. Taylor (U.S., 1856–1915), the creator of the theory known as "scientific management," who stressed specialization, elimination of all superfluous motion, and maximum utilization of plant and equipment. It was this system that made it possible for 15 million Model T's to roll out of the Ford factory between 1908 and 1927.

Gas turbine automobile (1950)

The first automobile powered by a gas turbine was built in 1950 by Rover, a British manufacturer. On June 26, 1952, one of these vehicles attained a speed of 150 mph. The gas turbine has an open circuit design, which incorporates a compressor, one or more compression chambers and the turbine itself. The turbine consists of two barrels: one that activates the compressor and keeps it at a constant speed and a second that transmits the power to the wheels by means of a speed reducer.

Self-parking automobile (1989)

At the Frankfurt Motor Show in 1989, German manufacturer Volkswagen presented the prototype of a self-parking automobile called Futura. To park the car the driver simply presses a button; laser sensors, four guiding wheels, an electronic accelerator, an automatic gearbox and power steering do the rest.

Twin-engined automobile (1990)

Constructed in collaboration with the German company Pöhlman, and based on the Audi 100, the Audi Duo has two engines: the first, a combustion engine (gasoline or diesel), drives the front wheels; the second, which is electric, drives the rear wheels.

Brake System

The brake (1895)

Automobile braking was first ensured by means of brake shoes such as those used in carts (1895). In 1899 the transmission shaft band and wheel brake appeared. These were commanded by a hand lever (brake drum).

The combined hydraulic (foot brake) and mechanical (hand brake) controls formed the subject of the 1924 Perrot-Lockheed patent. The Chrysler Corp. was the first company to utilize this patented system.

Disc brake (1902)

The disc brake, invented by Dr. Lanchester (Great Britain), was primarily used to equip military vehicles. The victory of Jaguar at the Le Mans 24-hour race in 1953 with a vehicle equipped with Dunlop disc brakes, which had been patented in 1945 and used in aeronautics, led to the spread of the invention.

ABS (1972)

The Anti-Blocking System (ABS) perfected by the German firm Bosch has been mass-produced since 1978. The ABS allows the driver, by slamming on the brakes, to stop the car in the shortest possible time, whether on a straight road or on a bend, whether the road is wet, graveled, icy or dry. This system, according to the specialists, represents the greatest step forward in safety since the invention of disc brakes and seat belts.

About a million cars had been fitted with ABS by 1988 and it is thought that that figure will have increased to five million by 1995.

Anti-skid system (1985)

Introduced in 1985 by the Swedish company Volvo, on its latest top-of-the-line models, the ETC (Electronic Traction Control) system intervenes when there is skidding during acceleration. As soon as a drive wheel turns more quickly than a front wheel, this control device reduces the supply of gas little by little until all four wheels are turning at the same speed. It thus considerably reduces the risk of loss of adhesion on a slippery road, even if the driver accelerates strongly. The driver is warned of the danger by means of a small light on the dashboard.

Transmission

Direct transmission (1899)

In 1899 Louis Renault (1877–1944) equipped his first car, completed in 1898, with a transmission coupled directly to the engine, and gearshifting by selector rod. The transmission on the 1899 Renault had three speeds and a reverse gear. The fastest speed, third gear, was reached directly, the primary and secondary propeller shafts turning at the same speed.

Transmission (1900)

It was in 1900 that Louis Bonneville (France) perfected the first "automatic transmission by epicyclic train," an invention that was mentioned in the August 18, 1900 issue of the American magazine *The Motor Car Journal*.

In 1950 Gaston Fleischel (France) invented and patented a complete range of possible controls for gearboxes with epicyclic trains, which the Specialty Equipment and Machinery Corp. of Maryland decided to use in that same year. Fleischel's patent led to a strongly disputed lawsuit dealing with industrial property, which ended in 1953 when a group of American car manufacturers bought all the shares of the Specialty Equipment and Machinery Corp.

Automatic gearbox (1910)

The automatic gearbox invented by Föttinger (Germany) in 1910 was nothing more than a torque converter.

Preselector gearbox (1917)

In 1917 Wilson, a major in the British army, invented the preselector gearbox for use in the battle tanks that had just been developed. After the war the box was fitted to all Armstrong-Siddeleys and, later on, to some Talbots in France. However, it was mainly used in large industrial vehicles and buses.

Fully automatic transmission (1971)

A belt-driven system called Variomatic, which provides fully automatic variations of gear ratio, appeared in 1971 on the Dutch car Daf before being fitted to the bottom-of-the-line Volvos and being tested at Fiat.

In 1987, after several Japanese cars were fitted with a CVT transmission derived from the Daf system, a Selecta version of the Fiat Uno range appeared in which the V belts of the old Van Dorne system were replaced by a continuous metal transmission. The Ford Fiestamatic is also fitted with this system.

In 1990 the Fiat Group, in association with the Japanese Fugi, transformed CVT transmission into ECVT (electromagnetic) transmission, which is lighter and more compact.

Electronic clutch (1988)

Officially introduced at the *Mondial de l'Automobile* in Paris, the Valéo electronic clutch couples the advantages of both the manual and the automatic gearboxes. By doing away with the third pedal, it frees the driver from having to operate the clutch while giving him complete freedom of choice when it comes to ratio, gear-shifting, level of acceleration and down-shifting with or without acceleration.

Steering

Differential (1827)

The differential was invented by Onésiphore Pecqueur (France) in November 1827 for a steam engine. In an automobile, the differential is the device that transmits the power from the engine to the wheels while allowing them to turn at different speeds as the car goes around bends. Then, the outside wheel has to turn faster than the inside wheel.

Front-wheel drive

Hooke-type universal joint (1926)

The invention of the Hooke-type universal joint Tracta by engineers Pierre Fenaille and Jean Grégoire (both France) in 1926 made front-wheel-drive cars possible. This joint allows transmission of the engine power to the front wheels.

The Citroën 7 (1934)

The true father of front-wheel drive is André Lefèbvre (France). Hired by André Citroën on March 1, 1933, he managed to perfect and build, in only one year, the first front-wheel-drive car. The Model 7 was officially introduced to Citroën agents on March 24, 1934. After the bodywork and the accessories were further improved, it won universal acclaim at the 1934 Paris Motor Show. The system has so many advantages that most cars now have front-wheel drive.

Four-wheel drive

Origins (c. 1920s)

The last phase of World War I created the need for an all-terrain vehicle. Therefore, in the early 1920s, French and German manufacturers tackled the problem. In 1926 Georges Latil introduced his T.L. tractor with four driving and directional wheels. The road model was soon adapted by foresters. For their part, Citroën and Unic were putting Adolphe Kégresse's patents into practice to produce vehicles with caterpillar tracks and driven front wheels.

Four-wheel-drive sedan (1983)

The first mass-produced all-weather (as opposed to all-purpose) sedan was the Audi 80 Quattro. Today most manufacturers have started to produce their own versions.

Four-wheel steering (1986)

This will be the next major revolution in the car industry. The four-wheel steering system (4WS) gives greatly increased comfort and safety. The ancestor of cars with four directional wheels is Amédée Bollée's steam car of 1876. After that, the same formula was used on a few prototypes. In 1967 Mickey Thompson (U.S.) raced a four-wheel-steering car at Indianapolis. In 1965 the Japanese firm Mazda took out its first patents. But it was in 1986 that the first commercial model was introduced: the Skyline from Nissan. In 1987 Honda offered the system as an option on its sports model Prelude XX.

Viscodrive (1986)

This system, which equips four-wheel-steering German cars (VW Golf Synchro and BMW 325 4 x 4), was invented by engineer Harry Ferguson (Great Britain). When the front wheels are skidding, Viscodrive takes over by increasing the power to the back wheels. To ensure satisfactory distribution of the torque, it can be incorporated into a transfer box or a differential.

Suspension

Hydropneumatic suspension (1924)

The first hydraulic suspension system was that of engineer Georges Messier (France), who, in 1924, made an "oleopneumatic suspension with position adjustment" (patented in 1920). It was fitted in 1926 on Messier cars without springs. It was in 1953 (20 years after Messier's death) that Citroën perfected its famous hydropneumatic suspension (combining a gas and an oil-based liquid), which was fitted first on 3,000 of its 15 CV front-wheel drive cars before being extended to its other models from 1955 onwards.

Volvo CCS suspension (1986)

Launched in Turin in 1986, the CCS suspension, created by Volvo, is controlled by a microprocessor that enables it to react 3,000 times per second, transmitting each impulse to the wheels, thus allowing them to adapt to the road. This new suspension keeps the vehicle steady in any conditions.

Hydroactive suspension (1989)

The hydroactive suspension of the Citroën XM, on the market since spring 1989, is controlled by an electronic calculator that instantaneously changes its setting to suit the road and the style of driving, using data provided by five sensors. Representing a new concept in active safety, this suspension automatically becomes firm before the driver suffers the drawbacks of too much softness, intelligently anticipating the car's reactions.

Bodywork and Accessories

Gas generator (1883)

The first gas generator that could be used to supply internal combustion gas engines was produced by engineer Emerson Dowson (Great Britain) in July 1883. A gas generator turns solid fuel into a gas fuel. Dowson's generator had a 60 percent efficiency. It was used by the Crossley brothers in England and by Deutz in Germany.

Pneumatic tire (1888)

A veterinary surgeon working in Belfast, John Boyd Dunlop (Great Britain, 1840–1921), invented the pneumatic tire in 1888. This was one of the most significant leaps forward as far as locomotion by wheels was concerned.

Dunlop had the idea of fitting air-filled tires on his son's bicycle.

The same idea had already been put forward by Dietz (Belgium) in 1836, and by engineer Robert W. Thompson (Great Britain) in 1845, but had not been put into practice. Abandoning his old profession, Dunlop patented his invention and founded the first tire factory, where he utilized Goodyear's vulcanization processs. Through the mediation of a German subsidiary, Dunlop tires were put on the first mass-produced motorcycle, the Hildebrand & Wolfmüller, in 1894. The Dunlop firm immediately received complete support from most manufacturers. However, it was the Michelin brothers, André (1853–1931) and Edouard (1859–1940) (both France) who in 1895 first used pneumatic tires on an automobile.

Removable tire (1891)

Invented in 1891 by the French firm Michelin, the removable tire proved to be revolutionary. A blowout, which formerly meant calling a specialized repairman, could now be fixed by the rider in less than 15 minutes. This invention was an immediate success.

Seat belt (1903)

The seat belt is derived from a patent registered in 1903 by Gustave Désiré Liebau (France) that dealt with "protective braces for use in motorcars and other vehicles," and from a slightly different model which a military doctor, Colonel Stapp (U.S.), tried out on a vehicle traveling at a speed of more than 124 mph. First used in aeronautics, the seat belt went through various stages before being fitted on mass-produced cars by Volvo after the firm conducted tests from 1959 to 1963 that led them to choose the three-point type.

Windshield (1903)

The first windshields appeared in 1903 and were generally very high, as the cars of the period reached a height of up to 6 ft 6 in. Made of ordinary glass, these early windshields were very dangerous and were considered optional accessories.

Bumpers (1905)

In 1905 F.R. Simms patented the first bumpers made from rubber. The Simms Manufacturing Co. of London, England fitted the bumpers onto a Simms-Welbeck in the summer of 1905. Bumpers had previously been fitted to a Czech vehicle, the Präsident, which was built in 1897. Unfortunately, the bumpers fell off after 9 miles, and were never replaced.

Rearview mirror (1906)

In 1906 Alfred Faucher (France) registered the first patent concerning a "warning mirror for motorcars." He had also fitted his car with a "hand to signal changes of direction," the ancestor of our direction indicators, and with the first rear warning light activated by touching the brake pedal. About 10 years later, side mirrors were introduced to complement the central rearview mirror that was fitted inside the car.

Windshield wiper (1916)

The first mechanical windshield wipers appeared in the United States in 1916. In 1921 W.M. Folberth (Great Britain) invented windshield wipers that worked automatically, using compressed air supplied by the engine. The first electric windshield wipers were manufactured in the United States by Berkshire.

Laminated windshield (1920)

The first windshields made of laminated glass (invented in 1909 by chemist E. Benedictus [France] and marketed as of 1920 under the name Triplex) were reserved for top-of-the-line models for some time. The first car manufacturer to use laminated glass windshields for a series model was Volvo in 1944 for the PV44.

Hatchback (1961)

The hatchback, which makes it possible to open touring cars from the back, the back shelf folding inwards, first appeared on the Renault 4 in September 1961. The Autobianchi Primula followed suit in 1963.

Airbag (1981)

The first "air pillow" dates to 1951. I.W. Hetrick (U.S.) received a U.S. patent for an "air pillow" that would open automatically in the event of the sudden deceleration of a vehicle. The following year, 1953, R.H. Hodges (U.S.) received a patent for an "inflatable bag" mounted on the dashboard. However, it wasn't until the late 1960s that Mercedes Benz stepped up research directed toward producing a commercial airbag. During the 1970s Mercedes's engineers perfected the system, and in 1981 Mercedes became the first company to equip certain models with this system.

Sensitive windshield wiper (1983)

The first windshield wiper to adjust its speed automatically to the intensity of the rain was developed in 1983 by the Japanese firm Nissan and fitted to all its cars.

Electronic antiglare rearview mirror (1988)

Perfected by Stewart Automotive Ltd. of Greenock, Scotland, the Eclipse rearview mirror, using microchip technology, automatically tilts within one-tenth of a second of being hit by the dazzle of headlights, going back to its original position only after the light conditions are normal again.

Automatic-release seat belt (1989)

In March 1989 Kim Nag-Hyun of the Seoul Polytechnic (South Korea) presented in New York an electric system that automatically releases the seat belt catch 30 seconds after the car has been stopped by an impact.

Integrated child seat (1990)

The first integrated child seat was produced by the French manufacturer Renault in 1990. It is a seat which, when not in use, is hidden in a retractable housing in the back seat. When it is in place it has the double advantage of enabling the child to look at the scenery as easily as an adult, and of allowing a conventional adult seat belt to be used, the lower strap being placed completely flat between the child's legs.

Procon Ten (1991)

In 1990 the German manufacturer Audi introduced a new system to reduce the chance of serious injury in front-end accidents: Procon Ten. This is a mechanical device triggered by the deformation of the front section of the car. When that happens, the engine and gearbox are pushed backwards toward the driver. This movement tightens a stainless steel cable that runs around the gearbox unit and immediately triggers the steering wheel to move forward into the dashboard, thus reducing the danger of the driver smashing his head into it. Simultaneously, the seat belts lock and so reduce the effects of whiplash.

BICYCLES

Celeripede and velocipede (1790)

The two-wheeled vehicle era started with Count de Sivrac's celeripede in 1790. This consisted of a two-wheeled wooden frame without a steering mechanism and propelled by no other means than the rider's feet pushing against the ground. The celeripede was renamed the velocipede, or dandy-horse, when attempts were made to improve its appearance by making it look like a lion, a horse or even a dragon.

Draisine (1817)

The Draisine was introduced in 1817 in the Luxembourg Gardens in Paris by Baron Karl

Seat belts for animals have been marketed since 1989. This "kitty sitter" should protect even the tiniest kitten. (Le Livre Mondial des Inventions)

von Drais von Sauerbronn (Germany). It brought two-wheelers back into fashion. The Draisine had a swiveling steering mechanism controlled by a sort of rudder, the ancestor of handlebars. It was propelled by being "walked" along the road. After some major improvements, the Draisine became quite popular, especially in England from 1819 on, where it was called a hobby-horse.

Around 1839 a blacksmith, Kirkpatrick Macmillan (Great Britain), added pedals that drove the rear wheel through a system of cranks.

Velocipede (1861)

In Paris in 1861 the blacksmith Pierre Michaux and his son Ernest had a brilliant idea. While repairing a dandy-horse, they decided to attach what was subsequently called a pedal-and-gear mechanism to the front-wheel axle. The innovation worked, and by 1865 the firm of Michaux & Co. had sold more than 400 vehicles.

Rover safety bicycle (1885)

In 1870 the first ordinary bicycle was built by James Starley in Coventry, England; it became known as the pennyfarthing because of its huge front wheel.

Harry J. Lawson patented his "safety" bicycle in 1876, which led to John Kemp Starley's Rover safety bicycle being designed in 1885. This model brought together the main features of the modern bike: wheels of equal size, geared-up chain drive, direct steering with inclined forks, and the diamond-shaped frame.

Dérailleur gears (1889)

The first two-speed gear-changing system fitted on the rear hub appeared in 1889 under the brand name The Cyclist. Tested by Paul de Vivie in 1905, it was improved in 1911 (Panel's patent for the rear *dérailleur*) and in 1925 (Raymond's patent for the front *dérailleur*).

MOTORCYCLES

Origins (1818)

On Sunday, April 5, 1818 in the Luxembourg Gardens in Paris, a Draisine fitted with a steam engine at the back was displayed. The only drawing of the period that has reached us, however, does not show how the power could be transmitted to the wheels. The official name of this astonishing vehicle was the *velocipedraisia vaporiana*.

The Italian Murnigotti was the first, in 1879, to register a patent for a two-wheeled vehicle with a 0.5 hp, four-stroke engine. The machine was never built.

Four-stroke motorcycle (1885)

In 1885 Wilhelm Maybach and Gottlieb Daimler (both Germany) built a motorcycle with a wooden frame and wooden wheels, powered by a

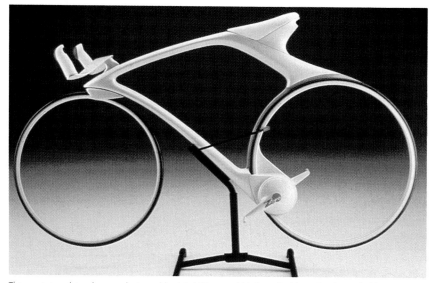

This prototype bicycle was designed by M. Mikita and H. Tsuzaki. The wheels are held in place by magnets, while magnetic forces ensure propulsion. (Sipa Press/Suu Irigoyen)

four-stroke internal combustion engine. The engine produced 0.5 hp and went at 11 mph.

First mass-produced motorcycle (1894)

In 1894 Heinrich Hildebrand and Alois Wolfmüller (both Germany) built a motorcycle that was mass-produced, with over a thousand units built. It was a two-cylinder, 1,488 cc motorcycle.

De Dion three-wheeler (1895)

The Marquis de Dion was the first person to see the potential that the Daimler engine could have on a light economical vehicle. The first tricycle with a four-stroke engine came out in 1895. It had a ¾ hp engine with electric ignition. Some 15,000 de Dion tricycles were produced up to 1902.

Motorbike (1897)

The motorbike, named the *Motocyclette* by its inventors, Eugène and Michel Werner (both France), was exhibited for the first time at the Paris Salon in 1897. These two Russian-born journalists had already produced several machines—a phonograph, a cine-projector and a typewriter—when in 1896 they undertook to mount a small engine, designed by H. Labitte, on a bicycle. First, they placed the engine horizontally above the back wheel, then in front of the handlebars, with a leather belt linking it to the front wheel to drive the bike. It was an immediate success, and thousands of these models were built from 1898 onwards in France and, under license, in England and Germany.

Two-stroke engine motorcycle (1900)

The first two-stroke engine fitted on a motorcycle was perfected by Cormery (France), who had the invention patented in Paris on August 20, 1900.

In 1901 another French manufacturer, Léon Cordonnier, registered a patent for his Ixion

engine, which also marked the beginning of the rotor arm. During the same period, Alfred A. Scott (Great Britain) was working on the first two-cylinder, two-stroke engine, which obtained its British patent on February 11, 1904 but was not built until 1908, when six were made.

It was not until 1911, when water-cooling appeared, that this vehicle reached its most competitve form. The two-stroke engine was only perfected in the 1930s because of research carried out by the German company DKW.

Finally, separate lubrication appeared on some makes, such as Scott in England in 1914 and DFR in France in 1924.

Four-cylinder motorcycle (1901)

Col. Holden (Great Britain) built a motorcycle with four opposed cylinders as early as 1901. Its connecting rods drove the back wheels without the use of a drive belt, like the connecting rods on a locomotive.

Motor scooter (1902)

The motor scooter first appeared in France in 1902, under the name of *Autofauteuil* (motor-armchair). It was a motorbike equipped with a protective "apron," small wheels and an open frame to allow the driver to be seated. Invented by Georges Gauthier, it was manufactured until 1914.

This type of vehicle caught on after 1919 and became very fashionable by 1946 with such models as the Italian Vespa. After a period of being out of favor, the motor scooter came back into fashion as a result of a Japanese offensive led by Honda and Yamaha from 1982 onwards.

Sidecar (c. 1910)

The idea of attaching a sidecar to a bike was discussed as early as April 29, 1894, in the magazine *Le Cycle*. But this addition had to wait until motorcycles became more solid and powerful; sidecars became popular around 1910. An articulated assembly was perfected in the United States in 1916. It allowed the motorcycle to lean when going into a curve or around a corner. A motorized sidecar wheel was developed in 1939 and adopted by the best-known makes in all industrial countries.

Motorcycle with reverse gear (1988)

The Goldwing 1 is the largest and most luxurious motorcycle ever built by Honda. This Rolls-Royce of the two-wheelers comes with a new six-cylinder, 1,520 cc, 100 hp engine. It is the only modern bike with a reverse gear (to make maneuvering easier).

Five-valve cylinder head (1988)

As early as 1977 Yamaha started research into a means of making four-stroke engines more efficient than two-stroke ones. This led them to look for a multivalve cylinder head. After many experiments they arrived at lentiform combustion chambers with five valves (three inlet valves and two exhaust valves). As opposed to the "roof-shaped" combustion chamber, Yamaha's five-valve chamber does not require a hemispherical piston head to achieve a high rate of compression, and the distance between the spark plug's electrode and the piston head remains generous. Maximum power is achieved and the torque curve is excellent. The five-valve cylinder head invented by Yamaha is fitted on the 750FZ and the 1000FZR Genesis.

Transmission

Chain (1897)

Adopted almost from the first days of the motorcycle (1897), it changed very little until 1972,

when the Duplex chain (a double chain), invented by Reynolds (Great Britain), appeared. In 1982 Yamaha's Tenéré was given an O-ring chain, which was waterproof and self-lubricating.

Transmission (c. 1900)

The drive belt, chain, and camshaft, which are the three main means of transmission of the engine's power to the back driving wheel, appeared with the first motorcycles, around 1900.

Shaft transmission (1900)

Shaft transmission was invented in 1900 by the Belgian company Delin, which first used it on a de Dion engine. However, it was not brought into mass production until 1923, when the first German BMW was put on the market. Not until the 1980s was this type of transmission perfected to become as smooth as the chain.

Variable transmission (1910)

As early as 1910, before gearboxes appeared, variable transmission by pulleys with variable cheek spacing appeared at Terrot's in France, and one year later at Rudge Witworth's in England.

This system was not suitable for increasingly powerful machines and was abandoned for motorcycles. An automatic version was fitted on mopeds, the first one being by Motobécane in 1966.

Gearbox (c. 1914)

True gearboxes became common on motorbikes just before World War I. At first the gearbox was controlled manually via a lever and a serrated quadrant fixed on the tank. The pedal control appeared in England in 1923 on the Vélocette but only took precedence after World War II.

Suspension

Front suspension (1903)

The first motorcycle front suspension to be marketed was the very complex Truffault fork, which was seen in December 1903 at the Paris Salon on a Peugeot motorcycle.

Rear suspension (1904)

The concept of rear suspension for velocipedes was invented as far back as 1898. For motorcycles, the first development was the French Stimula of 1904, which had rear suspension with a cantilevered rocking arm and a spring under the seat. In 1911 the German firm NSU inaugurated rear suspension with a rocking arm and two near-vertical shock absorbers with helicoidal springs, as used today. The English ASL of 1912 introduced pneumatic suspension, with inflatable front and rear shock absorbers. In addition, the seat contained an inflatable cushion.

All the basic principles of rear suspension had been invented by the beginning of the century, but the technology was not far enough advanced to apply them. It was only after World War II that sliding suspension appeared, then rocker suspension with greater and greater wheel clearance. Finally, in 1979 and 1980, the first variable geometric suspensions were marketed: Honda's Pro Link, Kawasaki's Uni Track, Suzuki's Full Floater, etc. These suspension systems contain a combination spring and shock absorber, activated by an intricate arrangement of articulated levers.

Telescopic fork (1904)

In 1904 a well-known French manufacturer, Terrot, patented what can be considered to be

The first motorcycle was called the *vélocipédraisiavaporiana*. This tendency for embellishment is still reflected in today's machines. (Ernoult)

the first telescopic fork. It was used until 1908, the year in which, in England, Scott also introduced a telescopic fork that did not have hydraulic dampers. The pendular fork, used by Terrot in France, then by Alcyon and Triumph in England, appeared in 1909.

Parallelogrammatic fork (1907)

The parallelogrammatic fork was the best-known type of front suspension. Invented in 1907, it was used until after World War I in various guises.

Telescopic fork with hydraulic damper (1935)

In 1935 the German firm BMW conceived the first telescopic fork with hydraulic damper. It was universally adopted when it came out and it is still being used. Only BMW, the firm that invented it, uses a different system, which it introduced in 1955—the Earles type suspension. That system was very popular until the 1960s, and was fitted on almost all motor scooters as well as on the first Hondas.

Other Systems and Accessories

Electric starter motor (1913)

In 1913 a U.S. firm, Indian, introduced the Hendee Special, with a V-shaped, two-cylinder, 998 cc engine. This was the first motorcycle equipped with an electric starter motor, the Dynastart. Too advanced for its time, the Hendee Special was a complete failure, and all Indian models with an electric starter motor were recalled to the factory for removal of this accessory, as unperfected as the fragile batteries supplying its current. The electric starter motor did not make its appearance commercially until the 1960s, on mass-produced Japanese motorcycles.

Cast wheels (1972)

Cast wheels appeared as early as 1972 thanks to Eric Offenstadt (France). They were cast in a magnesium alloy and gradually replaced those with spokes. They made possible, among other things, the use of tubeless tires, which are safer in the event of a puncture.

Turbocharger (1981)

The first mass-produced motorcycle with a turbocharger was the Honda CX500 Turbo in 1981.

ABS for motorcycles (1987)

The antiblocking brake system, perfected by the German firm Bosch for cars, was fitted for the first time by BMW in 1987 onto its top-of-the-line motorbikes. Several years were required to master a technique originally aimed at four-wheeled vehicles. But in both areas, the advent of the ABS system is certainly as impor-

tant as that of the disc brake was some 20 years ago.

Deltabox frame (1988)

A direct derivation from the one used on the 250 cc and 500 cc winners of the 1986 world championships, this frame consists of rectangular sections made from very high quality alloys. This technique gives optimum resistance to buckling and better road-holding. Strong and light (26 lb 14 oz), the Deltabox frame is used on the Yamaha 1000 FZR Genesis.

Two-wheel-drive motorbikes (1990)

Invented by David Watts (Great Britain) and developed by the company Sunshine Components, this motorbike was designed primarily for sand and snow riding, so is particularly well-suited to difficult terrain. Front braking is by means of a disc, mounted on the chain drive, that turns twice as fast as the wheel. With the clutch pedal system, it is impossible to lock the front wheel if the rear wheel does not come to a complete stop.

BALLOONS

Hot-air balloon (1783)

The first flight by a hot-air balloon took place at Annonay, near Lyons, France, on June 4, 1783. This hot-air balloon was constructed by two brothers, the paper manufacturers Joseph (1740–1810) and Etienne (1745–99) de Montgolfier. The *Montgolfière* was made of pack-cloth covered with paper. The balloon carried a portable stove in which wool and straw were burned to produce hot air, that is, a gas lighter than air. This first balloon attained an altitude of 3,300 ft and landed after 10 minutes. When the news of the flight reached Paris, it caused a sensation.

On September 19, 1783 the Montgolfier brothers repeated their first experiment in front of Louis XVI and his court at Versailles. This time the balloon carried a suspended cage containing the first air passengers: a sheep, a duck and a cock. This flight was also witnessed by Benjamin Franklin, then the United States' ambassador to France.

First human flight (1783)

Jean Pilâtre de Rozier (1756–85) and the Marquis d'Arlandes (1746–1809) made the first human flight on November 21, 1783. Ascending in a basket supported by a hot-air balloon, the first two aeronauts left the Bois de Boulogne, Paris and landed 25 minutes later close to the center of the city.

Pilâtre de Rozier, the first pilot, was also to become aviation's first victim. He was killed on June 15, 1785, while attempting to cross the English Channel. Soon after departure, the balloon caught fire and crashed 3 miles from Boulogne, France.

Hydrogen balloon (1783)

It was physicist Jacques Alexandre Charles (France, 1746–1823) who invented all the rules governing modern ballooning. The balloon he designed, inflated with hydrogen, went up in the Jardin des Tuileries in Paris on December 1, 1783, with Charles and Nicolas Robert on board. The American balloonist Wise perfected Charles's balloon by introducing the use of a rip cord. Modern sporting balloons differ from that of Charles only in the use of a nonflammable gas, helium, and in the quality of the covering used.

Airship (1852)

The airship was invented in 1852 by Henri Giffard (France), who perfected a balloon furnished with a means of propulsion. This hydrogen-filled airship was driven by a 3 hp steam engine, and it flew for the first time on September 24, 1852, covering a distance of 17 miles at a speed of 4.3 mph.

In 1883 the Tissendier brothers (both France) attached an electric motor to a conventional airship. It made two flights, but proved to be unreliable.

The first flight that returned to the takeoff point was accomplished on August 9, 1884 by the French Army captains Charles Renard and Arthur Krebs. Their airship, *la France*, was powered by an electric engine.

The Zeppelin (1890)

Count Ferdinand von Zeppelin (Germany) undertook experiments as early as 1890 and took out a series of patents for a streamlined dirigible that would not lose its shape but would remain rigid. A movable hangar enabled it to be taken out without risk, no matter what the wind direction was. The first ascent of the LZ1 took place on July 2, 1900.

This airship comprised a 420 ft cylinder with an aluminum frame covered with specially impregnated cotton.

Between 1900 and 1939, 52,000 people had traveled 1,250,000 miles by zeppelin. One accident brought the fashion to an end: the *Hindenburg* burst into flames on arriving at Lakehurst, N.J. on May 6, 1937.

The modern balloon (1963)

The revival of interest in balloons is due to research done by the U.S. Navy in the early 1950s, and it was in 1963 that touring balloons first appeared. Balloon coverings are now made of very light, synthetic materials; the basket is usually wicker, and the pilot heats the air with the help of a flame from a propane gas burner.

Skyship (1984)

The Skyship 600, fitted with a 39-ft-long gondola, can carry 12 to 15 passengers. Its manufacturer, Airship Industries, claims the airship can fly at a speed of 63 mph and has a 55-hour endurance and hence a range of 3,400 miles. Its polyester envelope is made in France by Zodiac. The craft is powered by two Porsche turbo engines.

AIRPLANES

Origins (1809)

Humankind has always dreamed of emulating birds. In the 15th century Leonardo da Vinci observed how birds flew and drew designs of artificial wings and even helicopters. His analysis was taken up by Borelli, in a study published in 1680.

Sir George Cayley (Great Britain, 1773–1857) is considered the father of airplane technology, pioneering the theory of heavier-than-air flight. In 1809 he perfected a fixed-wing engineless aircraft. In 1853 he built a fixed-wing glider that flew 1,640 feet. He is also credited with developing the idea of using propellers to obtain the necessary force to drive the plane.

In 1843 William Henson (Great Britain) patented a steam-powered flying machine, but it was his partner John Stringfellow who, in 1848, managed to make a model airplane fly a few dozen yards. Jean-Marie Le Bris (France) is generally credited with having made the first glider flight, in 1856. In 1871 Alphonse Pénaud (France) managed to make a model airplane propelled by a twisted rubber-band system fly more than 165 feet. This enabled him to set out flight equations for the first time.

"Flying leap" (1890)

The first piloted takeoff, generally referred to as a "flying leap," in an engine-powered airplane took place on October 9, 1890 at Armainvilliers, Saint-et-Marne, France. Clément Adler (France, 1841–1925) piloted the *Ecole*, whose wheels lifted a few inches off the ground for approximately 160 feet. The *Ecole* was a bat-shaped aircraft fitted with a 20 hp steam engine. In his patent for the machine, which was granted on April 19, 1890, Adler uses the word *avion* (airplane); this is believed to be the first time the word was used.

First flight (1903)

The world's first sustained powered flight was accomplished by the Wright brothers, Wilbur (U.S., 1867–1912), and Orville (U.S., 1871–1948). The brothers mounted a gasoline engine of their own design on a wood and fabric biplane, the *Flyer*, that they had previously used as a glider. The first flight took place on December 17, 1903 at Kitty Hawk, N.C. Orville piloted the craft, which flew 120 feet in 12 seconds at an average speed of 7.5 mph. Wilbur and Orville alternately accomplished two flights of 13 and 15 seconds each. During the fourth flight, Wilbur covered 930 feet in 59 seconds.

Seaplane (1910)

Henri Fabre (France, 1882–1984) is the father of marine aviation. He was the first to replace airplane wheels with floats, building a flat-bottomed seaplane with swivel floats. On March 28, 1910 Fabre piloted the seaplane in its first takeoff from the Etang de Berre in southern

Orville Wright achieved the first sustained flight at Kitty Hawk., N.C., on December 17, 1903. (J.L. Charnet)

France. The machine was of the canard type with wings and engine at the back.

Boeing 247 (1933)

The Boeing 247 was put into service by United Airlines in March 1933. A low-wing, twin-engine aircraft, it had retractable landing gear, wing de-icers, constant-speed, full-feathering propellers (which allowed the automatic pilot system to be operated) and a passenger capacity of 10 people. For the first time, travelers could cross the United States in less than 20 hours.

Douglas DC-3 (1935)

Equipped with the same advanced technology as the Boeing 247 but able to carry more passengers, the Douglas DC-3 was the first transport airplane to fly over the Himalayas, between

India and China. American Airways was the first company to put it into service, flying between New York and Chicago, in 1935.

Viscount V-630 (1948)

The Viscount V-630, constructed by the British company Vickers-Armstrong, was the first turboprop aircraft to be used for commercial service. Its maiden flight was made on July 29, 1948, and it was put into service on July 29, 1950. However the V-630 was in service for only two weeks, as it was dropped for the larger and more powerful Viscount V-700.

Havilland Comet 1 (1949)

The Comet 1, built by the British company De Havilland, made its maiden flight on July 27, 1949. The Comet was powered by four turbojet engines, each with 4,453 lb of thrust, and could cruise at 490 mph at an altitude of 39,360 feet. It entered service with BOAC on May 2, 1952, becoming the first turbojet airliner. The Comet was capable of flying from London, England to Johannesburg, South Africa (6,680 miles) in 17 hours 6 minutes. However, after a series of accidents the Comet was withdrawn from service.

Boeing 707 (1954)

The first trials of the B-367-80 (prototype of the Boeing 707) were made in Seattle, Wash. on July 15, 1954. The Boeing 707–120 aircraft made its first commercial flight with Pan American Airways on December 20, 1957. Powered by four turbojet engines, the wings were placed at a 35 degree sweep with an overall wingspan of 131 feet. The 707 carried 179 passengers and attained a cruising speed of 567 mph. Larger and more powerful than any airliner of the period, the 707 became the standard long-range airliner.

Caravelle (1955)

The revolutionary idea of mounting jet engines at the rear of the fuselage, rather than on the wings, originated with the French Caravelle, which made its first flight on May 27, 1955. Rear mounting of the jet engines allowed undisturbed airflow over the wings, increased aerodynamic efficiency and stability, and decreased cabin noise. The rear-mounted engine system was soon adopted by almost all manufacturers.

Boeing 747 (1969)

The first flight of the Boeing 747 took place on February 9, 1969. The aircraft was put into service by Pan American Airways on January 21, 1970. With the 747, Boeing launched a new generation of large-capacity planes that became known as jumbo jets. The aircraft has a wingspan of 197 feet and can cruise (with a full payload) over 4,600 miles at Mach 0.89.

Concorde (1969)

The Concorde, the first supersonic civil aircraft, is the fastest passenger aircraft in the world. A joint British–French project, the agreement to build the Concorde was signed by Aérospatiale and the British Aircraft Corp. on November 29, 1962. On March 2, 1969 the Concorde had its maiden flight. The first commercial flights took place on January 21, 1976—a British Airways flight from London to Bahrain, and an Air France flight from Paris to Rio de Janeiro, Brazil.

The Concorde has a wingspan of 83 feet 10 inches and is 203 feet 11 inches long. It can carry a maximum of 139 passengers and is capable of a speed of Mach 2.2 (1,448 mph). The Paris-to-New York route takes 3 hours 30 minutes, flying at an altitude of 59,000 feet.

On December 31, 1968 the supersonic Tupolev 144 made its maiden flight. Designed and built in the former Soviet Union, the Tupolev went into service on November 1, 1977. An accident in June 1978 halted commercial application of the aircraft. An upgraded version, the Tupolev 155, performed a 20-minute-long test flight using liquid natural gas on January 18, 1989. The test proved that it is possible to fly with this type of fuel, which is cheaper and less polluting than kerosene.

Pedal aircraft (1977)

The industrialist Paul McCready (U.S.) renewed popular interest in human propulsion for aircraft. His *Gossamer Condor* was, in 1977, the first aircraft in the world to give a convincing demonstration of human-powered flight.

On June 12, 1979 McCready's *Gossamer Albatross*, piloted and pedaled by Bryan Allen, crossed the English Channel, setting a record for pedal-powered aircraft.

Glasair (1979)

The Glasair was the first plane in kit form, and is still widely regarded as the best-performing plane of its type. Invented by Thomas S. Hamilton (U.S.) and Robert M. Gavinsky (U.S.) in 1979, the Glasair was designed for people who

wanted their own plane but couldn't afford to buy one.

Voyager (1986)

In December 1986 the twin-engine *Voyager*, piloted by Dick Rutan and Jeana Yeager (both U.S.), flew nonstop around the world, 24,987 miles, in a little over nine days, without refueling. Invented by Burt Rutan, Dick's brother, *Voyager* is a propeller plane consisting of little more than fuel tanks. Built from ultralight materials, *Voyager* was essentially an experiment to test these materials.

Airbus A320 (1988)

The Airbus is a European aircraft, conceived and built by a team of companies from France (Aérospatiale), Germany (MMB), Spain (CASA), Great Britain (British Aerospace) and Belgium (Belairbus) in the early 1970s. In April 1988 the Airbus A320 entered service equipped with more advanced technology than any other airliner. It was the first civil airliner to use "fly-by-wire" technology; the controls are driven by computers, easing the pilot's workload in routine situations; and the plane has built-in safety monitors to alert the pilot to potentially dangerous conditions. The aircraft was built using improved metal alloys and composites that aid safety and fuel economy.

Daedalus (1988)

Inspired by McCready's success with pedal-powered aircraft in the late 1970s, a team of engineers from MIT (Massachusetts Institute of Technology) developed a series of pedal-powered craft that set numerous distance records. The project's final goal was to recreate the mythical flight of Daedalus from Crete to the Greek mainland. On April 23, 1988, the MIT aircraft, dubbed *Daedalus*, took off from Heraklion in northern Crete, and 3 hours 55 minutes later crash-landed just off the island of Santorini, 73.3 miles away. *Daedalus* was piloted by a Greek racing cyclist, Kanellos Kanellopoulos. It had a wingspan of 112 feet, a wing area of 332 square feet, a length of 29 feet, and an unladen weight of 70 lb.

Miscellaneous Aircraft Developments

Parachute (1802)

In 1783 Sebastien Lenormand (France) dropped from a second-floor window holding a parasol in each hand. He dubbed the apparatus a *parachute* (*para* from parasol, and *chute* meaning "fall" in French). André-Jacques Garnerin (France, 1769–1823) was the first person to make a true parachute jump. On October 22, 1797 he went up in a balloon above the Parc Monceau in Paris, and at an altitude of 2,624 feet he cut the rope that held the balloon and the basket together. The basket descended hanging from a parachute. On October 11, 1802 Garnerin received a patent for his parachute.

The first flight of a Boeing 747, the jumbo jet, took place on February 9, 1969. (Boeing)

The first drop from an airplane was made by Capt. Albert Berry (U.S.), who jumped from a biplane above St. Louis, Mo. on March 1, 1912. In 1935, the former Soviet Union became the first country to use the parachute for military purposes.

Gyroscope (1852)

In 1852 the physicist Léon Foucault (France, 1819–68) set out to prove the earth's rotation. He hung a 179-ft-long pendulum from the center of the Pantheon's dome, thus demonstrating that a pendulum swings on a fixed plane. He then invented a mechanical device including a rotor and called it a *gyroscope*. At the beginning of the 20th century, gyroscopes were used as stabilizing devices on ships. These heavy and cumbersome sytems have nowadays been replaced by automatic pilots.

Gyrocompass (1904)

A true innovation in the domain of navigation was the gyrocompass, invented at the beginning of the 20th century. After Foucault's observations, G. Trouvé (France) made a spinning top powered by an electric motor in 1865. After that, the aim was to make gyroscopes for ships. Three names are linked with this development: Anschütz and Schüler (both Germany) and E. Sperry (U.S.). Anschütz's first gyrocompass was patented in 1904; in 1911 Sperry made a gyrocompass suspended by a wire. This type of equipment remained unchanged until World War II, from which time radionavigation began to be developed.

Joystick (1906)

It was the engineer and airman Robert Esnault-Pelterie (France, 1881–1957) who invented the control lever or joystick in 1906. Unfortunately he did not register a patent, and an American firm used his invention in spite of all his efforts to have his rights acknowledged.

Air speed indicator (1910)

After the pioneer era when pilots only used the controls as their instincts dictated, the factor that preoccupied the early pilots most was speed.

The first speed indicator was built by Captain Etévé in 1910. Perfected by the engineer Raoul Badin (1879–1963), it became a little clock called an *anemometer*, which measures the difference between the dynamic pressure of an aircraft moving through the atmosphere and the static pressure.

Current research, especially for large planes, is moving in the direction of the highly sensitive laser air speed indicator.

Retractable undercarriage (1911)

As is often the case, this idea was conceived in the first years of aeronautics: as early as 1876, the aviation pioneers Alphonse Pénaud and Paul Cauchot (both France) had thought of reducing the aerodynamic resistance produced by the wheels.

The first retractable undercarriage appeared in 1911, on the German monoplane Wiencziers, though the undercarriage was a folding one rather than a retractable one. A few years later, the pilot and engineer Glenn Martin (U.S.) fitted his Martin K-3 Kitten fighter with an undercarriage that could be retracted toward the rear. In 1920, on the American monoplane Dayton-Wright RB racer, the wheels disappeared up into the fuselage. The year 1922 saw the first plane with an undercarriage retracting into the wings: it was the American racer Verville-Sperry R3.

But it was in 1929 that Georges Messier (France) perfected the first retractable undercarriage operated by hydraulic controls.

Automatic pilot (1914)

The first night flights were made possible because of progress made in instrumentation and in the willingness to replace a human being at the controls of the plane. The first efficient system was produced by Elmer Sperry (U.S.) and further perfected by his son, Lawrence, on a Curtiss seaplane in 1912.

In 1914 Lawrence Sperry presented his device at a competition on airplane safety that took place in Paris. In order to demonstrate the stability of the plane, he made the flight with both arms in the air, while his passenger held on to the wing of the plane.

Pressurization (1920)

With the advent of jet transport and the consequent increase in flight altitudes, machines had to be pressurized so that passengers could breathe normally. The first airliner to be pressurized was the Boeing 307 Stratoliner, dating back to before World War II, but the first trials took place in 1920.

In-flight refueling (1923)

Wesley May (U.S.) should be credited with having performed the very first in-flight refueling. On November 12, 1921 May jumped from the wing of a Lincoln Standard to the wing of a JN-4 with a fuel tank strapped to his back. He then climbed on top of the engine and poured the fuel into the upper wing tank.

The first in-flight refueling using a pipe took place over San Diego, Calif., on June 26, 1923. An airplane piloted by U.S. Army Lt. Seifert refueled an airplane piloted by Capt. Smith and Lt. Richter.

From February 26–March 2, 1949, after flying exactly 94 hours 1 minute, U.S. Air Force Capt. James Gallagher completed the first nonstop around-the-world flight. His B-50 *Lucky Lady II* was refueled in the air several times during the flight.

Air hostess (1930)

The first air hostesses were in fact stewards. Before World War I, the large Zeppelin airships already had staff on board.

In 1919, at the beginning of commercial aviation, it was often the radio operators who served drinks or picnic-style meals. It was not until 1927–28 that the first stewards started to appear on British Imperial Airways aircraft.

But it was in May 1930 that Boeing Air Transport, which was to become United Airlines, hired stewardesses for the first time. Ellen Church and seven other young women made up the first team on the San Francisco to Chicago line. In Europe, the first air hostess was Nelly Diener, a Swiss woman hired in 1934 by Swissair.

Ejector seat (1946)

This system was invented with the high-speed plane, since jumping from one of these using a conventional parachute would be far too dangerous. Such a system was considered possible as early as 1918 by Col. Holt; preliminary designs were studied more closely in 1939 by the Germans and the Swedes.

The first experiment in which a man rather than a dummy was used was carried out on June 26, 1946 by Bernard Lynch (Great Britain), who jumped out of a Meteor in a seat built by the British company Martin-Baker. He was at an altitude of 8,200 ft and was flying at a speed exceeding 310 mph. The first pilot to be saved by his ejector seat was a Swede who had crashed into another plane on June 30, 1946.

The first time a pilot was ejected at supersonic speed was on February 26, 1955 from a F-100 Sabre.

Rocket belt (1961)

The rocket belt was perfected by the U.S. manufacturer Bell Aerosystem Co. and exhibited in 1961. The device was invented by Wendell F. Moore. To date, experimental flights with the belt have not exceeded 656 ft horizontally and 65 ft vertically. The rocket belt consists of two vertical tubes and a fuel tank strapped onto the user's back. Two motorcycle-type handles are used to control it. This belt allows vertical takeoffs and stationary flight, and it can rotate 360 degrees.

"Driven" by a "flying man," the rocket belt made a remarkable sight at the opening ceremonies of the Los Angeles Olympic Games in August 1984.

HELICOPTERS

Origins (1480)

The helicopter, in model form, flew for the first time in 1784. Launoy and Bienvenüe (both France) presented their model to the Academy of Science. This very simple machine consisted of two two-bladed propellers arranged at the opposite ends of a spindle so as to contra-rotate, powered by a taut whalebone bow.

In fact, as early as 1480, Leonardo da Vinci had designed a machine, a sort of airscrew, that had wings rotating around a vertical axis. Borelli in 1680 and Paucton in 1768 studied his theory. In 1862 Ponton d'Amécourt (France) (to whom we owe the word *helicopter*), and in 1877 Enrico Forlanini (Italy), built craft that were powered by steam engines. These experiments solved many problems and finally paved the way for making piloted machines.

First takeoff (1907)

The first takeoff by a manned helicopter was accomplished by Paul Cornu (France) on November 13, 1907 at Lisieux in France. The machine weighed 573 lb and was powered by a 24 hp Antoinette engine.

Rotor (1908)

The history of the rotor is intimately linked to that of the helicopter. In 1907 Paul Cornu (France) had hovered a few feet off the ground for a few seconds. In the United States in 1908 the aeronautical engineer Igor Sikorsky (b. Russia, 1889–1972) tackled the problem of the blade and rotor mechanism: the rotor ensuring both the lift and propulsion of the aircraft. This problem found many solutions during the evolution of the helicopter. A major invention was the variable cyclic pitch that makes it possible to change the position of the blades as they rotate so as to correct the uneven lift created by the forward motion of the craft.

In 1939 Sikorsky's work led him to fit the VS-300 with a single main rotor. This helicopter, in 1941, beat the world record for range with a one-and-a-half-hour flight. (In 1937 a two-rotor system had been fitted on the German helicopter, the Focke-Achgelis FA61.)

Since then there have been many different rotors: the first streamlined anti-torque rotor Fenestron, perfected by Aérospatiale in 1967; the Starflex, also from Aérospatiale (1973), with a rotor head made of a type of fiberglass and blades made of composites; the tilt-rotors that

allow the prototype Bell XV to perform as well as an airplane; Sikorsky's contra-rotating rotors, which are still in the experimental stage, etc.

Autogiro (1922)

As early as 1922 Juan de la Cierva (Spain, 1895–1936) had started to work on an autogiro. In 1924 he fitted a four-blade rotor above the cockpit of a Deperdussin monoplane. On September 18, 1928 la Cierva and a passenger, Henri Bouché, crossed the Channel from England to France, aboard the C811. The autogiro does not allow vertical flight but it was a first step in the tackling of slow flight. Many of these machines were built in England, France, the United States, the USSR and Japan.

First helicopter flight (1924)

Sixteen years after the airplane, the first helicopter to fly a distance of one kilometer over a closed circuit was the one flown by Etienne Oehmichen (France) on May 4, 1924. From 1920 to 1925 Paul Pescara (Spain) built three helicopters that managed to take off. It was the first time that the complete flight program of the helicopter, including autorotation, was studied and its principle established. The theory was put into practice only in 1936 when Louis Bréguet and René Dorand invented the Gyroplane Laboratoire, which, piloted by Maurice Claisse, went through the complete routine of hovering, flying sideways, long cruising flight and above all the first precision landing using autorotation with the engine off.

First operational helicopters (1940)

The first mass-produced helicopter was the Focke-Achgelis FA 223. The prototype's

maiden flight took place in 1940. The Bell 47 was the first helicopter in the world to receive a civil aviation certificate of airworthiness (March 8, 1946). The first operational Soviet helicopter was the MIL Mi-1, built by the Russian company Mikhail Mil and mass-produced from 1951.

Jet-powered helicopter (1953)

The only craft of this type to be mass-produced was the French SO 1221 Djinn, a two-seater with an unladen weight of 813 lb that flew for the first time in 1953.

Turbojet helicopter (1955)

The first helicopter to be powered by a gas turbine was the SO 1120 Ariel III. The flight took place at Villacoublay on April 18, 1951. But the turbojet's great popularity dates back to March 1955, when Jean Boulet took off for the first time aboard the *Alouette II* in France. Invented by Charles Marchetti and René Mouillé for Aérospatiale, the *Alouette II* is the first helicopter to be created around a turboshaft engine. It is a five-seater machine whose "offspring" are still in production.

Pedal helicopters (1989)

Called the *Da Vinci III*, this craft was built by a group of students from the California Institute of Technology. After a few successful liftoffs in November 1989, it achieved its first takeoff (seven seconds) on December 10 in the presence of the National Aeronautic Association (NAA), which recognized the Da Vinci as the first muscle-propelled helicopter. Research had begun in 1981.

The first takeoff by a manned helicopter was achieved by Paul Cornu (France) on November 13, 1907 at Lisieux, France. (Paul Cornu)

WHAT ON EARTH?

NOT ALL INVENTIONS CHANGE OUR LIVES, SOME JUST MAKE US SCRATCH OUR HEADS.

THE CONVERTIBLE

Owning a convertible is a dream of many drivers. Here is a selection of some convertibles that may strike your fancy: How about a "convertible suitcase?" Designed by Mazda engineer Yoshini Kanemoto, it weighs 70 lbs and reaches speeds of 12 mph. (Mazda) Perhaps a "convertible gateway" is more to your taste. Designed by Toyota engineer Ryugi Matsuzawa, it certainly solves parking problems. If neither of these is appealing, maybe the Cosmic Voyageur will relieve the tedium of the daily commute. Designed by Moru Umeda of Toyota, this car may have its up and downs, but it will certainly get you noticed. (Toyota)

SWEET-SMELLING ENGINES

The odors generated by automobile engines often invade the driving compartment of a car, and are rarely sweet-smelling or good for your health. Patrick Maître (France) has invented a potential solution to this problem, a smelling-kit that can be placed under the hood. This hydroelectric device, released by an interrupter, eliminates all noxious fumes and agreeably scents the driving environment. The kit has been available in France since 1992.

THE FIRE-BIKE

This is not the latest in daredevil motorcycle stunts, but a novel idea for a fire-fighting vehicle. Designed in France, the bike is equipped with a pump and a small fire hose that can be activated to contain a blaze if there is an adequate source of water. Because of its mobility and compact size, the bike can weave speedily in and out of traffic and reach the fire scene before conventional fire engines. A prototype is currently being built in France.

New ideas that may change the way we live

AUTOMOBILE CENTRAL HEATING

This car heater, independent and programmable, ensures an ideal temperature before starting the car. It was invented by a team of engineers of the German group Webasto, M.M. Weidemann and Grebe, and presented in 1991 at the Automobile Show of Frankfurt, Germany. It's the first miniature heater of its kind and can be installed in any car. Several patents have already been issued to protect this innovation, which will be much appreciated by drivers who, in winter, will find a warm interior and engine.

BLIND-SPOT-FREE REARVIEW MIRROR

Dubbed Asphenix, this new rearview mirror for automobiles, made up of two juxtaposed mirrors separated by a line, practically eliminates blind spots. The system was patented by Deutsche Spezialglas AG, a German company that is part of the Schott group. Volvo and Saab have mounted the mirror on certain 1993 models.

THE REVA

Invented by Raoul Parienti (France), the Reva is a small electric car (7 feet in length) designed as a means of individual public transportation. The car is parked at a public terminal that is opened by a memory card available to qualified drivers. When the driver has finished with the car, it is parked at the nearest terminal, and another driver can use it. The Reva is powered by an electric motor. Parienti has signed an agreement with a large French corporation to develop and market the car.

THE PROMETHEUS SYSTEM

The Prometheus system was launched in 1986 and is the most ambitious of all the in-car computer-guided driving systems currently being developed. A joint European effort, the goal of Prometheus is to reduce the problems of traffic congestion, pollution and safety. Three prototypes have been unveiled, including one system that could see through fog using an infrared camera and project onto the windshield road conditions ahead. A computer would assess whether the car was proceeding safely and would automatically slow it down if it believed the situation to be dangerous. Another function uses an on-board computer that logs into a city's system. This system would tell the driver which roads were congested, where parking is available and even which hotels had vacancies. Some of these devices could be ready by 1995, but it is expected that Prometheus will not be fully operational until the next century.

INTELLIGENT VEHICLE HIGHWAY SYSTEMS (IVHS)

A system similar to Prometheus being developed in the United States is the Intelligent Vehicle Highway Systems (IVHS). Several companies are testing IVHS throughout the country. In March 1992 a joint project of A.A.A., General Motors and the F.H.A. announced a one-year test trial in Orlando, Fla., for 75 Avis rental cars equipped with tracking devices and on-board computers. Using satellite signals and wheel sensors, the on-board computer generates a map on a video monitor showing the best route available.

In April 1992 AT&T and Lockheed announced an agreement to develop an IVHS.

Combining AT&T "smart card" technology and Lockheed's radio transmission systems, the IVHS would allow drivers to pay tolls without stopping, notify repair trucks of disabled vehicles and interact with other drivers through video displays in their cars. The card is inserted into a radio transponder as the tollbooth is approached, where receivers note the car and the amount paid. Similarly, parking fees can be paid this way. The radio transponder can also send and receive messages, such as notification of traffic congestion.

THE MAGLEV

The Maglev (Magnetic Levitation System) is a futuristic-looking high-speed magnetic train being developed in Japan. The train will be capable of covering the 340 miles from Tokyo to Osaka in one hour. A special track, 25 to 31 miles long, is being built to test the Maglev. It is projected that the train will be ready for service by 2001.

TEXAS SUPERTRAIN

The first high-speed rail transportation system to be built in the United States, the Texas Supertrain, is expected to start service between Dallas and Houston in July 1998. The proposed rail system will eventually link Dallas, Houston, Austin and San Antonio. The French-built trains consist of two electrically driven power cars and eight passenger cars. At speeds of up to 200 mph, the journey from Dallas to Houston will take two hours.

HYPERSONICS

Several European countries and the United States are funding projects to develop a hypersonic aircraft. In the United States, President Ronald Reagan drew national attention to the Orient Express, otherwise known as the X-30, which would make it possible to fly from Washington, D.C. to Tokyo, Japan in 2½ hours. These space aircraft projects raise numerous technical problems, notably the speed/overheating ratio, as the sound barrier is also the heat barrier. Another problem is propulsion. Engineers are currently studying the use of the ramjet engine as the best means to power a hypersonic craft. It is unlikely we will see such craft in operation before 2015.

IVHS technology will allow drivers to pay tolls using a radio transponder. (Lockheed)

MEDICINE AND HEALTH

EXAMINATION TECHNIQUES

Microscope (16th century)

The microscope appears to have been invented toward the end of the 16th century by the optician Hans Jansen (Netherlands) with the help of his son Zacharias. Described by Galileo in 1609, this microscope was quite basic and had minimal powers of magnification.

Antonie van Leeuwenhoek (Netherlands, 1632–1723) was the first to observe spermatozoa, muscular striation and certain oral bacteria, although magnification was still less than 200 times actual size. The first modern microscopes were constructed after 1880.

Thermometer (1626)

The first clinical thermometer was a water thermometer invented in 1626 by the physician Santorio (Italy), otherwise known as Sanctorius. The model of the modern clinical thermometer—a graduated glass tube containing mercury—was developed by the physician Sir Thomas Allbutt (Great Britain) in 1867.

There are now various types of medical thermometers available, including the disposable oral thermometer invented by Dr. Louis Weinstein (U.S.).

Percussion (1761)

Percussion was invented in 1761 by Dr. L. Auenbrügger (Austria). This clinical mode of exploration allows the condition of certain organs to be deduced by the noise obtained when they are tapped with the fingers. The system was improved by Baron Jean Corvisart (1755–1821), Napoleon's personal physician, and then by Joseph Skoda (Austria), who improved it considerably.

Auscultation (19th century)

With the exception of the medical observations of Hippocrates (Greece, 460–377 B.C.), the first true auscultation was performed by René Théophile Hyacinthe Laënnec (France, 1781–1826) using a makeshift stethoscope made from a sheet of paper rolled into a cylinder. He devised this method because of his embarrassment at having to place his ear on the naked chests of his female patients—the previous method of listening to the heart.

The stethoscope in the true sense of the word, from the Greek *stethos* meaning breast, was invented in 1815 when Laënnec replaced the sheet of paper with a wooden cylinder. The device was further modified and improved by Joseph Skoda (Austria) and Cammam (U.S.) to become the binaural stethoscope as we know it. The electron stethoscope was invented in 1980 by Groom and Boone (both U.S.).

Previous page: X-ray of a hand. (CNRI)

Measuring blood pressure (1819)

Taking the pulse has long been one of the main methods of making a diagnosis. In 1819 the doctor and physicist Jean-Louis Poiseuille (France, 1799–1869) invented the manometer, a mercury gauge for measuring blood pressure. It was succeeded by the sphygmomanometer, from the Greek *sphygmos* meaning pulse, which was a pulsometer developed by Dr. Siegfried Carl von Basch (Austria) in 1881, and by Dr. Pierre Potain (France) in 1889. This was followed by the broad armband, invented in 1896 by Scipione Riva-Rocci (Italy), which exerted a more consistent and reliable pressure. In 1905 Dr. N.S. Korotkov (Russia) perfected the method by developing a device that examined the arteries by means of auscultation rather than palpation.

Electrocardiograph (1887)

The first human electrocardiogram was recorded in 1887 by Augustus Désiré Waller (1856–1922), a physiologist from London University, born in Paris.

In 1901 Willem Einthoven, professor of physiology at the University of Leiden in Holland, and former colleague of the physicist and 1908 Nobel Prize-winner Gabriel Lippmann (France), developed the loop galvanometer. This made him the true inventor of the electrocardiograph (EKG), a piece of equipment that weighed 661 lb and required five people to operate it.

Carrying out an electrocardiogram is very straightforward, though interpreting the results is not. It is now possible for a pregnant woman to place an ultrasound probe on her abdomen to monitor her baby's heart. The result can then be sent by the woman by telephone to her doctor, who can then assess the health of the baby, thus saving everyone a great deal of time and effort.

Electron microscope (1926)

In 1926 Hans Busch (Germany) laid the theoretical foundations for the electron microscope. In 1928 two of his fellow countrymen, Max Knoll and Ernst Ruska, from the Technische Hochschule in Berlin, carried out experiments based on his research that led to the development of the first operational electron microscope in 1933. It was perfected by Ruska, who, with Heinrich Rohrer and Gerd Binnig, was awarded the Nobel Prize for Physics in 1986 for the invention of the tunnel effect miscroscope (see below).

Electroencephalogram (EEG) (1929)

In 1929 the spontaneous electrical activity of the brain was recorded for the first time by Hans Berger, professor of neuropsychiatry at the German University of Jena. But his recording was met with skepticism because of the weakness of the signal. It was not until the physiologist and 1932 Nobel Prize-winner Edgar Douglas Adrian (Great Britain) circulated the results in 1934 and defended Berger that the latter received the support of scientific and medical circles.

In 1984 Prof. Stores (Great Britain) carried out an experimental continuous recording of an electroencephalogram for a period of 24 hours.

Radioimmunology (1970s)

Radioimmunology, invented by Drs. Solomon Berson and Rosalyn Yalow (U.S.), for which the latter won the Nobel Prize for Medicine in 1977, is a combination of two techniques. The first, which is biological, uses the specificity of the immune reaction in order to identify a given organic substance, while the second is physical and marks these substances by introducing radioactive atoms into their molecules.

Tunnel effect microscope (1980)

In 1980 Gerd Binnig (West Germany) and Heinrich Rohrer (Switzerland), both working in the IBM research laboratory in Zurich, Switzerland, developed the tunnel effect microscope, for which they received the Nobel Prize for Physics in 1986. Based on a principle of quantum mechanics, anticipated at the end of the 1920s, it makes it possible for the surface of a sample to be viewed atom by atom, with a magnification of 100 million times.

Test for hepatitis-B (1984)

This test was developed in 1984 by a working party consisting of Diagnostic Pasteur and the French National Blood Transfusion Center. It was marked by Diagnostic Pasteur under the name Monolisa, *mono* for monoclonal antibody and *lisa* for the ELISA (enzyme *l*inked *i*mmuno *s*orbent *a*ssay) technique. It makes it possible for hepatitis-B to be traced quickly.

Three-dimensional electron microscope (1985)

Living cells could not be observed using the electron microscope, as the beam of electrons directed at the target had to circulate in a high vacuum. In 1985, scientists from the Massachusetts Institute of Technology, directed by Alan Nelson, invented a new process that consisted of placing the sample in a cavity that retained enough air to produce about 1/10th atmospheric pressure and so made it possible to keep the cells alive.

The second advantage of the process was that a three-dimensional image could be projected onto a television screen, by means of a technique based on medical X-ray scanners, which is why the procedure is known as scanning.

Diagnostic test for AIDS (1985)

The first diagnostic test for AIDS was devised in 1985 by Prof. Luc Montagnier (France) and his team at the Pasteur Institute in Paris. The detection kit used the sandwich-type immunoenzymatic technique known as ELISA, also used to develop the test for hepatitis-B.

In November 1990 the Japanese company NTT announced that it had perfected a diagnostic technique using lasers, which was a hundred times more sensitive than any method known at that time. It is based on the magnetic particles that stick to the virus, making it possible to detect the virus itself, rather than the antibodies produced in reaction to it.

During 1991 several U.S. drug companies unveiled research on mini-tests for seropositivity based on samples of saliva and urine. In 1992 Prof. Alexander Honigman of the Hebrew University in Jerusalem revealed a new method for early detection of AIDS, particularly in newborns, from observing fireflies. Fireflies owe their luminosity to a gene made up of an enzyme, luciferase. This gene can be incorporated with cells capable of recognizing the AIDS virus. In the presence of the virus, they emit a light that can be captured on sensitive film.

Algometer (1988)

Developed by the companies 3M and Racia and based on the work of Dr. Claude Willer of the Hôpital Saint-Antoine in Paris, the algometer, an instrument for measuring sensitivity to pain, measures the threshold above which a stimulus is experienced as pain. It has been tested on hundreds of patients and has been shown to be an objective and accurate method of measurement. It will be used to test the efficiency of certain medicines, to prescribe the required dosage of analgesics and to measure the level of analgesia during the administration of an anesthetic.

Rapid diagnosis of tuberculosis (1989)

Since November 1989 a technique for the rapid diagnosis of tuberculosis and other infections caused by mycobacteria has made it possible to detect the bacterium in three days as opposed to the previous minimum of six weeks. This process was developed jointly by the Pasteur Institute in Paris and Unit 82 of INSERM, the French national institute of health and medical research. The genetic material (DNA) of the bacteria is enlarged in vitro, and specific molecular probes make it possible to identify the type of mycobacteria in question.

Tracing hepatitis-C (1989)

A hepatitus virus that is neither A nor B, and that should therefore logically be referred to as hepatitis-C, has been identified in the blood by the research team of Dr. Qui-Lim-Choo of the Chiron Corp., a Californian biotechnology company. The hepatitis-C virus is the most common cause of the illnesses that tend to follow blood transfusions, such as hepatitis, cirrhosis and cancer of the liver. This is an important discovery that could permit the development of a vaccine. In November 1989 the virus was successfully traced for the first time.

Due to the rapid advances in virology, two further hepatitus viruses have been identified: D and E. Hepatitis-D is found only in B-infected people, while hepatitis-E is known as Epidemic Non A-Non B.

LipoScan (1989)

Anyone can now carry out on-the-spot cholesterol checks by using the LipoScan (TM)-TC, developed by Home Diagnostics Inc. and marketed in 1989.

A few years ago the same laboratory brought out a similar test, the DiaScan (TM)-S, which allowed diabetics to check the daily level of glucose in their blood.

Detection of Down's syndrome (1990)

Building on the work done by Prof. Bogart (U.S.), the geneticist Prof. André Boué (France) has developed a blood test that makes it possible to detect two-thirds of cases of Down's syndrome before birth. The HT21 test (developed by the Clonatec laboratory) is a blood marker that measures the levels of a particular hormone (HCG), the pregnancy hormone, in the blood. A very high level indicates, in two cases out of three, that the fetus is trisomic (i.e., having three chromosome No. 21s rather than two—any fetus with trisomy 21 will have Down's syndrome), although this initial diagnosis needs to be confirmed by a study of the chromosomes. The HT21 test must be carried out between the 15th and 17th week of pregnancy, since the levels of HCG are too low to be detectable any earlier. The test became available at the end of 1990.

Prenatal blood test (1990)

Fetal cells can be examined as early as the sixth week of pregnancy, simply by taking a blood sample from the mother. This technique, devised in 1990 by Prof. U. Mueller (Australia), uses monoclonal antibodies and PCR (polymerase chain reaction) to isolate fetal cells contained in the mother's blood. The test makes it possible to determine the sex of the child and to detect certain genetic disorders, such as cystic fibrosis and trisomy.

Detecting mental retardation (1992)

In 1992, Prof. Ted Brown and his team at North Shore University Hospital and Cornell University Medical College developed a technique based on PCR to detect the genetic mutation of the X chromosome that is the most frequent cause of hereditary mental retardation—the fragile-X syndrome.

MEDICAL PHOTOGRAPHY

Endoscope (1826)

This is a technique that allows organs to be examined internally, permitting the detection and even treatment of certain forms of damage. The first instrument was developed by Dr. Pierre Salomon Ségalas (France), who, in 1826, performed the first endoscopy of the bladder using a speculum lit by candles. In 1853 Dr. Antonin Desormeaux (France), performed the first rectal endoscopy. The first laryngoscopy was performed in 1829 using an instrument invented by Dr. Benjamin Babington (Great Britain). The first gastroscopy was performed in 1842; the first electric cystoscopy in 1878 by Dr. Max Nitze; the first tracheobronchoscopy in 1897, and the first arthroscopy in 1951 by Watanabe.

In the 1960s the range of investigations performed by endoscopy was greatly increased and extended because of the development of glass fiber instruments that are both extremely supple and excellent conductors of light.

Radiology (1895)

On November 8, 1895 the physicist Wilhelm Conrad Röntgen (Germany) discovered X-rays while working in his laboratory. On December 22, he X-rayed his wife's hand and was able to see the carpus, the phalanges, etc. In 1901 Röntgen received the Nobel Prize for Physics for his discovery.

In 1912 another physicist, Max von Laue (Germany), demonstrated that X-rays resemble visible light in that they are electromagnetic waves, but with a very short wavelength that enables them to pass through opaque matter.

Radiography was initially used for examining the skeleton, but was extended to the other organs by the use of injections of contrasting substances.

Tomography, a process by which a thin layer of an organ is X-rayed to a specific depth, was discovered by André Bocage (France) in 1915. The first tomographies were carried out in 1928.

The first X-ray of the skull was carried out by Walker in 1896; the first encephalogram, or X-ray photograph of the brain, by Dr. Walter Dandy (U.S.) in 1918; the first arteriogram by Dr. Antonio de Egas Moniz (Portugal) and Dr. Reynaldo Dos Santos in 1927; and the first X-ray of the pulmonary blood vessels and the cardiac chambers by Ameuille in 1938. Today, traditional radiology accounts for no more than half of medical photography.

Ultrasound (1952)

The principle of the echogram is the application of sonar to the human body. An ultrasonic source transmits a signal that is reflected by the obstacles in its path. Ultrasound was first used in medicine in 1952 by Dr. Robert Lee Wild (U.S.) and then by Dr. Leskell (U.S.), who was the first to observe the heart using ultrasound. In 1958 Dr. Ian Donald (Great Britain) carried out the first echogram of the uterus. The method was not widely used until after 1970, but today it can be used to examine any organ. It is used mainly in the fields of gynecology and cardiology.

Thermal analysis (1950s)

Thermal analysis is another painless and harmless method of examination developed during the 1950s by English and American scientists. It is a method of photographing the tissues using infrared rays that brings out the differences in temperature that result from changes in vascularization. It is used particularly as a means of checking for cysts and inflammation in the breasts, but is replaced by mammography for detecting malignant tumors. In 1980 the

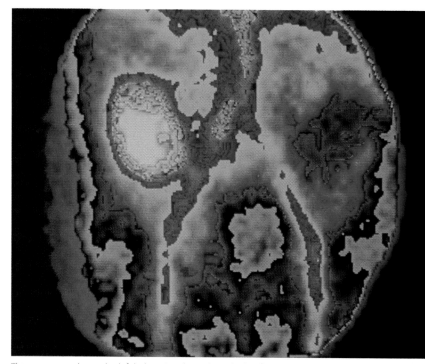

This scintiscan shows the left kidney (on the right), which is not working, and a new kidney, which has been transplanted (on the left) and is directly connected to the bladder. (CNRI)

microwave thermal analysis process was developed by a French research team led by Prof. Y. Leroy of Lille University of Science and Technology.

Scintiscanning (1961)

This technique of medical photography was used for the first time in 1961. It is based on the principle of introducing a radioactive substance such as phosphorus, iodine or thallium into the body, which then attaches itself to the organ to be examined. Nearly all organs can be scanned in this way, although the technique is currently used mainly for the thyroid gland and the bones. The method has great potential for the future. The use of computers since 1975 has enabled the resultant images to be improved.

Scanner (1972)

The scanner is the result of the combination of the X-ray and the computer. Perfected in 1972 by Sir Godfrey Newbold Hounsfield (Great Britain), an engineer working for EMI, the scanner or tomodensitometer makes it possible to take photographs of cross-sections of tissue in which the detail is 100 times larger than those produced by the traditional X-ray method.

Photography by magnetic resonance (1972)

The appearance of this technique in 1972 revolutionized the field of medical photography. It produced clearer and more detailed pictures than the scanner, with the added advantage that it did not use X-rays. The phenomenon of nuclear magnetic resonance (NMR) was discovered in 1948 by physicists Felix Bloch and

Edward Mills Purcell (both U.S.). In 1972 it was introduced into the medical world by P.C. Lauterbur, professor of chemistry at the State University of New York at Stony Brook, and biophysicist Raymond Damadian. The technique uses high frequency electromagnetic radiation that produces changes of energy within the cells which in turn enable the nature of the tissues being studied to be identified. The first pictures of the human body achieved in this way were obtained by Damadian in 1977. At present the technique is used mainly in the field of neurology, but it has other very promising possibilities.

Magnetic resonance angiography (1989)

This new system of creating magnetic resonance images makes it possible to measure the blood flow without injecting anything into the veins or arteries. It was first demonstrated in 1989 by scientists from the General Electric research and development laboratories. It works by creating a magnetic field. As the cells pass through the field they generate a current, and this current is then described pictorially on a television screen.

SQUID (1991)

A technique for recording magnetic fields in the brain using superconductor detectors was introduced in 1991 as the result of joint research between Siemens, Philips, Dornier and Biomagnetic Technologies. SQUIDs (superconducting *q*uantum *i*nterference *d*evices) make it possible to localize epileptogenic centers in the brain or sources of heartbeat irregularity with great precision.

VACCINATION

Variolation (11th century)

For centuries, smallpox epidemics had ravaged communities throughout Europe. The only known response had been to flee the area. Variolation, the first known immunization method, had, however, been used in Asia since the 11th century.

The principle behind variolation is that smallpox, like some other diseases, once contracted and cured, will not occur again in the same individual. Preventive variolation by the application of dried crusts of smallpox lesions to nasal mucous membranes (which Edward Jenner rediscovered in the late 18th century—see below) was used regularly in Asia in the 11th century, and was introduced to Europe in 1717 by Lady Mary Wortley Montagu (Great Britain), the wife of the British ambassador to Constantinople, when she revealed that her three-year-old son had been variolated.

Microbes (1762)

The first microbes were discovered by Dr. M.A. Plenciz (Austria, 1705–86), who published his *Medico-Physical Studies* in 1762.

Most of the microbes that we know had been discovered by the end of the 19th century.

Vaccination (1796)

On May 14, 1796, Edward Jenner (Great Britain, 1749–1823), having done considerable work on cowpox (a disease of the cow udder whose French name is *vaccine*), took a sample of the material from a pustule on the hand of a diarymaid, contaminated by the cows, and put it into the arm of a young boy named James Phipps. Ten days later, a pustule appeared on the boy and healed quite normally.

In a second experimental phase, Jenner inoculated the boy with smallpox; there was no harmful effeect. The experiment was a complete success, and in 1798 Jenner published his results. In 1799 he perfected his idea and his technique and called it *vaccination* after the disease initially treated.

The method spread widely in Europe, the East and the United States. Some 60 years later, Louis Pasteur (France, 1822–95) would make a discovery of still greater general interest in the area of disease prevention. However, although the biological principle was different, Pasteur kept the term vaccination, as a posthumous tribute to Jenner.

Assisted by his students, E. Roux and C. Chamberland, Pasteur first isolated a number of bacteria that cause disease in humans.

Pasteur made his first attempt at vaccination to fight the viral disease of rabies. On July 6, 1885 Pasteur injected Joseph Meister, who had been bitted by a rabid dog, with dried spinal marrow taken from rabbits he had inoculated with the virus. The result was conclusive.

In 1922 a veterinary surgeon, Gaston Ramon (France, 1886–1963), managed to isolate a diphtheria toxin and weakened it in formaldehyde. He thus paved the way for vaccines that cause no ill effects to the recipient.

Other parasites (1880)

Besides bacteria and viruses, a number of other disease-causing microorganisms exist.

In 1880 A. Laveran (France) identified the haematozoan, the protozoan responsible for malaria.

In 1881 R. Ross (Great Britain) and C. Finlay (Cuba) discovered the role of filariae (parasitic worms found in hot climates) in the transmission of malaria and yellow fever. In 1883 P. Manson (Great Britain) completed his studies by investigating the role of mosquitoes in the transmission of these filariae.

In 1895 D. Bruce (Australia) investigated the role of tsetse flies in the transmission of sleeping sickness.

Microbiology (19th century)

Robert Koch (Germany, 1843–1910) shares with Louis Pasteur the title of founder of the science of microbiology. Koch became famous in 1882 when he discovered the tuberculosis bacillus. In 1883 he detected the comma-shaped cholera bacillus *vibrio cholerae*. Koch had gone to Alexandria, Egypt, the center of a cholera epidemic, and made his discovery within a month of his arrival. He completed further research in India and concluded that the bacillus is transmitted via drinking water, food and clothing.

Serums (1890)

Serums, obtained by taking samples of blood serum from a diseased or vaccinated patient (serum which thus contains the desired antibodies), allow either preventative or curative action to be taken against numerous diseases and also against bites and stings from venomous animals, by providing the contaminated individual with protective antibodies.

The principal preventative serums were discovered before 1900:

- *Anti-diphtheria*: discovered in 1890 by E. von Behring (Germany), S. Kitasato (Japan), E. Roux, L. Martin and A. Chaillou (all France).
- *Anti-tetanus*: discovered in 1890 by Behring, Kitasato, Roux and Vaillard.
- *Anti-plague*: discovered in 1894 by A. Yersin (Switzerland).
- *Anti-anthrax*: discovered in 1895 by A. Sclavo (Italy) and E. Marchoux (France).
- *Anti-cholera*: discovered in 1896 by E. Roux (France), I Metchnikoff (Russia) and A. Salimbeni (Italy).

Viruses (1892)

The first virus to be characterized was detected in 1892 by microbiologist Dmitry Ivanovsky (Russia). It is the cause of tobacco mosaic, a disease that attacks a variety of plants.

Initially, the existence of viruses was only suspected, as they are not visible under the optical microscope (they can be several hundred times smaller than a red blood cell), but from 1933 onwards, with the development of the electron microscope, the list of identified viruses kept increasing. Today, certain viruses are identified even before the illnesses which they could cause have a chance to appear. In 1956 Werner christened them "orphan viruses"— that is, viruses that are looking for an illness.

Culture of hepatitis-B virus (1986)

The hepatitis-B virus, which is responsible for the most serious form of jaundice, has been cultivated in the laboratory since 1986. The success is due to a Franco-American team led by Prof. Max Essex of Harvard University. Tests and vaccines had already been developed, but the team's research has now made it possible to test antiviral medication, which is a major step forward in the fight against this extremely infectious disease.

Leishmaniasis vaccine (1989)

The first vaccine against leishmaniasis, a serious tropical disease transmitted by insects, which causes swelling of the liver and spleen, was developed in 1989. This vaccine was the culmination of 13 years of research by a team at the Institute of Biological Sciences of the University of Minas Gerais in Brazil, led by Prof. Wilson Marynk. Leishmaniasis is one of the five major endemic diseases targeted as priorities by the World Health Organization (WHO). The others are malaria, bilharzia, sleeping sickness and onchocerciasis.

THE HEART AND LUNGS

Blood circulation (13th century)

It is generally thought that the physicist William Harvey (England) discovered the circulation of blood in 1628. In fact, a 13th-century Arab physician, Ibn al-Nafis al-Quarashi, had already mentioned the existence of pulmonary circulation in a work dedicated to the Persian philosopher and scientist Ibn Sina or Avicenna. This work passed unnoticed until it was referred to in 1552 by theologian and physician Miguel Serveto (Spain) in his theological and medical work, *Restitutio Christianismi*, for which he was burned at the stake.

From 1550 onwards, several physiologists of the Paduan school, including Matteo Colombo, Carpi and Hieronymus Fabricius of Aquapendente, studied the problem. William Harvey based his work on that of his predecessors and had the inspired idea of considering the heart as a pump that was operated by muscular pressure. Proof of the existence of capillary vessels linking the arterial and venous systems was supplied in 1661 by the anatomist Marcello Malpighi (Italy).

Blood transfusion (1667)

There seems to be some question as to who should be given credit for the development and use of blood transfusion techniques. Early work in the field of blood transfusion was carried out in England by R. Lower, in France by J. Denis, in Germany by Mayor, and in Italy by F. Folli. Nevertheless, it is practically certain that Lower was the promoter of experimental transfusion in animals, and that Denis was the first to use it for humans. In 1667 Denis injected one liter of arterial blood taken from a lamb into a young man who had previously been bled. By virtue of its principle and because of the severe dangers inherent in its use, the method was immediately condemned and forbidden.

In 1821 the study of transfusion in animals was again taken up. The method was defined in 1875, but interhuman transfusion was developed only as of 1900, when the work of K. Landsteiner (Austria) demonstrated the existence of four large blood groups. In 1910 the serologist Jansky (Czechoslovakia) designated these groups by the letters A. B, AB and O.

William Haast has spent his life researching serums for snake bites. To immunize himself, he has had himself bitten on 148 occasions and then had a blood transfusion to help others. (Gamma-Liaison/Smart)

In 1940 Landsteiner crowned his achievements by identifying, with Wiener and Levine, the Rhesus factor. It is named after the kind of monkey in which it was first identified. The discovery provided an explanation for the hemolytic reaction in newborn babies.

Blood storage (1917)

At the beginning of this century the problem of blood storage and transportation was the subject of research by Arthus, Pages and Peckelharing. In 1914 Hustin made use of the anitcoagulant properties of sodium citrate.

In early 1917 Hédon, a doctor from Montpellier in southern France, demonstrated that the transfusion of blood with added sodium citrate was possible. On May 13 and 15 of the same year, Jeanbrau successfully performed the first three transfusions of stored blood.

Iron lung (1927)

Philip Drinken (U.S.), a professor at Harvard University, designed the iron lung in 1927. It was tested on a young girl at Boston Hospital on October 12, 1928.

The first model was made from bizarre objects: two vacuum cleaners alternately produced a positive and a negative pressure on the patient's thorax.

Plasmapheresis (1957)

Plasmapheresis is a method that consists of taking blood from a donor and separating the plasma from the corpuscles immediately so as to be able to return the latter to the donor. It was invented in 1957 by Profs. Stokes and Smolens, of the University of Pennsylvania.

Artificial heart (1957)

The artificial heart was invented by Willem Kolff, who began his research in 1957 at the Cleveland Clinic. In 1970 he joined scientists from other countries at the University of Utah, to develop models for the artificial heart.

In 1976 one of his colleagues, Dr. Robert Jarvik, invented the Jarvik 7, an artificial pneumatic heart that operated on compressed air and

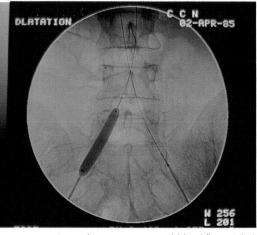

Angioplasty restores normal blood flow. A balloon is inserted into the artery and inflated to dilate it. (CNRI/CNN)

was connected, at the time, to a compressor that weighed 330 lb.

It is implanted in a patient in a situation where there is no alternative form of treatment. On December 2, 1982 the Jarvik 7 was implanted for the first time by Dr. William De Vries into a voluntary patient, Barney Clarke.

Since then some 90 Jarviks (the Jarvik 8 came out in 1986) have been implanted throughout the world. However, the benefits of the process have been widely disputed, even as an interim measure for those awaiting a heart transplant, and at the end of 1989 it was banned in the United States.

In addition to the Jarvik, other artificial hearts include the Pen State, developed by Dr. William Pierce, and the Buecherl System, developed by Prof. Emil S. Buecherl of Berlin, Germany. In July 1990 the American firm Novacor announced the development of a heart assistance device that performs the same function as an artificial heart. This is a miniature apparatus, which can be implanted directly into the patient's body.

Pacemaker (1958)

The cardiac pacemaker was invented in 1958 by Dr. Ake Senning (Sweden). The first implants took place in the early 1960s. The pacemaker is capable of stimulating other organs as well as the heart.

Angioplasty (1964)

In 1954 Dr. Charles Daughter (U.S.) had the idea of inserting a tiny balloon inside an artery and inflating it at the point at which the artery had become constricted. The idea was put into practice for the first time in Zurich, by Dr. Andreas Grüntzig (Switzerland) in 1964; since then the technique has been greatly improved.

Personal defibrillator (1970)

Certain irregularities in the muscular contractions of the heart cause what is known as ventricular fibrillation, i.e., uncontrolled contractions of the cardiac muscle. The defibrillator, developed in 1970 in the United States by Prof. Michel Mirowski, is implanted directly onto the heart, making it possible to identify any irregularity in the contractions and for immediate action to be taken. In this way the risks entailed in an emergency admission to hospital can be eliminated and the patient's chances of survival increased.

Artificial blood (1979)

In February 1979, Dr. Ryochi Naito (Japan) injected himself with 200 ml of artificial blood, fluosol DA. Fluosol DA, a totally synthetic derivative of petroleum and milky white in color, is capable of supplying essential hemoglobin, and thus makes artificial blood a viable possibility.

Previous attempts to produce artificial blood in the United States had encountered problems. In 1966 experiments with liquid perfluorocarbons at the University of Cincinnati proved that oxygen was present in the fluorocarbons. However, these fluorocarbons were incapable of mixing with blood. In 1967 Henry A. Slaviter (U.S.), a professor at the University of Pennsylvania, succeeded in emulsifying the perfluorocarbons by adding albumin, a natural protein found in blood. However, this emulsion

ran the risk of agglomerating and blocking some of the capillary vessels.

Naito's was the first successful human experiment. In April 1979, during an operation at the Fukushima Center, an emergency injection of fluosol DA was given to a man with a rare blood type. After 25 years' intensive experimentation, there are now two types of artificial blood in development: white blood, based on fluosol DA, and red blood, which is produced by the fragmentation and recovery of natural red corpuscles from expired blood donations. The red blood technique is still in the experimental stage.

TPA: the enzyme that prevents heart attacks (1984)

TPA (Tissue Plasminogen Activator) is an enzyme that has a thrombolytic effect, i.e., it dissolves blood clots that can damage the heart. It was produced in 1984 by the American company Genentech, based on the research of Dr. Collen of Louvain in Belgium. Its commercial production was undertaken in 1986 by Carl Thomas GmbH, a West German pharmaceutical company.

An international study in 1988 showed that if a patient was given TPA with aspirin within six hours of a heart attack, the damage done would be limited.

Cardiomyoplasty (1985)

On January 24, 1985 Prof. Alain Carpentier and his assistant, Dr. Carlos Chachques, a scientist at INSERM in Paris (both France) used, for the first time, a revolutionary technique which they had devised as an alternative to a heart transplant: cardiomyoplasty. This technique consists of replacing part of the defective cardiac muscle with another muscle that returns the contraction of the heart to as near normal as possible. For this to happen, the more rapid rhythm of the contractions of the booster muscle (in the case of this first operation it was a back muscle) has to be converted to the heart's unique rhythm of slow contractions. Only when the muscle has been re-educated can the operation take place. It is very lengthy and even more difficult than a transplant, but offers hope to all those patients who are unsuited to heart transplants or who cannot find suitable donors.

Pacemaker pill (1986)

In 1986 an American company, Arzco Medicals Electronics, brought out the first pacemaker "pill": an electrode contained in a gelatin capsule.

Programmed pacemaker (1986)

In 1986 a German company, Biotronik, developed a programmed cardiac pacemaker based on blood temperature, which is a good indicator of the level of activity of the patient. For example, as the patient climbs the stairs, the blood temperature rises and the device increases the heart rate accordingly.

Nuclear pacemaker (1988)

In November 1988 a 47-year-old man made history by being the first person ever to receive a double-pulse nuclear cardiac pacemaker. The Pulsar N-1, which operates by using a tiny pastille of plutonium coated with titanium, was implanted under the skin next to the chest. It should last for between 20 and 40 years, whereas single-pulse nuclear pacemakers, which act only on a single cardiac function, last for 16 years. Today, between 3,000 and 4,000 people are fitted with single-pulse pacemakers.

Hormone for the red corpuscles (1988)

For the first time a hormone that plays an essential part in the physiology of the blood—erythropoietin—is going to be produced commercially, as a result of the genetic engineering carried out by the Ortho-Cilag Laboratory. This is a medication that marks a major step forward in the treatment of patients suffering from renal insufficiency who are treated by dialysis, who are often unable to produce enough of this hormone. The result is anemia that requires continual blood transfusions.

Heart pump (1989)

The Hemopump, developed by Dr. Richard K. Wampler, is a miniature turbine that is designed to take over temporarily from the cardiac muscle in a situation where the latter is receiving an insufficient supply of blood. This temporary heart, 2.3 in. long and 2.3 in. in diameter, is inserted percutaneously and directed along the femoral artery to the left ventricle, which is responsible for pushing the blood into the aorta. Once in place, the pump, which is operated by an electric motor outside the body, rotates at a rate of 28,000 rmp to ensure a supply of blood. The Hemopump is extremely valuable in that it provides support at such critical moments as restarting the heart after a heart attack and recuperation after an operation. Its use is limited in that it can only be left in place for a maximum of six days.

IVOX (1990)

The first implantable Intra-Vascular Oxygenator (IVOX) was invented by Drs. J.D. Mortensen and M. Snider (both U.S.). It is a device consisting of microporous hollow fibers filled with oxygen. When installed in a blood vessel, it exchanges this oxygen for carbon dioxide diffused in the blood. This method of artificial oxygenation makes it possible to deal with critical phases of respiratory distress without recourse to mechanical ventilation. An IVOX implant was performed for the first time in the United States in 1990.

SURGERY

Origins (Neolithic times)

The first recorded surgical operation, an amputation, dates back to Neolithic times, between 5000 and 2500 B.C. But the skeleton of a Neanderthal man, about 45,000 years old, found in the Zagros Mountains in Iraq, seems also to have undergone an amputation. Its missing right arm was due neither to chance nor to an accident.

The sorcerers, doctors and surgeons of the time were also the first to perform trepanation (the removal of part of the skull) on living patients, some of whom appear to have survived this terrifying operation. In fact, some of the trepanned skulls show evidence of healing.

Dressings and Fractures

Treatment for fractures (3000 B.C.)

The Egyptians invented the earliest form of support for fractures. Around 3000 B.C. Athotis recommended strips of cloth soaked in mud.

Dressings and bandages (7th century B.C.)

The first evidence is recorded on slate tablets discovered during the digs in Assur and Nineveh in Assyria and written by one of the best-known medical practitioners of the 7th century B.C., Arad-Manai. In 1825 the surgeon Antoine Labarraque (France) introduced the chemical disinfection of wounds. In 1840 the physicians Sir Astley Cooper, Robert Liston, Syme and Macartnay (all Great Britain) introduced a new form of dressing, a piece of cotton cloth that had been moistened and covered with sticking plaster. In 1864 Dr. Joseph Lister (Great Britain) used dressings moistened with diluted carbolic acid, which acted as an antiseptic.

Plaster cast (1798)

In 1798 William Eton, a member of the British Consulate in Persia, noticed that plaster was used there to support fractures. In 1850 a Dutch military doctor from the Royal Hospital, Antonius Mathijsen, developed a method in which strips of linen sprinkled with dry plaster were prepared in advance and soaked when required.

Soluble dressings (1947)

The soluble dressing was invented simultaneously in 1947 by Jenkins in the United States and Robert Monod in France. It consists of a small gelatin sponge that can absorb 20 to 50 times its weight in blood, before gradually dissolving in the body.

Glass fiber and resin plaster (1982)

In 1982 the American company 3M developed the Scotchcast, a glass fiber strip impregnated with a polyurethane-based resin. This plaster-resin, which is extremely resistant, is waterproof and is only a third the weight of a traditional plaster cast.

Anesthesia

Origins (antiquity)

We know from very early documents that certain methods were used to suppress pain during medical operations. The Assyrians, for example, cut off the circulation to the brain by pressing on the carotid arteries while performing a circumcision.

During the 1st century A.D., Pliny the Elder referred to a method of making painless incisions and injections by the use of the mandrake. But before the discovery of anesthetics, the main obstacle to the surgeon's work was the pain suffered by the patient.

Anesthetic gases (1799)

In 1799 the chemist Sir Humphry Davy (Great Britain, 1778–1829) described the analgesic and laughter-provoking effect of nitrous oxide (laughing gas). To demonstrate these effects, he inhaled the gas to ease the pain brought on by an abscess on his tooth.

Some dentists, notably Horace Wells (U.S.) in 1844, used this chemical compound when extracting teeth. Wells said "A new era is beginning in dental surgery. It hurts no more than a pinprick." Wells died in 1848 from a wound to the femoral artery and, as a final recourse, inhaled the gas while dying.

General anesthesia (1842)

General anesthesia with ether was first used by C.W. Long (U.S.) in 1842. William Morton and John Collins Warren (both U.S.) operated on a neck tumor at Massachusetts General Hospital on October 14, 1846 after placing the patient under general anesthesia with ether. After their success, the use of ether spread throughout the United States, and Robert Liston, a surgeon (Great Britain), introduced it to Europe.

Chloroform became popular after ether. Dr. Simpson, a professor of obstetrics in Edinburgh, used the gas, which had been available since 1831, in a pure form in 1834. After Queen Victoria had been given chloroform during the delivery of her seventh child, anesthesia was adopted in all hospitals.

Local anesthetic (1884)

Local anesthetic was developed in 1884 using cocaine, by the ophthalmic surgeon Karl Köller (Austria). The effect of cocaine was subsequently improved by the addition of adrenaline in 1902, and then it was replaced in 1904 by lignocaine.

However, the earliest written record of local anesthetic dates back to Pliny the Elder, who, in his *Natural History*, gives the recipe for an anesthetic poultice made from crushed mandrake leaves mixed with polenta.

Epidural anesthetic (1885)

The epidural anesthetic was described for the first time in 1885 by neurologist J. Leonard Corning (U.S.). This regional anesthetic is carried out by injecting an analgesic into the epidural space, i.e., the space surrounding the spinal cord, between the eleventh dorsal and the fourth lumbar vertebrae. This deadens the pelvic organs (the uterus, kidneys, prostate, etc.). It was rediscovered in France in 1901 at the Hôpital Tenon by surgeon Fernand Cathelin (France) and physician Jean Athanase Sicard, and then neglected until 1970, when it began to be widely used, particularly in obstetrics.

Cryoanesthesia (1978)

According to 17th-century medical texts, doctors in Finland used a technique in which, in order to reduce fractures and to reposition joints, limbs were bathed in ice water. The process, known as cryoanesthesia, made the operation virtually painless. More recently, in 1978, the Spembly Llord Method has enabled an English manufacturer to market ST-2000 Neurostat equipment, which extends the range of this technique. These specially shaped cryosounds are able to reach deep-seated nerves and relieve very different types of pain such as backache, postoperative pain or pain resulting from a trapped nerve.

Plastic Surgery

Origins (3rd century B.C.)

The great progress made in the field of anatomy during the 3rd century B.C. in Alexandria encouraged surgeons to attempt the first operations in facial plastic surgery. Amynthas of Alexandria performed the first operation on a nose.

Plastic surgery as we know it appeared at around the same time on both sides of the Atlantic. In 1891 Roe (U.S.) and in 1898 Joseph (Germany) invented rhinoplastic surgery, that is, the alteration of the shape of the nose by surgery for purely esthetic reasons. In 1907 Dr. Hippolyte Morestin (France) described his method for the resection of enlarged breasts. In Vienna, in 1928 and 1930 respectively, H. Biesenberger and E. Schwarzmann made important contributions to mammary plastic surgery.

Facelift (1925)

In 1925 Dr. Suzanne Noël performed facelift operations under local anesthetic in the patient's home. Techniques and results in this field are improving all the time, thanks to the great demand for a younger look, especially in the United States, where it has become a billion-dollar business. It is Rio de Janeiro, however, that has the greatest density of plastic surgeons in the world.

Liposuction (1977)

In 1977 Dr. Yves-Gérard Illouz (France) perfected a technique for fat suction known as liposuction, which makes it possible to reduce the bulk of the stomach, the thighs, the hip and even the face without scarring. After a simple incision of 0.4 in, the fat is extracted using a foam-tipped canula connected to an aspirator.

Transplants

Origins (17th century)

In the 17th century the Boiani, a family of surgeons from southern Italy who practiced empirical medicine, developed a way of rebuilding the face based on the method of layering vines carried on in their region. They were the first surgeons to transplant skin tissue by a method still in use today, the skin graft.

But grafting was not developed further until 1958, with the discoveries relating to the HLA system made by hematologist and immunologist Prof. Jean-Baptiste Dausset, Nobel Prize-winner for Physiology and Medicine in 1980.

Skin culture (1950)

In 1950 Prof. Howard Green of the Massachusetts Institute of Technology discovered that the fibroblasts of human skin multiplied extremely well when a sort of "fertilizer" made from cancerous 3T3 cells was added. The cells were irradiated to prevent them from reproducing while at the same time allowing them to produce the required nutrient, with the result that cell culture was achieved.

As a result of this discovery, the research team led by Howard Green developed a technique that enabled 9.3 sq in. of skin to be cultured in 20 days from 1 mm^2 of skin taken from a newborn baby.

Kidney (1950)

On June 17, 1950, Ruth Tucker (U.S.), a 44-year-old woman whose kidneys were afflicted with cysts, underwent the ablation and replacement of one kidney with one taken from a cadaver. This medical first was the work of Dr. Richard H. Lawlor (U.S.). The surgery was performed at the Little Company of Mary Hospital in Chicago, Ill. The patient lived for five years.

Bone (1950)

Robert and Jean Judet (both France) performed the first human homograft of bone in 1950.

Hair (1959)

In 1959 Dr. Norman Orentreich (U.S.) invented the hair transplant method. Hairs are taken from the back of the scalp and transplanted in the bald areas. In 1985 Dr. Yamada (Japan) invented a technique for implanting artificial hairs into the scalp. The following year, Dr. Gilbert Ozun (France) introduced his technique of implanting into a cushion of air at the Hôpital Foch in Paris.

Limb (1962)

On May 23, 1962 at the Massachussetts General Hospital, Boston, Drs. Donald A. Malt and J. McKhann reattached the right arm of a 12-year-old boy, which had been severed at the shoulder.

Heart (1964)

The first heart transplant attempt took place on January 23, 1964. Dr. James D. Hardy (U.S.), at the Jackson University Hospital, Miss., transplanted the heart of a chimpanzee in Boyd Rush, a 58-year-old man. Rush survived for approximately three hours.

The first human heart transplant was performed by Dr. Christiaan Barnard (South Africa) in Cape Town, South Africa on December 3, 1967. The patient, Louis Washkansky, who was 54 years old, lived for 18 days.

Aortic valve (1965)

In 1965 J.P. Binet and A. Carpentier (both France) transplanted a pig aortic valve in a human. In 1970 the same surgeons inserted the first synthetic valve in a human.

Cyclosporin-A (1972)

In 1972 Dr. J.-F. Borel (Switzerland) of the Sandoz Laboratories in Basle, Switzerland discovered the immunosuppressive properties of cyclosporin-A. This is a substance found in a mushroom that grows on the Hardangervidda, a high plateau in southern Norway. The first tests on humans took place in 1978, and cyclosporin-A came into general use for bone marrow and organ transplants in 1983.

Brain (1982)

In January 1982, two teams led by Erik Backlund and Åka Seiger independently showed that embryonic brain tissue could be introduced into specific areas of the brain. Research in this area is mainly related to treatments for Parkinson's disease.

Synthetic skin (1986)

In 1986 Prof. John Burke (U.S.), a surgeon at Massachusetts General Hospital, and Prof. Ioanis Yannas (U.S.), of the Polymer Laboratory at MIT, saved several hopeless cases by performing synthetic skin grafts. Their work was based on the patent held by Howard Green and Eugene Bell (both U.S.), who created a second artificial layer of skin from beef collagen, which is well received by the human body, and from silicone plastic. This "skin" is then sterilized and frozen in alcohol. The technique enables epidermis to be recreated.

First in utero transplant (1989)

A world first took place at the Hôtel-Dieu hospital in Lyons, France in 1989, when Profs. Touraine and Raudran and their teams carried out an in utero transplant. It was performed on a 28-week-old fetus suffering from "bare lymphocyte syndrome," a rare disease characterized by a very serious immunity deficiency that requires the baby to be placed in an isolation tent from birth so as to avoid any possibility of infection; even a simple cold could be fatal as there are so few antibodies to combat it. While in the isolation tent the baby gradually builds up its immunities, and after several months is able to venture out into the world.

Hygiene, Instruments and Other Surgical Procedures

Appendectomy (1735)

The military surgeon Claudius Amyan (Great Britain) performed the first successful appendectomy in 1735.

On April 27, 1887 in Philadelphia, George Thomas Morton (the son of William Morton, one of the pioneers of anesthesia) operated on a young man who was suffering from acute appendicitis, thereby saving his life.

Sutures (1820)

Dr. Pierre-François Percy (France, 1754–1825) invented wire sutures in 1820. Catgut sutures appeared in 1920. It is interesting that the famous Hispano-Moorish surgeon Abulcasis was already using catgut in the 10th century, as he liked its suppleness, its strength and the fact that it is resorbent.

Terylene sutures were invented in 1950, and in 1964 the American company 3M invented the Steristrip, a type of dressing that knits the wound together but avoids stitch marks.

Asepsis (1844)

Asepsis, or medical and surgical hygiene, was invented by a physicist, Ignaz Phillip Semmelweis (Hungary) in 1844. Asepsis by boiling and by dry heat autoclave was first achieved by Dr. Octave Terrillon and Louis-Félix Terrier (France) in 1883. In 1889 Dr. William Stewart Halsted (U.S.) introduced the use of rubber gloves.

Antisepsis (1867)

The surgeon Joseph Lister (Great Britain, 1827–1912) concentrated his efforts on antiseptics. Prior to all operations, he sprayed carbolic acid in the room, and disinfected the instruments and the area of the patient's skin where the incision was to be made. He published the results of his work in the British medical journal *The Lancet* in 1867.

One of the first antiseptics was honey, which the Egyptians used on wounds.

Neurosurgery (1918)

Modern neurosurgery was first introduced in the United States in 1918 by Dr. Harvey Williams Cushing (U.S.). In 1936 Drs. Thierry de Martel and Clovis Vincent (both France) invented the technique of performing brain surgery while the patient remained seated. In the same year, Dr. Antonio de Egas Moniz (Portugal) invented arteriography.

In 1950, Talairach (France) invented stereotaxy, a method for detecting a point inside the brain that allows surgery to be performed via a simple hole drilled in the skull. One of the first applications of this process was in surgery for Parkinson's disease, performed by Dr. Fenelon (France).

In 1960 Dr. Guiot (France) operated on a tumor of the pituitary gland through the nose. In 1962 the radiologist Dr. Djindjian and the neurosurgeon Dr. Hudart performed the first arteriography of the spinal cord, which permitted the operation of angiomass in the marrow. In 1970 Dr. Serbedinko (USSR) eliminated the need for the operation by inserting a probe into the artery. At the end of a probe is a tiny balloon which the surgeon releases at the point chosen to block or embolize the artery.

Cryosurgery (c. 1960)

Cryosurgery is a method by which pathological tissue is destroyed by the use of extreme cold, i.e., below –40° F. It has the advantages of being painless and causing no risk of hemorrhage. In about 1960 Dr. Irving S. Cooper (U.S.), sponsored by Union Carbide, developed a cryosound using liquid nitrogen that reached a temperature of –292° F. Other instruments were used for cataract surgery, tumors of the larynx, and hemorrhoids. In 1964, Drs. M.J. Gonder and W.A. Soanes used cryosurgery to treat adenomas of the prostate gland. In 1975 A.J. Keller (Germany) invented cryocautery.

Cerebral radiotherapy (1982)

The multibeam convergent irradiation unit is a unique piece of equipment. It makes it possible to treat brain lesions that were previously inaccessible. The first version was invented in 1982 by Dr. Oswald Betti (Argentina).

Shock waves against kidney stones (1982)

In 1982 three German professors in Munich, Christian Chaussy, Egbert Schmied and Walter Brendel, working with the Dornier company (manufacturers of fighter planes), developed a device that can disintegrate kidney stones by shock waves. The stones are broken down into tiny grains of about 0.0585 in. which can then be removed during urination.

Treatment of gallstones by laser (1986)

In 1986 Dr. Ludwig Demling of the University Hospital of Nuremberg in West Germany obtained extremely interesting results by the internal use of a laser. An endoscope is inserted into the gallbladder, where it is directed at the stone or stones, and the surgeon fires a shot with the laser that destroys them without damaging the surrounding tissue.

Cryogenic probes (1986)

In 1986 Patrick Lepivert, a French doctor from Nice, in collaboration with the Center for Nuclear Research in Grenoble, developed tiny cryogenic probes that could be used in the treatment of varicose veins. These probes, which are adapted to the size of the veins, make it possible to operate without using an anesthetic, and to avoid postoperative complications and scars. The development of these micro-probes should permit them to be used in the same way as laser beams, and at a much lower cost, to destroy inoperable tumors in the colon and digestive tract.

Pencil-laser (1987)

This is a surgical laser which, according to its inventors, Prof. Jean Lemaire and his research team at the French University of Science and Technology in Lille, is as easy to use as a pencil. This CO_2 type laser, known as the Optro 20, was presented in 1987 as the first in Europe to combine the most recent developments in the fields of optics and electronics.

Transparent X-ray table (1989)

Orthopedic surgery, which is used, for example, when treating road accident victims, often uses X-ray treatment before, during and after operations. An invention has been available since 1989 that eliminates the visual obstacle of the operating table. It is a table made of composite materials that are completely transparent to X-rays. Developed jointly by Drs. Gindrey and Letourneur (both France), the table, known as the T 3000 and manufactured by Tasserit, has two positive advantages. By completely eliminating the image of the metal parts of the table, the intensity of the rays can be reduced by 50 percent. Also, the operation time is shorter, so the patient does not require such a strong anesthetic.

AUTOPSY

Origins (3rd century B.C.)

The study of anatomy began to develop as a result of the autopsy. Ancient religions prohibited the mutilation of the body. It was not until the 3rd century B.C., and during the reigns of Ptolemy I Soter and Ptolemy II Philadelphus, that the first examinations of a corpse were carried out in Alexandria by the famous Greek anatomists and physicians Herophilus and Erasistratus. For a long time after this the practice was prohibited.

Papal authorization (13th century)

It was not until the medical renaissance of the 13th and 14th centuries in Bologna and Padua, and then only with papal authorization, that the physician Mondino dei Liucci (Italy, c. 1270–c. 1362) was able to publish accounts of the dissections he had performed, in his *Anatomia*.

GYNECOLOGY

Menstrual Cycle

Sanitary napkins (1921)

The American company Kimberly-Clark of Wisconsin marketed the first commercial sanitary napkins under the name of Kotex in 1921.

This 15th-century miniature shows a cesarian delivery. The first Roman emperor was named Caesar because one of his forebears had given birth by this method. (Explorer/Charmet)

Sheath (16th century)

The invention of the sheath is attributed to Gabriele Fallopia (Italy, 1523–62), professor of anatomy at the University of Padua from 1551 to 1562. The sheath was made of cloth and was intended primarily as a means of combating veneral disease; its contraceptive value was secondary. Only when penicillin reduced the fear of syphilis in this century did the condom become used primarily for contraceptive purposes. Condom, a physician residing at the court of Charles II, was the inventor of the modern contraceptive that was named after him. Nowadays the contraceptive is widely available, and its importance as a protection against infection, and particularly against the spread of AIDS, has grown. The rubber sheath was first used in the 1870s.

Diaphragm (1881)

In 1881 in the Netherlands the first birth control clinic was opened under the direction of Drs. Rutgers and Aletta Jacobs. They advised women to use the diaphragm developed by Mensiga (Germany).

Coil (1928)

The first effective intrauterine device was the silver ring designed by Ernst Grafenberg (Germany) in 1928. Measuring 0.0585 in. in diameter, it was made of silver thread rolled into a spiral.

The pill (1954)

The pill was invented in 1954 by Gregory Pincus (U.S.) of the Worcester Foundation for Experimental Biology, Massachusetts, and John Rock. These doctors worked for five years to develop a definitive contraceptive that would be "without danger, sure, simple, practical, suitable for all women, and ethically acceptable for the couple." The initial clinical tests were performed in 1954, and the first large-scale experimentation took place in 1956 in San Juan, Puerto Rico with 1,308 female volunteers.

The first pill to be marketed was Enovid 10 in 1960, manufactured by G.D. Searle Inc. of Illinois. It became available in Great Britain in January 1961.

Ernest Mahler, a German chemist working in the United States, had invented a cotton substitute made from wood pulp to compensate for the lack of dressings in hospitals. Nurses acquired the habit of using these cellulose-padded dressings as hygienic menstrual napkins.

When the Kimberley-Clark company, which was already manufacturing cotton-wool bandages, learned of this, they began marketing them.

Tampons (1937)

In the 1930s Earl Hass (U.S.) thought of a way to modify the surgical tampon. He wanted to eliminate the inconvenience and embarrassment caused by use of the sanitary napkin. In 1937 he applied for a patent and founded the Tampax Co. After some improvements, the use of the tampon spread throughout the world after World War II.

Contraception

Origins (antiquity)

The vaginal tampon was already being used in Egypt in the time of the Pharaohs. Other Mediterranean peoples, such as the Syrians, used small sponges soaked in liquids such as spiced vinegar water which were supposed to have spermicidal properties. In 1984 there was a return to these origins when a sponge impregnated with spermicide came onto the market.

Modern spermicides, brought out in the 1970s in pessary or cream form, are 97 percent reliable. One of the most reliable of these products is Nonoxynol-9, which is also noted for its protection against AIDS.

Conception, Delivery and Neonatal Care

Feeding bottle (antiquity)

Feeding bottles have been used since antiquity. At first they were in the form of jugs with two openings, one to fill the container, and the other, in the shape of a beak, to feed the baby.

Until the end of the 18th century, the teat was made from a small piece of rolled linen, one end of which soaked in the container while the other was sucked by the child. Teats were also made of sponge, softened leather or dried cow udders.

When rubber was discovered in the second half of the 19th century, teats made from this new, hygienic material became popular.

Cesarean section (7th century B.C.)

The Cesarean is an operation that was first mentioned in a law set out by Numa Pompilius (715–672 B.C.), the legendary second king of Rome. According to his law, no woman who had died during her pregnancy could be buried until her infant had been removed via an abdominal incision. The name of the first of the Roman emperors, Caesar, is derived from the Latin word for cut, *caedere*, because one of his forebears had given birth by Cesarean section.

The first modern cesarean seems to have been performed in 1610 by surgeon Trautmann (Germany).

Obstetric forceps (17th century)

Obstetric forceps were invented in the 17th century by surgeon Peter Chamberlen (England). Until then, a kind of hook, known as a head-hook, had been used. The surgeon and obstetrician André Levret (France) improved the technique of the instrument, particularly the curve of the blades, in the 18th century. In 1838 there were 144 different types of forceps. After further improvements, the forceps of the obstetrician Stéphane Tarnier (France) were generally adopted.

Incubators (1880)

The incubator was invented by Budin of France in 1880. These first wooden incubators were heated by saucepans of hot water placed beneath them. In 1894 Lion, a French doctor from Nice, invented the first incubator for premature babies.

Test-tube babies (1978)

The first test-tube baby was Louise Brown, born on July 25, 1978 at Oldham Hospital, Lancashire, England. Louise's scientific "fathers" were Drs. Patrick Steptoe and Robert Edwards. They were the first to perform this scientific exploit. An ovum taken from the mother was fertilized in a test tube by spermatozoa from the father, and the resulting embryo was reimplanted in the mother's womb. Today, thousands of test-tube babies have been born throughout the world.

Frozen embryos (1984)

On April 11, 1984, Zoe, the first "frozen" baby, was born in Melbourne, Australia. This was made possible by Drs. Linda Mohr and Alan Frounson, biologists at the Queen Victoria Hospital. Zoe was born from an embryo formed in a test tube and preserved for two months in liquid nitrogen at a temperature of $-321°$ F.

Drugs and Treatment

Antipyretic agent (5th–4th century B.C.)

The first antipyretic agent (a remedy that lowers the temperature and relieves fever) was dis-covered by Hippocrates (Greece) and was based on camomile.

Sleeping pill (1st century B.C.)

The first sleeping pill was invented during early Roman times by the medical writer Celsus, who gave patients suffering from insomnia a pill made from mandrake and henbane. Today it is known that both these plants are narcotics.

Electrotherapy (1786)

In 1786 in Bologna, the anatomist Luigi Galvani established that, on contact with two different metals, the muscles of a frog twitched convulsively. He realized that this contraction was the result of an electric current passing through the frog. After the successful treatment in 1795 by J. Hallé (France) of a patient with facial paralysis, the laws of nerve stimulation were the subject of a great deal of research, notably by Magendie, Faraday and Du Bois-Reymond. This work led to the development of electrodiagnostics and electrotherapy.

From 1960 on, electrostimulation found a major application with the perfecting of the cardiac pacemaker.

Quinine (1820)

In the 17th century the Indians of Peru entrusted the secret of the "sacred bark," or cinchona bark, to the Jesuit missionaries who were both numerous and powerful in the country at the time. In 1820 the pharmacists Joseph Pelletier and Joseph Bienaimé Caventou (France) isolated the alkaloid contained in the cinchona bark: quinine. It was partially synthesized in 1931 by Rabe, but it was not until 1944 that total synthesis was achieved by Doering.

Aspirin (1853)

Aspirin or acetylsalicylic acid was synthesized by Charles Frederick von Gerhardt (France) at the University of Montpellier in 1853, but he was not particularly interested in its practical use.

In 1893 Felix Hoffman (Germany), a young chemist working at the Bayer company in Dusseldorf, rediscovered aspirin to treat his rheumatic father. Bayer began to market the drug in 1899 under the name Aspirin, formed from *a*cetyl + *spir*aeic + *in*, which was a popular ending for the names of medicines at the time. In the Treaty of Versailles in 1919 Germany surrendered the brand name to the Allies as part of its war reparations.

Antibiotics (1889)

In the course of his work, Louis Pasteur (France, 1822–95) noted the vital competition that makes some bacteria fight against each other. This fact was repeatedly confirmed and was attributed to the action of an *antibiote* by the scientist Vuillemin (France) in 1889. Penicillin was the first antibiotic discovered, and it remains the most important because of its curative effects and its almost complete absence of tox-icity (see Penicillin, p. 182).

Vitamins (1910)

Although the influence of vitamins on the body was demonstrated only in 1910, their effect had long been suspected, particularly in connection with deficiency diseases such as scurvy and beri-beri. The navigator Capt. James Cook (Great Britain) had been one of the first to mention them in a letter dated March 7, 1777 and addressed to the Royal Society of London.

In 1910 the chemist Casimir Funk (Poland) isolated vitamin B1 in unpolished rice and gave the name *vitamine* to this "amine" that was so essential to life (*vita* in Latin).

In 1936 the chemist Robert R. Williams (U.S.) synthesized vitamin B1, and in 1959 a physicist, Dieter Muting (Germany), invented an anti-mosquito pill based on vitamin B1. Vitamin C was isolated in 1928 by Saint Györgyi from the juice of the capsicum, and synthesized in 1933 by the chemist Tadeus Reichstein (Switzerland).

Insulin (1921)

Discovered by Paulesco (Romania) in 1921, insulin was isolated a few months later by the 1923 Nobel Prize-winners, the physiologists John James Macleod and Sir Frederick Grant Banting (Canada) of the University of Toronto, and the physiologist Charles Herbert Best (U.S.).

Synthetic insulin was obtained in 1964 by Panatotis and Kastoyannis of the University of Pittsburgh.

In 1978 the Eli Lilly Laboratories successfully synthesized the human insulin gene, which was a major step in the production of insulin by genetic engineering.

In 1982 the first human insulin obtained by genetic engineering appeared on the market.

Antihistamine (1937)

An antihistamine is a drug that combats the effects of histamine, an amine released by the body during allergic reactions, and is used especially to fight allergies, a type of condition that was discovered in 1906 by C. von Picquet (Austria). The first active antihistamine was discovered in 1937 by Bouet and Staub. The first synthesized antihistamine was created by Halpern (France) in 1942.

Cortisone (1948)

This steroid hormone was first synthesized by Edward Kendall (1886–1972) in 1948 after many years' work. This led to the discovery by his colleague, Philip Hench (1896–1965), that synthetic cortisone can be used to relieve the symptoms of rheumatoid arthritis. Further research established that it could also be used to treat asthma, skin diseases and leukemia, among other conditions. The chemist Tadeus Reichstein (Switzerland, b. Poland) also made important findings in this field, and the three men received the Nobel Prize for Medicine in 1950 for their work.

Polio vaccine (1953)

Polio was one of the most feared diseases in the United States during the first half of the 20th century. Several epidemics had infected thousands of children, often causing severe paralysis. Jonas Salk (U.S.) announced his trial vaccine in 1953. Salk's vaccine contained three types of known polio viruses killed with formaldehyde solution, mixed with a quantity of penicillin. In

1954 a mass trial of the vaccine proved hugely successful. In 1961 an oral vaccine developed by virologist Albert Sabin (U.S., b. Russia) was introduced.

Interferon (1957)

Interferon was first discovered in 1957 by a virologist, Alick Isaacs (Great Britain), and J. Lindenmann (Switzerland). It is one of the sub-stances (a protein) produced by an organism to combat viruses. In 1969 these substances, active in the immune system which is connected to the lymphatic system, were called *lymphokines*. Earlier, in 1966, J. David and V. Blum (both U.S.) had identified in a culture of T-lymphocytes (a type of white corpuscle) a factor that inhibited the migration of macrophages (another type of white corpuscle). This was the first in a series of discoveries that were extremely promising for the future of therapeutics.

Interferon was subsequently subdivided into categories and was not really developed further until it became possible to produce it by genetic engineering toward the end of the 1970s. Interferon 2A was marketed in 1987, after being tested for two years on tricholeucocyte leukemia and Kaposi's sarcoma.

Chemotherapy (1964)

Chemotherapy is the treatment of illnesses, particularly cancer, by chemical substances or drugs. In 1964 Prof. G. Rosen (U.S.) used chemotherapy for the first time, and before trying any other form of treatment, on two types of cancer. His work was based on experiments carried out on rats by Prof. Brooke.

A German surgeon working in Boston, Emil Frey, referred to the new technique as initial or neo-adjuvant chemotherapy.

Monoclonal antibodies (1975)

The first research on monoclonal antibodies was published in May 1975 by two immunologists, Georges Köhler (Germany) and César Milstein (Argentina), both working in Cambridge, England. In 1984 they were awarded the Nobel Prize for their research, which consisted of combining, in a test tube, lymphocytes from mice, which produce antibodies, with myeloma (cancer) cells. In this way they obtained hybrid cells or hybridomas that were able to survive indefinitely, continuously producing a single antibody specific to the illness against which the animal had been immunized. In therapeutics, monoclonal antibodies are able to direct a chemical substance against a given target located by the antibody which acts as a vector.

TNF (1975)

TNF, or Tumor Necrosis Factor, was discovered in 1975 by Carswell and his colleagues at the Sloan Kettering Memorial Institute in New York City. It is a protein produced by certain white corpuscles which selects and attacks tumorous cells. The production, study and classification of all these proteins has led to a review of knowledge in the field of immunology. These substances have potentially far-reaching effects and implications, not only in the fields of cancer research and virology, but also in the areas of parasitic, inflammatory, infectious and allergic diseases, and in vaccinations and transplants.

Interleukins (1979)

Other very well-known substances that act as a defense are the interleukins, so-called in 1979

Penicillin (1928): Sir Alexander Fleming

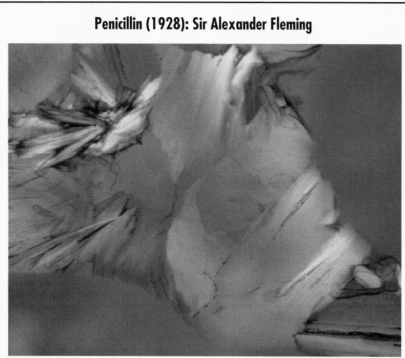

Penicillin as seen through polarization. (CNRI/Castano)

When Sir Alexander Fleming stumbled upon penicillin, he made the century's most important medical discovery. In fact, the story of penicillin is connected with centuries-old bits of folklore (some call them old wives' tales) that recommend moldy bread and cobwebs for festering wounds. Fleming was the first scientist to consider treating such wounds with mold, and his discovery has saved the lives of millions.

As a medical officer during World War I, Fleming was overwhelmed by the number of suppurating wounds he observed. After the war, he began the search for a drug that could attack bacterial disease without harming the tissue it lived in. In 1928, Fleming was studying staphylococci, a group of bacteria that causes septicemia, abscesses, and other diseases. After a few days away from the laboratory, Fleming returned to find that the lid had been left off one of the dishes where the staphylococcus cultures were growing. Exposed to the air, the culture had grown moldy.

Fleming moved to throw the dish away, then noticed that the bacteria cells had dissolved in the places where the mold was growing. In place of the yellow clumps of staphylococci, clear drops of a liquid like dew remained. The mold was a strain of the fungus *penicillium*, which secreted a substance that killed the bacteria. Fleming named his drug after its parent fungus.

There were problems ahead: penicillin proved very unstable, and Fleming could not grow and sustain enough of it. The threat of World War II was impetus for widespread research. In 1940 a pair of Oxford chemists, Howard Florey and Ernst Chain, succeeded in producing large volumes of pure powdered penicillin using the same freeze-dry method that is used to manufacture instant coffee.

During World War II, U.S. drug companies took over the manufacture of penicillin from Great Britain. The drug contributed to the recovery of 95 percent of wounded Allied soldiers. In 1945, Fleming, Florey and Chain shared the Nobel Prize for Medicine. Said Fleming: "Everywhere I go, people want to thank me for saving their lives. I really don't know why they do that. Nature created penicillin. I only found it."

because they act between lymphocytes (or lympholeukocytes), either causing the production of more lymphocytes or provoking the latter to produce other substances.

Patch (1981)

The first of these transdermal medicaments was developed by the Ciba-Geigy laboratories in Switzerland in conjunction with the American Alza Corp. Known as Scopoderm TTS (Transdermal Therapeutic System), and launched in the United States in 1981, it consists of a sticker containing a drug to combat seasickess and, as its name suggests, it is absorbed directly through the skin. Other patches have followed, one to treat angina, another to relieve symptons of menopause by hormone replacement, and the best-known patch: the nicotine patch. This patch uses transdermal technology to combat tobacco addiction by supplying small quantities of nicotine to those trying to give up smoking.

Interleukins 2 and 3 (1985 and 1986)

The most recently discovered of the interleukins, which are also subdivided into categories, is interleukin 3. It was discovered in 1986 by Drs. Steven Clark and Yu Chang Yan of the Genetic Institute in Cambridge, Mass. The anticancer effect of interleukin 2 was demonstrated in 1985 by Dr. Steven Rosenberg (U.S.). Although they provide an excellent defense against viruses, interleukins can have a toxic effect if they are administered in large quantities. For example, interleukin 2 has the side effect of giving people flu-like fever, but this can be easily controlled and is also a much less serious problem than the side effects of chemotherapy.

RU486 (1988)

Devised by Etienne-Emile Baulieu (France), the abortion pill RU486 was first authorized to be marketed in France on September 23, 1988. It works by blocking the receptors for progesterone in the uterus, thus making it impossible for the pregnancy to continue. RU486 does, however, have its limitations: it can be used only in the early stages of pregnancy and must be followed by a prostaglandin to make the uterus contract, which can lead to a sudden drop in blood pressure. This treatment has been the source of enormous controversy worldwide, and the drug has not been approved for use in the United States.

Panoject (1991)

Panoject is a wristwatch device that patients can use to inject themselves with the regular dosage of drugs they require. Developed by the Swiss watch company Swatch and the British company Elan, the Panoject has been available since 1991. The drugs are contained in the case of the watch, and they are injected (either continuously or in small doses) via an electronically controlled mini-syringe located under the watch case. The device is intended for patients

Imuran (1960): Gertrude Elion

Gertrude Elion. (Burroughs Wellcome)

Gertrude Elion has no Ph.D. She has a resumé that includes checking vanilla beans for freshness, fruit for mold, and mayonnaise for color. And she has a squeamish streak that led her to choose chemistry over biology, to avoid dissections.

Yet Elion's brilliant career climaxed with the winning of the Nobel Prize for Medicine in 1988, an honor she shared with Sir James W. Black of Great Britain and her erstwhile boss George H. Hitchings.

Hitchings hired Elion to work at the Burroughs Wellcome company in 1944, after World War II had opened the ranks of laboratory research—along with other businesses—to women. Watson and Crick had not yet decoded DNA, but scientists knew that nucleic acids held the key to genetics. The goal of Hitchings's research was to find ways to interfere with nucleic acid metabolism in cells in such a way as to block reproduction of bacteria, tumor, and virus cells without harming healthy cells.

Elion's role was the study of purines, a major category of nucleic acids. Following Hitchings's principles, Elion developed a compound that blocked metabolism in children with acute leukemia. In 1953, the Federal Drug Administration approved the drug, 6-MP (for 6-mercaptopurine). The drug was effective in prolonging life, and is still used today in combination with other cancer-fighting drugs.

Other researchers quickly picked up 6-MP and tested its scope. Robert Schwarz of the New England Medical Center found that 6-MP inhibited the growth of antibodies in rabbits. Roy Y. Calne, a British transplant surgeon, experimented with 6-MP as a preventor of transplant rejection. The drug worked initially, but soon became ineffective. Elion and Hitchings suggested a closely related purine, Imuran.

In 1960, Imuran was successfully used in a kidney transplant at Harvard Medical School. The patient was a collie dog named Lollipop. The first successful human kidney transplant took place in 1962. Imuran blocked the immune response, allowing the body to accept a foreign organ. Today, Imuran remains a key drug in transplants.

Elion, with Hitchings, continued to work in this way, using one discovery to open doors to others. She patented 45 compounds during her 39 years at Burroughs Wellcome. One was Zyloprim, used to treat gout as well as the excess uremic acid that results from chemotherapy and radiation treatment of cancer. Zovirax, another compound, is used to treat herpes.

Following in Hitchings' and Elion's huge footsteps, Burroughs Wellcome researchers used their methods and foundation research in discovering the use of the drug AZT as a treatment for AIDS.

Surely Elion has earned her place as the first woman inducted into the Inventors Hall of Fame.

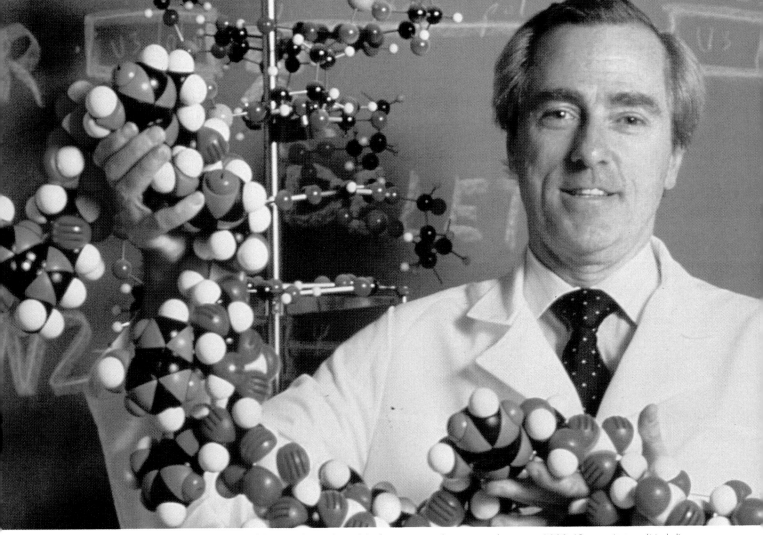

Dr. W. French Anderson was a member of the team that performed the first-ever gene therapy on a human, in 1990. (Gamma-Liaison/Markel)

requiring constant treatment, such as diabetics. A patch-type version is being researched which would eliminate the need for a needle.

THERAPEUTICS

Acupuncture (2000 B.C.)

The Chinese have been practicing acupuncture, one of the branches of their traditional medicine, since about 2000 B.C. The theory is that the cause of a disease can be explained by a disruption in the flow of energy, which can be remedied by action taken on one or more of the points situated along the meridians: pathways along which energy is transmitted around the body by oscillation and vibration. This action usually consists of the insertion of needles, but also of the application of heat (moxas) or massage. Today, even electric currents and laser beams are used.

Homeopathy (1796)

C.S. Hahnemann (Germany, 1755–1843) created homeopathy in 1796. In 1790 he had been struck by descriptions of the properties of the cinchona, a South American tree with medici-

nal bark, and by the incoherence of the explanations given for them, and decided to test its action on himself. He took large doses of cinchona over several days and indeed suffered the symptoms of an intermittent febrile state, identical to the fevers that cinchona cured.

Hahnemann then extended his experiments to deadly nightshade, digitalis, and mercury, and verified the law of similitude: any substance capable of inducing certain symptoms in a healthy person is also able to make the analogous symptoms disappear in a sick person.

Hahnemann based his theory on extensive experimentation with healthy subjects, and this led him to pronounce the second fundamental principle of homeopathy: the remedy acts not by virtue of its quantity, but in proportion to its dilution.

Psychoanalysis (1885)

Psychoanalysis is a method of understanding psychological and psychopathological phenomena, and at the same time a method of treating mental illness. It was developed around 1885 by Dr. Sigmund Freud (Austria, 1856–1939) in Vienna. Freud did not invent the idea of the psychic unconscious, but he undertook a systematic exploration of it.

At first received with considerable skepticism by the medical community because of its novel propositions regarding sexuality, psychoanaly-

sis has acquired a more and more important place in medicine and in psychology.

Osteopathy (1892)

Osteopathy entered the history of medicine in 1892, when a Missouri doctor, Andrew Taylor Still, founded the American School of Osteopathy. Osteopathy consists of using manual manipulation of the osteomuscular system, especially the spine, for therapeutic purposes. Today there are around 19,000 osteopaths in the United States.

Chiropractic (1897)

In 1897 a hypnotist, Daniel David Palmer, having discovered that he could cure patients by putting pressure on their backs and manipulating their spines, founded the first school of chiropractic, in Iowa.

The profession has been recognized since 1977 in the United States, where there are now 23,000 trained chiropractors.

Radiotherapy (1934)

Radiotherapy, the use of rays for therapeutic purposes, was developed after the discovery of X-rays in 1895, and of radioactivity. It became an area of specialization independent of radiodiagnosis in 1934 when the chemist Irène Joliot-Curie (France, 1897–1956) and her husband Jean-Frédéric Joliot (France, 1900–58) discovered artificial radioactivity. The first apparatus capable of transmitting radiation that could reach relatively deep-seated tumors was fed by a current of 250,000 volts. This method was gradually abandoned and replaced in 1956 by the cobalt bomb.

Gene therapy (1990)

On September 14, 1990 in Bethesda, Md., Drs. W. French Anderson, Michael Blaese and Kenneth Culver (all U.S.) performed the first-ever gene therapy on a human being. The patient was a four-year-old girl suffering from an extremely rare genetic disorder: a shortage of adenosine-deaminase. A healthy gene was grafted on to diseased cells using a harmless virus as a vector. The operation was the culmination of seven years of research in conjunction with a team led by Prof. Steven Rosenberg (U.S.).

INSTRUMENTS

Intravenous injection (16th century)

Elsholtz was the first to inject medicinal products into human veins, in the middle of the 16th century. However, we know that "intravenous infusions" had already been tested on animals.

In 1655 Schmidt treated syphilis by intravenous injection.

Syringe (1657)

The principle of the syringe was established by Gattinara (Italy) in the 15th century, but it was not until the 17th century that practical trials were carried out by C. Wren (England) and Robert Boyle (Ireland) in 1657.

Fergusson (Great Britain) was the first to use glass, whose transparency allowed the injection to be monitored. However, it was Luer (France) who produced the first all-glass syringe in 1869, and risks of infection fell as a result of its use.

Finally, it is to Rynd (Ireland) in 1845 and Wood (Great Britain) in 1853 that we owe the method of subcutaneous injection.

Anticholesterol machine (1986)

This process was invented in 1986 by biochemist Wilhelm Stoffel (Germany). It is based on hemodialysis, a system of filtering the blood, and is used for people whose kidneys do not function. It enables the particles of so-called bad cholesterol (Low Density Lipoprotein, LDL) to be eliminated, while the good cholesterol (High Density Lipoprotein, HDL) is completely restored to the patient after the filtering process. Such a technique can be applied to patients who suffer from inherited diseases resulting in an excess of cholesterol since birth and, regardless of diet, will give them a quality of life that would have been impossible until now.

Safety hypodermic (1987)

In 1987 Dr. Jean-Louis Brunet (France) of the Hôpital de la Croix-Rousse in Lyons patented a safety device that can be attached to hypodermic needles or vacutainers for taking blood samples. It eliminates any risk of contamination from the blood in illnesses such as AIDS and hepatitis.

The system enables the used needle to be automatically recapped as soon as it is withdrawn from the vein or muscle.

A similar type of invention in the same area is the disposable hypodermic that is impossible to reuse. It was invented by four Danish medical assistants working with drug users in Aarhus on the east coast of Denmark.

Jetnet (1988)

The handling of cutting instruments and hypodermics used in even minor operations is a source of contamination which, particularly in the case of AIDS, represents a very real danger for medical staff. A new system has been developed by 3M that ensures the complete isolation of used instruments and eliminates the need for direct contact. Presented in 1988, Jetnet consists of a hermetically sealed plastic receptacle with a cover in which there is a clamp-operated mechanism. Scalpel blades, needles and other instruments can be separated, kept in sealed receptacles, and then incinerated without ever being touched by the person using them. The cover can be sterilized and reused. The level of prevention achieved in this way is considered to be complete.

Novolet (1990)

This is the name of the new insulin syringe that is the smallest and lightest in the world. Developed by the Danish medical group Novo Nordisk, it is disposable and made from biodegradable plastic. It holds enough insulin to meet a diabetic's needs for three to seven days. The patient injects the necessary dose simply by pressure. When the syringe is empty, it is discarded.

The British have developed an insulin pen that gives a set dose and is easy to use. It won a design award.

VISION AND HEARING

Glasses

Eyeglasses (1280)

Very early on in history, various attempts were made to remedy sight defects. However, the magnifying glass was not invented until the 11th century.

In 1280 the Florentine physicist Salvino degli Armati (1245–1317) developed two eye glasses which, at a certain degree of thickness and with a certain curve, magnified objects. He can therefore be said to have invented eyeglasses. He told his secret to his friend Alessandro della Spina, a Dominican friar from the Monastery of Saint Catherine of Pisa, who subsequently revealed it. At this point the eyeglasses had convex lenses for far-sighted people.

Concave lenses for near-sighted people appeared at the end of the 15th century.

The first eyeglasses consisted of two lenses made of beryl, a sort of crystal, set in a circle of wood or horn. They were later joined by a stud.

Bifocals (1780)

Benjamin Franklin (U.S., 1706–90) invented bifocals for far-sighted people in 1780; in those days, bifocals were simply two lenses bound together by a metal frame. Bifocals made from one piece of glass were developed by Bentron and Emerson for the Carl Zeiss company in 1910. In 1908 J.L. Borsch had invented a process that allowed the two lenses to be soldered together.

Light-sensitive sunglasses (1938)

Dr. Edwin Land, the founder of the Polaroid company, invented polarizing sunglasses that eliminate reflections in 1938. As early as 1939 a chemist at Corning Glass, Dr. R.H. Dalton, had begun to develop glasses sensitive to variations in light. His invention, patented by Corning in 1964, was put on the market in 1967 as Photogray.

Varilux Pilote (1985)

The Varilux Pilote spectacles were invented in 1983 by Essilor Svenska, sponsored by the Swedish airline SAS, and have been on the market since 1985. They make it possible to see at close range not only by lowering the eyes, but also by raising them. This makes them extremely suitable for the professional activities of those who, like airline pilots, need to be able to see at close range above as well as below eye level.

Anti-rain glasses (1989)

Anyone who wears glasses and plays a sport knows only too well that, when it is raining or snowing, before long it becomes virtually impossible to see anything.

The unmarkable anti-rain lenses invented by Japanese researchers for Nikon are a real innovation. Water slides over the surface of the glass without clinging or leaving marks.

Contact Lenses

Origins (15th century)

The first person to think of contact lenses was Leonardo da Vinci. In his *Codex on the Eye*, he described an optical method for correcting refraction defects by immersing the eye in a water-filled tube that was sealed with a lens.

In 1686 René Descartes (France) performed the suggested experiment and it was performed again at the end of the 18th century by Thomas Young and John Herschel (both Great Britain). Herschel's experiment involved applying a layer of gelatin to the eye, held in place by a lens. This was to correct his astigmatism.

Contact lenses became more widely used during the period 1887–1892, due to the efforts of August Müller in Germany, A.E. Fick and Sulzer in Switzerland, and Kalt in France. The only material used at this time, and until the 1930s, was blown or molded glass, generally Zeiss glass.

Plexiglass lenses (1936)

The German company I.G. Farben made the first Plexiglass contact lens in 1936. This same material is used today for hard lenses.

Corneal lenses (1945)

The corneal lens was invented by Tuohy (U.S.) in 1964. The lens is designed to cover just the cornea of the eye.

Hydrophile lens (1964)

The academician Wichterle (Czechoslovakia) developed the hydrophile lens in 1964.

Holographic lenses (1987)

These lenses are for people who are both near- and far-sighted. They are called Diffrax, use a technique based on holography, and their entire surface corrects the vision. Even in half light they adapt to the vision of the wearer. They were invented by the English company Pilkington, which is well-known for its range of inventions in the field of glassware, and came onto the market at the beginning of 1987.

Disposable lenses (1989)

The first disposable contact lenses, developed by the American laboratory Vistakon, have been brought onto the market. They are designed to be worn continuously for a week at a time and then discarded and replaced by a new pair. They are suitable for mildly near-sighted people.

Eye Surgery

Cataract operation (1748)

The first description of a cataract operation by "lowering the cornea" was given by the surgeon Anthyllus in the 2nd century A.D.

In 1748 the ophthalmologist Jacques Daviel (France) performed the first cataract operation by extraction of the crystalline lens. At the time, the reputation of Daviel was equaled only by that of the surgeon William Cheselden (Great Britain), who had restored the sight of a patient who had been blind since birth.

Corneal graft (1949)

This form of treatment for certain types of myopia and severe hypermetropia is known as refractive lamellar keratoplasty and rectifies the curve of the cornea. The idea was first conceived in 1949 by the ophthalmic surgeon Prof. Barraquer of Bogotá, Colombia.

Since 1983 keratoplasty has been perfomed at the Rothschild Foundation in the departments run by Dr. Ganem and Prof. P. Couderc (both U.S.).

Artificial crystalline lens (1952)

Invented in 1952 by Dr. Harold Ridley (Great Britain), this polymethylmethacrylate (PMMA) or Plexiglas lens is placed behind the iris.

Incision of the cornea (1955)

This method of treatment, radial keratotomy, consists of making radial incisions on the inner surface of the cornea in order to correct myopia.

These contact lenses, patented by the American company Wesley-Jessen, turn brown eyes blue. (Gamma)

It is intended to replace the use of eyeglasses and contact lenses. It was developed in 1955 by T. Sato (Japan) only to be abandoned and then resumed in 1979 by Dr. Sviatoslav Fiodorov (USSR), who, with 50 surgeons, created a sort of production line in his hospital in Moscow that carried out 22,000 operations in one year. This system enables the most able specialists to concentrate on the important part of the operation, while the initial and final stages are supervised and dealt with by other practitioners.

Operation by ultrasound (1976)

In 1976 Charles Kelman (U.S.) invented an instrument that made it possible to remove a cataract through a tiny incision after fragmenting it with ultrasound. The operation was performed under local anesthetic.

In 1986 Dr. Kelman also invented a completely harmless, flexible ocular implant, which can be inserted into the eye by making a 1/8 in. incision in the cornea.

Operation by laser (1979)

In 1979 Prof. Danièle Aron-Rosa developed an operation technique using a super-quick-acting Yag laser that made it possible to operate without making an incision in the patient's eye.

Microlase (1987)

This is a new type of laser for treating eye diseases, including glaucoma and complications arising from diabetes. It uses laser diodes similar to those developed for the compact disc player. Since it produces neither sound signal nor light beam, patients are unaware of anything and can keep their eyes open during the operation. Invented in 1987 by Dr. Anthony Raven and Prof. John Marshall (both Great Britain), it has been available since 1989.

Multifocal crystalline lens (1989)

A new ocular implant has revolutionized cataract surgery by making it possible for the eye to accommodate without the patient having to wear eyeglasses.

Previously the artificial crystalline lens that replaces the opaque natural lens has restored the patient's vision without being able to accommodate. The lens is usually adjusted for long vision, so that the patient has had to wear eyeglasses for close work.

The multifocal intraocular implant developed by the 3M company diffracts the light in such a way that there are two focal points, one for long and one for short vision. This device, and other similar ones, is currently being studied in many centers throughout Europe and by the Food and Drug Administration.

Crystalline bifocals (1989)

Macular degeneration (the macula is a yellow spot on the retina where vision is especially good) associated with age is one of the primary causes of blindness in those over 60.

It is a slow deterioration of the central region of the retina, and there is no effective treatment

for it. Sufferers gradually become unable to read or write and are unable to see anything clearly. Magnifying glasses and other enlarging systems can be helpful but are often impractical for elderly people. Hence the idea of using a system based on Galileo's telescope, in which the eyepiece is made up of a bifocal implant, concave at the center, and the object-glass is in the form of a pair of glasses with very convex lenses.

This implant was devised by Profs. Ben-Sira and Lipshitz of the University of Jerusalem, in collaboration with the Israeli company Hanita, which has been manufacturing it since 1989. More than 500 implants have already been carried out worldwide.

Ocular endoscope (1990)

Until recently, 20 percent of the eye socket could not be examined, since it is hidden by the iris. In order to be able to see this part of the eye, Drs. Claude and Joseph Léon (both France) have developed the surgical ocular endoscope. This is the smallest endoscope there is, and is linked to a Bivision module, making it possible to incorporate the endoscopic image into the field of observation of an operating microscope. This means that during the operation surgeons can examine the images provided by the endoscope without taking their eyes from the microscope, and act accordingly. It was unveiled in 1990.

HEARING AIDS

Electric hearing aid (1901)

Miller Reese Hutchinson (U.S.) was 26 years old when he invented the first electro-acoustic apparatus designed to amplify sounds for the deaf. One of the first users of the invention was Queen Alexandra of Great Britain, consort to King Edward VII, who wore her Acousticon during the coronation ceremony. She presented a medal to the young inventor as a mark of her gratitude.

Implants for the severely deaf (1961)

In 1961 Georg von Békésy, a Hungarian physicist and physiologist living in the United States, was awarded the Nobel Prize for Physiology and Medicine for his discoveries concerning the stimulation mechanism of the inner ear or cochlea.

In 1973 the 3M company developed a cochlear implant that made it possible for severely deaf people to hear and interpret most sounds.

Scientists throughout the world have pursued similar lines of research with considerable success. In 1977 the Bertin implant was developed by Drs. Pialoux, Claude Chouard and MacLeod (all France), and in 1981 Prof. Graeme Clark (Australia) produced the "bionic ear." In 1988 the most recent model of the device was implanted in a five-year-old girl who had been completely deaf since birth. It was the first time that such an implant had been performed on a child of that age.

DENTISTRY

Dental Care

Crowns and bridges (3rd century B.C.)

A piece of a dental plate made of gold was found in Tanagra in Greece. The plate, which consisted of four elements, had been made to replace the two lateral incisors. It appears that the tomb in which it was found could date back to the 3rd century B.C. The two central incisors had bands around them and acted as a support for the extension of the false teeth which they held in place. This is the earliest existing evidence of a bridge.

In his Traité des Dents (Treatise on Teeth) the dentist Pierre Fauchard (France, 1678–1761) discusses different ways of achieving fixed dental plates, the bridges promoted by W.H. Dwinelle almost a century later in 1856.

Crowns made from porcelain or industrial resin, known as jacket crowns, appeared around 1895.

Toothpaste (1st century A.D.)

The earliest formula for toothpaste was given at the end of the 1st century A.D. by a Roman doctor, Scribonius Largus. It consisted of a mixture of vinegar, honey, salt and ground glass!

Pliny the Elder recommended urine as a mouthwash, and this use of urine, particularly as a treatment for dental caries, persisted until the 19th century. The explanation given was that urine, which was warm and acidic, neutralized the decaying action of the cold, damp secretions from the pituitary gland that flowed from the brain into the mouth.

Fillings (9th century)

The method of filling dental cavities resulting from dental caries is attributed to the famous 9th century Muslim physician Abu Zakariya Yuhanna Ibn Masawaih (776–855), also known as Mesuë Major, who used gold for his fillings. In the 15th century, important progress was made by the use of gold leaf, which made it possible to fill the cavities completely, a technique developed by the surgeon Giovanni Arcolani (Italy). In 1853 Makins replaced gold foil with porous gold. This was replaced by soft or noncohesive gold, and then by cohesive or adhesive gold, used by Arthur in 1955.

Dentures (16th century)

The earliest complete denture on record was found in a grave in Switzerland that dates from the early 16th century. The dentures appear to have been made from an ox femur that was cut and then carved. The upper and lower sections were joined by a metal wire.

Dentures were more widely used when it became possible to place the false teeth on a base that could then rest on the jawbone and adapt to its shape. In 1864 Goodyear brought out a vulcanized rubber that made it possible to produce this type of base.

False teeth (1788)

Until the 19th century, false teeth were made from the bones of familiar or exotic animals; hippopotamus bones were the most widely used as they were the strongest. But these teeth became worn, turning brown and giving off a nauseating smell, and had to be changed every 18 months to two years. So, different materials were sought.

As early as 1770 the apothecary A. Duchâteau (France) had tried to produce a complete denture made from a mineral paste.

In 1788 Dubois de Chemant, a Parisian dentist, produced hardwearing dentures by taking a wax impression from which he made a plaster model.

In 1817 the first porcelain teeth appeared in the United States, and in 1825 S.W. Stockton of Philadelphia commercialized what had previously been a rather unsophisticated process.

Amalgams (1819)

In 1819 Charles Bell recomended a mixture of mercury and silver to fill cavities. In 1850 Regnart suggested adding mercury to an alloy to lower the melting point.

Fillings with molten metal appeared in 1884, when they were used for inlays by Aguilhon de Sarran, and in 1886, when Litch used them for onlays.

Compounds (1963)

In 1963 Bowen of the United States discovered a formula for a synthetic resin for rebuilding and restoring teeth.

Since then, many improvements have been made in the fields of resistance to erosion and adhesive quality. Nowadays, adhesives are being used that prevent the recurrence of dental caries.

The use of ultraviolet rays, blue light and halogen lamps gives a better polymerization of the product. This also gives the dentist more time to concentrate on the delicate operation of putting the composite in place.

Dental implants (1965)

Dental implant as a method of treatment for people who have had all or some of their teeth removed has existed for the last 30 years. Pegs are inserted into the jaw to act as a support for false teeth. But it is a method which, over the years, has produced many failures. In 1965 positive progress was made as a result of a method of implantation developed by Prof. Per Ingvar Branemark (Sweden), a biologist at the University of Gothenburg. The method, which has a success rate of 81 percent for the upper jaw and 91 percent for the lower jaw, is the only one recognized by the American Dental Association.

Solid ceramic (1979)

This new type of ceramic, developed by Dr. Sozio (U.S.), makes it possible to construct artificial teeth that are superior to the original. The material is so solid that it does not require any reinforced metallic support.

Extraction of Teeth

Origins (2nd century B.C.)

In China the instruments preferred for pulling teeth were the fingers. For five or six hours a day, tooth-pullers practiced pulling out nails hammered into thick planks.

The invention of the first pair of dental pliers is traditionally attributed to the famous doctor and anatomist Erasistrates of Alexandria during the 2nd century B.C.

Celsus, the great Roman medical theoretician of the 1st century A.D., suggested placing a piece of flock soaked in the sap of tithymalis, a variety of euphorbia, in the painful cavity, a method that broke the tooth into pieces.

In the early 16th century, an instrument appeared that made it possible to extract teeth without the risk of crushing them or fracturing the crown. The invention was known as the pelican and was attributed to the surgeon Giovanni Arcolani (Italy). The first so-called anatomic forceps were designed by the London-based French surgeon J.-M. Everard (1800–82) in collaboration with Sir John Tomes (1815–59).

Dental transplants (11th century)

The Muslim physician and surgeon Abulcasis of Cordoba (Abul Kasim or Abu al-Qasim Khalaf ibn Abbas as-Zahrawi) advised that teeth that were knocked out accidentally should be reimplanted. He had them held in place for several weeks with ligatures that enabled them to re-root.

Toward the end of the 13th century Nicolas Falucci developed a transplantation technique in which teeth were taken from a donor, living or dead. During the 18th century, transplantations became very popular.

Oral anesthetic (14th century)

The first evidence of an oral anesthetic is provided by a surgeon from Padua, grandfather of the famous Italian religious and political reformer Girolamo Savonarola. He made his patients chew tiny cloth sachets filled with henbane, poppy seeds and mandrake. The sap from these plants produced an insensitivity of the mucous membrane that made it possible to make a painless incision.

Mouthwash (15th century)

In the 15th century an Italian surgeon from the Salerno School, Giovanni Plateario, was the first to recommend a mouthwash to accelerate postoperative healing. This was a major step forward at a time when the risk of oral sepsis, or infection, was extremely high.

Dental Equipment

Origins (11th century)

In his treatise on medicine and surgery, Abulcasis, the Muslim physician from Cordoba (see above), describes an impressive dental tool kit consisting of pliers, elevators and ligatures that has long been the arsenal of the dental surgeon.

The drill (1st century A.D.)

The first surgical drill dates back to the 1st century A.D. The Roman surgeon Archigenes developed an instrument that was set in motion by a rope and that drove a drill by rotation.

The dentist's chair (16th century)

In the early 16th century Giovanni Plateario abandoned the standard operating position in which the patient's head was held tightly between the surgeon's knees. He adopted a low chair with a shorter back rest that gave the dentist easier access to the patient's mouth.

The following dates represent the main stages in the development of the dentist's chair:
- *1810:* chair with a folding stool for the dentist;
- *1848:* the headrest;
- *1855:* the jack-operated chair invented by Ball;
- *1871:* the swivel chair invented by Harris;
- *1872:* the iron chair that was operated by a pneumatic jack and that could be tipped backwards, invented by Alexander Morrison;
- *1877:* the chair operated by hydraulic pump, invented by the Johnston brothers;
- *1950:* the electrically operated chair.

The mechanical drill (1864)

In 1864, Harrington (Great Britain) had the idea of activating a drill using a clock mechanism in which the spring could be wound up and then released.

In 1868, Green (U.S.) introduced a drill driven by pedal-operated bellows.

On February 7, 1871, J.B. Morrisson (U.S.) introduced a model that could achieve a speed of between 600 and 800 rpm. In 1874 Green constructed a system that was activated by an electric wheel and reached a rotational speed of between 1,200 and 4,000 rpm.

Since 1958, air-driven turbine-operated drills can reach a rotational speed of between 300,000 and 400,000 rpm.

Dental scanner (1987)

The dental scanner or T-Scan was invented by an information technologist named Rob Golden and a dentist named William Maness (both U.S.), who consider their invention the most important since the discovery of X-rays. The scanner is a small device shaped like a jawbone. As the patient "bites" the scanner, an image is simultaneously projected onto a screen that gives the dentist an immediate view of the teeth and enables him to see what treatment may be necessary. It provides a quick method of examination, which means treatment can be carried out without delay.

WHAT ON EARTH?

NOT ALL INVENTIONS CHANGE OUR LIVES, SOME JUST MAKE US SCRATCH OUR HEADS.

HAIR RESTORATIVE

▼ Methods to revive hair growth have not always been as sophisticated as current techniques. In 1955 Tony Voitechovsky, chairman of the London club called Curls, designed this apparatus to make hair grow again. The pumping action was designed to stimulate blood circulation around the bald patch. (Le Livre Mondial des Inventions)

PREGNANCY EMPATHY

▼ Psychotherapist Dan Neuhart and mother-to-be Linda Ware created this false stomach to help men understand the discomfort experienced by pregnant women. (Gamma-Liaison/ Kermani)

ALLERGY RECREATION

▲ For millions of allergy sufferers the great outdoors can be a nightmare rather than a pleasure. This air capsule device blocks out pollen and pumps in oxygen. It is ideal for leisurely outdoor pursuits such as croquet. (Sygma)

ANTI-SNORING PILLOW

The "anti-snoring" pillow was presented at an invention convention in Geneva, Switzerland by its creator, Lorenz Thomsen (Germany). When the "sleeping beauty" begins to snore, the awakened roommate activates a mini-pump placed near the bed; this inflates the central portion of the pillow; the head and body of the sleeper roll to the side and the snoring stops. The pillow deflates automatically after about three minutes and reinflates in the same manner if the snoring resumes.

SHOCK ABSORBERS FOR CRUTCHES

Having to walk with crutches is not just restrictive but also tiring, as the body absorbs shocks caused every time the crutches touch the ground. To alleviate this, Philippe Puyo (France) invented shock absorbers for crutches; these have been available since 1987. The end of each crutch has a spring that absorbs the shock and helps the crutch adhere more firmly to the ground, ensuring greater safety.

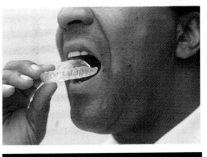

SNORING SHIELD

▲ This dental plate is another device aimed at stopping snoring. Invented by Prof. Morris Clark (U.S.), the shield pushes the jaw forward to improve air circulation. (Gamma-Liaison/ Springer)

TAGGING

To film the heart while it is functioning, without causing any disruption, is currently impossible. Echography has provided excellent images, but they lack realism. A new technique called *tagging*, developed by Dr. Zerhouni of Johns Hopkins Hospital, Baltimore, Md., might be the solution. Using this method the heart is rendered in three dimensions, appearing as if transparent behind its inner and outer walls. This technique, derived from magnetic resonance imagery, could revolutionize the study of the heart. Numerous applications are envisaged, in physiology as well as in pathology, particularly in the area of infarctions and cardiac weakness.

SYNTHETIC HEMOGLOBIN

The first clinical tests of a synthetic hemoglobin were performed on 30 patients in the United States in 1991 by Somatogen. The technology consists of grafting, through genetic manipulation, human hemoglobin genes onto certain bacteria that are thus capable of producing this essential protein. The process is still inhibited by the instability of synthetic hemoglobin, but researchers are hoping that this could eventually be the solution for transfusing blood.

GENETIC TREATMENT FOR MUSCOVISCIDOSIS (CYSTIC FIBROSIS)

Research undertaken by Prof. Roland Crystal (U.S.) in collaboration with Dr. Michel Perricaudet (France) has led to the successful grafting of the muscoviscidosis gene on the lungs of rats. This gene, introduced in an adenovirus, was able to insert itself in the cells of the pulmonary epithelium and produce the CFTR protein of muscoviscidosis, deficiency of which results in the disease. The reason for the interest in the adenovirus (which causes colds) is that it could be used in nasal sprays as part of a genetic treatment. Its safety and the risks of eventual contagion remain to be verified.

ELECTROSTATIC MICROMOTORS

The electrostatic micromotor has been in development since 1988. The tiny motor, built by Richard S. Muller (U.S.) of the University of Berkeley, California, measures 70 micrometers (0.003 in.) in diameter and is only a few micrometers thick. It was built with the same techniques used in electronics for the manufacture of integrated circuits. Most of the applications envisaged are still at the experimental stage, among them the making of instruments for microsurgery, and machines that would be able to move up and down the arteries to scrape off deposits, such as fat.

INSULIN-LIKE GROWTH FACTOR (IGF-1)

IGF-1 is a hormone that may be a possible treatment for nervous-system illnesses such as amyotrophic lateral sclerosis. The American company Cephalon Inc. obtained a U.S. patent for the hormone in 1992. Tests have indicated that IGF-1 may prolong the lifespan of a variety of nerve cells that are killed by nervous-system diseases. Limited trials on human patients began in the summer of 1992.

CILIARY NEUROTROPHIC PROTEIN (CNTF)

In May 1992 the Syntex-Synergen Neuroscience Joint Venture received FDA approval for human testing of CNTF, which may

New ideas that may change the way we live

be useful in preventing or slowing degeneration of the nerves. The joint venture between Synergen Inc. and Syntex Corp. was started in 1990, and it is hoped that CNTF will prove to be an effective treatment in such motor neuron diseases such as progressive bulbar palsy and amyotrophic lateral sclerosis.

TAXOL

Taxol is an anticancer drug that has been the subject of clinical studies since 1983. Two studies released in 1992 show that the drug may be effective in treating inoperable lung cancer and ovarian cancer. Taxol is extracted from the bark of the Pacific yew tree, *Taxus brevifolia*. Development of the drug has been slow because a large amount of bark is required to treat a single patient, and these rare yews are destroyed in the extraction process. The search for a substitute for the yew tree is ongoing. Researchers at the University of Kansas believe they have discovered a Himalayan tree, *Taxus baccata*, that can produce taxol and is in plentiful supply in the Himalayan region. Trials are being conducted to test this new source.

COOL STORAGE SKIN CULTURE

In recent years several companies have developed forms of artificial skin. The main limitation in developing this technology has been the short lifespan of the skin, usually less than eight hours, meaning that patients have to be near the production facility to receive the artificial skin graft. This problem may have been solved by BioSurface Technology Inc., which received a U.S. patent in 1992 for a "cool storage" technique that keeps the skin alive for up to 24 hours. For the first time it should be possible to ship artificial skin across the United States to any hospital location.

CATARACT DRUG

Researchers at the Oculon Corporation received a U.S. patent in 1992 for a cataract-inhibiting drug called OC-2. The drug contains pantethine, which is naturally present in the human body. Tests indicate that pantethine blocks proteins in the lens of the eye from clumping together, a process that leads to the formation of cataracts.

CARDIOPUMP

Devised by researchers at the University of California at San Francsico, the CardioPump is a device designed to improve standard CPR resuscitation techniques. The device operates on the principle of a plunger, alternately pushing down and pulling up. In tests, the CardioPump has proved more effective than CPR in reviving patients, since it both compresses and decompresses the chest, which allows more blood to be pumped through the coronary arteries while drawing air into the lungs.

The CardioPump, a CPR device. (Ambu Inc.)

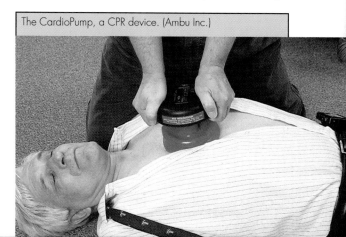

11 MEDIA AND COMMUNICATIONS

LANGUAGE AND WRITING

Origins (antiquity)

Writing seemed such an extraordinary invention that more than one civilization claimed it came from their gods. The three most ancient writing systems of which traces remain are cuneiform, hieroglyphics and ideograms, all of which appeared *c.* 3000 B.C.

Cuneiform (4th millennium B.C.)

Originally semipictographic, cuneiform is the most ancient writing system documented. It was developed by the Sumerians in the 4th and 3rd millennia B.C. The term *cuneiform* refers to the extremely angular aspect of the symbols. A young teacher from Göttingen in Germany, Georg Friedrich Grotenfend (1775–1853), was the first person, in 1802, to present a translation of cuneiform. Soon afterwards, Henry Creswicke Rawlinson (1810–95), a British major working for the East India Company, also solved the enigma.

Hieroglyphics (3rd millennium B.C.)

The appearance of hieroglyphics, the most ancient and characteristic form of Egyptian writing, coincided with the unification of Egypt around 3000 B.C. They remained in use until the 3rd century A.D.

Hieroglyphics are picture symbols; hieratic writing is a cursive form of hieroglyphics that was used by the priests until the 5th century A.D. Demotic writing also came from the same source and gave seven of its letters to the Coptic alphabet, which was used in Egypt after its conquest by the Arabs in A.D. 641.

In 1822 the Egyptologist J.F. Champollion (France, 1790–1832) deciphered the hieroglyphic and demotic characters inscribed on the Rosetta stone, a basalt slab dating from the reign of Ptolemy V (196 B.C.).

Ideograms (3rd millennium B.C.)

Chinese writing is said to have been invented by the country's emperors in the 3rd millennium B.C. The most ancient documents discovered date from between the 14th and 12th centuries B.C. Korea, Japan and Vietnam later adopted aspects of the language. Chinese is the only ancient language still in use, and its written characters often provide the only link among the billion Chinese who speak many different dialects.

The alphabet (2nd millennium B.C.)

These abstract signs representing language and thought date back to the second half of the 2nd millennium B.C. Discoveries made in Râs Shamrah in the Middle East confirm the theory that it was the Phoenicians who invented the alphabet during this period.

Comprising 22 signs, the Phoenician alphabet is the root of all Western alphabets.

Greek alphabet (c. 1000 B.C.)

The Greeks borrowed their alphabet from the Phoenicians and adapted it to their language around 1000 B.C. However, the fundamental innovation of the Greek alphabet was the introduction and rigorous notation of vowels. It is the first two letters in the Greek alphabet, *alpha* and *beta*, that are the root of the word *alphabet*.

Latin alphabet (c. 600 B.C.)

The earliest evidence of Latin writing we have dates back to the 7th and 6th centuries B.C. The Latin alphabet was derived originally from the Greek and was passed on by the Etruscans. The Roman Empire was to impose this alphabet on the whole of the Western world. A century before Christ, the Latin alphabet comprised 21 letters, to which *y* and *z* were added from the Ionian alphabet. In the Middle Ages, *j*, *u*, and *w* were introduced, to give us the alphabet we use today.

Arabic alphabet (512)

The first proven inscription in Arabic dates back to A.D. 512.

This language, which had Semitic origins and is the sister of Hebrew, is also related to Phoenician writing. The alphabet comprises 28 letters, all consonants, three of which serve as long vowels as well as diphthongs.

Cyrillic alphabet (862)

It was a theologian and missionary of Greek origin, Saint Cyril (*c.* A.D. 827–69), nicknamed

Tsang Kie, the hero with two pairs of eyes, is said to have created Chinese characters after studying traces left by birds' feet in the sand. (Le Livre Mondial des Inventions)

Previous page: "Body Building" is an artwork displayed in Haarlem, Netherlands. (Gamma/News)

This is a modern papyrus, but the art of making papyrus was discovered by the Egyptians long ago. (Le Livre Mondial des Inventions)

"the philosopher," who in 862 invented the Cyrillic alphabet for the purpose of translating the Bible for Slavic peoples to whom he wished to preach the Gospel.

This Glagolitic alphabet (from *glagolu*, meaning *word* in old Church Slavic) was modified towards the beginning of the 10th century through the introduction of 24 Greek letters. The present Russian alphabet derives from it.

The religious schism that occurred at the beginning of the 9th century gradually split the Slavic world into two alphabetic areas: Russians, Ukrainians, Bulgars and Serbs adopted the Cyrillic alphabet along with Greek Orthodoxy; the Poles, Czechs, Slovaks, Slovenes and Croatians adopted the Latin alphabet and Roman Catholicism.

Sign language (1620)

The first sign language alphabet was compiled in 1620 by J.P. Bonnet. He was a private tutor at the Spanish court, where, at that time, there were many deaf people.

Braille (1829)

In 1829 Louis Braille (France, 1809–52), a professor at the French Institute for the Blind, published a writing system based on raised dots. Braille had been accidentally blinded at the age of three by his father's tools.

Raised letters for the blind had been proposed by Valentin Hany (France) some years earlier, but Braille's system of six dots was easier to read with the fingertips.

Esperanto (1887)

Esperanto, the so-called international language, was invented by Lazarus L. Zamenhof (Poland, 1859–1917) in 1887.

Zamenhof wanted to promote the spirit of peace and communication between nations. The idea of a universal language was not new; in 1880 Johan Schleyer (Germany, 1831–1912) had invented Volapük. Esperanto replaced Volapük as the most widely spoken international language.

WRITING MATERIALS

Paper

Papyrus (c. 3000 B.C.)

The Egyptians are usually credited with the invention of papyrus around 3000 B.C. The stem of a reed cultivated in the Nile Valley constituted the raw material.

Parchment (2nd century B.C.)

It was, no doubt, the commercial and cultural rivalry between the Pharaoh Ptolemy and the King of Pergamum in Asia Minor which, between 197 and 156 B.C., brought about the invention of parchment. The pharaoh, taking umbrage at the growing reputation of Pergamum as a cultural center, must have stopped providing it with papyrus, thus obliging the scribes of Pergamum to invent a new material. Parchment is made from the skin of sheep, goats or calves (vellum).

Paper (2nd century B.C.)

The earliest example of paper was discovered in 1965 in a tomb excavated by archaeologists in the Xian region of China. Analysis has shown that this paper had been made from hemp fibers mixed with a small quantity of linen during the Han dynasty in the 2nd century B.C. However, it was not until the reign of Emperor Hedi (A.D. 88–106) that paper suitable for writing purposes began to be used. The inventor of this was Cai Lun, one of the emperor's eunuchs, who developed an inexpensive method using bark from trees, linen scraps, old rags and disused fishing nets.

The techniques rapidly improved, and paper reached neighboring countries first (Vietnam, Korea and Japan), and then Arab countries in the 8th century. It was the Arabs who introduced paper to Europe when they brought it to Spain.

The Silos missal, from near Burgos in Spain, is the oldest manuscript on European paper. It dates back to the beginning of the 11th century.

Very long paper (1799)

On January 18, 1799 Nicholas Robert, employed in Paris at the bookshop and printers François Didot, obtained a patent "for the manufacture of an extraordinary paper, measuring between 39 ft and 49 ft long, without the need for any workman and by purely mechanical means." This invention was improved by Bryan Donkin (Great Britain) in 1803. It enabled the paper mill to free itself from the traditional method of manufacturing paper—sheet by sheet in a tank.

Digital paper

Digital paper, sometimes called optical paper, is intended for use in data processing. Unlike traditional paper, it is composed of four layers of materials placed one on top of the other, including polyester, which is fine yet strong.

The first sheet of digital paper was manufactured in 1989 by the British company Image Data, a subsidiary of ICI.

WRITING IMPLEMENTS

Ink (2500 B.C.)

It was the Chinese who invented ink, in 2500 B.C. It was made with smoke, glue and aromatic substances.

Evidence has been found in Egyptian hypogea of papyrus covered in black or red ink applied with a reed and even a quill pen.

Pencil (16th century)

In 1564 the discovery of graphite in Cumbria, England led to the invention of lead pencils. In the 18th century the Cumbrian graphite mines had become a royal monopoly, the exploitation of which was subject to many rules since graphite was also used in cannon foundries. Each workman was searched upon leaving the works, and theft was a capital offense punishable by hanging.

The interruption of relations between Great Britain and France in 1792 led the engineer Jacques Nicolas Conté (France) to invent graphite and clay pencils covered with cedar wood. Demand crossed international borders, and his pencils were soon to reach all parts of the world.

Eraser (18th century)

Made from a rubber base that erases pen or pencil marks, the eraser is believed to have been invented in the mid-18th century by a physicist named Magalhaens, or Magellan (Portugal, 1722–90), who perfected numerous instruments for use in physics and astronomy. An eraser was mentioned for the first time in 1770 by the chemist J. Priestley (Great Britain). Today, plastic and synthetic rubber are commonly used to manufacture erasers.

Fountain pen (1884)

Nobody knows exactly how far back the revolutionary idea of adding an ink reservoir to a quill pen goes. In her *Memoirs*, Catherine the Great of Russia noted that she used an "endless quill" in 1748. Was she referring to one of the first pens?

Between 1880 and 1900, fountain pen inventions proliferated; more than 400 patents were registered.

The inventor of the first true fountain pen was Lewis E. Waterman (U.S.), an insurance broker, who had had enough of almost losing contracts due to malfunctioning pens. He threw himself into the task of solving the problem of ink flow and, on February 12, 1884, obtained the first patent for what was to become the Waterman Regular.

The ink cartridge was invented by M. Perrand, director of Jif-Waterman, in 1927, and patented in 1935.

Mechanical pencil (1915)

The first automatic mechanical pencil, called the Ever-Sharp Pencil, was invented in 1915 by Rokuji Hayakawa (Japan), founder in 1912 of a company to which the mechanical pencil gave its name. The Sharp Corporation has since broadened its activities, particularly in electronics.

Ballpoint pen (1938)

The ballpoint pen was invented in 1938 by Laszlo Biro (Hungary, 1899–1985), a journalist. During a visit to the print shop of the magazine for which he wrote, Biro was impressed by the advantage of quick-drying ink. He proceeded to make a prototype of a pen based on the same principle.

To escape the Nazi threat, he settled in Argentina in 1940 and there developed his invention. He patented it on June 10, 1943, and his pens were sold in Buenos Aires from 1945 on.

Bic (1953)

In 1953 a French baron, Bich, developed an industrial process for manufacturing ballpoint pens that dramatically lowered the cost of production. The Bic was born, and each year we buy three billion of them.

Felt-tipped pen (1963)

The Japanese firm Pentel was the first to develop a felt pen with an acrylic tip. It was invented and marketed in 1963.

Pentel also invented the first felt-tipped ballpoint pen in 1973, the Ball Pentel; and in 1981 it launched the first ceramic nib: the Ceramicron.

Erasable ballpoint pen (1979)

It was Gillette which, in 1979, launched the first erasable ballpoint pen, the Eraser Mate. One result of this product was that banks in the United States cautioned their depositors against using the pen to write checks.

Clean ink (1985)

In 1985 Rodger L. Gamblin (U.S.) patented an ink that does not run and does not soil readers' fingers. Its main use has been in printing newspapers.

Anti-fraud felt-tip pen (1985)

The French company Reynolds has, since 1985, sold a felt-tip (and ballpoint) anti-fraud pen that contains unerasable security ink. This pen was designed by Reynolds at the request of banks to make the falsification of checks more difficult.

WRITING TECHNIQUES

Shorthand (antiquity)

The invention of shorthand goes back to ancient times. Xenophon (Greece, c. 430–355 B.C.) could record his conversations with Socrates thanks to his semiology (writing by symbols). In Rome, Marcus Tullius Tiro developed one of the first systems for abridged writing in order to take down Cicero's speeches.

Use of shorthand disappeared subsequently, only to reemerge in the 17th century. The initiative came from England, where in 1602 J. Willis wrote a treatise on shorthand.

Various methods have since been introduced. Of these, the most famous are those by Isaac Pitman (1837) and John Robert Gregg (1888).

Punctuation (2nd century B.C.)

The invention of punctuation is credited to Aristophanes of Byzantium (257–180 B.C.). The Greek grammarian directed the famous library in Alexandria and developed a system comprising three signs corresponding to our period, semicolon and colon. It wasn't until the 16th century, however, with the invention of printing, that its usage was really respected. However, the rules of punctuation remained highly unreliable until the middle of the 19th century.

PRINTING

Origins (868)

Printing was already a widespread practice in China under the Tang dynasty (A.D. 618–907): books on magic, scholastic manuals and so on were produced. The discovery in the Dunhuang caves of a copy of the *Diamond Sutra* printed in 868 gives us the name of the printer, Wang Zhe.

Chinese printing prospered under the Sung dynasty (960–1279), and in the year 1000 an important Buddhist Sutra was published. In 1041 Bi Sheng (China) made movable characters out of fired clay. The casting of metal characters was developed mostly in Korea c. 1392.

Printing (c. 1447)

Around 1447 the printer Johannes Gensfleisch, called Gutenberg (Germany, c. 1398–1468) developed, along with his associates, the technique of movable characters. In addition, he perfected the material necessary for the quality and conservation of characters: an alloy of lead, antimony and tin.

Around 1455 in Mainz, Germany, Gutenberg printed the *Biblia sacra latina*, known as the 42-line-per-page Bible. It was the first Latin edition of the Bible printed in movable characters. Gutenberg's business partner, Johann Fust, took him to court for repayment of a loan advanced earlier, gained possession of the movable type characters, and took all the Bible's profits. However, Gutenberg was able to start up a new printing business by 1465. In 1477 William Caxton (c. 1422–91) set up the first printing press in England.

Around 1800 Lord Stanhope got rid of wood completely in presses and used metal instead. He multiplied newspaper productivity tenfold, reaching 3,000 sheets per day.

The first printing press run by a steam machine was developed by F. Koenig (Germany) in 1812. Later, Koenig, in association with A. Bauer, constructed the first cylinder press, which was followed by many others. In London, a single machine was able to print overnight the 4,000 copies of the London edition of *The Times*.

Printing Processes

Xylography (14th century)

This is one of the oldest and simplest methods of printing an illustration using a block of wood. Combined with typography, it led to the production of beautifully illustrated books at the end of the Middle Ages (14th to 15th centuries).

Printing was practiced in China as early as the 9th century. A modern press can print up to 22,155 impressions per hour. (I.O.S.)

Intaglio (1450)

This process uses engraved or etched surfaces to hold ink. The first method was copperplate engraving, whose discovery is credited to the jeweler Maso Finiguerra (Florence) in 1450. Finiguerra had the idea of inking an engraved silver plate and applying a sheet of paper to it in order to obtain a printed impression.

Aqua fortis (16th century)

Copperplates were first engraved using an etcher's needle in the Middle Ages. At the beginning of the 16th century, aqua fortis came into use. Aqua fortis (now called nitric acid) produces depressed lines in the copperplate at points where the protective varnish has been scraped away. Jacques Callot (France, 1592–1635) pioneered this technique, which he improved by covering copperplates with the hard varnish used by stringed-instrument makers.

Lithography (1796)

In 1796 the typographer Alois Senefelder (Germany, 1771–1834) invented lithography, a method of printing by transfer. He realized that a drawing done with a soft-lead pencil on limestone (the word *lithography* comes from the Greek *lithos*, meaning stone) is water-resistant. However, the unmarked stone absorbs water. If a coat of greasy ink is spread over the surface of the stone, it will not stick to the wet spots, only to the greased areas. The stone has therefore only to be placed in a press and it reproduces the initial drawings.

Senefelder rapidly improved his method. Instead of water, he used a solution of gum-arabic and nitric acid, which is completely impervious to printer's ink.

Photogravure (1822)

We owe the invention of photogravure, around 1822, to Nicéphore Niepce (France), who went on to invent photography. In fact, his invention first gave rise to a printing form (engraved copperplate) capable of producing existing images by means of a press. Replacing human-driven tools by light, photogravure contributed to the growth of typography and gave rise to heliogravure and offset printing.

Heliogravure (1875)

The heliogravure printing process was invented by Karl Klietsch (Austria) in 1875.

An industrial intaglio process, heliogravure became widely used in the printing of magazines and catalogs.

Offset (1904)

Invented by lithographer W. Rubel (U.S.) in 1904, offset came out of the lithographic process he perfected. The word *offset* covers the same transfer technique (direct apposition) as lithography. Offset is not done on stone but on a sheet of zinc.

Typesetting Machines

Movable characters (1041)

The first movable characters were made of clay. A Chinese invention, the first known movable type machine was built by Bi Sheng in 1041.

Metal characters (c. 1392)

The earliest evidence of metal characters is in machines used in Korea *c.* 1392. In 1433 a phonetic alphabet was introduced in Korea to make the characters easier to manipulate.

Linotype (1886)

A machine that made printing letters by casting characters line by line was built by Ottmar Mergenthaler (U.S.) in 1886. Mergenthaler's machine was built to an order placed by the editor of the *New York Herald Tribune*.

Monotype (1887)

In 1887 Tolbert Lanston (U.S.) invented a machine that could cast and typeset individual characters from hot metal. It permitted the typesetting of 9,000 characters per hour.

Photocomposition (1953)

The first phototypesetters were put into operation in the United States in 1953. They were invented by Louis Moyroud (France) and René Higonnet (France).

PUBLISHING

Book (2nd millennium B.C.)

Although the book first appeared in China in the 2nd millennium B.C., it was only between the 2nd and 4th centuries A.D. that it appeared in the West in the form we know. During this period, it went from being the volume (a scroll of papyrus or parchment), which was not very manageable, to the more portable codex (a volume of manuscripts in which sheets are inserted and folded together).

Library (1700 B.C.)

The first libraries appeared in Chaldea in 1700 B.C.; the "books" were baked clay tablets. In 540 B.C. Pisistratus endowed Athens with the first public library.

Book publishing (antiquity)

Genuine publishing houses already existed in ancient Greek and Roman times. Athens and Rome boasted printed works of which several hundred copies were published.

It was, of course, only with the invention of the industrial print shop that publishing really began to flourish, and the bookshop came soon

after. The latter was born in London with the bookstore of Wynkyn de Worde, successor to William Caxton, and publisher of the first book to be produced in English in England, in 1495.

But it was not until the late 16th century that bookshops began to specialize in selling books from one field or another, and it was only then that publishers charged them with the task of distributing their products.

Dictionary (600 B.C.)

The oldest dictionary to have been found dates back to 600 B.C. It comes from Mesopotamia and is written in Akkadian, the language of the Assyrians and the Babylonians. In China, the Hou Chin dictionary did not appear until 150 B.C.

In 1480 the printer William Caxton (England) published the first bilingual English-French dictionary for tourists. It had 36 pages.

The first polyglot dictionary, based on Latin and Italian, then extended to German, English and French, was the famous *Dictionary of the Latin Language* (1509). It was the work of the scholar Ambrogio Calepino (Italy).

In 1755 the English lexicographer Samuel Johnson (1709–84) produced *A Dictionary of the English Language*.

Encyclopedia (4th century B.C.)

The oldest known encyclopedia was written by Speusippus in Athens around 370 B.C. The most famous one in the English-speaking world is the *Encyclopaedia Britannica*, first published in Edinburgh in 1768. It now contains over 32,000 pages and 44 million words. Even this massive work is dwarfed by the Spanish *La Enciclopedia Universal Ilustrada Europeo-Americana*.

Newspaper (1605)

The first gazette to come out regularly appeared in Antwerp, Belgium in 1605 under the title *Nieuwe Tijdinghen*. Its creator was the printer Abraham Verhoeven.

It was widely imitated in Europe and, from 1609, two weekly gazettes appeared in Germany, one of which, *die Relation aller fürnemmen und gedenkwürdigen Historien*, published in Strasbourg, mentions in its 37th edition the invention of Galileo's telescope.

The first daily newspaper was published by Thimotheus Ritzch (Germany) in Leipzig. It appeared for the first time in 1650 under the title *Einkommende Zeitungen*. Subsequently called the *Leipzig Journal* (*Leipziger Zeitung*), it continued to appear until 1918!

Edible book (1992)

In 1992 a French publisher produced the world's first edible book, *Croqueland* ("Cookie-land"). A children's book, *Croqueland* contains 10 pages made from a sugar and fruit base. The author's words can now be digested in more ways than one.

MAIL DELIVERY

Postal service (6th century B.C.)

Cyrus the Great (558–528 B.C.), the founder of the Persian Empire, is said to have been the first to introduce a postal service. Cyrus had conquered a vast area and found that messengers bearing missives and information were inadequate, so he organized a postal service with staging posts at regular intervals where horses would be cared for after a reasonable day's journey.

The Romans copied this method of organization and created, during the reign of Augustus (27 B.C.–A.D. 14), the *Cursus publicus*. Military routes were marked with *mutationes*, which were staging posts providing rested horses, and *mansiones*, which were inns reserved for official travelers.

Directories (1785)

The first city directory was for the city and suburbs of Philadelphia, between 1st Street to the north and Maiden Street to the south, 10th Street to the west and Delaware Street to the east. Published by John Macpherson on October 1, 1785, it included 6,250 names and addresses.

Envelope (1820)

A Brighton, England resident named Brewer stated in 1820 that he had invented the envelope. However, several envelopes dating back to 1615 are preserved in Geneva, Switzerland. At that time a letter would be folded and covered with silk thread, with a wax stamp fixing the two ends together. Later the letter was wrapped in a folded white sheet on which the receiver's address would be written.

Stamps (1834)

James Chalmers (Great Britain) printed the first stamp in Dundee, Scotland in 1834, but it was not until 1840 that stamps were used, following the British postal reform carried out by Sir Rowland Hill (Great Britain, 1795–1879), who introduced penny postage.

The first adhesive stamp, which went into use in Great Britain on May 6, 1840, was the Penny Black, which bore the profile of Queen Victoria on a dark background.

Perforated stamps (1854)

The first apparatus for separating stamps was invented in 1847 by Henry Archer (Great Britain). It could only make slits, but its inventor perfected it one year later and the machine could then perforate a series of small holes. The first perforated stamp was the Penny Red, issued in February 1854.

Postcard (1861)

The postcard was invented in Philadelphia in 1861 by John P. Charlton, who obtained a copyright for it and then sold his rights to a stationer named Harry L. Lipman. The latter published the cards with a picture and the words "Lipman postcard, patent pending."

The prestamped postcard was conceived by Emmanuel Herrman (Austria) of the Neustadt Military Academy in Vienna. The first of these were made available on October 1, 1869.

TELEGRAPHY

Chappe's telegraph (1793)

After a preliminary demonstration in March 1791, an engineer, Claude Chappe (France), sent a telegraphic message a distance of about 9 miles between Saint-Martin-du-Tertre and Paris on July 12, 1793.

Chappe's telegraph was a relay of semaphore signals from stations positioned about 7½ miles apart at fairly high points so that someone with field-glasses could see the signals being made.

Electric telegraph (1833)

In 1827, Steinheil (Germany) discovered that a single grounded electric wire could be used as a transmission line. In 1933 the physicist Michael Faraday (Great Britain, 1791–1867) demonstrated that an electric current could be induced by moving a conductor within the field of influence of a magnet. If variants are used in accordance with a code common both to the sender and receiver, those two people will be able to send messages to each other.

It is on the basis of these principles that a diplomat, Pavel Schilling (Russia), created an experimental telegraph in St. Petersburg. His early death interrupted the experiment. Sir William Cooke (Great Britain, 1806–79), an Indian Army officer, and the great physicist Sir Charles Wheatstone (Great Britain, 1802–75), continued Schilling's work and patented the first electric signal in June 1837.

With the help of a telegraphic message, the police were able to arrest a murderer, John Tawell, traveling on the 7:42 train from Paddington on January 1, 1845. This arrest increased the popularity of the telegraph in Britain.

Morse telegraph (1837)

On September 28, 1837 Samuel F.B. Morse (U.S., 1791–1872) applied for a patent for electric telegraphy. However, his most original contribution was, without a doubt, the invention of Morse code, in which letters are translated by a succession of dots and dashes.

On December 30, 1842, after a great deal of effort, he managed to obtain a grant of $30,000 to build an experimental line from Washington, D.C. to Baltimore, which was opened on May 24, 1844. After a number of setbacks, Morse, who saw his invention being contested, had his rights confirmed by a judgment of the U.S. Supreme Court. The telegraph subsequently experienced enormous growth and Morse became rich and famous.

Although its only purpose now is to act as a support in the event of the failure of the radio system, the Morse code, 150 years after it was invented, is still taught to Navy radio controllers.

SOS (1906)

The most famous of all telegraphed messages, the SOS (three dots followed by three dashes, then three dots again) was first used in 1906 at the Berlin radio-telegraphic conference in Germany. The first SOS in the history of navigation was sent out by the Titanic on April 14, 1912. In 1999 the SOS is scheduled to be replaced by GMDSS, an alarm system that uses beacons, doubtless more efficient, but far less romantic.

Underwater Telegraphic Cable

Insulation (1847)

In 1847, Werner von Siemens (Germany) developed a machine that could apply gutta-percha (a rubberlike substance obtained from trees) onto cables, thereby ensuring that they were insulated.

Solid cable (1950)

After the rupture of the first telegraphic cable under the English Channel, on August 28, 1850, a cable made of four copper wires, each with a diameter of 1.65 mm, was used. The cable's wires were twisted into a single strand that was covered with tar-cloth and reinforced with 10 galvanized iron wires, each with a diameter of 7 mm.

Cable installation ships (1865)

After 1865, the first installation ships, which were simple steamboats equipped for the purpose, gave way to bigger, specifically equipped ships. These ships had cable tanks and winches for unrolling cable. The British ship *Great Eastern*, the largest ship of the time, was the prototype of the installation ship.

Transatlantic cable (1866)

On July 27, 1866 the first transatlantic telegraph cable was completed. Cyrus Field (U.S., 1819–92) had been the instigator of the operation, which cost him almost his entire fortune. The first four attempts, 1857–1865, had ended in failure.

TELEPHONE

Telephone (1876)

There are numerous claims for the title of inventor of the telephone, with each country claiming its own. Many researchers have described systems that in theory resemble some form of telephone system. Nonetheless, it is generally agreed that first operational telephone was made in the United States in 1876. Almost simultaneously, two men produced workable prototypes: Alexander Graham Bell (U.S., 1847–1922) and Elisha Gray (U.S., 1835–1901).

The earpieces of Bell's telephone. (J.R. Charmet)

On January 14, 1876, both Bell and Gray filed applications for patents at the Patent Office in New York City. Bell filed his application at noon; Gray filed his at 2 P.M. It was on the basis of this two hours' difference that the judges made a decision in Bell's favor after a long court case between the inventors.

In 1875 Bell was working with his assistant Thomas Watson towards improving the telegraph. On June 2, a decisive event took place. Bell in one room, Watson in another, were both working on their telegraph. Suddenly Watson made a mistake—a bad contact by a clamping screw that was too tight changed what should have been an intermittent transmission into a continuous current. Bell, who was at the other end of the wire, distinctly heard the sound of the contactor dropping. Bell spent the next winter making calculations and filed an application for a patent. It was not until March 6, 1876 that he succeeded in transmitting intelligible words to his colleague: "Come here, Watson, I want you."

The world learned of Bell's invention when he demonstrated it at the United States Centennial Exhibition held in Philadelphia in June 1876.

Telephone exchange (1878)

In 1878 the first manual telephone exchange opened in New Haven, Conn. It served 21 subscribers, one of whom was Mark Twain.

In 1891 Almon B. Strowger (U.S.), a funeral director from Kansas City, Mo., applied for a patent on the first automatic telephone exchange. Strowger's motive for his invention was purely business. He had discovered that his main business rival's wife, an operator at the local manual exchange, was the first to learn of deaths in the city and was directing Strowger's business to her husband.

Radiotelephone (1900)

The ancestor of the radiotelephone is Chichester Bell and Charles Sumner Tainter's graphophone. The first demonstration took place on February 15, 1885. Radiotelephony is a means of communication by radio waves rather than along telephone wires.

The first true radiotelephone was produced by Reginald A. Fessenden, who demonstrated the device in December 1900 at Cob Point, Maryland.

The first transatlantic transmission was made by AT&T in 1915 between Virginia and the Eiffel Tower in Paris.

Telex (1916)

The first teleprinter, which made it possible to send written messages through telephone lines, was invented in 1916 by Markrum Co. of Chicago. The system became operational in 1928 and was extended at a national level by the Bell Laboratories in 1931 under the name telex (from *tele*printer *ex*change). Today it is being overtaken by the fax machine.

Phototelegraphy (1924)

The first ancestor of the fax machine was A. Bain's (Great Britain) electrical picture transmitter in 1843. In 1906 Arthur Korn (Germany) transmitted a portrait of the crown prince by telephotography over a distance of 1,120 miles, and in 1907 the scientist Edouard Belin (France, 1876–1963) developed an apparatus that worked along similar lines, which he called the belinograph.

In 1924 Bell Laboratories carried out a preliminary demonstration of phototelegraphy.

Pay Telephones (1891): William Gray

One night in 1887, William Gray needed a telephone. His wife was critically ill. Gray begged for permission to use the phone at a nearby factory, and was refused. At last he convinced a company official to lend him the phone, and made his call. When the crisis had passsed, Gray set his sights on making telephones accessible to the public.

It wasn't a novel idea. The telephone company had tried to establish public telephone stations with paid attendants, but the expense was prohibitive, and service was thus limited. Gray came up with a design for a pay telephone with a slot for coins.

It wasn't Gray's first invention. A baseball fan, Gray had already patented an inflatable chest protector for catchers, and had sold Spalding a baseball bat with a sand handle for better gripping. Both inventions were enthusiastically backed by Charles Soby, a tobacco magnate and owner of the local ball club.

William Gray. (Connecticut Historical Society)

Gray was head of the polishing department at Pratt and Whitney, a machine manufacturer. He brought his pay phone design to Amos Whitney. Whitney assigned a 16-year-old apprentice, George A. Long, to build a model of the pay phone.

In 1891 the Gray Telephone Pay Station Company was formed, with Gray as inventor, Long as executor, Whitney as business executive, and Soby as financial backer. Gray continued working at Pratt and Whitney for 15 years before retiring to work exclusively on pay phones. From 1888 to 1902 he took out 23 separate patents for improvements on his original model.

Gray's invention did all he hoped for in bringing the telephone within reach of everyone. "Deposit five cents, please" became a catchphrase for generations. The pay phone brought in millions of dollars to fuel the young telephone industry and helped create a demand for household telephones.

This was a transmission by telephone of photographs from the Chicago and Cleveland conventions to New York when candidates for president were nominated. This method had been perfected by the engineers Ives and Gray of Bell Laboratories.

Visiophone (1929)

It was around 1929 that American engineers experimented with visiophone, a device that enables two speakers to see each other on a screen while on the telephone. During the 1970s Bell Laboratories marketed the Picturephone in the United States, but its exorbitant price led to its failure. Subsequently, numerous prototypes have emerged throughout the world, in particular in Japan (the Scopephone by NTT, for example).

Hertz relays (1942)

Telephone transmisison by ultra-short waves used in Hertz relays was perfected in the United States at the AT&T laboratories by Harold T. Friis around 1942. They were a direct result of the war effort made by Bell Laboratories.

Fax machine (1949)

The first facsimile machine (commonly known as the fax machine) was perfected and manufactured in 1947 by the British company Muirhead Ltd., a firm founded in 1846 by Alexander Muirhead and specializing in wireless telegraphy. The first experimental model was developed in collaboration with the press agency Associated Newspapers. In 1949 Muirhead installed the first fax system in Japan for the newspaper *Asahi Times.* The system became enormously successful in Japan, where it was manufactured on a large scale, facilitating the transmission of ideograms. It took much longer for the system to be adopted elsewhere. However, since the mid-1970s the market has expanded rapidly.

Communications terminal (1976)

This little radiocommunications apparatus is not really a telephone proper, since it only works in one direction, that is, receiving messages. Eurosignal—from the German company Bosch—was the first, invented in 1976. It makes it possible to receive messages at a distance, by using the telephone.

Portable radiotelephone (1979)

This apparatus, known as the cellular telephone, is causing a revolution in the field of communications.

It was in Sweden under the impetus of the Ericsson Co. that it first appeared in 1979. The area to be covered is divided into a certain number of small cells, each one served by a receiver. The unit is controlled by a data processing system.

Vocal control telephone (1983)

The first telephone unit to be controlled vocally was invented in June 1983 by Garth A. Clowes (U.S.) and then marketed in 1984 under the name TTC 6012. This is a device that responds to the sound of the voice, either directly or through a memory capable of storing 80 numbers. The device is able to recognize the voice of three different people.

A more recent development on this principle is a mobile telephone controlled by the human voice, developed by a Danish firm, Dancall, in cooperation with British Telecom in 1987.

Pocket telephone (1989)

Soon public telephones will be obsolete—all one will need will be a cordless telephone not much larger than a pack of cigarettes. Many companies are competing to get ahead in this market, which, by 1995, is estimated will be worth billions of dollars.

RADIO

Electromagnetic waves (1864)

It was the physicist James Clerk Maxwell (Great Britain, 1831–79) who first demonstrated the existence of electromagnetic waves. This discovery was at the root of the invention of radiotelegraphy, some 25 years later.

Maxwell demonstrated that light was the result of electromagnetic vibrations of a certain wavelength. His theory, put forward in 1864, allowed scientists to predict the propagation, reflection and diffraction of light. Moreover, it showed how electromagnetic waves other than light waves could be propagated.

Stereophony (1881)

The first transmission in stereo was arranged by Clément Ader, the pioneer of aviation, at the time of the first exhibition on electricity, held

Wireless Communication (1895): Guglielmo Marconi

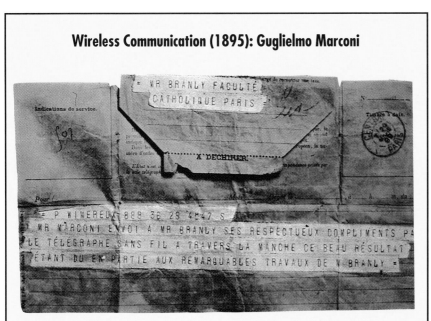

The first cross-Channel telegram, sent by Marconi to Branly on March 28, 1899. (Josse)

Guglielmo Marconi's mother knew her son was destined for great things. When he was born, the family's old gardener announced, "*Che orechi grandi ha!*" ("What big ears he has!") Signora Marconi responded, "With those ears, he'll be able to hear the still, small voices of the air."

While Marconi did not send voices through the air himself, he made many discoveries that were miraculous in themselves and that led to others' invention of voice radio.

In the late 19th century, electromagnetism was the hot new science. James Clerk Maxwell postulated that light was a series of waves of electromagnetic radiation. By 1888 Heinrich Hertz produced waves at a lower frequency than those of light. In 1895 Russia's Aleksandr Stepanovich Popov built a receiver to detect electromagnetism in the atmosphere. He predicted that his receiver could pick up generated signals.

It was Marconi, in 1895, who sent those signals. His first signal traveled the length of his mother's attic to make a bell tinkle at one end of the attic when he pushed a key at the other. Unable to win support from the Italian government, Marconi traveled to England. He carried his transmitter in a small black box. British customs officials confiscated it, breaking the mechanism. Marconi fixed it, and used it to set up a simple wireless communication system of transmitter, receiver and copper-strip antenna. This proved to be an effective system of sending Hertz's radiating waves, later called radio waves.

Encouraged by the British Post Office, Marconi improved his system and used it to send a signal nine miles across the Bristol Channel. In 1899 he set up a wireless station to communicate with a French station 31 miles across the English Channel. Before long the Marconi Wireless Telegraph and Signal Company had many such stations. Yet there were limits. Physicists believed that the earth's curve would prevent transmissions beyond 200 miles.

In 1901 Marconi proved them wrong with a signal sent from Cornwall to St. John's, Newfoundland, a distance of 2,000 miles. He continued to improve the reflectors he used to send signals and the antennae he used to receive them. By 1907 all large ocean liners carried Marconi radio equipment that allowed them to communicate in Morse code. The liners passed news to shore and to other liners, and radioed for help. When the *Titanic* struck an iceberg it radioed the *Carpathia*, 58 miles away; 705 people were saved in the *Carpathia*'s lifeboat. But another ship, 20 miles away, turned a deaf ear to the *Titanic*'s SOS—its radio operator had gone to bed.

In 1909, Marconi won the Nobel Prize for Physics. His inventions connected the world, and soon opened it to vocal communication.

in Paris in 1881. For the event, Ader had invented a telephonic "stereoscopic" system which, each evening, enabled an enthusiastic public to follow performances at the Opera, some 2 miles away.

However, stereophonic sound as we know it today emerged in the 1930s, when numerous systems were developed. After several experiments carried out during the decades that followed, the definitive method was adopted in 1964.

The Edison effect (1883)

In 1883 Thomas Alva Edison (U.S., 1847–1931) invented the first incandescent light bulb.

This bulb displays the Edison effect: a metal heated until it is red-hot emits an electron cloud. Radio tubes were able to make use of this effect in order to transmit sounds.

Hertzian waves (1888)

In 1888, at the age of 31, Heinrich Rudolf Hertz (Germany, 1857–94), professor of physics at the Polytechnic of Karlsruhe, detected, created and used electromagnetic waves. After becoming familiar with Maxwell's theories, Hertz manufactured a rudimentary transmitter called the *resonator*. With the help of this resonator Hertz verified all of Maxwell's theories. For the first time, waves, subsequently called Hertzian waves, were produced and then detected at a distance.

This invention was in turn to enable Guglielmo Marconi to invent the wireless.

Coherer (1888)

Edouard Branly (France, 1844–1940), doctor of sciences and medicine and professor of physics at the Catholic Institute in Paris, detected radio waves in 1888. After two years of research and improvements, he presented his radio detector to the Academy of Sciences on November 24, 1890. This device converted radio waves into usable electric current. Branly established that the radio waves could be detected tens of meters away and even through walls. Wireless telegraphy was about to be born.

Sir Oliver Lodge (Great Britain, 1851–1940) perfected and named the apparatus the *coherer*, and it is under this name that it has been passed down.

Syntony of circuits (1894)

In 1894 Sir Oliver Joseph Lodge (Great Britain), a professor at the University of Birmingham, England, introduced a new idea: tuning.

It seems obvious today that the receiver should be tuned to the wavelength of the transmitter from which one wishes to tap a signal. By applying the work of Lord Kelvin, Lodge, a pioneer in this field, established the system of tuning that for many years has been called *syntony*. A pioneer of syntony in the United States was Nicola Tesla (Croatia, 1856–1943).

Aerial (1895)

In 1895 Aleksandr Stepanovich Popov (Russia) invented the aerial.

As assistant professor at the School of Torpedos in Kronstadt, Russia, he had used the methods of Branly and Lodge for the purposes of detecting distant storms. He noticed that sensitivity was increased when he used a long vertical wire for the reception of waves produced by lightning. A lightning conductor was therefore the first aerial.

It is to Popov that we owe the first radio electric link in Morse code transmitted over a distance of 820 ft. The first words transmitted were "Heinrich Hertz" on March 24, 1896.

Although Popov was the inventor of the aerial, in 1891 Branly had shown that by equipping his apparatus with long metal rods he could improve their range.

Diode (1904)

Marconi's collaborator, Sir John Ambrose Fleming (Great Britain, 1849–1945), created the diode in 1904. He placed a plate in front of a heated wire (the filament) in a vacuum tube. The diode was the first radio tube, but it did not significantly advance the wireless sets of the time.

Triode (1906)

Lee De Forest (U.S., 1873–1961) invented the first triode in 1906 and named it the Audion.

With the Audion, the radio was equipped with an extremely sensitive apparatus. Because of the auxiliary electrode, it became possible to gauge transmission power with precision and thus to transmit voice vibrations, music and other sounds in all their subtle nuances.

De Forest's invention is the basis not only of radio but also of television, radar and the first computers.

Crystal set (1910)

In 1910, the work of two researchers, Dunwoody and Pickard (both U.S.) on crystals led to the invention of the crystal set, which was the first radio. Galena is a lead sulfur crystal that, combined with some simple elements, permitted thousands of amateurs to build their own wireless sets and to receive the first radio broadcasting transmissions.

Variable frequency receiver (1917)

This was invented in 1917 by Edwin H. Armstrong (U.S.). At the time, it was very difficult to achieve proper receiver adjustment since receivers were equipped with a great many buttons, and tuning in to a different frequency involved complicated manipulations. The superheterodyne, or variable frequency, receiver allowed the listener to search for stations with a single button. It considerably simplified receiver adjustments and also facilitated their industrial manufacture.

Presently, 99 percent of radio and television receivers, radar connections via satellite, etc. employ the principle of the superheterodyne.

Portable radio (1922)

It was in 1922 that J. McWilliams Stone of Chicago invented the Operadio, the first portable radio receiver. It cost $180 and weighed nearly 22 lb.

Car radio (1922)

The invention of the car radio can be attributed to George Frost (U.S.), who, in 1922, at the age of 18, installed a radio in a Model T Ford. The first industrially produced car radio was the Philco Transitone, manufactured by the Philadelphia Storage Battery Co. in 1927.

Frequency modulation (FM) (1933)

Edwin H. Armstrong (U.S.) began studying the principle of frequency modulation in 1925. This consists of modifying the frequency (or wavelength) of a transmission to adapt it to the rhythm of sound variations.

He studied the principal transmission and reception circuits in 1933 (his first patent was taken out on January 24, 1933) and he demonstrated that noise can be decreased by increasing the frequency band (contrary to what takes place in amplitude modulation). In 1938 General Electric installed the first transmitter of this type in Schenectady, New York, and this was followed by the Yankee Network. FM was also adopted in 1939 for police patrol radios in the United States.

Transistor (1948)

In 1948 three Bell Laboratories scientists, John Bardeen, Walter Brattain and William Shockley, published the results of the work that would win them the Nobel Prize for Physics in 1956. They had invented the transistor, which replaced the vacuum tube and revolutionized the field of electronics.

It took some years before the first transistor radio appeared. In August 1955 the Sony TR-55 was launched, soon to be followed by many more transistors, as the new radios were called.

TELEVISION

Nipkow scanning disc (1884)

It was a student, Paul Nipkow (Germany), who came up with the idea of cutting up images into lines. His "electric telescope," patented in 1884, was a pierced disc that turned in front of the object to be analyzed and detailed all its points, line by line. This method, called the Nipkow disc, was the basis of television.

Cathode-ray tube (1897)

It was in 1897 that the physicist Karl Ferdinand Braun (Germany, 1850–1919) invented the cathode-ray tube. It was a kind of vacuum tube in which a fluorescent screen is bombarded by a stream of high-energy electrons. This cath-

odic oscillator won him the Nobel Prize for Physics in 1909.

Mechanical television (1923)

The engineer John Logie Baird (Great Britain, 1888–1946) was one of the pioneers of television. In 1923 he applied for a patent for the use of the Nipkow disc within a mechanical television system. The first experiment was successfully carried out three years later, in 1926. The image obtained comprised only eight lines. He later invented the 240-line mechanically scanned system of television.

Mechanical television used a Nipkow disc (or one of its derivatives) for capturing images. For reception another disc was used that was synchronous with the first, linked to a neon bulb.

In 1928 Baird developed a television system in color, although it was still mechanical. In 1930 he established an experimental mechanical television network with the help of the BBC.

From 1930 onwards Baird marketed his Televisor, the first mass-market transmitter. However, his efforts proved unsuccessful.

Television camera (1923)

The iconoscope was the first television camera and was the result of the work of Vladimir Kosma Zworykin (U.S., b. Russia; 1889–1982). Zworykin conceived of an electronic analysis procedure that led to the creation of the iconoscope: a camera tube that converts an optical image into electrical pulses. For this he gained the title "father of television."

After having applied for a patent for the procedure in December 1923, Zworykin performed an initial demonstration of his invention in the RCA (Radio Corporation of America) electronic research laboratories in 1930. The iconoscope was developed as of 1933. It was used for experimental broadcasts carried out by RCA and NBC from the top of the Empire State Building in New York City in 1936.

Zworykin was also the inventor of a receiver tube called the cinescope, which appeared in 1929.

Electronic television (1926)

Virtually unknown in Europe, Kenjiro Takayanagi (Japan) almost certainly invented electronic television before Zworykin. In 1926 Takayanagi succeeded in transmitting and picking up the image of a Japanese character. The image comprised 40 lines and 14 frames per second. Only the camera used was mechanical.

The beginning of television (1932)

It was in London in 1932 that the BBC undertook to transmit the first regular television programs. These were based upon the mechanical method of John Logie Baird (Great Britain), perfected in 1932.

The first real television station was built in Berlin, Germany, in 1935, in anticipation of the Olympic Games. In 1936 in the United States, the Federal Communications Commission

The Video Walkman was first introduced in Japan in 1988. (Sony)

opted for a system of 441 lines. In the same year, NBC carried out experiments with the help of an iconoscope from the Empire State Building in New York City.

The first live journalistic reporting was undertaken in Great Britain by the BBC in 1937 at the coronation of King George VI.

Color televison (1954)

John Logie Baird (Great Britain) had demonstrated the possibility of color television in 1928. His color set was based on mechanical television technology. In 1949 David Sarnoff (U.S.) developed the first color tube, the Shadow Mask, in the RCA laboratories. However, the greatest advance in the development of color television came in 1954, when the National Television System Committee (NTSC), developed by scientists at Bell Laboratories, was adopted as the first practical nationwide color telecasting system.

In Europe, engineers were building systems different from the NTSC, but based on the same principles. In France, Henri de France (France) developed the SECAM (sequential color memory) procedure in 1956. The first SECAM color transmission took place in 1960 between London and Paris. In Germany, Walter Bruch (Germany) developed a PAL (phased alternate line) system. The first transmissions of color television using the PAL system took place in Germany in January 1967.

All three procedures for color television (NTSC, SECAM and PAL) are based on the same principle, using cathode tubes made up of a multitude of juxtaposed elements that give red, yellow or blue light via fluorescence. The tube comprises three electronic "cannons," each of which produces only a single color, due to a system of perforated masks.

Trinitron color tube (1968)

The Japanese company Sony developed Trinitron color tubes in 1968. Only one electronic tube and the center of a wide lens are used. There is also a grid for the selection of colors that permits a greater number of color beams to reach the screen in a more organized manner.

Pocket television (1984)

In 1984, several Japanese manufacturers began to market pocket television sets. The first was the Sony Watchman, which functions in black and white and has a 5 cm diagonal screen. Color sets were produced by various companies in 1985.

Rotating television (1989)

In 1989 the Danish manufacturer Bang & Olufsen developed the Biovision MX5000, a television set with a programmable motorized base. It can pivot up to 120 degrees, and can be adjusted to whatever position the viewer finds most comfortable.

Interactive TV (1990)

Originally developed by the Canadian network TV1, the principle of interactivity has been available to television viewers since 1990. For a single broadcast, viewers can choose among several options, accessible through remote control. For instance, during the retransmission of a football game, the viewer can watch the game, create slow-motion replays or follow an individual player. Similarly, with a news broadcast, the viewer can select the order in which the segments are broadcast from a menu that provides subject options. In the United States it is even possible to play cards and gamble against interactive TV.

Space System (1991)

The French company Thomson launched the Space System in 1991, the first of a new generation of television sets leading towards High Definition Television (HTV). Standard television sets project a rectangular image with a width:height ratio of 4:3. The Space System has a 16:9 ratio. It has the same height ratio but offers a broader image. This size screen is close to movie screen formats such as CinemaScope and Vistavision. A special zoom effect attachment to the Space System allows the Cinema-Scope image to be reproduced in full.

VIDEO

Video Recorders

First video recording (1951)

The first company to carry out a demonstration of black and white video recording was Mincom, a branch of the M/Scotch company, in the United States in 1951.

In 1954 the RCA Corp. built the first video recorder to be recognized as such. The following year, the BBC unveiled the VERA (Vision Electronic Recording Apparatus), a real monster that consumed 10½ miles of tape per hour!

Ampex solution (1953)

It was the Californian corporation Ampex which, in 1953, resolved the problem of tape consumption by adopting a system that made it possible to maintain an acceptable speed. This method is still in use today on professional or mass media video recorders.

The team of Ampex researchers was led by Charles P. Ginsberg and Charles E. Anderson.

They were joined by a 19-year-old student named Ray Dolby, who was soon to become a household name.

On March 2, 1955 Anderson carried out a very convincing demonstration of a method for recording sound by modulating the frequency. After further improvements, this video recorder was finally launched on the market in April 1956 under the name Ampex VR 1000.

First retransmisison of a recorded television program (1956)

This took place on November 30, 1956, on an Ampex VR 1000. On that day the CBS studio at Television City in Hollywood recorded the *Douglas Edwards and the News* program broadcast from New York, in order to retransmit it three hours later on the West Coast.

Magnetic videotape (1956)

The first videotape marketed was developed in 1956 by two researchers from 3M, Mel Sater and Joe Mazzitello. Working day and night the two men succeeded in unveiling their invention the very day that Ampex Corp. placed the first video recorder on the market. This first Scotch 179 reel was 2 in wide, nearly 875 yd long, and weighed 22 lb 8 oz.

Hair-thin optical fibers are replacing traditional coaxial cables. This technology will make it possible for viewers to participate in programs. (Cosmos/Walsh Science Photo Lab.)

First color video recorder (1958)

The first color video recorder was also built by Ampex. It was launched in 1958, two years after the first video recorder, under the name VR 1000 B. It was followed in 1963 by a transistor version, the VR 110.

Meanwhile the Japanese had been steadily working on video recorder technology:

In 1958 Toshiba announced the first single-head video recorder;

In 1959 JVC developed the first two-head video recorder, the KVI;

In 1962 Shiba Electric (now Hitachi), in co-operation with Asahi Broadcasting, presented a professional transistorized video recorder;

In 1964 Sony marketed the first video recorder for the general public.

Videocassette recorders (1970)

In addition to professional video recorders, manufacturers also designed models intended for the mass market. It was for this purpose that videocassette recorders were developed (as opposed to tapes).

Towards the end of the 1960s Matsushita, JVC and Sony together developed the standard U-Matic. The first models were launched on the market in 1970. Subsequently the standard U-Matic gained in prestige to the point where, today, it is considered to be the standard professional recorder.

Betamax (1975)

Invented by the Japanese company Sony, the Betamax was launched in 1975. Today Betamax has been almost completely abandoned, despite its technical superiority to VHS.

VHS (1975)

The VHS format (Video Home System) was launched by JVC in October 1975 and marketed from 1976. The VHS now holds a dominant position in the world market, with more than 80 percent of sales.

A variation of the VHS model, the VHS-C, was launched by JVC in 1982. It was then intended for the portable video and uses smaller videocassettes that can be reread on a traditional VHS recorder thanks to an adaptor.

In July 1985 JVC launched the VHS HQ (High Quality). In March 1987 JVC brought out a Super VHS in Japan that increased the number of horizontal lines on the image from 240 to 400.

The most modern VCRs, such as the Sony SLV-777, have Nicam stereo, jog and shuttle dials (which improve picture-search and freeze-frame control), inputs for camcorders and a built-in edit function which splits the TV screen into two pictures.

The 8 mm (1982)

On January 20, 1982 Sony, Hitachi, JVC, Matsushita and Philips signed an agreement for the joint establishment of standards for a new format called the 8 mm (because of the width of the tape), designed for camcorders.

Digital video recorder (1985)

In May 1985, at the Symposium of Montreux, Sony introduced the first video recorder with a digital recording facility. This model was solely for professional use.

Since then digital video recorders have become commonplace. The effects that can be produced are quite varied. For instance, it is possible to superimpose a reduced secondary image onto a corner of the screen. It is also possible to choose the speed of the tape, with faster and slower options, and so on.

Video Walkman (1988)

Like its audio predecessor, this is also a Sony invention. Marketed in Japan since August 1988, it is both a television receiver and an 8 mm format video recorder; and it weighs just 2½ lb. The latest version, the GV-300, has hi-fi stereo sound.

Video recorder with screen (1989)

Philips has launched the first video recorder that has integrated liquid crystal display (LCD). This allows you to play a cassette at the same time as watching a television channel or vice versa, to display settings, to check how a recording is progressing, and so on. Meanwhile, Panasonic has brought out the Maclord AV Gear, a portable video recorder with LCD, which is designed for S-VHS-C cassettes.

VHS/VHS-C recorder (1990)

To play VHS-C cassettes on a home video recorder, you used to have to use an adaptor. Now Panasonic and JVC have developed a recorder that is entirely compatible with both formats, and makes it possible to play either equally well with the same loading mechanism.

Panasonic went even further in 1991 with the NV-W1, which can play, record or copy in any format: PAL (the European TV format with 625 lines of resolution), NTSC (the American System with 525 lines) and the French Secam. It is, however, extremely expensive.

Double decker video (1990)

Amstrad's Double Decker DD8901 was the first two-deck video recorder. With this system, the user can watch a video on one deck while recording a TV program on the other. It is also possible to record two programs simultaneously or hook the system up to two separate sets and watch two videos at once. The user can program the system to record two to four hours of playing time, with the second deck taking over from the first.

Talking video recorder (1991)

In 1991 the Japanese company Panasonic unveiled the first video recorder that can be programmed orally, without a prerecorded voice. It confirms by voice synthesis all the instructions received: channel selection, date, time, etc.

Video Cameras and Camcorders

Betamovie (1982)

This was the first camcorder—a video camera and recorder combined. Launched at the Japan Electronic Show in Tokyo in October 1982 by Sony, it uses normal Betamax cassettes allowing up to 3 hours 35 minutes recording time.

8 mm camcorders (1983)

The first prototype 8 mm camcorders were brought out in the autumn of 1983 by Sanyo and Philips. However, the first one to go on the market was the Kodavision, launched in 1984 by Kodak, but produced by Matsushita.

In January 1985, Sony launched Video 8, which could record 90 minutes of images at normal speed and 180 at slow speed. In the same year Sony launched the Handycam, a very simple camcorder that only records, but is very compact and light (2 lb 14 oz). In 1991 Sony launched the MPK-TR, which will work up to 130 ft under water. Even the microphone is still effective at that depth.

Video-Movie (1984)

In Japan in 1984 JVC launched the Video-Movie, a VHS-C format camcorder, and in January 1986, in response to Sony's Handycam, it launched the GR-C7. This weighed 2 lb 14 oz, and offered CCD transducer, automatic focus, and recording and playback facilities. Then in September 1986 JVC announced the GR-C9, ultra-light (2 lb 3 oz with battery), with automatic focus and CCD transducer. Like the Handycam, it cannot play back recordings.

Folding camcorder (1990)

From Hitachi comes the VMC-1-S, the world's slimmest camcorder (2.7 in. thick). Very compact, it folds in on itself for storage, and records onto VHS-C utilizing the latest innovations—automatic focus, titling, automatic exposure program, and so on.

Concept C (1990)

In Japan in spring 1990, in the search for the ever smaller product, JVC launched a modular camcorder, the Concept C. In S-VHS-C format, it comprises a recording component, a camera-syntonizer component, an LCD screen and an electrical supply unit, which are all detachable.

Image stabilizer (1990)

The Panasonic PalmCorder NV-S1E was the first mini-camcorder equipped with a Digital Image Stabilizer (DES). The advantage of this system is that it dramatically reduces picture shake when shooting and, due to an integrated microprocessor, compensates electronically for unstable hand movement, which is considerable with this type of very compact apparatus.

Video Lens (VL) (1991)

In 1991 the Japanese manufacturing giants, Canon, Hitachi, Matsushita, Panasonic and Sony, agreed to adopt a common lens mount called Video Lens (VL). This move was aimed at equipping camcorders with interchangeable lenses.

Double image stabilizer (1992)

The Mitsubishi CX7 is a small pocket camcorder in the C-VHS-C format. To avoid trembles and shakes while shooting, it has a double stabilizer that measures and corrects irregularities along the vertical and horizontal axes of the image.

Dual usage (1992)

The Sharp VLMX 7S is a very small camcorder that benefits from dual uses. It can be used to vary the angle and depth of the image being taken without changing position. It can even combine two recordings in a single image and thus give the impression that the subject is being filmed from two separate cameras.

Videodiscs

Phonovision (1927)

John Logie Baird (Great Britain, 1888–1946) performed the first experiment using video signals on a disc to store images in 1928. He called his system *phonovision*.

Phonovoid (1965)

Phonovoid was launched by Westinghouse in 1965. The phonovoid method allowed storage of up to 200 still images per disc.

Teledec (1970)

The first commercial videodisc, the Teledec, was the product of a joint Anglo-German venture between AEG-Telefunken and Decca. Teledec was marketed in 1974, but proved to be a commercial failure.

Laservision (1972)

An improved version of laser-read videodisc technology developed by the Dutch company Philips N.V., laservision was first produced in 1972. The product was launched in the United States in 1980, and in Europe in 1982.

Selectavision (1974)

RCA developed a capacitance reading system called Selectavision in 1974. Launched in 1980, Selectavision was a commercial failure.

VHD (1978)

The Japanese company JVC developed a third videodisc system, the VHD (Very High Density) in 1978. VHD embodied a middle ground of technology between the Selectavision and Laservision systems. It was first marketed in 1983.

AHD (1983)

JVC developed the AHD (Audio High Density) system in 1983. Originally designed for audio-digital recording, the AHD procedure is completely compatible with the VHD because of its decoder.

Laservision (1984)

Sony and Hitachi produced the Laservision system in 1984. The first laservision videodisc with digital sound was produced by Pioneer. Not a popular success, the system is mainly used by "professional" users.

CDV (1987)

In 1987 Sony and Philips announced the development of the CDV (Compact Disc Video). The CDV offers a remarkably clear picture and digital hi-fi sound.

Laserdisc (1990)

A new application of the CDV, the first laserdiscs were marketed in 1990. The laserdisc has been used mainly as a medium for motion pictures.

COMMUNICATION CABLES

Cable television (1927)

The first cable television transmission was carried out in the United States by the Bell Telephone Co. in 1927. The experiment took place between Washington and New York. A Nipkow scanning disc was used for the transmission and another for the reception.

This cable technique was then taken up again for the purposes of reaching those areas without access to traditional Herzian transmission.

In 1949 a small town in Oregon suffered from bad reception of programs transmitted from Seattle because of the mountains that surrounded it. It was decided that a large aerial would be installed on high ground. From there a cable network transmitted programs, without any risk of parasitic oscillation.

It was not until the 1960s that cable television experienced real growth in the United States and Canada. Today over 22 million American households subscribe to cable systems (paid by subscription).

The development of optical fibers in place of traditional coaxial cable (invented by Affel and Espenschied [U.S.] in 1929) makes it possible to go from passive viewing of programs to active audience participation—users are able to choose their programs and to participate directly in their contents (quick surveys, questionnaires, games, etc.).

First transatlantic telephone cable (1956)

On September 26, 1956 the first cable telephonic transatlantic link was made. The cable made it possible to transmit 588 conversations—more than all radiotelephone traffic in the previous 10 days. In order to carry out this operation successfully, AT&T, the British GPO and the Canadian company Canadian Overseas Telecommunications worked together.

First fiber-optic transatlantic cable (1988)

The first fiber-optic transatlantic cable, the TAT-8, has linked the United States with Great Britain and France since 1988. The cable is 4,114 miles long and carries television, telephone and data processing signals. The partners in this venture are DGT (France), AT&T, and British Telecom International. It can handle 37,500 simultaneous conversations.

Communication Satellites

Telecommunications satellite (1960)

In 1945 the science fiction writer Arthur C. Clarke published the first theoretical analysis of an artificial satellite system, in the radio buffs' magazine *Wireless World*.

On August 12, 1960 NASA launched its first American telecommunications satellite, called *Echo 1*. It was simply a 98-ft-diameter balloon, the metallic surface of which reflected radio signals without either magnifying or diverting them. Unfortunately, *Echo 1* did not withstand meteorites for very long.

Telstar (1962)

On July 10, 1962 NASA launched the first truly efficient civil telecommunications satellite on behalf of AT&T: Telstar.

Satellite television (1962)

There are two types of satellites used in television: direct television satellites (DBS) and telecommunications satellites (still called "point-to-point" satellites), which are now very widespread. The first of these was Telstar, which was launched in 1962. However, the line between these two types of satellites is becoming blurred.

Teletext (1963)

Teletext, or broadcast videography, is a system for transmitting data sent as television signals to television receivers. The system is based on a demonstration that was made in 1963 by three French engineers, which showed the possibility of transmitting information using the vertical intervals between the video lines.

WHAT ON EARTH?

NOT ALL INVENTIONS CHANGE OUR LIVES, SOME JUST MAKE US SCRATCH OUR HEADS.

THE TANTRUM BRICK

If you have had it with the caliber of television programming you're watching, then William Johnson's latest invention is for you. It's the Tantrum brick: you pick it up, throw it at the TV set and presto, the TV switches itself off. There is no damage to the screen because the brick is made of foam. A micro-transmitter inside the brick transmits the message to the receiver (in this case the TV set), which picks up the signal. (Scientific Applied Research)

THE RECYCLED PENCIL

▲ Thousands of products have been proven detrimental to the environment in recent years. One of the more innovative environmentally conscious new inventions is the American EcoWriter pencil. Seen here with a standard pencil, the EcoWriter barrel is made entirely from recycled cardboard and newspaper fiber. It even has a green eraser. (Faber-Castell Corp.)

KARAOKE LASERDISC

Karaoke is a Japanese institution that is becoming increasingly popular in the United States. Karaoke systems are found mainly in bars, where patrons relax by singing their favorite songs, accompanied by a backing track and helped by a teleprompter. In 1991 Pioneer launched a Karaoke system that operates with a laserdisc. The audio/video amplifier provides an output of 2 x 120 W and has three microphone sockets. It also offers digital functions such as echo and reverberation effects.

BOOKSTAND FOR READING IN BED

Most people enjoy reading in bed, but often find it impossible to establish a comfortable position. Brothers Ernst and Thiemo Rosler (Germany) may have found the answer—an adjustable bookstand. It is a sort of lectern attached to a sliding and adjustable bar, suspended in the air, which makes it possible to read without getting tired from holding the book, even for long periods.

THE TWIN PHONE

▲ In 1989 Swatch, the famous watch manufacturer, introduced the Swatch Twin Phone. This phone enables two people using one phone set in one place to talk to a third person in another place. (P. Macor)

New ideas that may change the way we live

DIGITAL PRESS

In April 1992 a new digital printing press, the Electrobook Press, was unveiled. It was developed by a partnership of three companies: press manufacturer AM International Inc.; Printer R.R. Donnelly & Sons; and publisher McGraw-Hill. The press operates using digital electronic imaging and electrophotographic printing. Dubbed "electrostatic imaging," the system does not require printing plates and can print two sides of the paper simultaneously. The speed of the press is relatively slow, 350 feet per minute, and it is expected that it will be used for textbooks, business forms and similar mass-quantity items rather than newspapers, which require much faster presses.

IRIDIUM SYSTEM

The goal of the Iridium system is for users to be able to call from and to anywhere in the world, even from the middle of the Sahara Desert, from a Pacific Atoll, of from the heart of the Amazon rain forest. Under development by the electronics company Motorola, the Iridium system will be an international numerical communications system that utilizes satellite technology. Small portable terminals will link with a network of 77 orbiting satellites to ensure vocal communication, telecopy, data transmission and radio transmission to and from all points of the globe. Intended to be marketed to government agencies and multinational corporations, Iridium is not expected to be operational before the 21st century.

The CDL 300.
(Microcom Inc.)

CELLULAR DATA LINK

In 1992 Microcom launched the CDL 300, a cellular phone made by Mitsubishi with a Microcom modem housed inside it for linking portable computer users to their main office network system. The CDL 300 plugs into standard laptops and allows data transmission over the cellular network from almost any location.

UNDERWATER FIBER OPTICS

In June 1992 AT&T reported the successful testing of a new fiber-optic communications system that could revolutionize underwater cable system technology. Developed in conjunction with Japan's Kokusai Denshin Denwa Co. (KDD), the system, when operational, will be capable of carrying 600,000 simultaneous calls across the Pacific Ocean. The system uses wavelength division multiplexing (WDM) and optical amplifiers to boost light-wave signals traveling through the fiber. WDM involves the transmission of light pulses over various wavelengths of light. Optical amplifiers are spliced segments of optical fiber containing the rare earth element erbium. These amplifiers are set in the normal glass fiber system at regular intervals. Tests have been conducted with the amplifiers at distances ranging from 43 miles apart to 521 miles.

SPIRAL-MODE ANTENNA

Prof. Victor K. Tripp and Johnson K.H. Wang have applied for a patent for a spiral-mode antenna that eliminates the absorbent cavity that makes standard spiral antennas bulky and limits their application. The Wang-Tripp antenna is a mere three inches in diameter and less than a third of an inch deep. Among its numerous possible applications, this antenna can be molded to the surface of cars and aircraft, expanding the scope of radio and cellular transmissions to these vehicles.

THE CONFIDENTIAL FAX

Messages sent via fascimile machine are fast, inexpensive and convenient. They are also, however, readily available to anyone scanning the fax tray. Inventor Peter Castro received a U.S. patent in 1992 for a secure fax message system that may prove to be a practical solution to the problem of fax confidentiality. Castro's system, inspired by secret telegrams of the 1940s, sends a message printed in two layers. The bottom layer contains the message, while the top layer is imprinted with a pattern that obscures the message beneath. A custom preprinted label printed on the bottom layer is all that is exposed to the reader. The system even increases print quality, as the bottom layer uses plain paper that produces a finer image. Castro hopes to market his invention in 1993.

HIGH DEFINITION TELEVISION (HDTV)

Electronics companies in the United States, Japan and Europe have been developing HDTV technology for a number of years. The basic goal of this research is to produce a cost-effective, efficient television that produces a sharper image definition, a larger format and digital stereo by increasing the number of lines on the screen from 525 (NTSC standard) to as many as 1,250.

The economic stakes are considerable—700 million television sets will have to be changed in a market estimated at $200 billion by the year 2000. Already, measures are being considered in Europe and the United States that would protect domestic companies from overseas competition. The European Community has proposed a common standard transmission signal: the D2MAC Paquet invented by Telefunken in the mid-1970s. The D2MAC system is being upgraded to carry 1,250 lines, and will be known as HDMAC. The Japanese system MUSE carries 1,125 lines and will have to be adapted to work on European television sets. In the United States, lobbying groups have called for a U.S. standard similar to the European system that gives domestic manufacturers an advantage over their Japanese competition.

In the United States the debate also centers on the type of system being developed. Research underway at MIT has focused on the development of digitalization of the TV image. The signal is transformed into digital form for processing by computer. The compression and decompression techniques used in real time make it possible to reduce the amount of data needed by the digital memory for decoding and transmission. A few square inches of a microchip card will be sufficient to hold a television tuner that could easily be integrated into a computer. Experts claim this system is superior to HDTV, as it has a resolution of 2,000 lines; however, the technology is enormously expensive and federal funding has proved controversial. Both Philips and Thomson have made agreements to work on digitalization projects with American companies.

The implementation of HDTV systems may not be far off. Philips claims that it will have its version ready by 1994. Digitalization technology, however, is still in its infancy, and the earliest forecast for implementation is 1997.

CALCULATING MACHINES

The abacus (3000 B.C.)

The abacus, ancestor of the calculator and of the computer, is of Babylonian origin and dates from around 3000 B.C. The word *abacus* is derived from the Semitic term for dust. In its old form the abacus was in fact a slab of wood covered with fine sand on which figures were written with a stylus. The abacus later took the form of a bead frame. Nowadays, the bead frame is still used in India, China (*suan pan*), Japan (*soroban*) and Russia (*tschoty*). It is possible to perform four mathematical operations on an abacus: addition, subtraction, multiplication and division. The latter two by repetitive addition and subtraction.

Arithmetical machine (1624)

Wilhelm Schickard (Germany), a professor at the University of Heidelberg, built, in 1624, the first arithmetical machine capable of performing the four basic operations. He called it a calculator clock.

Pascaline (1642)

In 1642 Blaise Pascal (France, 1623–62) made the first calculating machine, which was the true ancestor of our modern pocket calculator. Pascal was a highly gifted young man, for he invented this machine at the age of 19, while working on conic sections, to help his father collect taxes in the central region of France. Counting whole numbers, cogwheels in a mechanical gear system performed additions or subtractions that could involve up to eight columns of figures at a time. This machine, which Pascal named the Pascaline in 1645, worked in the same way as a car odometer.

Stepped reckoner (1671)

In 1671 Gottfried Wilhelm von Leibnitz (Germany, 1646–1716), the philosopher and mathematician, invented a mechanical calculator

Jacquard's loom was the first machine to use numerical control. (Josse)

The modern pocket calculator traces its origin to Pascal's calculating machine, built in 1642. (Le Livre Mondial des Inventions)

that was similar to the Pascaline, but more refined. Pascal's machine could only count. Leibnitz's could multiply, divide and calculate square roots. However, both of these calculators were based on the same mechanical technique: "single step" calculation. They repeated the same operation, such as, for example, a series of additions. Many modern computer programs also work in this way.

Numerical control (1805)

Without realizing the importance of his invention, Joseph-Marie Jacquard (France, 1752–1834) used numerical control in the operation of a mechanical loom.

The Jacquard loom was, in 1805, the first machine to use a punched hole in a card to represent a number and thus control the pattern of its weave.

Previous page: A microphotograph of a human neuron developing on an integrated circuit. (Cosmos/Synaptery Science Photo Lab.)

Analytical engine (1835)

In 1835 Charles Babbage (Great Britain, 1792–1871), a professor of mathematics at Cambridge University, presented the concept of an "analytical engine." This machine, which was completely new, was in fact the world's first digital computer.

The first programs were written for this machine by Ada, Countess Lovelace (1815–52). Unfortunately, 19th-century technology was not sufficiently advanced to put most of Lovelace's and Babbage's brilliant concepts into practice. Only a rudimentary version of the analytical engine was built.

Electric totalizer (1886)

Hermann Hollerith (U.S., 1860–1929), a statistician, invented punch-card data processing to solve problems in compiling the 1890 census. In 1886, when he was working on the census, he tried placing punched cards over little bowls of mercury. He then dropped metal pins through the holes into the mercury, to complete an electrical circuit. This system of electromechanical detection enabled Hollerith's totalizer to classify data and enter it into a ledger. His systems were put to good use during the 1890 census.

Hollerith went on to develop punching and sorting machines, which were precursors of today's computer peripherals. In 1911 he helped set up the Computing Tabulating Recording Co., which became the International Business Machines Corporation (IBM) in 1957.

COMPUTERS

The Z1 (1931)

Early in the 1930s the engineer Konrad Zuse (Germany) made computers that operated in binary mode. The Z1 was followed by the mechanical Z2, then by the Z3, a relay computer that could perform a multiplication in three to four seconds.

Zuse was hindered by the slowness of his machines, and in 1940 he suggested to the German government that electromechanical relays should be replaced by electronic tubes. But Hitler, certain that the war would be won, reduced investment in this area. Zuse continued working and by 1944 was developing the Z4, but all his machines were destroyed in the bombardment of Berlin.

Binary computer (1939)

The first binary computer was made in 1939 by the mathematician George R. Stibitz (U.S.) at Bell Laboratories and was called the Model 1 Relay Computer or Complex Number Calculator.

It consisted of a logical mechanism in which the data output consisted of the sum of the data entered. Stibitz used telephone relays in his computer, which functioned in the binary "all or nothing" mode (in other words, it only used the digits 1 and 0), with the aim of developing

a universal computer. He assembled the computer in one weekend, using a few discarded relays, two lightbulbs and fragments of a tobacco jar.

The ABC tube computer (1939)

The idea was already there: a German, Schreyer (a friend of Zuse's), had obtained his doctorate by demonstrating the importance of vacuum tubes in digital calculation; but it was mathematician and physicist John Vincent Atanasoff who was the first to apply it. Assisted by one of his students, Clifford Berry, this professor at Iowa State College built a binary machine designed to solve the complex equations used in physics. It became known as the ABC (Atanasoff Berry Computer) and had no rivals until 1942. However, since neither Atanasoff nor Iowa State College registered a patent, the invention of the tube computer was long attributed to John W. Mauchly and J. Presper Eckert, although these two did in fact draw heavily on the ABC to build the ENIAC (*Electronic Numerical Integrator and Calculator*).

Colossus (1943)

Right from the start of World War II, British number theorists tried to find a way of decoding German messages. They put Dr. Alan Mathison Turing at the head of a team charged with solving this problem.

Before the war Turing had clarified the notion of calculability and adapted the notion of algorithms to calculate certain functions. He

had thus postulated the Turing machine, which was theoretically capable of calculating any calculable function. In 1941 the British government funded the project and in 1943 at Bletchley Park, England, the first electromechanical computer, Colossus, went into operation. It was formulated by Prof. Max H.A. Newman and built by T.H. Flowers. This computer contained more than 2,000 electronic tubes and could process 5,000 characters a second.

It was a specialized machine, which did its job very well: right until the end of the war, the British government was kept informed about German plans thanks to the decoding powers of Colossus.

Harvard Mark 1 (1944)

The first fully automatic calculator in the world was Harvard Mark 1, at that time called the IBM Automatic Sequence Controlled Calculator. The machine was presented by Howard Aiken of Harvard University, and its development had been encouraged and financed by T.J. Watson, then president of IBM. It weighed five metric tons and contained 500 miles of wire.

This calculator improved on Babbage's dream and included two innovations: a clock intended to synchronize the diverse sequences of operations, and the use of registers—an idea that was picked up by every other manufacturer.

A register is a device used by the computer to store information for high-speed access. The bits of data stored in the register could represent a binary number, an alphabetic character or a computer instruction.

The first fully automatic calculator was the Harvard Mark I, built by Howard Aiken in 1944. (IBM Corp.)

Universal electronic computer (1946)

After signing a contract in 1943 with the Ballistic Research Laboratory, John W. Mauchly and J. Presper Eckert (both U.S.), two scientists from the University of Pennsylvania, set to work. In 1946 they presented ENIAC (the acronym for *Electronic Numerical Integrator and Calculator*), the first universal computer. It weighed 30 metric tons, occupied a surface area of 1,720 sq ft and contained 18,000 electronic tubes. By means of electronics, it brought speed to the world of computers. It was used to calculate ballistic trajectories.

CONCEPTS

Algorithm (18th century B.C.)

In the 18th century B.C., Babylonian mathematicians of the time of Hammurabi formulated algorithms in order to solve certain numerical problems. An algorithm is a series of elementary actions designed to solve a problem.

The idea of mechanizing algorithms goes back to the year 1000, particularly to the work of Gerbert d'Aurillac (France, *c.* 938–1003), who became Pope Sylvester II.

A computer program is the translation of an algorithm into a well-defined language.

Mechanized calculation (1617)

In 1617 John Napier (Great Britain, 1550–1617) found a way of expressing division by a series of subtractions, and multiplication by a series of additions. He thus became the inventor of logarithms.

Napier's technique, which made it possible to perform any calculation simply by repeating the same operation several times, opened the way to calculation using mechanical means.

Computer program (1835)

While Charles Babbage was designing his analytic engine, Ada, Countess Lovelace (1815–52), was writing programs for it.

In fact it has recently be revealed that without the help of the Countess (who was the daughter of the famous poet Lord Byron), Babbage's machine would certainly not have been built.

The Countess Lovelace was thus the first programmer. Her work foreshadowed such techniques as subroutines and automatic programming.

Coding (19th century)

The invention of coding can be attributed to Hermann Hollerith (U.S.). The coding of punched cards is often called the Hollerith code, in memory of this scientific forerunner. Later notable contributions were made by Emile Baudot (France), who invented the telegraphic code that was patented in 1874. However, coding goes back to the first mechanisms to use punched cards: Jacquard's looms and Babbage's machine.

Binary logic (1859)

George Boole (Great Britain, 1815–64), a logician and mathematician, developed symbolic logic and, specifically, binary logic operations such as AND, OR, etc. Boole's rigorous system makes it possible to mechanize logic, operating with 0 and 1 only: 0 meaning off and 1 meaning on. This is how electronic logic circuits work in computers today.

Cybernetics (1940)

Cybernetics, as a science, was invented by Norbert Wiener (U.S.) in 1940, but the word was not coined until 1948 by Wiener and A. Rosenblueth. It comes from the Greek word *kubernétés* meaning a steersman or pilot.

Cybernetics is the study of automatic communication and control mechanisms in machines as well as in humans.

Neurocomputer science (1940s)

Neurocomputer science, the science of computers whose architecture is modeled on that of the brain, began in the 1940s. The first machine to be built was the Perceptron in 1949, which was designed by Frank Rosenblatt (U.S.). During the 1960s, engineers switched the focus of their research to artificial intelligence, which seemed a more promising field. Due to the work of John Hopefield (U.S.) in the 1980s and the discovery of learning algorithms, there has been a resurgence in neurocomputer research in recent years.

The importance of neuronal computers lies in the fact that they are able to work on imprecise data, e.g., the recognition of badly written manuscript figures, and they are capable of learning. Their "neurons" (simple components) are all interconnected and work in parallel, whereas traditional computers function sequentially—that is, one item of information follows another.

"Fail Safe" computing (1946)

A highly accurate computer, the BINAC (*Binary Automatic Computer*) was developed in 1946 by J.P. Eckert and J.W. Mauchly (both U.S.). It consisted of two computers that simultaneously carried out the same calculations, whose results were then compared. The BINAC was the first computer to work in real time.

Stored program computer (1948)

John von Neumann joined the team at the Institute of Advanced Study in Princeton, N.J., and it was here that the idea of a machine with a stored program was conceived. In 1946 Neumann, with Arthur W. Burks and H.H. Goldstine, published "Preliminary Discussion of the Logical Design of an Electronic Computing Instrument." This was a crucial document in the history of computer science: the program became a sequence of numbers stored in the computer's memory. EDVAC (Electronic Discrete Variable Automatic Computer) was capable of operating on and therefore changing the stored instructions, and was thus able to alter its own program.

The first machine to incorporate von Neumann's principles was built at Manchester University in 1948. In 1950 the first computer intended for business use came onto the market: the *Universal Automatic Computer* (UNIVAC I).

Byte (1961)

A byte is a group of eight bits, or eight binary elements. The byte appeared as a basic unit of information on the Stretch, a high-powered, transistorized computer built by IBM in 1961. Today the byte is universally used to represent a character (a letter or figure).

Computer capacity is usually given in kilobytes (one kb equals 1,024 bytes), megabytes (one Mb equals 1,024 kb), gigabytes (one Gb equals 1,024 Mb) or terabytes (one Tb equals 1,024 Gb).

Time-sharing system (1961)

A team headed by F. Corbato at the Massachusetts Institute of Technology designed, in 1961, the Compatible Time Sharing System (CTSS) for the exploitation of IBMs 700 and 7090. The first time-sharing system to be marketed was the PDP1 in 1962.

Work stations (1980)

A work station is a machine in the form of a microcomputer, designed to carry out a precise function—calculation or drawing (which requires a powerful processing capacity)—and linked to a central system and shared peripherals (file storage, flatbed plotters). The first work station was introduced by the American company Apollo in 1980.

SUPERCOMPUTERS

Cray X-MP (1982)

In 1982 Steve Chen, a Taiwanese immigrant to the United States, where he did his engineering studies, designed the world's first computer featuring parallel architecture, the Cray X-MP.

The Crays were overtaken by Control Data's Cyber 205, which performs 700 million operations a second.

Seymour Cray regained the advantage with the Cray 2, unveiled in 1986. It has a two gigabyte central memory and performs 1.6 billion operations a second. Its architecture is very compact to facilitate the movement of information, and to stop it from overheating it is submerged in a fluorocarbon fluid.

Connection machine (1987)

This fascinating supercomputer is the product of six years of research led by David Hills. Backed by a team of people who left MIT (which has continued to support them), he set up the Thinking Machines Corp. The Connection Machine works using parallel architecture, and it contains up to 64,000 processors. In

CRAY-1 Computer (1976): Seymour R. Cray

Cray-1 Computer System. (Cray Research Inc.)

When people with imagination, persistence, and technical prowess share a common vision, the result is often a head-to-head competition that yields a succession of inventions. Nowhere is this illustrated as clearly as in the computer industry.

The first modern machine for general-purpose computing was ENIAC (*E*lectronic *N*umerical *I*ntegrator *a*nd *C*alculator), a 1946 invention that weighed 30 tons, contained 500 miles of wire, and performed 100,000 operations per second. From then on, computers got smaller and faster at a rate that boggles the mind.

Transistors came along in 1947. Early computer builders used them as switches or amplifiers. Ten years later, American engineer Jack Kilby created the first integrated electronic circuits. The year 1971 saw production of microprocessor chips—tiny elements that form the core of every computer system.

Seymour Cray snapped up silicon chips and stuffed them into his 1976 computer, the Cray-1 Supercomputer. Cray had long been involved in the smaller, faster, better progression of computing. In 1957 he was one of the founders of Control Data Corporation (CDC), and designed the company's most successful large-scale computers. By 1972, Cray had been showered with awards for his contributions to the field. It was then that he left CDC to found Cray Research, Inc., to design and build the CRAY-1.

The CRAY-1 found a multitude of applications in many areas of research, including weather forecasting, petroleum research, automotive engineering, astronomy, economic analysis, medical research, seismic analysis, and particle physics. Before the CRAY-1's invention, solutions to the problems in these applications were not possible. The CRAY-1 allowed great quantities of information to be processed quickly and economically and has been invaluable in solving complex calculations.

Technological growth in silicon chips and other computer components has allowed for growth that is literally exponential. At this writing, the latest Cray computer, the CRAY 4-MP C90, had 250 times the memory of the CRAY-1.

themselves, none of these is particularly powerful, but they are all connected to each other. This provides incredible powers of calculation: more than 2 billion operations per second for the most powerful version.

Cray Y-MP (1988)

At the beginning of 1988, Cray, which still dominates the market with 60 percent of supercomputers in service (since Control Data left the field open to Cray Research by abandoning the ETA 10 and the supercomputer market), presented the Cray Y-MP. It is capable of performing 2 billion operations per second and costs $20 million. It is used by NASA, for instance, and in the biotechnologic, aerospace and chemical industries, which have applications that involve complex three-dimensional simulations requiring enormous computational workloads.

Supercomputers with superconductors (1989)

Superconductors allow the passage of electrons without resistance or heating, which are two of the fundamental problems for computer designers. On December 13, 1989, two Japanese scientists announced that they had succeeded in using superconductive materials to make microprocessors and memories; the latter must be kept at a temperature of –452° F.

These components are based on the Josephson effect: according to the physicist Brian Josephson (Great Britain), a current can pass between two superconductors if they are placed sufficiently close together.

Optical computer (1990)

A hand-held computer, weighing a few grams and containing billions of pieces of data, is now theoretically possible thanks to an invention by Alan Huang. This engineer at AT&T, the telecommunications giant, uses photons—light particles—to carry data, a technique that makes it possible to achieve calculation speeds a thousand times greater than that of usual electronic transport, without wasting energy.

It is not yet known whether this process—a prototype of which was presented in 1990—poses insurmountable technical problems. An answer is expected in the 21st century.

MICROCOMPUTERS

Micral (1971)

The first microcomputer in the world was French. At the end of 1971 François Gernelle, an engineer with R2E, designed it to respond to the French agricultural research institute's need for automatic regulation. R2E's chief, André Truong Trong Thi, a Frenchman of Vietnamese origins, was won over by the invention and decided to manufacture computers built around a single microprocessor. This very first microcomputer was called Micral. When

R2E was bought by Bull, all that remained of Micral was the brand name.

Electronic pocket calculator (1972)

The first electronic pocket calculator was developed by J.S. Kilby, J.D. Merryman and J.H. van Tassel (all U.S.) of Texas Instruments. The patent was applied for in 1972 and granted in 1978. The calculator is preserved at the Smithsonian Institution in Washington.

In 1973 Hewlett-Packard brought out pocket calculators that were programmed to suit the needs of a particular field (for example, finance or economics). In 1976 the same American company marketed the first programmable calculators, which were the true pocket computers.

Altair 8800 (1974)

Many companies have argued over who launched the first American microcomputer. But the one that really set things in motion was the Altair, produced by the company MITS, which was set up by H. Edward Roberts. In December 1974 the magazine *Popular Electronics* published a bombshell of an article: readers were invited to buy through the mail a kit with which they could build themselves a real computer, based on Intel's 8080 microprocessor. It cost $397 and was extremely basic compared to today's microcomputers. It had 25 console switches that had to be moved in a cumbersome sequence in order to start the machine, and it had a 256 byte internal memory (2,000 times less than many of today's PCs). Nonetheless, 200 orders were received on the first day.

Apple II (1977)

The Apple II, brought out for the first time in the United States in May 1977, was the first commercial product of the legendary company founded by Steve Jobs and Stephen Wozniak (both U.S.). It was an improvement on the first Apple, of which about 100 had been manufactured the previous year and which was simply a kit sold directly to members of the Home-Brew Club, the first computing club in the United Sates. The big advantage of the Apple was its user-friendliness.

IBM PC (1981)

It was on August 12, 1981 that the number one company in world computer science announced its entry into the microcomputing market with the IBM PC. The arrival of this microcomputer, designed by a team of young computer scientists headed by Philip Estridge, created a real standard throughout the world.

Apple Macintosh (1984)

At the beginning of 1984 Apple presented the Macintosh, the most original microcomputer and the one most likely to revolutionize the way in which nonspecialist users interact with their machines. The Apple team that developed the Macintosh, personally led by Steve Jobs, picked up ideas that had been used in the same company's Lisa in 1983: a mouse, a high defi-

nition screen, and graphic symbols representing programs and data.

These techniques had been outlined several years earlier at Rank Xerox's PARC Laboratory. They saved the user from having to be concerned with the internal workings of the computer.

NeXT (1989)

After leaving Apple, Steve Jobs came up with a new computer aimed at academics and researchers. This machine looks like a black cube and is produced by his company, NeXT. It uses a Motorola 68030 microprocessor and four coprocessors and has the first erasable optical disk as its mass memory, with a capacity of 256 Mb (millions of bytes or characters). Jobs joined forces with powerful allies (notably IBM and Canon) before announcing in 1990 that they were bringing the first machines onto the market. These are now aimed at all businesses.

SOFTWARE

Microcomputer Operating Systems

Origins (1954)

An operating system is software (or a program) that is used not by the person using the computer, but by the computer itself. It comes between the machine's electronic circuits and the application software with which the user is in contact.

It acts like the conductor of an orchestra, coordinating the functioning of the computer's different elements. In microcomputing it is also a tool for standardization, since it enables any software to function (with some modifications) on several different computers, provided they use the same operating system. Each one is designed for a particular type of microprocessor. The first operating sytem dates back to large computers: Gene Amdahl designed it in 1954 on an IBM 704.

Unix (1970)

The Unix operating system grew out of research done at Bell Laboratories and at the University of California at Berkeley. It was originally designed for minicomputers by Ken Thompson and Dennis Ritchie. Today there are versions of it for almost every sort of machine, from portables to supercomputers. The name Unix itself dates from 1970, and the first version was marketed in 1975.

The main advantage of this rather complex operating system on a microcomputer is that it is multitask, which explains its growing share of the market.

CP/M (1974)

In 1974 Gary Kildall invented the first operating system for microcomputers, which was mar-

keted in 1976. He was working on assembling systems for components of different origins and found it a tedious chore having to rewrite all his programs every time he tried to read different floppy disks on the same central unit. The adaptor software that he wrote at the time was the core for the CP/M (Control Program for Microcomputing) operating system. For some reason, Kildall chose to give his company the grandiose name of Intergalactic Digital Research. The fact remains that CP/M rose to the rank of standard operating system for eight-bit professional microcomputers equipped with a Zilog Z 80 microprocessor.

However, when IBM approached Intergalactic Digital Research to design the operating system for its PC (personal computer), the firm rejected the secrecy clause, thus unwittingly choosing the path that would lead it into decline. The market was taken over by Microsoft, which designed MS-DOS.

MS-DOS (1980)

In 1980 IBM asked Microsoft to provide it with an operating system for its future microcomputer, the PC. Bill Gates, Microsoft's owner, then bought Seattle Computer Products' Tim Patterson's 16-bit operating system SCP-DOS. Having adapted it, he christened it MS-DOS and delivered it to IBM (which calls it PC-DOS). MS-DOS has since been considerably improved and is today the most widely used operating system for professional microcomputers, since it is used by all IBM compatibles.

It was conceived and jointly launched by the two companies, under the direction of Bill Gates, to work with the PS/2.

OS/2 (1990)

In 1990 IBM launched OS/2 as a successor to MS-DOS. Designed to facilitate multi-tasking and client/server computing, OS/2 replaces the basic MS-DOS end-user interface with a graphical user interface (GUI). IBM had produced the initial version of OS/2 with Microsoft, but a split in their business relationship has led Microsoft to develop a competing operating system which will be known as Windows-NT. This is expected to be available in 1993.

Interface Software

Visi-On (1982)

The American company Visicorp was the first to come up with the idea of integrated software. Visi-On, which was first launched in November 1982, consisted of an integrating module onto which the required applications modules, such as word processing, spreadsheet, graphics, or file management applications, could be grafted. Visi-On could only use applications specifically designed for it, and ultimately failed.

Windows (1985)

This was launched in November 1985 by Microsoft. It required more than 50 person-

```
┌──────────────────────────────────────────────────────────────────┐
│                          MS-DOS Shell                              │
│  File   Options   View   Tree   Help              ▶                │
│  C:\DOS                                                            │
│  ⊟A   ⊟B   ■C   RAMD   RAM      NETH   NETI                         │
│ ┌──────────────────────┐ ┌─────┬────────────────────────────────┐ │
│ │    Directory Tree     │ │  Index       │    C:\DOS\*.*          │ │
│ │ 🗁 C:\                 │ │Keyboard    AMDRIVE.SYS   5,873  02-21-91│
│ │   🗁 ASTUFF            │ │Shell Basics BACKUP .BAT     214  02-22-91│
│ │     🗁 BONJOUR         │ │Commands    EADME  .TXT  26,992  02-21-91│
│ │     🗁 FANCY           │ │Procedures  EBUILD .COM  17,504  09-09-90│
│ │     🗁 NANCY           │ │Using Help  ECOVER .EXE   9,130  02-21-91│
│ │   🗁 DEMO              │ │            EMLINE .BAS  12,314  02-21-91│
│ │   🗁 DOS               │ │About Shell REPLACE.EXE  20,210  02-21-91│
│ │   🗁 ESTIMATE          │ │            RESTORE.EXE  38,262  02-21-91│
│ │     🗁 FY91            │ │         SELECT .HLP  28,695  11-30-88│
│ │       🗁 BUDGET91      │ │         SELECT .PRT   1,329  11-30-88│
│ │   🗁 FONTS             │ │         SETVER .EXE  12,007  02-21-91│
│ │   🗁 GRAPHS           ▼│ │         SHARE  .EXE  10,880  02-21-91 ▼│
│ ├──────────────────────┤ ├──────────────────────────────────────┤ │
│ │         Main          │ │          Active Task List            │ │
│ │ 🖵 Command Prompt    ▲│ │ Command Prompt                     ▲│ │
│ │ 🖵 MS-DOS Editor      │ │ Microsoft Works                     │ │
│ │ 🖵 MS-DOS QBasic      │ │ Microsoft Word                      │ │
│ │ 🖵 Microsoft Word     │ │ MS-DOS Editor                       │ │
│ │ 🖵 Microsoft Works    │ │                                     │ │
│ │ 🖵 Microsoft Learning DOS│ │                                  │ │
│ │ ⌨ Games              │ │                                     │ │
│ │ ⌨ Disk Utilities    ▼│ │                                    ▼│ │
│ └──────────────────────┘ └──────────────────────────────────────┘ │
│  F10=Actions   Shift+F9=Command Prompt                     3:49p   │
└──────────────────────────────────────────────────────────────────┘
```

MS-DOS is the most widely used microcomputer operating system. It was originally devised for the IBM PC. (Microsoft)

years of work. In April 1987 it was adopted as the standard integrator by IBM.

Windows 3-0 (1990)

Launched with great ceremony by Bill Gates on May 22, 1990, this integrating software makes it possible to use IBM PCs and compatibles with as much ease as an Apple; the different programs or options appear in windows on the screen, and can be called up using the keyboard. It is multitask and can even be used with some application softwares that were not specifically designed for it.

Windows 3-1 (1992)

This new model of the Windows system was launched in 1992. Windows 3-1 adds graphics and sound improvements to previous versions, making it a real multimedia tool.

Languages (Mainframe and Microcomputers)

All software, of whatever type, is written using a programming language, which has its own vocabulary (its instructions list) and syntax. The most basic language (from which all others are ultimately derived) is machine language, a series of binary or hexadecimal numbers that are directly comprehensible to the computer but hard for the programmer to manipulate.

Assembler (1950)

Assemblers are types of language close to machine language, but at a higher level, therefore easier to use. They are specific to a particular computer or microprocessor. Signs of the first assembler can be found in 1950 in the EDSAC, one of the ancestors of the large computers of today, which was developed in Cambridge, England, by M.V. Wilkes' team. The first commercial assembler was the SAP (Symbolic

Assembly Program), which was developed by the United Aircraft Corporation and installed on an IBM 704.

Artificial intelligence programming languages (1956)

Logical reasoning and formal calculus have led to entirely new programming methods. Today more than a hundred languages are used in the field of artificial intelligence (AI).

The first AI programming language, IPL (Information Processing Language), was invented in 1956 by scientists A. Newell, D. Shaw and H. Simon (all U.S.). It was developed specifically to write the LT (Logic Theorist) program, capable of resolving mathematical logic problems.

LISP (1958)

Although old by computer standards, LISP is the most commonly used language in artificial intelligence. As early as 1958, J. McCarthy had developed the particular concept of list processing that forms the basis of this language, whose name is a contraction of "list" and "processing." Since LISP needs a lot of memory, it generally requires fairly large computers to run properly, but microcomputer-based versions have been written.

COBOL (1959)

It was at a meeting at the University of Pennsylvania on April 8, 1959 that COBOL (*Common Business Oriented Language*) was launched. COBOL was designed as a common language for business applications that would not be directly associated with any manufacturer. Although a number of engineers were involved in the project, Capt. Grace M. Hopper (U.S., 1900–91) of the U.S. Navy is generally regarded as "the mother of COBOL." She invented Flow-Matic, the first data-processing compiler, without which COBOL could not have existed.

BASIC (1965)

Invented in 1965 at Dartmouth College, Hanover, N.H. by Thomas E. Kurtz and John G. Kemeny, BASIC was originally designed to help students to learn programming. BASIC stands for "*Beginners All-purpose Symbolic Instruction Code*." It was developed at a time when microcomputers did not exist and was adapted for use on them in 1974 by Bill Gates and Paul Allen, the founders of Microsoft. Today BASIC is the standard language of all home and office microcomputing, and its reputation as a beginner's language with little power is becoming increasingly unjustified.

Pascal (1969)

Named after the French mathematician, Pascal was developed in 1969 in the United States by Niklaus Wirth. The idea governing its design was to give programming students their own language, which was well structured and would instill good writing habits. It is more powerful than BASIC and is often used in microcomputing, in universities, and to write wide-circulation professional software.

C (1972)

This language is rapidly gaining popularity in the development of wide-distribution software applications. C was created in 1972 at Bell Laboratories by Dennis Ritchie—one of the inventors of the Unix operating systems—specifically to help the development of Unix. C has the innovative feature of mixing high-level code (which is easy to manipulate) with low-level code (which is efficient). It is based on BCPL, a language developed at the Massachusetts Institute of Technology and at Cambridge University in England.

PROLOG (1973)

One of the main languages adapted to artificial intelligence is French. PROLOG was designed in 1973 by Alain Colmerauer and his team at the University of Luminy-Marseilles, France. Its basic principle, which draws on mathematical logic, was revolutionary: instead of telling the computer how to solve a given problem—as happens with traditional languages, which are called procedural—the programmer simply sets out the data for the problem. PROLOG then gets on with finding the solution. Although PROLOG can function on supercomputers, it has recently come into use on microcomputers.

Ada (1979)

Ada was developed in 1979 after five years of effort by a team from CIL-Honeywell-Bull, headed by Jean Ichbiach (France).

This language takes its name from Ada, Countess Lovelace (1815–52), who may be regarded as the first programmer.

Ada has become a world standard. It is in general use for military and space applications, air control, etc.

Alsys, the company set up by Ichbiach in 1980, is involved in microcomputers too, and in 1987 produced Ada compilers for them.

Postscript (1985)

It was the American company Adobe Systems that developed the page description language Postscript, which was first used in microcomputing in Apple's Laserwriter printer, launched in January 1985.

It functions as an interface between the software and the laser printer, allowing the user to print directly onto the page. Its adoption by Apple, and then in March 1987 by IBM, ensured that it would be standard equipment.

Applications Software

The term applications software refers to programs that deliver a specific service directly to the user, such as word processing, printing paychecks or playing games.

Visicalc (1979)

Visicalc was invented by Dan Bricklin and Bob Frankston (both U.S.) and launched in 1979 on Apple computers. It was the world's first spreadsheet and an excellent example of how lively the minds of microcomputing inventors are. Certainly, before Visicalc, no programmer working on large computers had thought of such a program, which combines a table of figures with a table of formulas that determine the relations between the figures. As a result of these programs, it is possible to construct very complex models (for example, the provisional budget of a company), and to see in an instant what would happen if one of the hypotheses were changed: the spreadsheet automatically recalculates all the figures. Today spreadsheet programs are among the most widely used software on microcomputers, and there are hundreds of them. Similar tools have been developed for large computers.

Wordstar (1979)

The first major word-processing software for microcomputers was launched in 1979 by the American company Micropro. It is still on the

market today and has given rise to a whole host of programs of the same type.

dBase II (1980)

Launched in 1980 by the American firm Ashton-Tate, dBase II is the archetypal database management software for microcomputers. It makes it possible to classify, sort and select information according to numerous criteria. It was developed in October 1979 by C. Wayne Ratcliffe, who had marketed it under the name Vulcan before selling it to Ashton-Tate. New versions will soon be launched.

1-2-3 (1982)

This software, with its strange name, has given rise to a whole new generation of integrated software. It was designed by one man, Jonathan Sachs, and launched in October 1982 by the American company Lotus. Its particular feature is that it combines three functions in one microcomputer program. It is above all a very high-power spreadsheet, but is combined with a small file management facility and, most importantly, with a graphics module that makes it possible to visualize in curve form any group of figures presented in the spreadsheet. 1-2-3 is still one of the most widely used software products on PC compatibles.

Mac Paint (1984)

Written by Bill Atkinson in 1984, Mac Paint led to thousands of beginners' becoming interested in computers. This graphics software, specially designed for the Apple Macintosh, works on an instinctive basis: the user draws by moving the mouse on the desk after selecting one of the symbols—"pencil," "paintbrush," "spray" and even "eraser"—that are displayed on the screen and give lines of different appearance and thickness. The user simply selects a paint pot to color in a shape, the lasso to grasp part of the drawing and move it elsewhere, and so on. Since its creation, Mac Paint has had countless imitators.

Page Maker (1985)

On July 15, 1985 the American company Aldus perfected revolutionary software designed for the Apple Macintosh and called Page Maker. It was the first software to enable a single individual to write, lay out, paginate and print a newspaper or book, including illustrations, using only a microcomputer and a laser printer.

Since then the product has been much improved and, with version 3.0 in 1989, has become PC compatible.

Artificial Intelligence

Origins (c. 1953)

AI is a scientific discipline consisting of writing computer programs that attempt to model human intelligence. AI formalizes human knowledge and reasoning, whereas data processing merely manipulates information.

According to this definition, AI could date back to 450 B.C. when the Greek philosopher Socrates envisaged reducing all reasoning to a simple calculation in the form of something like geometry.

Fundamental papers relating to AI were published as early as 1953 in the United States. However, the term was used officially for the first time at the International Joint Conference on Artificial Intelligence held in Washington, D.C. in 1969.

Today, the most popular application of AI is in building expert systems.

Expert systems (1970s)

An expert system (ES) is a software program characterized by its ability to reason by logical inference starting from a problem set by the user. The system uses a base of knowledge and a set of rules called production rules, drawn up by a human expert.

In the early 1960s some researchers were already putting forward the idea that the laws of reason, combined with the power of a computer, could produce systems that go beyond the capacity of human experts. However, there are severe theoretical reservations.

The first operational ES appeared in the early 1970s. There are a great many of them today, in different domains.

Oldest expert system (1961)

In 1961 J.R. Slagle produced a thesis at the Massachusetts Institute of Technology on a heuristic program for solving problems related to symbolic mathematics. This was the beginning of SAINT (*Symbolic Automatic Integrator*), which culminated in MACSYMA, presented in 1971 by two MIT researchers, W.A. Martin and R.J. Fateman. Today an improved version of MACSYMA surpasses most human experts in performing symbolic differential and integral calculus. Today there are thousands of expert systems in such varied fields as medicine, chemistry, mining prospection, teaching, etc.

Fuzzy logic (1965)

Human speech is full of relative terms such as "quite good," "far," and "a little bit." Although these terms mean something to a human, a computer that understands only that 1 = yes and 0 = no finds them hard to comprehend. To fill this gap, Lofti Zadeh, a rsearcher at the University of California at Berkeley, invented Fuzzy Logic in 1965.

Zadeh's theory is based on the following principle: One doesn't say whether an element does or does not belong to a group but that it belongs to a certain degree, understood as being between 0 and 1. According to this principle, a set can be composed of young people aged between 0 and 45, within which a "baby" element will have a degree of belonging higher than that of an "adult" element.

In Japan, models drawn from Fuzzy Logic have been applied to financial systems analysis as well as to washing machines capable of detecting how dirty the laundry is.

COMPONENTS

Electronic tube (1906)

It was not until 1906 that inventor Lee De Forest (U.S., 1873–1961) developed the necessary element for the practical application of Boole's binary system. The electronic tube controlled the movement of electrons across a vacuum inside a hermetically sealed glass bulb. Also known as an "electronic valve," the main feature of this component was a direct current of electrons that produced the two conditions indispensable to binary logic: stop and go. On this basis, circuits could be produced according to binary logic, thus marking the dawn of the age of electronic computers.

Transistor (1947)

The transistor was invented at the end of 1947 by three physicsts at Bell Laboratories: William B. Shockley, John Bardeen and Walter H. Brattain. The transistor is a true semiconductor triode. It is the electronic component that characterized the second generation of computers. It was originally made with germanium, but after 1960 most transistors used silicon, which is more stable.

Transistors can detect, amplify and correct currents; they can also break them. They can produce very high-frequency electromagnetic waves and open or close circuits in the space of a millionth of a second. They have allowed advances to be made in information technology, communications, and aeronautics, and have also made electronic watches and pacemakers possible.

Internal memory (1947)

The internal memory of a computer is the mechanism that enables it provisionally to store information just before, during and after it is processed. In 1947, at Manchester University in England, F.C. Williams (Great Britain) experimented with electrostatic tubes used as a memory. In 1949, at Cambridge University in England, EDSAC, one of the computer's first ancestors, used delay lines. These were tubes filled with crystals that transformed electronic signals into sonic vibrations. Because sound travels more slowly than electricity, it was possible to store some information in them. Legend has it that Alan Turing advised putting gin in the delay lines. Then, in 1949, Jay Forrester used ferrite cores for the memory of the Whirlwind. Cores continued to be used until 1964, when they gave way to semiconductors.

Integrated circuit (1958)

On September 12, 1958 Jack St. Clair Kilby (U.S.), a young engineer from the University of Illinois who had recently been hired by Texas Instruments, showed the results of his work to some of his colleagues. He had assembled a few transistors and capacitors on a single support. This discovery was to revolutionze the electronics world. A patent for this first integrated circuit was applied for in 1959 and granted in 1964.

An integrated circuit is an electronic mechanism in which different components (transistors, resistances, capacitors, etc.) are diffused or implanted, then connected within a thin layer

The first integrated circuit (originally known as a single-crystal circuit) was invented by Jack Kilby of Texas Instruments in 1958. (Texas Instruments)

of semiconductor, such as silicon, permitting the formation of complex electronic circuits that carry out complete functions.

Microprocessor (1970)

Following court proceedings lasting 20 years, the U.S. Patent Office on July 17, 1990 recognized Gilbert Hyatt (U.S.) as the inventor of the microprocessor. His patent, deposited in December 1970, was the first to refer to a unique integrated circuit that contained all the necessary elements for the computer. Prior to the court's decision, the invention had been attributed to Marcian E. Hoff, Federico Faggin and Stanley Mazor of Intel Corp. These engineers did create the first commercial microchip in history in 1971—the Intel 4004—but their patents were related to particular aspects of the invention, and not to its general concept.

8080 (1974)

Launched by the American company Intel Corp. in 1974, the 8080 was the first 8 bit microprocessor. This technological advance was a commercial success and paved the way for personal computers.

Z 80 (1976)

In 1976 Zilog launched the Z80, a faster and cheaper version of the 8080. The capability and low price of the Z80 created a wider market for microcomputing in the 1970s. The operating system CP/M and leading software (Wordstar, dBase II) were written for this 8-bit processor.

6502 (1976)

In 1976 Chuck Peddle, one of microcomputing's great pioneers, developed the 6502, an 8-bit microprocessor marketed by the American company MOS Technologies. It was chosen by Stephen Wozniak and Steve Jobs to equip their first Apple II, and has had a fairytale career: it is still a core element in the latest versions of the Apple II, and an extraordinary software library has been designed around it.

8086 (1978)

In June 1978 Intel launched the first 16-bit microprocessor to be commercially successful, the 8086. It was devleoped by a team headed by Bill Pohlman. It has considerable strategic importance, since one of its versions, the 8088, an 8–16 bit processor, was chosen by IBM to equip its first microcomputer, the PC. Since then, IBM has bought part of Intel's capital, and all its microcomputers use Intel microprocessors.

68000 (1979)

In the United States in 1979 Motorola launched the 68000, the first of a series of microprocessors competing with those of Intel. This 16–32-bit processor is known above all for having been chosen by Apple for its Macintosh and, secondarily, by Atari for its ST series of personal microcomputers. It gave rise to several other versions, notably the 68020 used by the Macintosh II.

i386 (1985)

In 1985 Intel launched its 32-bit microprocessor, the i386, which offers microcomputers performance at the level of yesterday's minicomputers (it is capable of carrying out 3–4 million instructions a second), while being compatible with the software designed for its predecessors. The first microcomputers using the i386 appeared at the end of 1986.

Graphics processors (1986)

At first the main function of microprocessors was calculation. With the growing stress on user-friendliness, the manipulation of graphics has come to take up an increasing proportion of microcomputer power. This is why in 1986 Texas Instruments and Intel each separately launched graphics processors designed to ease the burden of the main processor. Texas's 34010 is particularly used in extension cards for IBM PC compatibles, and Intel's 82786 is its direct competitor.

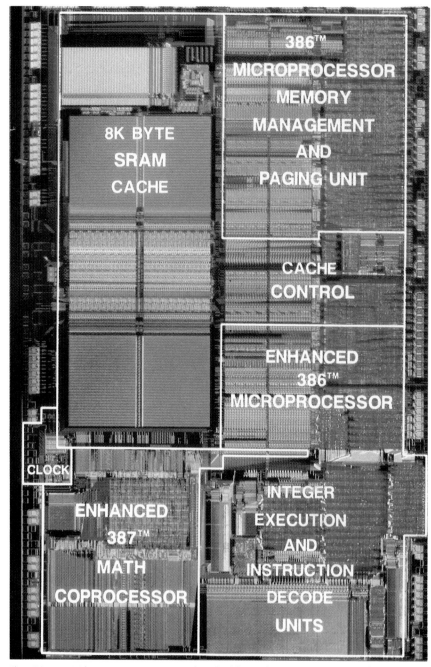

The i386, a 32-bit microprocessor, was launched by Intel in 1985. Capable of 3–4 million instructions per second, it was the most advanced of its kind. (Intel)

SRAM: 4-bit (1990)

The Japanese currently seem to be leading the field of SRAM, or Static Random Access Memory. Unlike a DRAM, an SRAM does not need constant reactivating to save the information in its millions of cells.

Sony, Hitachi and Toshiba have all independently announced the development of a new generation of 4-bit SRAMS; current SRAMS are 1-bit.

Synaptic microprocessor (1991)

Federico Faggin presented the first chip endowed with a synaptic internal logic system—that is, one mimicking the function of the human brain—in 1991. This Synaptics I 1000, intended for OCR (Optical Character Recognition), was able to read up to 20,000 characters per second without error.

Reflecting chips (1991)

A product of DMD (Deformable Mirror Device) technology, this chip contains a multitude of microoptic silicon mirrors mounted on pivots and activated by electric signals. Depending on its position, each mirror reflects or refracts light from its source, thus recreating part of an image. This technique, developed by Texas Instruments researchers in 1991, creates more viable, less energy-consuming and compact chips. The first commercial application of this invention was for a printer to be used by travel agents—the DMD2000. Thanks to optics, it contains 10 times fewer parts than a normal laser printer and has a longer lifespan.

INTEGRATION

Origins (1970s)

The integration of electronic components grew out of many different technologies, and its origins are thus hard to trace. The problem was to produce increasingly complex and small integrated circuits. In the case of a computer, the time taken by a signal to go from one circuit to the next limits its performance.

In the early 1970s engineers developed LSI (large scale integration), whereby a single chip could hold around 500 components. By the late 1970s LSI had been upgraded to VLSI (very large scale integration), which allowed up to 10,000 active elements.

The level of integration of components on single chips has continued to advance at an exponential rate. In 1992 a single chip is capable of containing 1 million active elements in the same space as that available in the 1970s.

Microframe (1989)

Developed in 1989, the Microframe contains a processor called SCAMP (Single Chip A Mainframe Processor) that contains as many circuits as a minicomputer, over 10 million transistors

The Gridpad, launched in 1990, was the first portable computer capable of recognizing handwriting. (Gamma-Liaison/Kermani)

in four square inches. Microframe was originally designed as a microcomputer, and is in fact very like one, while having the power of a mini.

COMPUTER PERIPHERALS

Speech synthesis (1933)

The first electric speech machine, the Voder (Voice Demonstrator), was built in 1933 by H.W. Dudley (U.S.). It was followed in 1939 by the Vocoder (Voice Coder). Speech synthesis is based on the theory of visible speech, formulated in 1948 by R.K. Potter, G.A. Kopp and H.C. Green (all U.S.), who showed how phonemes (vocal sounds) correspond to graphic traces.

Speech synthesis, which poses far fewer theoretical problems than speech recognition, is used in many domains, such as industry, cars and games.

The terminal (1940)

The first experiment that involved a terminal connected to a remote computer was conducted in 1940 by Bell Laboratories. The computer was in New York and the terminal at Dartmouth College, Hanover, N.H.

Speech recognition (1950)

The first machine to recognize 10 numbers pronounced by a human voice as a series of sonic signals was built at Bell Laboratories by K.H. Davies. That was in 1950. Since then progress has been slow.

Light pen (1963)

Light pens are accessories with which users can draw on their screens, as they would with a real pen. A light pen enables them to move part of a drawing, to "take" a color from a "palette" and use it to "paint" the surface they touch with the tip, and to command different functions. The first light pen was presented in 1963 at the Massachusetts Institute of Technology by I.E. Sutherland, who was associated with the conversational graphics system Sketchapad. Today this accessory is chiefly used on computer-aided design (CAD) consoles.

Mouse (1965)

The mouse is a small device that slides in all directions on a desk and makes it possible to interact naturally with the computer. Its use was popularized by Apple with the Lisa and the Macintosh models in 1983. However, it was the little-known American inventor Douglas Engelbart who conceived and designed it. His brilliant idea was to have the computer operator place his or her hand on a small box or mouse. A sphere on the underside of the mouse is used to measure movements, which are then transmitted to the computer via a lead—the tail of the mouse. These movements are translated to the cursor on the screen: if the mouse is pushed to the right the cursor goes to the right; if the mouse is pushed away from the user the cursor moves up, and so on. This revolutionary input device, originally found only on Apple computers, was adopted by IBM in 1987.

Tactile screen (1985)

In 1985 Zenith presented the first tactile screen system, based on surface acoustic wave technology: all the user has to do to give a command is touch a section of the screen.

The inventor of the floppy disk, Yoshiro Nakamats, displays one of his creations. (Sygma)

Eye control (1986)

In 1986 the American company Analytics Inc. developed a prototype computer that obeys sound and the eye. It uses an infrared beam to record eye movements. The user stares at a point on the screen, then gives a command to a micro and the machine carries it out immediately. This system could facilitate the control of robots or the selection of components on an assembly line.

Mouse-keyboard (1990)

A California computer scientist, Kirk MacKenzie, has invented a mouse equipped with a keyboard. The Power Mouse adapts to programs designed for use with a mouse, to which it brings keyboard facilitiies, or vice versa. It went on the market in spring 1990 in the United States.

Gridpad (1990)

The next concept for the portable computer is a machine that has no keyboard, but rather the user writes on the screen with an electronic pen. The computer recognizes handwriting and translates it into characters, functions and shapes. The first machine of this type was the Gridpad, invented by Jeff Hawkins (U.S.), and marketed in 1990.

MASS (PERIPHERAL) MEMORY

Origins (1805)

The first mass memory, in other words a medium allowing the permanent storage of data, was invented long before computer science, by Joseph-Marie Jacquard (France) in 1805. This was the punched card, and it was designed for his loom. Hermann Hollerith used it again in 1890 on his machine designed for the U.S. census. Then came magnetic tape, tested for the first time on an EDVAC in 1949, and removable disks, which were first marketed by IBM in 1962.

Floppy disks (1950)

Floppy disks, universally used on microcomputers, were invented in 1950 at the Imperial University in Tokyo by Dr. Yoshiro Nakamats, an inventor who boasts of having 2360 patents for objects as diverse as golf clubs and loudspeakers. He granted the sales license for the disk to IBM.

CD-ROM (1985)

The CD-ROM, invented by Philips and promoted throughout the world in collaboration with Sony, is simply a laser-read compact disc, similar to those used in hi-fi systems, but adapted to computing uses. It has the advantage of containing a thousand times more data than a diskette. Its disadvantage is that the data on it can be read, but new data cannot be written onto it. Developed in 1985, the CD-ROM began to take off in 1988.

WORM drive (1988)

Write once optical disks, called WORM (*Write Once Read Many* times), have been the object of much research. They have been marketed by IBM since 1988.

16 M-bit EPROM (1990)

In February 1990 the Japanese giant NEC announced the development of the first erasable and programmable 16 M-bit memory (EPROM). NEC has succeeded in putting 18 million transistors and other components on a 0.28 x 0.67 in. silicon chip.

Very high density diskette (1991)

Developed by the American company Insite Peripherals, the Floptical Disk Drive can store 20.8 megabytes on standard 3.5-inch diskettes. Moreover, it is fully compatible with earlier formats: 720 kilobytes and 1.44 megabytes. This achievement is due to the use of optical recording techniques. The Floptical has been available in the United States since March 1991.

Microchip diskette (1992)

Unlike standard chip diskettes, this new accessory doesn't contain magnetic disks, but a dedicated processor, the Motorola 68HC05 and myriad integrated circuits. Inserted in a standard disk reader, it stores data in a memory comparable to that of other computers. The advantage of this is that the processor renders the diskette intelligent, capable of assuming limited access functions or coding/decoding data.

Conceived by a subsidiary of the Innovatron group owned by Roland Moreno, the inventor of the microchip card, this diskette will have seven times the capacity of its magnetic equivalent.

PRINTERS

Origins (1953)

The printer allows data provided by the computer to be printed on paper. The first fast printer worthy of the name was developed in 1953 by Remington Rand. It printed 600 lines of 120 characters a minute.

The most widely used technologies fall into two types: impact printers (using dot matrix or daisy wheels) and nonimpact printers (thermal or laser transfer).

Dot matrix printer (1957)

Dot matrix printing is the method that has had the greatest success: the majority of printers use this principle. The print head has a vertical row of needles that are propelled forward electromagnetically as the head runs over each line. The first dot matrix printers were marketed by IBM in 1957.

Thermal printer (1966)

Invented in 1966 by Texas Instruments, thermal printing was first used for microcomputers. The print head is made of reistant needles that are heated when an electric current is passed through them. This technique requires special paper and gave way to "thermal transfer," in which the needle does not directly heat the paper but an inked ribbon. IBM retained this technology on its recent typewriter-printers.

Laser printer (1975)

The first laser pinter was introduced by IBM in 1975. It was an extremely expensive and bulky machine, designed for high-speed printing. In

1978 the IBM 3800 was followd by the ND2 from Siemens and the 9700 from Xerox, but it was not until 1984—with Hewlett-Packard's Laserjet—that the laser printer began to expand into the world of microcomputers. It works on a principle similar to that of offset printing: a laser beam "paints" the letters onto a roller, and the sheets of paper are printed by rotation. In 1988 color laser printers came on to the market.

Daisy wheel printer (1978)

The American company Diablo, since bought by Rank Xerox, invented this procedure, which was inspired by techniques used in typewriters.

APPLICATIONS

Computer graphics (1950)

The art of computer graphics can be traced back to the graphics made for wallpaper by Burnett in California from 1937 onwards. These graphics were based on Lissajous figures. But it was Ben F. Laposky who, in 1950, really founded the art of computer graphics.

Computer graphics are pure products of computer technology, and a few years ago still represented something of a feat (both technically and financially). Today, still graphics are quite common and can be produced on microcomputers. As for animated graphics—which are frequently used in television advertisements, for example—these can be so perfect and "real" that they are sometimes quite disturbing.

The work of the companies Robert Abel Associates, Digital Equipment Corporation and Sogitec (France) has now become famous in this field.

Automatic translation (1950)

In 1946 W. Weaver and A.D. Booth thought of using a computer to help with translation. But the techniques had not been perfected, and it was not until 1950 that Weaver and Booth could try out their idea.

Computer-generated 3-D images. (Jerrican/Nieto)

In 1970 Dr. P. Thomas developed a universal translation system, SYSTRAN. It was first put to spectacular use during the meeting of Apollo and Soyuz in 1975. It was adopted by the European Community in 1981.

There are some sytems that can translate in particular fields or with a limited vocabulary. But none of these systems can work without human intervention or error for any text of some difficulty.

Image animation (1951)

Computerized image animation was first experimented on at the Massachusetts Institute of Technology in 1951. But it was not until the early 1960s that the potential of the technique was fully understood. Today it is used in the fields of medicine, architecture (with models in three dimensions), space exploration and chemistry.

Music (1956)

Composers were the first creative artists to use computers in their work. The first of these were L. Hiller and M. Isaacson (both U.S.) in their composition *Iliac Suite* in 1956. Also important are the works of M. Phillipot and I. Xenakis, J. C. Risset and M. Matthews from Bell Laboratories, and those of the Vincennes Group.

At the end of the 1970s, computers became widely used in all fields of music, from pop music concerts to teaching.

Digital control (1956)

The digital control of machine tools first appeared in 1956, the year that the *Automatically Programmed Tools* (APT) language was created for the U.S. Air Force.

Computer-aided design (CAD) (1960)

Computer-aided design (CAD) began in the 1960s in the context of U.S. military aeronautics design programs.

The term refers to a set of techniques that can be used to create data that describe an object to be designed, to manipulate that data in a conversational mode and to arrive at a finished form of the design.

After its adoption by the military, CAD penetrated civil aeronautics and the auto and computing industries. It enables an object (for example, a car) to be drawn in three dimensions and to be examined in a great number of theoretical circumstances, even before the building has begun. Today CAD plays an essential role in almost all fields of industry.

Virtual Reality (1965)

It is possible today to be "absorbed" by a computer and move around in an imaginary and synthetic universe. This concept is called virtual reality. It is best known through its applications in the video game industry; however, its origins are in military applications. The concept is simple enough. On the one hand, a computer generates synthetic images, and on the other, the user controls these images through the intermediary of receptors placed in a glove

(Dataglove), and visualizes the result with stereoscopic glasses that have listening devices (Eyephone). Each movement of the fingers or the head is transmitted to the computer, which consequently interprets and modifies the surroundings. It is thus possible to touch or displace objects or to change the field of vision.

Eyephone (1965)

The Eyephone was developed by Ivan Sutherland (U.S.) in 1965 at MIT. The device was originally designed for use by the Army. Better known by the name HMD (Head Mounted Display), this helmet gives the operator an astonishing sense of immersion in an image. The image reacts to the movement of the head. Coupled with Dataglove (and connected to a powerful computer), it allows the operator to move objects visualized with the helmet by hand operation.

Dataglove (1982)

In the 1970s engineers were already researching methods that would make it possible to make the hand active in the virtual environment created by the computer. It was the Dataglove, invented by Thomas Zimmerman and Young Harvill, that made this idea a reality. The Dataglove was patented in 1982 and marketed by VPL Research in 1986.

Virtual Reality Systems (1989)

Artist and mathematician Jaron Lanier (U.S.) did not invent virtual reality, but he was the first to realize its potential beyond military applications. In 1989 he founded VPL Research and marketed virtual reality systems for such applications as video games, architecture and industrial design.

Motion pictures (1964)

The film industry was quick to grasp the possibilities of computer graphics. One interesting example is the pioneering work of Peter Foldes in his film *The Hunger*, but Steven Lisberger was the first to use all the computer's possibilities in the shooting of *Tron* in 1982.

Flight simulators (1970)

Around 1970 General Electric supplied NASA with the first flight simulation programs. The power of today's machines provides amazing possibilities, and all pilots are now trained on simulators. The advantages of this are obvious: pilots can try out difficult maneuvers without risk of losing their lives or destroying a plane.

ROBOTS

Automata

The first automata are to be found in antiquity at the time of Hero of Alexandria (1st century

A.D.). The Arabs kept the tradition going. In 1809 Sultan Harun ar-Rashid gave an animated clock to Charlemagne.

But it was not until the work of Jacques de Vaucanson (1709–82) that a machine was built that perfectly imitated natural animation. In Paris in 1738 Vaucanson exhibited an artificial duck that astounded everyone: it flapped its wings, swam, smoothed its feathers with its beak, drank and pecked; furthermore, after a certain time it evacuated the food it had taken in, in the form of a soft substance.

The torch was then taken up by Pierre and Henry-Louis Droz (both Switzerland). In 1773 they constructed a drawing machine. Their creation was so perfect that they were put on trial for witchcraft. Fortunately for them, there was growing public interest in scientific methods and the verdict was in their favor.

Robot patient (1980)

The first of these was the Japanese company Koken's robot patient in 1980, which was de-signed as a teaching aid in universities. The following year Michael Gordon, a professor of cardiology in Miami, created *Harvey*, a robot that could simulate 26 illnesses. Replicas of *Harvey* are widely available.

Robot nurse (1983)

Melkong (Medical Electric King Kong) was created by Prof. Hiroyasu Funakubo of Japan. It can hold a patient in its arms, wash him, put him to bed and tuck in the sheets!

Security robots (1983)

The American company Denning Mobile Robotics has been working on security robots since 1983. The Denning robots are capable of guarding factories and banks.

Walking robots (1983)

One of the major areas of research in robotics is that of giving robots the means of moving, in particular so that they can work in hostile environments where people cannot go.

There are many prototypes:

- *bipeds:* Certainly the most remarkable is the WHL-II, conceived by Ichiro Kato and built by Hitachi.
- *quadrupeds:* The Japanese Titan III can move over uneven ground and also climb stairs.
- *multilegged:* The most developed of these are undoubtedly Odex 1, 2, 3, from the American company Odetics, which can overcome obstacles while carrying a load of 1102 lb.

Domestic robots (1986)

Hero 2000 was born in 1986. Its big brother, Hero 1, was designed in 1982 by the American company Heathkit. The aim of both was educational: they were designed to initiate young people into robotics, but they can also teach languages. They can also carry out a number of useful tasks, such as carrying packages. Many less ambitious personal robots can be programmed to perform a certain number of tasks, but fundamentally these are just modern automata.

A robot for nuclear power plants (1988)

Using its two jointed caterpillar tracks, Centaur II, developed by the French Commission for Atomic Energy jointly with the Cyberg company, can move around in all sectors of nuclear installations in the event of incidents giving rise to dangerous radiation levels. It is autonomous and waterproof and can perform a certain number of simple operations.

Talking robot (1990)

The *Speech Activated Manipulator* (SAM) was launched in 1990 by Bell Labortories. It has a vocabulary of 127 current English words, enabling it to carry out its allotted tasks and talk about them. SAM combines the functions of several machines and can see, understand, touch and speak. SAM is designed to work in high-risk environments.

Robot (1961): Joseph F. Engelberger

The idea of robots is as old as mythology and as new as the latest industrial technology. A robot called the Golem is a monstrous mainstay of Jewish mythology. In 1738 a Parisian inventor created an artificial duck that ate grain, quacked, swam, and flapped its wings. Jules Verne wrote about artificial humans in the late 1800s. And the word *robot* was coined in 1923 in Karel Capek's play *R.U.R.* (*Rossum's Universal Robots*). The word *robot* is Czech for *worker*.

It was Isaac Asimov who in the 1940s created—in literature—the first benevolent robots whose purpose was to serve humans. Joseph F. Engelberger, a young physicist, was devoted to Asimov. He paid attention as well to the development

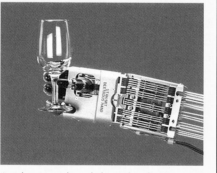

A robot extends a helping hand. (Cosmos/Woodifn, Camp & Assoc.)

of digital control, solid state electronics and servotheory, which had been used in World War II to aim guns fired from ships, automatically adapting to changes in the position of the ship and the motion of the water.

In 1956 Engelberger went to a cocktail party where he met George C. Devol, an inventor who had just applied for a patent for Programmed Article Transfer, a mechanism that Engelberger knew could be a robot. Together the two set out to create Unimates, robots that would take the place of humans in jobs that were tedious, limiting and dangerous. They sent out pamphlets about their robots, but they were turned down everywhere, until at last they found one manufacturer who was willing to put up $25,000 as an experiment.

The Unimate's first job was die casting. This robot did its job well, and won a berth in the Smithsonian Institution. Engelberger earned the title "Father of Robotics," and went on to create thousands of Unimates.

At first the business was not lucrative. Contrary to common opinion, the biggest obstacle was not labor or unions, but the skepticism of management. "We've only introduced 45,000 robots in the U.S. since the start," says Engelberger. "Japan has eight times as many. In just one year they build 55,000 robots. Our technology is still superior, but our industries took the short-range view on economics."

Nowadays Engelberger works to create and market robots that can conform to an economy that is now 75 percent service and just 25 percent industry. His robots are learning to sweep floors and clean toilets. A huge challenge is programming a robot to make a bed, which requires so many skills—anaylsis by touch, visual alignment, and esthetic judgments are just a few! One popular robot, the Helpmate, is an all-purpose hospital aide that delivers meals, mail and medicine, speaks English, runs errands, gives directions, and successfully navigates the hosptal corridors and elevators.

As always, Engelberger's robots conform to Isaac Asimov's Three Laws of Robotics:

1. A robot must not harm a human being, nor through inaction allow one to come to harm.
2. A robot must always obey human beings, unless that is in conflict with the first law.
3. A robot must protect itself from harm, unless that is in conflict with the first or second laws.

Accordingly, only three fatalities have been attributed to robots, while humans have been saved from countless injuries that might have occurred if people were doing the robots' jobs. As Engelberger says, "If a robot gets its hand caught in a press, it can be replaced or repaired. There's no replacing a human hand."

WHAT ON EARTH?

NOT ALL INVENTIONS CHANGE OUR LIVES, SOME JUST MAKE US SCRATCH OUR HEADS.

COMPUTER MODEL

▼ This is not a demonstration that computers have become so "user-friendly" that even a mannequin can operate one, but rather one of the latest in portable computers, the Lapbody. Designed by Hideji Takemasa of the Japanese company NEC, the lapbody attaches to the user, who can operate the machine in a standing or sitting position, and in any location. (Gamma/Kurita)

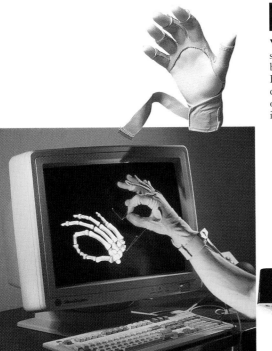

CYBERGLOVE

▲ CyberGlove is one of the latest advances in the rapidly growing field of virtual reality technology. Marketed by the American company Virtual Technologies, the CyberGlove is a lightweight flexible glove with 22 built-in sensors that reproduce the movements of the user's hand and fingers on a computer screen. It is used to create and edit 3-D virtual objects. (Virtual Technologies)

ROBOT SHEARER

In Australia there are 165 million sheep to shear; hence the need to invent a mechanized shearing procedure. After 10 years of research, the Australian company Merino Wool Harvesting has developed prototype robot shearers, capable of shearing a sheep in less than two minutes, which compares favorably with the three-minute average of a human shearer.

TEKODEX

▲ The first robotic vacuum cleaner, Tekodex was designed by Bernard and André Jonas (France) in 1990. The inventors claim Tekodex can reach all those difficult-to-reach places, yet it never succumbs to housemaid's knee. (Le Livre Mondial des Inventions)

ROBOTIC CARTRIDGE ACCESSOR

This dramatic-sounding robot is in fact an automated ▲ device for handling tape cartridges that store data for IBM's largest mainframe computers. This machine can store 18,920 cartridges of information (or 45 terabytes [trillions of bytes]). This is the equivalent of approximately 80 million books, each 350 pages long. (IBM Corp.)

A BULLETPROOF COMPUTER

An "armored" computer, designed for organizations threatened by criminal activity, such as banks, airlines and police stations, has been designed by Digital Equipment, which began marketing it in 1991. According to the manufacturers, even if it is fired on at point-blank range and some elements are destroyed, the computer will continue to function normally.

New ideas that may change the way we live

THE MOLECULAR COMPUTER

A team of Japanese engineers is developing a computer based on the stereochemical characteristics of certain molecules. It is estimated that if successful, the computer would have unlimited possibilities in terms of storage capacity and speed. Their research is already well advanced. The team has created a derivative of benzene, Ocah, whose optical properties change according to the angle formed by the eye and the two "poles" of the molecule, which means it can be either straight or bent, and its reaction to light is different in either case. Engineers then compared the two states, trans and cis, by binary means using a computer. The main problem with this was that the cis state is unstable and, consequently, memory was uncertain. This problem was solved by "balancing" the molecule by passing an electric current through it.

The implications of this technology are too broad to imagine them all. At an earlier stage, molecular electronics allowed calculations 10,000 times faster than the fastest computers. As for storage capacity, it will be hundreds of millions of bits per square inch in laser print, limited only to the size of the latter. Using procedures such as the tunnel effect, it may be possible to reach one billion bits on the same surface.

THE OPTICAL COMPUTER

The principle behind this computer is to replace electricity by light in order to convey information. Photons are much faster than electrons, and unlike the latter they don't "interfere": two lines can cross without affecting each other; therefore, significant levels in space and speed are gained. In France CNRS has patented a procedure for an optical computer. A preliminary prototype was presented in 1991.

For an optical computer to exist, components capable of reacting to light are needed as well. In a conventional microprocessor, it is transistors, in playing alternately the role of conductors or isolators, that allow for information processing. In 1990 John Hait (U.S.) of the Rocky Mountain Research Center invented an optical transistor. His invention is capable of performing logic functions such as "WHERE" and "AND," bases of information processing, from laser beams. Alan Huang (U.S.), director of the Optical Computing Research Department at the Bell AT&T Laboratories, produced a prototype for a similar device in February 1990.

Although the technology exists, much progress is still needed. At present, computation is too slow and uses too much energy, even though Bell has announced the invention of an electro-optic integrated circuit capable of computing in one-billionth of a second.

ELECTRONIC NEURONS

Peter Fromherz and Andreas Offenhäusser, of the University of Ulm, Germany, succeeded in 1991 in grafting neurons from leeches onto silicon oxide, the whole behaving like an electronic component controlled by the neuron. This discovery, despite its somewhat barbarous aspects, opened a field of vast exploration: interactions with the neurons of the human brain. At first it would further our understanding of the encephalus, but taken further, researchers have already begun to envision bioelectrical prostheses to enable the blind to recover sight, improved vision for fighter pilots, or even direct brain/computer transactions.

SILICON NEURONS

Still part of neuronal-computer science, but in an inverse sense, researchers at the California Institute of Technology at Pasadena presented in 1992 a "silicon neuron" as close as possible to the real thing. These analog chips open the road to a new generation of computers whose intelligence will bear a close resemblance to our own, and which, most notably, will be capable of reasoning based on approximations.

A 64-MBIT DRAM

In 1990 the German group Siemens, together with IBM, announced that they were joining forces to develop a 64-Mbit superchip. These new microprocessors should be produced and marketed by the mid-1990s.

FLASH MEMORY

In the mid-1980s the Japanese company Toshiba invented Flash Memory technology, a semiconductor memory chip that is small and stable. This technology has been developed dramatically by the American firm Intel, which recognized the technology's potential to replace the hard drive and create enormous possibilities in the portable computer market. In 1992 Intel introduced the "flash card," which holds 20 chips with 20 megabytes of memory on a board the size of a credit card. The card can retain information even when the machine is turned off, can store and retrieve information quickly and is less susceptible to damage or vibration than standard hard drives used in portable machines. This technology reduces the weight of a portable machine by as much as 4 lbs, and researchers believe that flash memory will lead to the development of an incredible range of small consumer gadgets, such as a wallet-sized personal stereo and even portable video players.

ACUMAX SYSTEM

The Acumax System is a portable and hands-free bar-code-based computer system designed to improve warehouse distribution systems. Designed by Symbol Technologies Inc., and EDS Corp., Acumax is a bar-code scanning glove with a display screen that is capable of data communication to the warehouse network. When shipments arrive at the loading area, workers point the device at the bar code on the boxes and the inventory information is recorded. Pen and paper are no longer required. A liquid-crystal display screen informs workers where items for an order are located, and even if they are stored in the wrong places.

The Acumax System uses a bar-code scanning glove to improve warehouse distribution systems. (Symbol Technologies, Inc.)

NOBEL PRIZE WINNERS

Nobel Prize Winners (1901–92)

The Nobel Prizes were established through a bequest of Alfred Nobel (Sweden, 1833–96), the inventor of dynamite. Supplemented by a gift from the Bank of Sweden, the prizes have been awarded annually since 1901 in the fields of chemistry, literature, peace, physics and physiology or medicine. In 1968, to mark the 300th anniversary of the Bank of Sweden, an additional prize for work in the field of economics was created, to be awarded from 1969 onward. The following is a complete list of award winners and their accomplishments in the three fields that apply to the topics of invention and discovery: chemistry, physics and physiology or medicine.

Chemistry

1901 Van't Hoff, Jacobus Henricus (Netherlands, 1952–1911)
For the discovery of the laws of chemical dynamics and osmotic pressure in solutions.

1902 Fischer, Hermann Emil (Germany, 1852–1919)
For his work on sugar and purine syntheses.

1903 Arrhenius, Svante August (Sweden, 1859–1927)
For his electrolytic theory of dissociation.

1904 Ramsay, Sir William (Great Britain, 1852–1916)
For the discovery of the inert gaseous elements in air, and his determination of their place in the periodic system.

1905 Von Baeyer, Johann Adolf (Germany, 1835–1916)
For his services in the advancement of organic chemistry and the chemical industry, through his work on organic dyes and hydroaromatic compounds.

1906 Moissan, Henri (France, 1852–1907)
For his investigation and isolation of the element fluorine, and for the adoption in the service of science of the electric furnace named after him.

1907 Buchner, Eduard (Germany, 1860–1917)
For his biochemical researches and his discovery of cell-free fermentation.

1908 Rutherford, Lord Ernest (Great Britain, 1871–1937)
For his investigations into the disintegration of the elements, and the chemistry of radioactive substances.

1909 Ostwald, Wilhelm (Germany, 1853–1932)
For his work on catalysis and for his investigations into the fundamental principles governing chemical equilibria and rates of reaction.

1910 Wallach, Otto (Germany, 1847–1931)
For his services to organic chemistry and the chemical industry by his pioneer work in the field of alicyclic compounds.

1911 Curie, Marie, née Sklodowska (France, 1867–1934)
For the discovery of the elements radium and polonium, by the isolation of radium and the study of the nature and compounds of this remarkable element.

1912 Grignard, Victor (France, 1871–1935)
For the discovery of the so-called Grignard reagent, which in recent years has greatly advanced the progress of organic chemistry.
Sabatier, Paul (France, 1854–1941)
For his method of hydrogenating organic compounds in the presence of finely disintegrated metals.

1913 Werner, Alfred (Switzerland, 1866–1919)
For his work on the linkage of atoms in molecules by which he has opened up new fields of research, especially in inorganic chemistry.

1914 Richards, Theodore William (U.S., 1868–1928)
For his accurate determinations of the atomic weight of a large number of chemical elements.

1915 Willstätter, Richard Martin (Germany, 1872–1942)
For his researches on plant pigments, especially chlorophyll.

1916–1917 Not awarded

1918 Haber, Fritz (Germany, 1868–1934)
For the synthesis of ammonia from its elements.

1919 Not awarded

1920 Nernst, Walther Hermann (Germany, 1864–1941)
For his work in thermochemistry.

1921 Soddy, Frederick (Great Britain, 1877–1956)
For his contributions to our knowledge of the chemistry of radioactive substances, and his investigations into the origin and nature of isotopes.

1922 Aston, Francis William (Great Britain, 1877–1945)
For his discovery, by means of his mass spectrograph, of isotopes, in a large number of nonradioactive elements, and for his enunciation of the whole-number rule.

1923 Pregl, Fritz (Austria, 1869–1930)
For his invention of the method of microanalysis of organic substances.

1924 Not awarded

1925 Zsigmondy, Richard Adolf (Germany, 1865–1929)
For his demonstration of the heterogeneous nature of colloid solutions and for the methods he used, which have since become fundamental in modern colloid chemistry.

1926 Svedberg, The (Theodor) (Sweden, 1884–1971)
For his work on disperse systems.

1927 Wieland, Heinrich Otto (Germany, 1877–1957)
For his investigations of the constitution of the bile acids and related substances.

1928 Windaus, Adolf Otto Reinhold (Germany, 1877–1959)
For his research into the constitution of the sterols and their connection with vitamins.

1929 Harden, Sir Arthur (Great Britain, 1865–1940)
Von Euler-Chelpin, Hans (Sweden, 1873–1964)
For their investigations on the fermentation of sugar and fermentative enzymes.

1930 Fischer, Hans (Germany, 1881–1945)
For his researches into the constitution of haemin and chlorophyll and especially for his synthesis of haemin.

1931 Bosch, Carl (Germany, 1874–1940)
Bergius, Friedrich (Germany, 1884–1949)
For their contributions to the invention and development of chemical high pressure methods.

1932 Langmuir, Irving (U.S., 1881–1957)
For his discoveries and investigations in surface chemistry.

1933 Not awarded

1934 Urey, Harold Clayton (U.S., 1893–1981)
For his discovery of heavy hydrogen.

1935 Joliot, Frédéric (France, 1900–58)
Joliot-Curie, Irène (France, 1897–1956)
For their synthesis of new radioactive elements.

1936 Debye, Petrus Josephus W. (Netherlands, 1894–1966)
For his contribution to our knowledge of molecular structure through his investigations on dipole moments and on the diffraction of X rays and electrons in gases.

1937 Haworth, Sir Walter Norman (Great Britain, 1883–1950)
For his investigations on carbohydrates and vitamin C.
Karrer, Paul (Switzerland, 1889–1971)
For his investigations on carotenoids, flavins and vitamins A and B2.

1938 Kuhn, Richard (Germany, 1900–67)
For his work on carotenoids and vitamins.

1939 Butenandt, Adolf Friedrich Johann (Germany, 1903–)
For his work on sex hormones.
Ruzicka, Leopold (Switzerland, 1887–1976)
For his work on polymethylenes and higher terpenes.

1940–42 Not awarded

1943 De Hevesy, George (Hungary, 1885–1966)
For his work on the use of isotopes as tracers in the study of chemical processes.

1944 Hahn, Otto (Germany, 1879–1968)
For his discovery of the fission of heavy nuclei.

1945 Virtanen, Artturi Ilmari (Finland, 1895–1973)
For his research and inventions in agricultural and nutrition chemistry, especially for his fodder preservation method.

1946 Sumner, James Batcheller (U.S., 1887–1955)
For his discovery that enzymes can be crystallized.
Northrop, John Howard (U.S., 1891–1987)
Stanley, Wendell Meredith (U.S., 1904–71)
For their preparation of enzymes and virus proteins in a pure form.

1947 Robinson, Sir Robert (Great Britain, 1886–1975)
For his investigations on plant products of biological importance, especially the alkaloids.

1948 Tiselius, Arne Wilhelm Kaurin (Sweden, 1902–71)
For his research on electrophoresis and absorption analysis, especially for his discoveries concerning the complex nature of the serum proteins.

1949 Giauque, William Francis (U.S., 1895–1982)
For his contributions in the field of chemical thermodynamics, particularly concerning the behavior of substances at extremely low temperatures.

1950 Diels, Otto (Germany, 1876–1954)
Alder, Kurt (Germany, 1902–58)
For their discovery and development of the diene synthesis.

1951 McMillan, Edwin Mattison (U.S., 1907–91)
Seaborg, Glenn Theodore (U.S., 1912–)
For their discoveries in the chemistry of the transuranium elements.

1952 Martin, Archer John Porter (Great Britain, 1910–)
Synge, Richard Laurence Millington (Great Britain, 1914–)
For their invention of partition chromatography.

1953 Staudinger, Hermann (Germany, 1881–1965)
For his discoveries in the field of macromolecular chemistry.

1954 Pauling, Linus Carl (U.S., 1901–)
For his research into the nature of the chemical bond and its application to the elucidation of the structure of complex substances.

1955 Du Vigneaud, Vincent (U.S., 1901–78)
For his work on biochemically important sulfur compounds, especially for the first synthesis of a polypeptide hormone.

1956 Hinshel Wood, Sir Cyril Norman (Great Britain, 1897–1967)
Semenov, Nikolaj Nikolajevic (USSR, 1896–1986)
For their researches into the mechanism of chemical reactions.

1957 Todd, Lord Alexander (Great Britain, 1907–)
For his work on nucleotides and nucleotide co-enzymes.

1958 Sanger, Frederick (Great Britain, 1918–)
For his work on the structure of proteins, especially that of insulin.

1959 Heyrovsky, Jaroslav (Czechoslovakia, 1890–1967)
For his discovery and development of the polarographic methods of analysis.

1960 Libby, Willard Frank (U.S., 1908–80)
For his method to use carbon-14 for age determination in archaeology and other branches of science.

1961 Calvin, Melvin (U.S., 1911–)
For his research on carbon dioxide assimilation in plants.

1962 Perutz, Max Ferdinand (Great Britain, 1914–)
Kendrew, Sir John Cowdery (Great Britain, 1917–)
For their studies of the structures of globular proteins.

1963 Ziegler, Karl (Germany, 1898–1973)
Natta, Giulio (Italy, 1903–79)
For their discoveries in the field of the chemistry and technology of high polymers.

1964 Hodgkin, Dorothy Crowfoot (Great Britain, 1910–)
For her determinations by X-ray techniques of the structures of important biochemical substances.

1965 Woodward, Robert Burns (U.S., 1917–79)
For his outstanding achievements in the art of organic synthesis.

1966 Mulliken, Robert S. (U.S., 1896–1986)
For his fundamental work concerning chemical bonds and the electronic structure of molecules by the molecular orbital method.

1967 Eigen, Manfred (Germany, 1927–)
Norrish, Ronald George Wreyford (Great Britain, 1897–1978)
Porter, Sir George (Great Britain, 1920–)
For their studies of extremely fast chemical reactions, effected by disturbing the equilibrium by means of very short pulses of energy.

1968 Onsager, Lars (U.S., 1903–76)
For the discovery of the reciprocal relations bearing his name, which are fundamental for the thermodynamics of irreversible processes.

1969 Barton, Sir Derek H. R. (Great Britain, 1918–)
Hassel, Odd (Norway, 1897–1981)
For their contributions to the development of the concept of conformation and its application in chemistry.

1970 Leloir, Luis F. (Argentina, 1906–87)
For his discovery of sugar nucleotides and their role in the biosynthesis of carbohydrates.

1971 Herzberg, Gerhard (Canada, 1904–)
For his contributions to the knowledge of electronic structure and geometry of molecules, particularly free radicals.

1972 Anfinsen, Christian B. (U.S, 1916–)
For his work on ribonuclease, especially concerning the connection between the amino acid sequence and the biologically active confirmation.
Moore, Stanford (U.S., 1913–82)
Stein, William H. (U.S., 1911–80)
For their contribution to the understanding of the connection between chemical structure and catalytic activity of the active center of the ribonuclease molecule.

1973 Fischer, Ernst Otto (Germany, 1918–)
Wilkinson, Sir Geoffrey (Great Britain, 1921–)
For their pioneering work, performed independently, on the chemistry of the organo-metallic, so-called sandwich, compounds.

1974 Flory, Paul J. (U.S., 1910–85)
For his fundamental achievements in the physical chemistry of the macromolecules.

1975 Cornforth, Sir John Warcup (Australia and Great Britain, 1917–)
For his work on the stereochemistry of enzyme-catalyzed reactions.
Prelog, Vladimir (Switzerland, 1906–)
For his research into the stereochemistry of organic molecules and reactions.

1976 Lipscomb, William N. (U.S., 1919–)
For his studies on the structure of boranes illuminating problems of chemical bonding.

1977 Prigogine, Ilya (Belgium, 1917–)
For his contributions to nonequilibrium thermodynamics, particularly the theory of dissipative structures.

1978 Mitchell, Peter D. (Great Britain, 1920–92)
For his contribution to the understanding of biological energy transfer through the formulation of the chemiosmotic theory.

1979 Brown, Herbert C. (U.S., 1912–)
Wittig, Georg (Germany, 1897–1987)
For their development of the use of boron- and phosphorus-containing compounds, respectively, into important reagents in organic synthesis.

1980 Berg, Paul (U.S., 1926–)
For his fundamental studies of the biochemistry of nucleic acids, with particular regard to recombinant-DNA.
Gilbert, Walter (U.S., 1932–)
Sanger, Frederick (Great Britain, 1918–)
For their contributions concerning the determination of base sequences in nucleic acids.

1981 Fukui, Kenichi (Japan, 1918–)
Hoffmann, Roald (U.S., 1937–)
For their theories, developed independently, concerning the course of chemical reactions.

1982 Klug, Aaron (Great Britain, 1926–)
For his development of crystallographic electron microscopy and his structural elucidation of biologically important nuclei acid-protein complexes.

1983 Taube, Henry (U.S., 1915–)
For his work on the mechanisms of electron transfer reactions, especially in metal complexes.

1984 Merrifield, Robert Bruce (U.S., 1921–)
For his development of methodology for chemical synthesis on a solid matrix.

1985 Hauptman, Herbert A. (U.S., 1917–)
Karle, Jerome (U.S., 1918–)
For their outstanding achievements in the development of direct methods for the determination of crystal structures.

1986 Herschbach, Dudley R. (U.S., 1932–)
Lee, Yuan T. (U.S., 1918–)
Polanyi, John C. (Canada, 1929–)
For their contributions concerning the dynamics of chemical elementary processes.

1987 Cram, Donald J. (U.S., 1919–)
Lehn, Jean-Marie (France, 1939–)
Pedersen, Charles J. (U.S., 1904–89)
For their development and use of molecules with structure-specific interactions of high selectivity.

1988 Deisenhofer, Johann (Germany, 1943–)
Huber, Robert (Germany, 1937–)
Michel, Hartmut (Germany, 1948–)
For the determination of the 3-D structure of a photosynthetic reaction center.

1989 Altman, Sidney (Canada, b. U.S.; 1939–)
Cech, Thomas R. (U.S., 1947–)
For their discovery of catalytic properties of RNA.

1990 Corey, Elias J. (U.S., 1928–)
For his development of the theory and methodology of organic synthesis.

1991 Ernst, Richard R. (Switzerland, 1933–)
For his contributions in refining the technology of nuclear magnetic resonance imaging.

1992 Marcus, Rudolph A. (U.S., 1923–)
For his mathematical analysis of the cause and effect of electrons jumping from one molecule to another.

Physics

1901 Röntgen, Wilhelm Conrad (Germany, 1845–1923)
For the discovery of the remarkable rays subsequently named after him.

1902 Lorentz, Hendrik Antoon (Netherlands, 1853–1928)
Zeeman, Pieter (Netherlands, 1865–1943)
For their researches into the influence of magnetism upon radiation phenomena.

1903 Becquerel, Antoine Henri (France, 1852–1908)
For his discovery of spontaneous radioactivity.
Curie, Pierre (France, 1859–1906)
Curie, Marie, née Sklodowska (France, 1867–1934)
For their joint researches on the radiation phenomena discovered by Professor Henri Becquerel.

1904 Rayleigh, Lord (John William Strutt) (Great Britain, 1842–1919)
For his investigations of the densities of the most important gases and for his discovery of argon.

1905 Lenard, Philipp Eduard Anton (Great Britain, 1862–1947)
For his work on cathode rays.

1906 Thomson, Sir Joseph John (Great Britain, 1856–1940)
For his theoretical and experimental investigations on the conduction of electricity by gases.

1907 Michelson, Albert Abraham (U.S., 1852–1931)
For his optical precision instruments and the spectroscopic and metrological investigations carried out with their aid.

1908 Lippmann, Gabriel (France, 1845–1921)
For reproducing colors photographically based on the phenomenon of interference.

1909 Marconi, Guglielmo (Italy, 1874–1937)
Braun, Karl Ferdinand (Germany, 1850–1918)
For their contributions to the development of wireless telegraphy.

1910 Van Der Waals, Johannes D. (Netherlands, 1837–1923)
For his work on the equation of state for gases and liquids.

1911 Wien, Wilhelm (Germany, 1864–1928)
For his discoveries regarding the laws governing the radiation of heat.

1912 Dalén, Nils Gustaf (Sweden, 1869–1937)
For his invention of automatic regulators for use in conjunction with gas accumulators for illuminating lighthouses and buoys.

1913 Kamerlingh-Onnes, Heike (Netherlands, 1853–1926)
For his investigations on the properties of matter at low temperatures which led, *inter alia*, to the production of liquid helium.

1914 Von Laue, Max (Germany, 1879–1960)
For his discovery of the diffraction of X rays by crystals.

1915 Bragg, Sir William Henry (Great Britain, 1862–1942)
Bragg, Sir William Lawrence (Great Britain, 1890–1971)
For their services in the analysis of crystal structure by means of X rays.

1916 Not awarded

1917 **Barkla, Charles Glover** (Great Britain, 1877–1944)
For his discovery of the characteristic Röntgen radiation of the elements.

1918 **Planck, Max Karl Ernst Ludwig** (Germany, 1858–1947)
For his discovery of energy quanta.

1919 **Stark, Johannes** (Germany, 1874–1957)
For his discovery of the Doppler effect in canal rays and the splitting of spectral lines in electric fields.

1920 **Guillaume, Charles Edouard** (Switzerland, 1861–1938)
For his discovery of anomalies in nickel steel alloys.

1921 **Einstein, Albert** (Germany and Switzerland, 1879–1955)
For his discovery of the law of the photoelectric effect.

1922 **Bohr, Niels** (Denmark, 1885–1962)
For his services in the investigation of the structure of atoms and of the radiation emanating from them.

1923 **Millikan, Robert Andrews** (Great Britain, 1868–1953)
For his work on the elementary charge of electricity and on the photoelectric effect.

1924 **Siegbahn, Karl Manne Georg** (Sweden, 1886–1978)
For his discoveries and research in the field of X-ray spectroscopy.

1925 **Franck, James** (Germany, 1882–1964)
Hertz, Gustav (Germany, 1887–1975)
For their discovery of the laws governing the impact of an electron upon an atom.

1926 **Perrin, Jean Baptiste** (France, 1870–1942)
For his work on the discontinuous structure of matter, and especially for his discovery of sedimentation equilibrium.

1927 **Compton, Arthur Holly** (U.S., 1892–1962)
For his discovery of the effect named after him.
Wilson, Charles Thomson Rees (Great Britain, 1869–1959)
For his method of making the paths of electrically charged particles visible by condensation of vapor.

1928 **Richardson, Sir Owen Willans** (Great Britain, 1879–1959)
For his work on the thermionic phenomenon and especially for the discovery of the law named after him.

1929 **De Broglie, Prince Louis-Victor** (France, 1892–1987)
For his discovery of the wave nature of electrons.

1930 **Rama, Sir Chandrasekhara Venkata** (India, 1888–1970)
For his work on the scattering of light and for the discovery of the effect named after him.

1931 Not awarded

1932 **Heisenberg, Werner** (Germany, 1901–76)
For the creation of quantum mechanics, the application of which has, *inter alia*, led to the discovery of the allotropic forms of hydrogen.

1933 **Schrödinger, Erwin** (Austria, 1887–1961)
Dirac, Paul Adrien Maurice (Great Britain, 1902–84)
For the discovery of new productive forms of atomic theory.

1934 Not awarded

1935 **Chadwick, Sir James** (Great Britain, 1891–1974)
For the discovery of the neutron.

1936 **Hess, Victor Franz** (Austria, 1883–1964)
For his discovery of cosmic radiation.
Anderson, Carl David (U.S., 1905–91)
For his discovery of the positron.

1937 **Davisson, Clinton Joseph** (U.S., 1881–1958)
Thomson, Sir George Paget (Great Britain, 1892–1975)
For their experimental discovery of the diffraction of electrons by crystals.

1938 **Fermi, Enrico** (Italy, 1901–54)
For his demonstrations of the existence of new radioactive elements produced by neutron irradiation, and for his related discovery of nuclear reactions brought about by slow neutrons.

1939 **Lawrence, Ernest Orlando** (U.S., 1901–58)
For the invention and development of the cyclotron and for results obtained with it, especially with regard to artificial radioactive elements.

1940–42 Not awarded

1943 **Stern, Otto** (U.S., 1888–1969)
For his contribution to the development of the molecular ray method and his discovery of the magnetic moment of the proton.

1944 **Rabi, Isidor Isaac** (U.S., 1898–1988)
For his resonance method for recording the magnetic properties of atomic nuclei.

1945 **Pauli, Wolfgang** (Austria, 1900–58)
For the discovery of the Pauli principle

1946 **Bridgman, Percy Williams** (U.S., 1882–1961)
For the invention of an apparatus to produce extremely high pressures, and the discoveries made therewith in the field of high pressure physics.

1947 **Appleton, Sir Edward Victor** (Great Britain, 1892–1965)
For his investigaitons of the physics of the upper atmosphere, especially for the discovery of the so-called Appleton layer.

1948 **Blackett, Lord Patrick Maynard Stuart** (Great Britain, 1897–1974)
For his development of the Wilson cloud chamber method, and his discoveries therewith in the fields of nuclear physics and cosmic radiation.

1949 **Yukawa, Hideki** (Japan, 1907–81)
For his prediction of the existence of mesons on the basis of theoretical work on nuclear forces.

1950 **Powell, Cecil Frank** (Great Britain, 1903–69)
For his development of the photographic method of studying nuclear processes and his discoveries regarding mesons made with this method.

1951 **Cockcroft, Sir John Douglas** (Great Britain, 1897–1967)
Walton, Ernest Thomas Sinton (Ireland, 1903–)
For their pioneer work on the transmutation of atomic nuclei by artificially accelerated atomic particles.

1952 Bloch, Felix (U.S., 1905–83)
Purcell, Edward Mills (U.S., 1912–)
For their development of new methods for nuclear magnetic precision measurements, and discoveries in connection therewith.

1953 Zernike, Frits (Frederik) (Netherlands, 1888–1966)
For his demonstration of the phase contrast method, especially for his invention of the phase contrast microscope.

1954 Born, Max (Great Britain, 1882–1970)
For his fundamental research in quantum mechanics, especially for his statistical interpretation of the wave function.
Bothe, Walther (Germany, 1891–1957)
For the coincidence method and his discoveries made therewith.

1955 Lamb, Willis Eugene (U.S., 1913–)
For his discoveries concerning the fine structure of the hydrogen spectrum.
Kusch, Polykarp (U.S., 1911–)
For his precision determination of the magnetic moment of the electron.

1956 Shockley, William (U.S., 1910–89)
Bardeen, John (U.S, 1908–92)
Brattain, Walter Houser (U.S., 1902–87)
For their researches on semiconductors and their discovery of the transistor effect.

1957 Yang, Cheng Ning (China, 1922–)
Lee, Tsung-Dao (China, 1926–)
For their penetrating investigation of the so-called parity laws, which has led to important discoveries regarding the elementary particles.

1958 Cerenkov, Pavel Aleksejvic (USSR, 1904–90)
Frank, Il'ja Michajlovic (USSR, 1908–90)
Tamm, Igor Jevgen'evic (USSR, 1895–1971)
For the discovery and the interpretation of the Cerenkov effect.

1959 Segrè, Emilio Gino (U.S., 1905–89)
Chamberlain, Owen (U.S., 1920–)
For their discovery of the antiproton.

1960 Glaser, Donald A. (U.S., 1926–)
For the invention of the bubble chamber.

1961 Hofstadter, Robert (U.S., 1915–90)
For his pioneering studies of electron scattering in atomic nuclei and his discoveries concerning the structure of the nucleons.
Mössbauer, Rudolf Ludvig (Germany, 1929–)
For his researches concerning the resonance absorption of gamma radiation and his discovery of the effect that bears his name.

1962 Landau, Lev Davidovic (USSR, 1908–68)
For his pioneering theories on condensed matter, especially liquid helium.

1963 Wigner, Eugene P. (U.S., 1902–)
For his contributions to the theory of the atomic nucleus and the elementary particles, particularly through the discovery and application of fundamental symmetry principles.
Goeppert-Mayer, Maria (U.S., 1906–72)
Jensen, J. Hans D. (Germany, 1907–73)
For their discoveries concerning nuclear shell structure.

1964 Townes, Charles Hard (U.S., 1915–)
Basov, Nicolai Gennadievic (USSR, 1922–)
Prochorov, Aleksandre Mikhailovic (USSR, 1916–)
For fundamental work in the field of quantum electronics, which has led to the construction of oscillators and amplifiers based on the maser-laser principle.

1965 Tomonaga, Sin-Itiro (Japan, 1906–79)
Schwinger, Julian (U.S., 1918–)
Feynman, Richard P. (U.S., 1918–88)
For their fundamental work in quantum electrodynamics, with deep-ploughing consequences for the physics of elementary particles.

1966 Kastler, Alfred (France, 1902–84)
For the discovery and development of optical methods for studying Hertzian resonances in atoms.

1967 Bethe, Hans Albrecht (U.S., 1906–)
For his contributions to the theory of nuclear reactions, especially his discoveries concerning the energy production in stars.

1968 Alvarez, Luis W. (U.S., 1911–)
For his decisive contributions to elementary particle physics, in particular the discovery of a large number of resonance states, made possible through his development of the technique of using hydrogen bubble chamber and data analysis.

1969 Gell-Mann, Murray (U.S., 1929–)
For his contributions and discoveries concerning the classification of elementary particles and their interactions.

1970 Alfvén, Hannes (Sweden, 1908–)
For fundamental work and discoveries in magnetohydrodynamics with fruitful applications in different parts of plasma physics.
Néél, Louis (France, 1904–)
For fundamental work and discoveries concerning anti-ferromagnetism and ferrimagnetism which have led to important applications in solid state physics.

1971 Gabor, Dennis (Great Britain, 1900–79)
For his invention and development of the holographic method.

1972 Bardeen, John (U.S., 1908–91)
Cooper, Leon N. (U.S., 1930–)
Schrieffer, J. Robert (U.S., 1931–)
For their jointly developed theory of superconductivity, usually called the BCS-theory.

1973 Esaki, Leo (Japan, 1925–)
Giaever, Ivar (U.S., 1929–)
For their experimental discoveries regarding tunneling phenomena in semiconductors and superconductors, respectively.
Josephson, Brian D. (Great Britain, 1940–)
For his theoretical predictions of the properties of a supercurrent through a tunnel barrier, especially the Josephson effects.

1974 Ryle, Sir Martin (Great Britain, 1918–84)
Hewish, Antony (Great Britain, 1924–)
For their pioneering research in radio astrophysics: Ryle for his observations and inventions of the aperture synthesis technique, and Hewish for his decisive role in the discovery of pulsars.

1975 Bohr, Aage (Denmark, 1922–)
Bottelson, Ben (Denmark, 1926–)
Rainwater, James (U.S., 1917–86)
For the discovery of the connection between collective motion and particle motion in atomic nuclei and the development of the theory of the structure of the atomic nucleus based on this connection.

1976   **Richter, Burton** (U.S., 1931–)
Ting, Samuel C. C. (U.S., 1936–)
For their pioneering work in the discovery of a heavy elementary particle of a new kind.

1977   **Anderson, Philip W.** (U.S., 1923–)
Mott, Sir Nevill F. (Great Britain, 1905–)
Van Vleck, John H. (U.S., 1899–1980)
For their fundamental theoretical investigations of the electronic structure of magnetic and disordered systems.

1978   **Kapitsa, Peter Leonidovitch** (USSR, 1894–1984)
For his basic inventions and discoveries in the area of low-temperature physics.
Penzias, Arno A. (U.S., 1933–)
Wilson, Robert W. (U.S., 1936–)
For their discovery of cosmic microwave background radiation.

1979   **Glashow, Sheldon L.** (U.S., 1932–)
Salam, Abdus (Pakistan, 1926–)
Weinberg, Steven (U.S., 1933–)
For their contributions to the theory of the unified weak and electromagnetic interation between elementary particles, including *inter alia* the prediction of the weak neutral current.

1980   **Cronin, James W.** (U.S., 1931–)
Fitch, Val L. (U.S., 1923–)
For the discovery of violations of fundamental symmetry principles in the decay of neutral K-mesons.

1981   **Bloembergen, Nicolaas** (U.S., 1920–)
Schawlow, Arthur L. (U.S., 1921–)
For their contribution to the development of laser spectroscopy.
Siegbahn, Kai M. (Sweden, 1918–)
For his contribution to the development of high-resolution electron spectroscopy.

1982   **Wilson, Kenneth G.** (U.S., 1936–)
For his theory on critical phenomena in connection with phase transitions.

1983   **Chandrasekhar, Subramanyan** (U.S., 1936–)
For his theoretical studies of the physical processes of importance to the structure and evolution of the stars.
Fowler, William A. (U.S., 1911–)
For his theoretical and experimental studies of the nuclear reactions of importance in the formation of the chemical elements in the universe.

1984   **Rubbia, Carlo** (Italy, 1934–)
Van Der Meer, Simon (Netherlands, 1925–)
For their decisive contributions to the large project that led to the discovery of the field particles W and Z, communicators of weak interaction.

1985   **Von Klitzing, Klaus** (Germany, 1943–)
For the discovery of the quantized Hall effect.

1986   **Ruska, Ernst** (Germany, 1906–88)
For his fundamental work in electron optics, and for the design of the first electron microscope.
Binnig, Gerd (Germany, 1947–)
Rohrer, Heinrich (Switzerland, 1933–)
For their design of the scanning tunneling microscope.

1987   **Bednorz, J. Georg** (Germany, 1950–)
Müller, K. Alexander (Switzerland, 1927–)

For their important breakthrough in the discovery of superconductivity in ceramic materials.

1988   **Lederman, Leon M.** (U.S., 1922–)
Schwartz, Melvin (U.S., 1932–)
Steinberger, Jack (U.S., 1921–)
For the neutrino beam method and the demonstration of the doublet structure of the leptons through the discovery of the muon neutrino.

1989   **Ramsey, Norman F.** (U.S., 1915–)
For the invention of the separated oscillatory fields method and its use in the hydrogen maser and other atomic clocks.
Dehmet, Hans G. (U.S., 1922–)
Paul, Wolfgang (Germany, 1913–)
For the development of the ion trap technique.

1990   **Friedman, Jerome I.** (U.S., 1930–)
Kendall, Henry W. (U.S., 1926–)
Taylor, Richard E. (Canada, 1929–)
For their pioneering investigations concerning deep inelastic scattering of electrons on protons and bound neutrons, which have been of essential importance for the development of the quark model in particle physics.

1991   **de Gennes, Pierre-Giles** (France, 1933–)
For his studies of the changes that take place in liquid crystals when the orientation of the molecules changes from a random, or "disordered," state to an aligned, or "ordered," state.

1992   **Charpak, George** (France, b. Poland, 1924–)
For devising an electronic detector that recorded the trajectories of sub-atomic particles in atom smashers.

Physiology or Medicine

1901   **Von Behring, Emil** (Germany, 1854–1917)
For his work on serum therapy, especially its application against diphtheria.

1902   **Ross, Sir Ronald** (Great Britain, 1857–1932)
For his work on malaria, showing how it enters the organism.

1903   **Finsen, Niels Ryberg** (Denmark, 1860–1904)
For his treatment of diseases, especially lupus vulgaris, with concentrated light radiation.

1904   **Pavlov, Ivan Petrovic** (Russia, 1849–1936)
For his work on the physiology of digestion.

1905   **Koch, Robert** (Germany, 1843–1910)
For his investigations and discoveries in relation to tuberculosis.

1906   **Golgi, Camillo** (Italy, 1843–1926)
Ramon Y Cajal, Santiago (Spain, 1852–1934)
For their work on the structure of the nervous system.

1907   **Laveran, Charles Louis Alphonse** (France, 1845–1922)
For his work on the role played by protozoa in causing diseases.

1908   **Mecnikov, Ilja Il'jic** (Russia, 1845–1916)
Ehrlich, Paul (Germany, 1854–1915)
For their work on immunity.

1909 Kocher, Emil Theodor (Switzerland, 1841–1927)
For his work on the physiology, pathology and surgery of the thyroid gland.

1910 Kossel, Albrecht (Germany, 1853–1927)
For contributions to our knowledge of cell chemistry made through his work on proteins, including the nucleic substances.

1911 Gullstrand, Allvar (Sweden, 1862–1930)
For his work on the dioptrics of the eye.

1912 Carrel, Alexis (France, 1873–1944)
For his work on vascular suture and the transplantation of blood vessels and organs.

1913 Richet, Charles Robert (France, 1950–1935)
For his work on anaphylaxis.

1914 Bárány, Robert (Austria, 1876–1936)
For his work on the physiology and pathology of the vestibular apparatus.

1915–1918 Not awarded

1919 Bordet, Jules (Belgium, 1870–1961)
For his discoveries relating to immunity.

1920 Krogh, Schack August Steenberger (Denmark, 1874–1949)
For his discovery of the capillary motor regulating mechanism.

1921 Not awarded

1922 Hill, Sir Archibald Vivian (Great Britain, 1886–1977)
For his discovery relating to the produciton of heat in the muscle.
Meyerhof, Otto Fritz (Germany, 1884–1951)
For his discovery of the fixed relationship between the consumption of oxygen and the metabolism of lactic acid in the muscle.

1923 Banting, Sir Frederick Grant (Canada, 1891–1941)
Macleod, John James Richard (Canada, 1876–1935)
For the discovery of insulin.

1924 Einthoven, Willem (Netherlands, 1860–1927)
For his discovery of the mechanism of the electrocardiogram.

1925 Not awarded

1926 Fibiger, Johannes Andreas Grib (Denmark, 1867–1928)
For his discovery of the Spiroptera carcinoma.

1927 Wagner-Jauregg, Julius (Austria, 1857–1940)
For his discovery of the therapeutic value of malaria inoculation in the treatment of dimentia paralytica.

1928 Nicolle, Charles Jules Henri (France, 1866–1936)
For his work on typhus.

1929 Eijkman, Christiaan (Netherlands, 1858–1930)
For his discovery of the anti-neuritic vitamin.
Hopkins, Sir Frederick Gowland (Great Britain, 1861–1947)
For his discovery of growth-stimulating vitamins.

1930 Landsteiner, Karl (Austria, 1868–1943)
For his discovery of human blood groups.

1931 Warburg, Otto Heinrich (Germany, 1883–1970)
For his discovery of the nature and mode of action of the respiratory enzyme.

1932 Sherrington, Sir Charles Scott (Great Britain, 1857–1952)
Adrian, Lord Edgar Douglas (Great Britain, 1889–1977)
For their discoveries regarding the functions of neurons.

1933 Morgan, Thomas Hunt (U.S., 1866–1945)
For his discoveries concerning the role played by the chromosome in heredity.

1934 Whipple, George Hoyt (U.S., 1878–1976)
Minot, George Richards (U.S., 1885–1950)
Murphy, William Parry (U.S., 1892–1987)
For their discoveries concerning liver therapy in cases of anemia.

1935 Spemann, Hans (Germany, 1869–1941)
For his discovery of the organizer effect in embryonic development.

1936 Dale, Sir Henry Hallett (Great Britain, 1875–1968)
Loewi, Otto (Austria, 1873–1961)
For their discoveries relating to chemical transmission of nerve impulses.

1937 Szent-Györgyi, Albert (Hungary, 1893–1986)
For his discoveries in connection with the biological combustion processes, with special reference to vitamin C and the catalysis of fumaric acid.

1938 Heymans, Corneille Jean (Belgium, 1892–1968)
For the discovery of the role played by the sinus and aortic mechanisms in the regulation of respiration.

1939 Domagk, Gerhard (Germany, 1895–1964)
For the discovery of the antibacterial effects of prontosil.

1940–42 Not awarded

1943 Dam, Henrik Carl Peter (Denmark, 1895–1976)
For his discovery of vitamin K.
Doisy, Edward Adelbert (U.S., 1893–1986)
For his discovery of the chemical nature of vitamin K.

1944 Erlanger, Joseph (U.S., 1874–1965)
Gasser, Herbert Spencer (U.S., 1888–1963)
For their discoveries relating to the highly differentiated functions of single nerve fibers.

1945 Fleming, Sir Alexander (Great Britain, 1881–1955)
Chain, Sir Ernst Boris (Great Britain, 1906–79)
Florey, Lord Howard Walter (Great Britain, 1898–1968)
For the discovery of penicillin and its curative effect in various infectious diseases.

1946 Muller, Hermann Joseph (U.S., 1890–1967)
For the discovery of the produciton of mutations by means of X-ray irradiation.

1947 Cori, Carl Ferdinand (U.S., 1896–1984)
Cori, Gerty Theresa, née Radnitz (U.S., 1896–1957)
For their discovery of the course of the catalytic conversion of glycogen.
Houssay, Bernardo Alberto (Argentina, 1887–1971)
For his discovery of the part played by the hormone of the anterior pituitary lobe in the metabolism of sugar.

1948 **Müller, Paul Hermann** (Switzerland, 1899–1965)
For his discovery of the high efficiency of DDT as a contact poison against several arthropods.

1949 **Hess, Walter Rudolf** (Switzerland, 1881–1973)
For his discovery of the functional organization of the interbrian as a coordinator of the activities of the internal organs.
Moniz, Antonio de Egas (Portugal, 1874–1955)
For his discovery of the therapeutic value of leucotomy in certain psychoses.

1950 **Kendall, Edward Calvin** (U.S., 1886–1972)
Reichstein, Tadeus (Switzerland, 1897–)
Hench, Philip Showalter (U.S., 1896–1965)
For their discoveries relating to the hormones of the adrenal cortex, their structure and biological effects.

1951 **Theiler, Max** (South Africa, 1899–1972)
For his discoveries concerning yellow fever and how to combat it.

1952 **Waksman, Selman Abraham** (U.S., 1888–1973)
For his discovery of streptomycin, the first antibiotic effective against tuberculosis.

1953 **Krebs, Sir Hans Adolf** (Great Britain, 1900–81)
For his discovery of the citric acid cycle.
Lipmann, Fritz Albert (U.S., 1899–1986)
For his discovery of co-enzyme A and its importance for intermediary metabolism.

1954 **Enders, John Franklin** (U.S., 1897–1985)
Weller, Thomas Huckle (U.S., 1915–)
Robbins, Frederick Chapman (U.S., 1916–)
For their discovery of the ability of poliomyelitis viruses to grow in cultures of various types of tissue.

1955 **Theorell, Axel Hugo Theodor** (Sweden, 1903–82)
For his discoveries concerning the nature and mode of action of oxidation enzymes.

1956 **Cournand, André Frédéric** (U.S., 1895–1988)
Forssmann, Werner (Germany, 1904–79)
Richards, Dickinson W. (U.S., 1895–1973)
For their discoveries concerning heart catheterization and pathological changes in the circulatory system.

1957 **Bovet, Daniel** (Italy, 1907–92)
For his discoveries relating to synthetic compounds that inhibit the action of certain body substances, and especially their action on the vascular system and the skeletal muscles.

1958 **Beadle, George Wells** (U.S., 1903–89)
Tatum, Edward Lawrie (U.S., 1909–75)
For their discovery that genes act by regulating definite chemical events.
Lederberg, Joshua (U.S., 1925–)
For his discoveries concerning genetic recombination and the organization of the genetic material of bacteria.

1959 **Ochoa, Severo** (U.S., 1905–)
Kornberg, Arthur (U.S., 1918–)
For their discovery of the mechanisms in the biological synthesis of ribonucleic acid and deoxiribonucleic acid.

1960 **Burnet, Sir Frank Macfarlane** (Australia, 1899–1985)
Medawar, Sir Peter Brian (Great Britain, 1915–87)
For discovery of acquired immunological tolerance.

1961 **Von Békésy, Georg** (U.S., 1899–1972)
For his discoveries of the physical mechanism of stimulation within the cochlea.

1962 **Crick, Francis Harry Compton** (Great Britain, 1916–)
Watson, James Dewey (U.S., 1928–)
Wilkins, Maurice Hugh Frederick (Great Britain, 1916–)
For their discoveries concerning the molecular structure of nuclear acids and its significance for information transfer in living material.

1963 **Eccles, Sir John Carew** (Australia, 1903–)
Hodgkin, Sir Alan Lloyd (Great Britain, 1914–)
Huxley, Sir Andrew Fielding (Great Britain, 1917–)
For their discoveries concerning the ionic mechanisms involved in excitation and inhibition in the peripheral and central portions of the nerve cell membrane.

1964 **Bloch, Konrad** (U.S., 1912–)
Lynen, Feodor (Germany, 1911–79)
For their discoveries concerning the mechanism and regulation of the cholesterol and fatty acid metabolism.

1965 **Jacob, François** (France, 1920–)
Lwoff, André (France, 1902–)
Monod, Jacques (France, 1910–76)
For their discoveries concerning genetic control of enzyme and virus synthesis.

1966 **Rous, Peyton** (U.S., 1879–1970)
For his discovery of tumor-inducing viruses.
Huggins, Charles Brenton (U.S., 1901–)
For his discoveries concerning hormonal treatment of prostatic cancer.

1967 **Granit, Ragnar** (Sweden, 1900–)
Hartline, Haldan Keffer (U.S., 1903–83)
Wald, George (U.S., 1906–)
For their discoveries concerning the primary physiological and chemical visual processes in the eye.

1968 **Holley, Robert W.** (U.S., 1922–)
Khorana, Har Gobind (U.S., 1922–)
Nirenberg, Marshall W. (U.S., 1927–)
For their interpretation of the genetic code and its function in protein synthesis.

1969 **Delbrück, Max** (U.S., 1906–81)
Hershey, Alfred D. (U.S., 1908–)
Luria, Salvador E. (U.S., 1912–91)
For their discoveries concerning the replication mechanism and the genetic structure of viruses.

1970 **Katz, Sir Bernard** (Great Britain, 1911–)
Von Euler, Ulf (Sweden, 1905–83)
Axelrod, Julius (U.S., 1912–)
For their discoveries concerning the humoral transmitters in the nerve terminals and the mechanism for their storage, release and inactivation.

1971 **Sutherland, Earl W. Jr.** (U.S., 1915–74)
For his discoveries concerning the mechanisms of the action of hormones.

1972 **Edelman, Gerald M.** (U.S., 1929–)
Porter, Rodney R. (Great Britain, 1917–85)
For their discoveries concerning the chemical structure of antibodies.

1973 Von Frisch, Karl (Germany, 1886–1982)
Lorenz, Konrad (Austria, 1903–89)
Tinbergen, Nikolaas (Great Britain, 1907–)
For their discoveries of the organization and elicitation of individual and social behavior patterns.

1974 Claude, Albert (Belgium, 1899–1983)
De Duve, Christian (Belgium, 1917–)
Palade, George E. (U.S., 1912–)
For their discoveries concerning the structural and functional organization of the cell.

1975 Baltimore, David (U.S., 1938–)
Dulbecco, Renato (U.S., 1914–)
Temin, Howard Martin (U.S., 1934–)
For their discoveries concerning the interaction between tumor viruses and the genetic material of the cell.

1976 Blumberg, Baruch S. (U.S., 1925–)
Gajdusek, D. Carleton (U.S., 1923–)
For their discoveries concerning new mechanisms for the origin and dissemination of infectious diseases.

1977 Guillemin, Roger (U.S., 1924–)
Schally, Andrew V. (U.S., 1926–)
For their discoveries concerning the peptide hormone production of the brain.
Yalow, Rosalyn (U.S., 1921–)
For the development of radio-immunoassays of peptide hormones.

1978 Arber, Werner (Switzerland, 1929–)
Nathans, Daniel (U.S., 1928–)
Smith, Hamilton O. (U.S., 1931–)
For the discovery of restriction enzymes and their application to problems of molecular genetics.

1979 Cormack, Allan M. (U.S., 1924–)
Hounsfield, Sir Godfrey N. (Great Britain, 1919–)
For the development of computer assisted tomography.

1980 Benacerraf, Baruj (U.S., 1920–)
Dausset, Jean (France, 1916–)
Snell, George D. (U.S., 1903–)
For their discoveries concerning genetically determined structures on the cell surface that regulate immunological reactions.

1981 Sperry, Roger W. (U.S., 1913–)
For his discoveries concerning the functional specialization of the cerebral hemispheres.
Hubel, David H. (U.S., 1926–)
Wiesel, Rorsten N. (Sweden, 1924–)
For their discoveries concerning information processing in the visual system.

1982 Bergström, Sune K. (Sweden, 1916–)
Samuelsson, Bengt I. (Sweden, 1934–)
Vane, Sir John R. (Great Britain, 1927–)
For their discoveries concerning prostaglandins and related biologically active substances.

1983 McClintock, Barbara (U.S., 1902–92)
For her discovery of mobile genetic elements.

1984 Jerne, Niels K. (Denmark, 1911–)
Köhler, Georges J. F. (Germany, 1946–)
Milstein, César (Great Britain and Argentina, 1927–)
For theories concerning the specificity in development and control of the immune system and the discovery of the principle for production of monoclonal antibodies.

1985 Brown, Michael S. (U.S, 1941–)
Goldstein, Joseph L. (U.S, 1940–)
For their discoveries concerning the regulation of cholesterol metabolism.

1986 Cohen, Stanley (U.S., 1922–)
Levi-Montalcini, Rita (Italy and U.S., 1909–)
For their discoveries of growth factors.

1987 Tonegawa, Susumu (Japan, 1939–)
For his discovery of the "genetic principle for generation of antibody diversity."

1988 Black, Sir James W. (Great Britain, 1924–)
Elion, Gertrude B. (U.S., 1918–)
Hitchings, George H. (U.S., 1905–)
For their discoveries of "important principles for drug treatment."

1989 Bishop, Michael J. (U.S., 1936–)
Varmus, Harold E. (U.S., 1939–)
For their discovery of the cellular origin of retroviral oncogenes.

1990 Murray, Joseph E. (U.S., 1919–)
Thomas, E. Donnall (U.S.,1920–)
For their discoveries concerning organ and cell transplantation in the treatment of human disease.

1991 Neher, Erwin (Germany, 1944–)
Sakmanna, Bert (Germany, 1942–)
For their work in uncovering basic cell functions.

1992 Fischer, Edmond H. (U.S., 1920–)
Krebs, Edwin G. (U.S., 1918–)
For their discovery in the 1950s of a cellular regulatory mechanism used to control a variety of metabolic processes.

Subject Index

Name Index